Political Philosophy

Essential Selections

Edited by

Aeon J. Skoble

Tibor R. Machan

Prentice Hall
Upper Saddle River, NJ 07458

Library of Congress Cataloging-in-Publication Data

Political philosophy : essential selections / edited by Aeon J. Skoble
and Tibor R. Machan.
    p.   cm.
   Includes bibliographical references (p.).
   ISBN 0–13–629577–0
   1. Political science—Philosophy. I. Skoble, Aeon J.
II. Machan, Tibor R.
JA71.P6224   1999
320′.01--dc21

98-5773
CIP

Editorial/production supervision
   and interior design: *Harriet Tellem*
Acquisitions editor: *Karita France*
Manufacturing buyer: *Tricia Kenny*
Editorial assistant: *Jennifer Ackerman*
Cover design: *Joe Sengotta*

This book was set in 10/12 New Baskerville by Pub-Set, Inc. and was printed
and bound by RR Donnelly, Harrisonburg. The cover was printed by Phoenix
Color Corp.

 © 1999 by Prentice-Hall, Inc.
Simon & Schuster/A Viacom Company
Upper Saddle River, New Jersey 07458

Printed in the United States of America
10 9 8 7 6 5 4 3 2 1

ISBN 0-13-629577-0

Prentice-Hall International (UK) Limited, *London*
Prentice-Hall of Australia Pty. Limited, *Sydney*
Prentice-Hall Canada, Inc., *Toronto*
Prentice-Hall Hispanoamericana, S.A., *Mexico*
Prentice-Hall of India Private Limited, *New Delhi*
Prentice-Hall of Japan, Inc., *Tokyo*
Simon & Schuster Asia Pte. Ltd., *Singapore*
Editora Prentice-Hall do Brasil, Ltda., *Rio de Janeiro*

For Lisa Bahnemann and Thomas Machan

Contents

Part III   Modern Political Philosophy   123

Part IV   Contemporary Political Philosophy   389

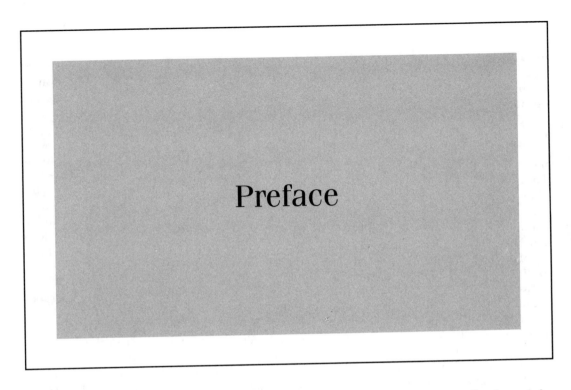

Preface

We might begin with a simple definition of "political philosophy" as the application of the tools of philosophical analysis to problems of politics. Philosophy asks questions about fundamentals, about justification, and typically seeks to use logical arguments to seek answers. Political philosophy, then, is concerned with questions such as "what is the nature of justice?" and "what sorts of social arrangements are best?" and "do I have an obligation to obey the law?".

Political scientists are sometimes concerned with these questions also, but as a formal discipline political science has come to be devoted more to empirical matters such as models of voting behavior or comparative world politics. These are hardly insignificant; we mention the distinction simply for the purpose of clarification. There are also some who think that political philosophy is concerned with something else, namely, how philosophers should deal with political regimes, but this meaning is a bit idiosyncratic, and used only in certain academic contexts.

In its most usual sense, political philosophy is a normative subject; it uses words like "best" and "right" and "good." Often, then, there is overlap between political philosophy and moral philosophy, for the basic concepts underlying words like that are the subject of the latter field. Nevertheless, political philosophy is its own distinctive area of inquiry, for theories about personal virtue or obligation may not answer all questions about social arrangements. We need some insights into moral philosophy to ask about the "most just government," but making progress towards an answer will take us beyond ethics. The question shifts from "how should I live my life?" to "how shall we arrange our society?".

One answer to the question of how best to arrange society is that "everyone should do as I command." This seems almost comical today, but for large bits of human history there has been little more that has served as a "guiding principle" for many societies. If my tribe has conquered yours, perhaps all in your tribe would recognize that mine should rule. But perhaps not. At some point, someone thought to ask about the justification of the power some held over others, and this remains a vexing question. The nature and justification of political authority, the proper relationship between the individual and society, the role of the divine in affairs of state—these and many other questions are the subject of the field we call political philosophy.

Not surprisingly, the ancient Greek philosophers Plato and Aristotle have much to say about these questions, but the debate continues today. It is often the case in philosophy that questions get revisited in each generation, in slightly different terms. This may be because relying merely on tradition is an unreliable guide. Still, some questions seem to have been answered with a virtual consensus: few today endorse the notion that trial-by-combat is a more reliable method of judicial inquiry than trial-by-jury, just as few defend the idea that kings have a divine right to absolute power over their subjects. Yet, although democracy has been challenged since its invention 2500 years ago, even in our own century it continues to be challenged by such recent competitors as Nazism and Communism. Within democracies, vital questions abound concerning the eternal conflict between the liberty of the individual and the will of the majority. Political philosophy remains an active field. But the debates of political philosophy are not merely academic: lives hang in the balance. Ideas shape political systems. From the wars between Greece and Persia to the 20th century battles among liberalism and fascism, political theory has played a role in shaping the fates of nations and of people. American independence is arguably the ultimate result of a radical argument put forward by a philosopher, as was Soviet Communism. Few could dispute that political philosophy is a subject which deserves attention.

Our goal in assembling this collection was to facilitate this attention. There have been many collections of political philosophy, but they tend to be either well-served in classical sources, with poor representation of contemporary debates, or vice versa. Our intention was a comprehensive collection, in one volume, of essential selections of political philosophy from the ancient world to the contemporary. Readings are presented in chronological order, grouped by period. Each reading is accompanied by a brief biographical sketch of the author, and each period is prefaced by a general historical overview, but we have endeavored to keep our own editorializing out. The thinkers represented here are perfectly capable of speaking for themselves, as are the professors who may be using this as a textbook. Since the readers, mostly students, need to have an in-depth encounter with these significant theorists, the selections ought to be approached on their own terms. Some guidance is called for, of course, but as students are likely to have such a guide in their teachers, the editors believe that adding additional commentary will tend to create confusion. A general bibliography is attached should the reader wish to pursue any of these matters.

We would like to thank all of those who continue to explore political philosophy and take it seriously. We also would like to express thanks to all of those who have helped us put this collection together and have shown us support. More specifically, we would like to thank Karita France, Harriet Tellem, and Bill McLane for their assistance. We would also like to thank J. Roger Lee, Douglas Rasmussen, Douglas Den Uyl, Tom Palmer, and Ralph Raico for their help. We are very grateful to Angela Stone for getting this project off the ground. Thank you to the reviewers of this book: Robert Westmoreland, University of Mississippi; and Cynthia Stark, University of Utah.

Part I

Ancient Political Philosophy

When we speak of "ancient Greece," we are of course speaking of a collection of societies quite different from one another in their social structure and conception of public virtue. The center of Greek philosophical activity was Athens, which prided itself on having developed a democracy. All the Greeks valued freedom in a certain sense, in that each city-state—or, organized, purposeful community—demanded and valued its own autonomy. But the Athenians extended this one step further and designed a system whereby each citizen could participate actively in the running of the city's affairs. Their democracy differed from ours in two crucial respects: first of all, they had a much more restricted franchise than we do. Only native-born male Athenian property-holders were enfranchised.

But it is the second significant difference between their democracy and ours which is the structural one. Theirs was a direct democracy rather than a representative democracy. Although we consider ourselves to be a democratic society, it is not the case that each citizen casts a vote on each matter to be decided, but rather that citizens get to vote democratically for delegates to a smaller body, which in turn makes decisions. In Athens, each citizen could participate in the decision making of the assembly. So when we say that the Athenians were democratic, we do not mean that their system was just like modern American government.

In any event, the Athenians prided themselves on their democracy, but some of the philosophers questioned whether it was indeed the best form of government. Socrates' inquiry into this and other matters was a contributing factor in his trial and execution, which suggests that democracy may not be perfect. Plato, appalled at the notion that a democracy could commit such an injustice, subjected theories of justice to as much philosophical scrutiny as anything else. So the fundamental question of political philosophy, "what is justice," has a pedigree extending back to Plato. Before we can decide whether democracy is just, we must know what justice is. The selections in this chapter include lengthy excerpts from Plato's famous work *Republic*, as well as selections from his work entitled *Statesman*. In *Republic*, Plato investigates the nature of justice, both in the moral sense and in the political sense, and the selection from *Statesman* offers some practical suggestions. Plato's inquiries on these matters set the stage for much of the history of these disputes, which is why the selections from *Republic* are so extensive.

Unsurprisingly, Aristotle also makes significant contributions to this field, in his essay *Politics*. Aristotle's theories became quite influential in Roman times, and influenced the framers of the American Constitution as well. This section also includes a fragment from the works of Xenophon.

Xenophon (426–354 B.C.E.)

Born in Athens during the Peloponnesian War, he made the acquaintance of the Athenian philosopher Socrates; Xenophon's *Apology, Symposium*, and *Memorabilia* form our chief alternative account of the historical Socrates to that of Plato. Xenophon was a soldier. In 401, after Sparta's victory over Athens, reportedly with the blessings of Socrates, Xenophon signed on as a soldier in the Achaemenid prince Cyrus the Younger's attempt to seize the throne of Persia. The enterprise ended with Cyrus' death in battle and with the killing of generals of the Greek mercenary army. It fell to younger soldiers, including Xenophon, to lead a year-long successful retreat through enemy territory from Baghdad, north to the Black Sea and west to Byzantium. Xenophon extended his military career in service to Sparta, triggering his official banishment from Athens. He settled in Scillus near Olympia and there raised a family and did most of his writing. Sparta's military reversals led to the loss of his estate in 371, and Xenophon spent the remainder of his life either in Corinth or perhaps, after legal rehabilitation, in Athens. Xenophon wrote histories, works on commanding cavalry forces and on horsemanship, and accounts of famous people. The following is an account of a conversation between the noted statesmen Pericles and Alcibiades.

From Memorabilia*

40. Alcibiades, it is said, before he was twenty years of age, held the following discourse with Pericles, who was his guardian, and chief ruler of the state about laws.

41. "Tell me," said he, "Pericles, can you teach me what a law is." "Certainly," replied Pericles. "Teach me then, in the name of the gods," said Alcibiades, "for I, hearing some persons praised as being obedient to the laws, consider that no one can fairly obtain such praise who does not know what a law is."

42. "You desire no very difficult matter, Alcibiades," said Pericles, "when you wish to know what a law is; for all those regulations are laws, which the people, on meeting together and approving them, have enacted, directing what we should do and what we should not do." "And whether do they direct that we should do good things, or that we should do bad things?" "Good, by Jupiter, my child," said he, "but bad by no means."

43. "And if it should not be the whole people, but a few, as where there is an oligarchy, that should meet together, and enact what we are to do, what are such enactments!" "Everything," replied Pericles, "which the supreme power in the state, on determining what the people ought to do, has enacted, is called a law." "And if a tyrant, holding rule over the state, prescribes to the citizens what they must do, is such prescription called a law?" "Whatever a tyrant in authority prescribes," returned Pericles, "is also called a law."

---

* An Excerpt.

44. "What then, Pericles," asked Alcibiades, "is force and lawlessness? Is it not when the stronger obliges the weaker, not by persuasion, but by compulsion, to do what he pleases?" "So it appears to me," replied Pericles. "Whatever then a tyrant compels the people to do, by enacting it without gaining their consent, is that an act of lawlessness?" "Yes," said Pericles, "it appears to me that it is, for I retract my admission that what a tyrant prescribes to the people without persuading them, is a law."

45. "But what the few enact, not from gaining the consent of the many, but from having superior power, should we say that that is force or that it is not?" "Everything," said Pericles, "which one man obliges another to do without gaining his consent, whether he enact it in writing or not, seems to me to be force rather than law." "Whatever, then, the whole people, when they are stronger than the wealthier class, enact without their consent, would be an act of force rather than a law?"

46. "Certainly, Alcibiades," said Pericles, "and I, when I was of your age, was very acute at such disquisitions; for we used to meditate and argue about such subjects as you now appear to meditate." "Would, therefore," said Alcibiades, "that I had conversed with you, Pericles, at the time when you were most acute in discussing such topics!"

47. When Alcibiades and Critias, therefore, began to think themselves superior to those who were then governing the state, they no longer attended Socrates (for he was not agreeable to them in other respects, and they were offended, if they went to him at all, at being reproved for any error that they had committed), but devoted themselves to political employments, with a view to which they had at first associated with Socrates. . . .

Plato (ca. 428–347 B.C.E.)

As a youth, Plato was one of the Athenians who thought Socrates was worth taking seriously, and perhaps as a result of their association, Plato devoted his life to the exploration and propagation of philosophy. In middle age he founded a school of philosophy in Athens, the Academy, where his pupils included Aristotle, and wrote many works of philosophy in dialogue form. Although the dialogues feature Socrates as a character, with the exception of Plato's account of the trial they do not purport to be transcripts of actual conversations. Since the Socratic method of philosophical exploration was dialectical, Plato chose the dialogue form as a vehicle for his written philosophy, although many scholars believe some of the shorter dialogues to more or less represent Socrates' views. Plato was profoundly disturbed by the Athenians' execution of Socrates; his skepticism of democracy and quest for an alternative to Athenian justice motivate Plato's political dialogues. He also wrote on metaphysics, epistemology, ethics, and art. The *Republic*, which we excerpt here, touches on all of these. It postulates an ideal, perfectly just city-state for the purpose of examining the nature of justice. Aware of the need for a more practical theory, Plato also discusses the necessary components of an obtainable, close-to-just state in the *Statesman*, excerpted here. For further reading, see *Laws*, *Minos*, and *Crito*.

From Republic*

Book II

. . . Glaucon and the rest entreated me by all means not to let the question drop, but to proceed in the investigation. They wanted to arrive at the truth, first, about the nature of justice and injustice, and secondly, about their relative advantages. I told them, what I—really thought, that the enquiry would be of a serious nature, and would require very good eyes. Seeing then, I said, that we are no great wits, I think that we had better adopt a method which I may illustrate thus; suppose that a short-sighted person had been asked by some one to read small letters from a distance; and it occurred to some one else that they might be found in another place which was larger and in which the letters were larger—if they were the same and he could read the larger letters first, and then proceed to the lesser—this would have been thought a rare piece of good fortune.

Very true, said Adeimantus; but how does the illustration apply to our enquiry?

I will tell you, I replied; justice, which is the subject of our enquiry, is, as you know, sometimes spoken of as the virtue of an individual, and sometimes as the virtue of a State.

True, he replied.

And is not a State larger than an individual?

It is.

---

*An Excerpt.

Then in the larger the quantity of justice is likely to be larger and more easily discernible. I propose therefore that we enquire into the nature of justice and injustice, first as they appear in the State, and secondly in the individual, proceeding from the greater to the lesser and comparing them.

That, he said, is an excellent proposal.

And if we imagine the State in process of creation, we shall see the justice and injustice of the State in process of creation also.

I dare say.

When the State is completed there may be a hope that the object of our search will be more easily discovered.

Yes, far more easily.

But ought we to attempt to construct one? I said; for to do so, as I am inclined to think, will be a very serious task. Reflect therefore.

I have reflected, said Adeimantus, and am anxious that you should proceed.

A State, I said, arises, as I conceive, out of the needs of mankind; no one is self-sufficing, but all of us have many wants. Can any other origin of a State be imagined?

There can be no other.

Then, as we have many wants, and many persons are needed to supply them, one takes a helper for one purpose and another for another; and when these partners and helpers are gathered together in one habitation the body of inhabitants is termed a State.

True, he said.

And they exchange with one another, and one gives, and another receives, under the idea that the exchange will be for their good.

Very true.

Then, I said, let us begin and create in idea a State; and yet the true creator is necessity, who is the mother of our invention.

Of course, he replied.

Now the first and greatest of necessities is food, which is the condition of life and existence.

Certainly.

The second is a dwelling, and the third clothing and the like.

True.

And now let us see how our city will be able to supply this great demand: We may suppose that one man is a husbandman, another a builder, some one else a weaver—shall we add to them a shoemaker, or perhaps some other purveyor to our bodily wants?

Quite right.

The barest notion of a State must include four or five men.

Clearly.

And how will they proceed? Will each bring the result of his labours into a common stock?—the individual husbandman, for example, producing for four, and labouring four times as long and as much as he need in the provision of food with which he supplies others as well as himself; or will he have nothing to do with others and not be at the trouble of producing for them, but provide for himself alone a fourth of the food in a fourth of the time, and in the remaining three-fourths of his time be employed in making a house or a coat or a pair of shoes, having no partnership with others, but supplying himself all his own wants?

Adeimantus thought that he should aim at producing food only and not at producing everything.

Probably, I replied, that would be the better way; and when I hear you say this, I am myself reminded that we are not all alike; there are diversities of natures among us which are adapted to different occupations.

Very true.

And will you have a work better done when the workman has many occupations, or when he has only one?

When he has only one.

Further, there can be no doubt that a work is spoilt when not done at the right time?

No doubt.

For business is not disposed to wait until the doer of the business is at leisure; but the doer must follow up what he is doing, and make the business his first object.

He must.

And if so, we must infer that all things are produced more plentifully and easily and of a better quality when one man does one thing which is natural to him and does it at the right time, and leaves other things.

Undoubtedly. . . .

Book IV

Here Adeimantus interposed a question: How would you answer, Socrates, said he, if a person were to say that you are making these people miserable, and that they are the cause of their own unhappiness; the city in fact belongs to them, but they are none the better for it; whereas other men acquire lands, and build large and handsome houses, and have everything handsome about them, offering sacrifices to the gods on their own account, and practising hospitality; moreover, as you were saying just now, they have gold and silver, and all that is usual among the favourites of fortune; but our poor citizens are no better than mercenaries who are quartered in the city and are always mounting guard?

Yes, I said; and you may add that they are only fed, and not paid in addition to their food, like other men; and therefore they cannot, if they would, take a journey of pleasure; they have no money to spend on a mistress or any other luxurious fancy, which, as the world goes, is thought to be happiness; and many other accusations of the same nature might be added.

But, said he, let us suppose all this to be included in the charge.

You mean to ask, I said, what will be our answer?

Yes.

If we proceed along the old path, my belief, I said, is that we shall find the answer. And our answer will be that, even as they are, our guardians may very likely be the happiest of men; but that our aim in founding the State was not the disproportionate happiness of any one class, but the greatest happiness of the whole; we thought that in a State which is ordered with a view to the good of the whole we should be most likely to find Justice, and in the ill-ordered State injustice: and, having found them, we might then decide which of the two is the happier. At present, I take it, we are fashioning the happy State, not piecemeal, or with a view of making a few happy citizens, but as a whole; and by-and-by we will proceed to view the opposite kind of State. Suppose that we were painting a statue, and some one came up to us and said, Why do you not put the most beautiful colours on the most beautiful parts of the body—the eyes ought to be purple, but you have made them black—to him we might fairly answer, Sir, you would not surely have us beautify the eyes to such a degree that they are no longer eyes; consider rather whether, by giving this and the other features their due proportion, we make the whole beautiful. And so I say to you, do not compel us to assign to the guardians a sort of happiness which will make them anything but guardians; for we too can clothe our husbandmen in royal apparel, and set crowns of gold on their heads, and bid them till the ground as much as they like, and no more. Our potters also might be allowed to repose on couches, and feast by the fireside, passing round the winecup, while their wheel is conveniently at hand, and working at pottery only as much as they like; in this way we might make every class happy—and then, as you imagine, the whole State would be happy. But do not put this idea into our heads; for, if we listen to you, the husbandman will be no longer a husbandman, the potter will cease to be a potter, and no one will have the character of any distinct class in the State. Now this is not of much consequence where the corruption of society, and pretension to be what you are not, is confined to cobblers; but when the guardians of the laws and of the government are only seemingly and not real guardians, then see how they turn the State upside down; and on the other hand they alone have the power of giving order and happiness to the State. We mean our guardians to be true saviours and not the destroyers of the State, whereas our opponent is thinking of peasants at a festival, who are enjoying a life of revelry, not of citizens who are doing their duty to the State. But, if so, we mean different things, and he is speaking of something which is not a State. And therefore we must consider whether in appointing our guardians we would look to their greatest happiness individually, or whether this principle of happiness does not rather reside in the State as a whole. But the latter be the truth, then the guardians and auxiliaries, and all others equally with them, must be compelled or induced to do their own work in the best way. And thus the whole State will grow up in a noble order, and the several classes will receive the proportion of happiness which nature assigns to them.

I think that you are quite right.

I wonder whether you will agree with another remark which occurs to me.

What may that be?

There seem to be two causes of the deterioration of the arts.

What are they?

Wealth, I said, and poverty.

How do they act?

The process is as follows: When a potter becomes rich, will he, think you, any longer take the same pains with his art?

Certainly not.

He will grow more and more indolent and careless?

Very true.

And the result will be that he becomes a worse potter?

Yes; he greatly deteriorates.

But, on the other hand, if he has no money, and cannot provide himself tools or instruments, he will not work equally well himself, nor will he teach his sons or apprentices to work equally well.

Certainly not.

Then, under the influence either of poverty or of wealth, workmen and their work are equally liable to degenerate?

That is evident.

Here, then, is a discovery of new evils, I said, against which the guardians will have to watch, or they will creep into the city unobserved.

What evils?

Wealth, I said, and poverty; the one is the parent of luxury and indolence, and the other of meanness and viciousness, and both of discontent.

That is very true, he replied; but still I should like to know, Socrates, how our city will be able to go to war, especially against an enemy who is rich and powerful, if deprived of the sinews of war.

There would certainly be a difficulty, I replied, in going to war with one such enemy; but there is no difficulty where there are two of them.

How so? he asked.

In the first place, I said, if we have to fight, our side will be trained warriors fighting against an army of rich men.

That is true, he said.

And do you not suppose, Adeimantus, that a single boxer who was perfect in his art would easily be a match for two stout and well-to-do gentlemen who were not boxers?

Hardly, if they came upon him at once.

What, not, I said, if he were able to run away and then turn and strike at the one who first came up? And supposing he were to do this several times under the heat of a scorching sun, might he not, being an expert, overturn more than one stout personage?

Certainly, he said, there would be nothing wonderful in that.

And yet rich men probably have a greater superiority in the science and practice of boxing than they have in military qualities.

Likely enough.

Then we may assume that our athletes will be able to fight with two or three times their own number?

I agree with you, for I think you right.

And suppose that, before engaging, our citizens send an embassy to one of the two cities, telling them what is the truth: Silver and gold we neither have nor are permitted to have, but you may; do you therefore come and help us in war, and take the spoils of the other city: Who, on hearing these words, would choose to fight against lean wiry dogs, rather than, with the dogs on their side, against fat and tender sheep?

That is not likely; and yet there might be a danger to the poor State if the wealth of many States were to be gathered into one.

But how simple of you to use the term State at all of any but our own!

Why so?

You ought to speak of other States in the plural number; not one of them is a city, but many cities, as they say in the game. For indeed any city, however small, is in fact divided into two, one the city of the poor, the other of the rich; these are at war with one another; and in either there are many smaller divisions, and you would be altogether beside the mark if you treated them all as a single State. But if you deal with them as many, and give the wealth or power or persons of the one to the others, you will always have a great many friends and not many enemies. And your State, while the wise order which has now been prescribed continues to prevail in her, will be the greatest of States, I do not mean to say in reputation or appearance, but in deed and truth, though she number not more than a thousand defenders. A single State which is her equal you will hardly find, either among Hellenes or barbarians, though many that appear to be as great and many times greater.

That is most true, he said.

And what, I said, will be the best limit for our rulers to fix when they are considering the size of the State and the amount of territory which they are to include, and beyond which they will not go?

What limit would you propose?

I would allow the State to increase so far as is consistent with unity; that, I think, is the proper limit.

Very good, he said.

Here then, I said, is another order which will have to be conveyed to our guardians: Let our city be accounted neither large nor small, but one and self-suffing.

And surely, said he, this is not a very severe order which we impose upon them.

And the other, said I, of which we were speaking before is lighter still—I mean the duty of degrading the offspring of the guardians when inferior, and of elevating into the rank of guardians the offspring of the lower classes, when naturally superior. The intention was that, in the case of the citizens generally, each individual should be put to the use for which nature intended him, one to one work, and then every man would do his own business, and be one and not many; and so the whole city would be one and not many.

Yes, he said; that is not so difficult.

The regulations which we are prescribing, my good Adeimantus, are not, as might be supposed, a number of great principles, but trifles all, if care be taken, as the saying is, of the one great thing—a thing, however, which I would rather call, not great, but sufficient for our purpose.

What may that be? he asked.

Education, I said, and nurture: If our citizens are well educated, and grow into sensible men, they will easily see their way through all these, as well as other matters which I omit; such, for example, as marriage, the possession of women and the procreation of children, which will all follow the general principle that friends have all things in common, as the proverb says.

That will be the best way of settling them.

Also, I said, the State, if once started well, moves with accumulating force like a wheel. For good nurture and education implant good constitutions, and these good constitutions taking root in a good education improve more and more, and this improvement affects the breed in man as in other animals. . . .

But where, amid all this, is justice? son of Ariston, tell me where. Now that our city has been made habitable, light a candle and search, and get your brother and Polemarchus and the rest of our friends to help, and let us see where in it we can discover justice and where injustice, and in what they differ from one another, and which of them the man who would be happy should have for his portion, whether seen or unseen by gods and men.

Nonsense, said Glaucon: did you not promise to search yourself, saying that for you not to help justice in her need would be an impiety?

I do not deny that I said so, and as you remind me, I will be as good as my word; but you must join.

We will, he replied.

Well, then, I hope to make the discovery in this way: I mean to begin with the assumption that our State, if rightly ordered, is perfect.

That is most certain.

And being perfect, is therefore wise and valiant and temperate and just.

That is likewise clear.

And whichever of these qualities we find in the State, the one which is not found will be the residue?

Very good.

If there were four things, and we were searching for one of them, wherever it might be, the one sought for might be known to us from the first, and there would be no further trouble; or we might know the other three first, and then the fourth would clearly be the one left.

Very true, he said.

And is not a similar method to be pursued about the virtues, which are also four in number?

Clearly.

First among the virtues found in the State, wisdom comes into view, and in this I detect a certain peculiarity.

What is that?

The State which we have been describing is said to be wise as being good in counsel?

Very true.

And good counsel is clearly a kind of knowledge, for not by ignorance, but by knowledge, do men counsel well?

Clearly.

And the kinds of knowledge in a State are many and diverse?

Of course.

There is the knowledge of the carpenter; but is that the sort of knowledge which gives a city the title of wise and good in counsel?

Certainly not; that would only give a city the reputation of skill in carpentering.

Then a city is not to be called wise because possessing a knowledge which counsels for the best about wooden implements?

Certainly not.

Nor by reason of a knowledge which advises about brazen pots, I said, nor as possessing any other similar knowledge?

Not by reason of any of them, he said.

Nor yet by reason of a knowledge which cultivates the earth; that would give the city the name of agricultural?

Yes.

Well, I said, and is there any knowledge in our recently founded State among any of the citizens which advises, not about any particular thing in the State, but about the whole, and considers how a State can best deal with itself and with other States?

There certainly is.

And what is knowledge, and among whom is it found? I asked.

It is the knowledge of the guardians, he replied, and found among those whom we were just now describing as perfect guardians.

And what is the name which the city derives from the possession of this sort of knowledge?

The name of good in counsel and truly wise.

And will there be in our city more of these true guardians or more smiths?

The smiths, he replied, will be far more numerous.

Will not the guardians be the smallest of all the classes who receive a name from the profession of some kind of knowledge?

Much the smallest.

And so by reason of the smallest part or class, and of the knowledge which resides in this presiding and ruling part of itself, the whole State, being thus constituted according to nature, will be wise; and this, which has the only knowledge worthy to be called wisdom, has been ordained by nature to be of all classes the least.

Most true.

Thus, then, I said, the nature and place in the State of one of the four virtues has somehow or other been discovered.

And, in my humble opinion, very satisfactorily discovered, he replied.

Again, I said, there is no difficulty in seeing the nature of courage; and in what part that quality resides which gives the name of courageous to the State.

How do you mean?

Why, I said, every one who calls any State courageous or cowardly, will be thinking of the part which fights and goes out to war on the State's behalf.

No one, he replied, would ever think of any other.

Certainly not.

The rest of the citizens may be courageous or may be cowardly but their courage or cowardice will not, as I conceive, have the effect of making the city either the one or the other.

The city will be courageous in virtue of a portion of herself which preserves under all circumstances that opinion about the nature of things to be feared and not to be feared in which our legislator educated them; and this is what you term courage.

I should like to hear what you are saying once more, for I do not think that I perfectly understand you.

I mean that courage is a kind of salvation.

Salvation of what?

Of the opinion respecting things to be feared, what they are and of what nature, which the law implants through education; and I mean by the words "under all circumstances" to intimate that in pleasure or in pain, or under the influence of desire or fear, a man preserves, and does not lose this opinion. Shall I give you an illustration?

If you please.

You know, I said, that dyers, when they want to dye wool for making the true sea-purple, begin by selecting their white colour first; this they prepare and dress with much care and pains, in order that the white ground may take the purple hue in full perfection. The dyeing then proceeds; and whatever is dyed in this manner becomes a fast colour, and no washing either with lyes or without them can take away the bloom. But, when the ground has not been duly prepared, you will have noticed how poor is the look either of purple or of any other colour.

Yes, he said; I know that they have a washed-out and ridiculous appearance.

Then now, I said, you will understand what our object was in selecting our soldiers, and educating them in music and gymnastic; we were contriving influences which would prepare them to take the dye of the laws in perfection, and the colour of their opinion about dangers and of every other opinion was to be indelibly fixed by their nurture and training, not to be washed away by such potent lyes as pleasure—mightier agent far in washing the soul than any soda or lye; or by sorrow, fear, and desire, the mightiest of all other solvents. And this sort of universal saving power of true opinion in conformity with law about real and false dangers I call and maintain to be courage, unless you disagree.

But I agree, he replied; for I suppose that you mean to exclude mere uninstructed courage, such as that of a wild beast or of a slave—this, in your opinion, is not the courage which the law ordains, and ought to have another name.

Most certainly.

Then I may infer courage to be such as you describe?

Why, yes, said I, you may, and if you add the words "of a citizen," you will not be far wrong;—hereafter, if you like, we will carry the examination further, but at present we are seeking not for courage but justice; and for the purpose of our enquiry we have said enough.

You are right, he replied.

Two virtues remain to be discovered in the State—first temperance, and then justice which is the end of our search.

Very true.

Now, can we find justice without troubling ourselves about temperance?

I do not know how that can be accomplished, he said, nor do I desire that justice should be brought to light and temperance lost sight of; and therefore I wish that you would do me the favour of considering temperance first.

Certainly, I replied, I should not be justified in refusing your request.

Then consider, he said.

Yes, I replied, I will; and as far as I can at present see, the virtue of temperance has more of the nature of harmony and symphony than the preceding.

How so? he asked.

Temperance, I replied, is the ordering or controlling of certain pleasures and desires; this is curiously enough implied in the saying of "a man being his own master" and other traces of the same notion may be found in language.

No doubt, he said.

There is something ridiculous in the expression "master of himself;" for the master is also the servant and the servant the master; and in all these modes of speaking the same person is denoted.

Certainly.

The meaning is, I believe, that in the human soul there is a better and also a worse principle; and when the better has the worse under control, then a man is said to be master of himself; and this is a term of praise: but when, owing to evil education or association, the better principle, which is also the smaller, is overwhelmed by the greater mass of the worse—in this case he is blamed and is called the slave of self and unprincipled.

Yes, there is reason in that.

And now, I said, look at our newly created State, and there you will find one of these two conditions realised; for the State, as you will acknowledge, may be justly called master of itself, if the words "temperance" and "self-mastery" truly express the rule of the better part over the worse.

Yes, he said, I see that what you say is true.

Let me further note that the manifold and complex pleasures and desires and pains are generally found in children and women and servants, and in the freemen so called who are of the lowest and more numerous class.

Certainly, he said.

Whereas the simple and moderate desires which follow reason, and are under the guidance of mind and true opinion, are to be found only in a few, and those the best born and best educated.

Very true.

These two, as you may perceive, have a place in our State; and the meaner desires of the many are held down by the virtuous desires and wisdom of the few.

That I perceive, he said.

Then if there be any city which may be described as master of its own pleasures and desires, and master of itself, ours may claim such a designation?

Certainly, he replied.

It may also be called temperate, and for the same reasons?

Yes.

And if there be any State in which rulers and subjects will be agreed as to the question who are to rule, that again will be our State?

Undoubtedly.

And the citizens being thus agreed among themselves, in which class will temperance be found—in the rulers or in the subjects?

In both, as I should imagine, he replied.

Do you observe that we were not far wrong in our guess that temperance was a sort of harmony?

Why so?

Why, because temperance is unlike courage and wisdom, each of which resides in a part only, the one making the State wise and the other valiant; not so temperance, which extends to the whole, and runs through all the notes of the scale, and produces a harmony of the weaker and the stronger and the middle class, whether you suppose them to be stronger or weaker in wisdom or power or numbers or wealth, or anything else. Most truly then may we deem temperance to be the agreement of the naturally superior and inferior, as to the right to rule of either, both in states and individuals.

I entirely agree with you.

And so, I said, we may consider three out of the four virtues to have been discovered in our State. The last of those qualities which make a state virtuous must be justice, if we only knew what that was.

The inference is obvious.

The time then has arrived, Glaucon, when, like huntsmen, we should surround the cover, and look sharp that justice does not steal away, and pass out of sight and escape us; for beyond a doubt she is somewhere in this country: watch therefore and strive to catch a sight of her, and if you see her first, let me know.

Would that I could! but you should regard me rather as a follower who has just eyes enough to see what you show him—that is about as much as I am good for.

Offer up a prayer with me and follow.

I will, but you must show me the way.

Here is no path, I said, and the wood is dark and perplexing; still we must push on.

Let us push on.

Here I saw something: Halloo! I said, I begin to perceive a track, and I believe that the quarry will not escape.

Good news, he said.

Truly, I said, we are stupid fellows.

Why so?

Why, my good sir, at the beginning of our enquiry, ages ago, there was justice tumbling out at our feet, and we never saw her; nothing could be more ridiculous. Like people who go about looking for what they have in their hands—that was the way with us—we looked not at what we were seeking, but at what was far off in the distance; and therefore, I suppose, we missed her.

What do you mean?

I mean to say that in reality for a long time past we have been talking of justice, and have failed to recognise her.

I grow impatient at the length of your exordium.

Well then, tell me, I said, whether I am right or not: You remember the original principle which we were always laying down at the foundation of the State, that one man should practise one thing only, the thing to which his nature was best adapted;—now justice is this principle or a part of it.

Yes, we often said that one man should do one thing only.

Further, we affirmed that justice was doing one's own business, and not being a busybody; we said so again and again, and many others have said the same to us.

Yes, we said so.

Then to do one's own business in a certain way may be assumed to be justice. Can you tell me whence I derive this inference?

I cannot, but I should like to be told.

Because I think that this is the only virtue which remains in the State when the other virtues of temperance and courage and wisdom are abstracted; and, that this is the ultimate cause and condition of the existence of all of them, and while remaining in them is also their preservative; and we were saying that if the three were discovered by us, justice would be the fourth or remaining one.

That follows of necessity.

If we are asked to determine which of these four qualities by its presence contributes most to the excellence of the State, whether the agreement of rulers and subjects, or the preservation in the soldiers of the opinion which the law ordains about the true nature of dangers, or wisdom and watchfulness in the rulers, or whether this other which I am mentioning, and which is found in children and women, slave and freeman, artisan, ruler, subject—the quality, I mean, of every one doing his own work, and not being a busybody, would claim the palm—the question is not so easily answered.

Certainly, he replied, there would be a difficulty in saying which.

Then the power of each individual in the State to do his own work appears to compete with the other political virtues, wisdom, temperance, courage.

Yes, he said.

And the virtue which enters into this competition is justice?

Exactly.

Let us look at the question from another point of view: Are not the rulers in a State those to whom you would entrust the office of determining suits at law?

Certainly.

And are suits decided on any other ground but that a man may neither take what is another's, nor be deprived of what is his own?

Yes; that is their principle.

Which is a just principle?

Yes.

Then on this view also justice will be admitted to be the having and doing what is a man's own, and belongs to him?

Very true.

Think, now, and say whether you agree with me or not. Suppose a carpenter to be doing the business of a cobbler, or a cobbler of a carpenter; and suppose them to exchange their implements or their duties, or the same person to be doing the work of both, or whatever be the change; do you think that any great harm would result to the State?

Not much.

But when the cobbler or any other man whom nature designed to be a trader, having his heart lifted up by wealth or strength or the number of his followers, or any like advantage, attempts to force his way into the class of warriors, or a warrior into that of legislators and guardians, for which he is unfitted, and either to take the implements or the duties of the other; or when one man is trader, legislator, and warrior all in one, then I think you will agree with me in saying that this interchange and this meddling of one with another is the ruin of the State.

Most true.

Seeing then, I said, that there are three distinct classes, any meddling of one with another, or the change of one into another, is the greatest harm to the State, and may be most justly termed evil-doing?

Precisely.

And the greatest degree of evil-doing to one's own city would be termed by you injustice?

Certainly.

This then is injustice; and on the other hand when the trader, the auxiliary, and the guardian each do their own business, that is justice, and will make the city just.

I agree with you. . . .

You will admit that the same education which makes a man a good guardian will make a woman a good guardian; for their original nature is the same?

Yes.

I should like to ask you a question.

What is it?

Would you say that all men are equal in excellence, or is one man better than another?

The latter.

And in the commonwealth which we were founding do you conceive the guardians who have been brought up on our model system to be more perfect men, or the cobblers whose education has been cobbling?

What a ridiculous question!

You have answered me, I replied: Well, and may we not further say that our guardians are the best of our citizens?

By far the best.

And will not their wives be the best women?

Yes, by far the best.

And can there be anything better for the interests of the State than that the men and women of a State should be as good as possible?

There can be nothing better.

And this is what the arts of music and gymnastic, when present in such manner as we have described, will accomplish?

Certainly.

Then we have made an enactment not only possible but in the highest degree beneficial to the State?

True. . . .

I was only going to ask whether, if we have discovered them, we are to require that the just man should in nothing fail of absolute justice; or may we be satisfied with an approximation, and the attainment in him of a higher degree of justice than is to be found in other men?

The approximation will be enough.

We are enquiring into the nature of absolute justice and into the character of the perfectly just, and into injustice and the perfectly unjust, that we might have an ideal. We were to look at these in order that we might judge of our own happiness and unhappiness according to the standard which they exhibited and the degree in which we resembled them, but not with any view of showing that they could exist in fact.

True, he said.

Would a painter be any the worse because, after having delineated with consummate art an ideal of a perfectly beautiful man, he was unable to show that any such man could ever have existed?

He would be none the worse.

Well, and were we not creating an ideal of a perfect State?

To be sure.

And is our theory a worse theory because we are unable to prove the possibility of a city being ordered in the manner described?

Surely not, he replied.

That is the truth, I said. But if, at your request, I am to try and show how and under what conditions the possibility is highest, I must ask you, having this in view, to repeat your former admissions.

What admissions?

I want to know whether ideals are ever fully realised in language? Does not the word express more than the fact, and must not the actual, whatever a man may think, always, in the nature of things, fall short of the truth? What do you say?

I agree.

Then you must not insist on my proving that the actual State will in every respect coincide with the ideal: if we are only able to discover how a city may be governed nearly as we proposed, you will admit that we have discovered the possibility which you demand; and will be contented. I am sure that I should be contented—will not you?

Yes, I will.

Let me next endeavour to show what is that fault in States which is the cause of their present maladministration, and what is the least change which will enable a State to pass into the truer form; and let the change, if possible, be of one thing only, or if not, of two; at any rate, let the changes be as few and slight as possible.

Certainly, he replied.

I think, I said, that there might be a reform of the State if only one change were made, which is not a slight or easy though still a possible one.

What is it? he said.

Now then, I said, I go to meet that which I liken to the greatest of the waves; yet shall the word be spoken, even though the wave break and drown me in laughter and dishonour; and do you mark my words.

Proceed.

I said: Until philosophers are kings, or the kings and princes of this world have the spirit and power of philosophy, and political greatness and wisdom meet in one, and those commoner natures who pursue either to the exclusion of the other are compelled to stand aside, cities will never have rest from their evils—nor the human race, as I believe—and then only will this our State have a possibility of life and behold the light of day. Such was the thought, my dear Glaucon, which I would fain have uttered if it had not seemed too extravagant; for to be convinced that in no other State can there be happiness private or public is indeed a hard thing.

Book VIII

And so, Glaucon, we have arrived at the conclusion that in the perfect State wives and children are to be in common; and that all education and the pursuits of war and peace are also to be common, and the best philosophers and the bravest warriors are to be their kings?

That, replied Glaucon, has been acknowledged.

Yes, I said; and we have further acknowledged that the governors, when appointed themselves, will take their soldiers and place them in houses such as we were describing, which are common to all, and contain nothing private, or individual; and about their property, you remember what we agreed?

Yes, I remember that no one was to have any of the ordinary possessions of mankind; they were to be warrior athletes and guardians, receiving from the other citizens, in lieu of annual payment, only their maintenance, and they were to take care of themselves and of the whole State.

True, I said; and now that this division of our task is concluded, let us find the point at which we digressed, that we may return into the old path.

There is no difficulty in returning; you implied, then as now, that you had finished the description of the State: you said that such a State was good, and that the man was good who answered to it, although, as now appears, you had more excellent things to relate both of State and man. And you said further, that if this was the true form, then the others were false; and of the false forms, you said, as I remember, that there were four principal ones, and that their defects, and the defects of the individuals corresponding to them, were worth examining. When we had seen all the individuals, and finally agreed as to who was the best and who was the worst of them, we were to consider whether the best was not also the happiest, and the worst the most miserable. I asked you what were the four forms of government of which you spoke, and then Polemarchus and Adeimantus put in their word; and you began again, and have found your way to the point at which we have now arrived.

Your recollection, I said, is most exact.

Then, like a wrestler, he replied, you must put yourself again in the same position; and let me ask the same questions, and do you give me the same answer which you were about to give me then.

Yes, if I can, I will, I said.

I shall particularly wish to hear what were the four constitutions of which you were speaking.

That question, I said, is easily answered: the four governments of which I spoke, so far as they have distinct names, are, first, those of Crete and Sparta, which are generally applauded; what is termed oligarchy comes next; this is not equally approved, and is a form of government which teems with evils; thirdly, democracy, which naturally follows oligarchy, although very different, and lastly comes tyranny, great and famous, which differs from them all, and is the fourth and worst disorder of a State. I do not know, do you? of any other constitution which can be said to have a distinct character. There are lordships and principalities which are bought and sold, and some other intermediate forms of government. But these are nondescripts and may be found equally among Hellenes and among barbarians.

Yes, he replied, we certainly hear of many curious forms of government which exist among them.

Do you know, I said, that governments vary as the dispositions of men vary, and that there must be as many of the one as there are of the other? For we cannot suppose that States are made of "oak and rock," and not out of the human natures which are in them, and which in a figure turn the scale and draw other things after them?

Yes, he said, the States are as the men are; they grow out of human characters.

Then if the constitutions of States are five, the dispositions of individual minds will also be five?

Certainly.

Him who answers to aristocracy, and whom we rightly call just and good, we have already described.

We have.

Then let us now proceed to describe the inferior sort of natures, being the contentious and ambitious, who answer to the Spartan polity; also the oligarchical, democratical, and tyrannical. Let us place the most just by the side of the most unjust, and when we see them we shall be able to compare the relative happiness or unhappiness of him who leads a life of pure justice or pure injustice. The enquiry will then be completed. And we shall know whether we ought to pursue injustice, as Thrasymachus advises, or in accordance with the conclusions of the argument to prefer justice.

Certainly, he replied, we must do as you say.

Shall we follow our old plan, which we adopted with a view to clearness, of taking the State first and then proceeding to the individual, and begin with the government of honour?—I know of no name for such a government other than timocracy, or perhaps timarchy. We will compare with this the like character in the individual; and, after that, consider oligarchical man; and then again we will turn our attention to democracy and the democratical man; and lastly, we will go and view the city of tyranny, and once more take a look into the tyrant's soul, and try to arrive at a satisfactory decision.

That way of viewing and judging of the matter will be very suitable.

First, then, I said, let us enquire how timocracy (the government of honour) arises out of aristocracy (the government of the best). Clearly, all political changes originate in divisions of the actual governing power; a government which is united, however small, cannot be moved.

Very true, he said. . . .

And the new government which thus arises will be of a form intermediate between oligarchy and aristocracy?

Very true.

Such will be the change, and after the change has been made, how will they proceed? Clearly, the new State, being in a mean between oligarchy and the perfect State, will partly follow one and partly the other, and will also have some peculiarities.

True, he said.

In the honour given to rulers, in the abstinence of the warrior class from agriculture, handicrafts, and trade in general, in the institution of common meals, and in the attention paid to gymnastics and military training—in all these respects this State will resemble the former.

True.

But in the fear of admitting philosophers to power, because they are no longer to be had simple and earnest, but are made up of mixed elements; and in turning from them to passionate and less complex characters, who are by nature fitted for war rather than peace; and in the value set by them upon military stratagems and contrivances, and in the waging of everlasting wars—this State will be for the most part peculiar.

Yes.

Yes, I said; and men of this stamp will be covetous of money, like those who live in oligarchies; they will have a fierce secret longing after gold and silver, which they will hoard in dark places, having magazines and treasuries of their own for the deposit and concealment of them; also castles which are just nests for their eggs, and in which they will spend large sums on their wives, or on any others whom they please.

That is most true, he said.

And they are miserly because they have no means of openly acquiring the money which they prize; they will spend that which is another man's on the gratification of their desires, stealing their pleasures and running away like children from the law, their father: they have been schooled not by gentle influences but by force, for they have neglected her who is the true Muse, the companion of reason and philosophy, and have honoured gymnastic more than music.

Undoubtedly, he said, the form of government which you describe is a mixture of good and evil.

Why, there is a mixture, I said; but one thing, and one thing only, is predominantly seen—the spirit of contention and ambition; and these are due to the prevalence of the passionate or spirited element.

Assuredly, he said.

Such is the origin and such the character of this State, which has been described in outline only; the more perfect execution was not required, for a sketch is enough to show the type of the most perfectly just and most perfectly unjust; and to go through all the States and all the characters of men, omitting none of them, would be an interminable labour.

Very true, he replied. . . .

I believe that oligarchy follows next in order.

And what manner of government do you term oligarchy?

A government resting on a valuation of property, in which the rich have power and the poor man is deprived of it.

I understand, he replied.

Ought I not to begin by describing how the change from timocracy to oligarchy arises?

Yes.

Well, I said, no eyes are required in order to see how the one passes into the other.

How?

The accumulation of gold in the treasury of private individuals is the ruin of timocracy; they invent illegal modes of expenditure; for what do they or their wives care about the law?

Yes, indeed.

And then one, seeing another grow rich, seeks to rival him, and thus the great mass of the citizens become lovers of money.

Likely enough.

And so they grow richer and richer, and the more they think of making a fortune the less they think of virtue; for when riches and virtue are placed together in the scales of the balance, the one always rises as the other falls.

True.

And in proportion as riches and rich men are honoured in the State, virtue and the virtuous are dishonoured.

Clearly.

And what is honoured is cultivated, and that which has no honour is neglected.

That is obvious.

And so at last, instead of loving contention and glory, men become lovers of trade and money; they honour and look up to the rich man, and make a ruler of him, and dishonour the poor man.

They do so.

They next proceed to make a law which fixes a sum of money as the qualification of citizenship; the sum is higher in one place and lower in another, as the oligarchy is more or less exclusive; and they allow no one whose property falls below the amount fixed to have any share in the government. These changes in the constitution they effect by force of arms, if intimidation has not already done their work.

Very true.

And this, speaking generally, is the way in which oligarchy is established.

Yes, he said; but what are the characteristics of this form of government, and what are the defects of which we were speaking?

First of all, I said, consider the nature of the qualification: just think what would happen if pilots were to be chosen according to their property, and a poor man were refused permission to steer, even though he were a better pilot?

You mean that they would shipwreck?

Yes; and is not this true of the government of anything?

I should imagine so.

Except a city? Or would you include a city?

Nay, he said, the case of a city is the strongest of all, inasmuch as the rule of a city is the greatest and most difficult of all.

This, then, will be the first great defect of oligarchy?

Clearly.

And here is another defect which is quite as bad.

What defect?

The inevitable division: such a State is not one, but two States, the one of poor, the other of rich men; and they are living on the same spot and always conspiring against one another.

That, surely, is at least as bad.

Another discreditable feature is, that, for a like reason, they are incapable of carrying on any war. Either they arm the multitude, and then they are more afraid of them than of the enemy; or, if they do not call them out in the hour of battle, they are oligarchs indeed, few to fight as they are few to rule. And at the same time their fondness for money makes them unwilling to pay taxes.

How discreditable!

And, as we said before, under such a constitution the same persons have too many callings—they are husbandmen, tradesmen, warriors, all in one. Does that look well?

Anything but well.

There is another evil which is, perhaps, the greatest of all, and to which this State first begins to be liable.

What evil?

A man may sell all that he has, and another may acquire his property; yet after the sale he may dwell in the city of which he is no longer a part, being neither trader, nor artisan, nor horseman, nor hoplite, but only a poor, helpless creature.

Yes, that is an evil which also first begins in this State.

The evil is certainly not prevented there; for oligarchies have both the extremes of great wealth and utter poverty.

True.

But think again: In his wealthy days, while he was spending his money, was a man of this sort a whit more good to the State for the purposes of citizenship? Or did he only seem to be a member of the ruling body, although in truth he was neither ruler nor subject, but just a spendthrift?

As you say, he seemed to be a ruler, but was only a spendthrift.

May we not say that this is the drone in the house who is like the drone in the honeycomb, and that the one is the plague of the city as the other is of the hive?

Just so, Socrates.

And God has made the flying drones, Adeimantus, all without stings, whereas of the walking drones he has made some without stings but others have dreadful stings; of the stingless class are those who in their old age end as paupers; of the stingers come all the criminal class, as they are termed.

Most true, he said.

Clearly then, whenever you see paupers in a State, somewhere in that neighborhood there are hidden away thieves, and cutpurses and robbers of temples, and all sorts of malefactors.

Clearly.

Well, I said, and in oligarchical States do you not find paupers?

Yes, he said; nearly everybody is a pauper who is not a ruler.

And may we be so bold as to affirm that there are also many criminals to be found in them, rogues who have stings, and whom the authorities are careful to restrain by force?

Certainly, we may be so bold.

The existence of such persons is to be attributed to want of education, ill-training, and an evil constitution of the State?

True.

Such, then, is the form and such are the evils of oligarchy; and there may be many other evils.

Very likely.

Then oligarchy, or the form of government in which the rulers are elected for their wealth, may now be dismissed. . . .

Next comes democracy; of this the origin and nature have still to be considered by us; and then we will enquire into the ways of the democratic man, and bring him up for judgement.

That, he said, is our method.

Well, I said, and how does the change from oligarchy into democracy arise? Is it not on this wise? The good at which such a State aims is to become as rich as possible, a desire which is insatiable?

What then?

The rulers, being aware that their power rests upon their wealth, refuse to curtail by law the extravagance of the spendthrift youth because they gain by their ruin; they take interest from them and buy up their estates and thus increase their own wealth and importance?

To be sure.

There can be no doubt that the love of wealth and the spirit of moderation cannot exist together in citizens of the same State to any considerable extent; one or the other will be disregarded.

That is tolerably clear.

And in oligarchical States, from the general spread of carelessness and extravagance, men of good family have often been reduced to beggary?

Yes, often.

And still they remain in the city; there they are, ready to sting and fully armed, and some of them owe money, some have forfeited their citizenship; a third class are in both predicaments; and they hate and conspire against those who have got their property, and against everybody else, and are eager for revolution.

That is true.

On the other hand, the men of business, stooping as they walk, and pretending not even to see those whom they have already ruined, insert their sting—that is, their money—into some one else who is not on his guard against them, and recover the parent sum many times over multiplied into a family of children: and so they make drone and pauper to abound in the State.

Yes, he said, there are plenty of them—that is certain.

The evil blazes up like a fire; and they will not extinguish it, either by restricting a man's use of his own property, or by another remedy.

What other?

One which is the next best, and has the advantage of compelling the citizens to look to their characters:—Let there be a general rule that every one shall enter into voluntary contracts at his own risk, and there will be less of this scandalous money-making, and the evils of which we were speaking will be greatly lessened in the State.

Yes, they will be greatly lessened.

At present the governors, induced by the motives which I have named, treat their subjects badly; while they and their adherents, especially the young men of the governing class, are habituated to lead a life of luxury and idleness both of body and mind; they do nothing, and are incapable of resisting either pleasure or pain.

Very true.

They themselves care only for making money, and are as indifferent as the pauper to the cultivation of virtue.

Yes, quite as indifferent.

Such is the state of affairs which prevails among them. And often rulers and their subjects may come in one another's way, whether on a pilgrimage or a march, as fellow-soldiers or fellow-sailors; aye, and they may observe the behaviour of each other in the very moment of danger—for where danger is, there is no fear that the poor will be despised by the rich—and very likely the wiry sunburnt poor man may be placed in battle at the side of a wealthy one who has never spoilt his complexion and has plenty of superfluous flesh—when he sees such an one puffing and at his wit's end, how can he avoid drawing the conclusion that men like him are only rich because no one has the courage to despoil them? And when they meet in private will not people be saying to one another "Our warriors are not good for much"?

Yes, he said, I am quite aware that this is their way of talking.

And, as in a body which is diseased the addition of a touch from without may bring on illness, and sometimes even when there is no external provocation a commotion may arise within—in the same way wherever there is weakness in the State there is also likely to be illness, of which the occasions may be very slight, the one party introducing from without their oligarchical, the other their democratical allies, and then the State falls sick, and is at war with herself; and may be at times distracted, even when there is no external cause.

Yes, surely.

And then democracy comes into being after the poor have conquered their opponents, slaughtering some and banishing some, while to the remainder they give an equal share of freedom and power; and this is the form of government in which the magistrates are commonly elected by lot.

Yes, he said, that is the nature of democracy, whether the revolution has been effected by arms, or whether fear has caused the opposite party to withdraw.

And now what is their manner of life, and what sort of a government have they? for as the government is, such will be the man.

Clearly, he said.

In the first place, are they not free; and is not the city full of freedom and frankness—a man may say and do what he likes?

'Tis said so, he replied.

And where freedom is, the individual is clearly able to order for himself his own life as he pleases?

Clearly.

Then in this kind of State there will be the greatest variety of human natures?

There will.

This, then, seems likely to be the fairest of States, being an embroidered robe which is spangled with every sort of flower. And just as women and children think a variety of colours to be of all things most charming, so there are many men to whom this State, which is spangled with the manners and characters of mankind, will appear to be the fairest of States.

Yes.

Yes, my good Sir, and there will be no better in which to look for a government.

Why?

Because of the liberty which reigns there—they have a complete assortment of constitutions; and he who has a mind to establish a State, as we have been doing, must go to a democracy as he would to a bazaar at which they sell them, and pick out the one that suits him; then, when he has made his choice, he may found his State.

He will be sure to have patterns enough.

And there being no necessity, I said, for you to govern in this State, even if you have the capacity, or to be governed, unless you like, or go to war when the rest go to war, or to be at peace when others are at peace, unless you are so disposed—there being no necessity also, because some law forbids you to hold office or be a dicast, that you should not hold office or be a dicast, if you have a fancy—is not this a way of life which for the moment is supremely delightful?

For the moment, yes.

And is not their humanity to the condemned in some cases quite charming? Have you not observed how, in a democracy, many persons, although they have been sentenced to death or exile, just stay where they are and walk about the world—the gentleman parades like a hero, and nobody sees or cares?

Yes, he replied, many and many a one.

See too, I said, the forgiving spirit of democracy, and the "don't care" about trifles, and the disregard which she shows of all the fine principles which we solemnly laid down at the foundation of the city—as when we said that, except in the case of some rarely gifted nature, there never will be a good man who has not from his childhood been used to play amid things of beauty and make of them a joy and a study—how grandly does she trample all these fine notions of ours under her feet, never giving a thought to the pursuits which make a statesman, and promoting to honour any one who professes to be the people's friend.

Yes, she is of a noble spirit.

These and other kindred characteristics are proper to democracy, which is a charming form of government, full of variety and disorder, and dispensing a sort of equality to equals and unequals alike.

We know her well. . . .

Last of all comes the most beautiful of all, man and State alike, tyranny and the tyrant; these we have now to consider.

Quite true, he said.

Say then, my friend, in what manner does tyranny arise?—that it has a democratic origin is evident.

Clearly.

And does not tyranny spring from democracy in the same manner as democracy from oligarchy—I mean, after a sort?

How?

The good which oligarchy proposed to itself and the means by which it was maintained was excess of wealth—am I not right?

Yes.

And the insatiable desire of wealth and the neglect of all other things for the sake of money-getting was also the ruin of oligarchy?

True.

And democracy has her own good, of which the insatiable desire brings her to dissolution?

What good?

Freedom, I replied; which, as they tell you in a democracy, is the glory of the State—and that therefore in a democracy alone will the freeman of nature deign to dwell.

Yes; the saying is in everybody's mouth.

I was going to observe, that the insatiable desire of this and the neglect of other things introduces the change in democracy, which occasions a demand for tyranny.

How so?

When a democracy which is thirsting for freedom has evil cupbearers presiding over the feast, and has drunk too deeply of the strong wine of freedom, then, unless her rulers are very amenable and give a plentiful draught, she calls them to account and punishes them, and says that they are cursed oligarchs.

Yes, he replied, a very common occurrence.

Yes, I said; and loyal citizens are insultingly termed by her slaves who hug their chains and men of naught; she would have subjects who are like rulers, and rulers who are like subjects: these are men after her own heart, whom she praises and honours both in private and public. Now, in such a State, can liberty have any limit?

Certainly not.

By degrees the anarchy finds a way into private houses, and ends by getting among the animals and infecting them.

How do you mean?

I mean that the father grows accustomed to descend to the level of his sons and to fear them, and the son is on a level with his father, he having no respect or reverence for either of his parents; and this is his freedom, and foreigner is equal with the citizen and the citizen with the foreigner, and the stranger is quite as good as either.

Yes, he said, that is the way.

And these are not the only evils, I said—there are several lesser ones: In such a state of society the master fears and flatters his scholars, and the scholars despise their masters and tutors; young and old are all alike; and the young man is on a level with the old, and is ready to compete with him in word or deed; and old men condescend to the young and are full of pleasantry and gaiety; they are loath to be thought morose and authoritative, and therefore they adopt the manners of the young.

Quite true, he said.

The last extreme of popular liberty is when the slave bought with money, whether male or female, is just as free as his or her purchaser; nor must I forget to tell of the liberty and equality of the two sexes in relation to each other.

Why not, as Aeschylus says, utter the word which rises to our lips?

That is what I am doing, I replied; and I must add that no one who does not know would believe, how much greater is the liberty which the animals who are under the dominion of man have in a democracy than in any other State: for truly, the she-dogs, as the proverb says, are as good as their she-mistresses, and the horses and asses have a way of marching along with all the rights and dignities of freemen; and they will run at anybody who comes in their way if he does not leave the road clear for them: and all things are just ready to burst with liberty.

When I take a country walk, he said, I often experience what you describe. You and I have dreamed the same thing.

And above all, I said, and as the result of all, see how sensitive the citizens become; they chafe impatiently at the least touch of authority and at length, as you know, they cease to care even for the laws, written or unwritten; they will have no one over them.

Yes, he said, I know it too well.

Such, my friend, I said, is the fair and glorious beginning out of which springs tyranny.

Glorious indeed, he said. But what is the next step?

The ruin of oligarchy is the ruin of democracy; the same disease magnified and intensified by liberty overmasters democracy—the truth being that the excessive increase of anything often causes a reaction in the opposite direction; and this is the case not only in the seasons and in vegetable and animal life, but above all in forms of government.

True.

The excess of liberty, whether in States or individuals, seems only to pass into excess of slavery.

Yes, the natural order.

And so tyranny naturally arises out of democracy, and the most aggravated form of tyranny and slavery out of the most extreme form of liberty?

As we might expect.

That, however, was not, as I believe, your question—you rather desired to know what is that disorder which is generated alike in oligarchy and democracy, and is the ruin of both?

Just so, he replied.

Well, I said, I meant to refer to the class of idle spendthrifts, of whom the more courageous are the leaders and the more timid the followers, the same whom we were comparing to drones, some stingless, and others having stings.

A very just comparison.

These two classes are the plagues of every city in which they are generated, being what phlegm and bile are to the body. And the good physician and lawgiver of the State ought, like the wise bee-master, to keep them at a distance and prevent, if possible, their ever coming in; and if they have anyhow found a way in, then he should have them and their cells cut out as speedily as possible.

Yes, by all means, he said.

Then, in order that we may see clearly what we are doing, let us imagine democracy to be divided, as indeed it is, into three classes; for in the first place freedom creates rather more drones in the democratic than there were in the oligarchical State.

That is true.

And in the democracy they are certainly more intensified.

How so?

Because in the oligarchical State they are disqualified and driven from office, and therefore they cannot train or gather strength; whereas in a democracy they are almost the entire ruling power, and while the keener sort speak and act, the rest keep buzzing about the beeman and do not suffer a word to be said on the other side; hence in democracies almost everything is managed by the drones.

Very true, he said.

Then there is another class which is always being severed from the mass.

What is that?

They are the orderly class, which in a nation of traders is sure to be the richest.

Naturally so.

They are the most squeezable persons and yield the largest amount of honey to the drones.

Why, he said, there is little to be squeezed out of people who have little.

And this is called the wealthy class, and the drones feed upon them.

That is pretty much the case, he said.

The people are a third class, consisting of those who work with their own hands; they are not politicians, and have not much to live upon. This, when assembled, is the largest and most powerful class in a democracy.

True, he said; but then the multitude is seldom willing to congregate unless they get a little honey.

And do they not share? I said. Do not their leaders deprive the rich of their estates and distribute them among the people; at the same time taking care to reserve the larger part for themselves?

Why, yes, he said, to that extent the people do share.

And the persons whose property is taken from them are compelled to defend themselves before the people as they best can?

What else can they do?

And then, although they may have no desire of change, the others charge them with plotting against the people and being friends of oligarchy?

True.

And the end is that when they see the people, not of their own accord, but through ignorance, and because they are deceived by informers, seeking to do them wrong, then at last they are forced to become oligarchs in reality; they do not wish to be, but the sting of the drones torments them and breeds revolution in them.

That is exactly the truth.

Then come impeachments and judgments and trials of one another.

True.

The people have always some champion whom they set over them and nurse into greatness.

Yes, that is their way.

This and no other is the root from which a tyrant springs; when he first appears above ground he is a protector.

Yes, that is quite clear.

How then does a protector begin to change into a tyrant? Clearly when he does what the man is said to do in the tale of the Arcadian temple of Lycaean Zeus.

What tale?

The tale is that he who has tasted the entrails of a single human victim minced up with the entrails of other victims is destined to become a wolf. Did you never hear it?

Oh, yes.

And the protector of the people is like him; having a mob entirely at his disposal, he is not restrained from shedding the blood of kinsmen; by the favourite method of false accusation he brings them into court and murders them, making the life of man to disappear, and with unholy tongue and lips tasting the blood of his fellow citizen; some he kills and others he banishes, at the same time hinting at the abolition of debts and partition of lands: and after this, what will be his destiny? Must he not either perish at the hands of his enemies, or from being a man become a wolf—that is, a tyrant?

Inevitably.

This, I said, is he who begins to make a party against the rich?

The same.

After a while he is driven out, but comes back, in spite of his enemies, a tyrant full grown.

That is clear.

And if they are unable to expel him, or to get him condemned to death by a public accusation, they conspire to assassinate him.

Yes, he said, that is their usual way.

Then comes the famous request for a bodyguard, which is the device of all those who have got thus far in their tyrannical career—"Let not the people's friend," as they say, "be lost to them."

Exactly.

The people readily assent; all their fears are for him—they have none for themselves.

Very true.

And when a man who is wealthy and is also accused of being an enemy of the people sees this, then, my friend, as the oracle said to Croesus,

By pebbly Hermus' shore he flees and rests not and is not ashamed to be a coward.

And quite right too, said he, for if he were, he would never be ashamed again.

But if he is caught he dies.

Of course.

And he, the protector of whom we spoke, is to be seen, not "larding the plain" with his bulk, but himself the overthrower of many, standing up in the chariot of State with the reins in his hand, no longer protector, but tyrant absolute.

No doubt, he said.

And now let us consider the happiness of the man, and also of the State in which a creature like him is generated.

Yes, he said, let us consider that.

At first, in the early days of his power, he is full of smiles, and he salutes every one whom he meets;—he to be called a tyrant, who is making promises in public and also in private! liberating debtors, and distributing land to the people and his followers, and wanting to be so kind and good to every one!

Of course, he said.

But when he has disposed of foreign enemies by conquest or treaty, and there is nothing to fear from them, then he is always stirring up some war or other, in order that the people may require a leader.

To be sure.

Has he not also another object, which is that they may be impoverished by payment of taxes, and thus compelled to devote themselves to their daily wants and therefore less likely to conspire against him?

Clearly.

And if any of them are suspected by him of having notions of freedom, and of resistance to his authority, he will have a good pretext for destroying them by placing them at the mercy of the enemy; and for all these reasons the tyrant must be always getting up a war.

He must.

Now he begins to grow unpopular.

A necessary result.

Then some of those who joined in setting him up, and who are in power, speak their minds to him and to one another, and the more courageous of them cast in his teeth what is being done.

Yes, that may be expected.

And the tyrant, if he means to rule, must get rid of them; he cannot stop while he has a friend or an enemy who is good for anything.

He cannot.

And therefore he must look about him and see who is valiant, who is high-minded, who is wise, who is wealthy; happy man, he is the enemy of them all, and must seek occasion against them whether he will or no, until he has made a purgation of the State.

Yes, he said, and a rare purgation.

Yes, I said, not the sort of purgation which the physicians make of the body; for they take away the worse and leave the better part, but he does the reverse.

If he is to rule, I suppose that he cannot help himself.

What a blessed alternative, I said:—to be compelled to dwell only with the many bad, and to be by them hated, or not to live at all!

Yes, that is the alternative.

And the more detestable his actions are to the citizens the more satellites and the greater devotion in them will he require?

Certainly.

And who are the devoted band, and where will he procure them?

They will flock to him, he said, of their own accord, if lie pays them.

By the dog! I said, here are more drones, of every sort and from every land.

Yes, he said, there are.

But will he not desire to get them on the spot?

How do you mean?

He will rob the citizens of their slaves; he will then set them free and enroll them in his bodyguard.

To be sure, he said; and he will be able to trust them best of all.

What a blessed creature, I said, must this tyrant be; he has put to death the others and has these for his trusted friends.

Yes, he said; they are quite of his sort.

Yes, I said, and these are the new citizens whom he has called into existence, who admire him and are his companions, while the good hate and avoid him.

Of course.

Verily, then, tragedy is a wise thing and Euripides a great tragedian.

Why so?

Why, because he is the author of the pregnant saying, "Tyrants are wise by living with the wise;" and he clearly meant to say that they are the wise whom the tyrant makes his companions.

Yes, he said, and he also praises tyranny as godlike; and many other things of the same kind are said by him and by the other poets.

And therefore, I said, the tragic poets being wise men will forgive us and any others who live after our manner if we do not receive them into our State, because they are the eulogists of tyranny.

Yes, he said, those who have the wit will doubtless forgive us.

But they will continue to go to other cities and attract mobs, and hire voices fair and loud and persuasive, and draw the cities over to tyrannies and democracies.

Very true.

Moreover, they are paid for this and receive honour—the greatest honour, as might be expected, from tyrants, and the next greatest from democracies; but the higher they ascend our constitution hill, the more their reputation fails, and seems unable from short-ness of breath to proceed further.

True.

But we are wandering from the subject: Let us therefore return and enquire how the tyrant will maintain that fair and numerous and various and ever-changing army of his.

If, he said, there are sacred treasures in the city, he will confiscate and spend them; and in so far as the fortunes of attainted persons may suffice, he will be able to diminish the taxes which he would otherwise have to impose upon the people.

And when these fail?

Why, clearly, he said, then he and his boon companions, whether male or female, will be maintained out of his father's estate.

You mean to say that the people, from whom he has derived his being, will main-tain him and his companions?

Yes, he said; they cannot help themselves.

But what if the people fly into a passion, and aver that a grown-up son ought not to be supported by his father, but that the father should be supported by the son? The father did not bring him into being, or settle him in life, in order that when his son became a man he should himself be the servant of his own servants and should support him and his rabble of slaves and companions; but that his son should protect him, and that by his help he might be emancipated from the government of the rich and aristocratic, as they are termed. And so he bids him and his companions depart, just as any other father might drive out of the house a riotous son and his undesirable associates.

By heaven, he said, then the parent will discover what a monster he has been fos-tering in his bosom; and, when he wants to drive him out, he will find that he is weak and his son strong.

Why, you do not mean to say that the tyrant will use violence? What! beat his father if he opposes him?

Yes, he will, having first disarmed him.

Then he is a parricide, and a cruel guardian of an aged parent; and this is real tyranny, about which there can be no longer a mistake: as the saying is, the people who would escape the smoke which is the slavery of freemen, has fallen into the fire which is the tyranny of slaves. Thus liberty, getting out of all order and reason, passes into the harshest and bitterest form of slavery.

True, he said.

Very well; and may we not rightly say that we have sufficiently discussed the nature of tyranny, and the manner of the transition from democracy to tyranny?

Yes, quite enough, he said. . . .

Book IX

I understand; you mean that [the just man] will be a ruler in the city of which we are the founders, and which exists in idea only; for I do not believe that there is such an one anywhere on earth?

In heaven, I replied, there is laid up a pattern of it, methinks, which he who desires may behold, and beholding, may set his own house in order. But whether such an one exists, or ever will exist in fact, is no matter; for he will live after the manner of that city, having nothing to do with any other.

I think so, he said.

From Statesman*

STRANGER: You are a little too quick for me, Socrates! I was just going to cross-examine you to see if you really accepted all I have said or felt some objection. I realize, however, from what you say that the point we are anxious to discuss in detail is this question whether a good governor can govern without laws.

YOUNG SOCRATES: Yes, it is.

STRANGER: In one sense it is evident that the art of kingship does include the art of lawmaking. But the political ideal is not full authority for laws but rather full authority for a man who understands the art of kingship and has kingly ability. Do you understand why?

YOUNG SOCRATES: No, please tell me why.

STRANGER: Law can never issue an injunction binding on all which really embodies what is best for each; it cannot prescribe with perfect accuracy what is good and right for each member of the community at any one time. The differences of human personality, the variety of men's activities, and the inevitable unsettlement attending all human experience make it impossible for any art whatsoever to issue unqualified rules holding good on all questions at all times. I suppose that so far we are agreed.

YOUNG SOCRATES: Most emphatically.

STRANGER: But we find practically always that the law tends to issue just this invariable kind of rule. It is like a self-willed, ignorant man who lets no one do anything but what he has ordered and forbids all subsequent questioning of his orders even if the situation has shown some marked improvement on the one for which he originally legislated.

YOUNG SOCRATES: Yes, that is just how the law treats us all.

STRANGER: It is impossible, then, for something invariable and unqualified to deal satisfactorily with what is never uniform and constant.

YOUNG SOCRATES: I am afraid it is impossible.

STRANGER: But why then must there be a system of laws, seeing that law is not the ideal form of control? We must find out why a legal system is necessary.

YOUNG SOCRATES: We must.

STRANGER: You have courses of training here in Athens, have you not, just as they have in other cities—courses in which pupils are trained in a group to fit themselves for athletic contests in running or in other sports?

YOUNG SOCRATES: Of course. We have quite a number of them.

---

*An Excerpt.

STRANGER: Let us call to mind the commands which professional trainers give to the athletes under their regimen in these courses.

YOUNG SOCRATES: In what particular?

STRANGER: The view such trainers take is that they cannot do their work in detail and issue special commands adapted to the condition of each member of the group. When they lay down rules for physical welfare they find it necessary to give bulk instructions having regard to the general benefit of the average pupil.

YOUNG SOCRATES: Quite so.

STRANGER: That is why we find them giving the same exercises to whole groups of pupils, starting or stopping all of them at the same time in their running, wrestling, or whatever it may be.

YOUNG SOCRATES: Yes.

STRANGER: Similarly we must expect that the legislator who has to give orders to whole communities of human creatures in matters of right and of mutual contractual obligation will never be able in the laws he prescribes for the whole group to give every individual his due with absolute accuracy.

YOUNG SOCRATES: Very probably not.

STRANGER: But we shall find him making the law for the generality of his subjects under average circumstances. Thus he will legislate for all individual citizens, but it will be by what may be called a "bulk" method rather than an individual treatment, and this method of "bulk" prescription will be followed by him whether he makes a written code of law or refrains from issuing such a code, preferring to legislate by using unwritten ancestral customs.

YOUNG SOCRATES: Yes, and quite rightly so.

STRANGER: Of course he is right, Socrates. How could any lawgiver be capable of prescribing every act of a particular individual and sit at his side, so to speak, all through his life and tell him just what to do? And if among the few who have really attained this true statesmanship there arose one who was free to give this detailed guidance to an individual, he would hardly put obstacles in his own way by deliberately framing legal codes of the kind we are criticizing.

YOUNG SOCRATES: That certainly follows, sir, from what has been said.

STRANGER: I would rather say, Socrates, that it follows from what is going to be said.

YOUNG SOCRATES: And what is that?

STRANGER: Let us put this case to ourselves. A doctor or trainer plans to travel abroad and expects to be away from his charges for quite a long time. The doctor might well think that his patients would forget any verbal instructions he gave and the trainer might think likewise. In these circumstances each might want to leave written reminders of his orders—do you not think so yourself, Socrates?

YOUNG SOCRATES: Exactly so, sir.

STRANGER: Well now, suppose our doctor did not stay abroad as long as he had expected and so came back the sooner to his patients. Would he hesitate to substitute different prescriptions for the original ones if his patients' condition happened to be better than anticipated because of a climatic improvement or some other unusual and unexpected development of that kind? Would the doctor feel it his duty to maintain stubbornly that there must be no transgression of the strict letter of those original prescriptions of his? Would he refuse to issue new prescriptions or conditions, or condemn a patient who was venturing to act contrary to the prescriptions he had written out for him? Would the doctor declare all such action must be wrong because those former prescriptions were the true canons of medicine and of health and therefore that all contravention of them must lead to disease and be contrary to medical science? Surely any such claims, in circumstances where a science is involved and a real art is at work, would only make the man who made the claim and his precious prescriptions supremely ridiculous.

YOUNG SOCRATES: Yes, it would indeed.

STRANGER: Imagine then the case of a scientific legislator. Suppose that by a written code or by support given to unwritten customs he has laid down what is just and honorable and what is not, and what benefits society and what hurts it. Suppose him to do this service for the several communities of the human flock who live in their cities as their appointed pasture shepherded by the codes their legislators have provided. If this man, who drew up his code by the art of statesmanship, wishes to amend it, or if another scientific legislator of this kind appears on the scene, will these be forbidden to enact new laws differing from the earlier ones? Surely such a prohibition would appear as ridiculous in the case of the legislator as it was in the case of the doctor, would it not?

YOUNG SOCRATES: Of course.

STRANGER: But are you familiar with the argument one usually hears advanced when an issue like this is raised?

YOUNG SOCRATES: No, I cannot remember it at the moment, at any rate.

STRANGER: It is quite a plausible argument, I grant that. They contend that if a man discovers better laws than those already enacted he is entitled to get them brought into effect, but only if in every instance he has first persuaded his own city to accept them.

YOUNG SOCRATES: But what of this? Surely this is a sound contention.

STRANGER: It may be, but answer this question. Suppose a man fails to persuade his city and forces his better laws upon it, what name are we to apply to force so used? But no, do not answer me that question yet, for there are others to be answered first.

YOUNG SOCRATES: What can they be?

STRANGER: Consider once more the case of the patient under the doctor's treatment. Suppose that the doctor fails to persuade the patient but has a mastery of medical knowledge, and suppose that he forces a particular course of treatment which goes against written prescription but is actually more salutary on a child patient, maybe, or on a man or a woman. What are we to call force of this kind? Whatever we decide to call it, we shall not call it "the sin against true medicine" or "a breach of the laws of health." Surely the very last thing a patient who is so constrained is entitled to say is that the doctor's act in applying the constraint was contrary to good medicine and an aggravation of his disease.

YOUNG SOCRATES: You are quite right.

STRANGER: By what name, then, do we call the sin against the art of statesmanship? Would it not be called dishonor, vice, injustice?

YOUNG SOCRATES: Assuredly.

STRANGER: What, then, shall we say of citizens of a state who have been forced to do things which are contrary to written laws and ancestral customs but are nevertheless juster, more effective, and more noble than the directions of these traditional authorities? How shall we regard censure by these citizens of the force which has applied in these circumstances? Unless they wish to appear ridiculous in the extreme there is one thing they must refrain from saying. They must not assert in any such instance that in being subjected to compulsion they have suffered disgrace, injustice, or evil at the hands of those who compelled them.

YOUNG SOCRATES: That is quite true.

STRANGER: Can it be the case that acts imposed under compulsion are right if the compeller is rich, but wrong if he is poor? Surely what matters is that with or without persuasion, rich or poor, according to a code or against it, the ruler does what is really beneficial. These are the real issues and all is well if he passes this test, the only genuine test of good government in a community and the only principle by which the understanding and upright ruler will administer the affairs of those whom he rules. The ship's captain fixes his attention on the real welfare at any given time of his ship and his crew. He lays down no written enactments but supplies a law in action by practical application of his knowledge of seamanship to the needs of the voyage. It is in this way that he preserves the lives of all in his ship. Would not a true constitution be just like this and work in the same way if the rulers really understood what government is and employed their art as a stronger power for good than any written laws? By rulers with this sound attitude of mind no wrong can possibly be done so long as they keep firmly to the one great principle, that they must always administer impartial justice to their subjects under the guidance of intelligence and the art of government. Then they will not only preserve the lives of their subjects but reform their characters too, so far as human nature permits of this.

YOUNG SOCRATES: There can be no objection to your last remarks at any rate.

STRANGER: No, nor can there be to my earlier ones either.

YOUNG SOCRATES: To which are you referring?

STRANGER: You remember that we said that in no community whatsoever could it happen that a large number of people received this gift of political wisdom and the power to govern by pure intelligence which would accompany it. Only in the hands of the select few or of the enlightened individual can we look for that right exercise of political power which is itself the one true constitution. For we must call all other constitutions mere imitations of this. Some are more perfect copies of it; others are grosser and less adequate imitations.

YOUNG SOCRATES: What do you really mean by this? For I must admit that I did not really understand what you said before about these "imitations."

STRANGER: But I must make you understand. It would be a serious failing to start a discussion of this issue and then simply drop it without exposing the error which is rampant today in all that is said about it.

YOUNG SOCRATES: And what is this error?

STRANGER: That is what we must now seek out, though it involves a search over unfamiliar ground and the error is hard to discover. We may say, then, that there is only one constitution in the true sense—the one we have described. For the rest of them owe their very preservation to their following a code of laws enacted for this true state and to a strict adherence to a rule which we admit to be desirable though it falls short of the ideal.

YOUNG SOCRATES: What rule is this?

STRANGER: The rule that none of the citizens may venture to do any act contrary to the laws, and that if any of them ventures to do such act, the penalty is to be death or the utmost rigor of punishment. This is the justest and most desirable course as a second best when the ideal we have just described has been set aside. We must now go on to say how this state of affairs we have just called second best is achieved in practice, must we not?

YOUNG SOCRATES: Yes, we must.

STRANGER: Let us go back once again to the parallel cases with which we have constantly to compare the ruler who really is a statesman.

YOUNG SOCRATES: Who are they?

STRANGER: Our good friend the ship's captain and the doctor "worth a dozen other men." Let us picture to ourselves a situation in which they might find themselves and see how it all works out in their case.

YOUNG SOCRATES: What situation?

STRANGER: Suppose we all suddenly decided that we are the victims of the worst possible outrages at their hands. Every doctor, you see, can preserve the life of any he will among us, and can hurt any he will by knife or cautery or by demanding fees which are nothing but imposed taxes—for only the tiniest proportion of them is spent on medicaments for the patient and all the rest goes to keep the doctor and his household. Their final enormity is to accept bribes from the patient's relations or from his enemies and put him to death. Ships' captains are guilty of a different set of crimes, but they are just as heinous. They will enter into a conspiracy to put out to sea with you and then leave you stranded, or else they will scuttle the ship and throw the passengers overboard—and these are not all their misdeeds. Suppose we formed this view of doctors and captains and then held a council at which the following decree was passed.

Neither medicine nor seamanship may be trusted in future with absolute control in its particular sphere, either over slaves or over free citizens. We therefore resolve to gather together an assembly of *all*, or *of the wealthy among*, the people. It shall be lawful for men of no calling or men of any other calling to advise this assembly on seamanship and medicine—that is to say, on the drugs and surgical instruments appropriate to the treatment of the sick, on ships and their tackle, on the handling of vessels, and on perils of the sea, including risks arising from wind and tide, risks arising from encountering pirates, and risks arising from maneuver of warships against enemy warships in the event of a naval engagement.

So much for the decree on these matters. The executive is to embody this decree of the assembly of the people—based, you remember, on the advice of a few doctors and sailors maybe, but certainly on the advice of many unqualified people too—in laws which they are to inscribe on tablets of wood and of stone, and in the case of some of the rules so resolved upon, they must see that they find their place among the unwritten ancestral customs. Thereafter forever medicine and navigation may only be practiced according to these laws and customs.

YOUNG SOCRATES: A pretty state of affairs this!

STRANGER: But we have not done yet. Suppose that they resolve further to appoint magistrates chosen by lot annually from the citizen body, whether from the wealthy only or from all citizens. Some of these magistrates, once they are appointed, are to take command of ships and navigate them; others are to cure the sick according to the written code.

YOUNG SOCRATES: This is getting worse!

STRANGER: But we have not done—see what follows. When the year of office of each of these magistrates expires, a court must be established and a jury chosen by lot, perhaps from among wealthier citizens whose names are on a list of previously selected jurors, perhaps from the people as a whole. The magistrates are to be summoned before this court and it is to subject them to audit. It is open to anyone to lay an accusation against them that during their year of office they failed to sail the ships according to the written laws or the ancient custom of our forebears. Similar charges may be brought concerning the healers of the sick. If the verdict goes against any of them, the court must assess the penalty or the fine the convicted parties must pay.

YOUNG SOCRATES: Well then, the man who took office voluntarily in such a society would deserve any punishment and any fine that might be imposed.

STRANGER: Then there can be further misdemeanors, and we must enact a law to provide against them. It will be a law against independent research. If a man be found guilty of inquiry into seamanship or medicine in contravention of this law—of inquiry into nautical practice, for instance, or into climatic influences and bodily temperatures, and especially if he be guilty of airing theories of his own on such things, action must be taken to suppress him. First we must deny him the title of "doctor" or "captain." Instead we must call him a man with his head in the clouds, one of these chattering Sophists. Furthermore it will be lawful for any citizen so desiring to indict him before a court of justice—or what passes for such a court—on the charge of corrupting the younger men and influencing them to go in for seamanship and medicine in an illegal manner by setting up as doctors or captains on their own authority. If he is found guilty of influencing young or old against the laws and written enactments, he shall suffer the utmost penalties. For there can be no claim to possess wisdom greater than the wisdom of the laws. No one need be ignorant of seamanship or medicine, of sailing regulations or health regulations. The laws are there written out for our conning; the ancient customs are firmly established in our midst. Any who really desire to learn may learn.

Suppose, Socrates, that all the arts are treated like this. How do you imagine that generalship and hunting in all its forms would be affected? What would happen to painting and other representational arts, or to building and manufacture of all types of implements under such conditions, and how could farming or any cultivation whatever be carried on? Imagine the rearing of horses and other animals tied down to legal prescription, or divination and similar ministerial functions so controlled. What would legally governed draughts be like or legal mathematics, whether simple arithmetic, plane geometry, stereometry, or kinematics? What would the world be like if everything worked on this principle, organized throughout according to written laws instead of according to the relevant arts?

YOUNG SOCRATES: It is quite clear that the arts as we know them would be annihilated and that they could never be resurrected because of this law which puts an embargo on all research. The result would be that life, which is hard enough as it is, would be quite impossible then and not to be endured.

STRANGER: Yes, but there is a further possible degradation to consider. Suppose we compel each of these arts to function according to a legal code and place a magistrate in charge of this code either by election or by the fall of the lot, and make him rule according to it. Suppose then that he has no regard for the code and acts only from motives of ambition and favoritism. He embarks on a course of action contrary to law but does not act on any basis of scientific knowledge. Evil as the former state was, will not this latter one be still worse?

YOUNG SOCRATES: It will indeed.

STRANGER: The laws which have been laid down represent the fruit of experience—one must admit that. Each of them has been put forward by some advocate who has been fortunate enough to hit on the right method of commending it and who has thus persuaded the public Assembly to enact it. Any man who dares by his action to infringe these laws is guilty of a wrong many times greater than the wrong done by strict laws, for such transgression, if tolerated, would do even more than a rigid code to pervert all ordered activity.

YOUNG SOCRATES: Yes, of course it would.

STRANGER: Then so long as men enact laws and written codes governing any department of life, our second-best method of government is to forbid any individual or any group to perform any act in contravention of these laws.

YOUNG SOCRATES: True.

STRANGER: Then laws would seem to be written copies of scientific truth in the various departments of life they cover, copies based as far as possible on the instructions received from those who really possess the scientific truth on these matters.

YOUNG SOCRATES: Yes, of course.

STRANGER: And yet we must never lose sight of the truth we stated before. The man with the real knowledge, the true statesman, will in many instances allow his activities to be dictated by his art and pay no regard to written prescriptions. He will do this whenever he is convinced that there are measures which are better than the instructions he previously wrote and sent to people at a time when he could not be there to control them personally.

YOUNG SOCRATES: Yes, that was what we said.

STRANGER: So an individual or a group who possess a code of laws but try to introduce some change in them because they consider it an improvement are doing the same thing according to their lights as the true statesman.

YOUNG SOCRATES: Yes.

STRANGER: But if they acted like this with minds unenlightened by knowledge, they would indeed try to copy the true original, but would copy it very badly. If on the other hand they possessed scientific knowledge, it would no longer be a case of copying at all; it would be the real and original statesmanship we are talking about.

YOUNG SOCRATES: Yes—or so I should say.

STRANGER: Now it has been argued already and we have agreed that no large group of men is capable of acquiring any art, be it what you will.

YOUNG SOCRATES: That stands as our agreed conclusion.

STRANGER: Granted then that an art of kingly rule exists, the wealthy group or the whole citizen body would never be able to acquire this scientific art of statesmanship.

YOUNG SOCRATES: How could they?

STRANGER: It seems to follow that there is an invariable rule which these imitative constitutions must obey if they mean to reproduce as far as they can that one real constitution, which is government by a real statesman using real statecraft. They must all keep strictly to the laws once they have been laid down and never transgress written enactments or established national customs.

YOUNG SOCRATES: Quite right.

STRANGER: When the wealthy seek to copy the ideal constitution we call the constitution which results "aristocracy," but when they disregard the laws, the constitution produced is "oligarchy."

YOUNG SOCRATES: I suppose so.

STRANGER: But when one individual governs according to laws, imitating the truly wise ruler, we call him "king." We make no difference in name between the individual ruler guided by political science and the individual ruler guided by a right opinion and acting according to the laws.

YOUNG SOCRATES: That seems to be so.

STRANGER: And so if there really were an example of a truly wise ruler in power his name would undoubtedly be the same—"the king"—it could not be anything else. So the total of the names of the constitutions now under consideration comes to five only.

YOUNG SOCRATES: So it seems.

STRANGER: But stay, what of the case where one man rules but does not govern his actions either by laws or by ancient customs, but claims falsely what only the truly wise ruler has a right to claim, and says that the "best" course must be taken in defiance of written codes? If in fact it is only his passion and his ignorance that lead him to attempt to copy the true statesman in this defiance of law, must we not call him and all like him by the name of tyrant?

YOUNG SOCRATES: Unquestionably.

STRANGER: So then we have the tyrant and the king, then oligarchy and aristocracy, then democracy, all of which arise when men turn down the idea of the one true and scientific ruler. Men doubt whether any man will ever be found fit to bear such perfect rule. They despair of finding any one man willing and able to rule with moral and intellectual insight and to render every man his due with strictest fairness. They feel sure that a man with such absolute power will be bound to employ it to the hurt and injury of his personal enemies and to put them out of the way. But it remains true that if the ideal ruler we have described were to appear on earth he would be acclaimed, and he would spend his days guiding in strictest justice and perfect felicity that one and only true commonwealth worthy of the name.

YOUNG SOCRATES: That is so of course.

STRANGER: We must take things as they are, however, and kings do not arise in cities in the natural course of things in the way the royal bee is born in a beehive—one individual obviously outstanding in body and mind and capable of taking charge of things at once. And therefore it seems men gather together and work out written codes, chasing as fast as they can the fading vision of the true constitution.

YOUNG SOCRATES: So it would seem.

STRANGER: Is it any wonder that under these makeshift constitutions of ours hosts of ills have arisen and more must be expected in the future? They all rest on the sandy foundation of action according to law and custom without real scientific insight. Another art that worked on such a foundation would obviously ruin all that it sought to build up. But something even more remarkable than these besetting ills is the sheer native strength a city possesses nevertheless. For all our cities, as we know, have been subject to such ills for many generations now, and yet some of them have not come to ruin but still stand firm. However, we see many instances of cities going down like sinking ships to their destruction. There have been such wrecks in the past and there surely will be others in the future, caused by the wickedness of captains and crews alike. For these are guilty men, whose sin is supreme ignorance of what matters most. They are men who know little or nothing of real political truth and yet they consider themselves to know it from end to end and suppose that they are better instructed in this art than in any other.

YOUNG SOCRATES: Very true.

STRANGER: All these imperfect constitutions are difficult to live under, but we might ask ourselves which of them is hardest to bear and which is most tolerable. Ought we perhaps to examine this matter, though it is not directly relevant to our appointed theme? After all one must remember that, speaking quite generally, the aim of all the actions of men everywhere is to secure for themselves the most tolerable life they can.

YOUNG SOCRATES: Then we can hardly help considering the question.

STRANGER: There is one of three constitutions which you must regard as being at once the hardest to live under and the easiest.

YOUNG SOCRATES: How do you mean?

STRANGER: I just want to remind you that at the beginning of this supplementary discussion we enumerated three constitutions—the rule of one, the rule of the few, and the rule of the many.

YOUNG SOCRATES: We did.

STRANGER: Dividing each of three into two let us make six, having first separated the true constitution from all, calling it the seventh.

YOUNG SOCRATES: How shall we divide the three others?

STRANGER: Under the rule of one we get kingly rule and tyranny; under the rule of the few, as we said, come the auspicious form of it, aristocracy, and also oligarchy. As for the subdividing of democracy, though we gave both forms of it one name previously, we must now treat it as twofold.

YOUNG SOCRATES: How is this? How can it be divided?

STRANGER: By the same division as the others, even though the word "democracy" proves to be doing double duty. Rule according to law is as possible under democracy as under the other constitutions.

YOUNG SOCRATES: Yes, it is.

STRANGER: This division of democracy into two kinds was not serviceable previously as we indicated at the time, for we were seeking then to define a perfect constitution. Now, however, we have excluded the perfect constitution from our reckoning and have before us those that have to serve us as constitutions in default of it. In this group we find the principle of obedience to law or contravention of law dividing each type of ruler into two types.

YOUNG SOCRATES: So it seems from the argument that was put forward just now.

STRANGER: The rule of one man, if it has been kept within the traces, so to speak, by the written rules we call laws, is the best of all the six. But when it is lawless it is hard, and the most grievous to have to endure.

YOUNG SOCRATES: So it would seem.

STRANGER: As for the rule of a few, just as the few constitute a middle term between the one and the many, so we must regard the rule of the few as of middle potency for good or ill. The rule of the many is weakest in every way; it is not capable of any real good or of any serious evil as compared with the other two. This is because in a democracy sovereignty has been divided out in small portions among a large number of rulers. If therefore all three constitutions are law-abiding, democracy is the worst of the three, but if all three flout the laws, democracy is the best of them. Thus if all constitutions are unprincipled the best thing to do is to live in a democracy. But when constitutions are lawful and ordered, democracy is the least desirable, and monarchy, the first of the six, is by far the best to live under—unless of course the seventh is possible, for that must always be exalted, like a god among mortals, above all other constitutions.

YOUNG SOCRATES: Things do seem to work out in this way, and so we must take your advice and act as you say.

STRANGER: Therefore all who take part in one of these governments—apart from the one based on real knowledge—are to be distinguished from the true statesman. They are not statesmen; they are party leaders, leaders of bogus governments and themselves as bogus as their systems. The supreme imitators and tricksters, they are of all Sophists the arch-Sophists.

YOUNG SOCRATES: It seems to me that the wheel has come full circle, now that the title of Sophist goes to those who most deserve it, to the men who get themselves called political leaders.

STRANGER: So this fantastic pageant that seemed like some strange masque of centaurs or some band of satyrs stands revealed for what it is. At much pains we have succeeded at last in distinguishing them and setting them apart, as we must, from all true practice of statesmanship.

YOUNG SOCRATES: So we see.

STRANGER: There remains another task, and it is even more difficult because the class to be set apart is closer akin to the kingly ruler and also in itself harder to discern clearly. It seems to me that we have reached a point where we have to act like gold refiners.

YOUNG SOCRATES: How so?

STRANGER: We are told that at the first stage of their work they separate off earth and stones and much else from the ore. When these are gone there still remain those precious substances akin to gold which are so combined with it as to be separable only in the furnace; I mean bronze and silver and sometimes adamant as well. These are removed only with difficulty as the metal is tried in the refining fire until at last the process yields the sight of unalloyed gold separated off by itself.

YOUNG SOCRATES: Yes, they do say that refining is done like that.

STRANGER: It looks as though we are in a like situation. We have separated off the elements which are quite different from statesmanship, the elements which are quite foreign and repugnant to it, but there still remain the precious elements which are akin to it. These include the art of generalship, the art of administering justice, and that department of the art of public speaking which is closely allied to the kingly art. This last persuades men to do what is right and therefore takes its share in controlling what goes on in a true community. How can we best separate these arts also from statesmanship and so bring out the nature of the statesman as such, in his essential character? That, after all, is our present object.

YOUNG SOCRATES: Clearly we must make the attempt by one means or another.

STRANGER: If trying will do it, he shall be shown in his true character. Music will provide us with an example which will help us in our task. I will begin by putting a question to you.

YOUNG SOCRATES: What is it?

STRANGER: There is such a thing as learning the principles of music or the principles of any of the crafts, is there not?

YOUNG SOCRATES: Yes.

STRANGER: But are we willing to admit that there exists an art of a higher order also concerned with this process of acquiring special skills? This second art is the one whose province is to decide whether or not we *ought* to learn any particular art.

YOUNG SOCRATES: Yes, we will attest the existence of an art of this higher order.

STRANGER: We must also agree then, that it is to be distinguished from all arts of the lower order.

YOUNG SOCRATES: Yes.

STRANGER: Ought there to be no priority at all as between these two orders of art? On the other hand, if there is to be priority, must the lower order control the higher or the higher guide and control the lower?

YOUNG SOCRATES: The higher order should control the lower.

STRANGER: Your decision is then, that the art which decides whether we learn a skill or not ought to have control of the art which actually teaches us that skill.

YOUNG SOCRATES: Yes, certainly.

STRANGER: Then in the same way the art which decides whether persuasion should or should not be used ought to control the operation of the art of persuasion itself.

YOUNG SOCRATES: Undoubtedly.

STRANGER: Which is the art to which we must assign the task of persuading the general mass of the population by telling them suitable stories rather than by giving them formal instruction?

YOUNG SOCRATES: I should say that it is obvious that this is the province to be assigned to rhetoric.

STRANGER: But to which art must we assign the function of deciding whether in any particular situation we must proceed by persuasion, or by coercive measures against a group of men, or whether it is right to take no action at all?

YOUNG SOCRATES: The art which can teach us how to decide that will be the art which controls rhetoric and the art of public speaking.

STRANGER: This activity can be none other than the work of the statesman, I suggest.

YOUNG SOCRATES: Excellent! That is exactly what it is.

STRANGER: Oratory, it seems, has been quickly set apart from statesmanship. It is distinct from statesmanship, and yet its auxiliary.

YOUNG SOCRATES: Yes.

STRANGER: Now we must consider the working of another art.

YOUNG SOCRATES: Which is that?

STRANGER: Consider the taking of decisions on military strategy once war has been declared by the state on an enemy state. What shall we say about this? Is such decision governed by no art at all, or shall we say that there is most certainly an art involved here?

YOUNG SOCRATES: How could we dream of saying that no art is concerned? Surely generalship and the whole art of warfare operates precisely in this field.

STRANGER: But which is the art which possesses the knowledge and capacity to form a reasoned decision whether to fight or settle a dispute on friendly terms? Is this the work of generalship or does it belong to another art?

YOUNG SOCRATES: Consistency to our earlier argument requires us to say that it is a different one which is involved.

STRANGER: So if our views here are to be consistent with our earlier views on the place of rhetoric, we must decide that this second art controls generalship.

YOUNG SOCRATES: I agree.

STRANGER: What art can we attempt to enthrone as queen over that mighty and dreadful art, the art of war in all its range, except the art of truly royal rule?

YOUNG SOCRATES: None other.

STRANGER: Then we must not describe the art that generals practice as statesmanship, for it proves to be but a servant of statesmanship.

YOUNG SOCRATES: Apparently that is so.

STRANGER: Now turn to another art and let us consider the activity of judges who make straight judgments.

YOUNG SOCRATES: By all means.

STRANGER: Does its province extend beyond the sphere of the mutual contractual obligations of the citizens? It has to act in this sphere by judging what is just or unjust according to the standards set up for it and embodied in the legal rules which it has received from the kingly lawgiver. It shows its peculiar virtue by coming to an impartial decision on the conflicting claims it examines, by refusing to pervert the lawgiver's ordinance through yielding to bribery or threats or sentimental appeals, and by rising above all considerations of personal friendship or enmity.

YOUNG SOCRATES: Yes, that is so. You have given us, sir, a succinct account of the jury-man's function and of his duty.

STRANGER: We find, then, that the power of the judges is a lesser thing than the power of the king. The judge guards the law and serves the king.

YOUNG SOCRATES: So it would seem.

STRANGER: If you will view the three arts we have spoken of as a group with a common character you will be bound to see that none of them has turned out to be itself the art of statesmanship. This is because it is not the province of the real kingly art to act for itself but rather to control the work of the arts which instruct us in the methods of action. The kingly art controls them according to its power to perceive the right occasions for undertaking and setting in motion the great enterprises of state. The other arts must do what they are told to do by the kingly art.

YOUNG SOCRATES: Precisely so.

STRANGER: The three arts we have just treated in detail may not control one another. They may not even control themselves, in fact. Each has its special field of action and each is entitled to the name which designates its proper sphere.

YOUNG SOCRATES: So it would seem.

STRANGER: There is an art which controls all these arts. It is concerned with the laws and with all that belongs to the life of the community. It weaves all into its unified fabric with perfect skill. It is a universal art and so we call it by a name of universal scope. That name is one which I believe to belong to this art and to this alone, the name of "statesmanship."

YOUNG SOCRATES: Yes, I agree absolutely.

STRANGER: Now that all the classes of arts active in the government of the state have been distinguished, shall we go on to scrutinize statesmanship and base our scrutiny of it on the art of weaving which provides our example for it?

YOUNG SOCRATES: Most certainly.

STRANGER: Then we must describe the kingly weaving process. What is it like? How is it done? What is the fabric that results from its labors?

YOUNG SOCRATES: These are just the questions we must answer.

STRANGER: The task of finding the answers is hard, but we cannot shirk it.

YOUNG SOCRATES: No, we must find them at all costs.

STRANGER: To say that "one kind of goodness clashes with another kind of goodness" is to preach a doctrine which is an easy target for the disputatious who appeal to commonly accepted ideas.

YOUNG SOCRATES: I do not follow you.

STRANGER: Then let me put the matter in this way. You regard courage as one part of virtue I suppose.

YOUNG SOCRATES: Surely.

STRANGER: Moderation differs from courage but is a specific kind of goodness just as courage is.

YOUNG SOCRATES: Yes.

STRANGER: We have now to be daring and make a startling statement about these two virtues.

YOUNG SOCRATES: What is it?

STRANGER: This pair of virtues are in a certain sense enemies from of old, ranged in opposition to each other in many realms of life.

YOUNG SOCRATES: What do you mean?

STRANGER: The doctrine is not a familiar one by any means. I suppose that the usual statement is that all the several parts of goodness are in mutual accord.

YOUNG SOCRATES: Yes.

STRANGER: Then we must give our very special attention to the matter. Is the position quite so simple as that? Is there not, on the contrary, something inherent in them which keeps alive a family quarrel among them?

YOUNG SOCRATES: Certainly we must consider this. Please tell us how we are to do so.

STRANGER: We must consider instances drawn from all levels of existence of things which we regard as excellent and yet classify as mutually opposed.

YOUNG SOCRATES: Please explain still more clearly.

STRANGER: Take swiftness and speed as an instance—swiftness of mind and body and rapid vibration of sound in a voice. Such swiftness may be seen in an actual living person or it may be represented in music or painting. Have you ever praised examples of such swiftness or listened with approval when one of your friends praised them?

YOUNG SOCRATES: Yes.

STRANGER: Do you happen to remember the way in which the approval is expressed in all these instances?

YOUNG SOCRATES: No, I can't say that I remember that in the least.

STRANGER: I wonder if I could really manage to put my thoughts on the subject into words and make them clear to you.

YOUNG SOCRATES: I am sure you could.

STRANGER: You seem to think it a light task! However, let us see the principle at work wherever those mutually opposite qualities are manifested. We admire speed and intensity and vivacity in many forms of action and under all kinds of circumstances. But whether the swiftness of mind or body or the vibrant power of the voice is being praised, we always find ourselves using one word to praise it—the word "vigorous."

YOUNG SOCRATES: How so?

STRANGER: "That is alert and vigorous," we say in the first instance, in another case, "That is speedy and vigorous," or, in yet another case, "That is intense and vigorous." In all the instances we use this epithet "vigorous," as applying in common to the people or things concerned, in order to express our approval of this quality in them.

YOUNG SOCRATES: True.

STRANGER: On the other hand, do we not quite often find ourselves approving gentleness and quietness when it is shown in many kinds of human behavior?

YOUNG SOCRATES: Yes, very decidedly.

STRANGER: Do we not describe this behavior by using an epithet which is the exact opposite of "vigorous," which was the term we applied to the other group of things?

YOUNG SOCRATES: How do you mean?

STRANGER: We constantly admire quietness and moderation, in processes of restrained thinking, in gentle deeds, in a smooth deep voice, in steady balance in movement, or in suitable restraint in artistic representation. Whenever we express such approval do we not use the expression "controlled" to describe all these excellences rather than the word "vigorous"?

YOUNG SOCRATES: Very true.

STRANGER: But when we find either of these kinds of behavior appearing out of its due time, we have different names for each of them and in that case we express our censure by attributing quite contrary qualities when we mention them.

YOUNG SOCRATES: How so?

STRANGER: If speed and swiftness are excessive and unseasonable and if the voice is harsh to the point of being violent we speak of all these as "excessive" and even "maniacal." Unseasonable heaviness, slowness, or softness we call "cowardly" or "indolent." One can generalize further. The very classes "energy" and "moderation" are ranged in mutual exclusiveness and in opposition to each other; it is not simply a case of conflict between these particular manifestations of them. They never meet in the activities of life without causing conflicts, and if we pursue the matter further, by studying people whose characters come to be dominated by either of them, we shall find inevitable conflict between them and people of the opposite type.

YOUNG SOCRATES: In what sphere do these conflicts occur?

STRANGER: In all the things we have just considered, of course. but in many others too, I think. Men react to situations in one way or another according to the affinities of their own dispositions. They favor some forms of action as being akin to their own character, and they recoil from acts arising from opposite tendencies as being foreign to themselves. Thus men come into violent conflict with one another on many issues.

YOUNG SOCRATES: Yes, they seem to do so.

STRANGER: Considered as a conflict of temperaments, this is a mere trifle, but when the conflict arises over matters of high public importance it becomes the most inimical of all the plagues which can threaten the life of a community.

YOUNG SOCRATES: What kind of evils do you mean?

STRANGER: Of course I mean all which concern the organization of the community as a whole. Men who are notable for moderation are always ready to support "peace and tranquillity." They want to keep themselves to themselves and to mind their own business. They conduct all their dealings with their fellow citizens on this principle and are prone to take the same line in foreign policy and preserve peace at any price with foreign states. Because of their indulgence of this passion for peace at the wrong times, whenever they are able to carry their policy into effect they become unwarlike themselves without being aware of it and render their young men unwarlike as well. Thus they are at the mercy of the chance aggressor. He swoops down on them and the result is that within a very few years they and their children and all the community to which they belong wake up to find that their freedom is gone and that they are reduced to slavery.

YOUNG SOCRATES: You have described a hard and bitter experience.

STRANGER: What then is the history of the party whose bent is rather toward strong action? Do we not find them forever dragging their cities into war and bringing them up against powerful foes on all sides just because they love a military existence too fiercely? And what is the result? Either they destroy their country altogether, or else they bring it into subjection to its enemies just as surely as the peace party did.

YOUNG SOCRATES: Yes, that is true too.

STRANGER: Can we deny, then, that in these high matters the two types of character concerned are bound to become hostile to one another and so take up opposing party lines?

YOUNG SOCRATES: We are bound to admit it.

STRANGER: We have discovered, then, the answer to the question into which we set out to inquire when we began this conversation. We find that important parts of goodness are at variance with one another and that they set at variance the men in whom they predominate.

YOUNG SOCRATES: So it seems.

STRANGER: There is a further point to consider.

YOUNG SOCRATES: What is it?

STRANGER: Does any art which works by combining materials deliberately choose to make any of its products, even the least important of them, out of a combination of good material with bad? Does not every art, whatever material it works in, reject bad material as far as possible and use what is good and serviceable? The materials may be alike or dissimilar, but surely it is desirable that they should be found, so that the art may combine them to form one product and fashion them to a structure proper to their specific function.

YOUNG SOCRATES: Yes.

STRANGER: Surely then the true and genuine statesmanship we are concerned with could never choose deliberately to construct the life of any community out of a combination of good characters with bad characters? Obviously it will first put the young children to the test in games. After this first test it will go on to entrust the young to competent educators trained to render this particular service, but it will retain direction and oversight of them all the time. This is exactly like weaving. The art of weaving hands over the materials it intends to use for the fabric to the carders and others concerned with preparatory processes, and yet it watches their work at every stage, retaining the direction and oversight itself and indicating to each auxiliary art such duties as it deems that each can usefully perform to make ready the threads for its own task of fashioning the web.

YOUNG SOCRATES: Precisely.

STRANGER: This is the way I see the true statesman dealing with those who rear and educate children according to the educational laws. He keeps the power of direction to himself. The only form of training he will permit is the one by which the educator produces the type of character fitted for his own task of weaving the web of state. He bids the educator encourage the young in these activities and in no others. Some pupils cannot be taught to be courageous and moderate and to acquire the other virtuous tendencies, but are impelled to godlessness and to vaunting pride and injustice by the drive of an evil nature. These the king expels from the community. He puts them to death or banishes them or else he chastises them by the severest public disgrace.

YOUNG SOCRATES: So one usually hears it stated.

STRANGER: Furthermore, he makes those who prove incapable of rising above ignorance and groveling subservience slaves to the rest of the community.

YOUNG SOCRATES: Quite rightly.

STRANGER: The statesman will then take over all the rest—all those who, under the training process, do in fact achieve sufficient nobility of character to stand up to the royal weaving process and yet to submit to it while it combines them all scientifically into a unity. Those in whom courage predominates will be treated by the statesman as having the firm warplike character as one might call it. The others will be used by him for what we may likewise call the supple, soft, wooflike strands of the web. He then sets about his task of combining and weaving together these two groups exhibiting their mutually opposed characters.

YOUNG SOCRATES: How does he do it?

STRANGER: He first unites that element in their souls which is supernatural by a divine bond, since this element in them is akin to the divine. After this supernatural link will come the natural bond, human ties to supplement the divine ones.

YOUNG SOCRATES: What do you mean by this? Once more I do not follow.

STRANGER: When there arises in the soul of men a right opinion concerning what is good, just, and profitable, and what is the opposite of these—an opinion based on absolute truth and settled as an unshakable conviction—I declare that such a conviction is a manifestation of the divine occurring in a race which is in truth of supernatural lineage.

YOUNG SOCRATES: It could not be more suitably described.

STRANGER: Do we realize that it is the true statesman, in that he is the good and true lawgiver, who alone is able—for who else should possess the power—to forge by the wondrous inspiration of the kingly art this bond of true conviction uniting the hearts of the young folk of whom we were speaking just now—the young folk who have profited as they should from their education?

YOUNG SOCRATES: That is certainly as one would expect.

STRANGER: The ruler who cannot weld that bond we will never honor with those glorious titles, "statesman" and "king."

YOUNG SOCRATES: Most rightly not.

STRANGER: Well then, will it not work out like this? The soul full of vigor and courage will be made gentle by its grasp of this truth and there is nothing as well calculated as this to make it a willing member of a community based on justice. If such a soul refused this gift, it will sink in the scale and become savage like a beast.

YOUNG SOCRATES: True.

STRANGER: What of the moderate soul? Sharing this firm conviction of truth, will it not be truly moderate and prudent, or at any rate prudent enough, to meet its public duties? But if it refuses to share this conviction, it deserves to be called foolish and our reproach of it is entirely proper.

YOUNG SOCRATES: It is indeed.

STRANGER: Do we agree then that this interweaving, this linking together, can never be lasting and permanent if vicious men are joined with other vicious men or good men with vicious? Surely no art would seriously try to forge such links where these faults of character exist?

YOUNG SOCRATES: How could it?

STRANGER: But in those of noble nature from their earliest days whose nurture too has been all it should be, the laws can foster the growth of this common bond of conviction and only in these. This is the talisman appointed for them by the design of pure intelligence. This most godlike bond alone can unite the elements of goodness which are diverse in nature and would else be opposing in tendency.

YOUNG SOCRATES: Most true.

STRANGER: There remain the other bonds, the human ones. When one sets to work with the divine link already forged it is not very difficult to see what these are and then to set about the forging of them.

YOUNG SOCRATES: But what are these links and how can they be forged?

STRANGER: They are forged by establishing intermarriage between the two types so that the children of the mixed marriages are so to speak shared between them and by restricting private arrangements for marrying off daughters. Most men make unsuitable matches from the point of view of the begetting of children of the best type of character.

YOUNG SOCRATES: What can you mean?

STRANGER: Would anyone think it worth while to censure in any respect the prevalent practice of pursuing wealth or influence when making such matches?

YOUNG SOCRATES: No, there is nothing very wrong in it.

STRANGER: But when we are specially concerned with the very people who make much of being "well connected," justice requires that we should be all the more outspoken if we find them acting unsuitably.

YOUNG SOCRATES: That is reasonable.

STRANGER: They do not act on any sound or self-consistent principle. See how they pursue the immediate satisfaction of their desire by hailing with delight those who are like themselves and by disliking those who are different. Thus they assign far too great an importance to their own likes and dislikes.

YOUNG SOCRATES: In what way?

STRANGER: The moderate natures look for a partner like themselves, and so far as they can, they choose their wives from women of this quiet type. When they have daughters to bestow in marriage, once again they look for this type of character in the prospective husband. The courageous class does just the same thing and looks for others of the same type. All this goes on, though both types should be doing exactly the opposite.

YOUNG SOCRATES: How can they, and why should they?

STRANGER: Because if a courageous character is reproduced for many generations without any admixture of the moderate type, the natural course of development is that at first it becomes superlatively powerful but in the end it breaks out into sheer fury and madness.

YOUNG SOCRATES: That is to be expected.

STRANGER: But the character which is too full of modest reticence and untinged by valor and audacity, if reproduced after its kind for many generations, becomes too dull to respond to the challenges of life and in the end becomes quite incapable of acting at all.

YOUNG SOCRATES: Yes, this is also the result one would expect.

STRANGER: I repeat what I was saying. There is no difficulty in forging these human bonds if the divine bond has been forged first. That bond is a conviction about values and standards shared by both types of character. There is one absorbing preoccupation for the kingly weaver as he makes the web of state. He must never permit the gentle characters to be separated from the brave ones; to avoid this he must make the fabric close and firm by working common convictions in the hearts of each type of citizen and making public honors and triumphs subserve this end, and finally, each must be involved with the other in the solemn pledges of matrimony. When he has woven his web smooth and "close-woven," as the phrase goes, out of men of these differing types, he must entrust the various offices of state to them to be shared in all cases between them.

YOUNG SOCRATES: How can he do this?

STRANGER: When a single magistrate happens to be needed, the statesman must choose a man possessing both characteristics and set him in authority. Where several magistrates are wanted he must bring together some representatives of each type to share the duties. Magistrates of the moderate type are exceedingly cautious, fair, and tenacious of precedent, but they lack pungency and the drive which makes for efficiency.

YOUNG SOCRATES: Yes, that certainly seems to be a fair summing up of the case.

STRANGER: The courageous type for their part have far less of the gifts of fairness and caution than their moderate brethren, but they have in a marked degree the drive that gets things done. A community can never function well either in the personal intercourse of its citizens or in its public activities unless both of these elements of character are present and active.

YOUNG SOCRATES: Of course that is so.

STRANGER: Now we have reached the appointed end of the weaving of the web of state. It is fashioned by the statesman's weaving; the strands run true, and these strands are the gentle and the brave. Here these strands are woven together into a unified character. For this unity is won where the kingly art draws the life of both types into a true fellowship by mutual concord and by ties of friendship. It is the finest and best of all fabrics. It infolds all who dwell in the city, bond or free, in its firm contexture. Its kingly weaver maintains his control and oversight over it, and it lacks nothing that makes for happiness so far as happiness is obtainable in a human community.

YOUNG SOCRATES: You have done what we requested of you, sir, and you have set beside your definition of the Sophist a picture drawn to perfection of the true king and statesman.

Aristotle (384–322 B.C.E.)

Born in Stagira, north of Athens, in the region of Macedon, Aristotle came to the Academy when he was 17, and stayed for 20 years. Over that time his relationship with Plato evolved from student to colleague, and while they agreed on many subjects, they also disagreed on many others. After Plato's death, the Academy was continued by more orthodox Platonists, and Aristotle returned to Macedon, where he was appointed by King Philip to be tutor to Philip's son Alexander (who would later be known as Alexander the Great). In 335 he returned to Athens and started his own school, the Lyceum. Aristotle wrote on an even wider variety of topics than did Plato, investigating what we would consider natural science as well as philosophy. His works range from logic to physics to animals to clouds to ethics. His dialogues are no longer extant, but we have many treatises, used in the Lyceum, and lecture notes. We excerpt here selections from the treatise on *Politics*.

From Politics*

1. Every state is a community of some kind, and every community is established with a view to some good; for everyone always acts in order to obtain that which they think good. But, if all communities aim at some good, the state or political community, which is the highest of all, and which embraces all the rest, aims at good in a greater degree than any other, and at the highest good.

Some people think that the qualifications of a statesman, king, householder, and master are the same, and that they differ, not in kind, but only in the number of their subjects. For example, the ruler over a few is called a master; over more, the manager of a household; over a still larger number, a statesman or king, as if there were no difference between a great household and a small state. The distinction which is made between the king and the statesman is as follows: When the government is personal, the ruler is a king; when, according to the rules of the political science, the citizens rule and are ruled in turn, then he is called a statesman.

But all this is a mistake, as will be evident to any one who considers the matter according to the method which has hitherto guided us. As in other departments of science, so in politics, the compound should always be resolved into the simple elements or least parts of the whole. We must therefore look at the elements of which the state is composed, in order that we may see in what the different kinds of rule differ from one another, and whether any scientific result can be attained about each one of them.

2. He who thus considers things in their first growth and origin, whether a state or anything else, will obtain the clearest view of them. In the first place there must be a

* An Excerpt.

union of those who cannot exist without each other; namely, of male and female, that the race may continue (and this is a union which is formed, not of choice, but because, in common with other animals and with plants, mankind have a natural desire to leave behind them an image of themselves), and of natural ruler and subject, that both may be preserved. For that which can foresee by the exercise of mind is by nature lord and master, and that which can with its body give effect to such foresight is a subject, and by nature a slave; hence master and slave have the same interest. Now nature has distinguished between the female and the slave. For she is not niggardly, like the smith who fashions the Delphian knife for many uses; she makes each thing for a single use, and every instrument is best made when intended for one and not for many uses. But among barbarians no distinction is made between women and slaves, because there is no natural ruler among them: they are a community of slaves, male and female. That is why the poets say,—

It is meet that Hellenes should rule over barbarians;

as if they thought that the barbarian and the slave were by nature one.

Out of these two relationships the first thing to arise is the family, and Hesiod is right when he says,—

First house and wife and an ox for the plough,

for the ox is the poor man's slave. The family is the association established by nature for the supply of men's everyday wants, and the members of it are called by Charondas, "companions of the cupboard," and by Epimenides the Cretan, "companions of the manger". But when several families are united, and the association aims at something more than the supply of daily needs, the first society to be formed is the village. And the most natural form of the village appears to be that of a colony from the family, composed of the children and grandchildren, who are said to be "suckled with the same milk." And this is the reason why Hellenic states were originally governed by kings; because the Hellenes were under royal rule before they came together, as the barbarians still are. Every family is ruled by the eldest, and therefore in the colonies of the family the kingly form of government prevailed because they were of the same blood. As Homer says:

Each one gives law to his children and to his wives.

For they lived dispersedly, as was the manner in ancient times. That is why men say that the Gods have a king, because they themselves either are or were in ancient times under the rule of a king. For they imagine not only the forms of the Gods but their ways of life to be like their own.

When several villages are united in a single complete community, large enough to be nearly or quite self-sufficing, the state comes into existence, originating in the bare needs of life, and continuing in existence for the sake of a good life. And therefore, if the earlier forms of society are natural, so is the state, for it is the end of them, and the nature of a thing is its end. For what each thing is when fully developed, we call its nature, whether we are speaking of a man, a horse, or a family. Besides, the final cause and end of a thing is the best, and to be self-sufficing is the end and the best.

Hence it is evident that the state is a creation of nature, and that man is by nature a political animal. And he who by nature and not by mere accident is without a state, is either a bad man or above humanity; he is like the

> Tribeless, lawless, hearthless one,

whom Homer denounces—the natural outcast is forthwith a lover of war; he may be compared to an isolated piece at draughts.

Now, that man is more of a political animal than bees or any other gregarious animals is evident. Nature, as we often say, makes nothing in vain, and man is the only animal who has the gift of speech. And whereas mere voice is but an indication of pleasure or pain, and is therefore found in other animals (for their nature attains to the perception of pleasure and pain and the intimation of them to one another, and no further), the power of speech is intended to set forth the expedient and inexpedient, and therefore likewise the just and the unjust. And it is a characteristic of man that he alone has any sense of good and evil, of just and unjust, and the like, and the association of living beings who have this sense makes a family and a state.

Further, the state is by nature clearly prior to the family and to the individual, since the whole is of necessity prior to the part; for example, if the whole body be destroyed, there will be no foot or hand, except homonymously, as we might speak of a stone hand; for when destroyed the hand will be no better than that. But things are defined by their function and power; and we ought not to say that they are the same when they no longer have their proper quality, but only that they are homonymous. The proof that the state is a creation of nature and prior to the individual is that the individual, when isolated, is not self-sufficing; and therefore he is like a part in relation to the whole. But he who is unable to live in society, or who has no need because he is sufficient for himself, must be either a beast or a god: he is no part of a state. A social instinct is implanted in all men by nature, and yet he who first founded the state was the greatest of benefactors. For man, when perfected, is the best of animals, but, when separated from law and justice, he is the worst of all; since armed injustice is the more dangerous, and he is equipped at birth with arms, meant to be used by intelligence and excellence, which he may use for the worst ends. That is why, if he has not excellence, he is the most unholy and the most savage of animals, and the most full of lust and gluttony. But justice is the bond of men in states; for the administration of justice, which is the determination of what is just, is the principle of order in political society. . . .

6. Having determined these questions, we have next to consider whether there is only one form of government or many, and if many, what they are, and how many, and what are the differences between them.

A constitution is the arrangement of magistracies in a state, especially of the highest of all. The government is everywhere sovereign in the state, and the constitution is in fact the government. For example, in democracies the people are supreme, but in oligarchies, the few; and, therefore, we say that these two constitutions also are different: and so in other cases.

First, let us consider what is the purpose of a state, and how many forms of rule there are by which human society is regulated. We have already said, in the first part of this treatise, when discussing household management and the rule of a master, that man is by nature a political animal. And therefore, men, even when they do not require one another's help, desire to live together; not but that they are also brought together by their common interests in so far as they each attain to any measure of well-being. This is certainly the chief end, both of individuals and of states. And mankind meet together and maintain the political community also for the sake of mere life (in which there is possibly some noble element so long as the evils of existence do not greatly overbalance the good). And we all see that men cling to life even at the cost of enduring great misfortune, seeming to find in life a natural sweetness and happiness.

There is no difficulty in distinguishing the various kinds of rule; they have been often defined already in our popular discussions. The rule of a master, although the slave by nature and the master by nature have in reality the same interests, is nevertheless exercised primarily with a view to the interest of the master, but accidentally considers the slave, since, if the slave perish, the rule of the master perishes with him. On the other hand, the government of a wife and children and of a household, which we have called household management, is exercised in the first instance for the good of the governed or for the common good of both parties, but essentially for the good of the governed, as we see to be the case in medicine, gymnastic, and the arts in general, which are only accidentally concerned with the good of the artists themselves. For there is no reason why the trainer may not sometimes practise gymnastics, and the helmsman is always one of the crew. The trainer or the helmsman considers the good of those committed to his care. But, when he is one of the persons taken care of, he accidentally participates in the advantage, for the helmsman is also a sailor, and the trainer becomes one of those in training. And so in politics: when the state is framed upon the principle of equality and likeness, the citizens think that they ought to hold office by turns. Formerly, as is natural, everyone would take his turn of service; and then again, somebody else would look after his interest, just as he, while in office, had looked after theirs. But nowadays, for the sake of the advantage which is to be gained from the public revenues and from office, men want to be always in office. One might imagine that the rulers, being sickly, were only kept in health while they continued in office; in that case we may be sure that they would be hunting after places. The conclusion is evident: that governments which have a regard to the common interest are constituted in accordance with strict principles of justice, and are therefore true forms; but those which regard only the interest of the rulers are all defective and perverted forms, for they are despotic, whereas a state is a community of freemen.

7. Having determined these points, we have next to consider how many forms of government there are, and what they are; and in the first place what are the true forms, for when they are determined the perversions of them will at once be apparent. The words constitution and government have the same meaning, and the government, which is the supreme authority in states, must be in the hands of one, or of a few, or of the many. The true forms of government, therefore, are those in which the one, or the few, or the many, govern with a view to the common interest; but governments which rule with a view to the private interest, whether of the one, or of the few, or of the many, are perversions. For the members of a state, if they are truly citizens, ought to participate in its advantages. Of forms of government in which one rules, we call that which regards the common interest, kingship; that in which more than one, but not many, rule, aristocracy; and it is so called, either because the rulers are the best men, or because they have at heart the best interests of the state and of the citizens. But when the many administer the state for the common interest, the government is called by the generic name—a constitution. And there is a reason for this use of language. One man or a few may excel in excellence; but as the number increases it becomes more difficult for them to attain perfection in every kind of excellence, though they may in military excellence, for this is found in the masses. Hence in a constitutional government the fighting-men have the supreme power, and those who possess arms are the citizens.

Of the above-mentioned forms, the perversions are as follows:—of kingship, tyranny; of aristocracy, oligarchy; of constitutional government, democracy. For tyranny is a kind of monarchy which has in view the interest of the monarch only; oligarchy has in view the interest of the wealthy; democracy, of the needy: none of them the common good of all.

8. But there are difficulties about these forms of government, and it will therefore be necessary to state a little more at length the nature of each of them. For he who would make a philosophical study of the various sciences, and is not only concerned with practice, ought not to overlook or omit anything, but to set forth the truth in every particular. Tyranny, as I was saying, is monarchy exercising the rule of a master over the political society; oligarchy is when men of property have the government in their hands; democracy, the opposite, when the indigent, and not the men of property, are the rulers. And here arises the first of our difficulties, and it relates to the distinction just drawn. For democracy is said to be the government of the many. But what if the many are men of property and have the power in their hands? In like manner oligarchy is said to be the government of the few; but what if the poor are fewer than the rich, and have the power in their hands because they are stronger? In these cases the distinction which we have drawn between these different forms of government would no longer hold good.

Suppose, once more, that we add wealth to the few and poverty to the many, and name the governments accordingly—an oligarchy is said to be that in which the few and the wealthy, and a democracy that in which the many and the poor are the rulers—there will still be a difficulty. For, if the only forms of government are the ones already mentioned, how shall we describe those other governments also just mentioned by us, in which the rich are the more numerous and the poor are the fewer, and both govern in their respective states?

The argument seems to show that, whether in oligarchies or in democracies, the number of the governing body, whether the greater number, as in a democracy, or the smaller number, as in an oligarchy, is an accident due to the fact that the rich everywhere are few, and the poor numerous. But if so, there is a misapprehension of the causes of the difference between them. For the real difference between democracy and oligarchy is poverty and wealth. Wherever men rule by reason of their wealth, whether they be few or many, that is an oligarchy, and where the poor rule, that is a democracy. But in fact the rich are few and the poor many; for few are well-to-do, whereas freedom is enjoyed by all, and wealth and freedom are the grounds on which the two parties claim power in the state.

9. Let us begin by considering the common definitions of oligarchy and democracy, and what is oligarchical and democratic justice. For all men cling to justice of some kind, but their conceptions are imperfect and they do not express the whole idea. For example, justice is thought by them to be, and is, equality—not, however, for all, but only for equals. And inequality is thought to be, and is, justice; neither is this for all, but only for unequals. When the persons are omitted, then men judge erroneously. The reason is that they are passing judgement on themselves, and most people are bad judges in their own case. And whereas justice implies a relation to persons as well as to things, and a just distribution, as I have already said in the *Ethics*, implies the same ratio between the persons and between the things, they agree about the equality of the things, but dispute about the equality of the persons, chiefly for the reason which I have just given—because they are bad judges in their own affairs; and secondly, because both the parties to the argument are speaking of a limited and partial justice, but imagine themselves to be speaking of absolute justice. For the one party, if they are unequal in one respect, for example wealth, consider themselves to be unequal in all; and the other party, if they are equal in one respect, for example free birth, consider themselves to be equal in all. But they leave out the capital point. For if men met and associated out of regard to wealth only, their share in the state would be proportioned to their property, and the oligarchical doctrine would then seem to carry the day. It would not be just that he who paid one mina should have the same share of a hundred minae, whether of the principal or of the profits, as he who paid the remaining ninety-nine. But a state exists for the sake of a good life, and not for the sake of life only: if life only were the object, slaves and brute animals might form a state, but they cannot, for they have no share in happiness or in a life based on choice. Nor does a state exist for the sake of alliance and security from injustice, nor yet for the sake of exchange and mutual intercourse; for then the Tyrrhenians and the Carthaginians, and all who have commercial treaties with one another, would be the citizens of one state. True, they have agreements about imports, and engagements that they will do no wrong to one another, and written articles of alliance. But there are no magistracies common to the contracting parties; different states have each their own magistracies. Nor does one state take care that the citizens of the other are such as they ought to be, nor see that those who come under the terms of the treaty do no wrong or wickedness at all, but only that they do no injustice to one another. Whereas, those who care for good government take into consideration political excellence and defect. Whence it may be further inferred that excellence must be the care of a state which is truly so called, and not merely enjoys the name: for without this end the community becomes a mere alliance which differs only in place from alliances of which the members live apart; and law is only a convention, "a surety to one another of justice," as the sophist Lycophron says, and has no real power to make the citizens good and just.

This is obvious; for suppose distinct places, such as Corinth and Megara, to be brought together so that their walls touched, still they would not be one city, not even if the citizens had the right to intermarry, which is one of the rights peculiarly characteristic of states. Again, if men dwelt at a distance from one another, but not so far off as to have no intercourse, and there were laws among them that they should not wrong each other in their exchanges, neither would this be a state. Let us suppose that one man is a carpenter, another a farmer, another a shoemaker, and so on, and that their number is ten thousand: nevertheless, if they have nothing in common but exchange, alliance, and the like, that would not constitute a state. Why is this? Surely not because they are at a distance from one another; for even supposing that such a community were to meet in one place, but that each man had a house of his own, which was in a manner his state, and that they made alliance with one another, but only against evil-doers; still an accurate thinker would not deem this to be a state, if their intercourse with one another was of the same character after as before their union. It is clear then that a state is not a mere society, having a common place, established for the prevention of mutual crime and for the sake of exchange. These are conditions without which a state cannot exist; but all of them together do not constitute a state, which is a community of families and aggregations of families in well-being, for the sake of a perfect and self-sufficing life. Such a community can only be established among those who live in the same place and intermarry. Hence there arise in cities family connexions, brotherhoods, common sacrifices, amusements which draw men together. But these are created by friendship, for to choose to live together is friendship. The end of the state is the good life, and these are the means towards it. And the state is the union of families and villages in a perfect and self-sufficing life, by which we mean a happy and honorable life.

Our conclusion, then, is that political society exists for the sake of noble actions, and not of living together. Hence they who contribute most to such a society have a greater share in it than those who have the same or a greater freedom or nobility of birth but are inferior to them in political excellence; or than those who exceed them in wealth but are surpassed by them in excellence.

From what has been said it will be clearly seen that all the partisans of different forms of government speak of a part of justice only.

10. There is also a doubt as to what is to be the supreme power in the state:—Is it the multitude? Or the wealthy? Or the good? Or the one best man? Or a tyrant? Any of these alternatives seems to involve disagreeable consequences. If the poor, for example, because they are more in number, divide among themselves the property of the rich—is not this unjust? No, by heaven (will be the reply), for the supreme authority justly willed it. But if this is not extreme injustice, what is? Again, when in the first division all has been taken, and the majority divide anew the property of the minority, is it not evident, if this goes on, that they will ruin the state? Yet surely, excellence is not the ruin of those who possess it, nor is justice destructive of a state; and therefore this law of confiscation clearly cannot be just. If it were, all the acts of a tyrant must of necessity be just; for he only coerces other men by superior power, just as the multitude coerce the rich. But is it just then that the few and the wealthy should be the rulers? And what if they, in like manner, rob and plunder the people—is this just? If so, the other case will likewise be just. But there can be no doubt that all these things are wrong and unjust.

Then ought the good to rule and have supreme power? But in that case everybody else, being excluded from power, will be dishonored. For the offices of a state are posts of honor; and if one set of men always hold them, the rest must be deprived of them.

Then will it be well that the one best man should rule? That is still more oligarchical, for the number of those who are dishonored is thereby increased. Someone may say that it is bad in any case for a man, subject as he is to all the accidents of human passion, to have the supreme power, rather than the law. But what if the law itself be democratic or oligarchical, how will that help us out of our difficulties? Not at all; the same consequences will follow.

11. Most of these questions may be reserved for another occasion. The principle that the multitude ought to be in power rather than the few best might seem to be solved and to contain some difficulty and perhaps even truth. For the many, of whom each individual is not a good man, when they meet together may be better than the few good, if regarded not individually but collectively, just as a feast to which many contribute is better than a dinner provided out of a single purse. For each individual among the many has a share of excellence and practical wisdom, and when they meet together, just as they become in a manner one man, who has many feet, and hands, and senses, so too with regard to their character and thought. Hence the many are better judges than a single man of music and poetry; for some understand one part, and some another, and among them they understand the whole. There is a similar combination of qualities in good men, who differ from any individual of the many, as the beautiful are said to differ from those who are not beautiful, and works of art from realities, because in them the scattered elements are combined, although, if taken separately, the eye of one person or some other feature in another person would be fairer than in the picture. Whether this principle can apply to every democracy, and to all bodies of men, is not clear. Or rather, by heaven, in some cases it is impossible to apply; for the argument would equally hold about brutes; and wherein, it will be asked, do some men differ from brutes? But there may be bodies of men about whom our statement is nevertheless true. And if so, the difficulty which has been already raised, and also another which is akin to it—viz, what power should be assigned to the mass of freemen and citizens, who are not rich and have no personal merit—are both solved. There is still a danger in allowing them to share the great offices of state, for their folly will lead them into error, and their dishonesty into crime. But there is a danger also in not letting them share, for a state in which many poor men are excluded from office will necessarily be full of enemies. The only way of escape is to assign to them some deliberative and judicial functions. For this reason Solon and certain other legislators give them the power of electing to offices, and of calling the magistrates to account, but they do not allow them to hold office singly. When they meet together their perceptions are quite good enough, and combined with the better class they are useful to the state (just as impure food when mixed with what is pure sometimes makes the entire mass more wholesome than a small quantity of the pure would be), but each individual, left to himself, forms an imperfect judgement. On the other hand, the popular form of government involves certain difficulties. In the first place, it might be objected that he who can judge of the healing of a sick man would be one who could himself heal his disease, and make him whole—that is, in other words, the physician; and so in all professions and arts. As, then, the physician ought to be called to account by physicians, so ought men in general to be called to account by their peers. But physicians are of three kinds:—there is the ordinary practitioner, and there is the master physician, and thirdly the man educated in the art: in all arts there is such a class; and we attribute the power of judging to them quite as much as to professors of the art. Secondly, does not the same principle apply to elections? For a right election can only be made by those who have knowledge; those who know geometry, for example, will choose a geometrician rightly, and those who know how to steer, a pilot; and, even if there be some occupations and arts in which private persons share in the ability to choose, they certainly cannot choose better than those who know. So that, according to this argument, neither the election of magistrates, nor the calling of them to account, should be entrusted to the many. Yet possibly these objections are to a great extent met by our old answer, that if the people are not utterly degraded, although individually they may be worse judges than those who have special knowledge, as a body they are as good or better. Moreover, there are some arts whose products are not judged of solely, or best, by the artists themselves, namely those arts whose products are recognized even by those who do not possess the art; for example, the knowledge of the house is not limited to the builder only; the user, or, in other words, the master, of the house will actually be a better judge than the builder, just as the pilot will judge better of a rudder than the carpenter, and the guest will judge better of a feast than the cook.

This difficulty seems now to be sufficiently answered, but there is another akin to it. That inferior persons should have authority in greater matters than the good would appear to be a strange thing, yet the election and calling to account of the magistrates is the greatest of all. And these, as I was saying, are functions which in some states are assigned to the people, for the assembly is supreme in all such matters. Yet persons of any age, and having but a small property qualification, sit in the assembly and deliberate and judge, although for the great officers of state, such as treasurers and generals, a high qualification is required. This difficulty may be solved in the same manner as the preceding, and the present practice of democracies may be really defensible. For the power does not reside in the juryman, or counsellor, or member of the assembly, but in the court, and the council, and the assembly, of which the aforesaid individuals—counsellor, assemblyman, juryman—are only parts or members. And for this reason the many may claim to have a higher authority than the few; for the people, and the council, and the courts consist of many persons, and their property collectively is greater than the property of one or of a few individuals holding great offices. But enough of this.

The discussion of the first question shows nothing so clearly as that laws, when good, should be supreme; and that the magistrate or magistrates should regulate those matters only on which the laws are unable to speak with precision owing to the difficulty of any general principle embracing all particulars. But what are good laws has not yet been clearly explained; the old difficulty remains. The goodness or badness, justice or injustice, of laws varies of necessity with the constitutions of states. This, however, is clear, that the laws must be adapted to the constitutions. But, if so, true forms of government will of necessity have just laws, and perverted forms of government will have unjust laws.

12. In all sciences and arts the end is a good, and the greatest good and in the highest degree a good in the most authoritative of all—this is the political science of which the good is justice, in other words, the common interest. All men think justice to be a sort of equality; and to a certain extent they agree with what we have said in our philosophical works about ethics. For they say that what is just is just *for* someone and that it should be equal for equals. But there still remains a question: equality or inequality of what? Here is a difficulty which calls for political speculation. For very likely some persons will say that offices of state ought to be unequally distributed according to superior excellence, in whatever respect, of the citizen, although there is no other difference between him and the rest of the community; for those who differ in any one respect have different rights and claims. But, surely, if this is true, the complexion or height of a man, or any other advantage, will be a reason for his obtaining a greater share of political rights. The error here lies upon the surface, and may be illustrated from the other arts and sciences. When a number of flute-players are equal in their art, there is no reason why those of them who are better born should have better flutes given to them; for they will not play any better on the flute, and the superior instrument should be reserved for him who is the superior artist. If what I am saying is still obscure, it will be made clearer as we proceed. For if there were a superior flute-player who was far inferior in birth and beauty, although either of these may be a greater good than the art of flute-playing and may excel flute-playing in a greater ratio than he excels the others in his art, still he ought to have the best flutes given to him, unless the advantages of wealth and birth contribute to excellence in flute-playing, which they do not. Moreover, upon this principle any good may be compared with any other. For if a given height may be measured against wealth and against freedom, height in general may be so measured. Thus if A excels in height more than B in excellence, even if excellence in general excels height still more, all goods will be comparable; for if a certain amount is better than some other, it is clear that some other will be equal. But since no such comparison can be made, it is evident that there is good reason why in politics men do not ground their claim to office on every sort of inequality. For if some be slow, and others swift, that is no reason why the one should have little and the others much; it is in gymnastic contests that such excellence is rewarded. Whereas the rival claims of candidates for office can only be based on the possession of elements which enter into the composition of a state. And therefore the well-born, or free-born, or rich, may with good reason claim office; for holders of offices must be freemen and tax-payers: a state can be no more composed entirely of poor men than entirely of slaves. But if wealth and freedom are necessary elements, justice and valor are equally so; for without the former qualities a state cannot exist at all, without the latter not well.

13. If the existence of the state is alone to be considered, then it would seem that all, or some at least, of these claims are just; but, if we take into account a good life, then, as I have already said, education and excellence have superior claims. As, however, those who are equal in one thing ought not to have an equal share in all, nor those who are unequal in one thing to have an unequal share in all, it is certain that all forms of government which rest on either of these principles are perversions. All men have a claim in a certain sense, as I have already admitted, but not all have an absolute claim. The rich claim because they have a greater share in the land, and land is the common element of the state; also they are generally more trustworthy in contracts. The free claim under the same title as the well-born; for they are nearly akin. For the well-born are citizens in a truer sense than the low-born, and good birth is always valued in a man's own home. Another reason is, that those who are sprung from better ancestors are likely to be better men, for good birth is excellence of race. Excellence, too, may be truly said to have a claim, for justice has been acknowledged by us to be a social excellence, and it implies all others. Again, the many may urge their claim against the few; for, when taken collectively, and compared with the few, they are stronger and richer and better. But, what if the good, the rich, the well-born, and the other classes who make up a state, are all living together in the same city, will there, or will there not, be any doubt who shall rule?— No doubt at all in determining who ought to rule in each of the above-mentioned forms of government. For states are characterized by differences in their governing bodies—one of them has a government of the rich, another of the good, and so on. But a difficulty arises when all these elements coexist. How are we to decide? Suppose the good to be very few in number: may we consider their numbers in relation to their duties, and ask whether they are enough to administer the state, or so many as will make up a state? Objections may be urged against all the aspirants to political power. For those who found their claims on wealth or family might be thought to have no basis of justice; on this principle, if any one person were richer than all the rest, it is clear that he ought to be ruler of them. In like manner he who is very distinguished by his birth ought to have the superiority over all those who claim on the ground that they are free-born. In an aristocracy a like difficulty occurs about excellence; for if one citizen is better than the other members of the government, however good they may be, he too, upon the same principle of justice, should rule over them. And if the people are to be supreme because they are stronger than the few, then if one man, or more than one, but not a majority, is stronger than the many, they ought to rule, and not the many.

All these considerations appear to show that none of the principles on which men claim to rule and to hold all other men in subjection to them are right. To those who claim to be masters of the government on the ground of their excellence or their wealth, the many might fairly answer that they themselves are often better and richer than the few—I do not say individually, but collectively. And another problem which is sometimes put forward may be met in a similar manner. Some persons doubt whether the legislator who desires to make the justest laws ought to legislate with a view to the good of the better or of the many, when the case which we have mentioned occurs. Now what is right must be construed as equally right, and what is equally right is to be considered with reference to the advantage of the state, and the common good of the citizens. And a citizen is one who shares in governing and being governed. He differs under different forms of government, but in the best state he is one who is able and chooses to be governed and to govern with a view to the life of excellence.

If, however, there be some one person, or more than one, although not enough to make up the full complement of a state, whose excellence is so pre-eminent that the excellence or the political capacity of all the rest admit of no comparison with his or theirs, he or they can be no longer regarded as part of a state; for justice will not be done to the superior, if he is reckoned only as the equal of those who are so far inferior to him in excellence and in political capacity. Such a man may truly be deemed a God among men. Hence we see that legislation is necessarily concerned only with those who are equal in birth and in capacity; and that for men of pre-eminent excellence there is no law—

they are themselves a law. Anyone would be ridiculous who attempted to make laws for them: they would probably retort what, in the fable of Antisthenes, the lions said to the hares, when in the council of the beasts the latter began haranguing and claiming equality for all. And for this reason democratic states have instituted ostracism, equality is above all things their aim, and therefore they ostracized and banished from the city for a time those who seemed to predominate too much through their wealth, or the number of their friends, or through any other political influence. Mythology tells us that the Argonauts left Heracles behind for a similar reason; the ship Argo would not take him because she feared that he would have been too much for the rest of the crew. That is why those who denounce tyranny and blame the counsel which Periander gave to Thrasybulus cannot be held altogether just in their censure. The story is that Periander, when the herald was sent to ask counsel of him, said nothing, but only cut off the tallest ears of corn till he had brought the field to a level. The herald did not know the meaning of the action, but came and reported what he had seen to Thrasybulus, who understood that he was to cut off the principal men in the state; and this is a policy not only expedient for tyrants or in practice confined to them, but equally necessary in oligarchies and democracies. Ostracism is a measure of the same kind, which acts by disabling and banishing the most prominent citizens. Great powers do the same to whole cities and nations, as the Athenians did to the Samians, Chians, and Lesbians; no sooner had they obtained a firm grasp of the empire, than they humbled their allies contrary to treaty; and the Persian king has repeatedly crushed the Medes, Babylonians, and other nations, when their spirit has been stirred by the recollection of their former greatness.

The problem is a universal one, and equally concerns all forms of government, true as well as false; for, although perverted forms with a view to their own interests may adopt this policy, those which seek the common interest do so likewise. The same thing may be observed in the arts and sciences; for the painter will not allow the figure to have a foot which, however beautiful, is not in proportion, nor will the ship-builder allow the stern or any other part of the vessel to be unduly large, any more than the chorus-master will allow anyone who sings louder or better than all the rest to sing in the choir. Monarchs, too, may practise compulsion and still live in harmony with their cities, if their own government is for the interest of the state. Hence where there is an acknowledged superiority the argument in favour of ostracism is based upon a kind of political justice. It would certainly be better that the legislator should from the first so order his state as to have no need of such a remedy. But if the need arises, the next best thing is that he should endeavour to correct the evil by this or some similar measure. The principle, however, has not been fairly applied in states; for, instead of looking to the good of their own constitution, they have used ostracism for factious purposes. It is true that under perverted forms of government, and from their special point of view, such a measure is just and expedient, but it is also clear that it is not absolutely just. . . .

Part II

Medieval Political Philosophy

One predominant medieval theory of government is not well represented in this collection, the notion that kings had a divine right to rule their subjects by inheritance. Since the prevailing rules of the time dictated that property was inherited by the first son, and since God gave the world to Adam, if a king could claim direct first-son descent from Adam, it would follow that the land was his by right. Needless to say, such genealogies were generally inauthentic. But there were complex tensions between the developing nation-states of the Middle Ages and the power of the Church. The king could claim a divine right to rule, but that put the Church in a position to dispute such claims. The resulting political intrigue is the subject of much historical study.

But the monastic philosophers contributed other significant theories to political philosophy, including the notion that the laws of God are of a higher priority than the laws of kings. What has come to be known as "natural law" theory, that civil laws must conform to natural moral principles, has its roots in ancient times, as some of the previous selections indicate, but it fell to medieval philosophers to incorporate Christian theology and expand the notion in many ways. The influence of these theorists may be seen in modern civil disobedience movements from British India to the American Civil Rights movement, and indeed in revolutionary struggles in America and France. This chapter includes seminal contributions from Saint Augustine of Hippo, Saint Thomas Aquinas, and Marsilius of Padua.

Saint Augustine of Hippo (Aurelius Augustinus) (354–430 C.E.)

Born in Tagaste in North Africa to a pagan father and a Christian mother, he studied law and Roman literature in Carthage (370-374) and initially taught rhetoric for a living. His career took him from Tagaste to Carthage, to Rome, and to Naples (374-391). In philosophy he first admired Roman skepticism, while in religion he was a Manichean, believing in two gods: one good, one evil. He later studied neo-Platonic philosophy and, under the guidance of Ambrose, the bishop of Milan, Christianity. He formally converted to Christianity in 386. In 391 he changed professions, becoming a priest of the Roman Catholic Church. From 395 to his death he was the bishop of Hippo, near Carthage. He wrote extensively throughout his clerical career, contributing to philosophy and to the literature distinguishing heresy from dogma in the Church. His writings on virtue set the stage for some key insights into political philosophy.

*The City of God**

Fallen Nature
and the Two Cities

God, desiring not only that the human race might be able by their similarity of nature to associate with one another, but also that they might be bound together in harmony and peace by the ties of relationship, was pleased to derive all men from one individual. And He created men with such a nature that the members of the race should not have died, had not the first two (of whom one was created out of nothing, and the other out of him) merited this with their disobedience; for by them so great a sin was committed, that by it the human nature was altered for the worse, and was transmitted also to their posterity. . . .

That the whole human race has been condemned in its first origin, this life itself, if life it is to be called, bears witness by the host of cruel ills with which it is filled. Is not this proved by the profound and dreadful ignorance which produces all the errors that enfold the children of Adam, and from which no man can be delivered without toil, pain, and fear? Is it not proved by his love of so many vain and hurtful things, which produces gnawing cares, disquiet, griefs, fears, wild joys, quarrels, law-suits, wars, treasons, angers, hatreds, deceit, flattery, fraud, theft, robbery, perfidy, pride, ambition, envy, murders, parricides, cruelty, ferocity, wickedness, luxury, insolence, impudence, shamelessness, fornications, adulteries, incests, and the numberless uncleannesses and unnatural acts of both sexes, which it is shameful so much as to mention; sacrileges, heresies, blasphemies, perjuries, oppression of the innocent, calumnies, plots, falsehoods, false witnessings, unrighteous judgments, violent deeds, plunderings, and innumerable other crimes that do

---

*Abridgement suggested by J.M. Porter.

not easily come to mind, but that never absent themselves from the actuality of human existence? These are indeed the crimes of wicked men, yet they spring from that root of error and misplaced love which is born with every son of Adam. For who is there that has not observed with what profound ignorance, manifesting itself even in infancy, and with what superfluity of foolish desires, beginning to appear in boyhood, man comes into this life, so that, were he left to live as he pleased, and to do whatever he pleased, he would plunge into all, or certainly into many of those crimes and iniquities which I mentioned, and could not mention?

But because God does not wholly desert those whom He condemns, nor shuts up in His anger His tender mercies, the human race is restrained by law and education, which keep guard against the ignorance that besets us, and oppose the assaults of vice, but are themselves full of labour and sorrow. For what mean those multifarious threats which are used to restrain the folly of children? What mean pedagogues, masters, the birch, the strap, the cane, the schooling which Scripture says must be given a child, "beating him on the sides lest he wax stubborn," and it be hardly possible or not possible at all to subdue him? Why all these punishments, save to overcome ignorance and bridle evil desires—these evils with which we come into the world? For why is it that we remember with difficulty, and without difficulty forget? learn with difficulty, and without difficulty remain ignorant? are diligent with difficulty, and without difficulty are indolent? Does not this show that vitiated nature inclines and tends to by its own weight, and what succour it needs if it is to be delivered? Inactivity, sloth, laziness, negligence, are vices which shun labour, since labour, though useful, is itself a punishment.

But, besides the punishments of childhood, without which there would be no learning of what the parents wish—and the parents rarely wish anything useful to be taught—who can describe, who can conceive the number and severity of the punishments which afflict the human race —pains which are not only the accompaniment of the wickedness of godless men, but are a part of the human condition and the common misery —what fear and what grief are caused by bereavement and mourning, by losses and condemnations, by fraud and falsehood, by false suspicions, and all the crimes and wicked deeds of other men? For at their hands we suffer robbery, captivity, chains, imprisonment, exile, torture, mutilation, loss of sight, the violation of chastity to satisfy the lust of the oppressor, and many other dreadful evils. What numberless casualties threaten our bodies from without—extremes of heat and cold, storms, floods, inundations, lightning, thunder, hail, earthquakes, houses falling; or from the stumbling, or shying, or vice of horses; from countless poisons in fruits, water, air, animals; from the painful or even deadly bites of wild animals; from the madness which a mad dog communicates, so that even the animal which of all others is most gentle and friendly to its own master, becomes an object of intenser fear than a lion or dragon, and the man whom it has by chance infected with this pestilential contagion becomes so rabid, that his parents, wife, children, dread him more than any wild beast! What disasters are suffered by those who travel by land or sea! What man can go out of his own house without being exposed on all hands to unforeseen accidents? Returning home sound in limb, he slips on his own door-step, breaks his leg, and never recovers. What can seem safer than a man sitting in his chair? Eli the priest fell from his, and broke his neck. How many accidents do farmers, or rather all men, fear that the crops may suffer from the weather, or the soil, or the ravages of destructive animals? Commonly they feel safe when the crops are gathered and housed. Yet, to my certain knowledge, sudden floods have driven the labourers away, and swept the barns clean of the finest harvest. Is innocence a sufficient protection against the various assaults of demons? That no man might think so, even baptized infants, who are certainly unsurpassed in innocence, are sometimes so tormented, that God, who permits it, teaches us hereby to bewail the calamities of this life, and to desire the felicity of the life to come. As to bodily diseases, they are so numerous that they cannot all be contained even in medical books. And in very many, or almost all of them, the cures and remedies are themselves tortures, so that men are delivered from a pain that destroys by a cure that pains. Has not the madness of thirst driven men to drink human urine, and even their own? Has not hunger driven men to eat human flesh, and that the flesh not of bodies found dead, but of bodies slain for the purpose? Have not the fierce pangs of famine driven mothers to eat their own children, incredibly savage as it seems? In fine sleep itself, which is justly called repose, how little of repose there sometimes is in it when disturbed with dreams and visions; and with what terror is the wretched mind overwhelmed by the appearances of things which are so presented, and which, as it were, so stand out before the senses, that we cannot distinguish them from realities! How wretchedly do false appearances distract men in certain diseases! With what astonishing variety of appearances are even healthy men sometimes deceived by evil spirits, who produce these delusions for the sake of perplexing the senses of their victims, if they cannot succeed in seducing them to their side!

From this hell upon earth, . . . the deserved penalty of sin would have hurled all headlong even into the second death, of which there is no end, had not the undeserved grace of God saved some therefrom. And thus it has come to pass, that though there are very many and great nations all over the earth, whose rites and customs, speech, arms, and dress, are distinguished by marked differences, yet there are no more than two kinds of human society, which we may justly call two cities, according to the language of our Scriptures. The one consists of those who wish to live after the flesh, the other of those who wish to live after the spirit.

First, we must see what it is to live after the flesh, and what to live after the spirit. For any one who either does not recollect, or does not sufficiently weigh, the language of sacred Scripture, may, on first hearing what we have said, suppose that the Epicurean philosophers live after the flesh, because they place man's highest good in bodily pleasure; and that those others do so who have been of the opinion that in some form or other bodily good is man's supreme good; and that the mass of men do so who, without dogmatizing or philosophizing on the subject, are so prone to lust that they cannot delight in any pleasure save such as they receive from bodily sensations: and he may suppose that the Stoics, who place the supreme good of men in the soul, live after the spirit; for what is man's soul, if not spirit? But in the sense of the divine Scripture both are proved to live after the flesh. For by flesh it means not only the body of a terrestrial and mortal animal, as when it says, "All flesh is not the same flesh, but there is one kind of flesh of men, another flesh of beasts, another of fishes, another of birds," but it uses this word in many other significations. . . . If we are to ascertain what it is to live after the flesh (which is certainly evil, though the nature of flesh is not itself evil), we must carefully examine that passage of the epistle which the Apostle Paul wrote to the Galatians, in which he says, "Now the works of the flesh are manifest, which are these: adultery, fornication, uncleanness, lasciviousness, idolatry, witchcraft, hatred, variance, emulations, wrath, strife, seditions, heresies, envyings, murders, drunkenness, revellings, and such like: of the which I tell you before, as I have also told you in time past, that they which do such things shall not inherit the Kingdom of God." This whole passage of the apostolic epistle being considered, so far as it bears on the matter in hand, will be sufficient to answer the question, what it is to live after the flesh. . . .

In enunciating this proposition of ours, then, that because some live according to the flesh and others according to the spirit there have arisen two diverse and conflicting cities, we might equally well have said, "because some live according to man, others according to God." For Paul says very plainly to the Corinthians, "For whereas there is among you envying and strife, are ye not carnal, and walk according to man?" So that to walk according to man and to be carnal are the same; for by *flesh*, that is, by a part of man, man is meant. . . .

But the character of the human will is of moment; . . . for the man who lives according to God, and not according to man, ought to be a lover of good, and therefore a hater of evil. And since no one is evil by nature, but whosoever is evil is evil by vice, he who lives according to God ought to cherish toward evil men a perfect hatred, so that he shall neither hate the man because of his vice, nor love the vice because of the man. For the vice being cursed, all that ought to be loved, and nothing that ought to be hated, will remain.

He who resolves to love God, and to love his neighbor as himself, not according to man but according to God, is on account of this love said to be of a good will; and this is in Scripture more commonly called charity, but it is also, even in the same books, called love. . . . The right will is, therefore, well-directed love, and the wrong will is ill-directed love. Love yearning to have what is loved, is desire; and having and enjoying it, is joy; fleeing what is opposed to it, is fear; and feeling what is opposed to it, when it has befallen it, is sadness. Now these motions are evil if the love is evil; good if the love is good. . . .

Two cities have been formed, therefore, by two loves: the earthly by love of self, even to contempt of God; the heavenly by love of God, even to contempt of self. The former glories in itself, the latter in the Lord. For the one seeks glory from men; but the greatest glory of the other is God, the witness of conscience. The one lifts up its head in its own glory; the other says to its God, "Thou art my glory, and the lifter up of mine head." In the one, the princes and the nations it subdues are ruled by the love of ruling; in the other, the princes and the subjects serve one another in love, the latter obeying, while the former take thought for all. The one delights in its own strength, represented in the persons of its rulers; the other says to its God, "I will love Thee, O Lord, my strength." And therefore the wise men of the one city, living according to man, have sought for profit to their own bodies or souls, or both, and those who have known God "glorified Him not as God, neither were thankful, but became vain in their imaginations, and their foolish hearts were darkened; professing themselves to be wise"—that is, glorying in their own wisdom, and being possessed by pride—"they became fools, and changed the glory of the incorruptible God into an image made like to corruptible man, and to birds, and four-footed beasts, and creeping things." For they were either leaders or followers of the people in adoring images, "and worshipped and served the creature more than the Creator, who is blessed for ever." But in the other city there is no human wisdom, but only godliness, which offers due worship to the true God, and looks for its reward in the society of the saints, of holy angels as well as holy men, "that God may be all in all." . . . And when these two cities severally achieve what they wish, they live in peace, each after its kind.

Now peace is a good so great, that even in this earthly and mortal life there is no word we hear with such pleasure, nothing we more strongly desire, or enjoy more thoroughly when it comes. So that if we dwell for a little longer on this subject, we shall not, in my opinion, be wearisome to our readers who will bear with us both for the sake of understanding what is the end of this city of which we speak, and for the sake of the sweetness of peace which is dear to all.

Everyone who has observed the conduct of men's affairs and common human nature will agree with me in this: that just as there is no man who does not long for joy, so there is no man who does not long for peace. Even those who want war, want it really only for victory's sake: that is, they want to attain a glorious peace by fighting. For what is victory if not the subjugation of those who resist us? And when this is done, peace follows.

It is therefore with the desire for peace that wars are waged, even by those who take pleasure in exercising their warlike nature in command and battle. And hence it is obvious that peace is the end sought for by war. For every man seeks peace by waging war, but no man seeks war by making peace. For even they who intentionally interrupt the peace in which they are living have no hatred of peace, but only wish it changed into a peace that suits them better. They do not, therefore, wish to have no peace, but only one more to their mind. And in the case of sedition, when men have separated themselves from the community, they yet do not effect what they wish, unless they maintain some kind of peace with their fellow-conspirators. And therefore even robbers take care to maintain peace with their comrades, that they may with greater effect and greater safety invade the peace of other men. And if an individual happens to be of such unrivalled strength, and to be so jealous of partnership, that he trusts himself with no comrades, but makes his own plots, and commits depredations and murders on his own account, yet he maintains some shadow of peace with such persons as he is unable to kill, and from whom he wishes to conceal his deeds. In his own home, too, he makes it his aim to be at peace with his wife and children, and any other members of his household; for unquestionably their prompt obedience to his every look is a source of pleasure to him. And if this be not rendered, he is angry, he chides and punishes; and even by this storm he secures the calm peace of his own home, as occasion demands. For he sees that peace cannot be maintained unless all the members of the same domestic circle be subject to one head, such as he himself is in his own house. And therefore if a city or nation offered to submit itself to him, to serve him in the same style as he had made his household serve him, he would no longer lurk in a brigand's hiding-places, but lift his head in open day as a king, though the same covetousness and wickedness should remain in him. And thus all men desire to have peace with their own circle whom they wish to govern as suits themselves. For even those whom they make war against they wish to make their own, and impose on them the laws of their own peace.

But let us suppose a man such as poetry and mythology speak of—a man so insociable and savage as to be called rather a semi-man than a man. Although, then, his kingdom was the solitude of a dreary cave, and he himself was so singularly bad-hearted that he was named Cacus, which is the Greek word for *bad*; though he had no wife to soothe him with endearing talk, no children to play with, no sons to do his bidding, no friend to enliven him with intercourse, not even his father Vulcan (though in one respect he was happier than his father, not having begotten a monster like himself); although he gave to no man, but took as he wished whatever he could, from whomsoever he could, when he could; yet in that solitary den, the floor of which, as Virgil says, was always reeking with recent slaughter, there was nothing else than peace sought, a peace in which no one should molest him, or disquiet him with any assault or alarm. With his own body he desired to be at peace; and he was satisfied only in proportion as he had this peace. For he ruled his members, and they obeyed him; and for the sake of pacifying his mortal nature, which rebelled when it needed anything, and of allaying the sedition of hunger which threatened to banish the soul from the body, he made forays, slew, and devoured, but used the ferocity and savageness he displayed in these actions only for the preservation of his own life's peace. So that, had he been willing to make with other men the same peace which he made with himself in his own cave, he would neither have been called bad, nor a monster, nor a semi-man. Or if the appearance of his body and his vomiting smoky fires frightened men from having any dealings with him, perhaps his fierce ways arose not from a desire to do mischief, but from the necessity of finding a living. But he may have had no existence, or, at least, he was not such as the poets fancifully describe him, for they had to exalt Hercules, and did so at the expense of Cacus. It is better, then, to believe that such a man or semi-man never existed, and that this, in common with many other fancies of the poets, is mere fiction. For the most savage animals (and he is said to have been almost a wild beast) encompass their own species with a ring of protecting peace. They cohabit, beget, produce, suckle, and bring up their young, though very many of them are not gregarious, but solitary—not like sheep, deer, pigeons, starlings, bees, but such as lions, foxes, eagles, bats. For what tigress does not gently purr over her cub, and lay aside her ferocity to fondle them? What kite, solitary as he is when circling over his prey, does not seek a mate, build a nest, hatch the eggs, bring up the young birds, and maintain with the mother of his family as peaceful a domestic alliance as he can? How much more powerfully do the laws of man's nature move him to hold fellowship and maintain peace with all men so far as in him lies, since even wicked men wage war to maintain the peace of their own circle, and wish that, if possible, all men belonged to them, that all men and things might serve but one head, and might, either through love or fear, yield themselves to peace with him! . . .

But the dominion of bad men harms themselves far more than their subjects, for they destroy their own souls in their greater license to exercise their lusts; while those who are put under them in service are not hurt except by their own iniquities. For to the just all the evils imposed on them by unjust rulers are not the punishment of crime, but the test of virtue. Therefore the good man, although he is a slave, is free; but the bad man, even if he reigns, is a slave, and that not of one man, but what is far more grievous, of as many masters as he has vices; of which vices where the divine Scripture treats, it says: "Of whatsoever a man is overcome, to that he is in bondage." . . .

This earthly city, which shall not be everlasting (for it will no longer be a city when it has been committed to perpetual pains) has all its good in this world, and rejoices in it with such joy as such things can afford. It is spread throughout the world in the most diverse places, and, though united by a common nature, is for the most part divided against itself, and the strongest oppress the others, because all follow after their own interests and lusts, while what is longed for either suffices for none, or not for all, because it is not the true good. . . . Each part of it that arms against another desires to be the world's master, whereas it is itself in bondage to vice. If, when it has conquered, it is inflated with pride, its victory is self-destroying; but if it turns its thoughts upon the common casualties of our mortal condition, and is rather anxious concerning the disasters that may befall it than elated with the successes already achieved, this victory, though of a higher kind, is still only short-lived; for it cannot abidingly rule over those whom it has subjugated by conquest. Yet one cannot say that the things this earthly city desires are not good, since it itself is, of its kind, better than all other human beings. For it desires earthly peace for the sake of enjoying earthly goods, and it makes war in order to attain this peace; since, if it has conquered, and there remains no one to resist it, it enjoys a peace which it had not while there were opposing parties to contest it for the enjoyment of those things which were too little to satisfy both.

And the vanquished readily succumb to the victors, preferring any sort of peace and safety to freedom itself; so that they who choose to die rather than be slaves have been greatly wondered at. For nature seems to cry out with one voice through all peoples of the world, that it is better to serve the conqueror than be destroyed by war. Thus it happens (but not without God's providence) that some are endowed with kingdoms and others made subject to kings.

True Justice:
Not of this World

Justinus, who wrote Greek or rather foreign history in Latin, and briefly, like Trogus Pompeius whom he followed, begins his work thus: "In the beginning of the affairs of peoples and nations the government was in the hands of kings, who were raised to the height of this majesty not by courting the people, but by the knowledge good men had of their moderation. The people were held bound by no laws; the decisions of the princes were instead of laws. It was the custom to guard rather than to extend the boundaries of the empire; and kingdoms were kept within the bounds of each ruler's native land. Ninus king of the Assyrians first of all, through new lust of empire, changed the old and, as it were, ancestral custom of nations. He first made war on his neighbours, and wholly subdued as far as to the frontiers of Libya the nations as yet untrained to resist." And a little after he says: "Ninus established by constant possession the greatness of the authority he had gained. Having mastered his nearest neighbours, he went on to others, strengthened by the accession of forces, and by making each fresh victory the instrument of that which followed, subdued the nations of the whole East." Now, with whatever fidelity to fact either he or Trogus may in general have written—for that they sometimes told lies is shown by other more trustworthy writers—yet it is agreed among other authors, that the kingdom of the Assyrians was extended far and wide by King Ninus. And it lasted so long, that the Roman empire has not yet attained the same age; for, as those write who have treated of chronological history, this kingdom endured for twelve hundred and forty years from the first year in which Ninus began to reign, until it was transferred to the Medes. But to make war on your neighbours, and thence to proceed to others, and through mere lust of dominion to crush and subdue people who do you no harm, what else is this to be called than great robbery? . . .

Indeed, without justice, what are kingdoms but great robberies? For what are robberies themselves, but little kingdoms? The band itself is made up of men; it is ruled by the authority of a prince, it is knit together by the pact of the confederacy; the booty is divided by the law agreed on. If, by the admittance of abandoned men, this evil increases to such a degree that it holds places, fixes abodes, takes possession of cities, and subdues peoples, it assumes the more plainly the name of a kingdom, because the reality is now manifestly conferred on it, not by the removal of covetousness, but by the addition of impunity. Indeed, that was an apt and true reply which was given to Alexander the Great by a pirate who had been seized. For when that king had asked the man what he meant by keeping hostile possession of the sea, he answered with bold pride, "What thou meanest by seizing the whole earth; but because I do it with a petty ship, I am called a robber, whilst thou who dost it with a great fleet art styled emperor." . . .

Yet, at the end of the second book of Cicero's *De Republica*, Scipio says: "As, among the different sounds which proceed from lyres, flutes, and the human voice, there must be maintained a certain harmony which a cultivated ear cannot endure to hear disturbed or jarring, but which may be elicited in full and absolute concord by the modulation even of voices very unlike one another; so where reason is allowed to modulate the diverse elements of the state, there is obtained a perfect concord from the upper, lower, and middle classes as from various sounds; and what musicians call harmony in singing, is concord in matters of state, which is the strictest bond and best security of any republic, and which by no ingenuity can be retained where justice has become extinct." Then, when he had expatiated somewhat more fully, and had more copiously illustrated the benefits of its presence and the ruinous effects of its absence upon a state, Pilus, one of the company present at the discussion, struck in and demanded that the question should be more thoroughly sifted, and that the subject of justice should be freely discussed for the sake of ascertaining what truth there was in the maxim which was then becoming daily more current, that "the republic cannot be governed without injustice." Scipio expressed his willingness to have this maxim discussed and sifted, and gave it as his opinion that it was baseless, and that no progress could be made in discussing the republic unless it was established, not only that this maxim, that "the republic cannot be governed without injustice," was false, but also that the truth is, that it cannot be governed without the most absolute justice. And the discussion of this question, being deferred till the next day, is carried on in the third book with great animation. For Pilus himself undertook to defend the position that the republic cannot be governed without injustice, at the same time being at special pains to clear himself of any real participation in that opinion. He advocated with great keenness the cause of injustice against justice, and endeavoured by plausible reasons and examples to demonstrate that the former is beneficial, the latter useless, to the republic. Then, at the request of the company, Laelius attempted to defend justice, and strained every nerve to prove that nothing is so hurtful to a state as injustice; and that without justice a republic can neither be governed, nor even continue to exist.

When this question has been handled to the satisfaction of the company, Scipio reverts to the original thread of discourse, and repeats with commendation his own brief definition of a republic, that it is the weal of the people. "The people" he defines as being not every assemblage or mob, but an assemblage associated by a common acknowledgement of law, and by a community of interests. Then he shows the use of definition in debate; and from these definitions of his own he gathers that a republic, or "weal of the people," then exists only when it is well and justly governed, whether by a monarch, or an aristocracy, or by the whole people. But when the monarch is unjust, or as the Greeks say, a tyrant; or the aristocrats are unjust, and form a faction; or the people themselves are unjust, and become, as Scipio for want of a better name calls them, themselves the tyrant, then the republic is not only blemished (as had been proved the day before), but by legitimate deduction from those definitions, it altogether ceases to be. For it could not be the people's weal when a tyrant factiously lorded it over the state; neither would the people be any longer a people if it were unjust, since it would no longer answer the definition of a people—"an assemblage associated by a common acknowledgement of law, and by a community of interests."

Cicero himself, speaking not in the person of Scipio or any one else, but uttering his own sentiments, uses the following language in the beginning of the fifth book, after quoting a line from the poet Ennius, in which he said, "Rome's severe morality and her citizens are her safeguard." "This verse," says Cicero, "seems to me to have all the sententious truthfulness of an oracle. For neither would the citizens have availed without the morality of the community, nor would the morality of the commons without outstanding men have availed either to establish or so long to maintain in vigour so grand a republic with so wide and just an empire. Accordingly, before our day, the hereditary usages formed our foremost men, and they on their part retained the usages and institutions of their fathers. But our age, receiving the republic as a *chef d'oeuvre* of another age which has already begun to grow old, has not merely neglected to restore the colours of the original, but has not even been at the pains to preserve so much as the general outline and most outstanding features. For what survives of that primitive morality which the poet called Rome's safeguard? It is so obsolete and forgotten, that, far from practising it, one does not even know it. And of the citizens what shall I say? Morality has perished through poverty of great men; a poverty for which we must not only assign a reason, but for the guilt of which we must answer as criminals charged with a capital crime. For it is through our vices, and not by any mishap, that we retain only the name of a republic, and have long since lost the reality."

This is the confession of Cicero, long indeed after the death of Africanus, whom he introduced as an interlocutor in his work *De Republica.* . . . But Rome's admirers have need to inquire whether, even in the days of primitive men and morals, true justice flourished in it; or was it not perhaps even then, to use the casual expression of Cicero, rather a coloured painting than the living reality? If God will, I mean in its own place to show that—according to the definitions in which Cicero himself, using Scipio as his mouthpiece, briefly propounded what a republic is, and what a people is, and according to many testimonies, both of his own lips and of those who took part in that same debate—Rome never was a republic, because true justice had never a place in it.

Away with deceitful masks, with deluding whitewashes; look at the naked deeds; weigh them naked, judge them naked! Sallust says that "equity and virtue prevailed among the Romans not more by force of laws than of nature."

Saint Thomas Aquinas (c. 1225–1274 C.E.)

One of the most influential of the medieval philosophers, Aquinas was the first to suc-cessfully integrate Aristotelian ideas into Catholic doctrine in a coherent and thorough way. He was canonized by Pope John XXII in 1323. He was an enormously prolific writer. We excerpt here the selections from his *Summa Theologica* which deal with the theory of "natural law." Natural law theory holds that laws of human construction must agree with certain natural principles in order to count as obligatory. This view has formed the basis of the modern civil disobedience tradition.

From The Treatise on Law*

Question 94

Of The Natural Law
(In Six Articles)

We must now consider the natural law; concerning which there are six points of inquiry: (1) What is the natural law? (2) What are the precepts of the natural law? (3) Whether all acts of virtue are prescribed by the natural law? (4) Whether the natural law is the same in all? (5) Whether it is changeable? (6) Whether it can be abolished from the heart of man?

First Article
Whether The Natural Law is a Habit?

We proceed thus to the First Article:—

Objection 1. It would seem that the natural law is a habit. Because, as the Philosopher says (*Ethic.* ii. 5), *there are three things in the soul, power, habit, and passion.* But the natural law is not one of the soul's powers: nor is it one of the passions; as we may see by going through them one by one. Therefore the natural law is a habit.

Obj. 2. Further, Basil says that the conscience or *synderesis is the law of our mind;* which can only apply to the natural law. But the *synderesis* is a habit, as was shown in the First Part. Therefore the natural law is a habit.

Obj. 3. Further, the natural law abides in man always, as will be shown further on (A. 6). But man's reason, which the law regards, does not always think about the nat-ural law. Therefore the natural law is not an act, but a habit.

On the contrary, Augustine says (*De Bono Conjug.* xxi) that *a habit is that whereby some-thing is done when necessary.* But such is not the natural law: since it is in infants and in the damned who cannot act by it. Therefore the natural law is not a habit.

---

*An Excerpt.

I answer that, A thing may be called a habit in two ways. First, properly and essentially: and thus the natural law is not a habit. For it has been stated above that the natural law is something appointed by reason, just as a proposition is a work of reason. Now that which a man does is not the same as that whereby he does it: for he makes a becoming speech by the habit of grammar. Since then a habit is that by which we act, a law cannot be a habit properly and essentially.

Secondly, the term habit may be applied to that which we hold by a habit: thus faith may mean that which we hold by faith. And accordingly, since the precepts of the natural law are sometimes considered by reason actually, while sometimes they are in the reason only habitually, in this way the natural law may be called a habit. Thus, in speculative matters, the indemonstrable principles are not the habit itself whereby we hold those principles, but are the principles the habit of which we possess.

Reply Obj. 1. The Philosopher proposes there to discover the genus of virtue; and since it is evident that virtue is a principle of action, he mentions only those things which are principles of human acts, viz., powers, habits and passions. But there are other things in the soul besides these three: there are acts; thus *to will* is in the one that wills; again, things known are in the knower; moreover its own natural properties are in the soul, such as immortality and the like.

Reply Obj. 2. *Synderesis* is said to be the law of our mind, because it is a habit containing the precepts of the natural law, which are the first principles of human actions.

Reply Obj. 3. This argument proves that the natural law is held habitually: and this is granted.

To the argument advanced in the contrary sense we reply that sometimes a man is unable to make use of that which is in him habitually, on account of some impediment; thus, on account of sleep, a man is unable to use the habit of science. In like manner, through the deficiency of his age, a child cannot use the habit of understanding of principles, or the natural law, which is in him habitually.

Second Article
Whether the Natural Law Contains Several
Precepts, or One Only?

We proceed thus to the Second Article:—

Objection 1. It would seem that the natural law contains, not several precepts, but one only. For law is a kind of precept, as stated above. If therefore there were many precepts of the natural law, it would follow that there are also many natural laws.

Obj. 2. Further, the natural law is consequent to human nature. But human nature, as a whole, is one; though, as to its parts, it is manifold. Therefore, either there is but one precept of the law of nature, on account of the unity of nature as a whole; or there are many, by reason of the number of parts of human nature. The result would be that even things relating to the inclination of the concupiscible faculty belong to the natural law.

Obj. 3. Further, law is something pertaining to reason, as stated above. Now reason is but one in man. Therefore there is only one precept of the natural law.

On the contrary, The precepts of the natural law in man stand in relation to practical matters, as the first principles to matters of demonstration. But there are several first indemonstrable principles. Therefore there are also several precepts of the natural law.

I answer that, As stated above, the precepts of the natural law are to the practical reason, what the first principles of demonstrations are to the speculative reason; because both are self-evident principles. Now a thing is said to be self-evident in two ways: first, in itself; secondly, in relation to us. Any proposition is said to be self-evident in itself, if its predicate is contained in the notion of the subject: although, to one who knows not the definition of the subject, it happens that such a proposition is not self-evident. For instance, this proposition, *Man is a rational being,* is, in its very nature, self-evident, since who says *man,* says *a rational being:* and yet to one who knows not what a man is, this proposition is not self-evident. Hence it is that, as Boethius says (*De Hebdom*), certain axioms or propositions are universally self-evident to all; and such are those propositions whose terms are known to all, as, *Every whole is greater than its part,* and, *Things equal to one and the same are equal to one another.* But some propositions are self-evident only to the wise, who understand the meaning of the terms of such propositions: thus to one who understands that an angel is not a body, it is self-evident that an angel is not circumscriptively in a place: but this is not evident to the unlearned, for they cannot grasp it.

Now a certain order is to be found in those things that are apprehended universally. For that which, before aught else, falls under apprehension, is *being,* the notion of which is included in all things whatsoever a man apprehends. Wherefore the first indemonstrable principle is that *the same thing cannot be affirmed and denied at the same time,* which is based on the notion of *being* and *not-being:* and on this principle all others are based, as is stated in *Metaph.* iv., text. 9. Now as *being* is the first thing that falls under the apprehension simply, so *good* is the first thing that falls under the apprehension of the practical reason, which is directed to action: since every agent acts for an end under the aspect of good. Consequently the first principle in the practical reason is one founded on the notion of good, viz., that *good is that which all things seek after.* Hence this is the first precept of law, that *good is to be done and ensued, and evil is to be avoided.* All other precepts of the natural law are based upon this: so that whatever the practical reason naturally apprehends as man's good (or evil) belongs to the precepts of the natural law as something to be done or avoided.

Since, however, good has the nature of an end, and evil, the nature of a contrary, hence it is that all those things to which man has a natural inclination, are naturally apprehended by reason as being good, and consequently as objects of pursuit, and their contraries as evil, and objects of avoidance. Wherefore according to the order of natural inclinations, is the order of the precepts of the natural law. Because in man there is first of all an inclination to good in accordance with the nature which he has in common with all substances: inasmuch as every substance seeks the preservation of its own being, according to its nature: and by reason of this inclination, whatever is a means of preserving human life, and of warding off its obstacles, belongs to the natural law. Secondly, there is in man an inclination to things that pertain to him more specially, according to that nature which he has in common with other animals: and in virtue of this inclination, those things are said to belong to the natural law, *which nature has taught to all animals,* such as sexual intercourse, education of offspring and so forth. Thirdly, there is in man an inclination to good, according to the nature of his reason, which nature is proper to him: thus man has a natural inclination to know the truth about God, and to live in society: and in this respect, whatever pertains to this inclination belongs to the natural law; for instance, to shun ignorance, to avoid offending those among whom one has to live, and other such things regarding the above inclination.

Reply Obj. 1. All these precepts of the law of nature have the character of one natural law, inasmuch as they flow from one first precept.

Reply Obj. 2. All the inclinations of any parts whatsoever of human nature, e.g., of the concupiscible and irascible parts, in so far as they are ruled by reason, belong to the natural law, and are reduced to one first precept, as stated above: so that the precepts of the natural law are many in themselves, but are based on one common foundation.

Reply Obj. 3. Although reason is one in itself, yet it directs all things regarding man; so that whatever can be ruled by reason, is contained under the law of reason.

Third Article
Whether All Acts of Virtue are Prescribed
by the Natural Law?

We proceed thus to the Third Article:—

Objection 1. It would seem that not all acts of virtue are prescribed by the natural law. Because, as stated above it is essential to a law that it be ordained to the common good. But some acts of virtue are ordained to the private good of the individual, as is evident especially in regard to acts of temperance. Therefore not all acts of virtue are the subject of natural law.

Obj. 2. Further, every sin is opposed to some virtuous act. If therefore all acts of virtue are prescribed by the natural law, it seems to follow that all sins are against nature: whereas this applies to certain special sins.

Obj. 3. Further, those things which are according to nature are common to all. But acts of virtue are not common to all: since a thing is virtuous in one, and vicious in another. Therefore not all acts of virtue are prescribed by the natural law.

On the contrary, Damascene says (*De Fide Orthod.* iii. 4) that *virtues are natural.* Therefore virtuous acts also are a subject of the natural law.

I answer that, We may speak of virtuous acts in two ways: first, under the aspect of virtuous; secondly, as such and such acts considered in their proper species. If then we speak of acts of virtue, considered as virtuous, thus all virtuous acts belong to the natural law. For it has been stated that to the natural law belongs everything to which a man is inclined according to his nature. Now each thing is inclined naturally to an operation that is suitable to it according to its form: thus fire is inclined to give heat. Wherefore, since the rational soul is the proper form of man, there is in every man a natural inclination to act according to reason: and this is to act according to virtue. Consequently, considered thus, all acts of virtue are prescribed by the natural law: since each one's reason naturally dictates to him to act virtuously. But if we speak of virtuous acts, considered in themselves, i.e., in their proper species, thus not all virtuous acts are prescribed by the natural law: for many things are done virtuously, to which nature does not incline at first; but which, through the inquiry of reason, have been found by men to be conducive to well-living.

Reply Obj. 1. Temperance is about the natural concupiscenses of food, drink and sexual matters, which are indeed ordained to the natural common good, just as other matters of law are ordained to the moral common good.

Reply Obj. 2. By human nature we may mean either that which is proper to man— and in this sense all sins, as being against reason, are also against nature, as Damascene states (*De Fide Orthod.* ii. 30): or we may mean that nature which is common to man and other animals; and in this sense, certain special sins are said to be against nature; thus contrary to sexual intercourse, which is natural to all animals, is unisexual lust, which has received the special name of the unnatural crime.

Reply Obj. 3. This argument considers acts in themselves. For it is owing to the various conditions of men, that certain acts are virtuous for some, as being proportionate and becoming to them, while they are vicious for others, as being out of proportion to them.

Fourth Article
Whether the Natural Law is the Same in All Men?

We proceed thus to the Fourth Article:—

Objection 1. It would seem that the natural law is not the same in all. For it is stated in the Decretals (*Dist.* i.) that *the natural law is that which is contained in the Law and the Gospel.* But this is not common to all men; because, as it is written (Rom. x. 16), *all do not obey the gospel.* Therefore the natural law is not the same in all men.

Obj. 2. Further, *Things which are according to the law are said to be just,* as stated in *Ethic.* v. But it is stated in the same book that nothing is so universally just as not to be subject to change in regard to some men. Therefore even the natural law is not the same in all men.

Obj. 3. Further, as stated above, to the natural law belongs everything to which a man is inclined according to his nature. Now different men are naturally inclined to different things; some to the desire of pleasures, others to the desire of honours, and other men to other things. Therefore there is not one natural law for all.

On the contrary, Isidore says (*Etym.* v. 4): *The natural law is common to all nations.*

I answer that, As stated above, to the natural law belongs those things to which a man is inclined naturally: and among these it is proper to man to be inclined to act according to reason. Now the process of reason is from the common to the proper. . . . The speculative reason, however, is differently situated in this matter, from the practical reason. For, since the speculative reason is busied chiefly with necessary things, which cannot be otherwise than they are, its proper conclusions, like the universal principles, contain the truth without fail. The practical reason, on the other hand, is busied with contingent matters, about which human actions are concerned: and consequently, although there is necessity in the general principles, the more we descend to matters of detail, the more frequently we encounter defects. Accordingly then in speculative matters truth is the same in all men, both as to principles and as to conclusions: although the truth is not known to all as regards the conclusions, but only as regards the principles which are called common notions. But in matters of action, truth or practical rectitude is not the same for all, as to matters of detail, but only as to the general principles: and where there is the same rectitude in matters of detail, it is not equally known to all.

It is therefore evident that, as regards the general principles whether of speculative or of practical reason, truth or rectitude is the same for all, and is equally known by all. As to the proper conclusions of the speculative reason, the truth is the same for all, but is not equally known to all: thus it is true for all that the three angles of a triangle are together equal to two right angles, although it is not known to all. But as to the proper conclusions of the practical reason, neither is the truth or rectitude the same for all, nor, where it is the same, is it equally known by all. Thus it is right and true for all to act according to reason: and from this principle it follows as a proper conclusion, that goods entrusted to another should be restored to their owner. Now this is true for the majority of cases: but it may happen in a particular case that it would be injurious, and therefore unreasonable, to restore goods held in trust; for instance if they are claimed for the purpose of fighting against one's country. And this principle will be found to fail the more, according as we descend further into detail, e.g., if one were to say that goods held in trust should be restored with such and such a guarantee, or in such and such a way; because the greater the number of conditions added, the greater the number of ways in which the principle may fail, so that it be not right to restore or not to restore.

Consequently we must say that the natural law, as to general principles, is the same for all, both as to rectitude and as to knowledge. But as to certain matters of detail, which are conclusions, as it were, of those general principles, it is the same for all in the majority of cases, both as to rectitude and as to knowledge; and yet in some few cases it may fail, both as to rectitude, by reason of certain obstacles (just as natures subject to generation and corruption fail in some few cases on account of some obstacle), and as to knowledge, since in some the reason is perverted by passion, or evil habit, or an evil disposition of nature; thus formerly, theft, although it is expressly contrary to the natural law, was not considered wrong among the Germans, as Julius Caesar relates.

Reply Obj. 1. The meaning of the sentence quoted is not that whatever is contained in the Law and the Gospel belongs to the natural law, since they contain many things that are above nature; but that whatever belongs to the natural law is fully contained in them. Wherefore Gratian, after saying that *the natural law is what is contained in the Law and the Gospel*, adds at once, by way of example, *by which everyone is commanded to do to others as he would be done by.*

Reply Obj. 2. The saying of the Philosopher is to be understood of things that are naturally just, not as general principles, but as conclusions drawn from them, having rectitude in the majority of cases, but failing in a few.

Reply Obj. 3. As, in man, reason rules and commands the other powers, so all the natural inclinations belonging to the other powers must needs be directed according to reason. Wherefore it is universally right for all men, that all their inclinations should be directed according to reason.

Fifth Article
Whether the Natural Law can be Changed?

We proceed thus to the Fifth Article:—

Objection 1. It would seem that the natural law can be changed. Because on Ecclus. xvii. 9, *He gave them instructions, and the law of life*, the gloss says: *He wished the law of the letter to be written, in order to correct the law of nature.* But that which is corrected is changed. Therefore the natural law can be changed.

Obj. 2. Further, the slaying of the innocent, adultery, and theft are against the natural law. But we find these things changed by God: as when God commanded Abraham to slay his innocent son (Gen. xxii. 2); and when He ordered the Jews to borrow and purloin the vessels of the Egyptians (Exod. xii. 35); and when He commanded Osee to take to himself *a wife of fornications* (Osee i. 2). Therefore the natural law can be changed.

Obj. 3. Further, Isidore says (*Etym.* v. 4) that *the possession of all things in common, and universal freedom, are matters of natural law.* But these things are seen to be changed by human laws. Therefore it seems that the natural law is subject to change.

On the contrary. It is said in the Decretals (*Dist.* v.): *The natural law dates from the creation of the rational creature. It does not vary according to time, but remains unchangeable.*

I answer that, A change in the natural law may be understood in two ways. First, by way of addition. In this sense nothing hinders the natural law from being changed: since many things for the benefit of human life have been added over and above the natural law, both by the Divine law and by human laws.

Secondly, a change in the natural law may be understood by way of subtraction, so that what previously was according to the natural law, ceases to be so. In this sense, the natural law is altogether unchangeable in its first principles: but in its secondary principles, which, as we have said, are certain detailed proximate conclusions drawn from the first principles, the natural law is not changed so that what it prescribes be not right in most cases. But it may be changed in some particular cases of rare occurrence, through some special causes hindering the observance of such precepts, as stated above.

Reply Obj. 1. The written law is said to be given for the correction of the natural law, either because it supplies what was wanting to the natural law; or because the natural law was perverted in the hearts of some men, as to certain matters, so that they esteemed those things good which are naturally evil; which perversion stood in need of correction.

Reply Obj. 2. All men alike, both guilty and innocent, die the death of nature: which death of nature is inflicted by the power of God on account of original sin, according to 1 Kings ii. 6: *The Lord killeth and maketh alive.* Consequently, by the command of God, death can be inflicted on any man, guilty or innocent, without any injustice whatever.—In like manner adultery is intercourse with another's wife; who is allotted to him by the law emanating from God. Consequently intercourse with any woman, by the command of God, is neither adultery nor fornication.—The same applies to theft, which is the taking of another's property. For whatever is taken by the command of God, to Whom all things belong, is not taken against the will of its owner, whereas it is in this that theft consists.—Nor is it only in human things, that whatever is commanded by God is right; but also in natural things, whatever is done by God, is, in some way, natural, as stated in the First Part.

Reply Obj. 3. A thing is said to belong to the natural law in two ways. First, because nature inclines thereto: e.g., that one should not do harm to another. Secondly, because nature did not bring in the contrary: thus we might say that for man to be naked is of the natural law, because nature did not give him clothes, but art invented them. In this sense, *the possession of all things in common and universal freedom* are said to be of the natural law, because, to wit, the distinction of possessions and slavery were not brought in by nature, but devised by human reason for the benefit of human life. Accordingly the law of nature was not changed in this respect, except by addition.

Sixth Article
Whether The Law of Nature Can Be Abolished from the Heart of Man?

We proceed thus to the Sixth Article:—

Objection 1. It would seem that the natural law can be abolished from the heart of man. Because on Rom. ii. 14, *When the Gentiles who have not the law*, etc., a gloss says that *the law of righteousness, which sin had blotted out, is graven on the heart of man when he is restored by grace.* But the law of righteousness is the law of nature. Therefore the law of nature can be blotted out.

Obj. 2. Further, the law of grace is more efficacious than the law of nature. But the law of grace is blotted out by sin. Much more therefore can the law of nature be blotted out.

Obj. 3. Further, that which is established by law is made just. But many things are enacted by men, which are contrary to the law of nature. Therefore the law of nature can be abolished from the heart of man.

On the contrary, Augustine says (*Conf.* ii.): *Thy law is written in the hearts of men, which iniquity itself effaces not.* But the law which is written in men's hearts is the natural law. Therefore the natural law cannot be blotted out.

I answer that, As stated above, there belong to the natural law, first, certain most general precepts, that are known to all; and secondly, certain secondary and more detailed precepts, which are, as it were, conclusions following closely from first principles. As to those general principles, the natural law, in the abstract, can nowise be blotted out from men's hearts. But it is blotted out in the case of a particular action, in so far as reason is hindered from applying the general principle to a particular point of practice, on account of concupiscence or some other passion, as stated above.—But as to the other, i.e., the secondary precepts, the natural law can be blotted out from the human heart, either by evil persuasions, just as in speculative matters errors occur in respect of necessary conclusions; or by vicious customs and corrupt habits, as among some men, theft, and even unnatural vices, as the Apostle states (Rom. i.), were not esteemed sinful.

Reply Obj. 1. Sin blots out the law of nature in particular cases, not universally, except perchance in regard to the secondary precepts of the natural law, in the way stated above.

Reply Obj. 2. Although grace is more efficacious than nature, yet nature is more essential to man, and therefore more enduring.

Reply Obj. 3. This argument is true of the secondary precepts of the natural law, against which some legislators have framed certain enactments which are unjust.

Question 95

Of Human Law
(In Four Articles)

We must now consider human law; and (1) this law considered in itself; (2) its power; (3) its mutability. Under the first head there are four points of inquiry: (1) Its utility. (2) Its origin. (3) Its quality. (4) Its division.

First Article
Whether it was Useful for Laws to be
Framed by Men?

We proceed thus to the First Article:—

Objection 1. It would seem that it was not useful for laws to be framed by men. Because the purpose of every law is that man be made good thereby, as stated above. But men are more to be induced to be good willingly by means of admonitions, than against their will, by means of laws. Therefore there was no need to frame laws.

Obj. 2. Further, as the Philosopher says (*Ethic.* v. 4), *men have recourse to a judge as to animate justice.* But animate justice is better than inanimate justice, which is contained in laws. Therefore it would have been better for the execution of justice to be entrusted to the decision of judges, than to frame laws in addition.

Obj. 3. Further, every law is framed for the direction of human actions, as is evident from what has been stated above. But since human actions are about singulars, which are infinite in number, matters pertaining to the direction of human actions cannot be taken into sufficient consideration except by a wise man, who looks into each one of them. Therefore it would have been better for human acts to be directed by the judgment of wise men, than by the framing of laws. Therefore there was no need of human laws.

On the contrary, Isidore says (*Etym.* v. 20): *Laws were made that in fear thereof human audacity might be held in check, that innocence might be safeguarded in the midst of wickedness, and that the dread of punishment might prevent the wicked from doing harm.* But these things are most necessary to mankind. Therefore it was necessary that human laws should be made.

I answer that, As stated above, man has a natural aptitude for virtue; but the perfection of virtue must be acquired by man by means of some kind of training. Thus we observe that man is helped by industry in his necessities, for instance, in food and clothing. Certain beginnings of these he has from nature, viz., his reason and his hands; but he has not the full complement, as other animals have, to whom nature has given sufficiency of clothing and food. Now it is difficult to see how man could suffice for himself in the matter of this training: since the perfection of virtue consists chiefly in withdrawing man from undue pleasures, to which above all man is inclined, and especially the young, who are more capable of being trained. Consequently a man needs to receive this training from another, whereby to arrive at the perfection of virtue. And as to those young people who are inclined to acts of virtue, by their good natural disposition, or by custom, or rather by the gift of God, paternal training suffices, which is by admonitions. But since some are found to be depraved, and prone to vice, and not easily amenable to words, it was necessary for such to be restrained from evil by force and fear, in order that, at least, they might desist from evildoing, and leave others in peace, and that they themselves, by being habituated in this way, might be brought to do willingly what hitherto they did from fear, and thus become virtuous. Now this kind of training, which compels through fear of punishment, is the discipline of laws. Therefore, in order that man might have peace and virtue, it was necessary for laws to be framed: for, as the Philosopher says (*Polit.* i. 2), *as man is the most noble of animals, if he be perfect in virtue, so is he the lowest of all, if he be severed from law and righteousness;* because man can use his reason to devise means of satisfying his lusts and evil passions, which other animals are unable to do.

Reply Obj. 1. Men who are well disposed are led willingly to virtue by being admonished better than by coercion: but men who are evilly disposed are not led to virtue unless they are compelled.

Reply Obj. 2. As the Philosopher says (*Rhet.* i. 1), *it is better that all things be regulated by law, than left to be decided by judges:* and this for three reasons. First, because it is easier to find a few wise men competent to frame right laws, than to find the many who would be necessary to judge aright of each single case.—Secondly, because those who make laws consider long beforehand what laws to make; whereas judgment on each single case has to be pronounced as soon as it arises: and it is easier for man to see what is right, by taking many instances into consideration, than by considering one solitary fact. —Thirdly, because lawgivers judge in the abstract and of future events; whereas those who sit in judgment judge of things present, towards which they are affected by love, hatred, or some kind of cupidity; wherefore their judgment is perverted.

Since then the animated justice of the judge is not found in every man, and since it can be deflected, it was necessary, whenever possible, for the law to determine how to judge, and for very few matters to be left to the decision of men.

Reply Obj. 3. Certain individual facts which cannot be covered by the law *have necessarily to be committed to judges,* as the Philosopher says in the same passage: for instance, *concerning something that has happened or not happened,* and the like.

Second Article
Whether Every Human Law is Derived from the Natural Law?

We proceed thus to the Second Article:—

Objection 1. It would seem that not every human law is derived from the natural law. For the Philosopher says (*Ethic.* v. 7) that *the legal just is that which originally was a matter of indifference.* But those things which arise from the natural law are not matters of indifference. Therefore the enactments of human laws are not all derived from the natural law.

Obj. 2. Further, positive law is contrasted with natural law, as stated by Isidore (*Etym.* v. 4) and the Philosopher (*Ethic.* v., loc. cit.) But those things which flow as conclusions from the general principles of the natural law belong to the natural law, as stated above. Therefore that which is established by human law does not belong to the natural law.

Obj. 3. Further, the law of nature is the same for all; since the Philosopher says (*Ethic.* v. 7) that *the natural just is that which is equally valid everywhere.* If therefore human laws were derived from the natural laws, it would follow that they too are the same for all: which is clearly false.

Obj. 4. Further, it is possible to give a reason for things which are derived from the natural law. But *it is not possible to give the reason for all the legal enactments of the lawgivers,* as the Jurist says. Therefore not all human laws are derived from the natural law.

On the contrary, Tully says (*Rhetor.* ii.): *Things which emanated from nature and were approved by custom, were sanctioned by fear and reverence for the laws.*

I answer that, As Augustine says (*De Lib. Arb.* i. 5), *that which is not just seems to be no law at all:* wherefore the force of a law depends on the extent of its justice. Now in human affairs a thing is said to be just, from being right, according to the rule of reason. But the first rule of reason is the law of nature, as is clear from what has been stated above. Consequently every human law has just so much of the nature of law, as it is derived from the law of nature. But if in any point it deflects from the law of nature, it is no longer a law but a perversion of law.

But it must be noted that something may be derived from the natural law in two ways: first, as a conclusion from premises, secondly, by way of determination of certain generalities. The first way is like to that by which, in sciences, demonstrated conclusions are drawn from the principles: while the second mode is likened to that whereby, in the arts, general forms are particularized as to details: thus the craftsman needs to determine the general form of a house to some particular shape. Some things are therefore derived from the general principles of the natural law, by way of conclusions; e.g., that *one must not kill* may be derived as a conclusion from the principle that *one should do harm to no man:* while some are derived therefrom by way of determination; e.g., the law of nature has it that the evildoer should be punished; but that he be punished in this or that way, is a determination of the law of nature.

Accordingly both modes of derivation are found in the human law. But those things which are derived in the first way, are contained in human law not as emanating therefrom exclusively, but have some force from the natural law also. But those things which are derived in the second way, have no other force than that of human law.

Reply Obj. 1. The Philosopher is speaking of those enactments which are by way of determination or specification of the precepts of the natural law.

Reply Obj. 2. This argument avails for those things that are derived from the natural law, by way of conclusions.

Reply Obj. 3. The general principles of the natural law cannot be applied to all men in the same way on account of the great variety of human affairs: and hence arises the diversity of positive laws among various people.

Reply Obj. 4. These words of the Jurist are to be understood as referring to decisions of rulers in determining particular points of the natural law: on which determinations the judgment of expert and prudent men is based as on its principles; in so far, to wit, as they see at once what is the best thing to decide.

Hence the Philosopher says (*Ethic.* vi. 11) that in such matters, *we ought to pay as much attention to the undemonstrated sayings and opinions of persons who surpass us in experience, age and prudence, as to their demonstrations.*

Third Article
Whether Isidore's Description of the Quality of Positive Law is Appropriate?

We proceed thus to the Third Article:—

Objection 1. It would seem that Isidore's description of the quality of positive law is not appropriate, when he says (*Etym.* v. 21): *Law shall be virtuous, just, possible to nature, according to the custom of the country, suitable to place and time, necessary, useful; clearly expressed, lest by its obscurity it lead to misunderstanding; framed for no private benefit, but for the common good.* Because he had previously expressed the quality of law in three conditions, saying that *law is anything founded on reason, provided that it foster religion, be helpful to discipline, and further the common weal.* Therefore it was needless to add any further conditions to these.

Obj. 2. Further, Justice is included in honesty, as Tully says (*De Offic.* vii.). Therefore after saying *honest* it was superfluous to add *just.*

Obj. 3. Further, written law is condivided with custom, according to Isidore (*Etym.* ii. 10). Therefore it should not be stated in the definition of law that it is *according to the custom of the country.*

Obj. 4. Further, a thing may be necessary in two ways. It may be necessary simply, because it cannot be otherwise: and that which is necessary in this way, is not subject to human judgment, wherefore human law is not concerned with necessity of this kind. Again a thing may be necessary for an end: and this necessity is the same as usefulness. Therefore it is superfluous to say both *necessary* and *useful.*

On the contrary stands the authority of Isidore.

I answer that, Whenever a thing is for an end, its form must be determined proportionately to that end; as the form of a saw is such as to be suitable for cutting (*Phys.* ii., text. 88). Again, everything that is ruled and measured must have a form proportionate to its rule and measure. Now both these conditions are verified of human law: since it is both something ordained to an end; and is a rule or measure ruled or measured by a higher measure. And this higher measure is twofold, viz., the Divine law and the natural law, as explained above. Now the end of human law is to be useful to man, as the Jurist states. Wherefore Isidore in determining the nature of law, lays down, at first, three conditions; viz., that it *foster religion,* inasmuch as it is proportionate to the Divine law; that it be *helpful to discipline,* inasmuch as it is proportionate to the natural law; and that it *further the common weal,* inasmuch as it is proportionate to the utility of mankind.

All the other conditions mentioned by him are reduced to these three. For it is called virtuous because it fosters religion. And when he goes on to say that it should be *just, possible to nature, according to the customs of the country, adapted to place and time,* he implies that it should be helpful to discipline. For human discipline depends first on the order of reason, to which he refers by saying *just:*—secondly, it depends on the ability of the agent; because discipline should be adapted to each one according to his ability, taking also into account the ability of nature (for the same burdens should be not laid on children as on adults); and should be according to human customs; since man cannot live alone in society, paying no heed to others:—thirdly, it depends on certain circumstances, in respect of which he says, *adapted to place and time.*—The remaining words, *necessary, useful, etc.*, mean that law should further the common weal: so that *necessity* refers to the removal of evils; *usefulness* to the attainment of good; *clearness of expression*, to the need of preventing any harm ensuing from the law itself.—And since, as stated above, law is ordained to the common good, this is expressed in the last part of the description.

This suffices for the Replies to the Objections.

Fourth Article
Whether Isidore's Division of Human Laws is Appropriate?

We proceed thus to the Fourth Article:—

Objection 1. It would seem that Isidore wrongly divided human statutes or human law (*Etym.* v. 4 *seqq.*). For under this law he includes the *law of nations*, so called, because, as he says, *nearly all nations use it.* But as he says, *natural law is that which is common to all nations.* Therefore the law of nations is not contained under positive human law, but rather under natural law.

Obj. 2. Further, those laws which have the same force, seem to differ not formally but only materially. But *statutes, decrees of the commonalty, senatorial decrees*, and the like which he mentions (ibid., 9), all have the same force. Therefore they do not differ, except materially. But art takes no notice of such a distinction: since it may go on to infinity. Therefore this division of human laws is not appropriate.

Obj. 3. Further, just as, in the state, there are princes, priests and soldiers, so are there other human offices. Therefore it seems that, as this division includes *military law*, and *public law*, referring to priests and magistrates; so also it should include other laws pertaining to other offices of the state.

Obj. 4. Further, those things that are accidental should be passed over. But it is accidental to law that it be framed by this or that man. Therefore it is unreasonable to divide laws according to the names of lawgivers, so that one be called the *Cornelian* law, another the *Falcidian* law, etc.

On the contrary, The authority of Isidore (Obj. 1) suffices.

I answer that, A thing can of itself be divided in respect of something contained in the notion of that thing. Thus a soul either rational or irrational is contained in the notion of animal: and therefore animal is divided properly and of itself in respect of its being rational or irrational; but not in the point of its being white or black, which are entirely beside the notion of animal. Now, in the notion of human law, many things are contained, in respect of any of which human law can be divided properly and of itself. For in the first place it belongs to the notion of human law, to be derived from the law of nature, as explained above. In this respect positive law is divided into the *law of nations* and *civil law*, according to the two ways in which something may be derived from the law of nature, as stated above. Because, to the law of nations belong those things which are derived from the law of nature, as conclusions from premises, e.g., just buyings and sellings, and the like, without which men cannot live together, which is a point of the law of nature, since man is by nature a social animal, as is proved in *Polit.* i. 2. But those things which are derived from the law of nature by way of particular determination, belong to the civil law, according as each state decides on what is best for itself.

Secondly, it belongs to the notion of human law, to be ordained to the common good of the state. In this respect human law may be divided according to the different kinds of men who work in a special way for the common good: e.g., priests, by praying to God for the people; princes, by governing the people; soldiers, by fighting for the safety of the people. Wherefore certain special kinds of law are adapted to these men.

Thirdly, it belongs to the notion of human law, to be framed by that one who governs the community of the state, as shown above. In this respect, there are various human laws according to the various forms of government. Of these, according to the Philosopher (*Polit.* iii. 10) one is *monarchy*, i.e., when the state is governed by one; and then we have *Royal Ordinances.* Another form is *aristocracy*, i.e., government by the best men or men of highest rank; and then we have the *Authoritative legal opinions* (*Responsa Prudentum*) and *Decrees of the Senate* (*Senatus consulta*). Another form is *oligarchy*, i.e., government by a few rich and powerful men; and then we have *Praetorian*, also called *Honorary*, law. Another form of government is that of the people, which is called democracy, and there we have *Decrees of the commonalty* (*Plebiscita*). There is also tyrannical government, which is altogether corrupt, which, therefore, has no corresponding law. Finally, there is a form of government made up of all these, and which is the best: and in this respect we have *law sanctioned by the Lords and Commons*, as stated by Isidore (loc. cit.).

Fourthly, it belongs to the notion of human law to direct human actions. In this respect, according to the various matters of which the law treats, there are various kinds of laws, which are sometimes named after their authors: thus we have the *Lex Julia* about adultery, the *Lex Cornelia* concerning assassins, and so on, differentiated in this way, not on account of the authors, but on account of the matters to which they refer.

Reply Obj. 1. The law of nations is indeed, in some way, natural to man, in so far as he is a reasonable being, because it is derived from the natural law by way of a conclusion that is not very remote from its premises. Wherefore men easily agreed thereto. Nevertheless it is distinct from the natural law, especially from that natural law which is common to all animals.

The Replies to the other Objections are evident from what has been said.

Question 96

Of the Power of Human Law
(In Six Articles)

We must now consider the power of human law. Under this head there are six points of inquiry: (1) Whether human law should be framed for the community? (2) Whether human law should repress all vices? (3) Whether human law is competent to direct all acts of virtue? (4) Whether it binds man in conscience? (5) Whether all men are subject to human law? (6) Whether those who are under the law may act beside the letter of the law?

First Article
Whether Human Law Should be Framed for the Community Rather than for the Individual?

We proceed thus to the First Article:—

Objection 1. It would seem that human law should be framed not for the community, but rather for the individual. For the Philosopher says (*Ethic.* v. 7) that *the legal just . . . includes all particular acts of legislation . . . and all those matters which are the subject of decrees,* which are also individual matters, since decrees are framed about individual actions. Therefore law is framed not only for the community, but also for the individual.

Obj. 2. Further, law is the director of human acts, as stated above. But human acts are about individual matters. Therefore human laws should be framed, not for the community, but rather for the individual.

Obj. 3. Further, law is a rule and measure of human acts, as stated above. But a measure should be most certain, as stated in *Metaph.* x. Since therefore in human acts no general proposition can be so certain as not to fail in some individual cases, it seems that laws should be framed not in general but for individual cases.

On the contrary, The Jurist says (*Pandect. Justin,* lib. i., tit. iii., art. ii., *De legibus,* etc.) that *laws should be made to suit the majority of instances; and they are not framed according to what may possibly happen in an individual case.*

I answer that, Whatever is for an end should be proportionate to that end. Now the end of law is the common good; because, as Isidore says (*Etym.* v. 21) that *law should be framed, not for any private benefit, but for the common good of all the citizens.* Hence human laws should be proportionate to the common good. Now the common good comprises many things. Wherefore laws should take account of many things, as to persons, as to matters, and as to times. Because the community of the state is composed of many persons; and its good is procured by many actions; nor is it established to endure for only a short time, but to last for all time by the citizens succeeding one another, as Augustine says (*De Civ. Dei* ii, 21; xxii. 6).

Reply Obj. 1. The Philosopher (*Ethic.* v. 7) divides the legal just, i.e., positive law, into three parts. For some things are laid down simply in a general way: and these are the general laws. Of these he says that *the legal is that which originally was a matter of indifference, but which, when enacted, is so no longer:* as the fixing of the ransom of a captive.—Some things affect the community in one respect, and individuals in another. These are called *privileges,* i.e., *private laws,* as it were, because they regard private persons, although their power extends to many matters; and in regard to these, he adds, *and further, all particular acts of legislation.*—Other matters are legal, not through being laws, but through being applications of general laws to particular cases: such are decrees which have the force of law; and in regard to these, he adds *all matters subject to decrees.*

Reply Obj. 2. A principle of direction should be applicable to many; wherefore (*Metaph.* x., text. 4) the Philosopher says that all things belonging to one genus, are measured by one, which is the principle in that genus. For if there were as many rules or measures as there are things measured or ruled, they would cease to be of use, since their use consists in being applicable to many things. Hence law would be of no use, if it did not extend further than to one single act. Because the decrees of prudent men are made for the purpose of directing individual actions; whereas law is a general precept, as stated above.

Reply Obj. 3. *We must not seek the same degree of certainty in all things* (*Ethic.* i. 3). Consequently in contingent matters, such as natural and human things, it is enough for a thing to be certain, as being true in the greater number of instances, though at times and less frequently it fail.

Second Article
Whether it Belongs to Human Law to Repress all Vices?

We proceed thus to the Second Article:—

Objection 1. It would seem that it belongs to human law to repress all vices. For Isidore says (*Etym.* v. 20) that *laws were made in order that, in fear thereof, man's audacity might be held in check.* But it would not be held in check sufficiently, unless all evils were repressed by law. Therefore human law should repress all evils.

Obj. 2. Further, the intention of the lawgiver is to make the citizens virtuous. But a man cannot be virtuous unless he forbear from all kinds of vice. Therefore it belongs to human law to repress all vices.

Obj. 3. Further, human law is derived from the natural law, as stated above. But all vices are contrary to the law of nature. Therefore human law should repress all vices.

On the contrary, We read in *De Lib. Arb.* i. 5: *It seems to me that the law which is written for the governing of the people rightly permits these things, and that Divine providence punishes them.* But Divine providence punishes nothing but vices. Therefore human law rightly allows some vices, by not repressing them.

I answer that. As stated above, law is framed as a rule or measure of human acts. Now a measure should be homogeneous with that which it measures, as stated in *Metaph.* x., text. 3, 4, since different things are measured by different measures. Wherefore laws imposed on men should also be in keeping with their condition, for, as Isidore says (*Etym.* v. 21), law should be *possible both according to nature, and according to the customs of the country.* Now possibility or faculty of action is due to an interior habit or disposition: since the same thing is not possible to one who has not a virtuous habit, as is possible to one who has. Thus the same is not possible to a child as to a full-grown man: for which reason the law for children is not the same as for adults, since many things are permitted to children, which in an adult are punished by law or at any rate are open to blame. In like manner many things are permissible to men not perfect in virtue, which would be intolerable in a virtuous man.

Now human law is framed for a number of human beings, the majority of whom are not perfect in virtue. Wherefore human laws do not forbid all vices, from which the virtuous abstain, but only the more grievous vices, from which it is possible for the majority to abstain; and chiefly those that are to the hurt of others, without the prohibition of which human society could not be maintained: thus human law prohibits murder, theft and suchlike.

Reply Obj. 1. Audacity seems to refer to the assailing of others. Consequently it belongs to those sins chiefly whereby one's neighbour is injured: and these sins are forbidden by human law, as stated.

Reply Obj. 2. The purpose of human law is to lead men to virtue, not suddenly, but gradually. Wherefore it does not lay upon the multitude of imperfect men the burdens of those who are already virtuous, viz., that they should abstain from all evil. Otherwise these imperfect ones, being unable to bear such precepts, would break out into yet greater evils: thus it is written (Prov. xxx. 33): *He that violently bloweth his nose, bringeth out blood;* and (Matth. ix. 17) that if *new wine,* i.e., precepts of a perfect life, is *put into old bottles,* i.e., into imperfect men, *the bottles break, and the wine runneth out,* i.e., the precepts are despised, and those men, from contempt, break out into evils worse still.

Reply Obj. 3. The natural law is a participation in us of the eternal law: while human law falls short of the eternal law. Now Augustine says (*De Lib. Arb.* i. 5): *The law which is framed for the government of states, allows and leaves unpunished many things that are punished by Divine providence. Nor, if this law does not attempt to do everything, is this a reason why it should be blamed for what it does.* Wherefore, too, human law does not prohibit everything that is forbidden by the natural law.

Third Article
Whether Human Law Prescribes Acts of All the Virtues?

We proceed thus to the Third Article:—

Objection 1. It would seem that human law does not prescribe acts of all the virtues. For vicious acts are contrary to acts of virtue. But human law does not prohibit all vices, as stated above. Therefore neither does it prescribe all acts of virtue.

Obj. 2. Further, a virtuous act proceeds from a virtue. But virtue is the end of law; so that whatever is from a virtue, cannot come under a precept of law. Therefore human law does not prescribe all acts of virtue.

Obj. 3. Further, law is ordained to the common good, as stated above. But some acts of virtue are ordained, not to the common good, but to private good. Therefore the law does not prescribe all acts of virtue.

On the contrary, the Philosopher says (*Ethic.* v. 1) that the law *prescribes the performance of the acts of a brave man, . . . and the acts of the temperate man, . . . and the acts of the meek man: and in like manner as regards the other virtues and vices, prescribing the former, forbidding the latter.*

I answer that, The species of virtues are distinguished by their objects, as explained above. Now all the objects of virtues can be referred either to the private good of an individual, or to the common good of the multitude: thus matters of fortitude may be achieved either for the safety of the state, or for upholding the rights of a friend, and in like manner with the other virtues. But law, as stated above is ordained to the common good. Wherefore there is no virtue whose acts cannot be prescribed by the law. Nevertheless human law does not prescribe concerning all the acts of every virtue: but only in regard to those that are ordainable to the common good,—either immediately, as when certain things are done directly for the common good,—or mediately, as when a lawgiver prescribes certain things pertaining to good order, whereby the citizens are directed in the upholding of the common good of justice and peace.

Reply Obj. 1. Human law does not forbid all vicious acts, by the obligation of a precept, as neither does it prescribe all acts of virtue. But it forbids certain acts of each vice, just as it prescribes some acts of each virtue.

Reply Obj. 2. An act is said to be an act of virtue in two ways. First, from the fact that a man does something virtuous; thus the act of justice is to do what is right, and an act of fortitude is to do brave things: and in this way law prescribes certain acts of virtue.—Secondly an act of virtue is when a man does a virtuous thing in a way in which a virtuous man does it. Such an act always proceeds from virtue: and it does not come under a precept of law, but is the end at which every lawgiver aims.

Reply Obj. 3. There is no virtue whose act is not ordainable to the common good, as stated above, either mediately or immediately.

Fourth Article
Whether Human Law Binds a Man in Conscience?

We proceed thus to the Fourth Article:—

Objection 1. It would seem that human law does not bind a man in conscience. For an inferior power has no jurisdiction in a court of higher power. But the power of a man, which frames human law, is beneath the Divine power. Therefore human law cannot impose its precept in a Divine court, such as is the court of conscience.

Obj. 2. Further, the judgment of conscience depends chiefly on the commandments of God. But sometimes God's commandments are made void by human laws, according to Matth. xv. 6: *You have made void the commandment of God for your tradition.* Therefore human law does not bind a man in conscience.

Obj. 3. Further, human laws often bring loss of character and injury on man, according to Isa. x. 1 *et seq.*: *Woe to them that make wicked laws, and when they write, write injustice; to oppress the poor in judgment, and do violence to the cause of the humble of My people.* But it is lawful for anyone to avoid oppression and violence. Therefore human laws do not bind man in conscience.

On the contrary, It is written (1 Pet. ii. 19): *This is thanksworthy, if for conscience . . . a man endure sorrows, suffering wrongfully.*

I answer that, Laws framed by man are either just or unjust. If they be just, they have the power of binding in conscience, from the eternal law whence they are derived, according to Prov. viii. 15: *By Me kings reign, and lawgivers decree just things.* Now laws are said to be just, both from the end, when, to wit, they are ordained to the common good,—and from their author, that is to say, when the law that is made does not exceed the power of the lawgiver,—and from their form, when, to wit, burdens are laid on the subjects, according to an equality of proportion and with a view to the common good. For, since one man is a part of the community, each man, in all that he is and has, belongs to the community; just as a part, in all that it is, belongs to the whole; wherefore nature inflicts a loss on the part, in order to save the whole: so that on this account, such laws as these, which impose proportionate burdens, are just and binding in conscience, and are legal laws.

On the other hand laws may be unjust in two ways: first, by being contrary to human good, through being opposed to the things mentioned above:—either in respect of the end, as when an authority imposes on his subjects burdensome laws, conducive, not to the common good, but rather to his own cupidity or vainglory;—or in respect of the author, as when a man makes a law that goes beyond the power committed to him;—or in respect of the form, as when burdens are imposed unequally on the community, although with a view to the common good. The like are acts of violence rather than laws; because as Augustine says (*De Lib. Arb.* i. 5): *a law that is not just, seems to be no law at all.* Wherefore such laws do not bind in conscience, except perhaps in order to avoid scandal or disturbance, for which cause a man should even yield his right, according to Matth. v. 40, 41: *If a man . . . take away thy coat, let go thy cloak also unto him; and whosoever will force thee one mile, go with him other two.*

Secondly, laws may be unjust through being opposed to the Divine good: such are the laws of tyrants inducing to idolatry, or to anything else contrary to the Divine law: and laws of this kind must nowise be observed, because, as stated in Acts v. 29, *we ought to obey God rather than men.*

Reply Obj. 1. As the Apostle says (Rom. xiii. 1, 2), all human power is from God . . . *therefore he that resisteth the power,* in matters that are within its scope, *resisteth the ordinance of God;* so that he becomes guilty according to his conscience.

Reply Obj. 2. This argument is true of laws that are contrary to the commandments of God, which is beyond the scope of (human) power. Wherefore in such matters human law should not be obeyed.

Reply Obj. 3. This argument is true of a law that inflicts unjust hurt on its subjects. The power that man holds from God does not extend to this: wherefore neither in such matters is man bound to obey the law, provided he avoid giving scandal or inflicting a more grievous hurt.

Fifth Article
Whether All are Subject to the Law?

We proceed thus to the Fifth Article:—

Objection 1. It would seem that not all are subject to the law. For those alone are subject to a law for whom a law is made. But the Apostle says (1 Tim. i. 9): *The law is not made for the just man.* Therefore the just are not subject to the law.

Obj. 2. Further, Pope Urban says: *He that is guided by the private law need not for any reason be bound by the public law.* Now all spiritual men are led by the private law of the

Holy Ghost, for they are the sons of God, of whom it is said (Rom. viii. 14): *Whosoever are led by the Spirit of God, they are the sons of God.* Therefore not all men are subject to human law.

Obj. 3. Further, the Jurist says that *the sovereign is exempt from the laws.* But he that is exempt from the law is not bound thereby. Therefore not all are subject to the law.

On the contrary, the Apostle says (Rom. xiii. 1): *Let every soul be subject to the higher powers.* But *subjection* to a power seems to imply subjection to the laws framed by that power. Therefore all men should be subject to human law.

I answer that, As stated above, the notion of law contains two things; first, that it is a rule of human acts; secondly, that it has coercive power. Wherefore a man may be subject to law in two ways. First, as the regulated is subject to the regulator: and, in this way, whoever is subject to a power, is subject to the law framed by that power. But it may happen in two ways that one is not subject to a power. In one way, by being altogether free from its authority: hence the subjects of one city or kingdom are not bound by the laws of the sovereign of another city or kingdom, since they are not subject to his authority. In another way, by being under a yet higher law; thus the subject of a proconsul should be ruled by his command, but not in those matters in which the subject receives his orders from the emperor: for in these matters, he is not bound by the mandate of the lower authority, since he is directed by that of a higher. In this way, one who is simply subject to a law, may not be subject thereto in certain matters, in respect of which he is ruled by a higher law.

Secondly, a man is said to be subject to a law as the coerced is subject to the coercer. In this way the virtuous and righteous are not subject to the law, but only the wicked. Because coercion and violence are contrary to the will: but the will of the good is in harmony with the law, whereas the will of the wicked is discordant from it. Wherefore in this sense the good are not subject to the law, but only the wicked.

Reply Obj. 1. This argument is true of subjection by way of coercion: for, in this way, *the law is not made for the just men:* because *they are a law to themselves,* since they *shew the work of the law written in their hearts,* as the Apostle says (Rom. ii. 14, 15). Consequently the law does not enforce itself upon them as it does on the wicked.

Reply Obj. 2. The law of the Holy Ghost is above all law framed by man: and therefore spiritual men, in so far as they are led by the law of the Holy Ghost, are not subject to the law in those matters that are inconsistent with the guidance of the Holy Ghost. Nevertheless the very fact that spiritual men are subject to law, is due to the leading of the Holy Ghost, according to 1 Pet. ii. 13: *Be ye subject . . . to every human creature for God's sake.*

Reply Obj. 3. The sovereign is said to be *exempt from the law,* as to its coercive power; since, properly speaking; no man is coerced by himself, and law has no coercive power save from the authority of the sovereign. Thus then is the sovereign said to be exempt from the law, because none is competent to pass sentence on him, if he acts against the law. Wherefore on Ps. L. 6: *To Thee only have I sinned,* a gloss says that *there is no man who can judge the deeds of a king.*—But as to the directive force of law, the sovereign is subject to the law by his own will, according to the statement (*Extra, De Constit.* cap. *Cum omnes*) that *whatever law a man makes for another, he should keep himself. And a wise authority says*: "*Obey the law that thou makest thyself.*" Moreover the Lord reproaches those who *say and do not;* and who *bind heavy burdens and lay them on men's shoulders, but with a finger of their own they will not move them* (Matth. xxiii. 3, 4). Hence, in the judgment of God, the sovereign is not exempt from the law, as to its directive force; but he should fulfil it of his own free-will and not of constraint.—Again the sovereign is above the law, in so far as, when it is expedient, he can change the law, and dispense in it according to time and place.

Sixth Article
Whether He Who is Under a Law May Act
Beside the Letter of the Law?

We proceed thus to the Sixth Article:—

Objection 1. It seems that he who is subject to a law may not act beside the letter of the law. For Augustine says (*De Vera Relig.* xxxi): *Although men judge about temporal laws when they make them, yet when once they are made they must pass judgment not on them, but according to them.* But if anyone disregard the letter of the law, saying that he observes the intention of the lawgiver, he seems to pass judgment on the law. Therefore it is not right for one who is under a law to disregard the letter of the law, in order to observe the intention of the lawgiver.

Obj. 2. Further, he alone is competent to interpret the law who can make the law. But those who are subject to the law cannot make the law. Therefore they have no right to interpret the intention of the lawgiver, but should always act according to the letter of the law.

Obj. 3. Further, every wise man knows how to explain his intention by words. But those who framed the laws should be reckoned wise: for Wisdom says (Prov. viii. 15): *By Me kings reign, and lawgivers decree just things.* Therefore we should not judge of the intention of the lawgiver otherwise than by the words of the law.

On the contrary, Hilary says (*De Trin.* iv.): *The meaning of what is said is according to the motive for saying it; because things are not subject to speech, but speech to things.* Therefore we should take account of the motive of the lawgiver, rather than of his very words.

I answer that, As stated above, every law is directed to the common weal of men, and derives the force and nature of law accordingly. Hence the Jurist says: *By no reason of law, or favour of equity, is it allowable for us to interpret harshly, and render burdensome, those useful measures which have been enacted for the welfare of man.* Now it happens often that the observance of some point of law conduces to the common weal in the majority of instances, and yet, in some cases, is very hurtful. Since then the lawgiver cannot have in view every single case, he shapes the law according to what happens most frequently, by directing his attention to the common good. Wherefore if a case arise wherein the observance of that law would be hurtful to the general welfare, it should not be observed. For instance, suppose that in a beseiged city it be an established law that the gates of the city are to be kept closed, this is good for public welfare as a general rule: but, if it were to happen that the enemy are in pursuit of certain citizens, who are defenders of the city, it would be a great loss to the city, if the gates were not opened to them: and so in that case the gates ought to be opened, contrary to the letter of the law, in order to maintain the common weal, which the lawgiver had in view.

Nevertheless it must be noted, that if the observance of the law according to the letter does not involve any sudden risk needing instant remedy, it is not competent for everyone to expound what is useful and what is not useful to the state: those alone can do this who are in authority, and who, on account of suchlike cases, have the power to dispense from the laws. If, however, the peril be so sudden as not to allow of the delay involved by referring the matter to authority, the mere necessity brings with it a dispensation, since necessity knows no law.

Reply Obj. 1. He who in case of necessity acts beside the letter of the law, does not judge of the law; but of a particular case in which he sees that the letter of the law is not to be observed.

Reply Obj. 2. He who follows the intention of the lawgiver, does not interpret the law simply; but in a case in which it is evident, by reason of the manifest harm, that the lawgiver intended otherwise. For if it be a matter of doubt, he must either act according to the letter of the law, or consult those in power.

Reply Obj. 3. No man is so wise as to be able to take account of every single case; wherefore he is not able sufficiently to express in words all those things that are suitable for the end he has in view. And even if a lawgiver were able to take all the cases into consideration, he ought not to mention them all, in order to avoid confusion: but should frame the law according to that which is of most common occurrence.

Marsilius of Padua (c. 1275–1342 C.E.)

Marsilius, an Italian political philosopher, taught at the University of Paris in the early 14th Century. He is thought to have begun his advanced education studying medicine. In his book *Defensor Pacis* (Defender of Peace), excerpted here, he embarked upon a criticism of absolute Papal authority—the doctrine of plenitude of power—for which the work was denounced by Pope John XXII, and Marsilius was branded a heretic. He had argued against the view that temporal authorities must be subject to papal edict, and for the idea that secular authority is higher because it represents the people. His book also describes his views on the proper scope for civil authorities. Marsilius left for Ludwig of Bavaria's Germany and lived there until his death in 1342.

From Defender of Peace*

Chapter II. On the First Questions in this Book, and the Distinction of the Various Meanings of the Term "State"

1. Entering upon our proposed task, we wish first to show what are the tranquillity and intranquillity of the state or city; and first the tranquillity, for if this be not clear, one is necessarily ignorant also of what is intranquillity. Since, however, both of these seem to be dispositions of the city or state (let this be assumed from Cassiodorus), we shall consequently make clear what must be revealed at the very outset; namely, what is the state or city, and why. Through this, the definitions of tranquillity and of its opposite will be more readily apparent.

2. Following the aforesaid order for the definition of the tranquillity of the city or state, we must notice, in order to prevent ambiguity from entering our project, that the term "state" (*regnum*) has many meanings. In one sense it means a number of cities (*civitatum*) or provinces contained under one regime; in which sense a state does not differ from a city with respect to species of polity but rather with respect to quantity. In another sense the term "state" signifies a certain species of temperate polity or regime, which Aristotle calls "temperate monarchy"; in this sense a state may consist in a single city as well as in many cities, as was the case around the time of the rise of civil communities, for then there was usually one king in a single city. The third and most familiar sense of this term is a combination of the first and the second. In its fourth sense it means something common to every species of temperate regime, whether in a single city or in many; it was in this sense that Cassiodorus used it in the passage we quoted at the beginning of this book, and this, too, is the sense in which we shall use the term in our discussions of the matters under inquiry.

---

*An Excerpt.

3. Now we must define tranquillity and its opposite. Let us assume with Aristotle in his *Politics* Book I, Chapter 2, and Book V, Chapter 3, that the city is like an animate nature or animal. For just as an animal well disposed in accordance with nature is composed of certain proportioned parts ordered to one another and communicating their functions mutually and for the whole, so too the city is constituted of certain such parts when it is well disposed and established in accordance with reason. The relation, therefore, of the city or state and its parts to tranquillity will be seen to be similar to the relation of the animal and its parts to health. The trustworthiness of this inference we can accept from what all men comprehend about each of these relations. For they think that health is the best disposition of an animal in accordance with nature, and likewise that tranquillity is the best disposition of a city established in accordance with reason. Health, moreover, as the more experienced physicists describe it, is the good disposition of the animal whereby each of its parts can perfectly perform the operations belonging to its nature; according to which analogy tranquillity will be the good disposition of the city or state whereby each of its parts will be able perfectly to perform the operations belonging to it in accordance with reason and its establishment. And since a good definition consignifies contraries, intranquillity will be the diseased disposition of the city or state, like the illness of an animal, whereby all or some of its parts are impeded from performing the operations belonging to them, either entirely or to the extent required for complete functioning.

In this general way, then, we have defined tranquillity and its opposite, intranquillity.

Chapter III. On the Origin of the Civil Community

1. Having defined tranquillity as the good disposition of the city for the functioning of its parts, we must now examine what the city is in itself, and why; what and how many are its primary parts; what is the function appropriate to each part, their causes, and their order in relation to one another. For these are the main points required for the perfect determination of tranquillity and its opposite.

2. However, before discussing the city and its species or modes, since the city is the perfect community we must first trace the origin of civil communities and of their regimes and modes of living. From the imperfect kinds, men have advanced to perfect communities, regimes, and modes of living in them. For from the less to the more perfect is always the path of nature and of its imitator, art. And men do not think that they have scientific knowledge of each thing unless they "know its first causes and first principles down to the elements."

3. Following this method, then, we must note that civil communities had small beginnings in diverse regions and times, and growing gradually came at length to completion, just as we said happens in every process of nature or of art. For the first and smallest combination of human beings, wherefrom the other combinations emerged, was that of male and female, as the foremost of the philosophers says in the *Politics*, Book I, Chapter 1, and as appears more fully from his *Economics*. From this combination there were generated other humans, who first occupied one household; from these, more combinations of the same kind were formed, and so great was the procreation of children that a single household did not suffice for them, but many households had to be made. A number of these households was called a village or hamlet, and this was the first community, as is also written in the above-cited treatise.

4. So long as men were in a single household, all their actions, especially those we shall henceforth call "civil," were regulated by the elder among them as being more discerning, but apart from laws or customs, because these could not yet have been discovered. Not only were the men of a single household ruled in this way, but the first community too, called the village, was ruled in almost the same manner, although in some things it was ruled differently. For although the head of a single household might have been allowed to pardon or to punish domestic injuries entirely according to his own will and pleasure, this would not have been allowed the head of the first community called the village. For in this community the elder had to regulate matters of justice and benefit by some reasonable ordinance or quasi-natural law, because thus it seemed appropriate to all by a certain equity, not as a result of prolonged inquiry, but solely by the common dictate of reason and a certain duty of human society.

The cause of this difference of regime in a single household and in a village is and was as follows. If someone in the single and first household or domestic family had killed or otherwise offended his brother, then the head of the household, if he so desired, was allowed not to give the wrongdoer the extreme penalty without any dangerous consequences resulting therefrom, because the injury seemed to have been done to the father alone, who forgave it; and because of the paucity of men; and again because it was less unfortunate and sorrowful for the father to lose one son than two. Our first ancestor, Adam, seems to have acted in this way when his first-born son, Cain, killed his brother Abel. For there is properly no civil justice of a father in relation to his son, as Aristotle wrote in Book IV of the *Ethics*, the treatise on justice. On the other hand, in the first community, the village or hamlet, such procedure was not and would not be allowed, because the case here was different from that of the family; indeed, unless injuries were avenged or equalized by the elder, there would have arisen fighting and the separation of the villagers.

Villages having multiplied and the community grown larger because of increasing procreation, they were still ruled by one man, either because of a lack of many prudent men or through some other cause, as is written in the *Politics*, Book III, Chapter 9. The ruler, however, was the elder or the man who was regarded as better, although the regulations of these communities were less imperfect than those by which the single village or hamlet was ordered. Those first communities, however, did not have so great a differentiation and ordering of parts, or so large a quantity of necessary arts and rules of living, as were gradually to be found afterwards in perfect communities. For sometimes the same man was both ruler and farmer or shepherd, like Abraham and several others after him; but in perfect communities this was not expedient nor would it be allowed.

5. These communities having gradually increased, men's experience became greater, more perfect arts and rules and ways of living were discovered, and also the parts of communities were more fully differentiated. Finally, the things which are necessary for living and for living well were brought to full development by men's reason and experience, and there was established the perfect community, called the city, with the differentiation of its parts, to the discussion of which we shall now proceed.

Let this much suffice, then, concerning the rise of the civil community.

Chapter IV. On the Final Cause of the City and of Its Civil Requirements, and the Differentiation in General of Its Parts

1. The city, according to Aristotle in the *Politics*, Book I, Chapter 1, is "the perfect community having the full limit of self-sufficiency, which came into existence for the sake of living, but exists for the sake of living well." This phrase of Aristotle—"came into existence for the sake of living, but exists for the sake of living well"—signifies the perfect final cause of the city, since those who live a civil life not only live, which beasts or slaves do too, but live well, having leisure for those liberal functions in which are exercised the virtues of both the practical and the theoretic soul.

2. Having thus determined the end of the city to be living and living well, we must treat first of living and its modes. For this, as we have said, is the purpose for the sake of which the city was established, and which necessitates all the things which exist in the city and are done by the association of men in it. Let us therefore lay this down as the principle of all the things which are to be demonstrated here, a principle naturally obtained, held, and freely granted by all: that all men not deformed or otherwise impeded naturally desire a sufficient life, and avoid and flee what is harmful thereto. This has been acknowledged not only with regard to man but also with regard to every genus of animals, according to Tully in his treatise *On Duties*, Book I, Chapter 3, where he says: "It is an original endowment which nature has bestowed upon every genus of living things, that it preserves itself, its body, and its life, that it avoids those things which seem harmful, and that it seeks and obtains all those things which are necessary for living." This principle can also be clearly grasped by everyone through sense induction.

3. But the living and living well which are appropriate to men fall into two kinds, of which one is temporal or earthly, while the other is usually called eternal or heavenly. However, this latter kind of living, the eternal, the whole body of philosophers were unable to prove by demonstration, nor was it self-evident, and therefore they did not concern themselves with the means thereto. But as to the first kind of living and living well or good life, that is, the earthly, and its necessary means, this the glorious philosophers comprehended almost completely through demonstration. Hence for its attainment they concluded the necessity of the civil community, without which this sufficient life cannot be obtained. Thus the foremost of the philosophers, Aristotle, said in his *Politics*, Book I, Chapter 1: "All men are driven toward such an association by a natural impulse." Although sense experience teaches this, we wish to bring out more distinctly that cause of it which we have indicated, as follows: Man is born composed of contrary elements, because of whose contrary actions and passions some of his substance is continually being destroyed; moreover, he is born "bare and unprotected" from excess of the surrounding air and other elements, capable of suffering and of destruction, as has been said in the science of nature. As a consequence, he needed arts of diverse genera and species to avoid the aforementioned harms. But since these arts can be exercised only by a large number of men, and can be had only through their association with one another, men had to assemble together in order to attain what was beneficial through these arts and to avoid what was harmful.

4. But since among men thus assembled there arise disputes and quarrels which, if not regulated by a norm of justice, would cause men to fight and separate and thus finally would bring about the destruction of the city, there had to be established in this association a standard of justice and a guardian or maker thereof. And since this guardian has to restrain excessive wrongdoers as well as other individuals both within and outside the city who disturb or attempt to oppress the community, the city had to have within it something by which to resist these. Again, since the community needs various conveniences, repairs, and protection of certain common things, and different things in time of peace and in time of war, it was necessary that there be in the community men to take care of such matters, in order that the common necessity might be relieved when it was expedient or needful. But beside the things which we have so far mentioned, which relieve only the necessities of the present life, there is something else which men associated in a civil community need for the status of the future world promised to the human race through God's supernatural revelation, and which is useful also for the status of the present life. This is the worship and honoring of God, and the giving of thanks both for benefits received in this world and for those to be received in the future one. For the teaching of these things and for the directing of men in them, the city had to designate certain teachers. The nature and qualities of all these and the other matters mentioned above will be treated in detail in the subsequent discussions.

5. Men, then, were assembled for the sake of the sufficient life, being able to seek out for themselves the necessaries enumerated above, and exchanging them with one another. This assemblage, thus perfect and having the limit of self-sufficiency, was called the city, whose final cause as well as that of its many parts has already been indicated by us in some measure, and will be more fully distinguished below. For since diverse things are necessary to men who desire a sufficient life, things which cannot be supplied by men of one order or office, there had to be diverse orders or offices of men in this association, exercising or supplying such diverse things which men need for sufficiency of life. But these diverse orders or offices of men are none other than the many and distinct parts of the city.

Let it suffice, then, to have covered thus in outline what the city is, why there came about such an association, and the number and division of its parts.

Chapter V. On the Differentiation of the Parts of the City, and the Necessity of Their Separate Existence for an End Discoverable by Man

1. We have now treated in general of the parts of the city, in whose perfect action and intercommunication, without external impediment, we have said that the tranquillity of the city consists. But we must now continue our discussion of them, since the fuller determination of these parts, with respect both to their functions or ends and to their other appropriate causes, will make more manifest the causes of tranquillity and of its opposite. Let us say, then, that the parts or offices of the city are of six kinds, as Aristotle said in the *Politics*, Book VII, Chapter 7: the agricultural, the artisan, the military, the financial, the priestly, and the judicial or deliberative. Three of these, the priestly, the warrior, and the judicial, are in the strict sense parts of the city, and in civil communities they are usually called the honorable class (*honorabilitatem*). The others are called parts only in the broad sense of the term, because they are offices necessary to the city according to the doctrine of Aristotle in the *Politics*, Book VII, Chapter 7. And the multitude belonging to these offices are usually called the vulgar. These, then, are the more familiar parts of the city or state, to which all the others can appropriately be reduced.

2. Although the necessity of these parts has been indicated to a certain extent in the preceding chapter, we wish to indicate it again more distinctly, assuming this proposition as having been previously demonstrated from what is self-evident, namely, that the city is a community established for the sake of the living and living well of the men in it. Of this "living" we have previously distinguished two kinds: one, the life or living of this world, that is, earthly; the other, the life or living of the other or future world. From these kinds of living, desired by man as ends, we shall indicate the necessity for the differentiation of the parts of the civil community. The first kind of human living, the earthly, is sometimes taken to mean the being of living things, as in Book II of the treatise *On the Soul*; "For living things, living is their being"; in which sense life is nothing other than soul. At other times, "living" is taken to mean the act, the action or passion, of the soul or of life. Again, each of these meanings is used in two ways, with reference either to the numerically same being or to the being that is common to many individuals and that is called specific. And although each of these kinds of living, both as proper to man and as common to him and to the other animate things, depends upon natural causes, yet we are not at present considering it in so far as it comes from these causes; the natural science of plants and animals deals with this. Rather, our present concern is with these causes in so far as they receive fulfilment "through art and reason," whereby "the human race lives."

3. Hence, we must note that if man is to live and to live well, it is necessary that his actions be done and be done well; and not only his actions but also his passions. By "well" I mean in proper proportion. And since we do not receive entirely perfect from nature the means whereby these proportions are fulfilled, it was necessary for man to go beyond natural causes to form through reason some means whereby to effect and preserve his actions and passions in body and soul. And these means are the various kinds of functions and products deriving from the virtues and arts both practical and theoretic.

4. Of human actions and passions, some come from natural causes apart from knowledge. Such are those which are effected by the contrariety of the elements composing our bodies, through their intermixture. In this class can properly be placed the actions of the nutritive part. Under this head also come actions effected by the elements surrounding our body through the alteration of their qualities; of this kind also are the alterations effected by things entering human bodies, such as food, drink, medicines, poisons, and other similar things. But there are other actions or passions which are performed by us or occur in us through our cognitive and appetitive powers. Of these some are called "immanent" because they do not cross over (*non transeunt*) into a subject other than the doer, nor are they exercised through any external organs or locomotive members; of this kind are the thoughts and desires or affections of men. But there are other actions and passions which are called "transitive" because they are opposed in either or in both respects to the kind which we have just described.

5. In order to proportion all these actions and passions, and to fulfil them in that to which nature could not lead, there were discovered the various kinds of arts and other virtues, as we said above, and men of various offices were established to exercise these for the purpose of supplying human needs. These orders are none other than the parts of the city enumerated above. For in order to proportion and preserve the acts of the nutritive part of the soul, whose cessation would mean the complete destruction of the animal both individually and as a species, agriculture and animal husbandry were established. To these may properly be reduced all kinds of hunting of land, sea, and air animals, and all other arts whereby food is acquired by some exchange or is prepared for eating, so that what is lost from the substance of our body may thereby be restored, and the body be continued in its immortal being so far as nature has permitted this to man.

6. In order to moderate the actions and passions of our body caused by the impressions of the elements which externally surround us, there was discovered the general class of mechanics, which Aristotle in the *Politics*, Book VII, Chapter 6, calls the "arts." To this class belong spinning, leathermaking, shoemaking, all species of housebuilding, and in general all the other mechanical arts which subserve the other offices of the city directly or indirectly, and which moderate not only men's touch or taste but also the other senses. These latter arts are more for pleasure and for living well than for the necessity of life, such as the painter's art and others similar to it, concerning which Aristotle says in the *Politics*, Book IV, Chapter 3: "Of these arts some must exist from necessity, and others are for pleasure and living well." Under this class is also placed the practice of medicine, which is in some way architectonic to many of the above-mentioned arts.

7. In order to moderate the excesses of the acts deriving from the locomotive powers through knowledge and desire, which we have called transitive acts and which can be done for the benefit or for the harm or injury of someone other than the doer for the status of the present world, there was necessarily established in the city a part or office by which the excesses of such acts are corrected and reduced to equality or due proportion. For without such correction the excesses of these acts would cause fighting and hence the separation of the citizens, and finally the destruction of the city and loss of the sufficient life. This part of the city, together with its subsidiaries, is called by Aristotle the "judicial" or "ruling" and "deliberative" part, and its function is to regulate matters of justice and the common benefit.

8. In addition, since the sufficient life cannot be led by citizens who are oppressed or cast into slavery by external oppressors, and also since the sentences of the judges against injurious and rebellious men within the city must be executed by coercive force, it was necessary to set up in the city a military or warrior part, which many of the mechanics also subserve. For the city was established for the sake of living and living well, as was said in the preceding chapter; but this is impossible for citizens cast into slavery. For this, as the excellent Aristotle said, is contrary to the nature of the city. Hence, indicating the necessity for this part, he said in the *Politics*, Book IV, Chapter 3: "There is a fifth class, that of the warriors, which is not less necessary than the others, if the citizens are not to be slaves of invaders. For nothing is more truly impossible than for that which is by nature slavish to be worthy of the name "city"; for a city is self-sufficient, but a slave is not self-sufficient." The necessity for this class because of internal rebels is treated by Aristotle in the *Politics*, Book VII, Chapter 6. We have omitted the quotation of this passage here for the sake of brevity, and because we shall quote it in Chapter XIV of this discourse, paragraph 8.

9. Again, since in some years on earth the harvests are large, and in others small; and the city is sometimes at peace with its neighbors, and sometimes not; and it is in need of various common services such as the construction and repair of roads, bridges, and other edifices, and similar things whose enumeration here would be neither appropriate nor brief—to provide all these things at the proper time it was necessary to establish in the city a treasure-keeping part, which Aristotle called the "money class." This part gathers and saves monies, coins, wines, oils, and other necessaries; it procures from all places things needed for the common benefit, and it seeks to relieve future necessities; it is also subserved by some of the other parts of the city. Aristotle called this the "money" part, since the saver of monies seems to be the treasurer of all things; for all things are exchanged for money.

10. It remains for us to discuss the necessity of the priestly part. All men have not thought so harmoniously about this as they have about the necessity of the other parts of the city. The cause of this difference was that the true and primary necessity of this part could not be comprehended through demonstration, nor was it self-evident. All nations, however, agreed that it was appropriate to establish the priesthood for the worship and honoring of God, and for the benefit resulting therefrom for the status of the present or the future world. For most laws or religions promise that in the future world God will distribute rewards to those who do good and punishment to doers of evil.

11. However, besides these causes of the laying down of religious laws, causes which are believed without demonstration, the philosophers, including Hesiod, Pythagoras, and several others of the ancients, noted appropriately a quite different cause or purpose for the setting forth of divine laws or religions—a purpose which was in some sense necessary for the status of this world. This was to ensure the goodness of human acts both individual and civil, on which depend almost completely the quiet or tranquillity of communities and finally the sufficient life in the present world. For although some of the philosophers who founded such laws or religions did not accept or believe in human resurrection and that life which is called eternal, they nevertheless feigned and persuaded others that it exists and that in it pleasures and pains are in accordance with the qualities of human deeds in this mortal life, in order that they might thereby induce in men reverence and fear of God, and a desire to flee the vices and to cultivate the virtues. For there are certain acts which the legislator cannot regulate by human law, that is, those acts which cannot be proved to be present or absent to someone, but which nevertheless cannot be concealed from God, whom these philosophers feigned to be the maker of such laws and the commander of their observance, under the threat or promise of eternal reward for doers of good and punishment for doers of evil. Hence, they said of the variously virtuous men in this world that they were placed in the heavenly firmament; and from this were perhaps derived the names of certain stars and constellations. These philosophers said that the souls of men who acted wrongly entered the bodies of various brutes; for example, the souls of men who had been intemperate eaters entered the bodies of pigs, those who were intemperate as regards [the pleasures of] the sense of touch and sexual matters entered the bodies of goats, and so on, according to the proportions of human vices to their condemnable properties. So too the philosophers assigned various kinds of torments to wrongdoers, like perpetual thirst and hunger for intemperate Tantalus: water and fruit were to be near him, but he was unable to drink or eat these, for they were always fleeing faster than he could pursue them. The philosophers also said that the infernal regions, the place of these torments, were deep and dark; and they painted all sorts of terrible and gloomy pictures of them. From fear of these, men eschewed wrongdoing, were instigated to perform virtuous works of piety and mercy, and were well disposed both in themselves and toward others. As a consequence, many disputes and injuries ceased in communities. Hence too the peace or tranquillity of cities and the sufficient life of men for the status of the present world were preserved with less difficulty; which was the end intended by these wise men in laying down such laws or religions.

12. Thus there existed a handing-down of such precepts by the gentile priests; and for the teaching of them they established in their communities temples in which their gods were worshiped. They also appointed teachers of these laws or traditions, whom they called priests (*sacerdotes*), because they handled the sacred objects of the temples, like the books, vases, and other such things subserving divine worship.

13. These affairs they arranged fittingly in accordance with their beliefs and rites. For as priests they appointed not anyone at all, but only virtuous and esteemed citizens who had held military, judicial, or deliberative office, and who had retired from secular affairs, being excused from civil burdens and offices because of age. For by such men, removed from passions, and in whose words greater credence was placed because of their age and moral dignity, it was fitting that the gods should be honored and their sacred objects handled, not by artisans or hirelings who had exercised lowly and defiling offices. Hence it is said in the *Politics*, Book VII, Chapter 7: "Neither a farmer nor an artisan should be made a priest."

14. Now correct views concerning God were not held by the gentile laws or religions and by all the other religions which are or were outside the catholic Christian faith or outside the Mosaic law which preceded it or the beliefs of the holy fathers which in turn preceded this—and, in general, by all those doctrines which are outside the tradition of what is contained in the sacred canon called the Bible. For they followed the human mind or false prophets or teachers of errors. Hence too they did not have a correct view about the future life and its happiness or misery, nor about the true priesthood established for its sake. We have, nevertheless, spoken of their rites in order to make more manifest their difference from the true priesthood, that of the Christians, and the necessity for the priestly part in communities.

Chapter VI. On the Final Cause of a Certain Part of the City, the Priesthood, Shown from the Immediate Teaching or Revelation of God, but Incapable of Being Proved by Human Reason

1. It remains now to discuss the final cause for which the true priesthood was established in communities of the faithful. This was in order to moderate human acts both immanent and transitive controlled by knowledge and desire, according as the human race is ordered by such acts toward the best life of the future world. Hence it must be noted that although the first man, Adam, was created principally for the glory of God, just as were the other creatures, nevertheless, unlike the other species of corruptible things, he was created uniquely in God's image and likeness, so that he might be capable of participating in eternal happiness after the life of the present world. Also he was created in a state of innocence or original justice and also of grace, as is plausibly said by some of the saints and certain leading teachers of the sacred Scriptures. Now if Adam had remained in this state, the establishment or differentiation of civil offices would not have been necessary for him or for his posterity, because nature would have produced for him the advantages and pleasures of the sufficiency of this life in the earthly or pleasurable paradise, without any suffering or fatigue on his part.

2. But because Adam corrupted his innocence or original justice and grace by eating of the forbidden fruit, transgressing thereby a divine commandment, he sank suddenly into guilt and misery, and was punished by being deprived of eternal happiness, the end to which he had been ordered with all his posterity by the beneficence of glorious God. His desert for transgressing this commandment was also to propagate all his posterity in lust. Every man after him was likewise conceived and born in lust, contracting therefrom the sin which in the law of the Christians is called "original." The only exception was Jesus Christ who, without any kind of sin or lust, was conceived by the Holy Spirit and born of the Virgin Mary; which came about when one of the three divine persons, the Son, true God in the unity of his person, assumed a human nature. As a result of this transgression of its first parents, the whole posterity of mankind was weakened in soul and is born weak, whereas it had previously been created in a state of perfect health, innocence, and grace. It was also because of this guilt that the human race was deprived of its best end to which it had been ordered.

3. But it is proper to God to have compassion for the human race, which He made in His own image, and which He had foreordained to a happy and eternal life. Hence God, who "never does anything in vain and never is lacking in necessaries," willed to remedy the human plight by giving certain commands which men were to obey and observe, and which would counteract the transgression and heal the disease of the guilt resulting from it. Like an expert physician, He proceeded in a very orderly manner from the easier to the more difficult steps. For He first commanded men to observe the rite of holocausts, sacrificing the first fruit of the earth and the first-born of the animals, as if He wanted to test human penitence and obedience. This rite the ancient fathers observed with reverence for God, with faith, obedience, and thankfulness, down to the time of Abraham. To him God gave an additional command, more difficult than the first: the circumcision of the whole male sex in the flesh of the foreskin. By this command God seemed again to be testing even more severely human penitence and obedience. These commands were observed by some men down to the time of Moses, through whom God handed down to the people of Israel a law wherein He set forth, in addition to the previous commands, further ones for the status of both the present and the future world; and He appointed priests and levites as ministers of this law. The utility of observing all the prior commands and the Mosaic law was that men would be purged of sin or guilt, both original and actual or freely committed, and would escape and be preserved from eternal and temporal sensory punishment of the other world, although by observing these commands they would not merit eternal happiness.

4. It was such happiness, however, to which merciful God had ordered the human race and which He wished to restore to it after leading it back from the fall, following the appropriate order. Hence, most recently of all, through His son Jesus Christ, true God and true man in unity of person, He handed down the evangelical law, containing commands and counsels of what must be believed, done, and avoided. By observance of these, not only are men preserved from sensory punishment, as they had been by observance of the prior commands, but also through God's gracious ordainment they merit, by a certain congruity, eternal happiness. And for this reason the evangelical law is called the law of grace, both because through the passion and death of Christ the human race was redeemed from its guilt and from the penalty of losing eternal beatitude which it had incurred as a result of the fall or sin of its first parents; and also because, by observing this law and receiving the sacraments established with it and in it, we are given divine grace, after it is given it is strengthened in us, and when we lose it, it is restored to us. Through this grace, by the ordainment of God and with the merit of the passion of Christ, our works come by a certain congruity (as we have said) to merit eternal happiness.

5. Through Christ's passion the grace whereby men are able to merit a blessed life was received not only by those who came after but also by those who had observed the first commands and the Mosaic law. Before Christ's advent, passion, death, and resurrection, they had been deprived of this beatitude in the other world, in the place called limbo. But through Christ, they received the promise given to them by God, although in the prior commands of the prophets and of the Mosaic law such a promise had been handed down to them in a veiled and enigmatic manner, for *all these things happened to them in figure* [1 Cor. 10:11], as the Apostle said to the Hebrews.

6. This divine procedure was very appropriate, for it went from the less to the more perfect and finally to the most perfect of the things appropriate to human salvation. Nor should it be thought that God could not have bestowed immediately at the outset, had

He so wished, a perfect remedy for the fall of man. But He acted as He did because He so willed it and it was fitting, as required by men's sin, lest a too easy pardon be the occasion for further sinning.

7. As teachers of this law, and as ministers of its sacraments, certain men in the communities were chosen, called priests and deacons or levites. It is their office to teach the commands and counsels of the Christian evangelical law, as to what must be believed, done, and spurned, to the end that a blessed state be attained in the future world, and the opposite avoided.

8. The end of the priesthood, therefore, is to teach and educate men in those things which, according to the evangelical law, it is necessary to believe, do, and omit in order to attain eternal salvation and avoid [eternal] misery.

9. To this office appropriately pertain all the disciplines, theoretic and practical, discovered by the human mind, which moderate human acts both immanent and transitive arising from desire and knowledge, and which make man well disposed in soul for the state of both the present and the future world. We have almost all these disciplines through the teaching of the admirable Philosopher and of other glorious men; however, we have omitted to enumerate them here, both for the sake of brevity and because it is not necessary to our present consideration.

10. With respect to this chapter and the one following, we must understand that the causes of the offices of the city, in respect of each kind of cause, differ according as they are offices of the city and according as they are habits of the human body or mind. For according as they are habits of the human body or soul, their final causes are the functions which are immediately and essentially forthcoming from them. For example, the final cause of the shipbuilding part of the city is a ship; of the military part, the use of arms and fighting; of the priesthood, the preaching of the divine law and the administration of the sacraments in accordance with it; and so on with all the rest. But according as they are offices determined and established in the city, their final causes are the benefits and sufficiencies which perfect human actions and passions, and which are forthcoming from the functions of the aforesaid habits, or which cannot be had without them. For example, from fighting, which is the act or end of the military habit, freedom is forthcoming and is preserved for men in the city, and this freedom is the end of the acts and functions of the military. So too from the function or end of the housebuilding part, which is a house, there is forthcoming to men or to the city protection from the harmful impressions of the air, the hot, the cold, the wet, or the dry, which protection is the final cause for whose sake the housebuilding office was established in the city. In the same way, from observance of the divine law, which is the end of the priesthood, eternal happiness is forthcoming to men. Similar considerations apply to all the other parts or offices of the city. And the other kinds of causes of these offices—the material, formal, and efficient causes—are distinguished in the same or a similar manner, as will appear in the following chapter.

We have now finished our discussion of the number of the parts of the city, their necessity, and their differentiation through the sufficiencies which are their ends.

Chapter VII. On the Other Kinds of Causes of the Separate Existence of the Parts of the City, and the Division of Each Kind in Two Ways Relevant to Our Purpose

1. We must now discuss the other causes of the offices or parts of the city. First we shall speak about their material and formal causes; then we shall inquire into their efficient cause. And since in things completed by the human mind the matter actually exists prior to the form, let us first discuss the material cause. The proper matter of the different offices, according as the offices mean habits of the soul, is men inclined from their generation or birth to different arts or disciplines. For "nature is not lacking in necessaries," and is more solicitous for what is more noble; among corruptible things, the most noble is the human species, which, perfected by different arts or disciplines, is the matter wherefrom must be established the city and its distinct parts necessary for the attainment of sufficiency of life, as was shown in Chapters IV and V of this discourse. Hence nature herself initiated this differentiation in the generation of men, producing some who in their natural dispositions were apt for and inclined toward farming, others toward military pursuits, and still others toward the other genera of arts and disciplines, but different men toward different ones. Nor did she incline only one individual toward one species of art or discipline, but rather many individuals toward the same species, to the extent necessary for sufficiency of life. Hence, she generated some men apt for prudence, since the judicial and deliberative part of the city must be composed of prudent men; some men apt for strength and courage, since the military part is appropriately composed of such men. So too she adapted the other men to the other genera of practical and theoretic habits which are necessary or appropriate for living and living well, so that out of the diversity of the natural inclinations toward habits of diverse genera and species in all men, she perfected what was necessary for the diversity of the parts of the city.

The material causes of the offices of the city, according as the offices mean parts of the city, are almost apparent already. For these are men habituated by the arts and disciplines of diverse genera and species, from whom the diverse orders or parts are established in the city for the sake of the sufficiencies or ends forthcoming from their arts and disciplines. Considered in this way, as having been established in the city for this purpose, the parts of the city are properly called offices, in the sense of services, for they are ordered toward human service.

2. The formal causes of the offices of the city, according as they are habits of the human mind, are none other than these very habits. For these habits are themselves the forms of those who have them; they fulfil or perfect the human inclinations which exist by nature. Hence it is said in the *Politics*, Book VII, last chapter: "Every art and discipline aims to supply what nature lacks." On the other hand, according as the offices of the city are established parts of the city, their formal causes are the commands which the efficient cause has given to or impressed upon the men who are appointed to exercise determinate functions in the city.

3. The efficient or productive causes of the offices, according as they mean habits of the soul, are the minds and wills of men through their thoughts and desires, individually or collectively. Also, in the case of certain offices, an added principle is the movement and exercise of the bodily organs. But the efficient cause of the offices, according as they are parts of the city, is frequently and in most cases the human legislator, although formerly, rarely and in very few cases, the immediate efficient cause was God, without human determination, as will be said in Chapter IX of this discourse and as will appear more fully from Chapter XII of this discourse and Chapter XV of Discourse II. With regard to the priesthood, however, there is a different manner of establishment, which will be sufficiently discussed in Chapters XV and XVII of Discourse II.

In this way, then, we have discussed the parts of the city and the necessity of their establishment from the three other kinds of cause.

Chapter VIII. On the Genera of Politics or Regimes, the Temperate and the Diseased, and the Division of Their Species

1. We must now show with greater certainty what was already shown to some extent above, that the establishment and differentiation of the parts of the city are brought about by an efficient cause which we have previously called the legislator. The same legislator establishes these parts, and differentiates and separates them as nature does with an animal, by first forming or establishing in the city one part which in Chapter V of this discourse we called the ruling or judicial part, and through this the other parts, as will be indicated more fully in Chapter XV of this discourse. Hence we must first say something concerning the nature of this ruling part. For since it is the first part of the city, as will appear below, the appropriate procedure will be to go from the indication of its efficient cause to the indication of the efficient cause which establishes and differentiates the other parts of the city.

2. There are two genera of ruling parts or governments, one well tempered, the other diseased. With Aristotle in the *Politics*, Book III, Chapter 5, I call that genus "well tempered" in which the ruler governs for the common benefit, in accordance with the will of the subjects; while the "diseased" genus is that which is deficient in this respect. Each of these genera, again, is divided into three species: the temperate into kingly monarchy, aristocracy, and polity; the diseased into the three opposite species of tyrannical monarchy, oligarchy, and democracy. And each of these again has sub-species, the detailed discussion of which is not part of our present task. For Aristotle gave a sufficient account of them in Books III and IV of his *Politics*.

3. To obtain a fuller knowledge of these species of government, which is necessary for the clear understanding of what follows, let us define each species in accordance with the view of Aristotle. A *kingly monarchy*, then, is a temperate government wherein the ruler is a single man who rules for the common benefit, and in accordance with the will or consent of the subjects. *Tyranny*, its opposite, is a diseased government wherein the ruler is a single man who rules for his own private benefit apart from the will of his subjects. *Aristocracy* is a temperate government in which the honorable class (*honorabilitas*) alone rules in accordance with the will or consent of the subjects and for the common benefit. *Oligarchy*, its opposite, is a diseased government in which some of the wealthier or more powerful rule for their own benefit apart from the will of the subjects. A *polity*, although in one sense it is something common to every genus or species of regime or government, means in another sense a certain species of temperate government, in which any citizen participates in some way in the government or in the deliberative function in turn according to his rank and ability or condition, for the common benefit and with the will or consent of the citizens. *Democracy*, its opposite, is a government in which the vulgar or the multitude of the needy establish the government and rule alone, apart from the will or consent of the other citizens and not entirely for the common benefit according to proper proportion.

4. As to which of the temperate governments is best or which of the diseased governments is worst, and the relative goodness or badness of the other species, the discussion of these points is not part of our present concern. Let it suffice to have said this much about the division of governments into their species and the definition of each.

Chapter IX. On the Methods of Establishing a Kingly Monarchy, and Which Method Is the More Perfect; Also on the Methods of Establishing the Other Kinds of Regime or Polity, Both Temperate and Diseased

1. Having determined these points, we must now discuss the methods of effecting or establishing the ruling part [of the city]. For from the better or worse nature of these methods, viewed as actions emerging from that nature to the civil regime, we must infer the efficient cause by which these methods and the ruling part established by them will emerge more advantageously to the polity.

2. In this book we are considering the causes and actions by which the ruling part must in most cases be established. First, however, we wish to indicate the method and cause by which this part has been established in the past, although rarely, in order to distinguish this method or action, and its immediate cause, from those by which the government must regularly and in most cases be established, and which we can prove by human demonstration. For of the former method no certain comprehension can be had through demonstration. This method or action, with its immediate cause, by which the ruling part and other parts of the city, especially the priesthood, were formed in the past, was the divine will commanding this either through the determinate oracle of some individual creature or else perhaps immediately through itself alone. It was by this method that the divine will established the government of the people of Israel in the person of Moses and of certain other judges after him, and also the priesthood in the person of Aaron and his successors. With respect to this cause and its free action, as to why it did or did not operate in one way or another, we can say nothing through demonstration, but we hold it by simple belief apart from reason. There is, however, another method of establishing governments which proceeds immediately from the human mind, although perhaps from God as remote cause, who grants all earthly rulership, as is said in the nineteenth chapter of John [cf. John 19:11], and as the Apostle clearly states in the thirteenth chapter of the epistle to the Romans [cf. Rom. 13:1] and St. Augustine in the *City of God*, Book V,

Chapter 21. However, God does not always act immediately; indeed in most cases, nearly everywhere, He establishes governments by means of human minds, to which He has granted the discretionary will for such establishment. And as for this latter cause, what it is, and by what kind of action it must establish such things, this can be indicated with human certainty from what is better or worse for the polity.

3. Omitting, then, that method of which we cannot attain certain knowledge through demonstration, we wish first to present those methods of establishing governments which are effected immediately by the human will; next we shall show which of these is the more certain and the simpler. Then, from the better nature of that method we shall infer the efficient cause from which alone it must and can emerge. From these points, consequently, will appear the cause which must move to the best establishment and determination of the other parts of the city. Finally we shall discuss the unity of the government, through which it will also be apparent what is the unity of the city or state.

4. In pursuit of this program, then, we shall first enumerate the methods of establishing kingly monarchy, by speaking of their origins. For this species of government seems rather kindred to us, and directly connected with the rule of the family, as is clear from what we said in Chapter III. After the determination of this point, the methods of establishing the other divisions of government will be made clear.

There are five methods of establishing kingly monarchies, according to Aristotle's *Politics*, Book III, Chapter 8. One is when the monarch is appointed for one determinate function with respect to the ruling of the community, such as the leadership of the army, either with hereditary succession or for his own lifetime only. It was by this method that Agamemnon was made leader of the army by the Greeks. In modern communities this office is called the captaincy or constabulary. This leader of the army had no judicial power in time of peace, but when the army was fighting a war he had the supreme authority to kill or otherwise punish transgressors.

Another method is that whereby certain monarchs rule in Asia; they receive their dominating authority through hereditary succession, and while they rule according to law, this law is like that of despots, being for the monarch's benefit rather than completely for the community's. The inhabitants of that region endure such rule "without protest," because of their barbaric and slavish nature and the influence of custom. This rule is kingly in that it is native to the country and is over voluntary subjects, because, for example, the monarch's ancestors had been the first inhabitants of the region. But it is also in a sense tyrannical, in that its laws are not completely for the common benefit but for that of the monarch.

A third method of kingly government is when the ruler receives his authority through election rather than hereditary succession, but governs according to a law which is not completely for the common benefit but rather for that of the monarch, like the law of tyrants. Aristotle, therefore, called this species of government an "elective tyranny," a tyranny because the law was despotic, and elective because it was not over involuntary subjects.

A fourth method is that whereby a ruler is elected with subsequent hereditary succession, and governs according to laws which are completely for the common benefit; this method was used "in heroic days," as Aristotle says in the chapter previously mentioned. Those days were called "heroic" either because the stars then produced men who were believed to be "heroes," that is, divine, on account of their exceeding virtue; or because such men and not others were named rulers on account of their exceeding virtues and beneficial deeds, in that they brought together a scattered multitude and assembled it into a civil community, or they freed the region of oppressors by fighting and strength of arms, or perhaps they bought the region or acquired it by some other appropriate method and divided it among the subjects. At any rate these men were made rulers with subsequent hereditary succession, because of their bestowal of great benefits or their excess of virtue over the rest of the multitude, as Aristotle also said in the *Politics*, Book V, Chapter 5. Under this species of monarchy, Aristotle perhaps included that in which someone is elected only for his own lifetime or a part of his lifetime; or else he designated it through the combination of this fourth species and the one called elective tyranny, because it shares features of both.

There is and was a fifth method of kingly monarchy, whereby the ruler is made lord (*dominus*) over everything in the community, disposing of things and persons according to his own will, just as the head of a family disposes at will of everything in his own household.

5. To make clearer these concepts of Aristotle, and to summarize all the methods of establishing the other kinds of government, we shall say that every government is over either voluntary or involuntary subjects. The first is the genus of well-tempered governments, the second of diseased governments. Each of these genera is divided into three species or modes, as was said in Chapter VIII. And since one of the species of well-tempered government, and perhaps the more perfect, is kingly monarchy, let us resume our previous statements about its various modes, by saying that the king or monarch either is named by the election of the inhabitants or citizens, or duly obtains the rulership without their election. If without the election of the citizens, this is either because he or his ancestors first inhabited the region, or because he bought the land and jurisdiction, or acquired it by a just war or by some other lawful method, such as by gift made to him for some great service. Each of these kinds of monarchy participates so much the more in true kingship, the more it is over voluntary subjects and according to law made for the common benefit of the subjects; and it savors so much the more of tyranny the more it departs from these features, that is, the consent of the subjects and law established for their common benefit. Hence it is written in the *Politics*, Book IV, Chapter 8: "These," that is, monarchies, "were kingly because they were according to law, and ruled voluntary subjects; but they were tyrannical because they ruled despotically and in accordance with their," that is, the monarchs', "own judgment." These two features, then, distinguish temperate from diseased government, as is apparent from the clear statement of Aristotle but absolutely or in greater degree it is the consent of the subjects which is the distinguishing criterion. Now if the ruling monarch is elected by the inhabitants, it is either with all his posterity succeeding him or not. If the latter, this may be in several ways, as he is named either for his own lifetime alone, or for his own lifetime and that of one or more of his successors, or not for the whole lifetime either of himself or of any of his successors but only for some determinate period, such as one or two years, more or less. Again, he is named to exercise either every judicial office, or only one office such as leading the army.

6. The elected and the non-elected kingly monarchs agree in that each rules voluntary subjects. They differ, however, in that the non-elected kings for the most part rule less voluntary subjects, and by laws which are less politic for the common benefit, as we said before in the case of the barbarians. The elected kings, on the other hand, rule more voluntary subjects, and by laws which are more politic, in that they are made for the common benefit, as we have said.

7. From these considerations it is clear, and will be even more apparent in the sequel, that the elected kind of government is superior to the non-elected. This is also the view of Aristotle in that passage of the *Politics*, Book III, Chapter 8, which we cited above with reference to those who were made rulers in the heroic days. Again, this method of establishing governments is more permanent in perfect communities. For at some time or other it becomes necessary to have recourse to this from among all the other methods of establishing governments, but not conversely. For example, if hereditary succession fails, or if for some reason the multitude cannot bear the excessive malice of that family's rule, they must then turn to the method of election, which can never fail so long as the generation of men does not fail. Moreover, by the method of election alone is the best ruler obtained. For it is expedient that the ruler be the best man in the polity, since he must regulate the civil acts of all the rest.

8. The method of establishing the other species of temperate government is usually election; in some cases the ruler is chosen by lot, without subsequent hereditary succession. Diseased governments, on the other hand, are usually established by fraud or force or both.

9. Which of the temperate governments is better, monarchy or one of the other two species, aristocracy or polity; and again, which of the monarchies is better, the elected or the non-elected; and moreover, which of the elected monarchies, that established with hereditary succession ensuing or that in which one man alone is named without such succession; which in turn is divided into the further alternatives of whether it is better to name the ruler for a whole lifetime, either of himself alone or of some of his successors also, or only for some determinate period, such as one or two years, more or less—in all these questions there is room for inquiry and reasonable doubt. It must be held without doubt, however, in accordance with the truth and the manifest view of Aristotle, that election is the more certain standard of government, as will be more fully shown in Chapters XII, XVI, and XVII, of this discourse.

10. We must not overlook, however, that different multitudes in different times and places are inclined toward different kinds of polity and government, as Aristotle says in the *Politics*, Book III, Chapter 9. Legislators and institutors of governments must hearken to this fact. For just as not every man is inclined toward the best discipline or study, whereupon it is appropriate that he be directed toward the acquisition not of that discipline but of some other good one for which he is more fitted, so too a multitude in some time or place may perhaps not be inclined to accept the best kind of government, and therefore recourse must first be had to that kind of temperate government which is more appropriate to it. For example, before the monarchy of Julius Caesar, the Roman people were for a long time unwilling to accept any definite monarch, either with hereditary succession or even one who was named only for his own lifetime. The reason for this was perhaps that there was a large number of heroic men worthy of rulership among them, both families and individuals.

11. From these conclusions, then, it emerges clearly that those who ask which monarch is better for a city or state, the one who rules through election or the one who rules through hereditary succession, do not put the question in the proper way. What they must correctly ask first is, which monarch is better, the elected or the non-elected. And if the elected, again which, the one who is named with hereditary succession ensuing or the one who is named without hereditary succession. For although a non-elected monarch almost always transmits the rulership to his heir, not every elected monarch does so, but only the one who is named to rule with hereditary succession ensuing.

Let these, then, be our conclusions about the methods of establishing governments, and that the absolutely better method is election.

Chapter X. On the Distinction of the Meaning of the Term "Law," and on the Meaning Which Is Most Proper and Intended by Us

1. Since we have said that election is the more perfect and better method of establishing governments, we shall do well to inquire as to its efficient cause, wherefrom it has to emerge in its full value; for from this will appear the cause not only of the elected government but also of the other parts of the polity. Now a government has to regulate civil human acts (as we demonstrated in Chapter V of this discourse), and according to a standard *regulam* which is and ought to be the form of the ruler, as such. We must, consequently, inquire into this standard, as to whether it exists, what it is, and why. For the efficient cause of this standard is perhaps the same as that of the ruler.

2. The existence of this standard, which is called a "statute" or "custom" and by the common term "law," we assume as almost self-evident by induction in all perfect communities. We shall show first, then, what law is; next we shall indicate its final cause or necessity; and finally we shall demonstrate by what person or persons and by what kind of action the law should be established; which will be to inquire into its legislator or efficient cause, to whom we think it also pertains to elect the government, as we shall show subsequently by demonstration. From these points there will also appear the matter or subject of the aforesaid standard which we have called law. For this matter is the ruling part, whose function it is to regulate the political or civil acts of men according to the law.

3. Following this procedure, then, we must first distinguish the meanings or intentions of this term "law," in order that its many senses may not lead to confusion. For in one sense it means a natural sensitive inclination toward some action or passion. This is the way the Apostle used it when he said in the seventh chapter of the epistle to the Romans: *I see another law in my members, fighting against the law of my mind* [Rom. 7:23]. In another sense this term "law" means any operative habit and in general every form, existing in the mind, of a producible thing, from which as from an exemplar or measure there emerge the forms of things made by art. This is the way in which the term was used in the forty-third chapter of Ezekiel: *This is the law of the house ... And these are the measurements of the altar* [Ezek. 43:12–13]. In a third sense "law" means the standard containing admonitions for voluntary human acts according as these are ordered toward glory or punishment in the future world. In this sense the "Mosaic Law" was in part called a law, just as the "Evangelical Law" in its entirety is called a law. Hence the Apostle said of these in his epistle to the Hebrews: *Since the priesthood has been changed, it is necessary that there be a change of the law also* [Heb. 7:12]. In this sense "law" was also used for the evangelic discipline in the first chapter of James: *He who has looked into the perfect law of liberty, and has continued therein ... this man shall be blessed in his deeds* [Jas. 1:25]. In this sense of the term law all religions, such as that of Muhammad or of the Persians, are called laws in whole or in part, although among these only the Mosaic and the evangelic, that is, the Christian, contain the truth. So too Aristotle called religions "laws" when he said, in the second book of his *Philosophy:* "The laws show how great is the power of custom"; and also in the twelfth book of the same work: "The other doctrines were added as myths to persuade men to obey the laws, and for the sake of expediency." In its fourth and most familiar sense, this term "law" means the science or doctrine or universal judgment of matters of civil justice and benefit, and of their opposites.

4. Taken in this last sense, law may be considered in two ways. In one way it may be considered in itself, as it only shows what is just or unjust, beneficial or harmful; and as such it is called the science or doctrine of right (*juris*). In another way it may be considered according as with regard to its observance there is given a command coercive through punishment or reward to be distributed in the present world, or according as it is handed down by way of such a command; and considered in this way it most properly is called, and is, a law. It was in this sense that Aristotle also defined it in the last book of the *Ethics*, Chapter 8, when he said: "Law has coercive force, for it is discourse emerging from prudence and understanding." Law, then, is a "discourse" or statement "emerging from prudence and" political "understanding," that is, it is an ordinance made by political prudence, concerning matters of justice and benefit and their opposites, and having "coercive force," that is, concerning whose observance there is given a command which one is compelled to observe, or which is made by way of such a command.

5. Hence not all true cognitions of matters of civil justice and benefit are laws unless a coercive command has been given concerning their observance, or they have been made by way of a command, although such true cognition is necessarily required for a perfect law. Indeed, sometimes false cognitions of the just and the beneficial become laws, when there is given a command to observe them, or they are made by way of a command. An example of this is found in the regions of certain barbarians, who cause it to be observed as just that a murderer be absolved of civil guilt and punishment on payment of a fine. This, however, is absolutely unjust, and consequently the laws of such barbarians are not absolutely perfect. For although they have the proper form, that is, a coercive command of observance, they lack a proper condition, that is, the proper and true ordering of justice.

6. Under this sense of law are included all standards of civil justice and benefit established by human authority, such as customs, statutes, plebiscites, decretals, and all similar rules which are based upon human authority as we have said.

7. We must not overlook, however, that both the evangelical law and the Mosaic, and perhaps the other religions as well, may be considered and compared in different ways in whole or in part, in relation to human acts for the status of the present or the future world. For they sometimes come, or have hitherto come, or will come, under the third sense of law, and sometimes under the last, as will be shown more fully in Chapters VIII and IX of Discourse II. Moreover, some of these laws are true, while others are false fancies and empty promises.

It is now clear, then, that there exists a standard or law of civil human acts, and what this is.

Chapter XI. On the Necessity for Making Laws (Taken in Their Most Proper Sense); and That No Ruler, However Virtuous or Just, Should Rule Without Laws

1. Having thus distinguished these various meanings of "law," we wish to show the end or necessity of law in its last and most proper sense. The principal end is civil justice and the common benefit; the secondary end is the security of rulers, especially those with hereditary succession, and the long duration of governments. The primary necessity of the law, then, is as follows: It is necessary to establish in the polity that without which civil judgments cannot be made with complete rightness, and through which these judgments are properly made and preserved from defect so far as it is humanly possible. Such a thing is the law, when the ruler is directed to make civil judgments in accordance with it. Therefore, the establishment of law is necessary in the polity. The major premise of this demonstration is almost self-evident, and is very close to being indemonstrable. Its certainty can and should be grasped from Chapter V, paragraph 7 of this discourse. The minor premise will now be proved in this way: To make a good judgment, there are required a right disposition (*affectio*) of the judges and a true knowledge of the matters to be judged; the opposites of which corrupt civil judgments. For if the judge has a perverted disposition, such as hate, love, or avarice, this perverts his desire. But such dispositions are kept away from the judgment, and it is preserved from them, when the judge or ruler is directed to make judgments according to the laws, because the law lacks all perverted disposition; for it is not made useful for friend or harmful for foe, but universally for all those who perform civil acts well or badly. For all other things are accidental to the law and are outside it; but they are not similarly outside the judge. Persons involved in a judgment can be friendly or inimical to the judge, helpful or harmful to him, by making him a gift or a promise; and in other ways too they can arouse in the judge a disposition which perverts his judgment. Consequently, no judgment, so far as possible, should be entrusted to the discretion of the judge, but rather it should be determined by law and pronounced in accordance with it.

2. This was also the view of the divine Aristotle in the *Politics*, Book III, Chapter 9, where he purposely asks whether it is better for a polity to be ruled by the best man without law or by the best laws; and he replies as follows: "That is better," that is, superior for judging, "which entirely lacks the passionate factor," that is, the disposition which may pervert the judgment, "than that to which passion is natural. But law does not have this," that is, passion or disposition, "while every human soul must necessarily have it"; and he said "every," not excepting anyone, however virtuous. He repeats this view in the *Rhetoric*, Book I, Chapter 1: "Most of all" is this required, that is, that nothing be left to the discretion of the judge, to be judged apart from the law, "because the judgment of the legislator," that is, the law, "is not partial," that is, it is not made on account of some one particular man, "but is concerned with future and universal matters. Now the judge and the magistrate judge about present and determinate matters, with which love and hate and private benefit are often involved, so that they cannot sufficiently see the truth, but instead have regard in their judgments to their own private pleasure and displeasure." He also makes this point in Book I, Chapter 2 of the same treatise: "We do not render the same judgments when we are pleased as when we are pained, when we love as when we hate."

3. A judgment is also corrupted through the ignorance of the judges, even if they be of good disposition or intention. This sin or defect is removed and remedied by the law, for in the law is determined well-nigh perfectly what is just or unjust, beneficial or harmful, with regard to each civil human act. Such determination cannot be made so adequately by any one man, however intelligent he may be. For no single man, and perhaps not even all the men of one era, could investigate or remember all the civil acts determined in the law; indeed, what was said about them by the first investigators and also by all the men of the same era who observed such acts was meager and imperfect, and attained its completion only subsequently through the additions made by later investigators. This can be sufficiently seen from experience, in the additions, subtractions, and complete changes sometimes made in the laws in different eras, or at different times within the same era.

Aristotle also attests to this in the *Politics*, Book II, Chapter 2, when he says: "We must not ignore that attention must be paid to the long time and many years of the past, in which it would not have remained unknown if these things were good," that is, the measures which are to be established as laws. He says the same thing in the *Rhetoric*, Book I, Chapter 1: "Laws are made after long study." This is also confirmed by reason, since the making of laws requires prudence, as we saw above from the definition of law, and prudence requires long experience, which, in turn, requires much time. Hence it is said in the sixth book of the *Ethics*: "A sign of what has been said is that while youths may become geometers, and be learned and wise in such sciences, they do not seem to become prudent. The cause is that prudence is of singular things which become known through experience; but a youth is not experienced, for experience requires a long time." Consequently, what one man alone can discover or know by himself, both in the science of civil justice and benefit and in the other sciences, is little or nothing. Moreover, what is observed by the men of one era is quite imperfect by comparison with what is observed in many eras, so that Aristotle, discussing the discovery of truth in every art and discipline, wrote as follows in the *Philosophy*, Book II, Chapter 1: "One man," that is, one discoverer of any art or discipline, "contributes to it," that is, discovers about it by himself alone, "little or nothing, but by the contributions of all a great deal is accomplished." This passage is clearer in the translation from the Arabic, in which it reads as follows: "Each of them," that is, each of the discoverers of any art or discipline, "comprehends little or nothing about the truth. But when a collection is made from among all who have achieved some comprehension, what is collected will be of considerable quantity." This may especially be seen in the case of astrology.

It is in this way, then, by men's mutual help and the addition of later to earlier discoveries, that all arts and disciplines have been perfected. Aristotle indicated this in a general way (*figuraliter*) with regard to the discovery of music in the same place cited above, when he said: "If there had been no Timotheus, we should be lacking much melody; but if there had been no Phrynes, there would have been no Timotheus"; that is, Timotheus would not have been so accomplished in melody if he had not had the melodies previously discovered by Phrynes. Averroes expounds these words as follows in the second book of his *Commentary:* "And what he," that is, Aristotle, "says in this chapter is clear. For no one can discover by himself the larger part of the practical or considerative," that is, theoretic, "arts, because these are completed only through the assistance which an earlier investigator gives to the one following him." And Aristotle says the same thing in the second book of the *Refutations*, last chapter, concerning the discovery of rhetoric and of all other disciplines, whatever the case may have been with regard to the discovery of logic, whose complete development he ascribed to himself alone without the discovery or assistance of any predecessor; in which he seems to have been unique among men. He also makes the same point in the *Ethics*, Book VIII, Chapter 1: "Two persons are better able to act and to understand" [than one alone]. But if two, then more than two, both simultaneously and successively, can do more than one man alone. And this is what Aristotle says with regard to our present subject in the *Politics*, Book III, Chapter 9: "It will appear most unreasonable if one man should perceive better, judging with only two eyes and two ears and acting with only two hands and feet, than many persons with many such organs."

Since, then, the law is an eye composed of many eyes, that is, the considered comprehension of many comprehenders for avoiding error in civil judgments and for judging rightly, it is safer that these judgments be made according to law than according to the discretion of the judge. For this reason it is necessary to establish the law, if politics are to be ordered for the best with regard to their civil justice and benefit; for through the law, civil judgments are preserved from the ignorance and perverted disposition of the judges. This was the minor premise of the demonstration by which we have tried from the beginning of this chapter to prove the necessity of the laws. As to the method by which a dispute or civil lawsuit is to be decided or judged when it is not determined by law, this will be discussed in Chapter XIV of this discourse. Laws, therefore, are necessary in order to exclude malice and error from the civil judgments or sentences of the judges.

4. For these reasons, Aristotle counseled that no judge or ruler should be granted the discretionary power to give judgments or commands without law, concerning those civil affairs which could be determined by law. Hence he said in the *Ethics*, Book IV, Chapter 5, the treatise on justice: "We must not allow man to rule, but" in accordance with "reason," that is, law; and Aristotle indicated the cause which we pointed out above, the perverted disposition which can be had by man. In the *Politics*, Book III, Chapter 6, he said: "The first question shows plainly above all that laws rightly made should govern," that is, that rulers should govern in accordance with laws. Again in the same treatise, Book III, Chapter 9, he said: "He who orders the mind to rule seems thereby to order God and the laws to rule; but he who orders man to rule," that is, without law, according to his own discretion, "instigates a beast"; and shortly thereafter he indicated the ground for this: "Hence the law is reason without appetite," as if to say that the law is reason or knowledge without appetite, that is, without any affective disposition. He repeated this view also in the *Rhetoric*, Book I, Chapter 1: "It is best, therefore, for rightly-made laws to determine as many matters as possible and to entrust as little as possible to the judges"; giving the reasons adduced above, the exclusion from civil judgments of the judges' malice and ignorance, which cannot arise in the law as they do in the judge, as we have shown above. And even more clearly Aristotle says in the *Politics*, Book IV, Chapter 4: "Where the laws do not govern," that is, where rulers do not govern in accordance with the laws, "there is no polity," that is, none which is temperate. "For the law should govern all things."

5. It still remains to show that all rulers should govern according to law and not without it, and especially those monarchs who rule with hereditary succession, in order that their governments may be more secure and longer lasting. This was the second reason for the necessity of laws which we indicated at the beginning of this chapter. This may be seen first of all from the fact that, when rulers govern according to law, their judgments are preserved from the defect which is caused by ignorance and perverted disposition. Hence the rulers are regulated both in themselves and in relation to their citizen subjects, and they suffer less from sedition and from the consequent destruction of their governments which they would incur if they acted badly according to their own discretion, as Aristotle clearly says in the *Politics*, Book V, Chapter 5: "For a kingdom is destroyed least of all by external forces: its destruction most usually comes from within itself. It is destroyed in two ways: one is when those who share the ruling power quarrel among themselves, the other is when they try to govern tyrannically, by controlling more things, and contrary to the law. Kingdoms no longer occur these days, but if monarchies occur, they are rather tyrannies."

6. Someone will raise an objection about the best man, who lacks ignorance and perverted disposition. As for us, however, we reply that such a man happens very rarely, and that even when he does he is not as free [from ignorance and passion] as the law itself, as we proved above from Aristotle, from reason, and from sense experience. For every soul sometimes has a vicious disposition. We can readily accept this from the thirteenth chapter of Daniel; for it is there written that *two elders came full of wicked device against Susanna, to put her to death* [Dan. 13:28]. Now these were old men and priests and judges of the people that year: nevertheless they bore false witness against her because she would not acquiesce to their vicious lust. If, then, old priests, about whom it would least be expected, were corrupted by carnal lust, what should be thought of other men, and how much more will they be corrupted by avarice and other vicious dispositions? Certainly, no one, however virtuous, can be so lacking in perverted passion and ignorance as is the law.

Therefore, it is safer that civil judgments be regulated by the law than that they be entrusted to the discretion of a judge, however virtuous he may be.

7. Let us assume, however, although it is most rare or impossible, that there is some ruler so heroic that in him neither passion nor ignorance finds a place. What shall we say of his sons, who are unlike him and who, ruling in accordance with their own discretion, will commit excesses which result in their being deprived of the rulership? Someone may say that the father, who is the best of men, will not hand over the government to such sons. This reply, however, is not to be granted, for two reasons: first, because it is not in the father's power to deprive his sons of the succession, since the rulership is a hereditary possession of his family, and second, because even if it were in the father's power to transfer the rulership to whomever he wanted, he would not deprive his sons of it no matter how vicious they were. Hence, Aristotle answers this objection as follows in the *Politics*, Book III, Chapter 9: "It is difficult to believe this," that is, that the father will deprive his sons of the rulership, "as it would require a greater virtue than human nature is capable of." For this reason it is more expedient for rulers that they be regulated and limited by law, than that they make civil judgments according to their own discretion. For when they act according to law, they will do nothing vicious or reprehensible, so that their rule will be made more secure and longer lasting.

8. This was the counsel which the distinguished Aristotle gave to all rulers, but to which they pay little heed. As he said in the *Politics*, Book V, Chapter 6: "The fewer things the rulers control," that is, without law, "the longer must every government endure, for they," that is, the rulers, "become less despotic, they are more moderate in their ways and are less hated by their subjects." And then Aristotle adduces the testimony of a certain very prudent king called Theopompus, who gave up some of the power which had been granted to him. We have thought it appropriate to quote Aristotle's words here because of this ruler's uniqueness and his outstanding virtue, almost unheard of in anyone else throughout the ages. This is what Aristotle said: "Theopompus exercised moderation," that is, he lessened his power, which may perhaps have seemed excessive, "among other ways by establishing the office of the ephors: for by diminishing his power he increased his kingdom in time," that is, he made it more durable; "hence in a way he made it not smaller but greater. When his wife asked him whether he was not ashamed to give his children a smaller kingdom than he had received from his father, he replied, 'Not at all, for the power I give to them will be more lasting.'" O heroic voice, proceeding from Theopompus' unheard-of prudence, a voice which should be heeded by all those who wish to wield plenitude of power over their subjects apart from laws! Many rulers, not heeding this voice, have been destroyed. And we ourselves have seen that from lack of attention to this voice not the least of kingdoms in modern times almost underwent a revolution, when its ruler wished to impose upon his subjects an unusual and illegal tax.

It is clear, then, from what we have said, that laws are necessary in politics if they are to be ordered with entire rightness and their governments are to be longer lasting.

Part III

Modern Political Philosophy

It is a peculiarity of the history of philosophy that the "modern" period is said to include 16th century thinkers but not 20th century thinkers. For historians of philosophy the modern period is generally understood to be from around the Renaissance through the Enlightenment. The 19th century philosophers are sometimes included in this category, other times not.

A host of intellectual developments came as Europe's medieval period gave way to what we now call the Renaissance. The development of a sizeable middle class, increased trade relations between nations, exploration, and developments in science and technology all created a climate in which many things taken for granted in the Middle Ages were called into question. The development of the printing press, for example, made possible a new high level of literacy and increased the spread of information astronomically. The Protestant Reformation called into question the authority of the Roman Catholic Church. Increased exploration led to an expanded conception of the world, not only with respect to its shape, but also its scope. Advances in medical science and astronomy led to radical rethinking about humanity and its place in the universe.

It is this intellectual climate which also produces a proliferation of new challenges to old ideas about justice and politics. The development, or in some cases significant refashioning, of such notions as government by consent, the social contract, individual rights, rights of women, socialism, anarchism, and liberalism, were all features of these centuries. It is our intention that this chapter introduce the reader to the many different theories that come from this period.

Niccolò Machiavelli (1469–1527 C.E.)

A Florentine, he spent the prime of his life in the public service of his state. On the ascent of the Medicis in 1512, he was removed from office, imprisoned, and tortured, but eventually retired without further prosecution. In retirement he wrote his best known work of political theory, *The Prince* (1513), from which this selection is taken. Dedicated to Lorenzo de Medici, its publication may have been an attempt to curry favor and appointment from the new Florentine government. If so, nothing came of it, and in continued retirement, he wrote another substantial contribution to political theory, *The Discourses on Livy* (1521).

From The Prince*

Chapter XV

Of the Means by which Men, and Especially Princes, Win Applause, or Incur Censure

It remains now to be seen in what manner a prince should conduct himself toward his subjects and his allies; and knowing that this matter has already been treated by many others, I apprehend that my writing upon it also may be deemed presumptuous, especially as in the discussion of the same I shall differ from the rules laid down by others. But as my aim is to write something that may be useful to him for whom it is intended, it seems to me proper to pursue the real truth of the matter, rather than to indulge in mere speculation on the same; for many have imagined republics and principalities such as have never been known to exist in reality. For the manner in which men live is so different from the way in which they ought to live, that he who leaves the common course for that which he ought to follow will find that it leads him to ruin rather than to safety. For a man who, in all respects, will carry out only his professions of good, will be apt to be ruined among so many who are evil. A prince therefore who desires to maintain himself must learn to be not always good, but to be so or not as necessity may require. Leaving aside then the imaginary things concerning princes, and confining ourselves only to the realities, I say that all men when they are spoken of, and more especially princes, from being in a more conspicuous position, are noted for some quality that brings them either praise or censure. Thus one is deemed liberal, another miserly (*misero*) to use a Tuscan expression (for avaricious is he who by rapine desires to gain, and miserly we call him who abstains too much from the enjoyment of his own). One man is esteemed generous, another rapacious; one cruel, another merciful; one faithless, and another faithful; one effeminate

---

*An Excerpt.

and pusillanimous, another ferocious and brave; one affable, another haughty; one las-civious, another chaste; one sincere, the other cunning; one facile, another inflexible; one grave, another frivolous; one religious, another sceptical; and so on.

I am well aware that it would be most praiseworthy for a prince to possess all of the above-named qualities that are esteemed good; but as he cannot have them all, nor en-tirely observe them, because of his human nature which does not permit it, he should at least be prudent enough to know how to avoid the infamy of those vices that would rob him of his state; and if possible also to guard against such as are likely to endanger it. But if that be not possible, then he may with less hesitation follow his natural inclinations. Nor need he care about incurring censure for such vices, without which the preservation of his state may be difficult. For, all things considered, it will be found that some things that seem like virtue will lead you to ruin if you follow them; while others, that apparently are vices, will, if followed, result in your safety and well-being.

Chapter XVI

Of Liberality and Parsimoniousness

To begin with the first of the above-named qualities, I say that it is well for a prince to be deemed liberal; and yet liberality, indulged in so that you will no longer be feared, will prove injurious. For liberality worthily exercised, as it should be, will not be recognized, and may bring upon you the reproach of the very opposite. For if you desire the reputa-tion of being liberal, you must not stop at any degree of sumptuousness; so that a prince will in this way generally consume his entire substance, and may in the end, if he wishes to keep up his reputation for liberality, be obliged to subject his people to extraordinary burdens, and resort to taxation, and employ all sorts of measures that will enable him to procure money. This will soon make him odious with his people; and when he becomes poor, he will be scorned by everybody; so that having by his prodigality injured many and benefited few, he will be the first to suffer every inconvenience, and be exposed to every danger. And when he becomes conscious of this and attempts to retrench, he will at once expose himself to the imputation of being a miser.

A prince then, being unable without injury to himself to practice the virtue of lib-erality in such manner that it may be generally recognized, should not, when he becomes aware of this and is prudent, mind incurring the charge of parsimoniousness. For after a while, when it is seen that by his prudence and economy he makes his revenues suffice him, and that he is able to provide for his defense in case of war, and engage in enter-prises without burdening his people, he will be considered liberal enough by all those from whom he takes nothing, and these are the many; while only those to whom he does not give, and which are the few, will look upon him as parsimonious.

In our own times we have not seen any great things accomplished except by those who were regarded as parsimonious; all others have been ruined. Pope Julius II, having been helped by his reputation of liberality to attain the pontificate, did not afterward care to keep up that reputation to enable him to engage in war against the King of France; and he carried on ever so many wars without levying any extraordinary taxes.

For his long-continued economy enabled him to supply the extraordinary expenses of his wars.

If the present King of Spain had sought the reputation of being liberal, he would not have been able to engage in so many enterprises, nor could he have carried them to a successful issue. A prince, then, who would avoid robbing his own subjects, and be able to defend himself, and who would avoid becoming poor and abject or rapacious should not mind incurring the reputation of being parsimonious; for that is one of those vices that will enable him to maintain his state. And should it be alleged that Julius Caesar attained the Empire by means of his liberality, and that many others by the same reputation have achieved the highest rank, then I reply, that you are either already a prince, or are in the way of becoming one; in the first case liberality would be injurious to you, but in the second it certainly is necessary to be reputed liberal. Now Cæsar was aiming to attain the Empire of Rome; but having achieved it, had he lived and not moderated his expenditures, he would assuredly have ruined the Empire by his prodigality.

And were any one to assert that there have been many princes who have achieved great things with their armies, and who were accounted most liberal, I answer that a prince either spends his own substance and that of his subjects, or that of others. Of the first two he should be very sparing, but in spending that of others he ought not to omit any act of liberality. The prince who in person leads his armies into foreign countries, and supports them by plunder, pillage, and exactions, and thus dispenses the substance of others, should do so with the greatest liberality, as otherwise his soldiers would not follow him. For that which belongs neither to him nor to his own subjects, a prince may spend most lavishly, as was done by Cyrus, Caesar, and Alexander. The spending of other people's substance will not diminish, but rather increase, his reputation; it is only the spending of his own that is injurious to a prince.

And there is nothing that consumes itself so quickly as liberality; for the very act of using it causes it to lose the faculty of being used, and will either impoverish you and make you despised, or it will make you rapacious and odious. And of all the things against which a prince should guard most carefully is incurring the hatred and contempt of his subjects. Now, liberality will bring upon you either the one or the other; there is therefore more wisdom in submitting to be called parsimonious, which may bring you blame without hatred, than, by aiming to be called liberal, to incur unavoidably the reputation of rapacity, which will bring upon you infamy as well as hatred.

Chapter XVII

Of Cruelty and Clemency, and Whether it is Better to be Loved than Feared

Coming down now to the other aforementioned qualities, I say that every prince ought to desire the reputation of being merciful, and not cruel; at the same time, he should be careful not to misuse that mercy. Cesare Borgia was reputed cruel, yet by his cruelty he reunited the Romagna to his states, and restored that province to order, peace, and loyalty; and if we carefully examine his course, we shall find it to have been really much more merciful than the course of the people of Florence, who, to escape the reputation of cruelty, allowed Pistoia to be destroyed. A prince, therefore, should not mind the ill repute of cruelty, when he can thereby keep his subjects united and loyal; for a few displays of severity will really be more merciful than to allow, by an excess of clemency, disorders to occur, which are apt to result in rapine and murder; for these injure a whole community, while the executions ordered by the prince fall only upon a few individuals. And, above all others, the new prince will find it almost impossible to avoid the reputation of cruelty, because new states are generally exposed to many dangers. It was on this account that Virgil made Dido to excuse the severity of her government, because it was still new, saying,—

"Res dura, et regni novitas me talia cogunt
Moliri, et late fines custode tueri."[1]

A prince, however, should be slow to believe and to act; nor should he be too easily alarmed by his own fears, and should proceed moderately and with prudence and humanity, so that an excess of confidence may not make him incautious, nor too much mistrust make him intolerant. This, then, gives rise to the question "whether it be better to be beloved than feared, or to be feared than beloved." It will naturally be answered that it would be desirable to be both the one and the other; but as it is difficult to be both at the same time, it is much more safe to be feared than to be loved, when you have to choose between the two. For it may be said of men in general that they are ungrateful and fickle, dissemblers, avoiders of danger, and greedy of gain. So long as you shower benefits upon them, they are all yours; they offer you their blood, their substance, their lives, and their children, provided the necessity for it is far off; but when it is near at hand, then they revolt. And the prince who relies upon their words, without having otherwise provided for his security, is ruined; for friendships that are won by rewards, and not by greatness and nobility of soul, although deserved, yet are not real, and cannot be depended upon in time of adversity.

Besides, men have less hesitation in offending one who makes himself beloved than one who makes himself feared; for love holds by a bond of obligation which, as mankind is bad, is broken on every occasion whenever it is for the interest of the obliged party to break it. But fear holds by the apprehension of punishment, which never leaves men. A prince, however, should make himself feared in such a manner that, if he has not won the affections of his people, he shall at least not incur their hatred; for the being feared, and not hated, can go very well together, if the prince abstains from taking the substance of his subjects, and leaves them their women. And if you should be obliged to inflict capital punishment upon any one, then be sure to do so only when there is manifest cause and proper justification for it; and, above all things, abstain from taking people's property,

---

[1]"My cruel fate,
And doubts attending an unsettled state,
Force me to guard my coasts from foreign foes."
—Dryden.

for men will sooner forget the death of their fathers than the loss of their patrimony. Besides, there will never be any lack of reasons for taking people's property; and a prince who once begins to live by rapine will ever find excuses for seizing other people's property. On the other hand, reasons for taking life are not so easily found, and are more readily exhausted. But when a prince is at the head of his army, with a multitude of soldiers under his command, then it is above all things necessary for him to disregard the reputation of cruelty; for without such severity an army cannot be kept together, nor disposed for any successful feat of arms.

Among the many admirable qualities of Hannibal, it is related of him that, having an immense army composed of a very great variety of races of men, which he led to war in foreign countries, no quarrels ever occurred among them, nor were there ever any dissensions between them and their chief, either in his good or in his adverse fortunes; which can only be accounted for by his extreme cruelty. This, together with his boundless courage, made him ever venerated and terrible in the eyes of his soldiers; and without that extreme severity all his other virtues would not have sufficed to produce that result.

Inconsiderate writers have, on the one hand, admired his great deeds, and, on the other, condemned the principal cause of the same. And the proof that his other virtues would not have sufficed him may be seen from the case of Scipio, who was one of the most remarkable men, not only of his own time, but in all history. His armies revolted in Spain solely in consequence of his extreme clemency, which allowed his soldiers more license than comports with proper military discipline. This fact was censured in the Roman Senate by Fabius Maximus, who called Scipio the corrupter of the Roman soldiers. The tribe of the Locrians having been wantonly destroyed by one of the lieutenants of Scipio, he neither punished him for that nor for his insolence,—simply because of his own easy nature; so that, when somebody wished to excuse Scipio in the Senate, he said, "that there were many men who knew better how to avoid errors themselves than to punish them in others." This easy nature of Scipio's would in time have dimmed his fame and glory if he had persevered in it under the Empire; but living as he did under the government of the Senate, this dangerous quality of his was not only covered up, but actually redounded to his honor.

To come back now to the question whether it be better to be beloved than feared, I conclude that, as men love of their own free will, but are inspired with fear by the will of the prince, a wise prince should always rely upon himself, and not upon the will of others; but, above all, should he always strive to avoid being hated, as I have already said above.

Chapter XVIII

In What Manner Princes Should
Keep Their Faith

It must be evident to every one that it is more praiseworthy for a prince always to maintain good faith, and practice integrity rather than craft and deceit. And yet the experience of our own times has shown that those princes have achieved great things who made small account of good faith, and who understood by cunning to circumvent the intelligence of others; and that in the end they got the better of those whose actions were dictated by loyalty and good faith. You must know, therefore, that there are two ways of carrying on a contest; the one by law, and the other by force. The first is practiced by men, and the other by animals; and as the first is often insufficient, it becomes necessary to resort to the second.

A prince then should know how to employ the nature of man, and that of the beasts as well. This was figuratively taught by ancient writers, who relate how Achilles and many other princes were given to Chiron the centaur to be nurtured, and how they were trained under his tutorship; which fable means nothing else than that their preceptor combined the qualities of the man and the beast; and that a prince, to succeed, will have to employ both the one and the other nature, as the one without the other cannot produce lasting results.

It being necessary then for a prince to know well how to employ the nature of the beasts, he should be able to assume both that of the fox and that of the lion; for while the latter cannot escape the traps laid for him, the former cannot defend himself against the wolves. A prince should be a fox, to know the traps and snares; and a lion, to be able to frighten the wolves; for those who simply hold to the nature of the lion do not understand their business.

A sagacious prince then cannot and should not fulfill his pledges when their observance is contrary to his interest, and when the causes that induced him to pledge his faith no longer exist. If men were all good, then indeed this precept would be bad; but as men are naturally bad, and will not observe their faith toward you, you must, in the same way, not observe yours to them; and no prince ever yet lacked legitimate reasons with which to color his want of good faith. Innumerable modern examples could be given of this; and it could easily be shown how many treaties of peace, and how many engagements, have been made null and void by the faithlessness of princes; and he who has best known how to play the fox has ever been the most successful.

But it is necessary that the prince should know how to color this nature well, and how to be a great hypocrite and dissembler. For men are so simple, and yield so much to immediate necessity, that the deceiver will never lack dupes. I will mention one of the most recent examples. Alexander VI never did nor ever thought of anything but to deceive, and always found a reason for doing so. No one ever had greater skill in pledging his word, no one affirmed his pledges with greater oaths, and observed them less, than Pope Alexander; and yet he was always successful in his deceits, because he knew the weakness of men in that particular.

It is not necessary, however, for a prince to possess all the above-mentioned qualities; but it is essential that he should at least seem to have them. I will even venture to say, that to have and to practice them constantly is pernicious, but to seem to have them is useful. For instance, a prince should seem to be merciful, faithful, humane, religious, and upright, and should even be so in reality; but he should have his mind so trained that, when occasion requires it, he may know how to change to the opposite. And it must be understood that a prince, and especially one who has but recently acquired his state, cannot perform all those things which cause men to be esteemed as good; he being often obliged, for the sake of maintaining his state, to act contrary to humanity, charity, and religion. And therefore is it necessary that he should have a versatile mind, capable of changing readily, according as the winds and changes of fortune bid him; and, as has been said above, not to swerve from the good if possible, but to know how to resort to evil if necessity demands it.

A prince then should be very careful never to allow anything to escape his lips that does not abound in the above-named five qualities, so that to see and to hear him he may seem all charity, integrity, and humanity, all uprightness, and all piety. And more than all else is it necessary for a prince to seem to possess the last quality; for mankind in general judge more by what they see than by what they feel, every one being capable of the former, and but few of the latter. Everybody sees what you seem to be, but few really feel what you are; and these few dare not oppose the opinion of the many, who are protected by the majesty of the state; for the actions of all men, and especially those of princes, are judged by the result, where there is no other judge to whom to appeal.

A prince then should look mainly to winning, and to the successful maintenance of his state. The means which he employs for this will always be accounted honorable, and will be praised by everybody; for the common people are always taken by appearances and by results, and it is the vulgar mass that constitutes the world. But a very few have rank and station, while the many have nothing to sustain them. A certain prince of our time, whom it is well not to name, never preached anything but peace and good faith; but if he had always observed either the one or the other, it would in most instances have cost him his reputation or his state.

Thomas Hobbes (1588–1679 C.E.)

Hand in hand with the Reformation, intellectuals throughout Europe had developed more and more of an interest in science. The English philosopher Thomas Hobbes, often regarded as the father of modern philosophy—and, indeed, very influential in forging the modern, social scientific view of humankind—was concerned with discovering principles of political science as rigorous and exacting as those in the natural sciences. Instead of simply declaring a divine right to rule, could the authority of monarchs be justified scientifically? Hobbes' famous work *Leviathan* (1651), excerpted here, attempts to answer this question. Hobbes, whose father had to flee his home of Malmesbury, England, was brought up by a well-to-do relative, and he began his formal education at Magdalene Hall, Oxford, at the age of 14. In subsequent visits abroad he learned that the Aristotelianism that had dissatisfied him at Oxford had lost prestige, and that science in the manner of Galileo had taken the intellectual center stage. He urgently wanted to teach England how to avoid internal strife, which he blamed mostly on the widespread ignorance of science. He was exiled to France and Holland from which, after serious medical problems, he returned to continue a vigorous intellectual and physical life. Hobbes was a scholar and translator of ancient classics. At age 86, shortly before his death, he produced verse translations of both the *Iliad* and the *Odyssey*.

From Leviathan*

Chap. XIII

Of the Naturall Condition of Mankind, as concerning their Felicity, and Misery

NATURE hath made men so equall, in the faculties of body, and mind; as that though there bee found one man sometimes manifestly stronger in body, or of quicker mind then another; yet when all is reckoned together, the difference between man, and man, is not so considerable, as that one man can thereupon claim to himselfe any benefit, to which another may not pretend, as well as he. For as to the strength of body, the weakest has strength enough to kill the strongest, either by secret machination, or by confederacy with others, that are in the same danger with himselfe.

And as to the faculties of the mind, (setting aside the arts grounded upon words, and especially that skill of proceeding upon generall, and infallible rules, called Science; which very few have, and but in few things; as being not a native faculty, born with us; nor attained, (as Prudence,) while we look after somewhat els,) I find yet a greater equality amongst men, than that of strength. For Prudence, is but Experience; which equall

---

*An Excerpt.

time, equally bestowes on all men, in those things they equally apply themselves unto. That which may perhaps make such equality incredible, is but a vain conceipt of ones owne wisdome, which almost all men think they have in a greater degree, than the Vulgar; that is, than all men but themselves, and a few others, whom by Fame, or for concurring with themselves, they approve. For such is the nature of men, that howsoever they may acknowledge many others to be more witty, or more eloquent, or more learned; Yet they will hardly believe there be many so wise as themselves: For they see their own wit at hand, and other mens at a distance. But this proveth rather that men are in that point equall, than unequall. For there is not ordinarily a greater signe of the equall distribution of any thing, than that every man is contented with his share.

From this equality of ability, ariseth equality of hope in the attaining of our Ends. And therefore if any two men desire the same thing, which neverthelesse they cannot both enjoy, they become enemies; and in the way to their End, (which is principally their owne conservation, and sometimes their delectation only,) endeavour to destroy, or subdue one an other. And from hence it comes to passe, that where an Invader hath no more to feare, than an other mans single power; if one plant, sow, build, or possesse a convenient Seat, others may probably be expected to come prepared with forces united, to dispossesse, and deprive him, not only of the fruit of his labour, but also of his life, or liberty. And the Invader again is in the like danger of another.

And from this diffidence of one another, there is no way for any man to secure himselfe, so reasonable, as Anticipation; that is, by force, or wiles, to master the persons of all men he can, so long, till he see no other power great enough to endanger him: And this is no more than his own conservation requireth, and is generally allowed. Also because there be some, that taking pleasure in contemplating their own power in the acts of conquest, which they pursue farther than their security requires; if others, that otherwise would be glad to be at ease within modest bounds, should not by invasion increase their power, they would not be able, long time, by standing only on their defence, to subsist. And by consequence, such augmentation of dominion over men, being necessary to a mans conservation, it ought to be allowed him.

Againe, men have no pleasure, (but on the contrary a great deale of griefe) in keeping company, where there is no power able to over-awe them all. For every man looketh that his companion should value him, at the same rate he sets upon himselfe: And upon all signes of contempt, or undervaluing, naturally endeavours, as far as he dares (which amongst them that have no common power, to keep them in quiet, is far enough to make them destroy each other,) to extort a greater value from his contemners, by dommage; and from others, by the example.

So that in the nature of man, we find three principall causes of quarrell. First, Competition; Secondly, Diffidence; Thirdly, Glory.

The first, maketh men invade for Gain; the second, for Safety; and the third, for Reputation. The first use Violence, to make themselves Masters of other mens persons, wives, children, and cattell; the second, to defend them; the third, for trifles, as a word, a smile, a different opinion, and any other signe of undervalue, either direct in their Persons, or by reflexion in their Kindred, their Friends, their Nation, their Profession, or their Name.

Hereby it is manifest, that during the time men live without a common Power to keep them all in awe, they are in that condition which is called Warre; and such a warre, is of every man, against every man. For WARRE, consisteth not in Battell onely, or the act of fighting; but in a tract of time, wherein the Will to contend by Battell is sufficiently known: and therefore the notion of *Time*, is to be considered in the nature of Warre; as it is in the nature of Weather. For as the nature of Foule weather, lyeth not in a showre or two of rain; but in an inclination thereto of many dayes together: So the nature of War, consisteth not in actuall fighting; but in the known disposition thereto, during all the time there is no assurance to the contrary. All other time is PEACE.

Whatsoever therefore is consequent to a time of Warre, where every man is Enemy to every man; the same is consequent to the time, wherein men live without other security, than what their own strength, and their own invention shall furnish them withall. In such condition, there is no place for Industry; because the fruit thereof is uncertain: and consequently no Culture of the Earth; no Navigation, nor use of the commodities that may be imported by Sea; no commodious Building; no Instruments of moving, and removing such things as require much force; no Knowledge of the face of the Earth; no account of Time; no Arts; no Letters; no Society; and which is worst of all, continuall feare, and danger of violent death; And the life of man, solitary, poore, nasty, brutish, and short.

It may seem strange to some man, that has not well weighed these things; that Nature should thus dissociate, and render men apt to invade, and destroy one another: and he may therefore, not trusting to this Inference, made from the Passions, desire perhaps to have the same confirmed by Experience. Let him therefore consider with himselfe, when taking a journey, he armes himselfe, and seeks to go well accompanied; when going to sleep, he locks his dores; when even in his house he locks his chests; and this when he knows there bee Lawes, and publike Officers, armed, to revenge all injuries shall bee done him; what opinion he has of his fellow subjects, when he rides armed; of his fellow Citizens, when he locks his dores; and of his children, and servants, when he locks his chests. Does he not there as much accuse mankind by his actions, as I do by my words? But neither of us accuse mans nature in it. The Desires, and other Passions of man, are in themselves no Sin. No more are the Actions, that proceed from those Passions, till they know a Law that forbids them: which till Lawes be made they cannot know: nor can any Law be made, till they have agreed upon the Person that shall make it.

It may peradventure be thought, there was never such a time, nor condition of warre as this; and I believe it was never generally so, over all the world: but there are many places, where they live so now. For the savage people in many places of *America*, except the government of small Families, the concord whereof dependeth on naturall lust, have no government at all; and live at this day in that brutish manner, as I said before. Howsoever, it may be perceived what manner of life there would be, where there were no common Power to feare; by the manner of life, which men that have formerly lived under a peacefull government, use to degenerate into, in a civill Warre.

But though there had never been any time, wherein particular men were in a condition of warre one against another; yet in all times, Kings, and Persons of Soveraigne authority, because of their Independency, are in continuall jealousies, and in the state and posture of Gladiators; having their weapons pointing, and their eyes fixed on one another; that is, their Forts, Garrisons, and Guns upon the Frontiers of their Kingdomes; and continuall Spyes upon their neighbours; which is a posture of War. But because they uphold thereby, the Industry of their Subjects; there does not follow from it, that misery, which accompanies the Liberty of particular men.

To this warre of every man against every man, this also is consequent; that nothing can be Unjust. The notions of Right and Wrong, Justice and Injustice have there no place. Where there is no common Power, there is no Law: where no Law, no Injustice. Force, and Fraud, are in warre the two Cardinall vertues. Justice, and Injustice are none of the Faculties neither of the Body, nor Mind. If they were, they might be in a man that were alone in the world, as well as his Senses, and Passions. They are Qualities, that relate to men in Society, not in Solitude. It is consequent also to the same condition, that there be no Propriety, no Dominion, no *Mine* and *Thine* distinct; but onely that to be every mans that he can get; and for so long, as he can keep it. And thus much for the ill condition, which man by meer Nature is actually placed in; though with a possiblity to come out of it, consisting partly in the Passions, partly in his Reason.

The Passions that encline men to Peace, are Feare of Death; Desire of such things as are necessary to commodious living; and a Hope by their Industry to obtain them. And Reason suggesteth convenient Articles of Peace, upon which men may be drawn to agreement. These Articles, are they, which otherwise are called the Lawes of Nature: whereof I shall speak more particularly, in the two following Chapters.

Chap. XIV

Of the first and second Naturall Lawes, and of Contracts

THE RIGHT OF NATURE, which Writers commonly call *Jus Naturale*, is the Liberty each man hath, to use his own power, as he will himselfe, for the preservation of his own Nature; that is to say, of his own Life; and consequently, of doing any thing, which in his own Judgement, and Reason, hee shall conceive to be the aptest means thereunto.

By LIBERTY, is understood, according to the proper signification of the word, the absence of externall Impediments: which Impediments, may oft take away part of a mans power to do what hee would; but cannot hinder him from using the power left him, according as his judgement, and reason shall dictate to him.

A LAW OF NATURE, (*Lex Naturalis*,) is a Precept, or generall Rule, found out by Reason, by which a man is forbidden to do, that, which is destructive of his life, or taketh away the means of preserving the same; and to omit, that, by which he thinketh it may be best preserved. For though they that speak of this subject, use to confound *jus*, and *Lex, Right* and *Law*; yet they ought to be distinguished; because RIGHT, consisteth in liberty to do, or to forbeare; Whereas LAW, determineth, and bindeth to one of them: so that Law, and Right, differ as much, as Obligation, and Liberty; which in one and the same matter are inconsistent.

And because the condition of Man, (as hath been declared in the precedent Chapter) is a condition of Warre of every one against every one; in which case every one is governed by his own Reason; and there is nothing he can make use of, that may not be a help unto him, in preserving his life against his enemyes; It followeth, that in such a condition, every man has a Right to every thing; even to one anothers body. And therefore, as long as this naturall Right of every man to every thing endureth, there can be no security to any man, (how strong or wise soever he be,) of living out the time, which Nature ordinarily alloweth men to live. And consequently it is a precept, or generall rule of Reason, *That every man, ought to endeavour Peace, as farre as he has hope of obtaining it; and when he cannot obtain it, that he may seek, and use, all helps, and advantages of Warre.* The first branch of which Rule, containeth the first, and Fundamentall Law of Nature; which is, *to seek Peace, and follow it.* The Second, the summe of the Right of Nature; which is, *By all means we can, to defend our selves.*

From this Fundamentall Law of Nature, by which men are commanded to endeavour Peace, is derived this second Law; *That a man be willing, when others are so too, as farre-forth, as for Peace, and defence of himselfe he shall think it necessary, to lay down this right to all things; and be contented with so much liberty against other men, as he would allow other men against himselfe.* For as long as every man holdeth this Right, of doing any thing he liketh; so long are all men in the condition of Warre. But if other men will not lay down their Right, as well as he; then there is no Reason for any one, to devest himselfe of his: For that were to expose himselfe to Prey, (which no man is bound to) rather than to dispose himselfe to Peace. This is that Law of the Gospel; *Whatsoever you require that others should do to you, that do ye to them.* And that Law of all men *Quod tibi fieri non vis, alteri ne feceris.*

To *lay downe* a mans *Right* to any thing, is to *devest* himselfe of the *Liberty*, of hindring another of the benefit of his own Right to the same. For he that renounceth, or passeth away his Right, giveth not to any other man a Right which he had not before; because there is nothing to which every man had not Right by Nature: but onely standeth out of his way, that he may enjoy his own originall Right, without hindrance from him; not without hindrance from another. So that the effect which redoundeth to one man, by another mans defect of Right, is but so much diminution of impediments to the use of his own Right originall.

Right is layd aside, either by simply Renouncing it; or by Transferring it to another. By *Simply* RENOUNCING; when he cares not to whom the benefit thereof redoundeth. By TRANSFERRING; when he intendeth the benefit thereof to some certain person, or persons. And when a man hath in either manner abandoned, or granted away his Right; then is he said to be OBLIGED, or BOUND, not to hinder those, to whom such Right is granted, or abandoned, from the benefit of it: and that he *Ought*, and it is his DUTY not to make voyd that voluntary act of his own: and that such hindrance is INJUSTICE and INJURY, as being *Sine Jure*; the Right being before renounced, or transferred. So that *Injury*, or *Injustice*, in the controversies of the world, is somewhat like to that, which in the disputations of Scholers is called *Absurdity*. For as it is there called an Absurdity, to contradict what one maintained in the Beginning: so in the world, it is called Injustice, and Injury, voluntarily to undo that, which from the beginning he had voluntarily done. The way by which a man either simply Renounceth, or Transferreth his Right, is a Declaration, or Signification, by some voluntary and sufficient signe, or signes, that he doth so Renounce, or Transferre; or hath so Renounced, or Transferred the same, to him that accepteth it. And these Signes are either Words onely, or Actions onely; or (as it happeneth most often) both Words and Actions. And the same are the BONDS by which men are bound, and obliged: Bonds, that have their strength, not from their own Nature, (for nothing is more easily broken then a mans word,) but from Feare of some evill consequence upon the rupture.

Whensoever a man Transferreth his Right, or Renounceth it; it is either in consideration of some Right reciprocally transferred to himselfe; or for some other good he hopeth for thereby. For it is a voluntary act: and of the voluntary acts of every man, the object is some *Good to himselfe*. And therefore there be some Rights, which no man can be understood by any words, or other signes, to have abandoned, or transferred. As first a man cannot lay down the right of resisting them, that assault him by force, to take away his life; because he cannot be understood to ayme thereby, at any Good to himselfe. The same may be sayd of Wounds, and Chayns, and Imprisonment; both because there is no benefit consequent to such patience; as there is to the patience of suffering another to be wounded, or imprisoned; as also because a man cannot tell, when he seeth men proceed against him by violence, whether they intend his death or not. And lastly the motive, and end for which this renouncing, and transferring of Right is introduced, is nothing else but the security of a mans person, in his life, and in the means of so preserving life, as not to be weary of it. And therefore if a man by words, or other signes, seem to despoyle himselfe of the End, for which those signes were intended; he is not to be understood as if he meant it, or that it was his will; but that he was ignorant of how such words and actions were to be interpreted.

The mutuall transferring of Right, is that which men call CONTRACT.

There is difference, between transferring of Right to the Thing; and transferring, or tradition, that is, delivery of the Thing it selfe. For the Thing may be delivered together with the Translation of the Right; as in buying and selling with ready mony; or exchange of goods, or lands: and it may be delivered some time after.

Again, one of the Contractors, may deliver the Thing contracted for on his part, and leave the other to perform his part at some determinate time after, and in the mean time be trusted; and then the Contract on his part, is called PACT or COVENANT Or both parts may contract now, to performe here-after: in which cases, he that is to performe in time to come, being trusted, his performance is called *Keeping of Promise*, or Faith; and the fayling of performance (if it be voluntary) *Violation of Faith*.

When the transferring of Right, is not mutuall; but one of the parties transferreth, in hope to gain thereby friendship, or service from another, or from his friends; or in hope to gain the reputation of Charity, or Magnanimity; or to deliver his mind from the pain of compassion; or in hope of reward in heaven; This is not Contract, but GIFT, FREE-GIFT, GRACE: which words signifie one and the same thing.

Signes of Contract, are either *Expresse*, or *by Inference*. Expresse, are words spoken with understanding of what they signifie: And such words are either of the time *Present*, or *Past*; as, *I Give, I Grant, I have Given, I have Granted, I will that this be yours:* Or of the future; as, *I will Give, I will Grant:* which words of the future, are called PROMISE.

Signes by Inference, are sometimes the consequence of Words; sometimes the consequence of Silence; sometimes the consequence of Actions; somtimes the consequence of Forbearing an Action: and generally a signe by Inference, of any Contract, is whatsoever sufficiently argues the will of the Contractor.

Words alone, if they be of the time to come, and contain a bare promise, are an insufficient signe of a Free-gift and therefore not obligatory. For if they be of the time to Come, as, *To morrow I Will Give*, they are a signe I have not given yet, and consequently that my right is not transferred, but remaineth till I transferre it by some other Act. But if the words be of the time Present, or Past, as, *I have given, or do give to be delivered to morrow*, then is my to morrows Right given away to day; and that by the vertue of the words, though there were no other argument of my will. And there is a great difference in the signification of these words, *Volc hoc tuum esse cras*, and *Cras dabo;* that is, between *I will that this be thine to morrow*, and, *I will give it thee to morrow:* For the word *I will*, in the former manner of speech, signifies an act of the will Present; but in the later, it signifies a promise of an act of the will to Come: and therefore the former words, being of the Present, transferre a future right; the later, that be of the Future, transferre nothing. But if there be other signes of the Will to transferre a Right, besides Words; then, though the gift be Free, yet may the Right be understood to passe by words of the future: as if a man propound a Prize to him that comes first to the end of a race, The gift is Free; and though the words be of the Future, yet the Right passeth: for if he would not have his words so be understood, he should not have let them runne.

In Contracts, the right passeth, not onely where the words are of the time Present, or Past; but also where they are of the Future: because all Contract is mutuall translation, or change of Right; and therefore he that promiseth onely, because he hath already received the benefit for which he promiseth, is to be understood as if he intended the Right should passe: for unlesse he had been content to have his words so understood, the other would not have performed his part first. And for that cause, in buying, and selling, and other acts of Contract, a Promise is equivalent to a Covenant; and therefore obligatory.

He that performeth first in the case of a Contract, is said to MERIT that which he is to receive by the performance of the other; and he hath it as *Due*. Also when a Prize is propounded to many, which is to be given to him onely that winneth; or mony is thrown amongst many, to be enjoyed by them that catch it; though this be a Free gift; yet so to Win, or so to Catch, is to *Merit*, and to have it as DUE For the Right is transferred in the Propounding of the Prize, and in throwing down the mony; though it be not determined to whom, but by the Event of the contention. But there is between these two sorts of Merit, this difference, that In Contract, I Merit by vertue of my own power, and the Contractors need; but in this case of Free gift, I am enabled to Merit onely by the benignity of the Giver: In Contract, I merit at the Contractors hand that hee should depart with his right; In this case of Gift, I Merit not that the giver should part with his right; but that when he has parted with it, it should be mine, rather than anothers. And this I think to be the meaning of that distinction of the Schooles, between *Meritum congrui,* and *Meritum condigni.* For God Almighty, having promised Paradise to those men (hoodwinkt with carnall desires,) that can walk through this world according to the Precepts, and Limits prescribed by him; they say, he that shall so walk, shall Merit Paradise *Ex congruo*. But because no man can demand a right to it, by his own Righteousnesse, or any other power in himselfe, but by the Free Grace of God onely; they say, no man can Merit Paradise *ex condigno*.

This I say, I think is the meaning of that distinction; but because Disputers do not agree upon the signification of their own termes of Art, longer than it serves their turn; I will not affirme any thing of their meaning: onely this I say; when a gift is given indefinitely, as a prize to be contended for, he that winneth Meriteth, and may claime the Prize as Due.

If a Covenant be made, wherein neither of the parties performe presently, but trust one another; in the condition of meer Nature, (which is a condition of Warre of every man against every man,) upon any reasonable suspition, it is Voyd: But if there be a common Power set over them both, with right and force sufficient to compell performance; it is not Voyd. For he that performeth first, has no assurance the other will performe after; because the bonds of words are too weak to bridle mens ambition, avarice, anger, and other Passions, without the feare of some coerceive Power; which in the condition of meer Nature, where all men are equall, and judges of the justnesse of their own fears cannot possibly be supposed. And therefore he which performeth first, does but betray himselfe to his enemy; contrary to the Right (he can never abandon) of defending his life, and means of living.

But in a civill estate, where there is a Power set up to constrain those that would otherwise violate their faith, that feare is no more reasonable; and for that cause, he which by the Covenant is to perform first, is obliged so to do.

The cause of feare, which maketh such a Covenant invalid, must be always something arising after the Covenant made; as some new fact, or other signe of the Will not to performe: else it cannot make the Covenant voyd. For that which could not hinder a man from promising, ought not to be admitted as a hindrance of performing.

He that transferreth any Right, transferreth the Means of enjoying it, as farre as lyeth in his power. As he that selleth Land, is understood to transfere the Herbage, and whatsoever growes upon it; Nor can he that sells a Mill turn away the Stream that drives it. And they that give to a man the Right of government in Soveraignty, are understood to give him the right of levying mony to maintain Souldiers; and of appointing Magistrates for the administration of Justice.

To make Covenant with bruit Beasts, is impossible; because not understanding our speech, they understand not, nor accept of any translation of Right; nor can translate any Right to another: and without mutuall acceptation, there is no Covenant.

To make Covenant with God, is impossible, but by Mediation of such as God speaketh to, either by Revelation supernaturall, or by his Lieutenants that govern under him, and in his Name: For otherwise we know not whether our Covenants be accepted, or not. And therefore they that Vow any thing contrary to any law of Nature, Vow in vain; as being a thing unjust to pay such Vow. And if it be a thing commanded by the Law of Nature, it is not the Vow, but the Law that binds them.

The matter, or subject of a Covenant, is alwayes something that falleth under deliberation; (For to Covenant, is an act of the Will; that is to say an act, and the last act, of deliberation;) and is therefore always understood to be something to come; and which is judged Possible for him that Covenanteth, to performe.

And therefore, to promise that which is known to be Impossible, is no Covenant. But if that prove impossible afterwards, which before was thought possible, the Covenant is valid, and bindeth, (though not to the thing it selfe,) yet to the value; or, if that also be impossible, to the unfeigned endeavour of performing as much as is possible: for to more no man can be obliged.

Men are freed of their Covenants two wayes; by Performing; or by being Forgiven. For Performance, is the naturall end of obligation; and Forgivenesse, the restitution of liberty; as being a retransferring of that Right, in which the obligation consisted.

Covenants entred into by fear, in the condition of meer Nature, are obligatory. For example, if I Covenant to pay a ransome, or service for my life, to an enemy; I am bound by it. For it is a Contract, wherein one receiveth the benefit of life; the other is to receive mony, or service for it; and consequently, where no other Law (as in the condition, of meer Nature) forbiddeth the performance, the Covenant is valid. Therefore Prisoners of warre, if trusted with the payment of their Ransome, are obliged to pay it: And if a weaker Prince, make a disadvantageous peace with a stronger, for feare; he is bound to keep it; unlesse (as hath been sayd before) there ariseth some new, and just cause of feare, to renew the war. And even in Common-wealths, if I be forced to redeem my selfe from a Theefe by promising him mony, I am bound to pay it, till the Civill Law discharge me. For whatsoever I may lawfully do without Obligation, the same I may lawfully Covenant to do through feare: and what I lawfully Covenant, I cannot lawfully break.

A former Covenant, makes voyd a later. For a man that hath passed away his Right to one man to day, hath it not to passe to morrow to another: and therefore the later promise passeth no Right, but is null.

A Covenant not to defend my selfe from force, by force, is alwayes voyd. For (as I have shewed before) no man can transferre, or lay down his Right to save himselfe from Death, Wounds, and Imprisonment, the avoyding whereof is the onely End of laying down any Right, and therefore the promise of not resisting force, in no Covenant transferreth any right; nor is obliging. For though a man may Covenant thus, *Unlesse I do so, or so, kill me;* he cannot Covenant thus, *Unlesse I do so, or so, I will not resist you, when you come to kill me.* For man by nature chooseth the lesser evill, which is danger of death in resisting; rather than the greater, which is certain and present death in not resisting. And this is granted to be true by all men, in that they lead Criminals to Execution, and Prison, with armed men, notwithstanding that such Criminals have consented to the Law, by which they are condemned.

A Covenant to accuse ones selfe, without assurance of pardon, is likewise invalide. For in the condition of Nature, where every man is Judge, there is no place for Accusation: and in the Civill State, the Accusation is followed with Punishment; which being Force, a man is not obliged not to resist. The same is also true, of the Accusation of those, by whose Condemnation a man falls into misery; as of a Father, Wife, or Benefactor. For the Testimony of such an Accuser, if it be not willingly given, is præsumed to be corrupted by Nature; and therefore not to be received: and where a mans Testimony is not to be credited, he is not bound to give it. Also Accusations upon Torture, are not to be reputed as Testimonies. For Torture is to be used but as means of conjecture, and light, in the further examination, and search of truth: and what is in that case confessed, tendeth to the ease of him that is Tortured; not to the informing of the Torturers: and therefore ought not to have the credit of a sufficient Testimony: for whether he deliver himselfe by true, or false Accusation, he does it by the Right of preserving his own life.

The force of Words, being (as I have formerly noted) too weak to hold men to the performance of their Covenants; there are in mans nature, but two imaginable helps to strengthen it. And those are either a Feare of the consequence of breaking their word; or a Glory, or Pride in appearing not to need to breake it. This later is a Generosity too rarely found to be presumed on, especially in the pursuers of Wealth, Command, or sensuall Pleasure; which are the greatest part of Mankind. The Passion to be reckoned upon, is Fear; whereof there be two very generall Objects: one, The Power of Spirits Invisible; the other, The Power of those men they shall therein Offend. Of these two, though the former be the greater Power, yet the feare of the later is commonly the greater Feare. The Feare of the former is in every man, his own Religion: which hath place in the nature of man before Civill Society. The later hath not so; at least not place enough, to keep men to their promises; because in the condition of meer Nature, the inequality of Power is not discerned, but by the event of Battell. So that before the time of Civill Society, or in the interruption thereof by Warre, there is nothing can strengthen a Covenant of Peace agreed on, against the temptations of Avarice, Ambition, Lust, or other strong desire, but the feare of that Invisible Power, which they every one Worship as God; and Feare as a Revenger of their perfidy. All therefore that can be done between two men not subject to Civill Power, is to put one another to swear by the God he feareth: Which *Swearing* or OATH, is a *Forme of Speech added to a Promise; by which he that promiseth, signifieth, that unlesse he performe, he renounceth the mercy of his God, or calleth to him for vengeance on himselfe.* Such was the Heathen Forme, *Let* Jupiter *kill me else, as I kill this Beast.* So is our Forme, *I shall do thus, and thus, so help me God.* And this, with the Rites and Ceremonies, which every one useth in his own Religion, that the feare of breaking faith might be the greater.

By this it appears, that an Oath taken according to any other Forme, or Rite, then his, that sweareth, is in vain; and no Oath: And that there is no Swearing by any thing which the Swearer thinks not God. For though men have sometimes used to swear by their Kings, for feare, or flattery; yet they would have it thereby understood, they attributed to them Divine honour. And that Swearing unnecessarily by God, is but prophaning of his name: and Swearing by other things, as men do in common discourse, is not Swearing, but an impious Custome, gotten by too much vehemence of talking.

It appears also, that the Oath addes nothing to the Obligation. For a Covenant, if lawfull, binds in the sight of God, without the Oath, as much as with it: if unlawfull, bindeth not at all; though it be confirmed with an Oath.

Chap. XV

Of other Lawes of Nature

FROM that law of Nature, by which we are obliged to transferre to another, such Rights, as being retained, hinder the peace of Mankind, there followeth a Third; which is this, *That men performe their Covenants made:* without which, Covenants are in vain, and but Empty words; and the Right of all men to all things remaining, wee are still in the condition of Warre.

And in this law of Nature, consisteth the Fountain and Originall of JUSTICE. For where no Covenant hath preceded, there hath no Right been transferred, and every man has right to every thing; and consequently, no action can be Unjust. But when a Covenant is made, then to break it is *Unjust:* And the definition of INJUSTICE, is no other than *the not Performance of Covenant.* And whatsoever is not Unjust, is *Just.*

But because Covenants of mutuall trust, where there is a feare of not performance on either part, (as hath been said in the former Chapter,) are invalid; though the Originall of Justice be the making of Covenants; yet Injustice actually there can be none, till the cause of such feare be taken away; which while men are in the naturall condition of Warre, cannot be done. Therefore before the names of Just, and Unjust can have place, there must be some coercive Power, to compell men equally to the performance of their Covenants, by the terrour of some punishment, greater than the benefit they expect by the breach of their Covenant; and to make good that Propriety, which by mutuall Contract men acquire, in recompence of the universall Right they abandon: and such power there is none before the erection of a Common-wealth. And this is also to be gathered out of the ordinary definition of Justice in the Schooles: For they say, that *Justice is the constant Will of giving to every man his own.* And therefore where there is no *Own,* that is, no Propriety, there is no Injustice; and where there is no coërceive Power erected, that is, where there is no Common-wealth, there is no Propriety; all men having Right to all things: Therefore where there is no Common-wealth, there nothing is Unjust. So that the nature of Justice, consisteth in keeping of valid Covenants: but the Validity of Covenants begins not but with the Constitution of a Civill Power, sufficient to compell men to keep them: And then it is also that Propriety begins.

The Foole hath sayd in his heart, there is no such thing as Justice; and sometimes also with his tongue; seriously alleaging, that every mans conservation, and contentment, being committed to his own care, there could be no reason, why every man might not do what he thought conduced thereunto: and therefore also to make, or not make; keep, or not keep Covenants, was not against Reason, when it conduced to ones benefit. He does not therein deny, that there be Covenants; and that they are sometimes broken, sometimes kept; and that such breach of them may be called Injustice, and the observance of them Justice: but he questioneth, whether Injustice, taking away the feare of God, (for the same Foole hath said in his heart there is no God,) may not sometimes stand with that Reason, which dictateth to every man his own good; and particularly then, when it conduceth to such a benefit, as shall put a man in a condition, to neglect not onely the dispraise, and revilings, but also the power of other men. The Kingdome of God is gotten by violence: but what if it could be gotten by unjust violence? were it against Reason so to get it, when it is impossible to receive hurt by it? and if it be not against Reason, it is not against Justice: or else Justice is not to be approved for good. From such reasoning as this, Succesfull wickednesse hath obtained the name of Vertue: and some that in all other things have disallowed the violation of Faith; yet have allowed it, when it is for the getting of a Kingdome. And the Heathen that believed, that *Saturn* was deposed by his son *Jupiter,* believed neverthelesse the same *Jupiter* to be the avenger of Injustice: Somewhat like to a piece of Law in *Cokes* Commentaries on *Litleton;* where he sayes, If the right Heire of the Crown be attainted of Treason; yet the Crown shall descend to him, and *eo instante* the Atteynder be voyd: From which instances a man will be very prone to inferre; that when the Heire apparent of a Kingdome, shall kill him that is in possession, though his father; you may call it Injustice, or by what other name you will; yet it can never be against Reason, seeing all the voluntary actions of men tend to the benefit of themselves; and those actions are most Reasonable, that conduce most to their ends. This specious reasoning is neverthelesse false.

For the question is not of promises mutuall, where there is no security of performance on either side; as when there is no Civill Power erected over the parties promising; for such promises are no Covenants: But either where one of the parties has performed already; or where there is a Power to make him performe; there is the question whether it be against reason, that is, against the benefit of the other to performe, or not. And I say it is not against reason. For the manifestation whereof, we are to consider; First, that when a man doth a thing, which notwithstanding any thing can be foreseen, and reckoned on, tendeth to his own destruction, howsoever some accident which he could not expect, arriving may turne it to his benefit; yet such events do not make it reasonably or wisely done. Secondly, that in a condition of Warre, wherein every man to every man, for want of a common Power to keep them all in awe, is an Enemy, there is no man can hope by his own strength, or wit, to defend himselfe from destruction, without the help of Confederates; where every one expects the same defence by the Confederation, that any one else does: and therefore he which declares he thinks it reason to deceive those that help him, can in reason expect no other means of safety, than what can be had from his own single Power. He therefore that breaketh his Covenant, and consequently declareth that he thinks he may with reason do so, cannot be received into any Society, that unite themselves for Peace and Defence, but by the errour of them that receive him; nor when he is received, be retayned in it, without seeing the danger of their errour; which errours a man cannot reasonably reckon upon as the means of his security: and therefore if he be left, or cast out of Society, he perisheth; and if he live in Society, it is by the errours of other men, which he could not foresee, nor reckon upon; and consequently against the reason of his preservation; and so, as all men that contribute not to his destruction, forbear him onely out of ignorance of what is good for themselves.

As for the Instance of gaining the secure and perpetuall felicity of Heaven, by any way; it is frivolous: there being but one way imaginable; and that is not breaking, but keeping of Covenant.

And for the other Instance of attaining Soveraignty by Rebellion; it is manifest, that though the event follow, yet because it cannot reasonably be expected, but rather the contrary; and because by gaining it so, others are taught to gain the same in like manner, the attempt thereof is against reason. Justice therefore, that is to say, Keeping of Covenant, is a Rule of Reason, by which we are forbidden to do any thing destructive to our life; and consequently a Law of Nature.

There be some that proceed further; and will not have the Law of Nature, to be those Rules which conduce to the preservation of mans life on earth; but to the attaining of an eternall felicity after death; to which they think the breach of Covenant may conduce; and consequently be just and reasonable; (such are they that think it a work of merit to kill, or depose, or rebell against, the Soveraigne Power constituted over them by their own consent.) But because there is no naturall knowledge of mans estate after death; much lesse of the reward that is then to be given to breach of Faith; but onely a beliefe grounded upon other mens saying, that they know it supernaturally, or that they know those, that knew them, that knew others, that knew it supernaturally; Breach of Faith cannot be called a Precept of Reason, or Nature.

Others, that allow for a Law of Nature, the keeping of Faith, do neverthelesse make exception of certain persons; as Heretiques, and such as use not to performe their Covenant to others: And this also is against reason. For if any fault of a man, be sufficient to discharge our Covenant made; the same ought in reason to have been sufficient to have hindred the making of it.

The names of Just, and Injust, when they are attributed to Men, signifie one thing; and when they are attributed to Actions, another. When they are attributed to Men, they signifie Conformity, or Inconformity of Manners, to Reason. But when they are attributed to Actions, they signifie the Conformity, or Inconformity to Reason, not of Manners, or manner of life, but of particular Actions. A Just man therefore, is he that taketh all the care he can, that his Actions may be all Just: and an Unjust man, is he that neglecteth it. And such men are more often in our Language stiled by the names of Righteous, and Unrighteous; then Just, and Unjust; though the meaning be the same. Therefore a Right-eous man, does not lose that Title, by one, or a few unjust Actions, that proceed from sudden Passion, or mistake of Things, or Persons: nor does an Unrighteous man, lose his character, for such Actions, as he does, or forbeares to do, for feare: because his Will is not framed by the Justice, but by the apparant benefit of what he is to do. That which gives to humane Actions the relish of Justice, is a certain Noblenesse or Gallantnesse of courage, (rarely found,) by which a man scorns to be beholding for the contentment of his life, to fraud, or breach of promise. This Justice of the Manners, is that which is meant, where Justice is called a Vertue; and Injustice a Vice.

But the Justice of Actions denominates men, not Just, but *Guiltlesse:* and the Injus-tice of the same, (which is also called Injury,) gives them but the name of *Guilty.*

Again, the Injustice of Manners, is the disposition, or aptitude to do Injurie; and is Injustice before it proceed to Act; and without supposing any individuall person injured. But the Injustice of an Action, (that is to say Injury,) supposeth an individuall person Injured; namely him, to whom the Covenant was made: And therefore many times the in-jury is received by one man, when the dammage redoundeth to another. As when the Master commandeth his servant to give mony to a stranger; if it be not done, the Injury is done to the Master, whom he had before Covenanted to obey; but the dammage re-doundeth to the stranger, to whom he had no Obligation; and therefore could not Injure him. And so also in Common-wealths, private men may remit to one another their debts; but not robberies or other violences, whereby they are endammaged; because the detain-ing of Debt, is an Injury to themselves; but Robbery and Violence, are Injuries to the Person of the Common-wealth.

Whatsoever is done to a man, conformable to his own Will signified to the doer, is no Injury to him. For if he that doeth it, hath not passed away his originall right to do what he please, by some Antecedent Covenant, there is no breach of Covenant; and therefore no Injury done him. And if he have; then his Will to have it done being sig-nified, is a release of that Covenant: and so again there is no Injury done him.

Justice of Actions, is by Writers divided into *Commutative,* and *Distributive:* and the for-mer they say consisteth in proportion Arithmeticall; the later in proportion Geometricall. Commutative therefore, they place in the equality of value of the things contracted for; And Distributive, in the distribution of equall benefit, to men of equall merit. As if it were Injustice to sell dearer than we buy; or to give more to a man than he merits. The value of all things contracted for, is measured by the Appetite of the Contractors: and therefore the just value, is that which they be contented to give. And Merit (besides that which is by Covenant, where the performance on one part, meriteth the performance of the other part, and falls under Justice Commutative, not Distributive,) is not due by Justice; but is rewarded of Grace onely. And therefore this distinction, in the sense wherein it useth to be expounded, is not right. To speak properly, Commutative Justice, is the Justice of a Contractor; that is, a Performance of Covenant, in Buying, and Selling; Hiring, and Let-ting to Hire; Lending, and Borrowing; Exchanging, Bartering, and other acts of Contract.

And Distributive Justice, the Justice of an Arbitrator; that is to say, the act of defin-ing what is Just. Wherein, (being trusted by them that make him Arbitrator,) if he per-forme his Trust, he is said to distribute to every man his own: and this is indeed Just Distribution, and may be called (though improperly) Distributive Justice; but more prop-erly Equity; which also is a Law of Nature, as shall be shewn in due place.

As Justice dependeth on Antecedent Covenant; so does GRATITUDE depend on Ante-cedent Grace; that is to say, Antecedent Free-gift: and is the fourth Law of Nature; which may be conceived in this Forme, *That a man which receiveth Benefit from another of meer Grace, Endeavour that he which giveth it, have no reasonable cause to repent him of his good will.* For no man giveth, but with intention of Good to himselfe; because Gift is Voluntary; and of all Voluntary Acts, the Object is to every man his own Good; of which if men see they shall be frustrated, there will be no beginning of benevolence, or trust; nor consequently of mu-tuall help; nor of reconciliation of one man to another; and therefore they are to remain still in the condition of *War;* which is contrary to the first and Fundamentall Law of Na-ture, which commandeth men to *Seek Peace.* The breach of this Law, is called *Ingratitude;* and hath the same relation to Grace, that Injustice hath to Obligation by Covenant.

A fifth Law of Nature, is COMPLEASANCE; that is to say, *That every man strive to accom-modate himselfe to the rest.* For the understanding whereof, we may consider, that there is in mens aptnesse to Society; a diversity of Nature, rising from their diversity of Affections; not unlike to that we see in stones brought together for building of an Ædifice. For as that stone which by the asperity, and irregularity of Figure, takes more room from others, than it selfe fills; and for the hardnesse, cannot be easily made plain, and thereby hin-dereth the building, is by the builders cast away as unprofitable, and troublesome: so also, a man that by asperity of Nature, will strive to retain those things which to himselfe are superfluous, and to others necessary; and for the stubbornness of his Passions, cannot be corrected, is to be left, or cast out of Society, as combersome thereunto. For seeing every man, not onely by Right, but also by necessity of Nature, is supposed to endeavour all he can, to obtain that which is necessary for his conservation; He that shall oppose himselfe against it, for things superfluous, is guilty of the warre that thereupon is to follow; and therefore doth that, which is contrary to the fundamentall Law of Nature, which commandeth *to seek Peace.* The observers of this Law, may be called SOCIABLE, (the Latines call them *Commodi:*) The contrary, *Stubborn, Insociable, Froward, Intractable.*

A sixth Law of Nature is this, *That upon caution of the Future time, a man ought to pardon the offences past of them that repenting, desire it.* For PARDON, is nothing but granting of Peace; which though granted to them that persevere in their hostility, be not Peace, but Feare; yet not granted to them that give caution of the Future time, is signe of an aversion to Peace; and therefore contrary to the Law of Nature.

A seventh is, *That in Revenges,* (that is, retribution of Evil for Evil,) *Men look not at the greatnesse of the evill past, but the greatnesse of the good to follow.* Whereby we are forbidden to inflict punishment with any other designe, than for correction of the offender, or direction of others. For this Law is consequent to the next before it, that commandeth Pardon, upon security of the Future time. Besides, Revenge without respect to the Example, and profit to come, is a triumph, or glorying in the hurt of another, tending to no end; (for the End is always somewhat to Come;) and glorying to no end, is vain-glory, and contrary to reason; and to hurt without reason, tendeth to the introduction of Warre; which is against the Law of Nature; and is commonly stiled by the name of *Cruelty.*

And because all signes of hatred, or contempt, provoke to fight; insomuch as most men choose rather to hazard their life, than not to be revenged; we may in the eighth place, for a Law of Nature, set down this Precept, *That no man by deed, word, countenance, or gesture, declare Hatred, or Contempt of another.* The breach of which Law, is commonly called *Contumely.*

The question who is the better man, has no place in the condition of meer Nature; where, (as has been shewn before,) all men are equall. The inequallity that now is, has bin introduced by the Lawes civill. I know that *Aristotle* in the first booke of his Politiques, for a foundation of his doctrine, maketh men by Nature, some more worthy to Command, meaning the wiser sort (such as he thought himselfe to be for his Philosophy;) others to Serve, (meaning those that had strong bodies, but were not Philosophers as he;) as if Master and Servant were not introduced by consent of men, but by difference of Wit: which is not only against reason; but also against experience. For there are very few so foolish, that had not rather governe themselves, than be governed by others: Nor when the wise in their own conceit, contend by force, with them who distrust their owne wisdome, do they alwaies, or often, or almost at any time, get the Victory. If Nature therefore have made men equall, that equalitie is to be acknowledged: or if Nature have made men unequall; yet because men that think themselves equall, will not enter into conditions of Peace, but upon Equall termes, such equalitie must be admitted. And therefore for the ninth law of Nature, I put this, *That every man acknowledge other for his Equall by Nature.* The breach of this Precept is *Pride.*

On this law, dependeth another, *That at the entrance into conditions of Peace, no man require to reserve to himselfe any Right, which he is not content should be reserved to every one of the rest.* As it is necessary for all men that seek peace, to lay down certaine Rights of Nature; that is to say, not to have libertie to do all they list: so is it necessarie for mans life, to retaine some; as right to governe their owne bodies; enjoy aire, water, motion, waies to go from place to place; and all things else without which a man cannot live, or not live well. If in this case, at the making of Peace, men require for themselves, that which they would not have to be granted to others, they do contrary to the precedent law, that commandeth the acknowledgment of naturall equalitie, and therefore also against the law of Nature. The observers of this law, are those we call *Modest,* and the breakers *Arrogant* men. The Greeks call the violation of this law πλεονεξία; that is, a desire of more than their share.

Also if *a man be trusted to judge between man and man,* it is a precept of the Law of Nature, *that he deale Equally between them.* For without that, the Controversies of men cannot be determined but by Warre. He therefore that is partiall in judgment, doth what in him lies, to deterre men from the use of Judges, and Arbitrators; and consequently, (against the fundamentall Lawe of Nature) is the cause of Warre.

The observance of this law, from the equall distribution to each man, of that which in reason belongeth to him, is called EQUITY, and (as I have sayd before) distributive Justice: the violation, *Acception of persons,* προσωποληψία.

And from this followeth another law, *That such things as cannot be divided, be enjoyed in Common, if it can be; and if the quantity of the thing permit, without Stint; otherwise Proportionably to the number of them that have Right.* For otherwise the distribution is Unequall, and contrary to Equitie.

But some things there be, that can neither be divided, nor enjoyed in common. Then, The Law of Nature, which prescribeth Equity, requireth, *That the Entire Right; or else, (making the use alternate,) the First Possession, be determined by Lot.* For equall distribution, is of the Law of Nature; and other means of equall distribution cannot be imagined.

Of *Lots* there be two sorts, *Arbitrary,* and *Naturall.* Arbitrary, is that which is agreed on by the Competitors: Naturall, is either *Primogeniture,* (which the Greek calls Κληρονομία, which signifies, *Given by Lot;*) or *First Seisure.*

And therefore those things which cannot be enjoyed in common, nor divided, ought to be adjudged to the First Possessor; and in some cases to the First-Borne, as acquired by Lot.

It is also a Law of Nature, *That all men that mediate Peace, be allowed safe Conduct.* For the Law that commandeth Peace, as the *End,* commandeth Intercession, as the *Means;* and to Intercession the Means is safe Conduct.

And because, though men be never so willing to observe these Lawes, there may neverthelesse arise questions concerning a mans action; First, whether it were done, or not done; Secondly (if done) whether against the Law, or not against the Law; the former whereof, is called a question *Of Fact;* the later a question *Of Right;* therefore unlesse the parties to the question, Covenant mutually to stand to the sentence of another, they are as farre from Peace as ever. This other, to whose Sentence they submit, is called an ARBITRATOR. And therefore it is of the Law of Nature, *That they that are at controversie, submit their Right to the judgement of an Arbitrator.*

And seeing every man is presumed to do all things in order to his own benefit, no man is a fit Arbitrator in his own cause: and if he were never so fit; yet Equity allowing to each party equall benefit, if one be admitted to be Judge, the other is to be admitted also; & so the controversie, that is, the cause of War, remains, against the Law of Nature.

For the same reason no man in any Cause ought to be received for Arbitrator, to whom greater profit, or honour, or pleasure apparently ariseth out of the victory of one party, than of the other: for hee hath taken (though an unavoydable bribe, yet) a bribe; and no man can be obliged to trust him. And thus also the controversie, and the condition of War remaineth, contrary to the Law of Nature.

And in a controversie of *Fact*, the Judge being to give no more credit to one, than to the other, (if there be no other Arguments) must give credit to a third; or to a third and fourth; or more: For else the question is undecided, and left to force, contrary to the Law of Nature.

These are the Lawes of Nature, dictating Peace, for a means of the conservation of men in multitudes; and which onely concern the doctrine of Civill Society. There be other things tending to the destruction of particular men; as Drunkenness, and all other parts of Intemperance; which may therefore also be reckoned amongst those things which the Law of Nature hath forbidden; but are not necessary to be mentioned, nor are pertinent enough to this place.

And though this may seem too subtile a deduction of the Lawes of Nature, to be taken notice of by all men; whereof the most part are too busie in getting food, and the rest too negligent to understand; yet to leave all men unexcusable, they have been contracted into one easie sum, intelligible, even to the meanest capacity; and that is, *Do not that to another, which thou wouldest not have done to thy selfe:* which sheweth him, that he has no more to do in learning the Lawes of Nature, but, when weighing the actions of other men with his own, they seem too heavy, to put them into the other part of the ballance, and his own into their place, that his own passions, and selfe-love, may adde nothing to the weight; and then there is none of these Lawes of Nature that will not appear unto him very reasonable.

The Lawes of Nature oblige *in foro interno;* that is to say, they bind to a desire they should take place: but *in foro externo;* that is, to the putting them in act, not alwayes. For he that should be modest, and tractable, and performe all he promises, in such time, and place, where no man els should do so, should but make himselfe a prey to others, and procure his own certain ruine, contrary to the ground of all Lawes of Nature, which tend to Natures preservation. And again, he that having sufficient Security, that others shall observe the same Lawes towards him, observes them not himselfe, seeketh not Peace, but War; & consequently the destruction of his Nature by Violence.

And whatsoever Lawes bind *in foro interno*, may be broken, not onely by a fact contrary to the Law but also by a fact according to it, in case a man think it contrary. For though his Action in this case, be according to the Law; yet his Purpose was against the Law; which where the Obligation is *in foro interno*, is a breach.

The Lawes of Nature are Immutable and Eternall; For Injustice, Ingratitude, Arrogance, Pride, Iniquity, Acception of persons, and the rest, can never be made lawfull. For it can never be that Warre shall preserve life, and Peace destroy it.

The same Lawes, because they oblige onely to a desire, and endeavour, I mean an unfeigned and constant endeavour, are easie to be observed. For in that they require nothing but endeavour; he that endeavoureth their performance, fulfilleth them; and he that fulfilleth the Law, is Just.

And the Science of them, is the true and onely Moral Philosophy. For Morall Philosophy is nothing else but the Science of what is *Good*, and *Evill*, in the conversation, and Society of mankind. *Good*, and *Evill*, are names that signifie our Appetites, and Aversions; which in different tempers, customes, and doctrines of men, are different: And divers men, differ not onely in their Judgement, on the senses of what is pleasant, and unpleasant to the tast, smell, hearing, touch, and sight; but also of what is conformable, or disagreeable to Reason, in the actions of common life. Nay, the same man, in divers times, differs from himselfe; and one time praiseth, that is, calleth Good, what another time he dispraiseth, and calleth Evil: From whence arise Disputes, Controversies, and at last War. And therefore so long a man is in the condition of meer Nature, (which is a condition of War,) as private Appetite is the measure of Good, and Evill: and consequently all men agree on this, that Peace is Good, and therefore also the way, or means of Peace, which (as I have shewed before) are *Justice, Gratitude, Modesty, Equity, Mercy,* & the rest of the Laws of Nature, are good; that is to say, *Morall Vertues;* and their contrarie *Vices,* Evill. Now the science of Vertue and Vice, is Morall Philosophie; and therfore the true Doctrine of the Lawes of Nature, is the true Morall Philosophie. But the Writers of Morall Philosophie, though they acknowledge the same Vertues and Vices; Yet not seeing wherein consisted their Goodnesse; nor that they come to be praised, as the meanes of peaceable, sociable, and comfortable living; place them in a mediocrity of passions: as if not the Cause, but the Degree of daring, made Fortitude; or not the Cause, but the Quantity of a gift, made Liberality.

These dictates of Reason, men use to call by the name of Lawes; but improperly: for they are but Conclusions, or Theoremes concerning what conduceth to the conservation and defence of themselves; wheras Law, properly is the word of him, that by right hath command over others. But yet if we consider the same Theoremes, as delivered in the word of God, that by right commandeth all things; then are they properly called Lawes.

Chap. XVI

Of Persons, Authors, and things Personated

A PERSON, is he *whose words or actions are considered, either as his own, or as representing the words or actions of an other man, or of any other thing to whom they are attributed, whether Truly or by Fiction.*

When they are considered as his owne, then is he called a *Naturall Person:* And when they are considered as representing the words and actions of an other, then is he a *Feigned* or *Artificiall person.*

The word Person is latine: insteed whereof the Greeks have πρόσωπον, which signifies the *Face*, as *Persona* in latine signifies the *disguise*, or *outward appearance* of a man, counterfeited on the Stage; and somtimes more particularly that part of it, which disguiseth the face, as a Mask or Visard: And from the Stage, hath been translated to any Representer of speech and action, as well in Tribunalls, as Theaters. So that a *Person*, is the same that an *Actor* is, both on the Stage and in common Conversation; and to *Personate*, is to *Act*, or *Represent* himselfe, or an other; and he that acteth another, is said to beare his

Person, or act in his name; (in which sence *Cicero* useth it where he saies, *Unus sustineo tres Personas; Mei, Adversarii, & Judicis.* I beare three Persons; my own, my Adversaries, and times, and in cases of the greatest consequence, a mute Person, and unapt, as for many things else, so for the government of a Multitude, especially in time of Warre.

Of Authors there be two sorts. The first simply so called; which I have before defined to be him, that owneth the Action of another simply. The second is he, that owneth an Action, or Covenant of another conditionally; that is to say, he undertaketh to do it, if the other doth it not, at, or before a certain time. And these Authors conditionall, are generally called SURETYES, in Latine *Fidejussores,* and *Sponsores;* and particularly for Debt, *Prædes;* and for Appearance before a Judge, or Magistrate, *Vades.*

Chap. XVII

Of the Causes, Generation, and Definition of a Common-Wealth

THE finall Cause, End, or Designe of men, (who naturally love Liberty, and Dominion over others,) in the introduction of that restraint upon themselves, (in which wee see them live in Common-wealths,) is the foresight of their own preservation, and of a more contented life thereby; that is to say, of getting themselves out from that miserable condition of Warre, which is necessarily consequent (as hath been shown) to the naturall Passions of men, when there is no visible Power to keep them in awe, and tye them by feare of punishment to the performance of their Covenants, and observation of those Lawes of Nature set down in the fourteenth and fifteenth Chapters.

For the Lawes of Nature (as *Justice, Equity, Modesty, Mercy,* and (in summe) *doing to others, as wee would be done to,*) of themselves, without the terrour of some Power, to cause them to be observed, are contrary to our naturall Passions, that carry us to Partiality, Pride, Revenge, and the like. And Covenants, without the Sword, are but Words, and of no strength to secure a man at all. Therefore notwithstanding the Lawes of Nature, (which every one hath then kept, when he has the will to keep them, when he can do it safely,) if there be no Power erected, or not great enough for our security; every man will and may lawfully rely on his own strength and art, for caution against all other men. And in all places, where men have lived by small Families, to robbe and spoyle one another, has been a Trade, and so farre from being reputed against the Law of Nature, that the greater spoyles they gained, the greater was their honour; and men observed no other Lawes therein, but the Lawes of Honour; that is, to abstain from cruelty, leaving to men their lives, and instruments of husbandry. And as small Familyes did then; so now do Cities and Kingdomes which are but greater Families (for their own security) enlarge their Dominions, upon all pretences of danger, and fear of Invasion, or assistance that may be given to Invaders, endeavour as much as they can, to subdue, or weaken their neighbours, by open force, and secret arts, for want of other Caution, justly; and are remembred for it in after ages with honour.

Nor is it the joyning together of a small number of men, that gives them this security; because in small numbers, small additions on the one side or the other, make the advantage of strength so great, as is sufficient to carry the Victory; and therefore gives encouragement to an Invasion. The Multitude sufficient to confide in for our Security, is not determined by any certain number, but by comparison with the Enemy we feare; and is then sufficient, when the odds of the Enemy is not of so visible and conspicuous moment, to determine the event of warre, as to move him to attempt.

And be there never so great a Multitude; yet if their actions be directed according to their particular judgements, and particular appetites, they can expect thereby no defence, nor protection, neither against a Common enemy, nor against the injuries of one another. For being distracted in opinions concerning the best use and application of their strength, they do not help, but hinder one another; and reduce their strength by mutuall opposition to nothing: whereby they are easily, not onely subdued by a very few that agree together; but also when there is no common enemy, they make warre upon each other, for their particular interests. For if we could suppose a great Multitude of men to consent in the observation of Justice, and other Lawes of Nature, without a common Power to keep them all in awe; we might as well suppose all Man-kind to do the same; and then there neither would be, nor need to be any Civill Government, or Commonwealth at all; because there would be Peace without subjection.

Nor is it enough for the security, which men desire should last all the time of their life, that they be governed, and directed by one judgement, for a limited time; as in one Battell, or one Warre. For though they obtain a Victory by their unanimous endeavour against a forraign enemy; yet afterwards, when either they have no common enemy, or he that by one part is held for an enemy, is by another part held for a friend, they must needs by the difference of their interests dissolve, and fall again into a Warre amongst themselves.

It is true, that certain living creatures, as Bees, and Ants, live sociably one with another, (which are therefore by *Aristotle* numbred amongst Politicall creatures;) and yet have no other direction, than their particular judgements and appetites; nor speech, whereby one of them can signifie to another, what he thinks expedient for the common benefit: and therefore some man may perhaps desire to know, why Man-kind cannot do the same. To which I answer,

First, that men are continually in competition for Honour and Dignity, which these creatures are not; and consequently amongst men there ariseth on that ground, Envy and Hatred, and finally Warre; but amongst these not so.

Secondly, that amongst these creatures, the Common good differeth not from the Private; and being by nature enclined to their private, they procure thereby the common benefit. But man, whose Joy consisteth in comparing himselfe with other men, can relish nothing but what is eminent.

Thirdly, that these creatures, having not (as man) the use of reason, do not see, nor think they see any fault, in the administration of their common businesse: whereas amongst men, there are very many, that thinke themselves wiser, and abler to govern the Publique, better than the rest; and these strive to reforme and innovate, one this way, another that way; and thereby bring it into Distraction and Civill warre.

Fourthly, that these creatures, though they have some use of voice, in making knowne to one another their desires, and other affections; yet they want that art of words, by which some men can represent to others, that which is Good, in the likenesse of Evill; and Evill, in the likenesse of Good; and augment, or diminish the apparent greatnesse of Good and Evill; discontenting men, and troubling, their Peace at their pleasure.

Fifthly, irrationall creatures cannot distinguish betweene *Injury,* and *Dammage;* therefore as long as they be at ease, they are not offended with their fellowes: whereas Man is then most troublesome, when he is most at ease: for then it is that he loves to shew his Wisdome, and controule the Actions of them that governe the Common-wealth.

Lastly, the agreement of these creatures is Naturall; that of men, is by Covenant only, which is Artificiall: and therefore it is no wonder if there be somewhat else required (besides Covenant) to make their Agreement constant and lasting; which is a Common Power, to keep them in awe, and to direct their actions to the Common Benefit.

The only way to erect such a Common Power, as may be able to defend them from the invasion of Forraigners, and the injuries of one another, and thereby to secure them in such sort, as that by their owne industrie, and by the fruites of the Earth, they may nourish themselves and live contentedly; is, to conferre all their power and strength upon one Man, or upon one Assembly of men, that may reduce all their Wills, by plurality of voices, unto one Will: which is as much as to say, to appoint one man, or Assembly of men, to beare their Person; and every one to owne, and acknowledge himselfe to be Author of whatsoever he that so beareth their Person, shall Act, or cause to be Acted, in those things which concerne the Common Peace and Safetie; and therein to submit their Wills, every one to his Will, and their Judgements, to his Judgment. This is more than Consent, or Concord; it is a reall Unitie of them all, in one and the same Person, made by Covenant of every man with every man, in such manner, as if every man should say to every man, *I Authorise and give up my Right of Governing my selfe, to this Man, or to this Assembly of men, on this condition, that thou give up thy Right to him, and Authorise all his Actions in like manner.* This done, the Multitude so united in one Person, is called a COMMON-WEALTH, in latine CIVITAS. This is the Generation of that great LEVIATHAN, or rather (to speake more reverently) of that *Mortall God,* to which wee owe under the *Immortall God,* our peace and defence. For by this Authoritie, given him by every particular man in the Common-Wealth, he hath the use of so much Power and Strength conferred on him, that by terror thereof, he is inabled to forme the wills of them all, to Peace at home, and mutuall ayd against their enemies abroad. And in him consisteth the Essence of the Common-wealth; which (to define it,) is *One Person, of whose Acts a great Multitude, by mutuall Covenants one with another, have made themselves every one the Author, to the end he may use the strength and means of them all, as he shall think expedient, for their Peace and Common Defence.*

And he that carryeth this Person, is called SOVERAIGNE, and said to have *Soveraigne Power;* and every one besides, his SUBJECT.

The attaining to this Soveraigne Power, is by two wayes. One, by Naturall force; as when a man maketh his children, to submit themselves, and their children to his government, as being able to destroy them if they refuse; or by Warre subdueth his enemies to his will, giving them their lives on that condition. The other, is when men agree amongst themselves, to submit to some Man, or Assembly of men, voluntarily, on confidence to be protected by him against all others. This later, may be called a Politicall Common-wealth or Common-wealth by *Institution;* and the former, a Common-wealth by *Acquisition.* And first, I shall speak of a Common-wealth by Institution.

Chap. XVIII

Of the Rights of Soveraignes by Institution

A *Common-wealth* is said to be *Instituted,* when a *Multitude* of men do Agree, and *Covenant, every one, with every one,* that to whatsoever *Man,* or *Assembly of Men,* shall be given by the major part, the *Right* to *Present* the Person of them all, (that is to say, to be their *Representative;*) every one, as well he that *Voted for it,* as he that *Voted against it,* shall *Authorise* all the Actions and Judgements, of that Man, or Assembly of men, in the same manner, as if they were his own, to the end, to live peaceably amongst themselves, and be protected against other men.

From this Institution of a Common-wealth are derived all the *Rights,* and *Facultyes* of him, or them, on whom the Soveraigne Power is conferred by the consent of the People assembled.

First, because they Covenant, it is to be understood, they are not obliged by former Covenant to any thing repugnant hereunto. And Consequently they that have already Instituted a Commonwealth, being thereby bound by Covenant, to own the Actions, and Judgements of one, cannot lawfully make a new Covenant, amongst themselves, to be obedient to any other, in any thing whatsoever, without his permission. And therefore, they that are subjects to a Monarch, cannot without his leave cast off Monarchy, and return to the confusion of a disunited Multitude; nor transferre their Person from him that beareth it, to another Man, or other Assembly of men: for they are bound, every man to every man, to Own, and be reputed Author of all, that he that already is their Soveraigne, shall do, and judge fit to be done: so that any one man dissenting, all the rest should break their Covenant made to that man, which is injustice: and they have also every man given the Soveraignty to him that beareth their Person; and therefore if they depose him, they take from him that which is his own, and so again it is injustice. Besides, if he that attempteth to depose his Soveraign, be killed, or punished by him for such attempt, he is author of his own punishment, as being by the Institution, Author of all his Soveraign shall do: And because it is injustice for a man to do any thing, for which he may be punished by his own authority, he is also upon that title, unjust. And whereas some men have pretended for their disobedience to their Soveraign, a new Covenant, made, not with men, but with God; this also is unjust: for there is no Covenant with God, but by mediation of some body that representeth Gods Person; which none doth but Gods Lieutenant, who hath the Soveraignty under God. But this pretence of Covenant with God, is so evident a lye, even in the pretenders own consciences, that it is not onely an act of an unjust, but also of a vile, and unmanly disposition.

Secondly, Because the Right of bearing the Person of them all, is given to him they make Soveraigne, by Covenant onely of one to another, and not of him to any of them; there can happen no breach of Covenant on the part of the Soveraigne; and consequently none of his Subjects, by any pretence of forfeiture, can be freed from his Subjection. That he which is made Soveraigne maketh no Covenant with his Subjects beforehand, is manifest; because either he must make it with the whole multitude, as one party to the Covenant; or he must make a severall Covenant with every man. With the whole, as one party, it is impossible; because as yet they are not one Person: and if he make so many severall Covenants as there be men, those Covenants after he hath the Soveraignty are voyd, because what act soever can be pretended by any one of them for breach thereof, is the act both of himselfe, and of all the rest, because done in the Person, and by the Right of every one of them in particular. Besides, if any one, or more of them, pretend a breach of the Covenant made by the Soveraigne at his Institution; and others, or one other of his Subjects, or himselfe alone, pretend there was no such breach, there is in this case, no Judge to decide the controversie: it returns therefore to the Sword again; and every man recovereth the right of Protecting himselfe by his own strength, contrary to the designe they had in the Institution. It is therefore in vain to grant Soveraignty by way of precedent Covenant. The opinion that any Monarch receiveth his Power by Covenant, that is to say on Condition, proceedeth from want of understanding this easie truth, that Covenants being but words, and breath, have no force to oblige, contain, constrain, or protect any man, but what it has from the publique Sword; that is, from the untyed hands of that Man, or Assembly of men that hath the Soveraignty, and whose actions are avouched by them all, and performed by the strength of them all, in him united. But when an Assembly of men is made Soveraigne; then no man imagineth any such Covenant to have past in the Institution; for no man is so dull as to say, for example, the People of *Rome*, made a Covenant with the Romans, to hold the Soveraignty on such or such conditions; which not performed, the Romans might lawfully depose the Roman People. That men see not the reason to be alike in a Monarchy, and in a Popular Government, proceedeth from the ambition of some, that are kinder to the government of an Assembly, whereof they may hope to participate, than of Monarchy, which they despair to enjoy.

Thirdly, because the major part hath by consenting voices declared a Soveraigne; he that dissented must now consent with the rest; that is, be contented to avow all the actions he shall do, or else justly be destroyed by the rest. For if he voluntarily entered into the Congregation of them that were assembled, he sufficiently declared thereby his will (and therefore tacitely covenanted) to stand to what the major part should ordayne: and therefore if he refuse to stand thereto, or make Protestation against any of their Decrees, he does contrary to his Covenant, and therfore unjustly. And whether he be of the Congregation, or not; and whether his consent be asked, or not, he must either submit to their decrees, or be left in the condition of warre he was in before; wherein he might without injustice be destroyed by any man whatsoever.

Fourthly, because every Subject is by this Institution Author of all the Actions, and Judgments of the Soveraigne Instituted; it followes, that whatsoever he doth, it can be no injury to any of his Subjects; nor ought he to be by any of them accused of Injustice. For he that doth any thing by authority from another, doth therein no injury to him by whose authority he acteth: But by this Institution of a Common-wealth, every particular man is Author of all the Soveraigne doth; and consequently he that complaineth of injury from his Soveraigne, complaineth of that whereof he himselfe is Author; and therefore ought not to accuse any man but himselfe; no nor himselfe of injury; because to do injury to ones selfe, is impossible. It is true that they that have Soveraigne power, may commit Iniquity; but not Injustice, or Injury in the proper signification.

Fiftly, and consequently to that which was sayd last, no man that hath Soveraigne power can justly be put to death, or otherwise in any manner by his Subjects punished. For seeing every Subject is Author of the actions of his Soveraigne; he punisheth another, for the actions committed by himselfe.

And because the End of this Institution, is the Peace and Defence of them all; and whosoever has right to the End, has right to the Means; it belongeth of Right, to whatsoever Man, or Assembly that hath the Soveraignty, to be Judge both of the meanes of Peace and Defence; and also of the hindrances, and disturbances of the same; and to do whatsoever he shall think necessary to be done, both before hand, for the preserving of Peace and Security, by prevention of Discord at home and Hostility from abroad; and, when Peace and Security are lost, for the recovery of the same. And therefore,

Sixtly, it is annexed to the Soveraignty, to be Judge of what Opinions and Doctrines are averse, and what conducing to Peace; and consequently, on what occasions, how farre, and what, men are to be trusted withall, in speaking to Multitudes of people; and who shall examine the Doctrines of all bookes before they be published. For the Actions of men proceed from their Opinions; and in the wel governing of Opinions, consisteth the well governing of mens Actions, in order to their Peace, and Concord. And though in matter of Doctrine, nothing ought to be regarded but the Truth; yet this is not repugnant to regulating of the same by Peace. For Doctrine repugnant to Peace, can no more be True, than Peace and Concord can be against the Law of Nature. It is true, that in a Common-wealth, where by the negligence, or unskilfullnesse of Governours, and Teachers, false Doctrines are by time generally received; the contrary Truths may be generally offensive: Yet the most sudden, and rough busling in of a new Truth, that can be, does never breake the Peace, but only somtimes awake the Warre. For those men that are so remissely governed, that they dare take up Armes, to defend, or introduce an Opinion, are still in Warre; and their condition not Peace, but only a Cessation of Armes for feare of one another; and they live as it were, in the procincts of battaile continually. It belongeth therefore to him that hath the Soveraign Power, to be Judge, or constitute all Judges of Opinions and Doctrines, as a thing necessary to Peace, thereby to prevent Discord and Civill Warre.

Seventhly, is annexed to the Soveraigntie, the whole power of prescribing the Rules, whereby every man may know, what Goods he may enjoy and what Actions he may doe, without being molested by any of his fellow Subjects: And this is it men call *Propriety.* For before constitution of Soveraign Power (as hath already been shewn) all men had right to all things; which necessarily causeth Warre: and therefore this Proprietie, being necessary to Peace, and depending on Soveraign Power, is the Act of that Power, in order to the publique peace. These Rules of Propriety (or *Meum* and *Tuum*) and of *Good, Evill, Lawfull,* and *Unlawfull* in the actions of Subjects, are the Civill Lawes, that is to say, the Lawes of each Common-wealth in particular; though the name of Civill Law be now restrained to the antient Civill Lawes of the City of *Rome;* which being the head of a great part of the World, her Lawes at that time were in these parts the Civill Law.

Eightly, is annexed to the Soveraigntie, the Right of Judicature; that is to say, of hearing and deciding all Controversies, which may arise concerning Law, either Civill, or Naturall, or concerning Fact. For without the decision of Controversies, there is no protection of one Subject, against the injuries of another; the Lawes concerning *Meum* and *Tuum* are in vaine; and to every man remaineth, from the naturall and necessary appetite of his own conservation, the right of protecting himselfe by his private strength, which is the condition of Warre; and contrary to the end for which every Common-wealth is instituted.

Ninthly, is annexed to the Soveraignty, the Right of making Warre, and Peace with other Nations, and Common-wealths; that is to say, of Judging when it is for the publique good, and how great forces are to be assembled, armed, and payd for that end; and to levy mony upon the Subjects, to defray the expenses thereof. For the Power by which the people are to be defended, consisteth in their Armies; and the strength of an Army, in the union of their strength under one Command; which Command the Soveraign Instituted, therefore hath; because the command of the *Militia*, without other Institution, maketh him that hath it Soveraign. And therefore whosoever is made Generall of an Army, he that hath the Soveraign Power is always Generallissimo.

Tenthly, is annexed to the Soveraignty, the choosing of all Councellours, Ministers, Magistrates, and Officers, both in Peace, and War. For seeing the Soveraign is charged with the End, which is the common Peace and Defence; he is understood to have Power to use such Means, as he shall think most fit for his discharge.

Eleventhly, to the Soveraign is committed the Power of Rewarding with riches, or honour; and of Punishing with corporall, or pecuniary punishment, or with ignominy every Subject according to the Law he hath formerly made; or if there be no Law made, according as he shall judge most to conduce to the encouraging of men to serve the Common-wealth, or deterring of them from doing dis-service to the same.

Lastly, considering what values men are naturally apt to set upon themselves; what respect they look for from others; and how little they value other men; from whence continually arise amongst them, Emulation, Quarrells, Factions, and at last Warre, to the destroying of one another, and diminution of their strength against a Common Enemy; It is necessary that there be Lawes of Honour, and a publique rate of the worth of such men as have deserved, or are able to deserve well of the Common-wealth; and that there be force in the hands of some or other, to put those Lawes in execution. But it hath already been shewn, that not onely the whole *Militia*, or forces of the Common-wealth; but also the judicature of all Controversies, is annexed to the Soveraignty. To the Soveraign therefore it belongeth also to give titles of Honour; and to appoint what Order of place, and dignity, each man shall hold; and what signes of respect, in publique or private meetings, they shall give to one another.

These are the Rights, which make the Essence of Soveraignty; and which are the markes, whereby a man may discern in what Man, or Assembly of men, the Soveraign Power is placed, and resideth. For these are incommunicable, and inseparable. The Power to coyn Mony; to dispose of the estate and persons of Infant heires; to have præemption in Markets; and all other Statute Prærogatives, may be transferred by the Soveraign; and yet the Power to protect his Subjects be retained. But if he transferre the *Militia*, he retains the Judicature in vain, for want of execution of the Lawes: Or if he grant away the Power of raising Mony; the *Militia* is in vain: or if he give away the government of Doctrines, men will be frighted into rebellion with the feare of Spirits. And so if we consider any one of the said Rights, we shall presently see, that the holding of all the rest, will produce no effect, in the conservation of Peace and Justice, the end for which all Common-wealths are Instituted. And this division is it, whereof it is said, *a Kingdome divided in it selfe cannot stand:* For unless this division precede, division into opposite Armies can never happen. If there had not first been an opinion received of the greatest part of *England,* that these Powers were divided between the King, and the Lords, and the House of Commons, the people had never been divided, and fallen into this Civill Warre; first between those that disagreed in Politiques; and after between the Dissenters about the liberty of Religion; which have so instructed men in this point of Soveraign Right, that there be few now (in *England,*) that do not see, that these Rights are inseparable, and will be so generally acknowledged, at the next return of Peace; and so continue, till their miseries are forgotten; and no longer, except the vulgar be better taught than they have hetherto been.

And because they are essentiall and inseparable Rights, it follows necessarily, that in whatsoever, words any of them seem to be granted away, yet if the Soveraign Power it selfe be not in direct termes renounced, and the name of Soveraign no more given by the Grantees to him that Grants them, the Grant is voyd: for when he has granted all he can, if we grant back the Soveraignty, all is restored, as inseparably annexed thereunto.

This great Authority being Indivisible, and inseparably annexed to the Soveraignty, there is little ground for the opinion of them, that say of Soveraign Kings, though they be *singulis majores* of greater Power than every one of their Subjects, yet they be *Universis minores* of lesse power than them all together. For if by *all together,* they mean not the collective body as one person, then *all together,* and *every one,* signifie the same; and the speech is absurd. But if by *all together,* they understand them as one Person (which person the Soveraign bears,) then the power of all together, is the same with the Soveraigns power; and so again the speech is absurd: which absurdity they see well enough, when the Soveraignty is in an Assembly of the people; but in a Monarch they see it not; and yet the power of Soveraignty is the same in whomsoever it be placed.

And as the Power, so also the Honour of the Soveraign, ought to be greater, than that of any, or all the Subjects. For in the Soveraignty is the fountain of Honour. The dignities of Lord, Earle, Duke, and Prince are his Creatures. As in the presence of the Master, the Servants are equall, and without any honour at all; So are the Subjects, in the presence of the Soveraign. And though they shine some more, some lesse, when they are out of his sight; yet in his presence, they shine no more than the Starres in presence of the Sun.

But a man may here object, that the Condition of Subjects is very miserable; as being obnoxious to the lusts, and other irregular passions of him, or them that have so unlimited a Power in their hands. And commonly they that live under a Monarch, think it the fault of Monarchy; and they that live under the government of Democracy, or other Soveraign Assembly, attribute all the inconvenience to that forme of Common-wealth; whereas the Power in all formes, if they be perfect enough to protect them, is the same; not considering that the estate of Man can never be without some incommodity or other; and that the greatest, that in any forme of Government can possibly happen to the people in generall, is scarce sensible, in respect of the miseries, and horrible calamities, that accompany a Civill Warre; or that dissolute condition of masterlesse men, without subjection to Lawes, and a coërcive Power to tye their hands from rapine, and revenge: nor considering that the greatest pressure of Soveraign Governours, proceedeth not from any delight, or profit they can expect in the dammage, or weakening of their Subjects, in whose vigor, consisteth their own strength and glory; but in the restiveness of themselves, that unwillingly contributing to their own defence, make it necessary for their Governours to draw from them what they can in time of Peace, that they may have means on any emergent occasion, or sudden need, to resist, or take advantage on their Enemies. For all men are by nature provided of notable multiplying glasses, (that is their Passions and Self-love,) through which, every little payment appeareth a great grievance; but are destitute of those prospective glasses, (namely Morall and Civill Science,) to see a farre off the miseries that hang over them, and cannot without such payments be avoyded.

Baruch Spinoza (1632–1677 C.E.)

Spinoza was born in Amsterdam to a family which, being Jewish, had been forced to leave Spain. He was later excommunicated by the Jewish community there because of his radically different conception of the divine, but he continued to live in Holland until his death at the age of forty-four. He was a student of Rationalist philosophy, and changed his given name to Benedict. He later supported himself through the profession of lens-grinding. Spinoza wrote many works which were published posthumously, but what he published while alive was sufficient to establish his reputation. He is famous for his "geometrical" style of writing, which proceeds in Euclidean fashion from axioms to theorems in rigorous order. His best known work, the *Ethics*, is a comprehensive account of God, the universe, human nature, and happiness. Spinoza also wrote on scientific matters, and on politics. His "Political Treatise" and "Theological-Political Treatise" (1670) set out some of the fundamental principles of what would be known later as liberalism.

From The Theological-Political Treatise*

Chapter XVI

Of the Foundations of a State; Of the Natural and Civil Rights of Individuals; and of the Rights of the Sovereign Power

Hitherto our care has been to separate philosophy from theology, and to show the freedom of thought which such separation insures to both. It is now time to determine the limits to which such freedom of thought and discussion may extend itself in the ideal state. For the due consideration of this question we must examine the foundations of a state, first turning our attention to the natural rights of individuals, and afterwards to religion and the state as a whole.

By the right and ordinance of nature, I merely mean those natural laws wherewith we conceive every individual to be conditioned by nature, so as to live and act in a given way. For instance, fishes are naturally conditioned for swimming, and the greater for devouring the less; therefore fishes enjoy the water, and the greater devour the less by sovereign natural right. For it is certain that nature, taken in the abstract, has sovereign right to do anything she can; in other words, her right is co-extensive with her power. The power of nature is the power of God, which has sovereign right over all things; and, inasmuch as the power of nature is simply the aggregate of the powers of all her individual components, it follows that every individual has sovereign right to do all that he can; in other words, the rights of an individual extend to the utmost limits of his power as it has been conditioned. Now it is the sovereign law and right of nature that each individual should

---

*An Excerpt.

endeavour to preserve itself as it is, without regard to anything but itself; therefore this sovereign law and right belongs to every individual, namely, to exist and act according to its natural conditions. We do not here acknowledge any difference between mankind and other individual natural entities, nor between men endowed with reason and those to whom reason is unknown; nor between fools, madmen, and sane men. Whatsoever an individual does by the laws of its nature it has a sovereign right to do, inasmuch as it acts as it was conditioned by nature, and cannot act otherwise. Wherefore among men, so long as they are considered as living under the sway of nature, he who does not yet know reason, or who has not yet acquired the habit of virtue, acts solely according to the laws of his desire with as sovereign a right as he who orders his life entirely by the laws of reason.

That is, as the wise man has sovereign right to do all that reason dictates, or to live according to the laws of reason, so also the ignorant and foolish man has sovereign right to do all that desire dictates, or to live according to the laws of desire. This is identical with the teaching of Paul, who acknowledges that previous to the law—that is, so long as men are considered of as living under the sway of nature, there is no sin.

The natural right of the individual man is thus determined, not by sound reason, but by desire and power. All are not naturally conditioned so as to act according to the laws and rules of reason; nay, on the contrary, all men are born ignorant, and before they can learn the right way of life and acquire the habit of virtue, the greater part of their life, even if they have been well brought up, has passed away. Nevertheless, they are in the meanwhile bound to live and preserve themselves as far as they can by the unaided impulses of desire. Nature has given them no other guide, and has denied them the present power of living according to sound reason; so that they are no more bound to live by the dictates of an enlightened mind, than a cat is bound to live by the laws of the nature of a lion.

Whatsoever, therefore, an individual (considered as under the sway of nature) thinks useful for himself, whether led by sound reason or impelled by the passions, that he has a sovereign right to seek and to take for himself as he best can, whether by force, cunning, entreaty, or any other means; consequently he may regard as an enemy anyone who hinders the accomplishment of his purpose.

It follows from what we have said that the right and ordinance of nature, under which all men are born, and under which they mostly live, only prohibits such things as no one desires, and no one can attain: it does not forbid strife, nor hatred, nor anger, nor deceit, nor, indeed, any of the means suggested by desire.

This we need not wonder at, for nature is not bounded by the laws of human reason, which aims only at man's true benefit and preservation; her limits are infinitely wider, and have reference to the eternal order of nature, wherein man is but a speck; it is by the necessity of this alone that all individuals are conditioned for living and acting in a particular way. If anything, therefore, in nature seems to us ridiculous, absurd, or evil, it is because we only know in part, and are almost entirely ignorant of the order and interdependence of nature as a whole, and also because we want everything to be arranged according to the dictates of our human reason; in reality that which reason considers evil, is not evil in respect to the order and laws of nature as a whole, but only in respect to the laws of our reason.

Nevertheless, no one can doubt that it is much better for us to live according to the laws and assured dictates of reason, for, as we said, they have men's true good for their object. Moreover, everyone wishes to live as far as possible securely beyond the reach of fear, and this would be quite impossible so long as everyone did everything he liked, and reason's claim was lowered to a par with those of hatred and anger; there is no one who is not ill at ease in the midst of enmity, hatred, anger, and deceit, and who does not seek to avoid them as much as he can. When we reflect that men without mutual help, or the aid of reason, must needs live most miserably, as we clearly proved in Chap. V., we shall plainly see that men must necessarily come to an agreement to live together as securely and well as possible if they are to enjoy as a whole the rights which naturally belong to them as individuals, and their life should be no more conditioned by the force and desire of individuals, but by the power and will of the whole body. This end they will be unable to attain if desire be their only guide (for by the laws of desire each man is drawn in a different direction); they must, therefore, most firmly decree and establish that they will be guided in everything by reason (which nobody will dare openly to repudiate lest he should be taken for a madman), and will restrain any desire which is injurious to a man's fellows, that they will do to all as they would be done by, and that they will defend their neighbour's rights as their own.

How such a compact as this should be entered into, how ratified and established, we will now inquire.

Now it is a universal law of human nature that no one ever neglects anything which he judges to be good, except with the hope of gaining a greater good, or from the fear of a greater evil; nor does anyone endure an evil except for the sake of avoiding a greater evil, or gaining a greater good. That is, everyone will, of two goods, choose that which he thinks the greatest; and, of two evils, that which he thinks the least. I say advisedly that which he thinks the greatest or the least, for it does not necessarily follow that he judges right. This law is so deeply implanted in the human mind that it ought to be counted among eternal truths and axioms.

As a necessary consequence of the principle just enunciated, no one can honestly promise to forego the right which he has over all things, and in general no one will abide by his promises, unless under the fear of a greater evil, or the hope of a greater good. An example will make the matter clearer. Suppose that a robber forces me to promise that I will give him my goods at his will and pleasure. It is plain (inasmuch as my natural right is, as I have shown, co-extensive with my power) that if I can free myself from this robber by stratagem, by assenting to his demands, I have the natural right to do so, and to pretend to accept his conditions. Or again, suppose I have genuinely promised someone that for the space of twenty days I will not taste food or any nourishment; and suppose I afterwards find that my promise was foolish, and cannot be kept without very great injury to myself; as I am bound by natural law and right to choose the least of two evils, I have complete right to break my compact, and act as if my promise had never been uttered. I say that I should have perfect natural right to do so, whether I was actuated by true and evident reason, or whether I was actuated by mere opinion in thinking I had promised rashly; whether my reasons were true or false, I should be in fear of a greater evil, which, by the ordinance of nature, I should strive to avoid by every means in my power.

We may, therefore, conclude that a compact is only made valid by its utility, without which it becomes null and void. It is, therefore, foolish to ask a man to keep his faith with us for ever, unless we also endeavour that the violation of the compact we enter into shall involve for the violator more harm than good. This consideration should have very great weight in forming a state. However, if all men could be easily led by reason alone, and could recognize what is best and most useful for a state, there would be no one who would not forswear deceit, for everyone would keep most religiously to their compact in their desire for the chief good, namely, the preservation of the state, and would cherish good faith above all things as the shield and buckler of the commonwealth. However, it is far from being the case that all men can always be easily led by reason alone; everyone is drawn away by his pleasure, while avarice, ambition, envy, hatred, and the like so engross the mind that reason has no place therein. Hence, though men make promises with all the appearances of good faith, and agree that they will keep to their engagement, no one can absolutely rely on another man's promise unless there is something behind it. Everyone has by nature a right to act deceitfully, and to break his compacts, unless he be restrained by the hope of some greater good, or the fear of some greater evil.

However, as we have shown that the natural right of the individual is only limited by his power, it is clear that by transferring, either willingly or under compulsion, this power into the hands of another, he in so doing necessarily cedes also a part of his right; and further, that the sovereign right over all men belongs to him who has sovereign power, wherewith he can compel men by force, or restrain them by threats of the universally feared punishment of death; such sovereign right he will retain only so long as he can maintain his power of enforcing his will; otherwise he will totter on his throne, and no one who is stronger than he will be bound unwillingly to obey him.

In this manner a society can be formed without any violation of natural right, and the covenant can always be strictly kept—that is, if each individual hands over the whole of his power to the body politic, the latter will then possess sovereign natural right over all things; that is, it will have sole and unquestioned dominion, and everyone will be bound to obey, under pain of the severest punishment. A body politic of this kind is called a Democracy, which may be defined as a society which wields all its power as a whole. The sovereign power is not restrained by any laws, but everyone is bound to obey it in all things; such is the state of things implied when men either tacitly or expressly handed over to it all their power of self-defence, or in other words, all their right. For if they had wished to retain any right for themselves, they ought to have taken precautions for its defence and preservation; as they have not done so, and indeed could not have done so without dividing and consequently ruining the state, they placed themselves absolutely at the mercy of the sovereign power; and, therefore, having acted (as we have shown) as reason and necessity demanded, they are obliged to fulfil the commands of the sovereign power, however absurd these may be, else they will be public enemies, and will act against reason, which urges the preservation of the state as a primary duty. For reason bids us choose the least of two evils.

Furthermore, this danger of submitting absolutely to the dominion and will of another, is one which may be incurred with a light heart: for we have shown that sovereigns only possess this right of imposing their will, so long as they have the full power to enforce it: if such power be lost their right to command is lost also, or lapses to those who have assumed it and can keep it. Thus it is very rare for sovereigns to impose thoroughly irrational commands, for they are bound to consult their own interests, and retain their power by consulting the public good and acting according to the dictates of reason, as Seneca says, "violenta imperia nemo continuit diu." No one can long retain a tyrant's sway.

In a democracy, irrational commands are still less to be feared: for it is almost impossible that the majority of a people, especially if it be a large one, should agree in an irrational design: and, moreover, the basis and aim of a democracy is to avoid the desires as irrational, and to bring men as far as possible under the control of reason, so that they may live in peace and harmony: if this basis be removed the whole fabric falls to ruin.

Such being the ends in view for the sovereign power, the duty of subjects is, as I have said, to obey its commands, and to recognize no right save that which it sanctions.

It will, perhaps, be thought that we are turning subjects into slaves: for slaves obey commands and free men live as they like; but this idea is based on a misconception, for the true slave is he who is led away by his pleasures and can neither see what is good for him nor act accordingly: he alone is free who lives with free consent under the entire guidance of reason.

Action in obedience to orders does take away freedom in a certain sense, but it does not, therefore, make a man a slave, all depends on the object of the action. If the object of the action be the good of the state, and not the good of the agent, the latter is a slave and does himself no good: but in a state or kingdom where the weal of the whole people, and not that of the ruler, is the supreme law, obedience to the sovereign power does not make a man a slave, of no use to himself, but a subject. Therefore, that state is the freest whose laws are founded on sound reason, so that every member of it may, if he will, be free; that is, live with full consent under the entire guidance of reason.

Children, though they are bound to obey all the commands of their parents, are yet not slaves: for the commands of parents look generally to the children's benefit.

We must, therefore, acknowledge a great difference between a slave, a son, and a subject; their positions may be thus defined. A slave is one who is bound to obey his master's orders, though they are given solely in the master's interest: a son is one who obeys his father's orders, given in his own interest; a subject obeys the orders of the sovereign power, given for the common interest, wherein he is included.

I think I have now shown sufficiently clearly the basis of a democracy: I have especially desired to do so, for I believe it to be of all forms of government the most natural, and the most consonant with individual liberty. In it no one transfers his natural right so absolutely that he has no further voice in affairs, he only hands it over to the majority of a society, whereof he is a unit. Thus all men remain, as they were in the state of nature, equals.

This is the only form of government which I have treated of at length, for it is the one most akin to my purpose of showing the benefits of freedom in a state.

I may pass over the fundamental principles of other forms of government, for we may gather from what has been said whence their right arises without going into its origin. The possessor of sovereign power, whether he be one, or many, or the whole body politic, has the sovereign right of imposing any commands he pleases: and he who has either voluntarily, or under compulsion, transferred the right to defend him to another, has, in so doing, renounced his natural right and is therefore bound to obey, in all things, the commands of the sovereign power; and will be bound so to do so long as the king, or nobles, or the people preserve the sovereign power which formed the basis of the original transfer. I need add no more.

The bases and rights of dominion being thus displayed, we shall readily be able to define private civil right, wrong, justice, and injustice, with their relations to the state; and also to determine what constitutes an ally, or an enemy, or the crime of treason.

By private civil right we can only mean the liberty every man possesses to preserve his existence, a liberty limited by the edicts of the sovereign power, and preserved only by its authority: for when a man has transferred to another his right of living as he likes, which was only limited by his power, that is, has transferred his liberty and power of self-defence, he is bound to live as that other dictates, and to trust to him entirely for his defence. Wrong takes place when a citizen, or subject, is forced by another to undergo some loss or pain in contradiction to the authority of the law, or the edict of the sovereign power.

Wrong is conceivable only in an organized community: nor can it ever accrue to subjects from any act of the sovereign, who has the right to do what he likes. It can only arise, therefore, between private persons, who are bound by law and right not to injure one another. Justice consists in the habitual rendering to every man his lawful due: injustice consists in depriving a man, under the pretence of legality, of what the laws, rightly interpreted, would allow him. These last are also called equity and iniquity, because those who administer the laws are bound to show no respect of persons, but to account all men equal, and to defend every man's right equally, neither envying the rich nor despising the poor.

The men of two states become allies, when for the sake of avoiding war, or for some other advantage, they covenant to do each other no hurt, but on the contrary, to assist each other if necessity arises, each retaining his independence. Such a covenant is valid so long as its basis of danger or advantage is in force: no one enters into an engagement, or is bound to stand by his compacts unless there be a hope of some accruing good, or the fear of some evil: if this basis be removed the compact thereby becomes void: this has been abundantly shown by experience. For although different states make treaties not to harm one another, they always take every possible precaution against such treaties being broken by the stronger party, and do not rely on the compact, unless there is a sufficiently obvious object and advantage to both parties in observing it. Otherwise they would fear a breach of faith, nor would there be any wrong done thereby: for who in his proper senses, and aware of the right of the sovereign power, would trust in the promises of one who has the will and the power to do what he likes, and who aims solely at the safety and advantage of his dominion? Moreover, if we consult loyalty and religion, we shall see that no one in possession of power ought to abide by his promises to the injury of his dominion; for he cannot keep such promises without breaking the engagement he made with his subjects, by which both he and they are most solemnly bound.

An enemy is one who lives apart from the state, and does not recognize its authority either as a subject or as an ally. It is not hatred which makes a man an enemy, but the rights of the state. The rights of the state are the same in regard to him who does not recognize by any compact the state authority, as they are against him who has done the state an injury: it has the right to force him as best it can, either to submit, or to contract an alliance.

Lastly, treason can only be committed by subjects, who by compact, either tacit or expressed, have transferred all their rights to the state: a subject is said to have committed this crime when he has attempted, for whatever reason, to seize the sovereign power, or to place it in different hands. I say, *has attempted,* for if punishment were not to overtake him till he had succeeded, it would often come too late, the sovereign rights would have been acquired or transferred already.

I also say, *has attempted, for whatever reason, to seize the sovereign power,* and I recognize no difference whether such an attempt should be followed by public loss or public gain. Whatever be his reason for acting, the crime is treason, and he is rightly condemned: in war, everyone would admit the justice of his sentence. If a man does not keep to his post, but approaches the enemy without the knowledge of his commander, whatever may be his motive, so long as he acts on his own motion, even if he advances with the design of defeating the enemy, he is rightly put to death, because he has violated his oath, and infringed the rights of his commander. That all citizens are equally bound by these rights in time of peace, is not so generally recognized, but the reasons for obedience are in both cases, identical. The state must be preserved and directed by the sole authority of the sovereign, and such authority and right have been accorded by universal consent to him alone: if, therefore, anyone else attempts, without his consent, to execute any public enterprise, even though the state might (as we said) reap benefit therefrom, such person has none the less infringed the sovereign's right, and would be rightly punished for treason.

In order that every scruple may be removed, we may now answer the inquiry, whether our former assertion that everyone who has not the practice of reason, may, in the state of nature, live by sovereign natural right, according to the laws of his desires, is not in direct opposition to the law and right of God as revealed. For as all men absolutely (whether they be less endowed with reason or more) are equally bound by the Divine command to love their neighbour as themselves, it may be said that they cannot, without wrong, do injury to anyone, or live according to their desires.

This objection, so far as the state of nature is concerned, can be easily answered, for the state of nature is, both in nature and in time, prior to religion. No one knows by nature that he owes any obedience to God, nor can he attain thereto by any exercise of his reason, but solely by revelation confirmed by signs. Therefore, previous to revelation, no one is bound by a Divine law and right of which he is necessarily in ignorance. The state of nature must by no means be confounded with a state of religion, but must be conceived as without either religion or law, and consequently without sin or wrong: this is how we have described it, and we are confirmed by the authority of Paul. It is not only in respect of ignorance that we conceive the state of nature as prior to, and lacking the Divine revealed law and right; but in respect of freedom also, wherewith all men are born endowed.

If men were naturally bound by the Divine law and right, or if the Divine law and right were a natural necessity, there would have been no need for God to make a covenant with mankind, and to bind them thereto with an oath and agreement.

We must, then, fully grant that the Divine law and right originated at the time when men by express covenant agreed to obey God in all things, and ceded, as it were, their natural freedom, transferring their rights to God in the manner described in speaking of the formation of a state.

However, I will treat of these matters more at length presently.

It may be insisted that sovereigns are as much bound by the Divine law as subjects: whereas we have asserted that they retain their natural rights, and may do whatever they like.

In order to clear up the whole difficulty, which arises rather concerning the natural right than the natural state, I maintain that everyone is bound, in the state of nature, to live according to Divine law, in the same way as he is bound to live according to the dictates of sound reason; namely, inasmuch as it is to his advantage, and necessary for his salvation; but, if he will not so live, he may do otherwise at his own risk. He is thus bound to live according to his own laws, not according to anyone else's, and to recognize no man as a judge, or as a superior in religion. Such, in my opinion, is the position of a sovereign, for he may take advice from his fellow-men, but he is not bound to recognize any as a judge, nor anyone besides himself as an arbitrator on any question of right, unless it be a prophet sent expressly by God and attesting his mission by indisputable signs. Even then he does not recognize a man, but God Himself as His judge.

If a sovereign refuses to obey God as revealed in His law, he does so at his own risk and loss, but without violating any civil or natural right. For the civil right is dependent on his own decree; and natural right is dependent on the laws of nature, which latter are not adapted to religion, whose sole aim is the good of humanity, but to the order of nature—that is, to God's eternal decree unknown to us.

This truth seems to be adumbrated in a somewhat obscurer form by those who maintain that men can sin against God's revelation, but not against the eternal decree by which He has ordained all things.

We may be asked, what should we do if the sovereign commands anything contrary to religion, and the obedience which we have expressly vowed to God? should we obey the Divine law or the human law? I shall treat of this question at length hereafter, and will therefore merely say now, that God should be obeyed before all else, when we have a certain and indisputable revelation of His will: but men are very prone to error on religious subjects, and, according to the diversity of their dispositions, are wont with considerable stir to put forward their own inventions, as experience more than sufficiently attests, so that if no one were bound to obey the state in matters which, in his own opinion concern religion, the rights of the state would be dependent on every man's judgment and passions. No one would consider himself bound to obey laws framed against his faith or superstition; and on this pretext he might assume unbounded license. In this way, the rights of the civil authorities would be utterly set at nought, so that we must conclude that the sovereign power, which alone is bound both by Divine and natural right to preserve and guard the laws of the state, should have supreme authority for making any laws about religion which it thinks fit; all are bound to obey its behests on the subject in accordance with their promise which God bids them to keep.

However, if the sovereign power be heathen, we should either enter into no engagements therewith, and yield up our lives sooner than transfer to it any of our rights;

or, if the engagement be made, and our rights transferred, we should (inasmuch as we should have ourselves transferred the right of defending ourselves and our religion) be bound to obey them, and to keep our word: we might even rightly be bound so to do, except in those cases where God, by indisputable revelation, has promised His special aid against tyranny, or given us special exemption from obedience. Thus we see that, of all the Jews in Babylon, there were only three youths who were certain of the help of God, and, therefore, refused to obey Nebuchadnezzar. All the rest, with the sole exception of Daniel, who was beloved by the king, were doubtless compelled by right to obey, perhaps thinking that they had been delivered up by God into the hands of the king, and that the king had obtained and preserved his dominion by God's design. On the other hand, Eleazar, before his country had utterly fallen, wished to give a proof of his constancy to his compatriots, in order that they might follow in his footsteps, and go to any lengths, rather than allow their right and power to be transferred to the Greeks, or brave any torture rather than swear allegiance to the heathen. Instances are occurring every day in confirmation of what I here advance. The rulers of Christian kingdoms do not hesitate, with a view to strengthening their dominion, to make treaties with Turks and heathen, and to give orders to their subjects who settle among such peoples not to assume more freedom, either in things secular or religious, than is set down in the treaty, or allowed by the foreign government. We may see this exemplified in the Dutch treaty with the Japanese, which I have already mentioned.

Chapter XVII

It is shown that no one can, or need, transfer all his rights to the sovereign power. Of the Hebrew republic, as it was during the lifetime of Moses, and after his death, till the foundation of the monarchy; and of its excellence. Lastly, of the causes why the theocratic republic fell, and why it could hardly have continued without dissension.

The theory put forward in the last chapter, of the universal rights of the sovereign power, and of the natural rights of the individual transferred thereto, though it corresponds in many respects with actual practice, and though practice may be so arranged as to conform to it more and more, must nevertheless always remain in many respects purely ideal. No one can ever so utterly transfer to another his power and, consequently, his rights, as to cease to be a man; nor can there ever be a power so sovereign that it can carry out every possible wish. It will always be vain to order a subject to hate what he believes brings him advantage, or to love what brings him loss, or not to be offended at insults, or not to wish to be free from fear, or a hundred other things of the sort, which necessarily follow from the laws of human nature. So much, I think, is abundantly shown by experience: for men have never so far ceded their power as to cease to be an object of fear to the rulers who received such power and right; and dominions have always been in as much danger from their own subjects as from external enemies. If it were really the case that men could be deprived of their natural rights so utterly as never to have any further influence on affairs, except with the permission of the holders of sovereign right, it would then be possible to maintain with impunity the most violent tyranny, which, I suppose, no one would for an instant admit.

We must, therefore, grant that every man retains some part of his right, in dependence on his own decision, and no one else's.

However, in order correctly to understand the extent of the sovereign's right and power, we must take notice that it does not cover only those actions to which it can compel men by fear, but absolutely every action which it can induce men to perform: for it is the fact of obedience, not the motive for obedience, which makes a man a subject.

Whatever be the cause which leads a man to obey the commands of the sovereign, whether it be fear or hope, or love of his country, or any other emotion—the fact remains that the man takes counsel with himself, and nevertheless acts as his sovereign orders. We must not, therefore, assert that all actions resulting from a man's deliberation with himself are done in obedience to the rights of the individual rather than the sovereign: as a matter of fact, all actions spring from a man's deliberation with himself, whether the determining motive be love or fear of punishment; therefore, either dominion does not exist, and has no rights over its subjects, or else it extends over every instance in which it can prevail on men to decide to obey it. Consequently, every action which a subject performs in accordance with the commands of the sovereign, whether such action springs from love, or fear, or (as is more frequently the case) from hope and fear together, or from reverence compounded of fear and admiration, or, indeed, any motive whatever, is performed in virtue of his submission to the sovereign, and not in virtue of his own authority.

This point is made still more clear by the fact that obedience does not consist so much in the outward act as in the mental state of the person obeying; so that he is most under the dominion of another who with his whole heart determines to obey another's commands; and consequently the firmest dominion belongs to the sovereign who has most influence over the minds of his subjects; if those who are most feared possessed the firmest dominion, the firmest dominion would belong to the subjects of a tyrant, for they are always greatly feared by their ruler. Furthermore, though it is impossible to govern the mind as completely as the tongue, nevertheless minds are, to a certain extent, under the control of the sovereign, for he can in many ways bring about that the greatest part of his subjects should follow his wishes in their beliefs, their loves, and their hates. Though such emotions do not arise at the express command of the sovereign they often result (as experience shows) from the authority of his power, and from his direction; in other words, in virtue of his right; we may, therefore, without doing violence to our understanding, conceive men who follow the instigation of their sovereign in their beliefs, their loves, their hates, their contempt, and all other emotions whatsoever.

Though the powers of government, as thus conceived, are sufficiently ample, they can never become large enough to execute every possible wish of their possessors. This, I think, I have already shown clearly enough. The method of forming a dominion which should prove lasting I do not, as I have said, intend to discuss, but in order to arrive at the object I have in view, I will touch on the teaching of Divine revelation to Moses in this respect, and we will consider the history and the success of the Jews, gathering therefrom what should be the chief concessions made by sovereigns to their subjects with a view to the security and increase of their dominion.

That the preservation of a state chiefly depends on the subjects' fidelity and constancy in carrying out the orders they receive, is most clearly taught both by reason and experience; how subjects ought to be guided so as best to preserve their fidelity and virtue is not so obvious. All, both rulers and ruled, are men, and prone to follow after their lusts. The fickle disposition of the multitude almost reduces those who have experience of it to despair, for it is governed solely by emotions, not by reason: it rushes headlong into every enterprise, and is easily corrupted either by avarice or luxury: everyone thinks himself omniscient and wishes to fashion all things to his liking, judging a thing to be just or unjust, lawful or unlawful, according as he thinks it will bring him profit or loss: vanity leads him to despise his equals, and refuse their guidance: envy of superior fame or fortune (for such gifts are never equally distributed) leads him to desire and rejoice in his neighbour's downfall. I need not go through the whole list, everyone knows already how much crime results from disgust at the present—desire for change, headlong anger, and contempt for poverty—and how men's minds are engrossed and kept in turmoil thereby.

To guard against all these evils, and form a dominion where no room is left for deceit; to frame our institutions so that every man, whatever his disposition, may prefer public right to private advantage, this is the task and this the toil. Necessity is often the mother of invention, but she has never yet succeeded in framing a dominion that was in less danger from its own citizens than from open enemies, or whose rulers did not fear the latter less than the former. Witness the state of Rome, invincible by her enemies, but many times conquered and sorely oppressed by her own citizens, especially in the war between Vespasian and Vitellius.

Alexander thought prestige abroad more easy to acquire than prestige at home, and believed that his greatness could be destroyed by his own followers. Fearing such a disaster, he thus addressed his friends: "Keep me safe from internal treachery and domestic plots, and I will front without fear the dangers of battle and of war. Philip was more secure in the battle array than in the theatre: he often escaped from the hands of the enemy, he could not escape from his own subjects. If you think over the deaths of kings, you will count up more who have died by the assassin than by the open foe."

For the sake of making themselves secure, kings who seized the throne in ancient times used to try to spread the idea that they were descended from the immortal gods, thinking that if their subjects and the rest of mankind did not look on them as equals, but believed them to be gods, they would willingly submit to their rule, and obey their commands. Thus Augustus persuaded the Romans that he was descended from Æneas, who was the son of Venus, and numbered among the gods. "He wished himself to be worshipped in temples, like the gods, with flamens and priests."

Alexander wished to be saluted as the son of Jupiter, not from motives of pride but of policy, as he showed by his answer to the invective of Hermolaus: "It is almost laughable," said he, "that Hermolaus asked me to contradict Jupiter, by whose oracle I am recognized. Am I responsible for the answers of the gods? It offered me the name of son; acquiescence was by no means foreign to my present designs. Would that the Indians also would believe me to be a god! Wars are carried through by prestige, falsehoods that are believed often gain the force of truth." In these few words he cleverly contrives to palm off a fiction on the ignorant, and at the same time hints at the motive for the deception.

Cleon, in his speech persuading the Macedonians to obey their king, adopted a similar device: for after going through the praises of Alexander with admiration, and recalling his merits, he proceeds, "the Persians are not only pious, but prudent in worshipping their kings as gods: for kingship is the shield of public safety," and he ends thus, "I, myself, when the king enters a banquet hall, should prostrate my body on the ground; other men should do the like, especially those who are wise." However, the Macedonians were more prudent—indeed, it is only complete barbarians who can be so openly cajoled, and can suffer themselves to be turned from subjects into slaves without interests of their own. Others, notwithstanding, have been able more easily to spread the belief that kingship is sacred, and plays the part of God on the earth, that it has been instituted by God, not by the suffrage and consent of men; and that it is preserved and guarded by Divine special providence and aid. Similar fictions have been promulgated by monarchs, with the object of strengthening their dominion, but these I will pass over, and in order to arrive at my main purpose, will merely recall and discuss the teaching on the subject of Divine revelation to Moses in ancient times.

. . . after the Hebrews came up out of Egypt they were not bound by the law and right of any other nation, but were at liberty to institute any new rites at their pleasure, and to occupy whatever territory they chose. After their liberation from the intolerable bondage of the Egyptians, they were bound by no covenant to any man; and, therefore, every man entered into his natural right, and was free to retain it or to give it up, and transfer it to another. Being, then, in the state of nature, they followed the advice of Moses, in whom they chiefly trusted, and decided to transfer their right to no human being, but only to God; without further delay they all, with one voice, promised to obey all the commands of the Deity, and to acknowledge no right that He did not proclaim as such by prophetic revelation. This promise, or transference of right to God, was effected in the same manner as we have conceived it to have been in ordinary societies, when men agree to divest themselves of their natural rights. It is, in fact, in virtue of a set covenant, and an oath, that the Jews freely, and not under compulsion or threats, surrendered their rights and transferred them to God. Moreover, in order that this covenant might be ratified and settled, and might be free from all suspicion of deceit, God did not enter into it till the Jews had had experience of His wonderful power by which alone they had been, or could be, preserved in a state of prosperity. It is because they believed that nothing but God's power could preserve them that they surrendered to God the natural power of self-preservation, which they formerly, perhaps, thought they possessed, and consequently they surrendered at the same time all their natural right.

God alone, therefore, held dominion over the Hebrews, whose state was in virtue of the covenant called God's kingdom, and God was said to be their king; consequently the enemies of the Jews were said to be the enemies of God, and the citizens who tried to seize the dominion were guilty of treason against God; and, lastly, the laws of the state were called the laws and commandments of God. Thus in the Hebrew state the civil and religious authority, each consisting solely of obedience to God, were one and the same.

The dogmas of religion were not precepts, but laws and ordinances; piety was regarded as the same as loyalty, impiety as the same as disaffection. Everyone who fell away from religion ceased to be a citizen, and was, on that ground alone, accounted an enemy: those who died for the sake of religion, were held to have died for their country; in fact, between civil and religious law and right there was no distinction whatever. For this reason the government could be called a Theocracy, inasmuch as the citizens were not bound by anything save the revelations of God.

However, this state of things existed rather in theory than in practice, for it will appear from what we are about to say, that the Hebrews, as a matter of fact, retained absolutely in their own hands the right of sovereignty: this is shown by the method and plan by which the government was carried on, as I will now explain.

Inasmuch as the Hebrews did not transfer their rights to any other person but, as in a democracy, all surrendered their rights equally, and cried out with one voice, "Whatsoever God shall speak (no mediator or mouthpiece being named) that will we do," it follows that all were equally bound by the covenant, and that all had an equal right to consult the Deity, to accept and to interpret His laws, so that all had an exactly equal share in the government. Thus at first they all approached God together, so that they might learn His commands, but in this first salutation, they were so thoroughly terrified and so astounded to hear God speaking, that they thought their last hour was at hand: full of fear, therefore, they went afresh to Moses, and said, "Lo, we have heard God speaking in the fire, and there is no cause why we should wish to die: surely this great fire will consume us: if we hear again the voice of God, we shall surely die. Thou, therefore, go near, and hear all the words of our God, and thou (not God) shalt speak with us: all that God shall tell us, that will we hearken to and perform."

They thus clearly abrogated their former covenant, and absolutely transferred to Moses their right to consult God and interpret His commands: for they do not here promise obedience to all that God shall tell them, but to all that God shall tell Moses. Moses, therefore, remained the sole promulgator and interpreter of the Divine laws, and consequently also the sovereign judge, who could not be arraigned himself, and who acted among the Hebrews the part of God; in other words, held the sovereign kingship: he alone had the right to consult God, to give the Divine answers to the people, and to see that they were carried out. I say he alone, for if anyone during the life of Moses was desirous of preaching anything in the name of the Lord, he was, even if a true prophet, considered guilty and a usurper of the sovereign right. We may here notice, that though the people had elected Moses, they could not rightfully elect Moses's successor; for having transferred to Moses their right of consulting God, and absolutely promised to regard him as a Divine oracle, they had plainly forfeited the whole of their right, and were bound to accept as chosen by God anyone proclaimed by Moses as his successor. If Moses had so chosen his successor, who like him should wield the sole right of government, possessing the sole right of consulting God, and consequently of making and abrogating laws, of deciding on peace or war, of sending ambassadors, appointing judges—in fact, discharging all the functions of a sovereign, the state would have become simply a monarchy, only differing from other monarchies in the fact, that the latter are, or should be, carried on in accordance with God's decree, unknown even to the monarch, whereas the

Hebrew monarch would have been the only person to whom the decree was revealed. A difference which increases, rather than diminishes the monarch's authority. As far as the people in both cases are concerned, each would be equally subject, and equally ignorant of the Divine decree, for each would be dependent on the monarch's words, and would learn from him alone, what was lawful or unlawful: nor would the fact that the people believed that the monarch was only issuing commands in accordance with God's decree revealed to him, make it less in subjection, but rather more. However Moses elected no such successor, but left the dominion to those who came after him in a condition which could not be called a popular government, nor an aristocracy, nor a monarchy, but a Theocracy. For the right of interpreting laws was vested in one man, while the right and power of administering the state according to the laws thus interpreted, was vested in another man.

In order that the question may be thoroughly understood, I will duly set forth the administration of the whole state.

First, the people were commanded to build a tabernacle, which should be, as it were, the dwelling of God—that is, of the sovereign authority of the state. This tabernacle was to be erected at the cost of the whole people, not of one man, in order that the place where God was consulted might be public property. The Levites were chosen as courtiers and administrators of this royal abode; while Aaron, the brother of Moses, was chosen to be their chief and second, as it were, to God their King, being succeeded in the office by his legitimate sons.

He, as the nearest to God, was the sovereign interpreter of the Divine laws; he communicated the answers of the Divine oracle to the people, and entreated God's favour for them. If, in addition to these privileges, he had possessed the right of ruling, he would have been neither more nor less than an absolute monarch; but, in respect to government, he was only a private citizen: the whole tribe of Levi was so completely divested of governing rights that it did not even take its share with the others in the partition of territory. Moses provided for its support by inspiring the common people with great reverence for it, as the only tribe dedicated to God.

Further, the army, formed from the remaining twelve tribes, was commanded to invade the land of Canaan, to divide it into twelve portions, and to distribute it among the tribes by lot. For this task twelve captains were chosen, one from every tribe, and were, together with Joshua and Eleazar, the high priest, empowered to divide the land into twelve equal parts, and distribute it by lot. Joshua was chosen for the chief command of the army, inasmuch as none but he had the right to consult God in emergencies, not like Moses, alone in his tent, or in the tabernacle, but through the high priest, to whom only the answers of God were revealed. Furthermore, he was empowered to execute, and cause the people to obey God's commands, transmitted through the high priests; to find, and to make use of, means for carrying them out; to choose as many army captains as he liked; to make whatever choice he thought best; to send ambassadors in his own name; and, in short, to have the entire control of the war. To his office there was no rightful successor—indeed, the post was only filled by the direct order of the Deity, on occasions of public emergency. In ordinary times, all the management of peace and war was vested in the captains of the tribes, as I will shortly point out. Lastly, all men between the ages of twenty and sixty were ordered to bear arms, and form a citizen army, owing allegiance, not to its general-in-chief, nor to the high priest, but to Religion and to God. The army, or the hosts, were called the army of God, or the hosts of God. For this reason God was called by the Hebrews the God of Armies; and the ark of the covenant was borne in the midst of the army in important battles, when the safety or destruction of the whole people hung upon the issue, so that the people might, as it were, see their King among them, and put forth all their strength.

From these directions, left by Moses to his successors, we plainly see that he chose administrators, rather than despots, to come after him; for he invested no one with the power of consulting God, where he liked and alone, consequently, no one had the power possessed by himself of ordaining and abrogating laws, of deciding on war or peace, of choosing men to fill offices both religious and secular: all these are the prerogatives of a sovereign. The high priest, indeed, had the right of interpreting laws, and communicating the answers of God, but he could not do so when he liked, as Moses could, but only when he was asked by the general-in-chief of the army, the council, or some similar authority. The general-in-chief and the council could consult God when they liked, but could only receive His answers through the high priest; so that the utterances of God, as reported by the high priest, were not decrees, as they were when reported by Moses, but only answers; they were accepted by Joshua and the council, and only then had the force of commands and decrees.

The high priest, both in the case of Aaron and of his son Eleazar, was chosen by Moses; nor had anyone, after Moses' death, a right to elect to the office, which became hereditary. The general-in-chief of the army was also chosen by Moses, and assumed his functions in virtue of the commands, not of the high priest, but of Moses: indeed, after the death of Joshua, the high priest did not appoint anyone in his place, and the captains did not consult God afresh about a general-in-chief, but each retained Joshua's power in respect to the contingent of his own tribe, and all retained it collectively, in respect to the whole army. There seems to have been no need of a general-in-chief, except when they were obliged to unite their forces against a common enemy. This occurred most frequently during the time of Joshua, when they had no fixed dwelling-place, and possessed all things in common. After all the tribes had gained their territories by right of conquest, and had divided their allotted gains, they became separated, having no longer their possessions in common, so that the need for a single commander ceased, for the different tribes should be considered rather in the light of confederated states than of bodies of fellow-citizens. In respect to their God and their religion, they were fellow-citizens; but, in respect to the rights which one possessed with regard to another, they were only confederated: they were, in fact, in much the same position (if one excepts the Temple common to all) as the United States of the Netherlands. The division of property held in common is only another phrase for the possession of his share by each of the owners singly, and the surrender by the others of their rights over such share. This is why Moses elected captains of the tribes—namely, that when the dominion was divided, each might take care of his own part; consulting God through the high priest on the affairs of his tribe, ruling over his army, building and fortifying cities, appointing judges, attacking the enemies of his own dominion, and having complete control over all civil and military affairs. He was not bound to acknowledge any superior judge save God, or a prophet whom God should expressly send. If he departed from the worship of God, the rest of the tribes did not arraign him as a subject, but attacked him as an enemy. Of this we have examples in Scripture. When Joshua was dead, the children of Israel (not a fresh general-in-chief) consulted God; it being decided that the tribe of Judah should be the first to attack its enemies, the tribe in question contracted a single alliance with the tribe of Simeon, for uniting their forces, and attacking their common enemy, the rest of the tribes not being included in the alliance. Each tribe separately made war against its own enemies, and, according to its pleasure, received them as subjects or allies, though it had been commanded not to spare them on any conditions, but to destroy them utterly. Such disobedience met with reproof from the rest of the tribes, but did not cause the offending tribe to be arraigned: it was not considered a sufficient reason for proclaiming a civil war, or interfering in one another's affairs. But when the tribe of Benjamin offended against the others, and so loosened the bonds of peace that none of the confederated tribes could find refuge within its borders, they attacked it as an enemy, and gaining the victory over it after three battles, put to death both guilty and innocent, according to the laws of war: an act which they subsequently bewailed with tardy repentance.

These examples plainly confirm what we have said concerning the rights of each tribe. Perhaps we shall be asked who elected the successors to the captains of each tribe; on this point I can gather no positive information in Scripture, but I conjecture that as the tribes were divided into families, each headed by its senior member, the senior of all these heads of families succeeded by right to the office of captain, for Moses chose from among these seniors his seventy coadjutors, who formed with himself the supreme council. Those who administered the government after the death of Joshua were called elders, and elder is a very common Hebrew expression in the sense of judge, as I suppose everyone knows; however, it is not very important for us to make up our minds on this point. It is enough to have shown that after the death of Moses no one man wielded all the power of a sovereign; as affairs were not all managed by one man, nor by a single council, nor by the popular vote, but partly by one tribe, partly by the rest in equal shares, it is most evident that the government, after the death of Moses, was neither monarchic, nor aristocratic, nor popular, but, as we have said, Theocratic. The reasons for applying this name are:

I. Because the royal seat of government was the Temple, and in respect to it alone, as we have shown, all the tribes were fellow-citizens,

II. Because all the people owed allegiance to God, their supreme Judge, to whom only they had promised implicit obedience in all things.

III. Because the general-in-chief or dictator, when there was need of such, was elected by none save God alone. This was expressly commanded by Moses in the name of God, and witnessed by the actual choice of Gideon, of Samson, and of Samuel; wherefrom we may conclude that the other faithful leaders were chosen in the same manner, though it is not expressly told us.

These preliminaries being stated, it is now time to inquire the effects of forming a dominion on this plan, and to see whether it so effectually kept within bounds both rulers and ruled, that the former were never tyrannical and the latter never rebellious.

Those who administer or possess governing power, always try to surround their high-handed actions with a cloak of legality, and to persuade the people that they act from good motives; this they are easily able to effect when they are the sole interpreters of the law; for it is evident that they are thus able to assume a far greater freedom to carry out their wishes and desires than if the interpretation of the law is vested in someone else, or if the laws were so self-evident that no one could be in doubt as to their meaning. We thus see that the Power of evil-doing was greatly curtailed for the Hebrew captains by the fact that the whole interpretation of the law was vested in the Levites, who, on their part, had no share in the government, and depended for all their support and consideration on a correct interpretation of the laws entrusted to them. Moreover, the whole people was commanded to come together at a certain place every seven years and be instructed in the law by the high-priest; further, each individual was bidden to read the book of the law through and through continually with scrupulous care.

The captains were thus for their own sakes bound to take great care to administer everything according to the laws laid down, and well known to all, if they wished to be held in high honour by the people, who would regard them as the administrators of God's dominion, and as God's vicegerents; otherwise they could not have escaped all the virulence of theological hatred. There was another very important check on the unbridled license of the captains, in the fact, that the army was formed from the whole body of the citizens, between the ages of twenty and sixty, without exception, and that the captains were not able to hire any foreign soldiery. This I say was very important, for it is well known that princes can oppress their peoples with the single aid of the soldiery in their pay; while there is nothing more formidable to them than the freedom of citizen soldiers, who have established the freedom and glory of their country by their valour, their toil, and their blood. Thus Alexander, when he was about to make war on Darius, a second time, after hearing the advice of Parmenio, did not chide him who gave the advice, but Polysperchon, who was standing by. For, as Curtius says, he did not venture to reproach Parmenio again after having shortly before reproved him too sharply. This freedom of the Macedonians, which he so dreaded, he was not able to subdue till after the number of captives enlisted in the army surpassed that of his own people: then, but not till then, he gave rein to his anger so long checked by the independence of his chief fellow-countrymen.

If this independence of citizen soldiers can restrain the princes of ordinary states who are wont to usurp the whole glory of victories, it must have been still more effectual against the Hebrew captains, whose soldiers were fighting, not for the glory of a prince, but for the glory of God, and who did not go forth to battle till the Divine assent had been given.

We must also remember that the Hebrew captains were associated only by the bonds of religion: therefore, if any one of them had transgressed, and begun to violate the Divine right, he might have been treated by the rest as an enemy and lawfully subdued.

An additional check may be found in the fear of a new prophet arising, for if a man of unblemished life could show by certain signs that he was really a prophet, he *ipso facto* obtained the sovereign right to rule, which was given to him, as to Moses formerly, in the name of God, as revealed to himself alone; not merely through the high priest, as in the case of the captains. There is no doubt that such an one would easily be able to enlist an oppressed people in his cause, and by trifling signs persuade them of anything he wished: on the other hand, if affairs were well ordered, the captain would be able to make provision in time; that the prophet should be submitted to his approval, and be examined whether he were really of unblemished life, and possessed indisputable signs of his mission: also, whether the teaching he proposed to set forth in the name of the Lord agreed with received doctrines, and the general laws of the country; if his credentials were insufficient, or his doctrines new, he could lawfully be put to death, or else received on the captain's sole responsibility and authority.

Again, the captains were not superior to the others in nobility or birth, but only administered the government in virtue of their age and personal qualities. Lastly, neither captains nor army had any reason for preferring war to peace. The army, as we have stated, consisted entirely of citizens, so that affairs were managed by the same persons both in peace and war. The man who was a soldier in the camp was a citizen in the market-place, he who was a leader in the camp was a judge in the law courts, he who was a general in the camp was a ruler in the state. Thus no one could desire war for its own sake, but only for the sake of preserving peace and liberty; possibly the captains avoided change as far as possible, so as not to be obliged to consult the high priest and submit to the indignity of standing in his presence.

So much for the precautions for keeping the captains within bounds. We must now look for the restraints upon the people: these, however, are very clearly indicated in the very groundwork of the social fabric.

Anyone who gives the subject the slightest attention, will see that the state was so ordered as to inspire the most ardent patriotism in the hearts of the citizens, so that the latter would be very hard to persuade to betray their country, and be ready to endure anything rather than submit to a foreign yoke. After they had transferred their right to God, they thought that their kingdom belonged to God, and that they themselves were God's children. Other nations they looked upon as God's enemies, and regarded with intense hatred (which they took to be piety): nothing would have been more abhorrent to them than swearing allegiance to a foreigner, and promising him obedience: nor could they conceive any greater or more execrable crime than the betrayal of their country, the kingdom of the God whom they adored.

It was considered wicked for anyone to settle outside of the country, inasmuch as the worship of God by which they were bound could not be carried on elsewhere: their own land alone was considered holy, the rest of the earth unclean and profane.

David, who was forced to live in exile, complained before Saul as follows: "But if they be the children of men who have stirred thee up against me, cursed be they before the Lord; for they have driven me out this day from abiding in the inheritance of the Lord, saying, Go, serve other gods." For the same reason no citizen, as we should especially remark, was ever sent into exile: he who sinned was liable to punishment, but not to disgrace.

Thus the love of the Hebrews for their country was not only patriotism, but also piety, and was cherished and nurtured by daily rites till, like their hatred of other nations, it must have passed into their nature. Their daily worship was not only different from that of other nations (as it might well be, considering that they were a peculiar people and entirely apart from the rest), it was absolutely contrary. Such daily reprobation naturally gave rise to a lasting hatred, deeply implanted in the heart: for of all hatreds none is more deep and tenacious than that which springs from extreme devoutness or piety, and is itself cherished as pious. Nor was a general cause lacking for inflaming such hatred more and more, inasmuch as it was reciprocated; the surrounding nations regarding the Jews with a hatred just as intense.

How great was the effect of all these causes, namely, freedom from man's dominion; devotion to their country; absolute rights over all other men; a hatred not only permitted but pious; a contempt for their fellow-men; the singularity of their customs and religious rites; the effect, I repeat, of all these causes in strengthening the hearts of the Jews to bear all things for their country, with extraordinary constancy and valour, will at once be discerned by reason and attested by experience. Never, so long as the city was standing, could they endure to remain under foreign dominion; and therefore they called Jerusalem "a rebellious city." Their state after its reestablishment (which was a mere shadow of the first, for the high priests had usurped the rights of the tribal captains) was, with great difficulty, destroyed by the Romans, as Tacitus bears witness:—"Vespasian had closed the war against the Jews, abandoning the siege of Jerusalem as an enterprise difficult and arduous, rather from the character of the people and the obstinacy of their superstition, than from the strength left to the besieged for meeting their necessities." But besides these characteristics, which are merely ascribed by an individual opinion, there was one feature peculiar to this state and of great importance in retaining the affections of the citizens, and checking all thoughts of desertion, or abandonment of the country: namely, self-interest, the strength and life of all human action. This was peculiarly engaged in the Hebrew state, for nowhere else did citizens possess their goods so securely as did the subjects of this community, for the latter possessed as large a share in the land and the fields as did their chiefs, and were owners of their plots of ground in perpetuity; for if any man was compelled by poverty to sell his farm or his pasture, he received it back again intact at the year of jubilee: there were other similar enactments against the possibility of alienating real property.

Again, poverty was nowhere more endurable than in a country where duty towards one's neighbour, that is, one's fellow-citizen, was practised with the utmost piety, as a means of gaining the favour of God the King. Thus the Hebrew citizens would nowhere be so well off as in their own country; outside its limits they met with nothing but loss and disgrace.

The following considerations were of weight, not only in keeping them at home, but also in preventing civil war and removing causes of strife: no one was bound to serve his equal, but only to serve God, while charity and love towards fellow-citizens was accounted the highest piety; this last feeling was not a little fostered by the general hatred with which they regarded foreign nations and were regarded by them. Furthermore, the strict discipline of obedience in which they were brought up, was a very important factor; for they were bound to carry on all their actions according to the set rules of the law: a man might not plough when he liked, but only at certain times, in certain years, and with one sort of beast at a time; so, too, he might only sow and reap in a certain method and season—in fact, his whole life was one long school of obedience; such a habit was thus engendered, that conformity seemed freedom instead of servitude, and men desired what was commanded rather than what was forbidden. This result was not a little aided by the fact that the people were bound, at certain seasons of the year, to give themselves up to rest and rejoicing, not for their own pleasure, but in order that they might worship God cheerfully.

Three times in the year they feasted before the Lord; on the seventh day of every week they were bidden to abstain from all work and to rest; besides these, there were other occasions when innocent rejoicing and feasting were not only allowed but enjoined. I do not think any better means of influencing men's minds could be devised; for there is no more powerful attraction than joy springing from devotion, a mixture of admiration and love. It was not easy to be wearied by constant repetition, for the rites on the various festivals were varied and recurred seldom. We may add the deep reverence for the Temple which all most religiously fostered, on account of the peculiar rites and duties that they were obliged to perform before approaching thither. Even now, Jews cannot read without horror of the crime of Manasseh, who dared to place an idol in the Temple. The laws, scrupulously preserved in the inmost sanctuary, were objects of equal reverence to the people. Popular reports and misconceptions were, therefore, very little to be feared in this quarter, for no one dared decide on sacred matters, but all felt bound to obey, without consulting their reason, all the commands given by the answers of God received in the Temple, and all the laws which God had ordained.

I think I have now explained clearly, though briefly, the main features of the Hebrew commonwealth. I must now inquire into the causes which led the people so often to fall away from the law, which brought about their frequent subjection, and, finally, the complete destruction of their dominion. Perhaps I shall be told that it sprang from their hardness of heart; but this is childish, for why should this people be more hard of heart than others; was it by nature?

But nature forms individuals, not peoples; the latter are only distinguishable by the difference of their language, their customs, and their laws; while from the two last—*i.e.,* customs and laws,—it may arise that they have a peculiar disposition, a peculiar manner of life, and peculiar prejudices. If, then, the Hebrews were harder of heart than other nations, the fault lay with their laws or customs.

This is certainly true, in the sense that, if God had wished their dominion to be more lasting, He would have given them other rites and laws, and would have instituted a different form of government. We can, therefore, only say that their God was angry with them, not only, as Jeremiah says, from the building of the city, but even from the founding of their laws.

This is borne witness to by Ezekiel: "Wherefore I gave them also statutes that were not good, and judgments whereby they should not live; and I polluted them in their own gifts, in that they caused to pass through the fire all that openeth the womb; that I might make them desolate, to the end that they might know that I am the Lord."

In order that we may understand these words, and the destruction of the Hebrew commonwealth, we must bear in mind that it had at first been intended to entrust the whole duties of the priesthood to the firstborn, and not to the Levites. It was only when all the tribes, except the Levites, worshipped the golden calf, that the firstborn were rejected and defiled, and the Levites chosen in their stead. When I reflect on this change,

I feel disposed to break forth with the words of Tacitus. God's object at that time was not the safety of the Jews, but vengeance. I am greatly astonished that the celestial mind was so inflamed with anger that it ordained laws, which always are supposed to promote the honour, well-being, and security of a people, with the purpose of vengeance, for the sake of punishment; so that the laws do not seem so much laws—that is, the safeguard of the people—as pains and penalties.

The gifts which the people were obliged to bestow on the Levites and priests—the redemption of the firstborn, the poll-tax due to the Levites, the privilege possessed by the latter of the sole performance of sacred rites—all these, I say, were a continual reproach to the people, a continual reminder of their defilement and rejection. Moreover, we may be sure that the Levites were for ever heaping reproaches upon them: for among so many thousands there must have been many importunate dabblers in theology. Hence the people got into the way of watching the acts of the Levites, who were but human; of accusing the whole body of the faults of one member, and continually murmuring.

Besides this, there was the obligation to keep in idleness men hateful to them, and connected by no ties of blood. Especially would this seem grievous when provisions were dear. What wonder, then, if in times of peace, when striking miracles had ceased, and no men of paramount authority were forthcoming, the irritable and greedy temper of the people began to wax cold, and at length to fall away from a worship, which, though Divine, was also humiliating, and even hostile, and to seek after something fresh; or can we be surprised that the captains, who always adopt the popular course, in order to gain the sovereign power for themselves by enlisting the sympathies of the people, and alienating the high priest, should have yielded to their demands, and introduced a new worship? If the state had been formed according to the original intention, the rights and honour of all the tribes would have been equal, and everything would have rested on a firm basis. Who is there who would willingly violate the religious rights of his kindred? What could a man desire more than to support his own brothers and parents, thus fulfilling the duties of religion? Who would not rejoice in being taught by them the interpretation of the laws, and receiving through them the answers of God?

The tribes would thus have been united by a far closer bond, if all alike had possessed the right to the priesthood. All danger would have been obviated, if the choice of the Levites had not been dictated by anger and revenge. But, as we have said, the Hebrews had offended their God, Who, as Ezekiel says, polluted them in their own gifts by rejecting all that openeth the womb, so that He might destroy them.

This passage is also confirmed by their history. As soon as the people in the wilderness began to live in ease and plenty, certain men of no mean birth began to rebel against the choice of the Levites, and to make it a cause for believing that Moses had not acted by the commands of God, but for his own good pleasure, inasmuch as he had chosen his own tribe before all the rest, and had bestowed the high priesthood in perpetuity on his own brother. They, therefore, stirred up a tumult, and came to him, crying out that all men were equally sacred, and that he had exalted himself above his fellows wrongfully. Moses was not able to pacify them with reasons; but by the intervention of a miracle, in proof of the faith, they all perished. A fresh sedition then arose among the whole people, who believed that their champions had not been put to death by the judgment of God, but by the device of Moses. After a great slaughter, or pestilence, the rising subsided from inanition, but in such a manner that all preferred death to life under such conditions.

We should rather say that sedition ceased than that harmony was re-established. This is witnessed by Scripture, where God, after predicting to Moses that the people after his death will fall away from the Divine worship, speaks thus: "For I know their imagination which they go about, even now before I have brought them into the land which I sware;" and, a little while after, Moses says: "For I know thy rebellion and thy stiff neck: behold, while I am yet alive with you this day, ye have been rebellious against the Lord; and how much more after my death!"

Indeed, it happened according to his words, as we all know. Great changes, extreme license, luxury, and hardness of heart grew up; things went from bad to worse, till at last the people, after being frequently conquered, came to an open rupture with the Divine right, and wished for a mortal king, so that the seat of government might be the Court, instead of the Temple, and that the tribes might remain fellow-citizens in respect to their king, instead of in respect to Divine right and the high priesthood.

A vast material for new seditions was thus produced, eventually resulting in the ruin of the entire state. Kings are above all things jealous of a precarious rule, and can in no-wise brook a dominion within their own. The first monarchs, being chosen from the ranks of private citizens, were content with the amount of dignity to which they had risen; but their sons, who obtained the throne by right of inheritance, began gradually to introduce changes, so as to get all the sovereign rights into their own hands. This they were generally unable to accomplish, so long as the right of legislation did not rest with them, but with the high priest, who kept the laws in the sanctuary, and interpreted them to the people. The kings were thus bound to obey the laws as much as were the subjects, and were unable to abrogate them, or to ordain new laws of equal authority; moreover, they were prevented by the Levites from administering the affairs of religion, king and subject being alike unclean. Lastly, the whole safety of their dominion depended on the will of one man, if that man appeared to be a prophet; and of this they had seen an example, namely, how completely Samuel had been able to command Saul, and how easily, because of a single disobedience, he had been able to transfer the right of sovereignty to David. Thus the kings found a dominion within their own, and wielded a precarious sovereignty.

In order to surmount these difficulties, they allowed other temples to be dedicated to the gods, so that there might be no further need of consulting the Levites; they also sought out many who prophesied in the name of God, so that they might have creatures of their own to oppose to the true prophets. However, in spite of all their attempts, they never attained their end. For the prophets, prepared against every emergency, waited for a favourable opportunity, such as the beginning of a new reign, which is always precarious, while the memory of the previous reign remains green. At these times they could easily pronounce by Divine authority that the king was tyrannical, and could produce a champion of distinguished virtue to vindicate the Divine right, and lawfully to claim dominion, or a share in it. Still, not even so could the prophets effect much. They could, indeed, remove a tyrant; but there were reasons which prevented them from doing more than setting up, at great cost of civil bloodshed, another tyrant in his stead. Of discords and civil wars there was no end, for the causes for the violation of Divine right remained always the same, and could only be removed by a complete remodelling of the state.

We have now seen how religion was introduced into the Hebrew commonwealth, and how the dominion might have lasted for ever, if the just wrath of the Lawgiver had allowed it. As this was impossible, it was bound in time to perish. I am now speaking only of the first commonwealth, for the second was a mere shadow of the first, inasmuch as the people were bound by the rights of the Persians to whom they were subject. After the restoration of freedom, the high priests usurped the rights of the secular chiefs, and thus obtained absolute dominion. The priests were inflamed with an intense desire to wield the powers of the sovereignty and the high priesthood at the same time. I have, therefore, no need to speak further of the second commonwealth. Whether the first, in so far as we deem it to have been durable, is capable of imitation, and whether it would be pious to copy it as far as possible, will appear from what follows. I wish only to draw attention, as a crowning conclusion, to the principle indicated already—namely, that it is evident, from what we have stated in this chapter, that the Divine right, or the right of religion, originates in a compact: without such compact, none but natural rights exist. The Hebrews were not bound by their religion to evince any pious care for other nations not included in the compact, but only for their own fellow-citizens.

John Locke (1632–1704 C.E.)

A tremendous influence on Britain's Glorious Revolution, and the American and French revolutions, this English philosopher was the first to produce a thorough and coherent account of government by consent. Rejecting the theories of monarchical divine right, Locke argued that the only basis for one person having dominion over another was consent. Locke's theories of rights, property, and consent remain influential today, and together with Adam Smith's *Wealth of Nations*, have formed the basis for modern democratic capitalism. Locke's *First Treatise of Civil Government* was a specific refutation of the theory of the divine right of kings. The following is from the *Second Treatise of Government* (c. 1688), which discusses the nature of legitimate political authority.

From Second Treatise of Government*

Chapter III

Of the State of War

16. The *state of war* is a state of *enmity* and *destruction:* And therefore declaring by word or action, not a passionate and hasty, but a sedate settled design upon another man's life, *puts him in a state of war* with him against whom he has declared such an intention, and so has exposed his life to the other's power to be taken away by him, or any one that joins with him in his defence, and espouses his quarrel: it being reasonable and just I should have a right to destroy that which threatens me with destruction. For *by the fundamental law of nature, man being to be preserved* as much as possible, when all cannot be preserved, the safety of the innocent is to be preferred: And one may destroy a man who makes war upon him, or has discovered an enmity to his being, for the same reason that he may kill a *wolf* or a *lion*; because such men are not under the ties of the common law of reason, have no other rule, but that of force and violence, and so may be treated as beasts of prey, those dangerous and noxious creatures, that will be sure to destroy him whenever he falls into their power.

17. And hence it is, that he who attempts to get another man into his absolute power, does thereby *put himself into a state of war* with him; it being to be understood as a declaration of a design upon his life. For I have reason to conclude, that he who would get me into his power without my consent, would use me as he pleased when he got me there, and destroy me too when he had a fancy to it; for no body can desire to *have me in his absolute power* unless it be to compel me by force to that which is against the right of my freedom, i.e. make me a slave. To be free from such force is the only security of my preservation; and reason bids me look on him, as an enemy to my preservation, who

---

*An Excerpt.

would take away that freedom which is the fence to it; so that he who makes an *attempt to enslave* me, thereby puts himself into a state of war with me. He that, in the state of nature, *would take away the freedom* that belongs to any one in that state, must necessarily be supposed to have a design to take away every thing else, that *freedom* being the foundation of all the rest: As he that, in the state of society, would take away the freedom belonging to those of that society or commonwealth, must be supposed to design to take away from them every thing else, and so be looked on as *in a state of war*.

18. This makes it lawful for a man to *kill a thief*, who has not in the least hurt him, nor declared any design upon his life, any farther, than by the use of force, so to get him in his power, as to take away his money, or what he pleases, from him; because using force, where he has no right, to get me into his power, let his pretence be what it will, I have no reason to suppose, that he, who would *take away my liberty*, would not, when he had me in his power, take away every thing else. And therefore it is lawful for me to treat him as one who has put *himself into a state of war* with me, i.e. kill him if I can; for to that hazard does he justly expose himself, whoever introduces a state of war, and is aggressor in it.

19. And here we have the plain *difference between the state of nature and the state of war;* which however some men have confounded, are as far distant, as a state of peace, good will, mutual assistance and preservation, and a state of enmity, malice, violence and mutual destruction, are one from another. Men living together according to reason, without a common superior on earth, with authority to judge between them, is *properly the state of nature*. But force, or a declared design of force, upon the person of another, where there is no common superior on earth to appeal to for relief, *is the state of war:* And it is the want of such an appeal gives a man the right of war even against an aggressor, though he be in society and a fellow subject. Thus a *thief,* whom I cannot harm, but by appeal to the law, for having stolen all that I am worth, I may kill, when he sets on me to rob me but of my horse or coat; because the law, which was made for my preservation, where it cannot interpose to secure my life from present force, which, if lost, is capable of no reparation, permits me my own defence, and the right of war, a liberty to kill the aggressor, because the aggressor allows not time to appeal to our common judge, nor the decision of the law, for remedy in a case where the mischief may be irreparable. *Want of a common judge with authority, puts all men in a state of nature: Force without right, upon a man's person, makes a state of war,* both where there is, and is not, a common judge.

20. But when the actual force is over, the *state of war ceases* between those that are in society, and are equally on both sides subjected to the fair determination of the law; because then there lies open the remedy of appeal for the past injury, and to prevent future harm: but where no such appeal is, as in the state of nature, for want of positive laws, and judges with authority to appeal to, *the state of war once begun, continues* with a right to the innocent party to destroy the other whenever he can, until the aggressor offers peace, and desires reconciliation on such terms as may repair any wrongs he has already done, and secure the innocent for the future: nay, where an appeal to the law, and constituted judges, lies open, but the remedy is denied by a manifest perverting of justice, and a barefaced wresting of the laws to protect or indemnify the violence or injuries of some men, or party of men, *there* it *is* hard to imagine any thing but *a state of war*. For wherever violence is used, and injury done, though by hands appointed to administer justice, it is still violence and injury, however coloured with the name, pretences, or forms of law, the end whereof being to protect and redress the innocent, by an unbiassed application of it, to all who are under it; wherever that is not *bona fide* done, *war is made* upon the sufferers, who having no appeal on earth to right them, they are left to the only remedy in such cases, an appeal to heaven.

21. To avoid this *state of war* (wherein there is no appeal but to heaven, and wherein every the least difference is apt to end, where there is no authority to decide between the contenders) is one great *reason of men's putting themselves into society,* and quitting the state of nature. For where there is an authority, a power on earth, from which relief can be had by *appeal,* there the continuance of the *state of war* is excluded, and the controversy is decided by that power. Had there been any such court, any superior jurisdiction on earth, to determine the right between Jephthah and the Ammonites, they had never come to a *state of war:* But we see he was forced to appeal to heaven. "The Lord the Judge," says he, "be judge this day, between the children of Israel and the children of Ammon," and then prosecuting, and relying on his appeal, he leads out his army to battle: and therefore in such controversies, where the question is put, *who shall be judge?* it cannot be meant, who shall decide the controversy; every one knows what Jephthah here tells us, that "the Lord the Judge" shall judge. Where there is no judge on earth, the appeal lies to God in heaven. That question then cannot mean, who shall judge? whether another hath put himself in a *state of war* with me, and whether I may, as Jephthah did, *appeal to heaven* in it? of that I myself can only be judge in my own conscience, as I will answer it, at the great day, to the supreme judge of all men.

Chapter IV

Of Slavery

22. The *natural liberty* of man is to be free from any superior power on earth, and not to be under the will or legislative authority of man, but to have only the law of nature for his rule. The *liberty of man* in society, is to be under no other legislative power, but that established, by consent, in the commonwealth; nor under the dominion of any will, or restraint of any law, but what that legislative shall enact, according to the trust put in it. Freedom then is not what Sir Robert Filmer tells us, "a liberty for every one to do what he lists, to live as he pleases, and not to be tied by any laws:" But *freedom of men under government,* is, to have a standing rule to live by, common to every one of that society, and made by the legislative power erected in it; a liberty to follow my own will in all things, where the rule prescribes not; and not to be subject to the inconstant, uncertain, unknown, arbitrary will of another man: As *freedom of nature* is, to be under no other restraint but the law of nature.

23. This freedom from absolute, arbitrary power, is so necessary to, and closely joined with a man's preservation, that he cannot part with it, but by what forfeits his preservation and life together. For a man, not having the power of his own life, cannot, by compact, or his own consent, enslave himself to any one, nor put himself under the absolute, arbitrary power of another, to take away his life, when he pleases. No body can give more power than he has himself; and he that cannot take away his own life, cannot give another power over it. Indeed, having by his fault forfeited his own life, by some act that deserves death; he, to whom he has forfeited it, may (when he has him in his power) delay to take it, and make use of him to his own service, and he does him no injury by it. For, whenever he finds the hardship of his slavery outweigh the value of his life, it is in his power, by resisting the will of his master, to draw on himself the death he desires.

24. This is the perfect condition of *slavery*, which is nothing else, but *the state of war continued, between a lawful conqueror and a captive.* For, if once compact enter between them, and make an agreement for a limited power on the one side, and obedience on the other, the state of war and slavery ceases, as long as the compact endures. For, as has been said, no man can, by agreement, pass over to another that which he hath not in himself, a power over his own life.

I confess, we find among the Jews, as well as other nations, that men did sell themselves; but, it is plain, this was only to *drudgery, not to slavery.* For it is evident, the person sold was not under an absolute, arbitrary, despotical power. For the master could not have power to kill him, at any time, whom, at a certain time, he was obliged to let go free out of his service: and the master of such a servant was so far from having an arbitrary power over his life, that he could not, at pleasure, so much as maim him, but the loss of an eye, or tooth, set him free.

Chapter V

Of Property

25. Whether we consider natural *reason*, which tells us, that men, being once born, have a right to their preservation, and consequently to meat and drink, and such other things as nature affords for their subsistence: or *revelation*, which gives us an account of those grants God made of the world to Adam, and to Noah, and his sons, it is very clear, that God, as King David says, "has given the earth to the children of men," given it to mankind in common. But this being supposed, it seems to some a very great difficulty how any one should ever come to have a *property* in any thing: I will not content myself to answer, that if it be difficult to make out *property*, upon a supposition, that God gave the world to Adam, and his posterity in common; it is impossible that any man, but one universal monarch, should have any property upon a supposition, that God gave the world to Adam, and his heirs in succession, exclusive of all the rest of his posterity. But I shall endeavour to shew, how men might come to have a *property* in several parts of that which God gave to mankind in common, and that without any express compact of all the commoners.

26. God, who hath given the world to men in common, hath also given them reason to make use of it to the best advantage of life, and convenience. The earth, and all that is therein, is given to men for the support and comfort of their being. And though all the fruits it naturally produces, and beasts it feeds, belong to mankind in common, as they are produced by the spontaneous hand of nature; and no body has originally a private dominion, exclusive of the rest of mankind, in any of them, as they are thus in their natural state: yet being given for the use of men, there must of necessity be *a means to appropriate* them some way or other, before they can be of any use, or at all beneficial to any particular man. The fruit, or venison, which nourishes the wild Indian, who knows no enclosure, and is still a tenant in common, must be his, and so his, i.e. a part of him, that another can no longer have any right to it, before it can do him any good for the support of his life.

27. Though the earth, and all inferior creatures, be common to all men, yet every man has a property in his own person: this no body has any right to but himself. The labour of his body, and the work of his hands, we may say, are properly his. Whatsoever then he removes out of the state that nature hath provided, and left it in, he hath mixed his labour with, and joined to it something that is his own, and thereby makes it his property. It being by him removed from the common state nature hath placed it in, it hath by this labour something annexed to it, that excludes the common right of other men. For this labour being the unquestionable property of the labourer, no man but he can have a right to what that is once joined to, at least where there is enough, and as good, left in common for others.

28. He that is nourished by the acorns he picked up under an oak, or the apples he gathered from the trees in the wood, has certainly appropriated them to himself. No body can deny but the nourishment is his. I ask then, when did they begin to be his? When he digested? Or when he eat? Or when he boiled? Or when he brought them home? Or when he picked them up? And it is plain, if the first gathering made them not his, nothing else could. That *labour* put a distinction between them and common: that added something to them more than nature, the common mother of all, had done; and so they became his private right. And will any one say he had no right to those acorns or apples he thus appropriated, because he had not the consent of all mankind to make them his? Was it a robbery thus to assume to himself what belonged to all in common? If such a consent as that was necessary, man had starved, notwithstanding the plenty God had given him. We see in *commons*, which remain so by compact, that it is the taking any part of what is common, and removing it out of the state nature leaves it in, which *begins the property;* without which the common is of no use. And the taking of this or that part does not depend on the express consent of all the commoners. Thus the grass my horse has bit; the turfs my servant has cut; and the ore I have digged in any place, where I have a right to them in common with others, become my *property*, without the assignation or consent of any body. The *labour* that was mine, removing them out of that common state they were in, hath *fixed* my *property* in them.

29. By making an explicit consent of every commoner necessary to any one's appropriating to himself any part of what is given in common, children or servants could not cut the meat, which their father or master had provided for them in common, without assigning to every one his peculiar part. Though the water running in the fountain be every one's, yet who can doubt, but that in the pitcher is his only who drew it out? His

labour hath taken it out of the hands of nature, where it was common, and belonged equally to all her children, and *hath* thereby *appropriated* it to himself.

30. Thus this law of reason makes the deer that Indian's who hath killed it; it is allowed to be his goods, who hath bestowed his labour upon it, though before it was the common right of every one. And amongst those who are counted the civilized part of mankind, who have made and multiplied positive laws to determine *property*, this original law of nature, for the *beginning of property*, in what was before common, still takes place; and by virtue thereof, what fish any one catches in the ocean, that great and still remaining common of mankind; or what ambergreise any one takes up here, is *by* the *labour* that removes it out of that common state nature left it in, *made* his *property* who takes that pains about it. And even amongst us, the hare that any one is hunting, is thought his who pursues her during the chase. For being a beast that is still looked upon as common, and no man's private possession; whoever has employed so much *labour* about any of that kind, as to find and pursue her, has thereby removed her from the state of nature, wherein she was common, and hath *begun a property*.

31. It will perhaps be objected to this, that *if gathering the acorns, or other fruits of the earth, &c.* makes a right to them, then any one may engross as much as he will. To which I answer, Not so. The same law of nature, that does by this means give us property, does also *bound* that *property* too. "God has given us all things richly," is the voice of reason confirmed by inspiration. But how far has he given it us? *To enjoy.* As much as any one can make use of to any advantage of life before it spoils, so much he may by his labour fix a property in: whatever is beyond this, is more than his share, and belongs to others. Nothing was made by God for man to spoil or destroy. And thus, considering the plenty of natural provisions there was a long time in the world, and the few spenders; and to how small a part of that provision the industry of one man could extend itself, and engross it to the prejudice of others; especially keeping within the *bounds* set by reason, *of* what might serve for his *use;* there could be then little room for quarrels or contentions about property so established.

32. But the *chief matter of property* being now not the fruits of the earth, and the beasts that subsist on it, but the *earth it self;* as that which takes in, and carries with it all the rest: I think it is plain, that *property* in that too is acquired as the former. *As much land* as a man tills, plants, improves, cultivates, and can use the product of, so much is his *property*. He by his labour does, as it were, enclose it from the common. Nor will it invalidate his right, to say every body else has an equal title to it; and therefore he cannot appropriate, he cannot enclose, without the consent of all his fellow commoners, all mankind. God, when he gave the world in common to all mankind, commanded man also to labour, and the penury of his condition required it of him. God and his reason commanded him to subdue the earth, i.e. improve it for the benefit of life, and therein lay out something upon it that was his own, his labour. He that, in obedience to this command of God, subdued, tilled, and sowed any part of it, thereby annexed to it something that was his *property*, which another had no title to, nor could without injury take from him.

33. Nor was this *appropriation* of any parcel of *land,* by improving it, any prejudice to any other man, since there was still enough, and as good left; and more than the yet unprovided could use. So that, in effect, there was never the less left for others because of his enclosure for himself. For he that leaves as much as another can make use of, does as good as take nothing at all. No body could think himself injured by the drinking of another man, though he took a good draught, who had a whole river of the same water left him to quench his thirst: And the case of land and water, where there is enough of both, is perfectly the same.

34. God gave the world to men in common; but since he gave it them for their benefit, and the greatest conveniences of life they were capable to draw from it, it cannot be supposed he meant it should always remain common and uncultivated. He gave it to the use of the industrious and rational, (and *labour* was to be *his title* to it) not to the fancy or covetousness of the quarrel some and contentious. He that had as good left for his improvement, as was already taken up, needed not complain, ought not to meddle with what was already improved by another's labour: If he did, it is plain he desired the benefit of another's pains, which he had no right to, and not the ground which God had given him in common with others to labour on, and whereof there was as good left, as that already possessed, and more than he knew what to do with, or his industry could reach to.

35. It is true, in *land* that is *common* in England, or any other country, where there is plenty of people under government, who have money and commerce, no one can enclose or appropriate any part, without the consent of all his fellow-commoners: Because this is left common by compact, i.e. by the law of the land, which is not to be violated. And though it be common, in respect of some men, it is not so to all mankind, but is the joint property of this country, or this parish. Besides, the remainder, after such enclosure, would not be as good to the rest of the commoners, as the whole was when they could all make use of the whole: whereas in the beginning and first peopling of the great common of the world, it was quite otherwise. The law man was under, was rather for appropriating. God commanded, and his wants forced him to *labour.* That was his *property* which could not be taken from him wherever he had fixed it. And hence subduing or cultivating the earth, and having dominion, we see are joined together. The one gave title to the other. So that God, by commanding to subdue, gave authority so far to *appropriate.* And the condition of human life, which requires labour and materials to work on, necessarily introduces private possessions.

36. The *measure of property* nature has well set by the extent of men's *labour, and the conveniences of life:* No man's labour could subdue or appropriate all; nor could his enjoyment consume more than a small part; so that it was impossible for any man, this way, to intrench upon the right of another, or acquire to himself a property, to the prejudice of his neighbour, who would still have room for as good, and as large a possession (after the other had taken out his) as before it was appropriated. This *measure* did confine every man's *possession* to a very moderate proportion, and such as he might appropriate to himself, without injury to any body, in the first ages of the world, when men were more in danger to be lost, by wandering from their company, in the then vast wilderness of the earth, than to be straitened for want of room to plant in. And the same measure may be allowed still without prejudice to any body, as full as the world seems. For supposing a man, or family, in the state they were at first peopling of the world by the children of Adam, or Noah; let him plant in some inland, vacant places of America, we shall find that the *possessions* he could make himself, upon the *measures* we have given, would not be very large, nor, even to this day, prejudice the rest of mankind, or give them reason to complain, or think themselves injured by this man's encroachment, though the race of men have now spread themselves to all the corners of the world, and do infinitely exceed the small number was at the beginning. Nay, the extent of *ground* is of so little value, *without labour*, that I have heard it affirmed, that in Spain itself a man may be permitted to plough, sow, and reap, without being disturbed, upon land he has no other title to, but only his making use of it. But, on the contrary, the inhabitants think themselves beholden to him, who by his industry on neglected and consequently waste land, has increased the stock of corn, which they wanted. But be this as it will, which I lay no stress on; this I dare boldly affirm, that the same *rule of propriety*, (*viz.*) that every man should have as much as he could make use of, would hold still in the world, without straitening any body, since there is land enough in the world to suffice double the inhabitants, had not the *invention of money*, and the tacit agreement of men to put a value on it, introduced (by consent) larger possessions, and a right to them; which, how it has done, I shall by and by shew more at large.

37. This is certain, that in the beginning, before the desire of having more than man needed had altered the intrinsic value of things, which depends only on their usefulness to the life of man; or had *agreed, that a little piece of yellow metal*, which would keep without wasting or decay, should be worth a great piece of flesh, or a whole heap of corn; though men had a right to appropriate, by their labour, each one to himself as much of the things of nature as he could use: yet this could not be much, nor to the prejudice of others, where the same plenty was still left to those who would use the same industry. To which let me add, that he who appropriates land to himself by his labour, does not lessen, but increase the common stock of mankind. For the provisions serving to the support of human life, produced by one acre of enclosed and cultivated land, are (to speak much within compass) ten times more than those which are yielded by an acre of land of an equal richness lying waste in common. And therefore he that encloses land, and has a greater plenty of the conveniencies of life from ten acres, than he could have from an hundred left to nature, may truly be said to give ninety acres to mankind. For his labour now supplies him with provisions out of ten acres, which were by the product of an hundred lying in common. I have here rated the improved land very low, in making its product but as ten to one, when it is much nearer an hundred to one. For I ask, whether in the wild woods and uncultivated waste of America, left to nature, without any improvement, tillage, or husbandry, a thousand acres yield the needy and wretched inhabitants as many conveniencies of life, as ten acres equally fertile land do in Devonshire, where they are well cultivated?

Before the appropriation of land, he who gathered as much of the wild fruit, killed, caught, or tamed, as many of the beasts as he could; he that so employed his pains about any of the spontaneous products of nature, as any way to alter them from the state which nature put them in, *by* placing any of his *labour* on them, did thereby *acquire a propriety in them;* but if they perished, in his possession, without their due use; if the fruits rotted, or the venison putrified, before he could spend it, he offended against the common law of nature, and was liable to be punished; he invaded his neighbour's share, for he had *no right, farther than his use* called for any of them, and they might serve to afford him conveniences of life.

38. The same *measures* governed the *possession of land* too: whatsoever he tilled and reaped, laid up and made use of, before it spoiled, that was his peculiar right; whatsoever he enclosed, and could feed, and make use of, the cattle and product was also his. But if either the grass of his inclosure rotted on the ground, or the fruit of his planting perished without gathering, and laying up, this part of the earth, notwithstanding his inclosure, was still to be looked on as waste, and might be the possession of any other. Thus at the beginning, Cain might take as much ground as he could till, and make it his own land, and yet leave enough to Abel's sheep to feed on; a few acres would serve for both their possessions. But as families increased, and industry enlarged their stocks, their *possessions enlarged* with the need of them; but yet it was commonly *without any fixed property in the ground* they made use of, till they incorporated, settled themselves together, and built cities, and then, by consent, they came in time to set out the *bounds of their distinct territories,* and agree on limits between them and their neighbours; and by laws within themselves settled the *properties* of those of the same society. For we see, that in that part of the world which was first inhabited, and therefore like to be best peopled, even as low down as Abraham's time, they wandered with their flocks, and their herds, which was their substance, freely up and down; and this Abraham did, in a country where he was a stranger. Whence it is plain, that at least a great part of the *land lay in common;* that the inhabitants valued it not, nor claimed property in any more than they made use of. But when there was not room enough in the same place, for their herds to feed together, they by consent, as Abraham and Lot did, separated and enlarged their pasture, where it best liked them. And for the same reason Esau went from his father, and his brother, and planted in Mount Seir.

39. And thus, without supposing any private dominion, and property in Adam, over all the *world,* exclusive of all other men, which can no way be proved, nor any one's property be made out from it; but supposing the *world* given, as it was, to the children of men *in common,* we see how *labour* could make men distinct titles to several parcels of it, for their private uses; wherein there could be no doubt of right, no room for quarrel.

40. Nor is it so strange, as perhaps before consideration it may appear, that the *property of labour* should be able to over-balance the community of land. For it is *labour* indeed that *puts the difference of value* on every thing; and let any one consider what the difference is between an acre of land planted with tobacco or sugar, sown with wheat or barley, and an acre of the same land lying in common, without any husbandry upon it, and he will find, that the improvement of *labour makes* the far greater part of the value. I think it will be but a very modest computation to say, that of the *products* of the earth useful to the life of man, nine tenths are the *effects of labour;* nay, if we will rightly estimate things as they come to our use, and cast up the several expences about them, what in them is purely owing to *nature* and what to *labour*, we shall find, that in most of them ninety-nine hundredths are wholly to be put on the account of *labour*.

41. There cannot be a clearer demonstration of any thing, than several nations of the Americans are of this, who are rich in land, and poor in all the comforts of life; whom nature having furnished as liberally as any other people, with the materials of plenty, i.e. a fruitful soil, apt to produce in abundance what might serve for food, raiment, and delight; yet *for want of improving it by labour*, have not one hundredth part of the conveniencies we enjoy; and a king of a large and fruitful territory there feeds, lodges, and is clad worse than a day labourer in England.

42. To make this a little clearer, let us but trace some of the ordinary provisions of life, through their several progresses, before they come to our use, and see how much they receive of their *value from human industry*. Bread, wine, and cloth, are things of daily use, and great plenty, yet notwithstanding, acorns, water, and leaves, or skins, must be our bread, drink, and cloathing, did not labour furnish us with these more useful commodities. For whatever bread is more worth than acorns, wine than water, and *cloth* or *silk*, than leaves, skins, or moss, that is *wholly owing to labour* and *industry*. The one of these being the food and raiment which unassisted nature furnishes us with; the other, provisions which our industry and pains prepare for us, which how much they exceed the other in value, when any one hath computed, he will then see how much *labour makes the far greatest part of the value* of things we enjoy in this world; and the ground which produces the materials, is scarce to be reckoned in, as any, or, at most, but a very small part of it: so little, that even amongst us, land that is left wholly to nature, that hath no improvement of pasturage, tillage, or planting, is called, as indeed it is, *waste*; and we shall find the benefit of it amount to little more than nothing.

This shews how much numbers of men are to be preferred to largeness of dominions; and that the increase of lands, and the right of employing of them, is the great art of government; and that prince, who shall be so wise and godlike, as by established laws of liberty to secure protection and encouragement to the honest industry of mankind, against the oppression of power and narrowness of party, will quickly be too hard for his neighbours; but this by the by. To return to the argument in hand.

43. An acre of land, that bears here twenty bushels of wheat, and another in America, which, with the same husbandry, would do the like, are, without doubt, of the same natural intrinsic value: but yet the benefit mankind receives from the one in a year, is worth £5 and from the other possibly not worth a penny, if all the profit an Indian received from it were to be valued, and sold here; at least, I may truly say, not one thousandth. It is *labour* then which *puts the greatest part of the value upon land*, without which it would scarcely be worth any thing; it is to that we owe the greatest part of all its useful products; for all that the straw, bran, bread, of that acre of wheat, is more worth than the product of an acre of as good land, which lies waste, is all the effect of labour. For it is not barely the ploughman's pains, the reaper's and thresher's toil, and the baker's sweat is to be counted into the *bread* we eat, the labour of those who broke the oxen, who digged and wrought the iron and stones, who felled and framed the timber employed about the plough, mill, oven, or any other utensils, which are a vast number requisite to this corn, from its being seed to be sown, to its being made bread, must all be *charged on* the account of *labour*, and received as an effect of that: nature and the earth furnished only the almost worthless materials, as in themselves. It would be a strange *catalogue of things, that industry provided and made use of, about every loaf of bread*, before it came to our use, if we could trace them; iron, wood, leather, bark, timber, stone, bricks, coals, lime, cloth, dying drugs, pitch, tar, masts, ropes, and all the materials made use of in the ship, that brought any of the commodities made use of by any of the workmen, to any part of the work, all which it would be almost impossible, at least too long, to reckon up.

44. From all which it is evident, that though the things of nature are given in common yet man, by being master of himself, and *proprietor of his own person, and the actions or labour of it, had still in himself the great foundation of property;* and that which made up the great part of what he applied to the support or comfort of his being, when invention and arts had improved the conveniencies of life, was perfectly his own, and did not belong in common to others.

45. Thus *labour*, in the beginning, *gave a right of property*, wherever any one was pleased to employ it upon what was common, which remained a long while the far greater part, and is yet more than mankind makes use of. Men, at first, for the most part, contented themselves with what unassisted nature offered to their necessities: and though afterwards, in some parts of the world, (where the increase of people and stock, with the *use of money*, had made land scarce, and so of some value) the several *communities* settled the bounds of their distinct territories, and by laws within themselves regulated the properties of the private men of their society, and so, by *compact* and agreement, *settled the property* which labour and industry began; and the leagues that have been made between several states and kingdoms, either expressly or tacitly disowning all claim and right to the land in the others possession, have by common consent, given up their pretences to their natural common right, which originally they had to those countries, and so have, by *positive agreement, settled a property* amongst themselves, in distinct parts and parcels of the earth; yet there are still *great tracts of ground* to be found, which (the inhabitants thereof not having joined with the rest of mankind, in the consent of the use of their common money) *lie waste*, and are more than the people who dwell on it do, or can make use of, and so still lie in common. Though this can scarce happen amongst that part of mankind that have consented to the use of money.

46. The greatest part of *things really useful* to the life of man, and such as the necessity of subsisting made the first commoners of the world look after, as it doth the Americans now, *are* generally things of *short duration;* such as, if they are not consumed by use, will decay and perish of themselves: gold, silver, and diamonds, are things that fancy or agreement hath put the value on, more than real use, and the necessary support of life. Now of those good things which nature hath provided in common, every one had a right, (as hath been said) to as much as he could use, and property in all that he could affect with his labour; all that his *industry* could extend to, to alter from the state nature had put it in, was his. He that *gathered* a hundred bushels of acorns or apples, had thereby a *property* in them, they were his goods as soon as gathered. He was only to look, that he used them before they spoiled, else he took more than his share, and robbed others. And indeed it was a foolish thing, as well as dishonest, to hoard up more than he could make use of. If he gave away a part to any body else, so that it perished not uselessly in his possession, these he also made use of. And if he also bartered away plums, that would have rotted in a week, for nuts that would last good for his eating a whole year, he did no injury; he wasted not the common stock; destroyed no part of the portion of goods that belonged to others, so long as nothing perished uselessly in his hands. Again, if he would give his nuts for a piece of metal, pleased with its colour; or exchange his sheep for shells, or wool for a sparkling pebble or a diamond, and keep those by him all his life, he invaded not the right of others, he might heap up as much of these durable things as he pleased; the *exceeding of the bounds of* his *just property* not lying in the largeness of his possession, but the perishing of any thing uselessly in it.

47. And thus *came in the use of money*, some lasting thing that men might keep without spoiling, and that by mutual consent men would take in exchange for the truly useful, but perishable supports of life.

48. And as different degrees of industry were apt to give men possessions in different proportions, so this *invention of money* gave them the opportunity to continue and enlarge them. For supposing an island, separate from all possible commerce with the rest of the world, wherein there were but an hundred families, but there were sheep, horses, and cows, with other useful animals, wholesome fruits, and land enough for corn for a hundred thousand times as many, but nothing in the island, either because of its commonness, or perishableness, fit to supply the place of *money:* What reason could any one have there to enlarge his possessions beyond the use of his family and a plentiful supply to its *consumption*, either in what their own industry produced, or they could barter for like perishable, useful commodities with others? Where there is not something, both lasting and scarce, and so valuable to be hoarded up, there men will not be apt to enlarge their *possessions of land*, were it never so rich, never so free for them to take. For I ask, what would a man value ten thousand, or an hundred thousand acres of excellent *land*, ready cultivated and well stocked too with cattle, in the middle of the inland parts of America, where he had no hopes of commerce with other parts of the world, to draw *money* to him by the sale of the product? It would not be worth the enclosing, and we should see him give up again to the wild common of nature, whatever was more than would supply the conveniencies of life to be had there for him and his family.

49. Thus in the beginning all the world was America, and more so than that is now; for no such thing as *money* was any where known. Find out something that hath the *use and value of money* amongst his neighbours, you shall see the same man will begin presently to *enlarge* his possessions.

50. But since gold and silver, being little useful to the life of man in proportion to food, raiment, and carriage, has its *value* only from the consent of men, whereof *labour* yet *makes*, in great part, the *measure*, it is plain, that men have agreed to a disproportionate and unequal *possession of the earth*, they having, by a tacit and voluntary consent, found out a way how a man may fairly possess more land than he himself can use the product of, by receiving in exchange for the overplus, gold and silver, which may be hoarded up without injury to any one; these metals not spoiling or decaying in the hands of the possessor. This partage of things in an inequality of private possessions, men have made practicable out of the bounds of society, and without compact, only by putting a value on gold and silver, and tacitly agreeing in the use of money. For in governments, the laws regulate the right of property, and the possession of land is determined by positive constitutions.

51. And thus, I think, it is very easy to conceive, without any difficulty *how labour could at first begin a title of property* in the common things of nature, and how the spending it upon our uses bounded it. So that there could then be no reason of quarrelling about title, nor any doubt about the largeness of possession it gave. Right and conveniency went together; for as a man had a right to all he could employ his labour upon, so he had no temptation to labour for more than he could make use of. This left no room for controversy about the title, nor for encroachment on the right of others; what portion a man carved to himself, was easily seen; and it was useless, as well as dishonest, to carve himself too much, or take more than he needed.

Chapter VII

Of Political or Civil Society

77. God having made man such a creature, that in his own judgment, it was not good for him to be alone, put him under strong obligations of necessity, convenience, and inclination, to drive him into society, as well as fitted him with understanding and language to continue and enjoy it. The first society was between man and wife, which gave beginning to that between parents and children; to which, in time, that between master and servant came to be added; and though all these might, and commonly did meet together, and make up but one family, wherein the master or mistress of it had some sort of rule proper to a family; each of these, or all together, came short of *political society*, as we shall see, if we consider the different ends, ties, and bounds of each of these. . . .

87. Man being born, as has been proved, with a title to perfect freedom, and an uncontrolled enjoyment of all the rights and privileges of the law of nature, equally with any other man, or number of men in the world, hath by nature a power, not only to preserve his property, that is, his life, liberty, and estate, against the injuries and attempts of other men; but to judge of and punish the breaches of that law in others, as he is persuaded the offence deserves, even with death itself, in crimes where the heinousness of the fact, in his opinion, requires it. But because no *political* society can be, nor subsist, without having in itself the power to preserve the property, and, in order thereunto, punish the offences of all those of that society; there and there only is *political society*, where every one of the members hath quitted his natural power, resigned it up into the hands of the community in all cases that excludes him not from appealing for protection to the law established by it. And thus all private judgment of every particular member being excluded, the community comes to be umpire by settled standing rules, indifferent, and the same to all parties; and by men having authority from the community, for the execution of those rules, decides all the differences that may happen between any members of that society concerning any matter of right; and punishes those offences which any member hath committed against the society, with such penalties as the law has established, whereby it is easy to discern, who are, and who are not, in *political society* together. Those who are united into one body, and have a common established law and judicature to appeal to, with authority to decide controversies between them, and punish offenders, *are in civil society* one with another: but those who have no such common appeal, I mean on earth, are still in the state of nature, each being, where there is no other, judge for himself, and executioner: which is, as I have before shewed, the perfect *state of nature.*

88. And thus the commonwealth comes by a power to set down what punishment shall belong to the several transgressions which they think worthy of it, committed amongst the members of that society, (which is the *power of making laws*) as well as it has the power to punish any injury done unto any of its members, by any one that is not of it, (which is the power of war and peace,) and all this for the preservation of the property of all the members of that society, as far as is possible. But though every man who has entered into civil society, and is become a member of any commonwealth, has thereby quitted his power to punish offences against the law of nature, in prosecution of his own private judgment; yet with the judgment of offences, which he has given up to the legislative in all cases, where he can appeal to the magistrate, he has given a right to the commonwealth to employ his force, for the execution of the judgments of the commonwealth whenever he shall be called to it; which indeed are his own judgments, they being made by himself, or his representative. And herein we have the original of the legislative and executive power of civil society, which is to judge by standing laws, how far offences are to be punished, when committed within the commonwealth; and also to determine, by occasional judgments founded on the present circumstances of the fact, how far injuries from without are to be vindicated; and in both these to employ all the force of all the members, when there shall be need.

89. Whenever therefore any number of men are so united into one society, as to quit every one his executive power of the law of nature, and to resign it to the public, there and there only is a political, or civil society. And this is done, wherever any number of men, in the state of nature, enter into society to make one people, one body politic, under one supreme government; or else when any one joins himself to, and incorporates with any government already made. For hereby he authorizes the society, or, which is all one, the legislative thereof, to make laws for him, as the public good of the society shall require; to the execution whereof, his own assistance (as to his own degrees) is due. And this puts men out of a state of nature into that of a commonwealth, by setting up a judge on earth, with authority to determine all the controversies, and redress the injuries that may happen to any member of the commonwealth: which judge is the legislative, or magistrate appointed by it. And wherever there are any number of men, however associated, that have no such decisive power to appeal to, there they are still in the state of nature.

90. Hence it is evident, that absolute monarchy, which by some men is counted the only government in the world, is indeed inconsistent with civil society, and so can be no form of civil government at all; for the end of civil society being to avoid and remedy these inconveniencies of the state of nature, which necessarily follow from every man's being judge in his own case, by setting up a known authority, to which every one of that society may appeal upon any injury received, or controversy that may arise, and which every one of the society ought to obey; wherever any persons are, who have not such an authority to appeal to for the decision of any difference between them, there those persons are still *in the state of nature*. And so is every *absolute prince*, in respect of those who are under his dominion.

91. For he being supposed to have all, both legislative and executive power in himself alone, there is no judge to be found, no appeal lies open to any one, who may fairly, and indifferently, and with authority decide, and from whose decision relief and redress may be expected of any injury or inconveniency that may be suffered from the prince, or by his order: so that such a man, however intitled, *czar*, or *grand seignior*, or how you please, is as much *in the state of nature*, with all under his dominion, as he is with the rest of mankind. For wherever any two men are, who have no standing rule, and common judge to appeal to on earth, for the determination of controversies of right betwixt them, there they are still *in the state of nature*, and under all the inconveniencies of it, with only this woful difference to the subject, or rather slave of an absolute prince; that whereas in the ordinary state of nature he has a liberty to judge of his right, and, according to the best of his power, to maintain it; now, whenever his property is invaded by the will and order of his monarch, he has not only no appeal, as those in society ought to have, but, as if he were degraded from the common state of rational creatures, is denied a liberty to judge of, or to defend his right; and so is exposed to all the misery and inconveniencies that a man can fear from one, who being in the unrestrained state of nature, is yet corrupted with flattery, and armed with power.

92. For he that thinks *absolute power purifies men's blood*, and corrects the baseness of human nature, need read but the history of this or any other age, to be convinced of the contrary. He that would have been so insolent and injurious in the woods of America, would not probably be much better in a throne; where perhaps learning and religion shall be found out to justify all that he shall do to his subjects, and the sword presently silence all those that dare question it. For what the *protection of absolute monarchy* is, what kind of fathers of their countries it makes princes to be, and to what a degree of happiness and security it carries civil society, where this sort of government is grown to perfection; he that will look into the late relation of Ceylon, may easily see.

93. *In absolute monarchies*, indeed, as well as other governments of the world, the subjects have an appeal to the law, and judges to decide any controversies, and restrain any violence that may happen betwixt the subjects themselves, one amongst another. This every one thinks necessary, and believes he deserves to be thought a declared enemy to society and mankind, who should go about to take it away. But whether this be from a true love of mankind and society, and such a charity as we all owe one to another, there is reason to doubt. For this is no more than what every man, who loves his own power, profit, or greatness, may and naturally must do, keep those animals from hurting, or destroying one another, who labour and drudge only for his pleasure and advantage; and so are taken care of, not out of any love the master has for them, but love of himself, and the profit they bring him. For if it be asked, what security, what fence is there, in such a state, *against the violence and oppression of this absolute ruler?* the very question can scarce be borne. They are ready to tell you, that it deserves death only to ask after safety. Betwixt subject and subject, they will grant, there must be measures, laws, and judges, for their mutual peace and security: but as for the ruler he ought to be *absolute,* and is above all such circumstances; because he has power to do more hurt and wrong, it is right when he does it. To ask how you may be guarded from harm, or injury, on that side where the strongest hand is to do it, is presently the voice of faction and rebellion: as if when men quitting the state of nature entered into society, they agreed that all of them but one should be under the restraint of laws, but that he should still retain all the liberty of the state of nature, increased with power, and made licentious by impunity. This is to think, that men are so foolish, that they take care to avoid what mischiefs may be done them by *pole cats,* or *foxes;* but are content, nay think it safety, to be devoured by *lions.*

94. But whatever flatterers may talk to amuse people's understandings, it hinders not men from feeling; and when they perceive, that any man, in what station soever, is out of the bounds of the civil society which they are of, and that they have no appeal on earth against any harm they may receive from him, they are apt to think themselves in the state of nature, in respect of him whom they find to be so: and to take care, as soon as they can, to have that *safety and security in civil society,* for which it was instituted, and for which only they entered into it. And therefore, though perhaps at first, (as shall be shewed more at large hereafter in the following part of this discourse) some one good and excellent man having got a pre-eminency amongst the rest, had this deference paid to his goodness and virtue, as to a kind of natural authority, that the chief rule, with arbitration of their differences, by a tacit consent devolved into his hands, without any other caution, but the assurance they had of his uprightness and wisdom; yet when time, giving authority, and (as some men would persuade us) sacredness to customs, which the negligent and unforeseen innocence of the first ages began, had brought in successors of another stamp, the people finding their properties not secure under the government, as then it was, (whereas government has no other end but the preservation of property) could never be safe nor at rest, *nor think themselves in civil society,* till the legislature was placed in collective bodies of men, call them senate, parliament, or what you please. By which means every single person became subject, equally with other the meanest men, to those laws, which he himself, as part of the legislative, had established; nor could any one, by his own authority, avoid the force of the law, when once made; nor by any pretence of superiority plead exemption, thereby to license his own, or the miscarriages of any of his dependents. *No man in civil society can be exempted from the laws of it.* For if any man may do what he thinks fit, and there be no appeal on earth, for redress or security against any harm he shall do; I ask, whether he be not perfectly still in the state of nature, and so can be *no part or member of that civil society:* unless any one will say, the state of nature and civil society are one and the same thing, which I have never yet found any one so great a patron of anarchy as to affirm.

Chapter VIII

Of the Beginning of Political Societies

95. Men being, as has been said, by nature, all free, equal, and independent, no one can be put out of this estate, and subjected to the political power of another, without his own consent. The only way, whereby any one divests himself of his natural liberty, and puts on the *bonds of civil society,* is by agreeing with other men to join and unite into a community, for their comfortable, safe, and peaceable living one amongst another, in a secure enjoyment of their properties, and a greater security against any, that are not of it. This any number of men may do, because it injures not the freedom of the rest; they are left as they were in the liberty of the state of nature. When any number of men have so *consented to make one community or government,* they are thereby presently incorporated, and make *one body politic,* wherein the *majority* have a right to act and conclude the rest.

96. For when any number of men have, by the consent of every individual, made a *community,* they have thereby made that *community* one body, with a power to act as one body, which is only by the will and determination of the majority. For that which acts any community, being only the *consent* of the individuals of it, and it being necessary to that which is one body to move one way; it is necessary the body should move that way whither the greater force carries it, which is the *consent of the majority:* or else it is impossible it should act or continue one body, one community, which the consent of every individual that united into it, agreed that it should; and so every one is bound by that consent to be concluded by the majority. And therefore we see, that in assemblies, impowered to act by positive laws, where no number is set by that positive law which impowers them, the *act of the majority* passes for the act of the whole, and of course determines, as having, by the law of nature and reason, the power of the whole.

97. And thus every man, by consenting with others to make one body politic under one government, puts himself under an obligation, to every one of that society, to submit to the determination of the majority, and to be concluded by it; or else this *original compact,* whereby he with others incorporate into one society, would signify nothing, and be no compact, if he be left free, and under no other ties than he was in before in the state of nature. For what appearance would there be of any compact? What new engagement if he were no farther tied by any decrees of the society, than he himself thought fit, and did actually consent to? This would be still as great a liberty, as he himself had before his compact, or any one else in the state of nature hath, who may submit himself, and consent to any acts of it if he thinks fit.

98. For if *the consent of the majority* shall not, in reason, be received as *the act of the whole,* and conclude every individual; nothing but the consent of every individual can make any thing to be the act of the whole: But such a consent is next to impossible ever to be had, if we consider the infirmities of health, and avocations of business, which in a number, though much less than that of a commonwealth, will necessarily keep many away from the public assembly. To which if we add the variety of opinions, and contrariety of interests, which unavoidably happen in all collections of men, the coming into society upon such terms would be only like Cato's coming into the theatre, only to go out again. Such a constitution as this would make the mighty *leviathan* of a shorter duration, than the feeblest creatures, and not let it outlast the day it was born in: which cannot be supposed, till we can think, that rational creatures should desire and constitute societies only to be dissolved. For where the majority cannot conclude the rest, there they cannot act as one body, and consequently will be immediately dissolved again.

99. Whosoever therefore out of a state of nature unite into a community, must be understood to give up all the power, necessary to the ends for which they unite into society, to the majority of the community, unless they expressly agreed in any number greater than the majority. And this is done by barely agreeing to *unite into one political society*, which is *all the compact* that is, or needs be, between the individuals, that enter into, or make up a commonwealth. And thus that, which begins and actually *constitutes any political society*, is nothing, but the consent of any number of freemen capable of a majority, to unite and incorporate into such a society. And this is that, and that only, which did, or could give beginning to any lawful government in the world.

100. To this I find two objections made.

First, *That there are no instances to be found in story, of a company of men independent and equal one amongst another, that met together, and in this way began and set up a government.*

Secondly, *It is impossible of right, that men should do so, because all men being born under government, they are to submit to that, and are not at liberty to begin a new one.*

101. To the first there is this to answer, That it is not at all to be wondered, that *history* gives us but a very little account of *men, that lived together in the state of nature.* The inconveniencies of that condition and the love and want of society, no sooner brought any number of them together, but they presently united and incorporated, if they designed to continue together. And if we may not suppose men ever to have been *in the state of nature*, because we hear not much of them in such a state, we may as well suppose the armies of Salmanasser or Xerxes were never children, because we hear little of them, till they were men, and embodied in armies. Government is every where antecedent to records, and letters seldom come in amongst a people till a long continuation of civil society has, by other more necessary arts, provided for their safety, ease, and plenty. And then they begin to look after the history of their founders, and search into their original, when they have outlived the memory of it. For it is with commonwealths, as with particular persons, they are commonly *ignorant of their own births and infancies:* and if they know any thing of their original, they are beholden for it to the accidental records that others have kept of it. And those that we have of the beginning of any politics in the world, excepting that of the Jews, where God himself immediately interposed, and which favours not at all paternal dominion, are all either plain instances of such a beginning as I have mentioned, or at least have manifest footsteps of it.

102. He must shew a strange inclination to deny evident matter of fact, when it agrees not with his hypothesis, who will not allow, that the *beginning* of Rome and Venice were by the uniting together of several men free and independent one of another, amongst whom there was no natural superiority or subjection. And if Josephus Acosta's word may be taken, he tells us, that in many parts of America there was no government at all. "There are great and apparent conjectures," says he, "that these men, speaking of those of Peru, for a long time had neither kings nor commonwealths, but lived in troops, as they do this day in Florida, the Cheriquanas, those of Brasil, and many other nations, which have no certain kings, but as occasion is offered, in peace or war, they choose their captains as they please." If it be said, that every man there was born subject to his father, or the head of his family. That the subjection due from a child to a father took not away his freedom of uniting into what political society he thought fit, has been already proved. But be that as it will, these men, it is evident, were actually free; and whatever superiority some politicians now would place in any of them, they themselves claimed it not, but by consent were all equal, till by the same consent they set rulers over themselves. So that their politic societies all began from a voluntary union, and the mutual agreement of men freely acting in the choice of their governors, and forms of government.

103. And I hope those who went away from Sparta with Palantus, mentioned by Justin, will be allowed to have been freemen, *independent* one of another, and to have set up a government over themselves, by their own consent. Thus I have given several examples out of history, of *people free and in the state of nature*, that being met together, incorporated and *began a commonwealth*. And if the want of such instances be an argument to prove that governments were not, nor could not be so begun, I suppose the contenders for paternal empire were better let it alone, than urge it against natural liberty. For if they can give so many instances out of history, of governments begun upon paternal right, I think (though at best an argument from what has been to what should of right be, has no great force) one might, without any great danger, yield them the cause. But if I might advise them in the case, they would do well not to search too much into the *original of governments*, as they have begun *de facto*, lest they should find, at the foundation of most of them, something very little favourable to the design they promote, and such a power as they contend for.

104. But to conclude, reason being plain on our side, that men are naturally free, and the examples of history shewing, that the governments of the world, that were begun in peace, had their beginning laid on that foundation, and were *made by the consent of the people;* there can be little room for doubt, either where the right is, or what has been the opinion, or practice of mankind, about the *first erecting of governments*.

105. I will not deny, that if we look back as far as history will direct us, towards the *original of commonwealths*, we shall generally find them under the government and administration of one man. And I am also apt to believe, that where a family was numerous enough to subsist by itself, and continued entire together, without mixing with others, as it often happens, where there is much land, and few people, the government commonly began *in the father.* For the father having, by the law of nature, the same power with every man else to punish, as he thought fit, any offences against that law, might thereby punish his transgressing children, even when they were men, and out of their pupilage; and they were very likely to submit to his punishment, and all join with him against the offender, in their turns, giving him thereby power to execute his sentence against any transgression, and so in effect make him the law maker, and governour over all that remained in conjunction with his family. He was fittest to be trusted; paternal affection secured their property and interest under his care; and the custom of obeying him, in their childhood, made it easier to submit to him, rather than to any other. If, therefore, they must have one to rule them, as government is hardly to be avoided amongst men that live together; who so likely to be the man as he that was their common father; unless negligence, cruelty, or any other defect of mind or body made him unfit for it? But when either the father died, and left his next heir, for want of age, wisdom, courage, or any other qualities, less fit for rule; or where several families met, and consented to continue together; there, it is not to be doubted, but they used their natural freedom to set up him whom they judged the ablest, and most likely to rule well over them. Conformable hereunto we find the people of America, who (living out of the reach of the conquering swords, and spreading domination of the two great empires of Peru and Mexico) enjoyed their own natural freedom, though, *caeteris paribus*, they commonly prefer the heir of their deceased king; yet, if they find him any way weak, or incapable, they pass him by, and set up the stoutest and bravest man for their ruler.

106. Thus, though looking back as far as records give us any account of peopling the world, and the history of nations, we commonly find the government to be in one hand; yet it destroys not that which I affirm, viz. that the *beginning of politic society* depends upon the consent of the individuals, to join into, and make one society; who, when they are thus incorporated, might set up what form of government they thought fit. But this having given occasion to men to mistake, and think, that by nature government was monarchical, and belonged to the father; it may not be amiss here to consider, why people in the beginning generally pitched upon this form; which though perhaps the father's pre-eminency might, in the first institution of some commonwealth give rise to, and place in the beginning the power in one hand; yet it is plain that the reason, that continued the form of *government in a single person*, was not any regard or respect to paternal authority; since all petty monarchies, that is, almost all monarchies, near their original, have been commonly, at least upon occasion, *elective*.

107. First then, in the beginning of things, the father's government of the childhood of those sprung from him, having accustomed them to the *rule of one man*, and taught them that where it was exercised with care and skill, with affection and love to those under it, it was sufficient to procure and preserve to men all the political happiness they sought for in society. It was no wonder that they should pitch upon, and naturally run into that form of government, which from their infancy they had been all accustomed to; and which, by experience, they had found both easy and safe. To which, if we add, that monarchy being simple, and most obvious to men, whom neither experience had instructed in forms of government, nor the ambition or insolence of empire had taught to beware of the encroachments of prerogative, or the inconveniencies of absolute power, which monarchy in succession was apt to lay claim to, and bring upon them; it was not at all strange, that they should not much trouble themselves to think of methods of restraining any exorbitancies of those to whom they had given the authority over them, and of balancing the power of government, by placing several parts of it in different hands. They had neither felt the oppression of tyrannical dominion, nor did the fashion of the age, nor their possessions, or way of living, (which afforded little matter for covetousness or ambition) give them any reason to apprehend or provide against it; and therefore it is no wonder they put themselves into such a *frame of government,* as was not only, as I said, most obvious and simple, but also best suited to their present state and condition; which stood more in need of defence against foreign invasions and injuries, than of multiplicity of laws. The equality of a simple poor way of living, confining their desires within the narrow bounds of each man's small property, made few controversies, and so no need of many laws to decide them, or variety of officers to superintend the process, or look after the execution of justice, where there were but few trespasses, and few offenders. Since then those, who liked one another so well as to join into society, cannot but be supposed to have some acquaintance and friendship together, and some trust one in another; they could not but have greater apprehensions of others, than of one another: and therefore their first care and thought cannot but be supposed to be, how to secure themselves against foreign force. It was natural for them to put themselves under a *frame of government* which might best serve to that end, and choose the wisest and bravest man to conduct them in their wars, and lead them out against their enemies, and in this chiefly be their *ruler.*

108. Thus we see, that the *kings* of the Indians in America, which is still a pattern of the first ages in Asia and Europe, whilst the inhabitants were too few for the country, and want of people and money gave men no temptation to enlarge their possessions of land, or contest for wider extent of ground, are little more than *generals of their armies;* and though they command absolutely in war, yet at home and in time of peace they exercise very little dominion, and have but a very moderate sovereignty; the resolutions of peace and war being ordinarily either in the people, or in a council. Though the war itself, which admits not of plurality of governors, naturally devolves the command into the *king's sole authority.*

109. And thus, in Israel itself, the *chief business of their judges, and first kings,* seems to have been *to be captains in war,* and leaders of their armies; which (besides what is signified by *going out and in before the people,* which was to march forth to war, and home again at the heads of their forces) appears plainly in the story of Jephthah. The Ammonites making war upon Israel, the Gileadites in fear sent to Jephthah, a bastard of their family whom they had cast off, and article with him, if he will assist them against the Ammonites, to make him their ruler; which they do in these words, "And the people made him head and captain over them," which was, as it seems, all one as to be judge. "And he judged Israel," that is, was their captain-general, *six years.* So when Jotham upbraids the Shechemites with the obligation they had to Gideon, who had been their judge and ruler, he tells them, "He fought for you, and adventured his life far, and delivered you out of the hands of Midian." Nothing is mentioned of him, but what he did as a *general:* and indeed that is all is found in his history, or in any of the rest of the judges. And Abimelech particularly is called *king,* though at most he was but their *general.* And when, being weary of the ill conduct of Samuel's sons, the children of Israel desired a king, "like all the nations, to judge them, and to go out before them, and to fight their battles." God granting their desire, says to Samuel. "I will send thee a man, and thou shalt anoint him to be captain over my people Israel, that he may save my people out of the hands of the Philistines." As if the only *business of a king* had been to lead out their armies, and fight in their defence; and accordingly at his inauguration, pouring a vial of oil upon him, declares to Saul, that "the Lord had anointed him to be captain over his inheritance." And therefore those who, after Saul's being solemnly chosen and saluted *king* by the *tribes* of Mispah, were unwilling to have him their king, made no other objection but this, "How shall this man save us?" as if they should have said, this man is unfit to be our *king*, not having skill and conduct enough in war to be able to defend us. And when God resolved to transfer the government to David, it is in these words, "But now thy kingdom shall not continue: the Lord hath sought him a man after his own heart, and the Lord hath commanded him to be captain over his people." As if the whole kingly authority were nothing else but to be their general: and therefore the tribes who had stuck to Saul's family, and opposed David's reign, when they came to Hebron with terms of submission to him, they tell him, amongst other arguments, they had to submit to him as their king, that he was in effect their king in Saul's time, and therefore they had no reason but to receive him as their king now. "Also" (say they,) "in time past, when Saul was king over us, thou wast he that leddest out, and broughtest in Israel, and the Lord said unto thee, Thou shalt feed my people Israel, and thou shalt be a captain over Israel."

110. Thus, whether a family by degrees *grew up into a commonwealth*, and the fatherly authority being continued on to the elder son, every one in his turn growing up under it, tacitly submitted to it; and the easiness and equality of it not offending any one, every one acquiesced, till time seemed to have confirmed it, and settled a right of succession by prescription: or whether several families, or the descendants of several families, whom chance, neighbourhood, or business brought together, *uniting into society*, the need of a general, whose conduct might defend them against their enemies in war, and the great confidence the innocence and sincerity of that poor but virtuous age (such as are almost all those which begin governments, that ever come to last in the world), gave men of one another, made the first beginners of commonwealths generally put the rule into one man's hand, without any other express limitation or restraint, but what the nature of the thing and the end of government required: Whichever of those it was that at first put the rule into the hands of a single person, certain it is that no body was entrusted with it but for the public good and safety, and to those ends, in the infancies of commonwealths, those who had it, commonly used it. And unless they had done so, young societies could not have subsisted; without such nursing fathers tender and careful of the public weal, all governments would have sunk under the weakness and infirmities of their infancy, and the prince and the people had soon perished together.

111. But though the *golden age* (before vain ambition, and *amor sceleratus habendi*, evil concupiscence, had corrupted men's minds into a mistake of true power and honour) had more virtue, and consequently better governors, as well as less vicious subjects; and there was then *no stretching prerogative* on the one side, to oppress the people; nor consequently on the other, any *dispute about privilege*, to lessen or restrain the power of the magistrate; and so no contest betwixt rulers and people about governors or government: yet when ambition and luxury in future ages would retain and increase the power, without doing the business for which it was given; and, aided by flattery, taught princes to have distinct and separate interests from their people; men found it necessary to examine more carefully the original and rights of government, and to find out ways to *restrain the exorbitancies*, and prevent the abuses of that power, which they having entrusted in another's hands only for their own good, they found was made use of to hurt them.

112. Thus we may see how probable it is, that people that were naturally free, and by their own consent either submitted to the government of their father, or united together out of different families to make a government, should generally put the *rule into one man's hands*, and choose to be under the conduct of a single person, without so much as by express conditions limiting or regulating his power, which they thought safe enough in his honesty and prudence. Though they never dreamed of monarchy being *jure divino*, which we never heard of among mankind, till it was revealed to us by the divinity of this last age; nor ever allowed paternal power to have a right to dominion, or to be the foundation of all government. And thus much may suffice to shew, that, as far as we have any light from history, we have reason to conclude, that all peaceful beginnings of government have been *laid in the consent of the people*. I say peaceful, because I shall have occasion in another place to speak of conquest, which some esteem a way of beginning of governments.

The other objection I find urged against the beginning of polities, in the way I have mentioned, is this, viz.

113. *That all men being born under government, some or other, it is impossible any of them should ever be free, and at liberty to unite together, and begin a new one, or ever be able to erect a lawful government.*

If this argument be good, I ask, how came so many lawful monarchies into the world? for if any body, upon this supposition, can shew me any one man in any age of the world free to begin a lawful monarchy, I will be bound to shew him ten other *free men* at liberty at the same time to unite and begin a new government under a regal or any other form. It being demonstration, that if any one, *born under the dominion* of another, may be so free as to have a right to command others in a new and distinct empire, every one that is *born under the dominion* of another may be so free too, and may become a ruler, or subject of a distinct separate government. And so by this their own principle, either all men, however born, are free, or else there is but one lawful prince, one lawful government in the world. And then they have nothing to do, but barely to shew us which that is; which when they have done, I doubt not but all mankind will easily agree to pay obedience to him.

114. Though it be a sufficient answer to their objection, to shew that it involves them in the same difficulties that it doth those they use it against; yet I shall endeavour to discover the weakness of this argument a little farther.

"All men," say they, "are born under government, and therefore they cannot be at liberty to begin a new one. Every one is born a subject to his father, or his prince, and is therefore under the perpetual tie of subjection and allegiance." It is plain mankind never owned nor considered any such natural *subjection that they were born in*, to one or to the other, that tied them, without their own consents, to a subjection to them and their heirs.

115. For there are no examples so frequent in history, both sacred and profane, as those of men withdrawing themselves, and their obedience from the jurisdiction they were born under, and the family or community they were bred up in, and *setting up new governments* in other places, from whence sprang all that number of petty commonwealths in the beginning of ages, and which always multiplied as long as there was room enough, till the stronger, or more fortunate, swallowed the weaker; and those great ones again breaking to pieces, dissolved into lesser dominions. All which are so many testimonies against paternal sovereignty, and plainly prove, that it was not the natural right of the father descending to his heirs, that made governments in the beginning, since it was impossible, upon that ground, there should have been so many little kingdoms; all must have been but only one universal monarchy, if men had not been *at liberty to separate themselves* from their families, and the government, be it what it will, that was set up in it, and go and make distinct commonwealths and other governments, as they thought fit.

116. This has been the practice of the world from its first beginning to this day; nor is it now any more hindrance to the freedom of mankind, that they are *born under constituted and ancient polities,* that have established laws, and set forms of government, than if they were born in the woods, amongst the unconfined inhabitants, that run loose in them. For those who would persuade us, that, *by being born under any government, we are naturally subjects to it,* and have no more any title or pretence to the freedom of the state of nature; have no other reason (bating that of paternal power, which we have already answered) to produce for it, but only, because our fathers or progenitors passed away their natural liberty, and thereby bound up themselves and their posterity to a perpetual subjection to the government which they themselves submitted to. It is true, that whatever engagements or promises any one has made for himself, he is under the obligation of them, but cannot, by any compact whatsoever, bind his children or posterity. For his son, when a man, being altogether as free as the father, any *act of the father can no more give away the liberty of the son,* than it can of any body else: he may indeed annex such conditions to the land he enjoyed as a subject of any commonwealth, as may oblige his son to be of that community, if he will enjoy those possessions which were his father's; because that estate being his father's property, he may dispose, or settle it, as he pleases.

117. And this has generally given the occasion to mistake in this matter; because commonwealths not permitting any part of their dominions to be dismembered, nor to be enjoyed by any but those of their community, the son cannot ordinarily enjoy the possessions of his father, but under the same terms his father did, by becoming a member of the society; whereby he puts himself presently under the government he finds there established, as much as any other subject of that commonwealth. And thus *the consent of freemen, born under government, which only makes them members of it,* being given separately in their turns, as each comes to be of age, and not in a multitude together; people take no notice of it, and thinking it not done at all, or not necessary, conclude they are naturally subjects as they are men.

118. But, it is plain, governments themselves understand it otherwise; they claim *no power over the son, because of that they had over the father;* nor look on children as being their subjects, by their fathers being so. If a subject of England have a child, by an English woman in France, whose subject is he? Not the king of England's; for he must have leave to be admitted to the privileges of it. Nor the king of France's: for how then has his father a liberty to bring him away, and breed him as he pleases? And who ever was judged as a traitor or deserter, if he left, or warred against a country, for being barely born in it of parents that were aliens there? It is plain then, by the practice of governments themselves, as well as by the law of right reasons, that *a child is born a subject of no country or government.* He is under his father's tuition and authority, till he comes to age of discretion; and then he is a freeman, at liberty what government he will put himself under, what body politic he will unite himself to. For if an Englishman's son, born in France, be at liberty, and may do so, it is evident there is no tie upon him by his father's being a subject of this kingdom; nor is he bound up by any compact of his ancestors. And why then hath not his son, by the same reason, the same liberty, though he be born any where else? Since the power that a father hath naturally over his children is the same, wherever they be born, and the ties of natural obligations are not bounded by the positive limits of kingdoms and commonwealths.

119. Every man being, as has been shewed, naturally free, and nothing being able to put him into subjection to any earthly power, but only his own consent; it is to be considered, what shall be understood to be a *sufficient declaration of* a man's *consent, to make him subject* to the laws of any government. There is a common distinction of an express and a tacit consent, which will concern our present case. No body doubts but an express consent, of any man entering into any society, makes him a perfect member of that society, a subject of that government. The difficulty is, what ought to be looked upon as a *tacit consent,* and how far it binds, i.e. how far any one shall be looked on to have consented, and thereby submitted to any government, where he has made no expressions of it at all. And to this I say, that every man, that hath any possessions, or enjoyment of any part of the dominions of any government, doth thereby give his *tacit consent,* and is as far forth obliged to obedience to the laws of that government, during such enjoyment, as any one under it; whether this his possession be of land, to him and his heirs for ever, or a lodging only for a week; or whether it be barely travelling freely on the highway: and, in effect, it reaches as far as the very being of any one within the territories of that government.

120. To understand this the better, it is fit to consider, that every man, when he at first incorporates himself into any commonwealth, he, by his uniting himself thereunto, annexed also, and submits to the community, those possessions which he has, or shall acquire, that do not already belong to any other government. For it would be a direct contradiction, for any one to enter into society with others for the securing and regulating of property, and yet to suppose, his land, whose property is to be regulated by the laws of the society, should be exempt from the jurisdiction of that government, to which he himself, the proprietor of the land, is a subject. By the same act therefore, whereby any one unites his person, which was before free, to any commonwealth; by the same he unites his possessions, which were before free, to it also: and they become, both of them, person and possession, subject to the government and dominion of that commonwealth, as long as it hath a being. Whoever therefore, from thenceforth, by inheritance, purchase, permission, or otherways, *enjoys any part of the land* so annexed to, and under the government *of that commonwealth, must take it with the condition* it is under; that is, *of submitting to the government of the commonwealth,* under whose jurisdiction it is, as far forth as any subject of it.

121. But since the government has a direct jurisdiction only over the land, and reaches the possessor of it, (before he has actually incorporated himself in the society) only as he dwells upon, and enjoys that; the obligation any one is under, by virtue of such enjoyment, to *submit to the government, begins and ends with the enjoyment:* so that whenever the owner, who has given nothing but such a tacit consent to the government, will, by donation, sale, or otherwise, quit the said possession, he is at liberty to go and incorporate himself into any other commonwealth; or to agree with others to begin a new one, *in vacuis locis,* in any part of the world they can find free and unpossessed: whereas he, that has once, by actual agreement, and any express declaration, given his *consent* to be of any commonwealth, is perpetually and indispensably obliged to be, and remain unalterably a subject to it, and can never be again in the liberty of the state of nature; unless, by any calamity, the government he was under comes to be dissolved, or else by some public act cuts him off from being any longer a member of it.

122. But submitting to the laws of any country, living quietly, and enjoying privileges and protection under them, *makes not a man a member of that society:* this is only a local protection and homage due to and from all those, who, not being in a state of war, come within the territories belonging to any government, to all parts whereof the force of its laws extends. But this no more *makes a man a member of that society,* a perpetual subject of that commonwealth, than it would make a man a subject to another, in whose family he found it convenient to abide for some time, though, whilst he continued in it, he were obliged to comply with the laws, and submit to the government he found there. And thus we see, that foreigners, by living all their lives under another government, and enjoying the privileges and protection of it, though they are bound, even in conscience, to submit to its administration, as far forth as any denison; yet do not thereby come to be *subjects or members of that commonwealth.* Nothing can make any man so, but his actually entering into it by positive engagement, and express promise and compact. This is that, which I think, concerning the beginning of political societies, and that *consent which makes any one a member of any commonwealth.*

Chapter IX

Of the Ends of Political Society and Government

123. If man in the state of nature be so free, as has been said; if he be absolute lord of his own person and possessions, equal to the greatest, and subject to no body, why will he part with his freedom? why will he give up this empire, and subject himself to the dominion and control of any other power? To which it is obvious to answer, that though in the state of nature he hath such a right, yet the enjoyment of it is very uncertain, and constantly exposed to the invasion of others. For all being kings as much as he, every man his equal, and the greater part no strict observers of equity and justice, the enjoyment of the property he has in this state is very unsafe, very unsecure. This makes him willing to quit this condition, which, however free, is full of fears and continual dangers: and it is not without reason, that he seeks out, and is willing to join in society with others, who are already united, or have a mind to unite, for the mutual preservation of their lives, liberties, and estates, which I call by the general name, property.

124. The great and *chief end*, therefore, of men's uniting into commonwealths, and putting themselves under government, *is the preservation of their property*. To which in the state of nature there are many things wanting.

First, There wants an established, settled, known law, received and allowed by common consent to be the standard of right and wrong, and the common measure to decide all controversies between them. For though the law of nature be plain and intelligible to all rational creatures; yet men being biassed by their interest, as well as ignorant for want of studying it, are not apt to allow of it as a law binding to them in the application of it to their particular cases.

125. Secondly, In the state of nature there wants *a known and indifferent judge*, with authority to determine all differences according to the established law. For every one in that state being both judge and executioner of the law of nature, men being partial to themselves, passion and revenge is very apt to carry them too far, and with too much heat, in their own cases; as well as negligence, and unconcernedness, to make them too remiss in other men's.

126. Thirdly, In the state of nature, there often wants power to back and support the sentence when right, and to give it due execution. They who by any injustice offended, will seldom fail, where they are able, by force to make good their injustice; such resistance many times makes the punishment dangerous, and frequently destructive, to those who attempt it.

127. Thus mankind, notwithstanding all the privileges of the state of nature, being but in an ill condition, while they remain in it, are quickly driven into society. Hence it comes to pass that we seldom find any number of men live any time together in this state. The inconveniencies that they are therein exposed to, by the irregular and uncertain exercise of the power every man has of punishing the transgressions of others, make them take sanctuary under the established laws of government, and therein seek *the preservation of their property*. It is this makes them so willingly give up every one his single power of punishing, to be exercised by such alone, as shall be appointed to it amongst them; and by such rules as the community, or those authorized by them to that purpose, shall agree on. And in this we have the original *right and rise of both the legislative and executive power*, as well as of the governments and societies themselves.

128. For in the state of nature, to omit the liberty he has of innocent delights, a man has two powers.

The first is to do whatsoever he thinks fit for the preservation of himself and others within the permission of the *law of nature* by which law, common to them all, he and all the rest of *mankind are one community*, make up one society, distinct from all other creatures. And, were it not for the corruption and viciousness of degenerate men, there would be no need of any other; no necessity that men should separate from this great and natural community, and by positive agreements combine into smaller and divided associations.

The other power a man has in the state of nature, is the *power to punish the crimes* committed against that law. Both these he gives up, when he joins in a private, if I may so call it, or particular politic society, and incorporates into any commonwealth, separate from the rest of mankind.

129. The first *power,* viz. *of doing whatsoever he thought fit for the preservation of himself,* and the rest of mankind, *he gives up* to be regulated by laws made by the society, so far forth as the preservation of himself and the rest of that society shall require; which laws of the society in many things confine the liberty he had by the law of nature.

130. *Secondly,* The *power of punishing he wholly gives up,* and engages his natural force, (which he might before employ in the execution of the law of nature, by his own single authority, as he thought fit) to assist the executive power of the society, as the law thereof shall require. For being now in a new state, wherein he is to enjoy many conveniencies, from the labour, assistance, and society of others in the same community, as well as protection from its whole strength; he is to part also, with as much of his natural liberty, in providing for himself, as the good, prosperity, and safety of the society shall require; which is not only necessary, but just, since the other members of the society do the like.

131. But though men, when they enter into society, give up the equality, liberty, and executive power they had in the state of nature, into the hands of the society, to be so far disposed of by the legislative, as the good of the society shall require; yet it being only with an intention in every one the better to preserve himself, his liberty and property; (for no rational creature can be supposed to change his condition with an intention to be worse) the power of the society, or legislative constituted by them, *can never be supposed to extend farther, than the common good;* but is obliged to secure every one's property, by providing against those three defects above mentioned, that made the state of nature so unsafe and uneasy. And so whoever has the legislative or supreme power of any commonwealth, is bound to govern by established standing laws, promulgated and known to the people, and not by extemporary decrees; by indifferent and upright judges, who are to decide controversies by those laws; and to employ the force of the community at home, *only in the execution of such laws;* or abroad to prevent or redress foreign injuries, and secure the community from inroads and invasion. And all this to be directed to no other *end,* but the *peace, safety,* and *public good* of the people.

Chapter X

Of the Forms of a Commonwealth

132. The majority having, as has been shewed, upon men's first uniting into society, the whole power of the community naturally in them, may employ all that power in making laws for the community from time to time, and executing those laws by officers of their own appointing; and then the *form* of the government is a perfect *democracy:* or else may put the power of making laws into the hands of a few select men, and their heirs or successors; and then it is an *oligarchy:* or else into the hands of one man, and then it is a *monarchy:* if to him and his heirs, it is an *hereditary monarchy:* if to him only for life, but upon his death the power only of nominating a successor to return to them; an *elective monarchy.* And so accordingly of these the community may make compounded and mixed forms of government, as they think good. And if the legislative power be at first given by the majority to one or more persons only for their lives, or any limited time, and then the supreme power to revert to them again; when it is so reverted, the community may dispose of it again anew into what hands they please, and so constitute a new form of government. For the *form of government depending upon the placing* the supreme power, which is the *legislative* (it being impossible to conceive that an inferiour power should prescribe to a superiour, or any but the supreme make laws), according as the power of making laws is placed, such is the *form of the commonwealth.*

133. By commonwealth, I must be understood all along to mean, not a democracy, or any form of government, but *any independent community,* which the Latines signified by the word *civitas;* to which the word which best answers in our language, is *commonwealth,* and most properly expresses such a society of men, which community or city in English does not. For there may be subordinate communities in government; and city amongst us has quite a different notion from commonwealth: and therefore, to avoid ambiguity, I crave leave to use the word *commonwealth* in that sense, in which I find it used by King *James the first;* and I take it to be its genuine signification; which if any body dislike, I consent with him to change it for a better.

David Hume (1711–1776 c.e.)

The Scottish philosopher and historian Hume was initially headed toward the profession of law. After he finished his studies at Edinburgh University in his middle teens, he began an intensive program of self-education. By age twenty-eight he produced, anonymously, his most important book, in which he applied the new skepticism afforded by Newtonian science to a variety of matters ranging from the nature of knowledge to the psychological foundations of morals. Hume is famous for advancing an argument against rationalistic ethics that still, today, energizes the thinking of many philosophers. In political theory, Hume was skeptical about social contract theory, and argued for a different conception of justice, based on his understanding of human motivation. The selections that follow are from his youthful but radical work, *A Treatise of Human Nature* (1739). Hume is one of the most intriguing philosophers, whose thinking is still the subject of numerous studies and varied interpretations. He ended his work in philosophy quite early and turned, instead, to the history of Great Britain. He was never an academician and took an active role in public life, such as serving as charge d'affaires in Paris from 1763 to 1766. Despite his change in career, academic philosophers since Immanuel Kant have regarded him as a source of many philosophical challenges.

From A Treatise of Human Nature*

Part II
Of Justice and Injustice

Section I
Justice, whether a natural or artificial virtue?

I have already hinted, that our sense of every kind of virtue is not natural; but that there are some virtues, that produce pleasure and approbation by means of an artifice or contrivance, which arises from the circumstances and necessity of mankind. Of this kind I assert *justice* to be; and shall endeavour to defend this opinion by a short, and, I hope, convincing argument, before I examine the nature of the artifice, from which the sense of that virtue is derived.

'Tis evident, that when we praise any actions, we regard only the motives that produced them, and consider the actions as signs or indications of certain principles in the mind and temper. The external performance has no merit. We must look within to find the moral quality. This we cannot do directly; and therefore fix our attention on actions, as on external signs. But these actions are still considered as signs; and the ultimate object of our praise and approbation is the motive, that produc'd them.

---

*An Excerpt.

After the same manner, when we require any action, or blame a person for not performing it, we always suppose, that one in that situation shou'd be influenc'd by the proper motive of that action, and we esteem it vicious in him to be regardless of it. If we find, upon enquiry, that the virtuous motive was still powerful over his breast, tho' check'd in its operation by some circumstances unknown to us, we retract our blame, and have the same esteem for him, as if he had actually perform'd the action, which we require of him.

It appears, therefore, that all virtuous actions derive their merit only from virtuous motives, and are consider'd merely as signs of those motives. From this principle I conclude, that the first virtuous motive, which bestows a merit on any action, can never be a regard to the virtue of that action, but must be some other natural motive or principle. To suppose, that the mere regard to the virtue of the action, may be the first motive, which produc'd the action, and render'd it virtuous, is to reason in a circle. Before we can have such a regard, the action must be really virtuous; and this virtue must be deriv'd from some virtuous motive: And consequently the virtuous motive must be different from the regard to the virtue of the action. A virtuous motive is requisite to render an action virtuous. An action must be virtuous, before we can have a regard to its virtue. Some virtuous motive, therefore, must be antecedent to that regard.

Nor is this merely a metaphysical subtilty; but enters into all our reasonings in common life, tho' perhaps we may not be able to place it in such distinct philosophical terms. We blame a father for neglecting his child. Why? because it shews a want of natural affection, which is the duty of every parent. Were not natural affection a duty, the care of children cou'd not be a duty; and 'twere impossible we cou'd have the duty in our eye in the attention we give to our offspring. In this case, therefore, all men suppose a motive to the action distinct from a sense of duty.

Here is a man, that does many benevolent actions; relieves the distress'd, comforts the afflicted, and extends his bounty even to the greatest strangers. No character can be more amiable and virtuous. We regard these actions as proofs of the greatest humanity. This humanity bestows a merit on the actions. A regard to this merit is, therefore, a secondary consideration, and deriv'd from the antecedent principle of humanity, which is meritorious and laudable.

In short, it may be establish'd as an undoubted maxim, *that no action can be virtuous, or morally good, unless there be in human nature some motive to produce it, distinct from the sense of its morality.*

But may not the sense of morality or duty produce an action, without any other motive? I answer, It may: But this is no objection to the present doctrine. When any virtuous motive or principle is common in human nature, a person, who feels his heart devoid of that motive, may hate himself upon that account, and may perform the action without the motive, from a certain sense of duty, in order to acquire by practice, that virtuous principle, or at least, to disguise to himself, as much as possible, his want of it. A man that really feels no gratitude in his temper, is still pleas'd to perform grateful actions, and thinks he has, by that means, fulfill'd his duty. Actions are at first only consider'd as signs of motives: But 'tis usual, in this case, as in all others, to fix our attention on the signs, and neglect, in some measure, the thing signify'd. But tho', on some occasions, a person may perform an action merely out of regard to its moral obligation, yet still this supposes in human nature some distinct principles, which are capable of producing the action, and whose moral beauty renders the action meritorious.

Now to apply all this to the present case; I suppose a person to have lent me a sum of money, on condition that it be restor'd in a few days; and also suppose, that after the expiration of the term agreed on, he demands the sum: I ask, *What reason or motive have I to restore the money?* It will, perhaps, be said, that my regard to justice, and abhorrence of villainy and knavery, are sufficient reasons for me, if I have the least grain of honesty, or sense of duty and obligation. And this answer, no doubt, is just and satisfactory to man in his civiliz'd state, and when train'd up according to a certain discipline and education. But in his rude and more *natural* condition, if you are pleas'd to call such a condition natural, this answer wou'd be rejected as perfectly unintelligible and sophistical. For one in that situation wou'd immediately ask you, *Wherein consists this honesty and justice, which you find in restoring a loan, and abstaining from the property of others?* It does not surely lie in the external action. It must, therefore, be plac'd in the motive, from which the external action is deriv'd. This motive can never be a regard to the honesty of the action. For 'tis a plain fallacy to say, that a virtuous motive is requisite to render an action honest, and at the same time that a regard to the honesty is the motive of the action. We can never have a regard to the virtue of an action, unless the action be antecedently virtuous. No action can be virtuous, but so far as it proceeds from a virtuous motive. A virtuous motive, therefore, must precede the regard to the virtue; and 'tis impossible, that the virtuous motive and the regard to the virtue can be the same.

'Tis requisite, then, to find some motive to acts of justice and honesty, distinct from our regard to the honesty; and in this lies the great difficulty. For shou'd we say, that a concern for our private interest or reputation is the legitimate motive to all honest actions; it wou'd follow, that wherever that concern ceases, honesty can no longer have place. But 'tis certain, that self-love, when it acts at its liberty, instead of engaging us to honest actions, is the source of all injustice and violence; nor can a man ever correct those vices, without correcting and restraining the *natural* movements of that appetite.

But shou'd it be affirm'd, that the reason or motive of such actions is the *regard to publick interest,* to which nothing is more contrary than examples of injustice and dishonesty; shou'd this be said, I wou'd propose the three following considerations, as worthy of our attention. *First,* public interest is not naturally attach'd to the observation of the rules of justice; but is only connected with it, after an artificial convention for the establishment of these rules, as shall be shewn more at large hereafter. *Secondly,* if we suppose, that the loan was secret, and that it is necessary for the interest of the person, that the money be restor'd in the same manner (as when the lender wou'd conceal his riches) in that case the example ceases, and the public is no longer interested in the actions of the borrower; tho' I suppose there is no moralist, who will affirm, that the duty and obligation ceases. *Thirdly,* experience sufficiently proves, that men, in the ordinary conduct of life, look not so far as the public interest, when they pay their creditors, perform their promises, and abstain from theft, and robbery, and injustice of every kind. That is a motive too remote and too sublime to affect the generality of mankind, and operate with any force in actions so contrary to private interest as are frequently those of justice and common honesty.

In general, it may be affirm'd, that there is no such passion in human minds, as the love of mankind, merely as such, independent of personal qualities, of services, or of relation to ourself. 'Tis true, there is no human, and indeed no sensible, creature, whose happiness or misery does not, in some measure, affect us, when brought near to us, and represented in lively colours: But this proceeds merely from sympathy, and is no proof of such an universal affection to mankind, since this concern extends itself beyond our own species. An affection betwixt the sexes is a passion evidently implanted in human nature; and this passion not only appears in its peculiar symptoms, but also in inflaming every other principle of affection, and raising a stronger love from beauty, wit, kindness, than what wou'd otherwise flow from them. Were there an universal love among all human creatures, it wou'd appear after the same manner. Any degree of a good quality wou'd cause a stronger affection than the same degree of a bad quality wou'd cause hatred; contrary to what we find by experience. Men's tempers are different, and some have a propensity to the tender, and others to the rougher, affections: But in the main, we may affirm, that man in general, or human nature, is nothing but the object both of love and hatred, and requires some other cause, which by a double relation of impressions and ideas, may excite these passions. In vain wou'd we endeavour to elude this hypothesis. There are no phænomena that point out any such kind affection to men, independent of their merit, and every other circumstance. We love company in general; but 'tis as we love any other amusement. An *Englishman* in *Italy* is a friend: A *Europæan* in *China*; and perhaps a man wou'd be belov'd as such, were we to meet him in the moon. But this proceeds only from the relation to ourselves; which in these cases gathers force by being confined to a few persons.

If public benevolence, therefore, or a regard to the interests of mankind, cannot be the original motive to justice, much less can *private benevolence*, or a *regard to the interests of the party concern'd*, be this motive. For what if he be my enemy, and has given me just cause to hate him? What if he be a vicious man, and deserves the hatred of all mankind? What if he be a miser, and can make no use of what I wou'd deprive him of? What if he be a profligate debauchee, and wou'd rather receive harm than benefit from large possessions? What if I be in necessity, and have urgent motives to acquire something to my family? In all these cases, the original motive to justice wou'd fail; and consequently the justice itself, and along with it all property, right, and obligation.

A rich man lies under a moral obligation to communicate to those in necessity a share of his superfluities. Were private benevolence the original motive to justice, a man wou'd not be oblig'd to leave others in the possession of more than he is oblig'd to give them. At least the difference wou'd be very inconsiderable. Men generally fix their affections more on what they are possess'd of, than on what they never enjoy'd: For this reason, it wou'd be greater cruelty to dispossess a man of any thing, than not to give it him. But who will assert, that this is the only foundation of justice?

Besides, we must consider, that the chief reason, why men attach themselves so much to their possessions is, that they consider them as their property, and as secur'd to them inviolably by the laws of society. But this is a secondary consideration, and dependent on the preceding notions of justice and property.

A man's property is suppos'd to be fenc'd against every mortal, in every possible case. But private benevolence is, and ought to be, weaker in some persons, than in others: And in many, or indeed in most persons, must absolutely fail. Private benevolence, therefore, is not the original motive of justice.

From all this it follows, that we have no real or universal motive for observing the laws of equity, but the very equity and merit of that observance; and as no action can be equitable or meritorious, where it cannot arise from some separate motive, there is here an evident sophistry and reasoning in a circle. Unless, therefore, we will allow, that nature has establish'd a sophistry, and render'd it necessary and unavoidable, we must allow, that the sense of justice and injustice is not deriv'd from nature, but arises artificially, tho' necessarily from education, and human conventions.

I shall add, as a corollary to this reasoning, that since no action can be laudable or blameable, without some motives or impelling passions, distinct from the sense of morals, these distinct passions must have a great influence on that sense. 'Tis according to their general force in human nature, that we blame or praise. In judging of the beauty of animal bodies, we always carry in our eye the œconomy of a certain species; and where the limbs and features observe that proportion, which is common to the species, we pronounce them handsome and beautiful. In like manner we always consider the *natural* and *usual* force of the passions, when we determine concerning vice and virtue; and if the passions depart very much from the common measures on either side, they are always disapprov'd as vicious. A man naturally loves his children better than his nephews, his nephews better than his cousins, his cousins better than strangers, where every thing else is equal. Hence arise our common measures of duty, in preferring the one to the other. Our sense of duty always follows the common and natural course of our passions.

To avoid giving offence, I must here observe, that when I deny justice to be a natural virtue, I make use of the word, *natural*, only as oppos'd to *artificial*. In another sense of the word; as no principle of the human mind is more natural than a sense of virtue; so no virtue is more natural than justice. Mankind is an inventive species; and where an invention is obvious and absolutely necessary, it may as properly be said to be natural as any thing that proceeds immediately from original principles, without the intervention of thought or reflexion. Tho' the rules of justice be *artificial*, they are not *arbitrary*. Nor is the expression improper to call them *Laws of Nature;* if by natural we understand what is common to any species, or even if we confine it to mean what is inseparable from the species.

Section II
Of the origin of justice and property

We now proceed to examine two questions, viz. *concerning the manner, in which the rules of justice are establish'd by the artifice of men;* and *concerning the reasons, which determine us to attribute to the observance or neglect of these rules a moral beauty and deformity.* These questions will appear afterwards to be distinct. We shall begin with the former.

Of all the animals, with which this globe is peopled, there is none towards whom nature seems, at first sight, to have exercis'd more cruelty than towards man, in the numberless wants and necessities, with which she has loaded him, and in the slender means, which she affords to the relieving these necessities. In other creatures these two particulars generally compensate each other. If we consider the lion as a voracious and carnivorous animal, we shall easily discover him to be very necessitous; but if we turn our eye to his make and temper, his agility, his courage, his arms, and his force, we shall find, that his advantages hold proportion with his wants. The sheep and ox are depriv'd of all these advantages; but their appetites are moderate, and their food is of easy purchase. In man alone, this unnatural conjunction of infirmity, and of necessity, may be observ'd in its greatest perfection. Not only the food, which is requir'd for his sustenance, flies his search and approach, or at least requires his labour to be produc'd, but he must be possess'd of cloaths and lodging, to defend him against the injuries of the weather; tho' to consider him only in himself, he is provided neither with arms, nor force, nor other natural abilities, which are in any degree answerable to so many necessities.

'Tis by society alone he is able to supply his defects, and raise himself up to an equality with his fellow-creatures, and even acquire a superiority above them. By society all his infirmities are compensated; and tho' in that situation his wants multiply every moment upon him, yet his abilities are still more augmented, and leave him in every respect more satisfied and happy, than 'tis possible for him, in his savage and solitary condition, ever to become. When every individual person labours a-part, and only for himself, his force is too small to execute any considerable work; his labour being employ'd in supplying all his different necessities, he never attains a perfection in any particular art; and as his force and success are not at all times equal, the least failure in either of these particulars must be attended with inevitable ruin and misery. Society provides a remedy for these *three* inconveniences. By the conjunction of forces, our power is augmented: By the partition of employments, our ability encreases: And by mutual succour we are less expos'd to fortune and accidents. 'Tis by this additional *force, ability*, and *security*, that society becomes advantageous.

But in order to form society, 'tis requisite not only that it be advantageous, but also that men be sensible of these advantages; and 'tis impossible, in their wild uncultivated state, that by study and reflexion alone, they should ever be able to attain this knowledge. Most fortunately, therefore, there is conjoin'd to those necessities, whose remedies are remote and obscure, another necessity, which having a present and more obvious remedy, may justly be regarded as the first and original principle of human society. This necessity is no other than that natural appetite betwixt the sexes, which unites them together, and preserves their union, till a new tye takes place in their concern for their common offspring. This new concern becomes also a principle of union betwixt the parents and offspring, and forms a more numerous society; where the parents govern by the advantage of their superior strength and wisdom, and at the same time are restrain'd in the exercise of their authority by that natural affection, which they bear their children. In a little time, custom and habit operating on the tender minds of the children, makes them sensible of the advantages, which they may reap from society, as well as fashions them by degrees for it, by rubbing off those rough corners and untoward affections, which prevent their coalition.

For it must be confest, that however the circumstances of human nature may render an union necessary, and however those passions of lust and natural affection may seem to render it unavoidable; yet there are other particulars in our *natural temper*, and in our *outward circumstances*, which are very incommodious, and are even contrary to the requisite conjunction. Among the former, we may justly esteem our *selfishness* to be the most considerable. I am sensible, that, generally speaking, the representations of this quality have been carried much too far; and that the descriptions, which certain philosophers delight so much to form of mankind in this particular, are as wide of nature as any accounts of monsters, which we meet with in fables and romances. So far from thinking, that men have no affection for any thing beyond themselves, I am of opinion, that tho' it be rare to meet with one, who loves any single person better than himself; yet 'tis as rare to meet with one, in whom all the kind affections, taken together, do not overbalance all the selfish. Consult common experience: Do you not see, that tho' the whole expence of the family be generally under the direction of the master of it, yet there are few that do not bestow the largest part of their fortunes on the pleasures of their wives, and the education of their children, reserving the smallest portion for their own proper use and entertainment. This is what we may observe concerning such as have those endearing ties; and may presume, that the case would be the same with others, were they plac'd in a like situation.

But tho' this generosity must be acknowledg'd to the honour of human nature, we may at the same time remark, that so noble an affection, instead of fitting men for large societies, is almost as contrary to them, as the most narrow selfishness. For while each person loves himself better than any other single person, and in his love to others bears the greatest affection to his relations and acquaintance, this must necessarily produce an opposition of passions, and a consequent opposition of actions; which cannot but be dangerous to the new-establish'd union.

'Tis however worth while to remark, that this contrariety of passions wou'd be attended with but small danger, did it not concur with a peculiarity in our *outward circumstances*, which affords it an opportunity of exerting itself. There are three different species of goods, which we are possess'd of; the internal satisfaction of our minds, the external advantages of our body, and the enjoyment of such possessions as we have acquir'd by our industry and good fortune. We are perfectly secure in the enjoyment of the first. The second may be ravish'd from us, but can be of no advantage to him who deprives us of them. The last only are both expos'd to the violence of others, and may be transferr'd without suffering any loss or alteration; while at the same time, there is not a sufficient quantity of them to supply every one's desires and necessities. As the improvement, therefore, of these goods is the chief advantage of society, so the *instability* of their possession, along with their *scarcity*, is the chief impediment.

In vain shou'd we expect to find, in *uncultivated nature*, a remedy to this inconvenience; or hope for any inartificial principle of the human mind, which might controul those partial affections, and make us overcome the temptations arising from our circumstances. The idea of justice can never serve to this purpose, or be taken for a natural principle, capable of inspiring men with an equitable conduct towards each other. That virtue, as it is now understood, wou'd never have been dream'd of among rude and savage men. For the notion of injury or injustice implies an immorality or vice committed against some other person: And as every immorality is deriv'd from some defect or unsoundness of the passions, and as this defect must be judg'd of, in a great measure, from the ordinary course of nature in the constitution of the mind; 'twill be easy to know, whether we be guilty of any immorality, with regard to others, by considering the natural, and usual force of those several affections, which are directed towards them. Now it appears, that in the original frame of our mind, our strongest attention is confin'd to ourselves; our next is extended to our relations and acquaintance; and 'tis only the weakest which reaches to strangers and indifferent persons. This partiality, then, and unequal affection, must not only have an influence on our behaviour and conduct in society, but even on our ideas of vice and virtue; so as to make us regard any remarkable transgression of such a degree of partiality, either by too great an enlargement, or contraction of the affections, as vicious and immoral. This we may observe in our common judgments concerning actions, where we blame a person, who either centers all his affections in his family, or is so regardless of them, as, in any opposition of interest, to give the preference to a stranger, or mere chance acquaintance. From all which it follows, that our natural uncultivated ideas of morality, instead of providing a remedy for the partiality of our affections, do rather conform themselves to that partiality, and give it an additional force and influence.

The remedy, then, is not deriv'd from nature, but from *artifice;* or more properly speaking, nature provides a remedy in the judgment and understanding, for what is irregular and incommodious in the affections. For when men, from their early education in society, have become sensible of the infinite advantages that result from it, and have besides acquir'd a new affection to company and conversation; and when they have observ'd, that the principal disturbance in society arises from those goods, which we call external, and from their looseness and easy transition from one person to another; they must seek for a remedy, by putting these goods, as far as possible, on the same footing with the fix'd and constant advantages of the mind and body. This can be done after no other manner, than by a convention enter'd into by all the members of the society to bestow stability on the possession of those external goods, and leave every one in the peaceable enjoyment of what he may acquire by his fortune and industry. By this means, every one knows what he may safely possess; and the passions are restrain'd in their partial and contradictory motions. Nor is such a restraint contrary to these passions; for if so, it cou'd never be enter'd into, nor maintain'd; but it is only contrary to their heedless and impetuous movement. Instead of departing from our own interest, or from that of our nearest friends, by abstaining from the possessions of others, we cannot better consult both these interests, than by such a convention; because it is by that means we maintain society, which is so necessary to their well-being and subsistence, as well as to our own.

This convention is not of the nature of a *promise:* For even promises themselves, as we shall see afterwards, arise from human conventions. It is only a general sense of common interest; which sense all the members of the society express to one another, and which induces them to regulate their conduct by certain rules. I observe, that it will be for my interest to leave another in the possession of his goods, *provided* he will act in the same manner with regard to me. He is sensible of a like interest in the regulation of his conduct. When this common sense of interest is mutually express'd, and is known to both, it produces a suitable resolution and behaviour. And this may properly enough be call'd a convention or agreement betwixt us, tho' without the interposition of a promise; since the actions of each of us have a reference to those of the other, and are perform'd upon the supposition, that something is to be perform'd on the other part. Two men, who pull the oars of a boat, do it by an agreement or convention, tho' they have never given promises to each other. Nor is the rule concerning the stability of possession the less deriv'd from human conventions, that it arises gradually, and acquires force by a slow progression, and by our repeated experience of the inconveniences of transgressing it. On the contrary, this experience assures us still more, that the sense of interest has become common to all our fellows, and gives us a confidence of the future regularity of their conduct: And 'tis only on the expectation of this, that our moderation and abstinence are founded. In like manner are languages gradually establish'd by human conventions without any promise. In like manner do gold and silver become the common measures of exchange, and are esteem'd sufficient payment for what is of a hundred times their value.

After this convention, concerning abstinence from the possessions of others, is enter'd into, and every one has acquir'd a stability in his possessions, there immediately arise the ideas of justice and injustice; as also those of *property, right,* and *obligation.* The latter are altogether unintelligible without first understanding the former. Our property is nothing but those goods, whose constant possession is establish'd by the laws of society; that is, by the laws of justice. Those, therefore, who make use of the words *property,* or *right,* or *obligation,* before they have explain'd the origin of justice, or even make use of them in that explication, are guilty of a very gross fallacy, and can never reason upon any solid foundation. A man's property is some object related to him. This relation is not natural, but moral, and founded on justice. 'Tis very preposterous, therefore, to imagine, that we can have any idea of property, without fully comprehending the nature of justice, and shewing its origin in the artifice and contrivance of men. The origin of justice explains that of property. The same artifice gives rise to both. As our first and most natural sentiment of morals is founded on the nature of our passions, and gives the preference to ourselves and friends, above strangers; 'tis impossible there can be naturally any such thing as a fix'd right or property, while the opposite passions of men impel them in contrary directions, and are not restrain'd by any convention or agreement.

No one can doubt, that the convention for the distinction of property, and for the stability of possession, is of all circumstances the most necessary to the establishment of human society, and that after the agreement for the fixing and observing of this rule, there remains little or nothing to be done towards settling a perfect harmony and concord. All the other passions, beside this of interest, are either easily restrain'd, or are not of such pernicious consequence, when indulg'd. *Vanity* is rather to be esteem'd a social passion, and a bond of union among men. *Pity* and *love* are to be consider'd in the same light. And as to *envy* and *revenge,* tho' pernicious, they operate only by intervals, and are directed against particular persons, whom we consider as our superiors or enemies. This avidity alone, of acquiring goods and possessions for ourselves and our nearest friends, is insatiable, perpetual, universal, and directly destructive of society. There scarce is any one, who is not actuated by it; and there is no one, who has not reason to fear from it, when it acts without any restraint, and gives way to its first and most natural movements. So that upon the whole, we are to esteem the difficulties in the establishment of society, to be greater or less, according to those we encounter in regulating and restraining this passion.

'Tis certain, that no affection of the human mind has both a sufficient force, and a proper direction to counter-balance the love of gain, and render men fit members of society, by making them abstain from the possessions of others. Benevolence to strangers is too weak for this purpose; and as to the other passions, they rather inflame this avidity, when we observe, that the larger our possessions are, the more ability we have of gratifying all our appetites. There is no passion, therefore, capable of controlling the interested affection, but the very affection itself, by an alteration of its direction. Now this alteration must necessarily take place upon the least reflection; since 'tis evident, that the passion is much better satisfy'd by its restraint, than by its liberty, and that in preserving society, we make much greater advances in the acquiring possessions, than in the solitary and forlorn condition, which must follow upon violence and an universal licence. The question, therefore, concerning the wickedness or goodness of human nature, enters not in the least into that other question concerning the origin of society; nor is there any thing to be consider'd but the degrees of men's sagacity or folly. For whether the passion of self-interest be esteemed vicious or virtuous, 'tis all a case; since itself alone restrains it: So that if it be virtuous, men become social by their virtue; if vicious, their vice has the same effect.

Now as 'tis by establishing the rule for the stability of possession, that this passion restrains itself; if that rule be very abstruse, and of difficult invention; society must be esteem'd, in a manner, accidental, and the effect of many ages. But if it be found, that nothing can be more simple and obvious than that rule; that every parent, in order to preserve peace among his children, must establish it; and that these first rudiments of justice must every day be improv'd, as the society enlarges: If all this appear evident, as it certainly must, we may conclude, that 'tis utterly impossible for men to remain any considerable time in that savage condition, which precedes society; but that his very first state and situation may justly be esteem'd social. This, however, hinders not, but that philosophers may, if they please, extend their reasoning to the suppos'd *state of nature;* provided they allow it to be a mere philosophical fiction, which never had, and never cou'd have any reality. Human nature being compos'd of two principal parts, which are requisite in all its actions, the affections and understanding; 'tis certain, that the blind motions of the former, without the direction of the latter, incapacitate men for society: And it may be allow'd us to consider separately the effects, that result from the separate operations of these two component parts of the mind. The same liberty may be permitted to moral, which is allow'd to natural philosophers; and 'tis very usual with the latter to consider any motion as compounded and consisting of two parts separate from each other, tho' at the same time they acknowledge it to be in itself uncompounded and inseparable.

This *state of nature,* therefore, is to be regarded as a mere fiction, not unlike that of the *golden age,* which poets have invented; only with this difference, that the former is describ'd as full of war, violence and injustice; whereas the latter is painted out to us, as the most charming and most peaceable condition, that can possibly be imagin'd. The seasons, in that first age of nature, were so temperate, if we may believe the poets, that there was no necessity for men to provide themselves with cloaths and houses as a security against the violence of heat and cold. The rivers flow'd with wine and milk: The oaks yielded honey; and nature spontaneously produc'd her greatest delicacies. Nor were these the chief advantages of that happy age. The storms and tempests were not alone remov'd from nature; but those more furious tempests were unknown to human breasts, which now cause such uproar, and engender such confusion. Avarice, ambition, cruelty, selfishness, were never heard of: Cordial affection, compassion, sympathy, were the only movements, with which the human mind was yet acquainted. Even the distinction of *mine* and *thine* was banish'd from that happy race of mortals, and carry'd with them the very notions of property and obligation, justice and injustice.

This, no doubt, is to be regarded as an idle fiction; but yet deserves our attention, because nothing can more evidently shew the origin of those virtues, which are the subjects of our present enquiry. I have already observ'd, that justice takes its rise from human conventions; and that these are intended as a remedy to some inconveniences, which proceed from the concurrence of certain *qualities* of the human mind with the *situation* of external objects. The qualities of the mind are *selfishness* and *limited generosity:* And the situation of external objects is their *easy change,* join'd to their *scarcity* in comparison of the wants and desires of men. But however philosophers may have been bewilder'd in those speculations, poets have been guided more infallibly, by a certain taste or common instinct, which in most kinds of reasoning goes farther than any of that art and philosophy, with which we have been yet acquainted. They easily perceiv'd, if every man had a tender regard for another, or if nature supplied abundantly all our wants and desires, that the jealousy of interest, which justice supposes, could no longer have place; nor would there be any occasion for those distinctions and limits of property and possession, which at present are in use among mankind. Encrease to a sufficient degree the benevolence of men, or the bounty of nature, and you render justice useless, by supplying its place with much nobler virtues, and more valuable blessings. The selfishness of men is animated by the few possessions we have, in proportion to our wants; and 'tis to restrain this selfishness, that men have been oblig'd to separate themselves from the community, and to distinguish betwixt their own goods and those of others.

Nor need we have recourse to the fictions of poets to learn this; but beside the reason of the thing, may discover the same truth by common experience and observation. 'Tis easy to remark, that a cordial affection renders all things common among friends; and that married people in particular mutually lose their property, and are unacquainted with the *mine* and *thine*, which are so necessary, and yet cause such disturbance in human society. The same effect arises from any alteration in the circumstances of mankind; as when there is such a plenty of any thing as satisfies all the desires of men: In which case the distinction of property is entirely lost, and every thing remains in common. This we may observe with regard to air and water, tho' the most valuable of all external objects; and may easily conclude, that if men were supplied with every thing in the same abundance, or if *every one* had the same affection and tender regard for *every one* as for himself; justice and injustice would be equally unknown among mankind.

Here then is a proposition, which, I think, may be regarded as certain, *that 'tis only from the selfishness and confin'd generosity of men, along with the scanty provision nature has made for his wants, that justice derives its origin.* If we look backward we shall find, that this proposition bestows an additional force on some of those observations, which we have already made on this subject.

First, we may conclude from it, that a regard to public interest, or a strong extensive benevolence, is not our first and original motive for the observation of the rules of justice;

since 'tis allow'd, that if men were endow'd with such a benevolence, these rules would never have been dreamt of.

Secondly, we may conclude from the same principle, that the sense of justice is not founded on reason, or on the discovery of certain connexions and relations of ideas, which are eternal, immutable, and universally obligatory. For since it is confest, that such an alteration as that above-mention'd, in the temper and circumstances of mankind, wou'd entirely alter our duties and obligations, 'tis necessary upon the common system, *that the sense of virtue is deriv'd from reason,* to shew the change which this must produce in the relations and ideas. But 'tis evident, that the only cause, why the extensive generosity of man, and the perfect abundance of every thing, wou'd destroy the very idea of justice, is because they render it useless; and that, on the other hand, his confin'd benevolence, and his necessitous condition, give rise to that virtue, only by making it requisite to the publick interest, and to that of every individual. 'Twas therefore a concern for our own, and the publick interest, which made us establish the laws of justice; and nothing can be more certain, than that it is not any relation of ideas, which gives us this concern, but our impressions and sentiments, without which every thing in nature is perfectly indifferent to us, and can never in the least affect us. The sense of justice, therefore, is not founded on our ideas, but on our impressions.

Thirdly, we may farther confirm the foregoing proposition, *that those impressions, which give rise to this sense of justice, are not natural to the mind of man, but arise from artifice and human conventions.* For since any considerable alteration of temper and circumstances destroys equally justice and injustice; and since such an alteration has an effect only by changing our own and the publick interest; it follows, that the first establishment of the rules of justice depends on these different interests. But if men pursu'd the publick interest naturally, and with a hearty affection, they wou'd never have dream'd of restraining each other by these rules; and if they pursu'd their own interest, without any precaution, they wou'd run head-long into every kind of injustice and violence. These rules, therefore, are artificial, and seek their end in an oblique and indirect manner; nor is the interest, which gives rise to them, of a kind that cou'd be pursu'd by the natural and inartificial passions of men.

To make this more evident, consider, that tho' the rules of justice are establish'd merely by interest, their connexion with interest is somewhat singular, and is different from what may be observ'd on other occasions. A single act of justice is frequently contrary to *public interest;* and were it to stand alone, without being follow'd by other acts, may, in itself, be very prejudicial to society. When a man of merit, of a beneficent disposition, restores a great fortune to a miser, or a seditious bigot, he has acted justly and laudably, but the public is a real sufferer. Nor is every single act of justice, consider'd apart, more conducive to private interest, than to public; and 'tis easily conceiv'd how a man may impoverish himself by a signal instance of integrity, and have reason to wish, that with regard to that single act, the laws of justice were for a moment suspended in the universe. But however single acts of justice may be contrary, either to public or private interest, 'tis certain, that the whole plan or scheme is highly conducive, or indeed absolutely requisite, both to the support of society, and the well-being of every individual. 'Tis impossible to separate the good from the ill. Property must be stable, and must be fix'd by general rules. Tho' in one instance the public be a sufferer, this momentary ill is amply compensated by the steady prosecution of the rule, and by the peace and order, which it establishes in society. And even every individual person must find himself a gainer, on ballancing the account; since, without justice, society must immediately dissolve, and every one must fall into that savage and solitary condition, which is infinitely worse than the worst situation that can possibly be suppos'd in society. When therefore men have had experience enough to observe, that whatever may be the consequence of any single act of justice, perform'd by a single person, yet the whole system of actions, concurr'd in by the whole society, is infinitely advantageous to the whole, and to every part; it is not long before justice and property take place. Every member of society is sensible of this interest: Every one expresses this sense to his fellows, along with the resolution he has taken of squaring his actions by it, on condition that others will do the same. No more is requisite to induce any one of them to perform an act of justice, who has the first opportunity. This becomes an example to others. And thus justice establishes itself by a kind of convention or agreement; that is, by a sense of interest, suppos'd to be common to all, and where every single act is perform'd in expectation that others are to perform the like. Without such a convention, no one wou'd ever have dream'd, that there was such a virtue as justice, or have been induc'd to conform his actions to it. Taking any single act, my justice may be pernicious in every respect; and 'tis only upon the supposition, that others are to imitate my example, that I can be induc'd to embrace that virtue; since nothing but this combination can render justice advantageous, or afford me any motives to conform my self to its rules. . . .

Section III
Of the rules, which determine property

Tho' the establishment of the rule, concerning the stability of possession, be not only useful, but even absolutely necessary to human society, it can never serve to any purpose. while it remains in such general terms. Some method must be shewn, by which we may distinguish what particular goods are to be assign'd to each particular person, while the rest of mankind are excluded from their possession and enjoyment. Our next business, then, must be to discover the reasons which modify this general rule, and fit it to the common use and practice of the world.

'Tis obvious, that those reasons are not deriv'd from any utility or advantage, which either the *particular* person or the public may reap from his enjoyment of any *particular* goods, beyond what wou'd result from the possession of them by any other person. 'Twere better, no doubt, that every one were possess'd of what is most suitable to him, and proper for his use: But besides, that this relation of fitness may be common to several at once, 'tis liable to so many controversies, and men are so partial and passionate in judging of these controversies, that such a loose and uncertain rule wou'd be absolutely incompatible with the peace of human society. The convention concerning the stability of possession is enter'd into, in order to cut off all occasions of discord and contention; and this end wou'd never be attain'd, were we allow'd to apply this rule differently in every particular case, according to every particular utility, which might be discover'd in such an application. Justice, in her decisions, never regards the fitness or unfitness of objects to particular persons, but conducts herself by more extensive views. Whether a man be generous, or a miser, he is equally well receiv'd by her, and obtains with the same facility a decision in his favour, even for what is entirely useless to him.

It follows, therefore, that the general rule, *that possession must be stable*, is not apply'd by particular judgments, but by other general rules, which must extend to the whole society, and be inflexible either by spite or favour. To illustrate this, I propose the following instance. I first consider men in their savage and solitary condition; and suppose, that being sensible of the misery of that state, and foreseeing the advantages that wou'd result from society, they seek each other's company, and make an offer of mutual protection and assistance. I also suppose, that they are endow'd with such sagacity as immediately to perceive, that the chief impediment to this project of society and partnership lies in the avidity and selfishness of their natural temper; to remedy which, they enter into a convention for the stability of possession, and for mutual restraint and forbearance. I am sensible, that this method of proceeding is not altogether natural; but besides that I here only suppose those reflexions to be form'd at once, which in fact arise insensibly and by degrees; besides this, I say, 'tis very possible, that several persons, being by different accidents separated from the societies, to which they formerly belong'd, may be oblig'd to form a new society among themselves; in which case they are entirely in the situation above-mention'd.

'Tis evident, then, that their first difficulty, in this situation, after the general convention for the establishment of society, and for the constancy of possession, is, how to separate their possessions, and assign to each his particular portion, which he must for the future inalterably enjoy. This difficulty will not detain them long; but it must immediately occur to them, as the most natural expedient, that every one continue to enjoy what he is at present master of, and that property or constant possession be conjoin'd to the immediate possession. Such is the effect of custom, that it not only reconciles us to any thing we have long enjoy'd, but even gives us an affection for it, and makes us prefer it to other objects, which may be more valuable, but are less known to us. What has long lain under our eye, and has often been employ'd to our advantage, *that* we are always the most unwilling to part with; but can easily live without possessions, which we never have enjoy'd, and are not accustom'd to. 'Tis evident, therefore, that men wou'd easily acquiesce in this expedient, *that every one continue to enjoy what he is at present possess'd of;* and this is the reason, why they wou'd so naturally agree in preferring it.

But we may observe, that tho' the rule of the assignment of property to the present possessor be natural, and by that means useful, yet its utility extends not beyond the first formation of society; nor wou'd any thing be more pernicious, than the constant observance of it; by which restitution wou'd be excluded, and every injustice wou'd be authoriz'd and rewarded. We must, therefore, seek for some other circumstance, that may give rise to property after society is once establish'd; and of this kind, I find four most considerable, *viz.* Occupation, Prescription, Accession, and Succession. We shall briefly examine each of these, beginning with *Occupation.*

The possession of all external goods is changeable and uncertain; which is one of the most considerable impediments to the establishment of society, and is the reason why, by universal agreement, express or tacite, men restrain themselves by what we now call the rules of justice and equity. The misery of the condition, which precedes this restraint, is the cause why we submit to that remedy as quickly as possible; and this affords us an easy reason, why we annex the idea of property to the first possession, or to *occupation*. Men are unwilling to leave property in suspence, even for the shortest time, or open the least door to violence and disorder. To which we may add, that the first possession always engages the attention most; and did we neglect it, there wou'd be no colour of reason for assigning property to any succeeding possession.

There remains nothing, but to determine exactly, what is meant by possession; and this is not so easy as may at first sight be imagin'd. We are said to be in possession of any thing, not only when we immediately touch it, but also when we are so situated with respect to it, as to have it in our power to use it; and may move, alter, or destroy it, according to our present pleasure or advantage. This relation, then, is a species of cause and effect; and as property is nothing but a stable possession, deriv'd from the rules of justice, or the conventions of men, 'tis to be consider'd as the same species of relation. But here we may observe, that as the power of using any object becomes more or less certain, according as the interruptions we may meet with are more or less probable; and as this probability may increase by insensible degrees; 'tis in many cases impossible to determine when possession begins or ends; nor is there any certain standard, by which we can decide such controversies. A wild boar, that falls into our snares, is deem'd to be in our possession, if it be impossible for him to escape. But what do we mean by impossible? How do we separate this impossibility from an improbability? And how distinguish that exactly from a probability? Mark the precise limits of the one and the other, and shew the standard, by which we may decide all disputes that may arise, and, as we find by experience, frequently do arise upon this subject.

But such disputes may not only arise concerning the real existence of property and possession, but also concerning their extent; and these disputes are often susceptible of no decision, or can be decided by no other faculty than the imagination. A person who lands on the shore of a small island, that is desart and uncultivated, is deem'd its possessor from the very first moment, and acquires the property of the whole; because the object is there bounded and circumscrib'd in the fancy, and at the same time is proportion'd to the new possessor. The same person landing on a desart island, as large as *Great Britain*, extends his property no farther than his immediate possession; tho' a numerous colony are esteem'd the proprietors of the whole from the instant of their debarkment.

But it often happens, that the title of first possession becomes obscure thro' time; and that 'tis impossible to determine many controversies, which may arise concerning it. In that case long possession or *prescription* naturally takes place, and gives a person a sufficient property in any thing he enjoys. The nature of human society admits not of any great accuracy; nor can we always remount to the first origin of things, in order to determine their present condition. Any considerable space of time sets objects at such a distance, that they seem, in a manner, to lose their reality, and have as little influence on the mind, as if they never had been in being. A man's title, that is clear and certain at present, will seem obscure and doubtful fifty years hence, even tho' the facts, on which it is founded, shou'd be prov'd with the greatest evidence and certainly. The same facts have not the same influence after so long an interval of time. And this may be receiv'd as a convincing argument for our preceding doctrine with regard to property and justice. Possession during a long tract of time conveys a title to any object. But as 'tis certain, that, however every thing be produc'd in time, there is nothing real, that is produc'd by time; it follows, that property being produc'd by time, is not any thing real in the objects, but is the offspring of the sentiments, on which alone time is found to have any influence.

We acquire the property of objects by *accession*, when they are connected in an intimate manner with objects that are already our property, and at the same time are inferior to them. Thus the fruits of our garden, the offspring of our cattle, and the work of our slaves, are all of them esteem'd our property, even before possession. Where objects are connected together in the imagination, they are apt to be put on the same footing, and are commonly suppos'd to be endow'd with the same qualities. We readily pass from one to the other, and make no difference in our judgments concerning them; especially if the latter be inferior to the former.

The right of *succession* is a very natural one, from the presum'd consent of the parent or near relation, and from the general interest of mankind, which requires, that men's possessions shou'd pass to those, who are dearest to them, in order to render them more industrious and frugal. Perhaps these causes are seconded by the influence of *relation*, or the association of ideas, by which we are naturally directed to consider the son after the parent's decease, and ascribe to him a title to his father's possessions. Those goods must become the property of some body: But *of whom* is the question. Here 'tis evident the persons children naturally present themselves to the mind; and being already connected to those possessions by means of their deceas'd parent, we are apt to connect them still farther by the relation of property. Of this there are many parallel instances.

Immanuel Kant (1724–1804 C.E.)

Kant was born and lived his entire life in Königsberg, East Prussia. From 1746 to 1755 he worked as a private tutor, and in 1755 became lecturer in the Philosophy faculty of the university there. It was not until 1770, however, that he was appointed to a paying professorship at the university. He held his professorship until poor health led to his retirement from teaching in 1797. His condition allowed some writing for two years but not for his last five years. Kant was a bachelor of exceedingly regular habits and was known to keep a fine table with good conversation. His major works are all considered essential parts of the philosophical landscape in metaphysics, epistemology, aesthetics, and ethics. The *Critique of Pure Reason* (1781, rev. 1787) presents views on the metaphysics, scope, and methods of knowledge which remain central to philosophy. The *Groundwork for the Metaphysics of Morals* (1785) and the *Critique of Practical Reason* (1788) extended his metaphysical position to form a stance on moral philosophy which figures in his political theory. The following excerpt is from "Perpetual Peace" (1795).

From Perpetual Peace: A Philosophical Sketch*

The Perpetual Peace

A Dutch innkeeper once put this satirical inscription on his signboard, along with the picture of a graveyard. We shall not trouble to ask whether it applies to men in general, or particularly to heads of state (who can never have enough of war), or only to the philosophers who blissfully dream of perpetual peace. The author of the present essay does, however, make one reservation in advance. The practical politician tends to look down with great complacency upon the political theorist as a mere academic. The theorist's abstract ideas, the practitioner believes, cannot endanger the state, since the state must be founded upon principles of experience; it thus seems safe to let him fire off his whole broadside, and the *worldly-wise* statesman need not turn a hair. It thus follows that if the practical politician is to be consistent, he must not claim, in the event of a dispute with the theorist, to scent any danger to the state in the opinions which the theorist has randomly uttered in public. By this saving clause, the author of this essay will consider himself expressly safeguarded, in correct and proper style, against all malicious interpretation.

First Section
Which Contains the Preliminary Articles of a Perpetual Peace Between States

1. 'No conclusion of peace shall be considered valid as such if it was made with a secret reservation of the material for a future war.'

---

*An Excerpt.

For if this were the case, it would be a mere truce, a suspension of hostilities, not a *peace*. Peace means an end to all hostilities, and to attach the adjective 'perpetual' to it is already suspiciously close to pleonasm. A conclusion of peace nullifies all existing reasons for a future war, even if these are not yet known to the contracting parties, and no matter how acutely and carefully they may later be pieced together out of old documents. It is possible that either party may make a mental reservation with a view to reviving its old pretensions in the future. Such reservations will not be mentioned explicitly, since both parties may simply be too exhausted to continue the war, although they may nonetheless possess sufficient ill will to seize the first favourable opportunity of attaining their end. But if we consider such reservations in themselves, they soon appear as Jesuitical casuistry; they are beneath the dignity of a ruler, just as it is beneath the dignity of a minister of state to comply with any reasoning of this kind.

But if, in accordance with 'enlightened' notions of political expediency, we believe that the true glory of a state consists in the constant increase of its power by any means whatsoever, the above judgement will certainly appear academic and pedantic.

2. 'No independently existing state, whether it be large or small, may be acquired by another state by inheritance, exchange, purchase or gift.'

For a state, unlike the ground on which it is based, is not a possession (*patrimonium*). It is a society of men, which no-one other than itself can command or dispose of. Like a tree, it has its own roots, and to graft it on to another state as if it were a shoot is to terminate its existence as a moral personality and make it into a commodity. This contradicts the idea of the original contract, without which the rights of a people are unthinkable. Everyone knows what danger the supposed right of acquiring states in this way, even in our own times, has brought upon Europe (for this practice is unknown in other continents). It has been thought that states can marry one another, and this has provided a new kind of industry by which power can be increased through family alliances, without expenditure of energy, while landed property can be extended at the same time. It is the same thing when the troops of one state are hired to another to fight an enemy who is not common to both; for the subjects are thereby used and misused as objects to be manipulated at will.

3. 'Standing armies (*miles perpetuus*) will gradually be abolished altogether.'

For they constantly threaten other states with war by the very fact that they are always prepared for it. They spur on the states to outdo one another in arming unlimited numbers of soldiers, and since the resultant costs eventually make peace more oppressive than a short war, the armies are themselves the cause of wars of aggression which set out to end burdensome military expenditure. Furthermore, the hiring of men to kill or to be killed seems to mean using them as mere machines and instruments in the hands of someone else (the state), which cannot easily be reconciled with the rights of man in one's own person. It is quite a different matter if the citizens undertake voluntary military training from time to time in order to secure themselves and their fatherland against attacks from outside. But it would be just the same if wealth rather than soldiers were accumulated, for it would be seen by other states as a military threat; it might compel them to mount preventive attacks, for of the three powers within a state—the *power of the army,* the *power of alliance* and the *power of money*—the third is probably the most reliable instrument of war. It would lead more often to wars if it were not so difficult to discover the amount of wealth which another state possesses.

4. 'No national debt shall be contracted in connection with the external affairs of the state.'

There is no cause for suspicion if help for the national economy is sought inside or outside the state (e.g., for improvements to roads, new settlements, storage of foodstuffs for years of famine, etc.). But a credit system, if used by the powers as an instrument of aggression against one another, shows the power of money in its most dangerous form. For while the debts thereby incurred are always secure against present demands (because not all the creditors will demand payment at the same time), these debts go on growing indefinitely. This ingenious system, invented by a commercial people in the present century, provides a military fund which may exceed the resources of all the other states put together. It can only be exhausted by an eventual tax-deficit, which may be postponed for a considerable time by the commercial stimulus which industry and trade receive through the credit system. This ease in making war, coupled with the warlike inclination of those in power (which seems to be an integral feature of human nature), is thus a great obstacle in the way of perpetual peace. Foreign debts must therefore be prohibited by a preliminary article of such a peace, otherwise national bankruptcy, inevitable in the long run, would necessarily involve various other states in the resultant loss without their having deserved it, thus inflicting upon them a public injury. Other states are therefore justified in allying themselves against such a state and its pretensions.

5. 'No state shall forcibly interfere in the constitution and government of another state.'

For what could justify such interference? Surely not any sense of scandal or offence which a state arouses in the subjects of another state. It should rather serve as a warning to others, as an example of the great evils which a people has incurred by its lawlessness. And a bad example which one free person gives to another (as a *scandalum acceptum*) is not the same as an injury to the latter. But it would be a different matter if a state, through internal discord, were to split into two parts, each of which set itself up as a separate state and claimed authority over the whole. For it could not be reckoned as interference in another state's constitution if an external state were to lend support to one of them, because their condition is one of anarchy. But as long as this internal conflict is not yet decided, the interference of external powers would be a violation of the rights of an independent people which is merely struggling with its internal ills. Such interference would be an active offence and would make the autonomy of all other states insecure.

6. 'No state at war with another shall permit such acts of hostility as would make mutual confidence impossible during a future time of peace. Such acts would include the employment of *assassins (percussores)* or *poisoners (venefici)*, *breach of agreements, the instigation of treason (perduellio)* within the enemy state, etc.'

These are dishonourable stratagems. For it must still remain possible, even in wartime, to have some sort of trust in the attitude of the enemy, otherwise peace could not be concluded and the hostilities would turn into a war of extermination (*bellum internecinum*). After all, war is only a regrettable expedient for asserting one's rights by force within a state of nature, where no court of justice is available to judge with legal authority. In such cases, neither party can be declared an unjust enemy, for this would already presuppose a judge's decision; only the *outcome* of the conflict, as in the case of a so-called 'judgement of God', can decide who is in the right. A war of punishment (*bellum punitivum*) between states is inconceivable, since there can be no relationship of superior to inferior among them. It thus follows that a war of extermination, in which both parties and right itself might all be simultaneously annihilated, would allow perpetual peace only on the vast graveyard of the human race. A war of this kind and the employment of all means which might bring it about must thus be absolutely prohibited. But the means listed above would inevitably lead to such a war, because these diabolical arts, besides being intrinsically despicable, would not long be confined to war alone if they were brought into use. This applies, for example, to the employment of spies (*uti exploratoribus*), for it exploits only the dishonesty of others (which can never be completely eliminated). Such practices will be carried over into peace-time and will thus completely vitiate its purpose.

All of the articles listed above, when regarded objectively or in relation to the intentions of those in power, are *prohibitive laws* (*leges prohibitivae*). Yet some of them are of the *strictest* sort (*leges strictae*), being valid irrespective of differing circumstances, and they require that the abuses they prohibit should be abolished *immediately* (Nos. 1, 5, and 6). Others (Nos. 2, 3, and 4), although they are not exceptions to the rule of justice, allow some *subjective* latitude according to the circumstances in which they are applied (*leges latae*). The latter need not necessarily be executed at once, so long as their ultimate purpose (e.g. the *restoration* of freedom to certain states in accordance with the second article) is not lost sight of. But their execution may not be *put off* to a non-existent date (*ad calendas graecas*, as Augustus used to promise), for any delay is permitted only as a means of avoiding a premature implementation which might frustrate the whole purpose of the article. For in the case of the second article, the prohibition relates only to the *mode of acquisition*, which is to be forbidden hereforth, but not to the present *state of political possessions*. For although this present state is not backed up by the requisite legal authority, it was considered lawful in the public opinion of every state at the time of the putative acquisition.

Second Section
Which Contains the Definitive Articles of a Perpetual Peace Between States

A state of peace among men living together is not the same as the state of nature, which is rather a state of war. For even if it does not involve active hostilities, it involves a constant threat of their breaking out. Thus the state of peace must be *formally instituted*, for a suspension of hostilities is not in itself a guarantee of peace. And unless one neighbour gives a guarantee to the other at his request (which can happen only in a *lawful* state), the latter may treat him as an enemy.

First Definitive Article of a Perpetual Peace:
The Civil Constitution of Every State shall be Republican

A *republican constitution* is founded upon three principles: firstly, the principle of *freedom* for all members of a society (as men); secondly, the principle of the *dependence* of everyone upon a single common legislation (as subjects); and thirdly, the principle of legal *equality* for everyone (as citizens). It is the only constitution which can be derived from the idea of an original contract, upon which all rightful legislation of a people must be founded. Thus as far as right is concerned, republicanism is in itself the original basis of every kind of civil constitution, and it only remains to ask whether it is the only constitution which can lead to a perpetual peace.

The republican constitution is not only pure in its origin (since it springs from the pure concept of right); it also offers a prospect of attaining the desired result, i.e. a perpetual peace, and the reason for this is as follows.—If, as is inevitably the case under this constitution, the consent of the citizens is required to decide whether or not war is to be declared, it is very natural that they will have great hesitation in embarking on so dangerous an enterprise. For this would mean calling down on themselves all the miseries of war, such as doing the fighting themselves, supplying the costs of the war from their own resources, painfully making good the ensuing devastation, and, as the crowning evil, having to take upon themselves a burden of debt which will embitter peace itself and which can never be paid off on account of the constant threat of new wars. But under a constitution where the subject is not a citizen, and which is therefore not republican, it is the simplest thing in the world to go to war. For the head of state is not a fellow citizen, but the owner of the state, and a war will not force him to make the slightest sacrifice so far as his banquets, hunts, pleasure palaces and court festivals are concerned. He can thus decide on war, without any significant reason, as a kind of amusement, and unconcernedly leave it to the diplomatic corps (who are always ready for such purposes) to justify the war for the sake of propriety.

The following remarks are necessary to prevent the republican constitution from being confused with the democratic one, as commonly happens. The various forms of state (*civitas*) may be classified either according to the different persons who exercise supreme authority, or according to the way in which the nation is governed by its ruler, whoever he may be. The first classification goes by the form of sovereignty (*forma imperii*), and only three such forms are possible, depending on whether the ruling power is in the hands of an *individual*, of *several persons* in association, or of *all* those who together constitute civil society (i.e. *autocracy, aristocracy* and *democracy*—the power of a prince, the power of a nobility, and the power of the people). The second classification depends on the form of government (*forma regiminis*), and relates to the way in which the state, setting out from its constitution (i.e. an act of the general will whereby the mass becomes a people), makes use of its plenary power. The form of government, in this case, will be either *republican* or *despotic. Republicanism* is that political principle whereby the executive power (the government) is separated from the legislative power. Despotism prevails in a state if the laws are made and arbitrarily executed by one and the same power, and it reflects the will of the people only in so far as the ruler treats the will of the people as his own private will. Of the three forms of sovereignty, *democracy,* in the truest sense of the word, is necessarily a *despotism,* because it establishes an executive power through which all the citizens may make decisions about (and indeed against) the single individual without his consent, so that decisions are made by all the people and yet not by all the people; and this means that the general will is in contradiction with itself, and thus also with freedom.

For any form of government which is not *representative* is essentially an *anomaly,* because one and the same person cannot at the same time be both the legislator and the executor of his own will, just as the general proposition in logical reasoning cannot at the same time be a secondary proposition subsuming the particular within the general. And even if the other two political constitutions (i.e. autocracy and aristocracy) are always defective in as much as they leave room for a despotic form of government, it is at least possible that they will be associated with a form of government which accords with the *spirit* of a representative system. Thus Frederick II at least *said* that he was merely the highest servant of the state, while a democratic constitution makes this attitude impossible, because everyone under it wants to be a ruler. We can therefore say that the smaller the number of ruling persons in a state and the greater their powers of representation, the more the constitution will approximate to its republican potentiality, which it may hope to realise eventually by gradual reforms. For this reason, it is more difficult in an aristocracy than in a monarchy to reach this one and only perfectly lawful kind of constitution, while it is possible in a democracy only by means of violent revolution. But the people are immensely more concerned with the mode of government than with the form of the constitution, although a great deal also depends on the degree to which the constitution fits the purpose of the government. But if the mode of government is to accord with the concept of right, it must be based on the representative system. This system alone makes possible a republican state, and without it, despotism and violence will result, no matter what kind of constitution is in force. None of the so-called 'republics' of antiquity employed such a system, and they thus inevitably ended in despotism, although this is still relatively bearable under the rule of a single individual.

Second Definitive Article of a Perpetual Peace: The Right of Nations shall be based on a Federation of Free States

Peoples who have grouped themselves into nation states may be judged in the same way as individual men living in a state of nature, independent of external laws; for they are a standing offence to one another by the very fact that they are neighbours. Each nation, for the sake of its own security, can and ought to demand of the others that they should enter along with it into a constitution, similar to the civil one, within which the rights of each could be secured. This would mean establishing a *federation of peoples.* But a federation of this sort would not be the same thing as an international state. For the idea of an international state is contradictory, since every state involves a relationship between a superior (the legislator) and an inferior (the people obeying the laws), whereas a number of nations forming one state would constitute a single nation. And this contradicts our initial assumption, as we are here considering the right of nations in relation to one another in so far as they are a group of separate states which are not to be welded together as a unit.

We look with profound contempt upon the way in which savages cling to their lawless freedom. They would rather engage in incessant strife than submit to a legal constraint which they might impose upon themselves, for they prefer the freedom of folly to the freedom of reason. We regard this as barbarism, coarseness, and brutish debasement of humanity. We might thus expect that civilised peoples, each united within itself as a state, would hasten to abandon so degrading a condition as soon as possible. But instead of doing so, each *state* sees its own majesty (for it would be absurd to speak of the majesty of a *people*) precisely in not having to submit to any external legal constraint, and the glory of its ruler consists in his power to order thousands of people to immolate themselves for a cause which does not truly concern them, while he need not himself incur any danger whatsoever. And the main difference between the savage nations of Europe and those of America is that while some American tribes have been entirely eaten up by their enemies, the Europeans know how to make better use of those they have defeated than merely by making a meal of them. They would rather use them to increase the number of their own subjects, thereby augmenting their stock of instruments for conducting even more extensive wars.

Although it is largely concealed by governmental constraints in law-governed civil society, the depravity of human nature is displayed without disguise in the unrestricted relations which obtain between the various nations. It is therefore to be wondered at that the word *right* has not been completely banished from military politics as superfluous pedantry, and that no state has been bold enough to declare itself publicly in favour of doing so. For Hugo Grotius, Pufendorf, Vattel and the rest (sorry comforters as they are) are still dutifully quoted in *justification* of military aggression, although their philosophically or diplomatically formulated codes do not and cannot have the slightest *legal* force, since states as such are not subject to a common external constraint. Yet there is no instance of a state ever having been moved to desist from its purpose by arguments supported by the testimonies of such notable men. This homage which every state pays (in words at least) to the concept of right proves that man possesses a greater moral capacity, still dormant at present, to overcome eventually the evil principle within him (for he cannot deny that it exists), and to hope that others will do likewise. Otherwise the word *right* would never be used by states which intend to make war on one another, unless in a derisory sense, as when a certain Gallic prince declared: 'Nature has given to the strong the prerogative of making the weak obey them.' The way in which states seek their rights can only be by war, since there is no external tribunal to put their claims to trial. But rights cannot be decided by military victory, and a *peace treaty* may put an end to the current war, but not to that general warlike condition within which pretexts can always be found for a new war. And indeed, such a state of affairs cannot be pronounced completely unjust, since it allows each party to act as judge in its own cause. Yet while natural right allows us to say of men living in a lawless condition that they ought to abandon it, the right of nations does not allow us to say the same of states. For as states, they already have a lawful internal constitution, and have thus outgrown the coercive right of others to subject them to a wider legal constitution in accordance with their conception of right. On the other hand, reason, as the highest legislative moral power, absolutely condemns war as a test of rights and sets up peace as an immediate duty. But peace can neither be inaugurated nor secured without a general agreement between the nations; thus a particular kind of league, which we might call a *pacific federation* (*foedus pacificum*), is required. It would differ from a *peace treaty* (*pactum pacis*) in that the latter terminates *one* war, whereas the former would seek to end *all* wars for good. This federation does not aim to acquire any power like that of a state, but merely to preserve and secure the *freedom* of each state in itself, along with that of the other confederated states, although this does not mean that they need to submit to public laws and to a coercive power which enforces them, as do men in a state of nature. It can be shown that this idea of *federalism*, extending gradually to encompass all states and thus leading to perpetual peace, is practicable and has objective reality. For if by good fortune one powerful and enlightened nation can form a republic (which is by its nature inclined to seek perpetual peace), this will provide a focal point for federal association among other states. These will join up with the first one, thus securing the freedom of each state in accordance with the idea of international right, and the whole will gradually spread further and further by a series of alliances of this kind.

It would be understandable for a people to say: 'There shall be no war among us; for we will form ourselves into a state, appointing for ourselves a supreme legislative, executive and juridical power to resolve our conflicts by peaceful means.' But if this state says: 'There shall be no war between myself and other states, although I do not recognise any supreme legislative power which could secure my rights and whose rights I should in turn secure', it is impossible to understand what justification I can have for placing any confidence in my rights, unless I can rely on some substitute for the union of civil society, i.e. on a free federation. If the concept of international right is to retain any meaning at all, reason must necessarily couple it with a federation of this kind.

The concept of international right becomes meaningless if interpreted as a right to go to war. For this would make it a right to determine what is lawful not by means of universally valid external laws, but by means of one-sided maxims backed up by physical force. It could be taken to mean that it is perfectly just for men who adopt this attitude to destroy one another, and thus to find perpetual peace in the vast grave where all the horrors of violence and those responsible for them would be buried. There is only one rational way in which states coexisting with other states can emerge from the lawless condition of pure warfare. Just like individual men, they must renounce their savage and lawless freedom, adapt themselves to public coercive laws, and thus form an *international state* (*civitas gentium*), which would necessarily continue to grow until it embraced all the peoples of the earth. But since this is not the will of the nations, according to their present conception of international right (so that they reject *in hypothesi* what is true *in thesi*), the positive idea of a *world republic* cannot be realised. If all is not to be lost, this can at best find a negative substitute in the shape of an enduring and gradually expanding *federation* likely to prevent war. The latter may check the current of man's inclination to defy the law and antagonise his fellows, although there will always be a risk of it bursting forth anew. *Furor impius intus—fremit horridus ore cruento* (Virgil).

Third Definitive Article of a Perpetual Peace: Cosmopolitan Right shall be limited to Conditions of Universal Hospitality

As in the foregoing articles, we are here concerned not with philanthropy, but with *right*. In this context, *hospitality* means the right of a stranger not to be treated with hostility when he arrives on someone else's territory. He can indeed be turned away, if this can be done without causing his death, but he must not be treated with hostility, so long as he behaves in a peaceable manner in the place he happens to be in. The stranger cannot claim the *right of a guest* to be entertained, for this would require a special friendly agreement whereby he might become a member of the native household for a certain time. He may only claim a *right of resort*, for all men are entitled to present themselves in the society of others by virtue of their right to communal possession of the earth's surface. Since the earth is a globe, they cannot disperse over an infinite area, but must necessarily tolerate one another's company. And no-one originally has any greater right than anyone else to occupy any particular portion of the earth. The community of man is divided by uninhabitable parts of the earth's surface such as oceans and deserts, but even then, the *ship* or the *camel* (the ship of the desert) make it possible for them to approach their fellows over these ownerless tracts, and to utilise as a means of social intercourse that *right to the earth's surface* which the human race shares in common. The inhospitable behaviour of coastal dwellers (as on the Barbary coast) in plundering ships on the adjoining seas or enslaving stranded seafarers, or that of inhabitants of the desert (as with the Arab Bedouins), who regard their proximity to nomadic tribes as a justification for plundering them, is contrary to natural right. But this natural right of hospitality, i.e. the right of strangers, does not extend beyond those conditions which make it possible for them to *attempt* to enter into relations with the native inhabitants. In this way, continents distant from each other can enter into peaceful mutual relations which may eventually be regulated by public laws, thus bringing the human race nearer and nearer to a cosmopolitan constitution.

If we compare with this ultimate end the *inhospitable* conduct of the civilised states of our continent, especially the commercial states, the injustice which they display in *visiting* foreign countries and peoples (which in their case is the same as *conquering* them) seems appallingly great. America, the negro countries, the Spice Islands, the Cape, etc. were looked upon at the time of their discovery as ownerless territories; for the native inhabitants were counted as nothing. In East India (Hindustan), foreign troops were brought in under the pretext of merely setting up trading posts. This led to oppression of the natives, incitement of the various Indian states to widespread wars, famine, insurrection, treachery and the whole litany of evils which can afflict the human race.

China and Japan (Nippon), having had experience of such guests, have wisely placed restrictions on them. China permits contact with her territories, but not entrance into them, while Japan only allows contact with a single European people, the Dutch, although they are still segregated from the native community like prisoners. The worst (or from the point of view of moral judgements, the best) thing about all this is that the commercial states do not even benefit by their violence, for all their trading companies are on the point of collapse. The Sugar Islands, that stronghold of the cruellest and most calculated slavery, do not yield any real profit; they serve only the indirect (and not entirely laudable) purpose of training sailors for warships, thereby aiding the prosecution of wars in Europe. And all this is the work of powers who make endless ado about their piety, and who wish to be considered as chosen believers while they live on the fruits of iniquity.

The peoples of the earth have thus entered in varying degrees into a universal community, and it has developed to the point where a violation of rights in *one* part of the world is felt *everywhere*. The idea of a cosmopolitan right is therefore not fantastic and overstrained; it is a necessary complement to the unwritten code of political and international right, transforming it into a universal right of humanity. Only under this condition can we flatter ourselves that we are continually advancing towards a perpetual peace.

First Supplement: On the Guarantee of a Perpetual Peace

Perpetual peace is *guaranteed* by no less an authority than the great artist *Nature* herself (*natura daedala rerum*). The mechanical process of nature visibly exhibits the purposive plan of producing concord among men, even against their will and indeed by means of their very discord. This design, if we regard it as a compelling cause whose laws of operation are unknown to us, is called *fate*. But if we consider its purposive function within the world's development, whereby it appears as the underlying wisdom of a higher cause, showing the way towards the objective goal of the human race and predetermining the world's evolution, we call it *providence*. We cannot actually observe such an agency in the artifices of nature, nor can we even *infer* its existence from them. But as with all relations between the form of things and their ultimate purposes, we can and must *supply it mentally* in order to conceive of its possibility by analogy with human artifices. Its relationship to and conformity with the end which reason directly prescribes to us (i.e. the end of morality) can only be conceived of as an idea. Yet while this idea is indeed far-fetched in *theory*, it does possess dogmatic validity and has a very real foundation in *practice*, as with the concept of *perpetual peace*, which makes it our duty to promote it by using the natural mechanism described above. But in contexts such as this, where we are concerned purely with theory and not with religion, we should also note that it is more in keeping with the limitations of human reason to speak of *nature* and not of *providence*, for reason, in dealing with cause and effect relationships, must keep within the bounds of possible experience. *Modesty* forbids us to speak of providence as something we can recognise, for this would mean donning the wings of Icarus and presuming to approach the mystery of its inscrutable intentions.

But before we define this guarantee more precisely, we must first examine the situation in which nature has placed the actors in her great spectacle, for it is this situation which ultimately demands the guarantee of peace. We may next enquire in what manner the guarantee is provided.

Nature's provisional arrangement is as follows. Firstly, she has taken care that human beings are able to live in all the areas where they are settled. Secondly, she has driven them in all directions by means of *war*, so that they inhabit even the most inhospitable regions. And thirdly, she has compelled them by the same means to enter into more or less legal relationships. It is in itself wonderful that moss can still grow in the cold wastes around the Arctic Ocean; the *reindeer* can scrape it out from beneath the snow, and can thus itself serve as nourishment or as a draft animal for the Ostiaks or Samoyeds. Similarly, the sandy salt deserts contain the *camel*, which seems as if it had been created for travelling over them in order that they might not be left unutilised. But evidence of design in nature emerges even more clearly when we realise that the shores of the Arctic Ocean are inhabited not only by fur-bearing animals, but also by seals, walrusses and whales, whose flesh provides food and whose fat provides warmth for the native inhabitants. Nature's care arouses most admiration, however, by carrying driftwood to these treeless regions, without anyone knowing exactly where it comes from. For if they did not have this material, the natives would not be able to construct either boats or weapons, or dwellings in which to live. And they have enough to do making war on the animals to be able to live in peace among themselves. But it was probably nothing but war which *drove* them into these regions. And the first *instrument of war* among all the animals which man learned to domesticate in the course of peopling the earth was the *horse*. For the elephant belongs to that later age of luxury which began after states had been established. The same applies to the art of cultivating certain kinds of grasses known as *cereals*, whose original nature is now unknown to us, and to the production and refinement of various *fruits* by transplanting and grafting (in Europe, perhaps only two species were involved, the crab-apple and the wild pear). Such arts could arise only within established states in which landed property was secure, after men had made the transition to an *agricultural* way of life, abandoning the lawless freedom they had enjoyed in their previous existence as hunters, fishers and shepherds. *Salt* and *iron* were next discovered, and were perhaps the first articles of trade between nations to be in demand everywhere. In this way, nations first entered into *peaceful relations* with one another, and thus achieved mutual understanding, community of interests and peaceful relations, even with the most distant of their fellows.

In seeing to it that men *could* live everywhere on earth, nature has at the same time despotically willed that they *should* live everywhere, even against their own inclinations. And this obligation does not rest upon any concept of duty which might bind them to fulfil it in accordance with a moral law; on the contrary, nature has chosen war as a means of attaining this end.

We can observe nations which reveal the unity of their descent by the unity of their language. This is the case with the *Samoyeds* on the Arctic Ocean and another people with a similar language living two hundred miles away in the Altai Mountains; another people of Mongol extraction, given to horsemanship and hence to warlike pursuits, has pushed its way between them, thus driving the one part of the tribe far away from the other into the most inhospitable Arctic regions, where it would certainly not have gone by its own inclinations. In the same way, the Finns in the northernmost region of Europe (where they are known as Lapps) are now far separated from the Hungarians, to whom they are linguistically related, by Gothic and Sarmatian peoples who have pushed their way in between them. And what else but war, nature's means of peopling the whole earth, can have driven the Eskimos so far North—for they are quite distinct from all other American races, and are perhaps descended from European adventurers of ancient times; the Pesherae have been driven South into Tierra del Fuego in the same manner. War itself, however, does not require any particular kind of motivation, for it seems to be ingrained in human nature, and even to be regarded as something noble to which man is inspired by his love of honour, without selfish motives. Thus warlike courage, with the American savages as with their European counterparts in medieval times, is held to be of great and immediate value—and not just *in times of war* (as might be expected), but also *in order that* there may be war. Thus wars are often started merely to display this quality, so that war itself is invested with an inherent *dignity;* for even philosophers have eulogised it as a kind of ennobling influence on man, forgetting the Greek saying that 'war is bad in that it produces more evil people than it destroys'. So much, then, for what nature does to further *her own end* with respect to the human race as an animal species.

We now come to the essential question regarding the prospect of perpetual peace. What does nature do in relation to the end which man's own reason prescribes to him as a duty, i.e. how does nature help to promote his *moral purpose?* And how does nature guarantee that what man *ought* to do by the laws of his freedom (but does not do) will in fact be done through nature's compulsion, without prejudice to the free agency of man? This question arises, moreover, in all three areas of public right—in *political, international* and *cosmopolitan right.* For if I say that nature *wills* that this or that should happen, this does not mean that nature imposes on us a *duty* to do it, for duties can only be imposed by practical reason, acting without any external constraint. On the contrary, nature does it herself, whether we are willing or not: *fata volentem ducunt, nolentem trahunt.*

1. Even if people were not compelled by internal dissent to submit to the coercion of public laws, war would produce the same effect from outside. For in accordance with the natural arrangement described above, each people would find itself confronted by another neighbouring people pressing in upon it, thus forcing it to form itself internally into a *state* in order to encounter the other as an armed *power.* Now the *republican* constitution is the only one which does complete justice to the rights of man. But it is also the most difficult to establish, and even more so to preserve, so that many maintain that it would only be possible within a state of *angels,* since men, with their self-seeking inclinations, would be incapable of adhering to a constitution of so sublime a nature. But in fact, nature comes to the aid of the universal and rational human will, so admirable in itself but so impotent in practice, and makes use of precisely those self-seeking inclinations in order to do so. It only remains for men to create a good organisation for the state, a task which is well within their capability, and to arrange it in such a way that their self-seeking energies are opposed to one another, each thereby neutralising or eliminating the destructive effects of the rest. And as far as reason is concerned, the result is the same as if man's selfish tendencies were non-existent, so that man, even if he is not morally good in himself, is nevertheless compelled to be a good citizen. As hard as it may sound, the problem of setting up a state can be solved even by a nation of devils (so long as they possess understanding). It may be stated as follows: 'In order to organise a group of rational beings who together require universal laws for their survival, but of whom each separate individual is secretly inclined to exempt himself from them, the constitution must be so designed that, although the citizens are opposed to one another in their private attitudes, these opposing views may inhibit one another in such a way that the public conduct of the citizens will be the same as if they did not have such evil attitudes.' A problem of this kind must be soluble. For such a task does not involve the moral improvement of man; it only means finding out how the mechanism of nature can be applied to men in such a manner that the antagonism of their hostile attitudes will make them compel one another to submit to coercive laws, thereby producing a condition of peace within which the laws can be enforced. We can even see this principle at work among the actually existing (although as yet very imperfectly organised) states. For in their external relations, they have already approached what the idea of right prescribes, although the reason for this is certainly not their internal moral attitudes. In the same way, we cannot expect their moral attitudes to produce a good political constitution; on the contrary, it is only through the latter that the people can be expected to attain a good level of moral culture. Thus that mechanism of nature by which selfish inclinations are naturally opposed to one another in their external relations can be used by reason to facilitate the attainment of its own end, the reign of established right. Internal and external peace are thereby furthered and assured, so far as it lies within the power of the state itself to do so. We may therefore say that nature *irresistibly wills* that right should eventually gain the upper hand. What men have neglected to do will ultimately happen of its own accord, albeit with much inconvenience. As Bouterwek puts it: 'If the reed is bent too far, it breaks; and he who wants too much gets nothing.'

2. The idea of international right presupposes the separate existence of many independent adjoining states. And such a state of affairs is essentially a state of war, unless there is a federal union to prevent hostilities breaking out. But in the light of the idea of reason, this state is still to be preferred to an amalgamation of the separate nations under a single power which has overruled the rest and created a universal monarchy. For the laws progressively lose their impact as the government increases its range, and a soulless despotism, after crushing the germs of goodness, will finally lapse into anarchy. It is nonetheless the desire of every state (or its ruler) to achieve lasting peace by thus dominating the whole world, if at all possible. But *nature* wills it otherwise, and uses two means to separate the nations and prevent them from intermingling—*linguistic* and *religious* differences. These may certainly occasion mutual hatred and provide pretexts for wars, but as culture grows and men gradually move towards greater agreement over their principles, they lead to mutual understanding and peace. And unlike that universal despotism which saps all man's energies and ends in the graveyard of freedom, this peace is created and guaranteed by an equilibrium of forces and a most vigorous rivalry.

3. Thus nature wisely separates the nations, although the will of each individual state, even basing its arguments on international right, would gladly unite them under

its own sway by force or by cunning. On the other hand, nature also unites nations which the concept of cosmopolitan right would not have protected from violence and war, and does so by means of their mutual self-interest. For the *spirit of commerce* sooner or later takes hold of every people, and it cannot exist side by side with war. And of all the powers (or means) at the disposal of the power of the state, *financial power* can probably be relied on most. Thus states find themselves compelled to promote the noble cause of peace, though not exactly from motives of morality. And wherever in the world there is a threat of war breaking out, they will try to prevent it by mediation, just as if they had entered into a permanent league for this purpose; for by the very nature of things, large military alliances can only rarely be formed, and will even more rarely be successful.

In this way, nature guarantees perpetual peace by the actual mechanism of human inclinations. And while the likelihood of its being attained is not sufficient to enable us to *prophesy* the future theoretically, it is enough for practical purposes. It makes it our duty to work our way towards this goal, which is more than an empty chimera.

Second Supplement: Secret Article of a Perpetual Peace

In transactions involving public right, a secret article (regarded objectively or in terms of its content) is a contradiction. But in subjective terms, i.e. in relation to the sort of person who dictates it, an article may well contain a secret element, for the person concerned may consider it prejudicial to his own dignity to name himself publicly as its originator.

The only article of this kind is embodied in the following sentence: '*The maxims of the philosophers on the conditions under which public peace is possible shall be consulted by states which are armed for war.*'

Although it may seem humiliating for the legislative authority of a state, to which we must naturally attribute the highest degree of wisdom, to seek instruction from *subjects* (the philosophers) regarding the principles on which it should act in its relations with other states, it is nevertheless extremely advisable that it should do so. The state will therefore invite their help *silently*, making a secret of it. In other words, it will *allow them to speak* freely and publicly on the universal maxims of warfare and peace-making, and they will indeed do so of their own accord if no-one forbids their discussions. And no special formal arrangement among the states is necessary to enable them to agree on this issue, for the agreement already lies in the obligations imposed by universal human reason in its capacity as a moral legislator. This does not, however, imply that the state must give the principles of the philosopher precedence over the pronouncements of the jurist (who represents the power of the state), but only that the philosopher should be given a *hearing*. The jurist, who has taken as his symbol the scales of right and the sword of justice, usually uses the latter not merely to keep any extraneous influences away from the former, but will throw the *sword* into one of the *scales* if it refuses to sink (*vae victis!*). Unless the jurist is at the same time a philosopher, at any rate in moral matters, he is under the greatest temptation to do this, for his business is merely to apply existing laws, and not to enquire whether they are in need of improvement. He acts as if this truly low rank of his faculty were in fact one of the higher ones, for the simple reason that it is accompanied by power (as is also the case with two of the other faculties). But the philosophical faculty occupies a very low position in face of the combined power of the others. Thus we are told, for instance, that philosophy is the *handmaid* of theology, and something similar in relation to the others. But it is far from clear whether this handmaid bears the torch before her gracious lady, or carries the train behind.

It is not to be expected that kings will philosophise or that philosophers will become kings; nor is it to be desired, however, since the possession of power inevitably corrupts the free judgement of reason. Kings or sovereign peoples (i.e. those governing themselves by egalitarian laws) should not, however, force the class of philosophers to disappear or to remain silent, but should allow them to speak publicly. This is essential to both in order that light may be thrown on their affairs. And since the class of philosophers is by nature incapable of forming seditious factions or clubs, they cannot incur suspicion of disseminating propaganda.

Jean-Jacques Rousseau (1712–1778 C.E.)

Rousseau was born in Geneva, raised by an aunt and an unruly father. After being introduced to novels and biographies, Rousseau did not receive a formal education, but studied to be a notary and acquired skills as an engraver. He eventually lived most of his life in France, often under the financial care of Mme. De Warens, a converted Roman Catholic whose influence on Rousseau had been considerable, including leading him to convert to the same faith. He was later invited by David Hume to stay in England, but his emotional imbalance led him to regard Hume as an enemy. Rousseau was an associate of the well-known French *philosophes* of that time and a contributor to the famous *Encyclopedia*. In the later periods of his life, Rousseau suffered much emotional turmoil, fearing conspiracies against him everywhere. He finally came to reside in Paris, where he died abruptly, but not before he converted back to Protestantism. He is most famous for his theories of the social contract and of human nature. The following excerpt is from his 1762 work *On the Social Contract*.

From On The Social Contract*

Chapter I
Subject of the First Book

Man was born free, and everywhere he is in chains. Many a one believes himself the master of others, and yet he is a greater slave than they. How has this change come about? I do not know. What can render it legitimate? I believe that I can settle this question.

If I considered only force and the results that proceed from it, I should say that so long as a people is compelled to obey and does obey, it does well; but that, so soon as it can shake off the yoke and does shake it off, it does better; for, if men recover their freedom by virtue of the same right by which it was taken away, either they are justified in resuming it, or there was no justification for depriving them of it. But the social order is a sacred right which serves as a foundation for all others. This right, however, does not come from nature. It is therefore based on conventions. The question is to know what these conventions are. Before coming to that, I must establish what I have just laid down.

Chapter II

Primitive Societies

The earliest of all societies, and the only natural one, is the family; yet children remain attached to their father only so long as they have need of him for their own preservation. As soon as this need ceases, the natural bond is dissolved. The children being freed from

---

*An Excerpt.

the obedience which they owed to their father, and the father from the cares which he owed to his children, become equally independent. If they remain united, it is no longer naturally but voluntarily; and the family itself is kept together only by convention.

This common liberty is a consequence of man's nature. His first law is to attend to his own preservation, his first cares are those which he owes to himself; and as soon as he comes to years of discretion, being sole judge of the means adapted for his own preservation, he becomes his own master.

The family is, then, if you will, the primitive model of political societies; the chief is the analogue of the father, while the people represent the children; and all, being born free and equal, alienate their liberty only for their own advantage. The whole difference is that, in the family, the father's love for his children repays him for the care that he bestows upon them; while, in the State, the pleasure of ruling makes up for the chief's lack of love for his people.

Grotius denies that all human authority is established for the benefit of the governed, and he cites slavery as an instance. His invariable mode of reasoning is to establish right by fact. A juster method might be employed, but none more favorable to tyrants.

It is doubtful, then, according to Grotius, whether the human race belongs to a hundred men, or whether these hundred men belong to the human race; and he appears throughout his book to incline to the former opinion, which is also that of Hobbes. In this way we have mankind divided like herds of cattle, each of which has a master, who looks after it in order to devour it.

Just as a herdsman is superior in nature to his herd, so chiefs, who are the herdsmen of men, are superior in nature to their people. Thus, according to Philo's account, the Emperor Caligula reasoned, inferring truly enough from this analogy that kings are gods, or that men are brutes.

The reasoning of Caligula is tantamount to that of Hobbes and Grotius. Aristotle, before them all, had likewise said that men are not naturally equal, but that some are born for slavery and others for dominion.

Aristotle was right, but he mistook the effect for the cause. Every man born in slavery is born for slavery; nothing is more certain. Slaves lose everything in their bonds, even the desire to escape from them; they love their servitude as the companions of Ulysses loved their brutishness. If, then, there are slaves by nature, it is because there have been slaves contrary to nature. The first slaves were made such by force; their cowardice kept them in bondage.

I have said nothing about King Adam nor about Emperor Noah, the father of three great monarchs who shared the universe, like the children of Saturn with whom they are supposed to be identical. I hope that my moderation will give satisfaction; for, as I am a direct descendant of one of these princes, and perhaps of the eldest branch, how do I know whether, by examination of titles, I might not find myself the lawful king of the human race? Be that as it may, it cannot be denied that Adam was sovereign of the world, as Robinson was of his island, so long as he was its sole inhabitant; and it was an agreeable feature of that empire that the monarch, secure on his throne, had nothing to fear from rebellions, or wars, or conspirators.

Chapter III

The Right of the Strongest

The strongest man is never strong enough to be always master, unless he transforms his power into right, and obedience into duty. Hence the right of the strongest—a right apparently assumed in irony, and really established in principle. But will this phrase never be explained to us? Force is a physical power; I do not see what morality can result from its effects. To yield to force is an act of necessity, not of will; it is at most an act of prudence. In what sense can it be a duty?

Let us assume for a moment this pretended right. I say that nothing results from it but inexplicable nonsense; for if force constitutes right, the effect changes with the cause, and any force which overcomes the first succeeds to its rights. As soon as men can disobey with impunity, they may do so legitimately; and since the strongest is always in the right, the only thing is to act in such a way that one may be the strongest. But what sort of a right is it that perishes when force ceases? If it is necessary to obey by compulsion, there is no need to obey from duty; and if men are no longer forced to obey, obligation is at an end. We see, then, that this word *right* adds nothing to force; it here means nothing at all.

Obey the powers that be. If that means, Yield to force, the precept is good but superfluous; I reply that it will never be violated. All power comes from God, I admit; but every disease comes from Him too; does it follow that we are prohibited from calling in a physician? If a brigand should surprise me in the recesses of a wood, am I bound not only to give up my purse when forced, but am I also morally bound to do so when I might conceal it? For, in effect, the pistol which he holds is a superior force.

Let us agree, then, that might does not make right, and that we are bound to obey none but lawful authorities. Thus my original question ever recurs.

Chapter IV

Slavery

Since no man has any natural authority over his fellow men, and since force is not the source of right, conventions remain as the basis of all lawful authority among men.

If an individual, says Grotius, can alienate his liberty and become the slave of a master, why should not a whole people be able to alienate theirs, and become subject to a king? In this there are many equivocal terms requiring explanation; but let us confine ourselves to the word *alienate*. To alienate is to give or sell. Now, a man who becomes another's slave does not give himself; he sells himself at the very least for his subsistence. But why does a nation sell itself? So far from a king supplying his subjects with their subsistence, he draws his from them; and, according to Rabelais, a king does not live on a little. Do subjects, then, give up their persons on condition that their property also shall be taken? I do not see what is left for them to keep.

It will be said that the despot secures to his subjects civil peace. Be it so; but what do they gain by that, if the wars which his ambition brings upon them, together with his insatiable greed and the vexations of his administration, harass them more than their own dissensions would? What do they gain by it if this tranquillity is itself one of their miseries? Men live tranquilly also in dungeons; is that enough to make them contented there? The Greeks confined in the cave of the Cyclops lived peacefully until their turn came to be devoured.

To say that a man gives himself for nothing is to say what is absurd and inconceivable; such an act is illegitimate and invalid, for the simple reason that he who performs it is not in his right mind. To say the same thing of a whole nation is to suppose a nation of fools; and madness does not confer rights.

Even if each person could alienate himself, he could not alienate his children; they are born free men; their liberty belongs to them, and no one has a right to dispose of it except themselves. Before they have come to years of discretion, the father can, in their name, stipulate conditions for their preservation and welfare, but not surrender them irrevocably and unconditionally; for such a gift is contrary to the ends of nature, and exceeds the rights of paternity. In order, then, that an arbitrary government might be legitimate, it would be necessary that the people in each generation should have the option of accepting or rejecting it; but in that case such a government would no longer be arbitrary.

To renounce one's liberty is to renounce one's quality as a man, the rights and also the duties of humanity. For him who renounces everything there is no possible compensation. Such a renunciation is incompatible with man's nature, for to take away all freedom from his will is to take away all morality from his actions. In short, a convention which stipulates absolute authority on the one side and unlimited obedience on the other is vain and contradictory. Is it not clear that we are under no obligations whatsoever towards a man from whom we have a right to demand everything? And does not this single condition, without equivalent, without exchange, involve the nullity of the act? For what right would my slave have against me, since all that he has belongs to me? His rights being mine, this right of me against myself is a meaningless phrase.

Grotius and others derive from war another origin for the pretended right of slavery. The victor having, according to them, the right of slaying the vanquished, the latter may purchase his life at the cost of his freedom; an agreement so much the more legitimate that it turns to the advantage of both.

But it is manifest that this pretended right of slaying the vanquished in no way results from the state of war. Men are not naturally enemies, if only for the reason that, living in their primitive independence, they have no mutual relations sufficiently durable to constitute a state of peace or a state of war. It is the relation of things and not of men which constitutes war; and since the state of war cannot arise from simple personal relations, but only from real relations, private war—war between man and man—cannot exist either in the state of nature, where there is no settled ownership, or in the social state, where everything is under the authority of the laws.

Private combats, duels, and encounters are acts which do not constitute a state of war; and with regard to the private wars authorized by the Establishments of Louis IX, king of France, and suspended by the Peace of God, they were abuses of the feudal government, an absurd system if ever there was one, contrary both to the principles of natural right and to all sound government.

War, then, is not a relation between man and man, but a relation between State and State, in which individuals are enemies only by accident, not as men, nor even as citizens,* but as soldiers; not as members of the fatherland, but as its defenders. In short, each State can have as enemies only other States and not individual men, inasmuch as it is impossible to fix any true relation between things of different kinds.

This principle is also conformable to the established maxims of all ages and to the invariable practice of all civilized nations. Declarations of war are not so much warnings to the powers as to their subjects. The foreigner, whether king, or nation, or private person, that robs, slays, or detains subjects without declaring war against the government, is not an enemy, but a brigand. Even in open war, a just prince, while he rightly takes possession of all that belongs to the State in an enemy's country, respects the person and property of individuals; he respects the rights on which his own are based. The aim of war being the destruction of the hostile State, we have a right to slay its defenders so long as they have arms in their hands; but as soon as they lay them down and surrender, ceasing to be enemies or instruments of the enemy, they become again simply men, and no one has any further right over their lives. Sometimes it is possible to destroy the State without killing a single one of its members; but war confers no right except what is necessary to its end. These are not the principles of Grotius; they are not based on the authority of poets, but are derived from the nature of things, and are founded on reason.

With regard to the right of conquest, it has no other foundation than the law of the strongest. If war does not confer on the victor the right of slaying the vanquished, this right, which he does not possess, cannot be the foundation of a right to enslave them. If we have a right to slay an enemy only when it is impossible to enslave him, the right to enslave him is not derived from the right to kill him; it is, therefore, an iniquitous bargain to make him purchase his life, over which the victor has no right, at the cost of his liberty. In establishing the right of life and death upon the right of slavery, and the right of slavery upon the right of life and death, is it not manifest that one falls into a vicious circle?

Even if we grant this terrible right of killing everybody, I say that a slave made in war, or a conquered nation, is under no obligation at all to a master, except to obey him so far as compelled. In taking an equivalent for his life the victor has conferred no favor on the slave; instead of killing him unprofitably, he has destroyed him for his own advantage. Far, then, from having acquired over him any authority in addition to that of force, the state of war subsists between them as before, their relation even is the effect of it; and the exercise of the rights of war supposes that there is no treaty of peace. They have

---

*The Romans, who understood and respected the rights of war better than any nation in the world, carried their scruples so far in this respect that no citizen was allowed to serve as a volunteer without enlisting expressly against the enemy, and by name against a certain enemy. A legion in which Cato the younger made his first campaign under Popilius having been re-formed, Cato the elder wrote to Popilius that, if he consented to his son's continuing to serve under him, it was necessary that he should take a new military oath, because, the first being annulled, he could no longer bear arms against the enemy (Cicero, *De Officiis* I, 11). And Cato also wrote to his son to abstain from appearing in battle until he had taken this new oath. I know that it will be possible to urge against me the siege of Clusium and other particular cases; but I cite laws and customs (Livy, V. 35-37). No nation has transgressed its laws less frequently than the Romans, and no nation has had laws so admirable.

made a convention. Be it so; but this convention, far from terminating the state of war, supposes its continuance.

Thus, in whatever way we regard things, the right of slavery is invalid, not only because it is illegitimate, but because it is absurd and meaningless. These terms, *slavery* and *right*, are contradictory and mutually exclusive. Whether addressed by a man to a man, or by a man to a nation, such a speech as this will always be equally foolish: "I make an agreement with you wholly at your expense and wholly for my benefit, and I shall observe it as long as I please, while you also shall observe it as long as I please."

Chapter V

That It Is Always Necessary to Go Back to a First Convention

If I should concede all that I have so far refuted, those who favor despotism would be no farther advanced. There will always be a great difference between subduing a multitude and ruling a society. When isolated men, however numerous they may be, are subjected one after another to a single person, this seems to me only a case of master and slaves, not of a nation and its chief; they form, if you will, an aggregation, but not an association, for they have neither public property nor a body politic. Such a man, had he enslaved half the world, is never anything but an individual; his interest, separated from that of the rest, is never anything but a private interest. If he dies, his empire after him is left disconnected and disunited, as an oak dissolves and becomes a heap of ashes after the fire has consumed it.

A nation, says Grotius, can give itself to a king. According to Grotius, then, a nation is a nation before it gives itself to a king. This gift itself is a civil act, and presupposes a public resolution. Consequently, before examining the act by which a nation elects a king, it would be proper to examine the act by which a nation becomes a nation; for this act, being necessarily anterior to the other, is the real foundation of the society.

In fact, if there were no anterior convention, where, unless the election were unanimous, would be the obligation upon the minority to submit to the decision of the majority? And whence do the hundred who desire a master derive the right to vote on behalf of ten who do not desire one? The law of the plurality of votes is itself established by convention, and presupposes unanimity once at least.

Chapter VI

The Social Pact

I assume that men have reached a point at which the obstacles that endanger their preservation in the state of nature overcome by their resistance the forces which each individual can exert with a view to maintaining himself in that state. Then this primitive condition can no longer subsist, and the human race would perish unless it changed its mode of existence.

Now, as men cannot create any new forces, but only combine and direct those that exist, they have no other means of self-preservation than to form by aggregation a sum of forces which may overcome the resistance, to put them in action by a single motive power, and to make them work in concert.

This sum of forces can be produced only by the combination of many; but the strength and freedom of each man being the chief instruments of his preservation, how can he pledge them without injuring himself, and without neglecting the cares which he owes to himself? This difficulty, applied to my subject, may be expressed in these terms:—

"To find a form of association which may defend and protect with the whole force of the community the person and property of every associate, and by means of which each, coalescing with all, may nevertheless obey only himself, and remain as free as before." Such is the fundamental problem of which the social contract furnishes the solution.

The clauses of this contract are so determined by the nature of the act that the slightest modification would render them vain and ineffectual; so that, although they have never perhaps been formally enunciated, they are everywhere the same, everywhere tacitly admitted and recognized, until, the social pact being violated, each man regains his original rights and recovers his natural liberty, while losing the conventional liberty for which he renounced it.

These clauses, rightly understood, are reducible to one only, viz., the total alienation to the whole community of each associate with all his rights; for, in the first place, since each gives himself up entirely, the conditions are equal for all; and, the conditions being equal for all, no one has any interest in making them burdensome to others.

Further, the alienation being made without reserve, the union is as perfect as it can be, and an individual associate can no longer claim anything; for, if any rights were left to individuals, since there would be no common superior who could judge between them and the public, each, being on some point his own judge, would soon claim to be so on all; the state of nature would still subsist, and the association would necessarily become tyrannical or useless.

In short, each giving himself to all, gives himself to nobody; and as there is not one associate over whom we do not acquire the same rights which we concede to him over ourselves, we gain the equivalent of all that we lose, and more power to preserve what we have.

If, then, we set aside what is not of the essence of the social contract, we shall find that it is reducible to the following terms: "Each of us puts in common his person and his whole power under the supreme direction of the general will; and in return we receive every member as an indivisible part of the whole."

Forthwith, instead of the individual personalities of all the contracting parties, this act of association produces a moral and collective body, which is composed of as many members as the assembly has voices, and which receives from this same act its unity, its common self (*moi*), its life, and its will. This public person, which is thus formed by the union of all the individual members, formerly took the name of *city* and now takes that of *republic* or *body politic*, which is called by its members *State* when it is passive, *sovereign* when it is active, *power* when it is compared to similar bodies. With regard to the associates, they take collectively the name of *people*, and are called individually *citizens*, as participating in the sovereign power, and *subjects*, as subjected to the laws of the State. But these terms are often confused and are mistaken one for another; it is sufficient to know how to distinguish them when they are used with complete precision.

Chapter VII

The Sovereign

We see from this formula that the act of association contains a reciprocal engagement between the public and individuals, and that every individual, contracting so to speak with himself, is engaged in a double relation, viz., as a member of the sovereign towards individuals, and as a member of the State towards the sovereign. But we cannot apply here the maxim of civil law that no one is bound by engagements made with himself; for there is a great difference between being bound to oneself and to a whole of which one forms part.

We must further observe that the public resolution which can bind all subjects to the sovereign in consequence of the two different relations under which each of them is regarded cannot, for a contrary reason, bind the sovereign to itself; and that accordingly it is contrary to the nature of the body politic for the sovereign to impose on itself a law which it cannot transgress. As it can only be considered under one and the same relation, it is in the position of an individual contracting with himself; whence we see that there is not, nor can be, any kind of fundamental law binding upon the body of the people, not even the social contract. This does not imply that such a body cannot perfectly well enter into engagements with others in what does not derogate from this contract; for, with regard to foreigners, it becomes a simple being, an individual.

But the body politic or sovereign, deriving its existence only from the sanctity of the contract, can never bind itself, even to others, in anything that derogates from the original act, such as alienation of some portion of itself, or submission to another sovereign. To violate the act by which it exists would be to annihilate itself; and what is nothing produces nothing.

So soon as the multitude is thus united in one body, it is impossible to injure one of the members without attacking the body, still less to injure the body without the members feeling the effects. Thus duty and interest alike oblige the two contracting parties to give mutual assistance; and the men themselves should seek to combine in this twofold relationship all the advantages which are attendant on it.

Now, the sovereign, being formed only of the individuals that compose it, neither has nor can have any interest contrary to theirs; consequently the sovereign power needs no guarantee towards its subjects, because it is impossible that the body should wish to injure all its members; and we shall see hereafter that it can injure no one as an individual. The sovereign, for the simple reason that it is so, is always everything that it ought to be.

But this is not the case as regards the relation of subjects to the sovereign, which, notwithstanding the common interest, would have no security for the performance of their engagements, unless it found means to ensure their fidelity.

Indeed, every individual may, as a man, have a particular will contrary to, or divergent from, the general will which he has as a citizen; his private interest may prompt him quite differently from the common interest; his absolute and naturally independent existence may make him regard what he owes to the common cause as a gratuitous contribution, the loss of which will be less harmful to others than the payment of it will be burdensome to him; and, regarding the moral person that constitutes the State as an imaginary being because it is not a man, he would be willing to enjoy the rights of a citizen without being willing to fulfil the duties of a subject. The progress of such injustice would bring about the ruin of the body politic.

In order, then, that the social pact may not be a vain formulary, it tacitly includes this engagement, which can alone give force to the others—that whoever refuses to obey the general will shall be constrained to do so by the whole body; which means nothing else than that he shall be forced to be free; for such is the condition which, uniting every citizen to his native land, guarantees him from all personal dependence, a condition that ensures the control and working of the political machine, and alone renders legitimate civil engagements, which, without it, would be absurd and tyrannical, and subject to the most enormous abuses.

Chapter VIII

The Civil State

The passage from the state of nature to the civil state produces in man a very remarkable change, by substituting in his conduct justice for instinct, and by giving his actions the moral quality that they previously lacked. It is only when the voice of duty succeeds physical impulse, and law succeeds appetite, that man, who till then had regarded only himself, sees that he is obliged to act on other principles, and to consult his reason before listening to his inclinations. Although, in this state, he is deprived of many advantages that he derives from nature, he acquires equally great ones in return; his faculties are exercised and developed; his ideas are expanded; his feelings are ennobled; his whole soul is exalted to such a degree that, if the abuses of this new condition did not often degrade him below that from which he has emerged, he ought to bless without ceasing the happy moment that released him from it for ever, and transformed him from a stupid and ignorant animal into an intelligent being and a man.

Let us reduce this whole balance to terms easy to compare. What man loses by the social contract is his natural liberty and an unlimited right to anything which tempts him and which he is able to attain; what he gains is civil liberty and property in all that he possesses. In order that we may not be mistaken about these compensations, we must clearly distinguish natural liberty, which is limited only by the powers of the individual, from civil liberty, which is limited by the general will; and possession, which is nothing but the result of force or the right of first occupancy, from property, which can be based only on a positive title.

Besides the preceding, we might add to the acquisitions of the civil state moral freedom, which alone renders man truly master of himself; for the impulse of mere appetite is slavery, while obedience to a self-prescribed law is liberty. But I have already said too much on this head, and the philosophical meaning of the term *liberty* does not belong to my present subject.

Chapter IX

Real Property

Every member of the community at the moment of its formation gives himself up to it, just as he actually is, himself and all his powers, of which the property that he possesses forms part. By this act, possession does not change its nature when it changes hands, and become property in those of the sovereign; but, as the powers of the State (*cité*) are incomparably greater than those of an individual, public possession is also, in fact, more secure and more irrevocable, without being more legitimate, at least in respect of foreigners; for the State, with regard to its members, is owner of all their property by the social contract, which, in the State, serves as the basis of all rights; but with regard to other powers, it is owner only by the right of first occupancy which it derives from individuals.

The right of first occupancy, although more real than that of the strongest, becomes a true right only after the establishment of that of property. Every man has by nature a right to all that is necessary to him; but the positive act which makes him proprietor of certain property excludes him from all the residue. His portion having been allotted, he ought to confine himself to it, and he has no further right to the undivided property. That is why the right of first occupancy, so weak in the state of nature, is respected by every member of a State. In this right men regard not so much what belongs to others as what does not belong to themselves.

In order to legalize the right of first occupancy over any domain whatsoever, the following conditions are, in general, necessary: first, the land must not yet be inhabited by any one; secondly, a man must occupy only the area required for his subsistence; thirdly, he must take possession of it, not by an empty ceremony, but by labor and cultivation, the only mark of ownership which, in default of legal title, ought to be respected by others.

Indeed, if we accord the right of first occupancy to necessity and labor, do we not extend it as far as it can go? Is it impossible to assign limits to this right? Will the mere setting foot on common ground be sufficient to give an immediate claim to the ownership of it? Will the power of driving away other men from it for a moment suffice to deprive them for ever of the right of returning to it? How can a man or a people take possession of an immense territory and rob the whole human race of it except by a punishable usurpation, since other men are deprived of the place of residence and the sustenance which nature gives to them in common? When Núñez de Balboa on the seashore took possession of the Pacific Ocean and of the whole of South America in the name of the crown of Castille, was this sufficient to dispossess all the inhabitants, and exclude from it all the princes in the world? On this supposition, such ceremonies might have been multiplied vainly enough; and the Catholic king in his cabinet might, by a single stroke, have taken possession of the whole world, only cutting off afterwards from his empire what was previously occupied by other princes.

We perceive how the lands of individuals, united and contiguous, become public territory, and how the right of sovereignty, extending itself from the subjects to the land which they occupy, becomes at once real and personal; which places the possessors in greater dependence, and makes their own powers a guarantee for their fidelity—an advantage which ancient monarchs do not appear to have clearly perceived, for, calling themselves only kings of the Persians or Scythians or Macedonians, they seem to have regarded themselves as chiefs of men rather than as owners of countries. Monarchs of today call themselves more cleverly kings of France, Spain, England, etc.; in thus holding the land they are quite sure of holding its inhabitants.

The peculiarity of this alienation is that the community, in receiving the property of individuals, so far from robbing them of it, only assures them lawful possession, and changes usurpation into true right, enjoyment into ownership. Also, the possessors being considered as depositaries of the public property, and their rights being respected by all the members of the State, as well as maintained by all its power against foreigners, they have, as it were, by a transfer advantageous to the public and still more to themselves, acquired all that they have given up—a paradox which is easily explained by distinguishing between the rights which the sovereign and the proprietor have over the same property, as we shall see hereafter.

It may also happen that men begin to unite before they possess anything, and that afterwards occupying territory sufficient for all, they enjoy it in common, or share it among themselves, either equally or in proportions fixed by the sovereign. In whatever way this acquisition is made, the right which every individual has over his own property is always subordinate to the right which the community has over all; otherwise there would be no stability in the social union, and no real force in the exercise of sovereignty.

I shall close this chapter and this book with a remark which ought to serve as a basis for the whole social system; it is that instead of destroying natural equality, the fundamental pact, on the contrary, substitutes a moral and lawful equality for the physical inequality which nature imposed upon men, so that, although unequal in strength or intellect, they all become equal by convention and legal right.*

From Book II

Chapter IV

The Limits of the Sovereign Power

If the State or city is nothing but a moral person, the life of which consists in the union of its members, and if the most important of its cares is that of self-preservation, it needs a universal and compulsive force to move and dispose every part in the manner most expedient for the whole. As nature gives every man an absolute power over all his limbs, the social pact gives the body politic an absolute power over all its members; and it is this same power which, when directed by the general will, bears, as I said, the name of sovereignty.

But besides the public person, we have to consider the private persons who compose it, and whose life and liberty are naturally independent of it. The question, then, is to dis-

---

*Under bad governments this equality is only apparent and illusory; it serves only to keep the poor in their misery and the rich in their usurpations. In fact, laws are always useful to those who possess and injurious to those that have nothing; whence it follows that the social state is advantageous to men only so far as they all have something, and none of them has too much.

tinguish clearly between the respective rights of the citizens and of the sovereign, as well as between the duties which the former have to fulfill in their capacity as subjects and the natural rights which they ought to enjoy in their character as men.

It is admitted that whatever part of his power, property, and liberty each one alienates by the social compact is only that part of the whole of which the use is important to the community; but we must also admit that the sovereign alone is judge of what is important.

All the services that a citizen can render to the State he owes to it as soon as the sovereign demands them; but the sovereign, on its part, cannot impose on its subjects any burden which is useless to the community; it cannot even wish to do so, for, by the law of reason, just as by the law of nature, nothing is done without a cause.

The engagements which bind us to the social body are obligatory only because they are mutual; and their nature is such that in fulfilling them we cannot work for others without also working for ourselves. Why is the general will always right, and why do all invariably desire the prosperity of each, unless it is because there is no one but appropriates to himself this word *each* and thinks of himself in voting on behalf of all? This proves that equality of rights and the notion of justice that it produces are derived from the preference which each gives to himself, and consequently from man's nature; that the general will, to be truly such, should be so in its object as well as in its essence; that it ought to proceed from all in order to be applicable to all; and that it loses its natural rectitude when it tends to some individual and determinate object, because in that case, judging of what is unknown to us, we have no true principle of equity to guide us.

Indeed, so soon as a particular fact or right is in question with regard to a point which has not been regulated by an anterior general convention, the matter becomes contentious; it is a process in which the private persons interested are one of the parties and the public the other, but in which I perceive neither the law which must be followed, nor the judge who should decide. It would be ridiculous in such a case to wish to refer the matter for an express decision of the general will, which can be nothing but the decision of one of the parties, and which, consequently, is for the other party only a will that is foreign, partial, and inclined on such an occasion to injustice as well as liable to error. Therefore, just as a particular will cannot represent the general will, the general will in turn changes its nature when it has a particular end, and cannot, as general, decide about either a person or a fact. When the people of Athens, for instance, elected or deposed their chiefs, decreed honors to one, imposed penalties on another, and by multitudes of particular decrees exercised indiscriminately all the functions of government, the people no longer had any general will properly so called; they no longer acted as a sovereign power, but as magistrates. This will appear contrary to common ideas, but I must be allowed time to expound my own.

From this we must understand that what generalizes the will is not so much the number of voices as the common interest which unites them; for, under this system, each necessarily submits to the conditions which he imposes on others—an admirable union of interest and justice, which gives to the deliberations of the community a spirit of equity that seems to disappear in the discussion of any private affair, for want of a common interest to unite and identify the ruling principle of the judge with that of the party.

By whatever path we return to our principle we always arrive at the same conclusion, viz., that the social compact establishes among the citizens such an equality that they all pledge themselves under the same conditions and ought all to enjoy the same rights. Thus, by the nature of the compact, every act of sovereignty, that is, every authentic act of the general will, binds or favors equally all the citizens; so that the sovereign knows only the body of the nation, and distinguishes none of those that compose it.

What, then, is an act of sovereignty properly so called? It is not an agreement between a superior and an inferior, but an agreement of the body with each of its members; a lawful agreement, because it has the social contract as its foundation; equitable, because it is common to all; useful, because it can have no other object than the general welfare; and stable, because it has the public force and the supreme power as a guarantee. So long as the subjects submit only to such conventions, they obey no one, but simply their own will; and to ask how far the respective rights of the sovereign and citizens extend is to ask up to what point the latter can make engagements among themselves, each with all and all with each.

Thus we see that the sovereign power, wholly absolute, wholly sacred, and wholly inviolable as it is, does not, and cannot, pass the limits of general conventions, and that every man can fully dispose of what is left to him of his property and liberty by these conventions; so that the sovereign never has a right to burden one subject more than another, because then the matter becomes particular and his power is no longer competent.

These distinctions once admitted, so untrue is it that in the social contract there is on the part of individuals any real renunciation, that their situation, as a result of this contract, is in reality preferable to what it was before, and that, instead of an alienation, they have only made an advantageous exchange of an uncertain and precarious mode of existence for a better and more assured one, of natural independence for liberty, of the power to injure others for their own safety, and of their strength, which others might overcome, for a right which the social union renders inviolable. Their lives, also, which they have devoted to the State, are continually protected by it; and in exposing their lives for its defense, what do they do but restore what they have received from it? What do they do but what they would do more frequently and with more risk in the state of nature, when, engaging in inevitable struggles, they would defend at the peril of their lives their means of preservation? All have to fight for their country in case of need, it is true; but then no one ever has to fight for himself. Do we not gain, moreover, by incurring, for what insures our safety, a part of the risks that we should have to incur for ourselves individually, as soon as we were deprived of it?

Edmund Burke (1729–1797 C.E.)

Born in Dublin, Ireland, he was educated at Trinity College there (1743–48). From 1759 to 1764 he was secretary to William Hamilton and involved in the political administration of Ireland. In 1755 he became secretary to the Marquis of Rockingham, leader of the Whig party. Elected to Parliament in 1765, Burke served there until 1794. He was chief articulator of Whig policy in this period. He advocated government by parliamentary committee against pressure from the Crown's administration, urged reform of the British administration of Ireland, favored toleration of religious differences, and counseled moderation in the negotiations with the contentious American colonies on issues of taxation. His most famous work, *Reflections on the Revolution in France* (1790) argues that the excesses of the French Revolution and The Terror violate the natural organic principles of governance of states–natural society.

From Reflections on the Revolution in France*

. . . Far am I from denying in theory, full as far is my heart from withholding in practice, (if I were of power to give or to withhold,) the *real* rights of men. In denying their false claims of right, I do not mean to injure those which are real, and are such as their pretended rights would totally destroy. If civil society be made for the advantage of man, all the advantages for which it is made become his right. It is an institution of beneficence; and law itself is only beneficence acting by a rule. Men have a right to live by that rule; they have a right to do justice, as between their fellows, whether their fellows are in public function or in ordinary occupation. They have a right to the fruits of their industry; and to the means of making their industry fruitful. They have a right to the acquisitions of their parents; to the nourishment and improvement of their offspring; to instruction in life, and to consolation in death. Whatever each man can separately do, without trespassing upon others, he has a right to do for himself; and he has a right to a fair portion of all which society, with all its combinations of skill and force, can do in his favour. In this partnership all men have equal rights; but not to equal things. He that has but five shillings in the partnership, has as good a right to it, as he that has five hundred pounds has to his larger proportion. But he has not a right to an equal dividend in the product of the joint stock; and as to the share of power, authority, and direction which each individual ought to have in the management of the state, that I must deny to be amongst the direct original rights of man in civil society; for I have in my contemplation the civil social man, and no other. It is a thing to be settled by convention.

If civil society be the offspring of convention, that convention must be its law. That convention must limit and modify all the descriptions of constitution which are formed under it. Every sort of legislative, judicial, or executory power are its creatures. They can have no being in any other state of things; and how can any man claim under the con-

---

*An Excerpt.

ventions of civil society, rights which do not so much as suppose its existence? rights which are absolutely repugnant to it? One of the first motives to civil society, and which becomes one of its fundamental rules, is, *that no man should be judge in his own cause.* By this each person has at once divested himself of the first fundamental right of uncovenanted man, that is, to judge for himself, and to assert his own cause. He abdicates all rights to be his own governor. He inclusively, in a great measure, abandons the right of self-defence, the first law of nature. Men cannot enjoy the rights of an uncivil and of a civil state together. That he may obtain justice, he gives up his right of determining what it is in points the most essential to him. That he may secure some liberty, he makes a surrender in trust of the whole of it.

Government is not made in virtue of natural rights, which may and do exist in total independence of it; and exist in much greater clearness, and in a much greater degree of abstract perfection: but their abstract perfection is their practical defect. By having a right to everything they want everything. Government is a contrivance of human wisdom to provide for human *wants*. Men have a right that these wants should be provided for by this wisdom. Among these wants is to be reckoned the want, out of civil society, of a sufficient restraint upon their passions. Society requires not only that the passions of individuals should be subjected, but that even in the mass and body, as well as in the individuals, the inclinations of men should frequently be thwarted, their will controlled, and their passions brought into subjection. This can only be done *by a power out of themselves;* and not, in the exercise of its function, subject to that will and to those passions which it is its office to bridle and subdue. In this sense the restraints on men, as well as their liberties, are to be reckoned among their rights. But as the liberties and the restrictions vary with times and circumstances, and admit of infinite modifications, they cannot be settled upon any abstract rule; and nothing is so foolish as to discuss them upon that principle.

The moment you abate anything from the full rights of men, each to govern himself, and suffer any artificial, positive limitation upon those rights, from that moment the whole organization, of government becomes a consideration of convenience. This it is which makes the constitution of a state, and the due distribution of its powers, a matter of the most delicate and complicated skill. It requires a deep knowledge of human nature and human necessities, and of the things which facilitate or obstruct the various ends, which are to be pursued by the mechanism of civil institutions. The state is to have recruits to its strength, and remedies to its distempers. What is the use of discussing a man's abstract right to food or medicine? The question is upon the method of procuring and administering them. In that deliberation I shall always advise to call in the aid of the farmer and the physician, rather than the professor of metaphysics.

The science of constructing a commonwealth, or renovating it, or reforming it, is, like every other experimental science, not to be taught *à priori*. Nor is it a short experience that can instruct us in that practical science; because the real effects of moral causes are not always immediate; but that which in the first instance is prejudicial may be excellent in its remoter operation; and its excellence may arise even from the ill effects it produces in the beginning. The reverse also happens: and very plausible schemes, with very pleasing commencements, have often shameful and lamentable conclusions. In states there are often some obscure and almost latent causes, things which appear at first view of little moment, on which a very great part of its prosperity or adversity may most essentially depend. The science of government being therefore so practical in itself, and intended for such practical purposes, a matter which requires experience, and even more experience than any person can gain in his whole life, however sagacious and observing he may be, it is with infinite caution that any man ought to venture upon pulling down an edifice, which has answered in any tolerable degree for ages the common purposes of society, or on building it up again, without having models and patterns of approved utility before his eyes.

These metaphysic rights entering into common life, like rays of light which pierce into a dense medium, are, by the laws of nature, refracted from their straight line. Indeed in the gross and complicated mass of human passions and concerns, the primitive rights of men undergo such a variety of refractions and reflections, that it becomes absurd to talk of them as if they continued in the simplicity of their original direction. The nature of man is intricate; the objects of society are of the greatest possible complexity: and therefore no simple disposition or direction of power can be suitable either to man's nature, or to the quality of his affairs. When I hear the simplicity of contrivance aimed at and boasted of in any new political constitutions, I am at no loss to decide that the artificers are grossly ignorant of their trade, or totally negligent of their duty. The simple governments are fundamentally defective, to say no worse of them. If you were to contemplate society in but one point of view, all these simple modes of polity are infinitely captivating. In effect each would answer its single end much more perfectly than the more complex is able to attain all its complex purposes. But it is better that the whole should be imperfectly and anomalously answered, than that, while some parts are provided for with great exactness, others might be totally neglected, or perhaps materially injured, by the over-care of a favourite member.

The pretended rights of these theorists are all extremes: and in proportion as they are metaphysically true, they are morally and politically false. The rights of men are in a sort of *middle,* incapable of definition, but not impossible to be discerned. The rights of men in governments are their advantages; and these are often in balances between differences of good; in compromises sometimes between good and evil, and sometimes between evil and evil. Political reason is a computing principle; adding, subtracting, multiplying, and dividing, morally and not metaphysically, or mathematically, true moral denominations.

By these theorists the right of the people is almost always sophistically confounded with their power. The body of the community, whenever it can come to act, can meet with no effectual resistance; but till power and right are the same, the whole body of them has no right inconsistent with virtue, and the first of all virtues, prudence. Men have no right to what is not reasonable, and to what is not for their benefit; for though a pleasant writer said, *Liceat perire poetis,* when one of them, in cold blood, is said to have leaped into the flames of a volcanic revolution, *Ardentem frigidus Ætnam insiluit,* I consider such a frolic rather as an unjustifiable poetic license, than as one of the franchises of Parnassus; and whether he were poet, or divine, or politician, that chose to exercise this kind of right, I think that more wise, because more charitable, thoughts would urge me rather to save the man, than to preserve his brazen slippers as the monuments of his folly.

The kind of anniversary sermons to which a great part of what I write refers, if men are not shamed out of their present course, in commemorating the fact, will cheat many out of the principles, and deprive them of the benefits, of the revolution they commemorate. I confess to you, Sir, I never liked this continual talk of resistance, and revolution, or the practice of making the extreme medicine of the constitution its daily bread. It renders the habit of society dangerously valetudinary: it is taking periodical doses of mercury sublimate, and swallowing down repeated provocatives of cantharides to our love of liberty.

This distemper of remedy, grown habitual, relaxes and wears out, by a vulgar and prostituted use, the spring of that spirit which is to be exerted on great occasions. It was in the most patient period of Roman servitude that themes of tyrannicide made the ordinary exercise of boys at school—*cum perimit sævos classis numerosa tyrannos.* In the ordinary state of things, it produces in a country like ours the worst effects, even on the cause of that liberty which it abuses with the dissoluteness of an extravagant speculation. Almost all the high-bred republicans of my time have, after a short space, become the most decided, thorough-paced courtiers; they soon left the business of a tedious, moderate, but practical resistance, to those of us whom, in the pride and intoxication of their theories, they have slighted as not much better than Tories. Hypocrisy, of course, delights in the most sublime speculations; for, never intending to go beyond speculation, it costs nothing to have it magnificent. But even in cases where rather levity than fraud was to be suspected in these ranting speculations, the issue has been much the same. These professors, finding their extreme principles not applicable to cases which call only for a qualified, or, as I may say, civil and legal resistance, in such cases employ no resistance at all. It is with them a war or a revolution, or it is nothing. Finding their schemes of politics not adapted to the state of the world in which they live, they often come to think lightly of all public principle; and are ready, on their part, to abandon for a very trivial interest what they find of very trivial value. Some indeed are of more steady and persevering natures; but these are eager politicians out of parliament, who have little to tempt them to abandon their favourite projects. They have some change in the church or state, or both, constantly in their view. When that is the case, they are always bad citizens, and perfectly unsure connexions. For, considering their speculative designs as of infinite value, and the actual arrangement of the state as of no estimation, they are at best indifferent about it. They see no merit in the good, and no fault in the vicious, management of public affairs; they rather rejoice in the latter, as more propitious to revolution. They see no merit or demerit in any man, or any action, or any political principle, any further than as they may forward or retard their design of change: they therefore take up, one day, the most violent and stretched prerogative, and another time the wildest democratic ideas of freedom, and pass from the one to the other without any sort of regard to cause, to person, or to party. . . .

The Federalist Papers

The Federalist Papers is the collective name given to a series of essays written by *John Jay* (1745–1829 C.E.), *Alexander Hamilton* (1755-1804), and *James Madison* (1751–1836) in support of the newly proposed federal constitution for the United States of America. Using the pseudonym "Publius," the three wrote a series of letters addressed to the public in New York newspapers between October 1787 and August 1788. Their intention was to explain to the people the ideas behind the final product of the Constitutional Convention of 1787. Although this was aimed at raising support for ratification, they serve today to provide insight into the different ideas being considered as operative political theories. All three men had been delegates to the Constitutional Convention in Philadelphia. Jay, a lawyer, was the principal author of the Constitution of the State of New York (1777), and later was Chief Justice of the Supreme Court. Hamilton, also a lawyer, went on to serve as Secretary of the Treasury in the Washington administration, and was an influential force on early federal policy. He was slain by Aaron Burr in a duel in 1804. Madison served in the newly designed Congress for eight years, then became Secretary of State in the Jefferson administration. He was elected President in 1808.

From The Federalist Papers*

No. 10: Madison

Among the numerous advantages promised by a well-constructed Union, none deserves to be more accurately developed than its tendency to break and control the violence of faction. The friend of popular governments never finds himself so much alarmed for their character and fate as when he contemplates their propensity to this dangerous vice. He will not fail, therefore, to set a due value on any plan which, without violating the principles to which he is attached, provides a proper cure for it. The instability, injustice, and confusion introduced into the public councils have, in truth, been the mortal diseases under which popular governments have everywhere perished, as they continue to be the favorite and fruitful topics from which the adversaries to liberty derive their most specious declamations. The valuable improvements made by the American constitutions on the popular models, both ancient and modern, cannot certainly be too much admired; but it would be an unwarrantable partiality to contend that they have as effectually obviated the danger on this side, as was wished and expected. Complaints are everywhere heard from our most considerate and virtuous citizens, equally the friends of public and private faith and of public and personal liberty, that our governments are too unstable, that the public good is disregarded in the conflicts of rival parties, and that measures are too often decided, not according to the rules of justice and the rights of the minor party, but by

---

*An Excerpt.

the superior force of an interested and overbearing majority. However anxiously we may wish that these complaints had no foundation, the evidence of known facts will not permit us to deny that they are in some degree true. It will be found, indeed, on a candid review of our situation, that some of the distresses under which we labor have been erroneously charged on the operation of our governments; but it will be found, at the same time, that other causes will not alone account for many of our heaviest misfortunes; and, particularly, for that prevailing and increasing distrust of public engagements and alarm for private rights which are echoed from one end of the continent to the other. These must be chiefly, if not wholly, effects of the unsteadiness and injustice with which a factious spirit has tainted our public administration.

By a faction I understand a number of citizens, whether amounting to a majority or minority of the whole, who are united and actuated by some common impulse of passion, or of interest, adverse to the rights of other citizens, or to the permanent and aggregate interests of the community.

There are two methods of curing the mischiefs of faction: the one, by removing its causes; the other, by controlling its effects.

There are again two methods of removing the causes of faction: the one, by destroying the liberty which is essential to its existence; the other, by giving to every citizen the same opinions, the same passions, and the same interests.

It could never be more truly said than of the first remedy that it was worse than the disease. Liberty is to faction what air is to fire, an ailment without which it instantly expires. But it could not be a less folly to abolish liberty, which is essential to political life, because it nourishes faction than it would be to wish the annihilation of air, which is essential to animal life, because it imparts to fire its destructive agency.

The second expedient is as impracticable as the first would be unwise. As long as the reason of man continues fallible, and he is at liberty to exercise it, different opinions will be formed. As long as the connection subsists between his reason and his self-love, his opinions and his passions will have a reciprocal influence on each other; and the former will be objects to which the latter will attach themselves. The diversity in the faculties of men, from which the rights of property originate, is not less an insuperable obstacle to a uniformity of interests. The protection of these faculties is the first object of government. From the protection of different and unequal faculties of acquiring property, the possession of different degrees and kinds of property immediately results; and from the influence of these on the sentiments and views of the respective proprietors ensues a division of the society into different interests and parties.

The latent causes of faction are thus sown in the nature of man; and we see them everywhere brought into different degrees of activity, according to the different circumstances of civil society. A zeal for different opinions concerning religion, concerning government, and many other points, as well of speculation as of practice; an attachment to different leaders ambitiously contending for pre-eminence and power; or to persons of other descriptions whose fortunes have been interesting to the human passions, have, in turn, divided mankind into parties, inflamed them with mutual animosity, and rendered them much more disposed to vex and oppress each other than to co-operate for their common good. So strong is this propensity of mankind to fall into mutual animosities that where no substantial occasion presents itself the most frivolous and fanciful distinctions have been sufficient to kindle their unfriendly passions and excite their most violent conflicts. But the most common and durable source of factions has been the verious and unequal distribution of property. Those who hold and those who are without property have ever formed distinct interests in society. Those who are creditors, and those who are debtors, fall under a like discrimination. A landed interest, a manufacturing interest, a mercantile interest, a moneyed interest, with many lesser interests, grow up of necessity in civilized nations, and divide them into different classes, actuated by different sentiments and views. The regulation of these various and interfering interests forms the principal task of modern legislation and involves the spirit of party and faction in the necessary and ordinary operations of government.

No man is allowed to be a judge in his own cause, because his interest would certainly bias his judgment, and, not improbably, corrupt his integrity. With equal, nay with greater reason, a body of men are unfit to be both judges and parties at the same time; yet what are many of the most important acts of legislation but so many judicial determinations, not indeed concerning the rights of single persons, but concerning the rights of large bodies of citizens? And what are the different classes of legislators but advocates and parties to the causes which they determine? Is a law proposed concerning private debts? It is a question to which the creditors are parties on one side and the debtors on the other. Justice ought hold the balance between them. Yet, the parties are, and must be, themselves the judges; and the most numerous party, or in other words, the most powerful faction must be expected to prevail. Shall domestic manufacturers be encouraged and in what degree, by restrictions on foreign manufacturers? are questions which would be differently decided by the landed and the manufacturing classes, and probably by neither with a sole regard to justice and the public good. The apportionment of taxes on the various descriptions of property is an act which seems to require the most exact impartiality; yet there is, perhaps, no legislative act in which greater opportunity and temptation are given to a predominant party to trample on the rules of justice. Every shilling with which they overburden the inferior number is a shilling saved to their own pockets.

It is in vain to say that enlightened statesmen will be able to adjust these clashing interests and render them all subservient to the public good. Enlightened statesmen will not always be at the helm. Nor, in many cases, can such an adjustment be made at all without taking into view indirect and remote considerations, which will rarely prevail over the immediate interest which one party may find in disregarding the rights of another or the good of the whole.

The inference to which we are brought is that the *causes* of faction cannot be removed and that relief is only to be sought in the means of controlling its *effects*.

If a faction consists of less than a majority, relief is supplied by the republican principle, which enables the majority to defeat its sinister views by regular vote. It may clog the administration, it may convulse the society; but it will be unable to execute and mask its violence under the forms of the Constitution. When a majority is included in a faction, the form of popular government, on the other hand, enables it to sacrifice to its ruling passion or interest both the public good and the rights of other citizens. To secure the public good and private rights against the danger of such a faction, and at the same time to preserve the spirit and the form of popular government, is then the great object to which our inquiries are directed. Let me add that it is the great desideratum by which alone this form of government can be rescued from the opprobrium under which it has so long labored and be recommended to the esteem and adoption of mankind.

By what means is this object attainable? Evidently by one of two only. Either the existence of the same passion or interest in a majority at the same time must be prevented, or the majority, having such coexistent passion or interest, must be rendered, by their number and local situation, unable to concert and carry into effect schemes of oppression. If the impulse and the opportunity be suffered to coincide, we well know that neither moral nor religious motives can be relied on as an adequate control. They are not found to be such on the injustice and violence of individuals, and lose their efficacy in proportion to the number combined together, that is, in proportion as their efficacy becomes needful.

From this view of the subject it may be concluded that a pure democracy, by which I mean a society consisting of a small number of citizens, who assemble and administer the government in person, can admit of no cure for the mischiefs of faction. A common passion or interest will, in almost every case, be felt by a majority of the whole; a communication and concert results from the form of government itself; and there is nothing to check the inducements to sacrifice the weaker party or an obnoxious individual. Hence it is that such democracies have ever been spectacles of turbulence and contention; have ever been found incompatible with personal security or the rights of property; and have in general been as short in their lives as they have been violent in their deaths. Theoretic politicians, who have patronized this species of government, have erroneously supposed that by reducing mankind to a perfect equality in their political rights, they would at the same time be perfectly equalized and assimilated in their possessions, their opinions, and their passions.

A republic, by which I mean a government in which the scheme of representation takes place, opens a different prospect and promises the cure for which we are seeking. Let us examine the points in which it varies from pure democracy, and we shall comprehend both the nature of the cure and the efficacy which it must derive from the Union.

The two great points of difference between a democracy and a republic are: first, the delegation of the government, in the latter, to a small number of citizens elected by the rest; secondly, the greater number of citizens and greater sphere of country over which the latter may be extended.

The effect of the first difference is, on the one hand, to refine and enlarge the public views by passing them through the medium of a chosen body of citizens, whose wisdom may best discern the true interest of their country and whose patriotism and love of justice will be least likely to sacrifice it to temporary or partial considerations. Under such a regulation it may well happen that the public voice, pronounced by the representatives of the people, will be more consonant to the public good than if pronounced by the people themselves, convened for the purpose. On the other hand, the effect may be inverted. Men of factious tempers, of local prejudices, or of sinister designs, may, by intrigue, by corruption, or by other means, first obtain the suffrages, and then betray the interests of the people. The question resulting is whether small or extensive republics are most favorable to the election of proper guardians of the public weal; and it is clearly decided in favor of the latter by two obvious considerations.

In the first place it is to be remarked that however small the republic may be the representatives must be raised to a certain number in order to guard against the cabals of a few; and that however large it may be they must be limited to a certain number in order to guard against the confusion of a multitude. Hence, the number of representatives in the two cases not being in proportion to that of the constituents, and being proportionally greatest in the small republic, it follows that if the proportion of fit characters be not less in the large than in the small republic, the former will present a greater option, and consequently a greater probability of a fit choice.

In the next place, as each representative will be chosen by a greater number of citizens in the large than in the small republic, it will be more difficult for unworthy candidates to practise with success the vicious arts by which elections are too often carried; and the suffrages of the people being more free, will be more likely to center on men who possess the most attractive merit and the most diffusive and established characters.

It must be confessed that in this, as in most other cases, there is a mean, on both sides of which inconveniencies will be found to lie. By enlarging too much the number of electors, you render the representative too little acquainted with all their local circumstances and lesser interests; as by reducing it too much, you render him unduly attached to these, and too little fit to comprehend and pursue great and national objects. The federal Constitution forms a happy combination in this respect; the great and aggregate interests being referred to the national, the local and particular to the State legislatures.

The other point of difference is the greater number of citizens and extent of territory which may be brought within the compass of republican than of democratic government; and it is this circumstance principally which renders factious combinations less to be dreaded in the former than in the latter. The smaller the society, the fewer probably will be the distinct parties and interests composing it; the fewer the distinct parties and interests, the more frequently will a majority be found of the same party; and the smaller the number of individuals composing a majority, and the smaller the compass within which they are placed, the more easily will they concert and execute their plans of oppression. Extend the sphere and you take in a greater variety of parties and interests; you make it less probable that a majority of the whole will have a common motive to invade the rights of other citizens; or if such a common motive exists, it will be more difficult for all who feel it to discover their own strength and to act in unison with each other. Besides other impediments, it may be remarked that, where there is a consciousness of unjust or dishonorable purposes, communication is always checked by distrust in proportion to the number whose concurrence is necessary.

Hence, it clearly appears that the same advantage which a republic has over a democracy in controlling the effects of faction is enjoyed by a large over a small republic—is enjoyed by the Union over the States composing it. Does this advantage consist in the substitution of representatives whose enlightened views and virtuous sentiments render them superior to local prejudices and to schemes of injustice? It will not be denied that the representation of the Union will be most likely to possess these requisite endowments. Does it consist in the greater security afforded by a greater variety of parties, against the event of any one party being able to outnumber and oppress the rest? In an equal degree does the increased variety of parties comprised within the Union increase this security. Does it, in fine, consist in the greater obstacles opposed to the concert and accomplishment of the secret wishes of an unjust and interested majority? Here again the extent of the Union gives it the most palpable advantage.

The influence of factious leaders may kindle a flame within their particular States but will be unable to spread a general conflagration through the other States. A religious sect may degenerate into a political faction in a part of the Confederacy; but the variety of sects dispersed over the entire face of it must secure the national councils against any danger from that source. A rage for paper money, for an abolition of debts, for an equal division of property, or for any other improper or wicked project, will be less apt to pervade the whole body of the Union than a particular member of it, in the same proportion as such a malady is more likely to taint a particular county or district than an entire State.

In the extent and proper structure of the Union, therefore, we behold a republican remedy for the diseases most incident to republican government. And according to the degree of pleasure and pride we feel in being republicans ought to be our zeal in cherishing the spirit and supporting the character of federalists. PUBLIUS

No. 15: Hamilton

In the course of the preceding papers I have endeavored, my fellow-citizens, to place before you in a clear and convincing light the importance of Union to your political safety and happiness. I have unfolded to you a complication of dangers to which you would be exposed, should you permit that sacred knot which binds the people of America together to be severed or dissolved by ambition or by avarice, by jealousy or by misrepresentation. In the sequel of the inquiry through which I propose to accompany you, the truths intended to be inculcated will receive further confirmation from facts and arguments hitherto unnoticed. If the road over which you will still have to pass should in some places appear to you tedious or irksome, you will recollect that you are in quest of information on a subject the most momentous which can engage to attention of a free people, that the field through which you have to travel is in itself spacious, and that the difficulties of the journey have been unnecessarily increased by the mazes with which sophistry has beset the way. It will be my aim to remove the obstacles to your progress in as compendious a manner as it can be done, without sacrificing utility to dispatch.

In pursuance of the plan which I have laid down for the discussion of the subject, the point next in order to be examined is the "insufficiency of the present Confederation to the preservation of the Union." It may perhaps be asked what need there is of reasoning or proof to illustrate a position which is not either controverted or doubted, to which the understandings and feelings of all classes of men assent, and which in substance is admitted by the opponents as well as by the friends of the new Constitution. It must in truth be acknowledged that, however these may differ in other respects, they in general appear to harmonize in this sentiment at least: that there are material imperfections in our national system and that something is necessary to be done to rescue us from impending anarchy. The facts that support this opinion are no longer objects of speculation.

They have forced themselves upon the sensibility of the people at large, and have at length extorted from those, whose mistaken policy has had the principal share in precipitating the extremity at which we are arrived, a reluctant confession of the reality of those defects in the scheme of our federal government which have been long pointed out and regretted by the intelligent friends of the Union.

We may indeed with propriety be said to have reached almost the last stage of national humiliation. There is scarcely anything that can wound the pride or degrade the character of an independent nation which we do not experience. Are there engagements to the performance of which we are held by every tie respectable among men? These are the subjects of constant and unblushing violation. Do we owe debts to foreigners and to our own citizens contracted in a time of imminent peril for the preservation of our political existence? These remain without any proper or satisfactory provision for their discharge. Have we valuable territories and important posts in the possession of a foreign power which, by express stipulations, ought long since to have been surrendered? These are still retained to the prejudice of our interests, not less than of our rights. Are we in a condition to resent or to repel the aggression? We have neither troops, nor treasury, nor government.* Are we even in a condition to remonstrate with dignity? The just imputations on our own faith in respect to the same treaty ought first to be removed. Are we entitled by nature and compact to a free participation in the navigation of the Mississippi? Spain excludes us from it. Is public credit an indispensable resource in time of public danger? We seem to have abandoned its cause as desperate and irretrievable. Is commerce of importance to national wealth? Ours is at the lowest point of declension. Is respectability in the eyes of foreign powers a safeguard against foreign encroachments? The imbecility of our government even forbids them to treat with us. Our ambassadors abroad are the mere pageants of mimic sovereignty. Is a violent and unnatural decrease in the value of land a symptom of national distress? The price of improved land in most parts of the country is much lower than can be accounted for by the quantity of waste land at market, and can only be fully explained by that want of private and public confidence, which are so alarmingly prevalent among all ranks and which have a direct tendency to depreciate property of every kind. Is private credit the friend and patron of industry? That most useful kind which relates to borrowing and lending is reduced within the narrowest limits, and this still more from an opinion of insecurity than from a scarcity of money. To shorten an enumeration of particulars which can afford neither pleasure nor instruction, it may in general be demanded, what indication is there of national disorder, poverty, and insignificance that could befall a community so peculiarly blessed with natural advantages as we are, which does not form a part of the dark catalogue of our public misfortunes?

This is the melancholy situation to which we have been brought by those very maxims and counsels which would now deter us from adopting the proposed Constitution; and which, not content with having conducted us to the brink of a precipice, seem resolved to plunge us into the abyss that awaits us below. Here, my countrymen, impelled by every motive that ought to influence an enlightened people, let us make a firm stand

---

*"I mean for the Union."

for our safety, our tranquillity, our dignity, our reputation. Let us at last break the fatal charm which has too long seduced us from the paths of felicity and prosperity.

It is true, as has been before observed, that facts too stubborn to be resisted have produced a species of general assent to the abstract proposition that there exist material defects in our national system; but the usefulness of the concession on the part of the old adversaries of federal measures is destroyed by a strenuous opposition to a remedy upon the only principles that can give it a chance of success. While they admit that the government of the United States is destitute of energy, they contend against conferring upon it those powers which are requisite to supply that energy. They seem still to aim at things repugnant and irreconcilable; at an augmentation of federal authority without a diminution of State authority; at sovereignty in the Union and complete independence in the members. They still, in fine, seem to cherish with blind devotion the political monster of an *imperium in imperio*. This renders a full display of the principal defects of the Confederation necessary in order to show that the evils we experience do not proceed from minute or partial imperfections, but from fundamental errors in the structure of the building, which cannot be amended otherwise than by an alteration in the first principles and main pillars of the fabric.

The great and radical vice in the construction of the existing Confederation is in the principle of LEGISLATION for STATES or GOVERNMENTS, in their CORPORATE or COLLECTIVE CAPACITIES, and as contradistinguished from the INDIVIDUALS of whom they consist. Though this principle does not run through all the powers delegated to the Union, yet it pervades and governs those on which the efficacy of the rest depends. Except as to the rule of apportionment, the United States have an indefinite discretion to make requisitions for men and money; but they have no authority to raise either by regulations extending to the individual citizens of America. The consequence of this is that though in theory their resolutions concerning those objects are laws constitutionally binding on the members of the Union, yet in practice they are mere recommendations which the States observe or disregard at their option.

It is a singular instance of the capriciousness of the human mind that after all the admonitions we have had from experience on this head, there should still be found men who object to the new Constitution for deviating from a principle which has been found the bane of the old and which is in itself evidently incompatible with the idea of GOVERNMENT; a principle, in short, which, if it is to be executed at all, must substitute the violent and sanguinary agency of the sword to the mild influence of the magistracy.

There is nothing absurd or impracticable in the idea of a league or alliance between independent nations for certain defined purposes precisely stated in a treaty regulating all the details of time, place, circumstance, and quantity, leaving nothing to future discretion, and depending for its execution on the good faith of the parties. Compacts of this kind exist among all civilized nations, subject to the usual vicissitudes of peace and war, of observance and nonobservance, as the interests or passions of the contracting powers dictate. In the early part of the present century there was an epidemical rage in Europe for this species of compacts, from which the politicians of the times fondly hoped for benefits which were never realized. With a view to establishing the equilibrium of power and the peace of that part of the world, all the resources of negotiations were exhausted, and triple and quadruple alliances were formed; but they were scarcely formed before they were broken, giving an instructive but afflicting lesson to mankind how little dependence is to be placed on treaties which have no other sanction than the obligations of good faith, and which oppose general considerations of peace and justice to the impulse of any immediate interest or passion.

If the particular States in this country are disposed to stand in a similar relation to each other, and to drop the project of a general DISCRETIONARY SUPERINTENDENCE, the scheme would indeed be pernicious and would entail upon us all the mischiefs which have been enumerated under the first head; but it would have the merit of being, at least, consistent and practicable. Abandoning all views towards a confederate government, this would bring us to a simple alliance offensive and defensive; and would place us in a situation to be alternate friends and enemies of each other, as our mutual jealousies and rivalships, nourished by the intrigues of foreign nations, should prescribe to us.

But if we are unwilling to be placed in this perilous situation; if we still will adhere to the design of a national government, or, which is the same thing, of a superintending power under the direction of a common council, we must resolve to incorporate into our plan those ingredients which may be considered as forming the characteristic difference between a league and a government; we must extend the authority of the Union to the persons of the citizens—the only proper objects of government.

Government implies the power of making laws. It is essential to the idea of a law that it be attended with a sanction; or, in other words, a penalty or punishment for disobedience. If there be no penalty annexed to disobedience, the resolutions or commands which pretend to be laws will, in fact, amount to nothing more than advice or recommendation. This penalty, whatever it may be, can only be inflicted in two ways: by the agency of the courts and ministers of justice, or by military force; by the COERCION of the magistracy, or by the COERCION of arms. The first kind can evidently apply only to men; the last kind must of necessity be employed against bodies politic, or communities, or States. It is evident that there is no process of a court by which the observance of the laws can in the last resort be enforced. Sentences may be denounced against them for violations of their duty; but these sentences can only be carried into execution by the sword. In an association where the general authority is confined to the collective bodies of the communities that compose it, every breach of the laws must involve a state of war; and military execution must become the only instrument of civil obedience. Such a state of things can certainly not deserve the name of government, nor would any prudent man choose to commit his happiness to it.

There was a time when we were told that breaches by the States of the regulations of the federal authority were not to be expected; that a sense of common interest would preside over the conduct of the respective members, and would beget a full compliance with all the constitutional requisitions of the Union. This language, at the present day, would appear as wild as a great part of what we now hear from the same quarter will be thought, when we shall have received further lessons from that best oracle of wisdom, experience. It at all times betrayed an ignorance of the true springs by which human conduct is actuated, and belied the original inducements to the establishment of civil power. Why has government been instituted at all? Because the passions of men will not conform to the dictates of reason and justice without constraint. Has it been found that bodies of men act with more rectitude or greater disinterestedness than individuals? The contrary of this has been inferred by all accurate observers of the conduct of mankind; and the inference is founded upon obvious reasons. Regard to reputation has a less active influence when the infamy of a bad action is to be divided among a number than when it is to fall singly upon one. A spirit of faction, which is apt to mingle its poison in the deliberations of all bodies of men, will often hurry the persons of whom they are composed into improprieties and excesses for which they would blush in a private capacity.

In addition to all this, there is in the nature of sovereign power an impatience of control that disposes those who are invested with the exercise of it to look with an evil eye upon all external attempts to restrain or direct its operations. From this spirit it happens that in every political association which is formed upon the principle of uniting in a common interest a number of lesser sovereignties, there will be found a kind of eccentric tendency in the subordinate or inferior orbs by the operation of which there will be a perpetual effort in each to fly off from the common center. This tendency is not difficult to be accounted for. It has its origin in the love of power. Power controlled or abridged is almost always the rival and enemy of that power by which it is controlled or abridged. This simple proposition will teach us how little reason there is to expect that the persons intrusted with the administration of the affairs of the particular members of a confederacy will at all times be ready with perfect good humor and an unbiased regard to the public weal to execute the resolutions or decrees of the general authority. The reverse of this results from the constitution of man.

If, therefore, the measures of the Confederacy cannot be executed without the intervention of the particular administrations, there will be little prospect of their being executed at all. The rulers of the respective members, whether they have a constitutional right to do it or not, will undertake to judge of the propriety of the measures themselves. They will consider the conformity of the thing proposed or required to their immediate interests or aims; the momentary conveniences or inconveniences that would attend its adoption. All this will be done; and in a spirit of interested and suspicious scrutiny, without that knowledge of national circumstances and reasons of state, which is essential to a right judgment, and with that strong predilection in favor of local objects, which can hardly fail to mislead the decision. The same process must be repeated in every member of which the body is constituted; and the execution of the plans, framed by the councils of the whole, will always fluctuate on the discretion of the ill-informed and prejudiced opinion of every part. Those who have been conversant in the proceedings of popular assemblies; who have seen how difficult it often is, when there is no exterior pressure of circumstances, to bring them to harmonious resolutions on important points, will readily conceive how impossible it must be to induce a number of such assemblies, deliberating at a distance from each other, at different times and under different impressions, long to co-operate in the same views and pursuits.

In our case the concurrence of thirteen distinct sovereign wills is requisite under the Confederation to the complete execution of every important measure that proceeds from the Union. It has happened as was to have been foreseen. The measures of the Union have not been executed; and the delinquencies of the States have step by step matured themselves to an extreme, which has, at length, arrested all the wheels of the national government and brought them to an awful stand. Congress at this time scarcely possess the means of keeping up the forms of administration, till the States can have time to agree upon a more substantial substitute for the present shadow of a federal government. Things did not come to this desperate extremity at once. The causes which have been specified produced at first only unequal and disproportionate degrees of compliance with the requisitions of the Union. The greater deficiencies of some States furnished the pretext of example and the temptation of interest to the complying, or to the least delinquent States. Why should we do more in proportion than those who are embarked with us in the same political voyage? Why should we consent to bear more than our proper share of the common burden? There were suggestions which human selfishness could not withstand, and which even speculative men, who looked forward to remote consequences, could not without hesitation combat. Each State yielding to the persuasive voice of immediate interest or convenience has successively withdrawn its support, till the frail and tottering edifice seems ready to fall upon our heads and to crush us beneath its ruins.   PUBLIUS

No. 31: Hamilton

In disquisitions of every kind there are certain primary truths, or first principles, upon which all subsequent reasonings must depend. These contain an internal evidence which, antecedent to all reflection or combination, commands the assent of the mind. Where it produces not this effect, it must proceed either from some disorder in the organs of perception, or from the influence of some strong interest, or passion, or prejudice. Of this nature are the maxims in geometry that the whole is greater than its parts; that things equal to the same are equal to one another; that two straight lines cannot enclose a space; and that all right angles are equal to each other. Of the same nature are these other maxims in ethics and politics, that there cannot be an effect without a cause; that the means ought to be proportioned to the end; that every power ought to be commensurate with its object; that there ought to be no limitation of a power destined to effect a purpose which is itself incapable of limitation. And there are other truths in the two latter sciences which, if they cannot pretend to rank in the class of axioms, are yet such direct inferences from them, and so obvious in themselves, and so agreeable to the natural and unsophisticated dictates of common sense that they challenge the assent of a sound and unbiased mind with a degree of force and conviction almost equally irresistible.

The objects of geometrical inquiry are so entirely abstracted from those pursuits which stir up and put in motion the unruly passions of the human heart that mankind, without difficulty, adopt not only the more simple theorems of the science, but even those abstruse paradoxes which, however they may appear susceptible of demonstration, are at variance with the natural conceptions which the mind, without the aid of philosophy, would be led to entertain upon the subject. The INFINITE DIVISIBILITY of matter, or, in other words, the INFINITE divisibility of a FINITE thing, extending even to the minutest atom, is a point agreed among geometricians, though not less incomprehensible to common sense that any of those mysteries in religion against which the batteries of infidelity have been so industriously leveled.

But in the sciences of morals and politics, men are found far less tractable. To a certain degree it is right and useful that this should be the case. Caution and investigation are a necessary armor against error and imposition. But this untractableness may be carried too far, and may degenerate into obstinacy, perverseness, or disingenuity. Though it cannot be pretended that the principles of moral and political knowledge have, in general, the same degree of certainty with those of the mathematics, yet they have much better claims in this respect than to judge from the conduct of men in particular situations we should be disposed to allow them. The obscurity is much oftener in the passions and prejudices of the reasoner than in the subject. Men, upon too many occasions, do not give their own understandings fair play; but, yielding to some untoward bias, they entangle themselves in words and confound themselves in subtleties.

How else could it happen (if we admit the objectors to be sincere in their opposition) that positions so clear as those which manifest the necessity of a general power of taxation in the government of the Union should have to encounter any adversaries among men of discernment? Though these positions have been elsewhere fully stated, they will perhaps not be improperly recapitulated in this place as introductory to an examination of what may have been offered by way of objection to them. They are in substance as follows:

A government ought to contain in itself every power requisite to the full accomplishment of the objects committed to its care, and to the complete execution of the trusts for which it is responsible, free from every other control but a regard to the public good and to the sense of the people.

As the duties of superintending the national defense and of securing the public peace against foreign or domestic violence involve a provision for casualties and dangers to which no possible limits can be assigned, the power of making that provision ought to know no other bounds than the exigencies of the nation and the resources of the community.

As revenue is the essential engine by which the means of answering the national exigencies must be procured, the power of procuring that article in its full extent must necessarily be comprehended in that of providing for those exigencies.

As theory and practice conspire to prove that the power of procuring revenue is unavailing when exercised over the States in their collective capacities, the federal government must of necessity be invested with an unqualified power of taxation in the ordinary modes.

Did not experience evince the contrary, it would be natural to conclude that the propriety of a general power of taxation in the national government might safely be permitted to rest on the evidence of these propositions, unassisted by any additional arguments or illustrations. but we find, in fact, that the antagonists of the proposed Constitution, so far from acquiescing in their justness or truth, seem to make their principal and most zealous effort against this part of the plan. It may therefore be satisfactory to analyze the arguments with which they combat it.

Those of them which have been most labored with that view seem in substance to amount to this: "It is not true, because the exigencies of the Union may not be susceptible of limitation, that its power of laying taxes ought to be unconfined. Revenue is as requisite to the purposes of the local administrations as to those of the Union; and the former are at least of equal importance with the latter to the happiness of the people. It is, there-fore, as necessary that the State governments should be able to command the means of supplying their wants, as that the national government should possess the like faculty in respect to the wants of the Union. But an indefinite power of taxation in the *latter* might, and probably would, in time, deprive the *former* of the means of providing for their own necessities; and would subject them entirely to the mercy of the national legislature. As the laws of the Union are to become the supreme law of the land, as it is to have power to pass all laws that may be NECESSARY for carrying into execution the authorities with which it is proposed to vest it, the national government might at any time abolish the taxes imposed for State objects upon the pretense of an interference with its own. It might allege a necessity of doing this in order to give efficacy to the national revenues. And thus all the resources of taxation might by degrees become the subjects of federal monopoly to the entire exclusion and destruction of the State governments."

This mode of reasoning appears sometimes to turn upon the supposition of usur-pation in the national government; at other times it seems to be designed only as a deduction from the constitutional operation of its intended powers. It is only in the lat-ter light that it can be admitted to have any pretensions to fairness. The moment we launch into conjectures about the usurpations of the federal government, we get into an unfathomable abyss and fairly put ourselves out of the reach of all reasoning. Imagina-tion may range at pleasure till it gets bewildered amidst the labyrinths of an enchanted castle, and knows not on which side to turn to escape from the apparitions which itself has raised. Whatever may be the limits or modifications of the powers of the Union, it is easy to imagine an endless train of possible dangers; and by indulging an excess of jealousy and timidity, we may bring ourselves to a state of absolute skepticism and irreso-lution. I repeat here what I have observed in substance in another place, that all obser-vations founded upon the danger of usurpation ought to be referred to the composition and structure of the government, not to the nature or extent to its powers. The State governments by their original constitutions are invested with complete sovereignty. In what does our security consist against usurpations from that quarter? Doubtless in the manner of their formation, and in due a dependence of those who are to adminis-ter them upon the people. If the proposed construction of the federal government be found, upon an impartial examination of it, to be such as to afford to a proper ex-tent the same species of security, all apprehensions on the score of usurpation ought to be discarded.

It should not be forgotten that a disposition in the State governments to encroach upon the rights of the Union is quite as probable as a disposition in the Union to en-croach upon the rights of the State governments. What side would be likely to prevail in such a conflict must depend on the means which the contending parties could employ towards insuring success. As in republics strength is always on the side of the people, and as there are weighty reasons to induce a belief that the State governments will commonly possess most influence over them, the natural conclusion is that such contests will be most apt to end to the disadvantage of the Union; and that there is greater probability of en-croachments by the members upon the federal head than by the federal head upon the members. But it is evident that all conjectures of this kind must be extremely vague and fallible: and that it is by far the safest course to lay them altogether aside and to confine our attention wholly to the nature and extent of the powers as they are delineated in the Constitution. Everything beyond this must be left to the prudence and firmness of the people; who, as they will hold the scales in their own hands, it is to be hoped will always take care to preserve the constitutional equilibrium between the general and the State governments. Upon this ground, which is evidently the true one, it will not be difficult to obviate the objections which have been made to an indefinite power of taxation in the United States.   PUBLIUS

No. 37: Madison

In reviewing the defects of the existing Confederation and showing that they cannot be supplied by a government of less energy than that before the public, several of the most important principles of the latter fell of course under consideration. But as the ultimate object of these papers is to determine clearly and fully the merits of this Constitution, and the expediency of adopting it, our plan cannot be completed without taking a more critical and thorough survey of the work of the convention, without examining it on all its sides, comparing it in all its parts, and calculating its probable effects. That this remaining task may be executed under impressions conducive to a just and fair result, some reflections must in this place be indulged, which candor previously suggests.

It is a misfortune, inseparable from human affairs, that public measures are rarely investigated with that spirit of moderation which is essential to a just estimate of their real tendency to advance or obstruct the public good; and that this spirit is more apt to be diminished than promoted by those occasions which require an unusual exercise of it. To those who have been led by experience to attend to this consideration, it could not appear surprising that the act of the convention, which recommends so many important changes and innovations, which may be viewed in so many lights and relations, and which touches the springs of so many passions and interests, should find or excite dispositions unfriendly, both on one side and on the other, to a fair discussion and accurate judgment of its merits. In some, it has been too evident from their own publications that they have scanned the proposed Constitution, not only with a predisposition to censure, but with a predetermination to condemn; as the language held by others betrays an opposite predetermination or bias, which must render their opinions also of little moment in the question. In placing, however, these different characters on a level with respect to the weight of their opinions I wish not to insinuate that there may not be a material difference in the purity of their intentions. It is but just to remark in favor of the latter description that as our situation is universally admitted to be peculiarly critical, and to require indispensably that something should be done for our relief, the predetermined patron of what has been actually done may have taken his bias from the weight of these considerations, as well as from considerations of a sinister nature. The predetermined adversary, on the other hand, can have been governed by no venial motive whatever. The intentions of the first may be upright, as they may on the contrary be culpable. The views of the last cannot be upright, and must be culpable. But the truth is that these papers are not addressed to persons falling under either of these characters. They solicit the attention of those only who add to a sincere zeal for the happiness of their country, a temper favorable to a just estimate of the means of promoting it.

Persons of this character will proceed to an examination of the plan submitted by the convention, not only without a disposition to find or to magnify faults; but will see the propriety of reflecting that a faultless plan was not to be expected. Not will they barely make allowances for the errors which may be chargeable on the fallibility to which the convention, as a body of men, were liable; but will keep in mind that they themselves also are but men and ought not to assume an infallibility in rejudging the fallible opinions of others.

With equal readiness will it be perceived that besides these inducements to candor, many allowances ought to be made for the difficulties inherent in the very nature of the undertaking referred to the convention.

The novelty of the undertaking immediately strikes us. It has been shown in the course of these papers that the existing Confederation is founded on principles which are fallacious; that we must consequently change this first foundation, and with it the superstructure resting upon it. It has been shown that the other confederacies which could be consulted as precedents have been vitiated by the same erroneous principles, and can therefore furnish no other light than that of beacons, which give warning of the course to be shunned, without pointing out that which ought to be pursued. The most that the convention could do in such a situation was to avoid the errors suggested by the past experience of other countries, as well as of our own; and to provide a convenient mode of rectifying their own errors, as future experience may unfold them.

Among the difficulties encountered by the convention, a very important one must have lain in combining the requisite stability and energy in government with the inviolable attention due to liberty and to the republican form. Without substantially accomplishing this part of their undertaking, they would have very imperfectly fulfilled the object of their appointment, or the expectation of the public; yet that it could not be easily accomplished will be denied by no one who is unwilling to betray his ignorance of the subject. Energy in government is essential to that security against external and internal danger and to that prompt and salutary execution of the laws which enter into the very definition of good government. Stability in government is essential to national character and to the advantages annexed to it, as well as to that repose and confidence in the minds of the people, which are among the chief blessings of civil society. An irregular and mutable legislation is not more an evil in itself than it is odious to the people; and it may be pronounced with assurance that the people of this country, enlightened as they are with regard to the nature, and interested, as the great body of them are, in the effects of good government, will never be satisfied till some remedy be applied to the vicissitudes and uncertainties which characterize the State administrations. On comparing, however, these valuable ingredients with the vital principles of liberty, we must perceive at once the difficulty of mingling them together in their due proportions. The genius of republican liberty seems to demand on one side not only that all power should be derived from the people, but that those intrusted with it should be kept in dependence on the people by a short duration of their appointments; and that even during this short period the trust should be placed not in a few, but a number of hands. Stability, on the contrary, requires that the hands in which power is lodged should continue for a length of time the same.

A frequent change of men will result from a frequent return of elections; and a frequent change of measures from a frequent change of men: whilst energy in government requires not only a certain duration of power, but the execution of it by a single hand.

How far the convention may have succeeded in this part of their work will better appear on a more accurate view of it. From the cursory view here taken, it must clearly appear to have been an arduous part.

Not less arduous must have been the task of marking the proper line of partition between the authority of the general and that of the State governments. Every man will be sensible of this difficulty in proportion as he has been accustomed to contemplate and discriminate objects extensive and complicated in their nature. The faculties of the mind itself have never yet been distinguished and defined with satisfactory precision by all the efforts of the most acute and metaphysical philosophers. Sense, perception, judgment, desire, volition, memory, imagination are found to be separated by such delicate shades and minute gradations that their boundaries have eluded the most subtle investigations, and remain a pregnant source of ingenious disquisition and controversy. The boundaries between the great kingdom of nature, and, still more, between the various provinces and lesser portions into which they are subdivided afford another illustration of the same important truth. The most sagacious and laborious naturalists have never yet succeeded in tracing with certainty the line which separates the district of vegetable life from the neighboring region of unorganized matter, or which marks the termination of the former and the commencement of the animal empire. A still greater obscurity lies in the distinctive characters by which the objects in each of these great departments of nature have been arranged and assorted.

When we pass from the works of nature, in which all the delineations are perfectly accurate and appear to be otherwise only from the imperfection of the eye which surveys them, to the institutions of man, in which the obscurity arises as well from the object itself as from the organ by which it is contemplated, we must perceive the necessity of moderating still further our expectations and hopes from the efforts of human sagacity. Experience has instructed us that no skill in the science of government has yet been able to discriminate and define, with sufficient certainty, its three great provinces—the legislative, executive, and judiciary; or even the privileges and powers of the different legislative branches. Questions daily occur in the course of practice which prove the obscurity which reigns in these subjects, and which puzzle the greatest adepts in political science.

The experience of ages, with the continued and combined labors of the most enlightened legislators and jurists. has been equally unsuccessful in delineating the several objects and limits of different codes of laws and different tribunals of justice. The precise extent of the common law, and the statute law, the maritime law, the ecclesiastical law, the law of corporations, and other local laws and customs, remains still to be clearly and finally established in Great Britain, where accuracy in such subjects has been more industriously pursued than in any other part of the world. The jurisdiction of her several courts, general and local, of law, of equity, of admiralty, etc., is not less a source of frequent and intricate discussions, sufficiently denoting the indeterminate limits by which they are respectively circumscribed. All new laws, though penned with the greatest technical skill and passed on the fullest and most mature deliberation, are considered as more or less obscure and equivocal, until their meaning be liquidated and ascertained by a se-ries of particular discussions and adjudications. Besides the obscurity arising from the complexity of objects and the imperfection of the human faculties, the medium through which the conceptions of men are conveyed to each other adds a fresh embarrassment. The use of words is to express ideas. Perspicuity, therefore, requires not only that the ideas should be distinctly formed, but that they should be expressed by words distinctly and exclusively appropriate to them. But no language is so copious as to supply words and phrases for every complex idea, or so correct as not to include many equivocally denot-ing different ideas. Hence it must happen that however accurately objects may be discrim-inated in themselves, and however accurately the discrimination may be considered, the definition of them may be rendered inaccurate by the inaccuracy of the terms in which it is delivered. And this unavoidable inaccuracy must be greater or less, according to the complexity and novelty of the objects defined. When the Almighty himself condescends to address mankind in their own language, his meaning, luminous as it must be, is ren-dered dim and doubtful by the cloudy medium through which it is communicated.

Here, then, are three sources of vague and incorrect definitions: indistinctness of the object, imperfection of the organ of conception, inadequateness of the vehicle of ideas. Any one of these must produce a certain degree of obscurity. The convention, in delineating the boundary between the federal and State jurisdictions, must have experi-enced the full effect of them all.

To the difficulties already mentioned may be added the interfering pretensions of the larger and smaller States. We cannot err in supposing that the former would contend for a participation in the government, fully proportioned to their superior wealth and importance; and that the latter would not be less tenacious of the equality at present en-joyed by them. We may well suppose that neither side would entirely yield to the other, and consequently that the struggle could be terminated only by compromise. It is ex-tremely probable, also, that after the ratio of representation had been adjusted, this very compromise must have produced a fresh struggle between the same parties to give such a turn to the organization of the government and to the distribution of its powers as would increase the importance of the branches, in forming which they had respectively obtained the greatest share of influence. There are features in the Constitution which war-rant each of these suppositions; and as far as either of them is well founded, it shows that the convention must have been compelled to sacrifice theoretical propriety to the force of extraneous considerations.

Nor could it have been the large and small States only which would marshal them-selves in opposition to each other on various points. Other combinations, resulting from a difference of local position and policy, must have created additional difficulties. As every State may be divided into different districts, and its citizens into different classes, which give birth to contending interests and local jealousies, so the different parts of the United States are distinguished from each other by a variety of circumstances, which produce a like effect on a larger scale. And although this variety of interests, for reasons sufficiently explained in a former paper, may have a salutary influence on the administration of the government when formed, yet every one must be sensible of the contrary influence which must have been experienced in the task of forming it.

Would it be wonderful if, under the pressure of all these difficulties, the convention should have been forced into some deviations from that artificial structure and regular symmetry which an abstract view of the subject might lead an ingenious theorist to bestow on a Constitution planned in his closet or in his imagination. The real wonder is that so many difficulties should have being surmounted, and surmounted with a unanimity almost as unprecedented as it must have been unexpected. It is impossible for any man of candor to reflect on this circumstance without partaking of the astonishment. It is impossible for the man of pious reflection not to perceive in it a finger of that Almighty hand which has been so frequently and signally extended to our relief in the critical stages of the revolution.

We had occasion in a former paper to take notice of the repeated trials which have been unsuccessfully made in the United Netherlands for reforming the baneful and notorious vices of their constitution. The history of almost all the great councils and consultations held among mankind for reconciling their discordant opinions, assuaging their mutual jealousies and adjusting their respective interests, is a history of factions, contentions, and disappointments, and may be classed among the most dark and degrading pictures which display the infirmities and depravities of the human character. If in a few scattered instances a brighter aspect is presented, they serve only as exceptions to admonish us of the general truth; and by their luster to darken the gloom of the adverse prospect to which they are contrasted. In resolving the causes from which these exceptions result, and applying them to the particular instances before us, we are necessarily led to two important conclusions. The first is that the convention must have enjoyed, in a very singular degree, an exemption from the pestilential influence of party animosities—the disease most incident to deliberative bodies and most apt to contaminate their proceedings. The second conclusion is that all the deputations composing the convention were either satisfactorily accommodated by the final act, or were induced to accede to it by a deep conviction of the necessity of sacrificing private opinions and partial interests to the public good, and by a despair of seeing this necessity diminished by delays or by new experiments.   PUBLIUS

No. 49: Madison

The author of the *Notes on the State of Virginia,* quoted in the last paper, has subjoined to that valuable work the draught of a constitution, which had been prepared in order to be laid before a convention expected to be called in 1783, by the legislature, for the establishment of a constitution for that commonwealth. The plan, like everything from the same pen, marks a turn of thinking, original, comprehensive, and accurate; and is the more worthy of attention as it equally displays a fervent attachment to republican government and an enlightened view of the dangerous propensities against which it ought to be guarded. One of the precautions which he proposes, and on which he appears ultimately to rely as a palladium to the weaker departments of power against the invasions of the stronger, is perhaps altogether his own, and as it immediately relates to the subject of our present inquiry, ought not to be overlooked.

His proposition is "that whenever any two of the three branches of government shall concur in opinion, each by the voices of two thirds of their whole number, that a convention is necessary for altering the Constitution, or *correcting breaches of it,* a convention shall be called for the purpose."

As the people are the only legitimate fountain of power, and it is from them that the constitutional charter, under which the several branches of government hold their power, is derived, it seems strictly consonant to the republican theory to recur to the same original authority, not only whenever it may be necessary to enlarge, diminish, or new-model the powers of government, but also whenever any one of the departments may commit encroachments on the chartered authorities of the others. The several departments being perfectly co-ordinate by the terms of their common commission, neither of them, it is evident, can pretend to an exclusive or superior right of settling the boundaries between their respective powers; and how are the encroachments of the stronger to be prevented, or the wrongs of the weaker to be redressed, without an appeal to the people themselves, who, as the grantors of the commission, can alone declare its true meaning, and enforce its observance?

There is certainly great force in this reasoning, and it must be allowed to prove that a constitutional road to the decision of the people ought to be marked out and kept open, for certain great and extraordinary occasions. But there appear to be insuperable objections against the proposed recurrence to the people, as a provision in all cases for keeping the several departments of power within their constitutional limits.

In the first place, the provision does not reach the case of a combination of two of the departments against the third. If the legislative authority, which possesses so many means of operating on the motives of the other departments, should be able to gain to its interest either of the others, or even one third of its members, the remaining department could derive no advantage from this remedial provision. I do not dwell, however, on this objection, because it may be thought to lie rather against the modification of the principle, than against the principle itself.

In the next place, it may be considered as an objection inherent in the principle that as every appeal to the people would carry an implication of some defect in the government, frequent appeals would, in great measure, deprive the government of that veneration which time bestows on everything, and without which perhaps the wisest and freest governments would not possess the requisite stability. If it be true that all governments rest on opinion, it is no less true that the strength of opinion in each individual, and its practical influence on his conduct, depend much on the number which he supposes to have entertained the same opinion. The reason of man, like man himself, is timid and cautious when left alone, and acquires firmness and confidence in proportion to the number with which it is associated. When the examples which fortify opinion are *ancient* as well as *numerous,* they are known to have a double effect. In a nation of philosophers, this consideration ought to be disregarded. A reverence for the laws would be sufficiently inculcated by the voice of an enlightened reason. But a nation of philosophers is as little to be expected as the philosophical race of kings wished for by Plato. And in every other nation, the most rational government will not find it a superfluous advantage to have the prejudices of the community on its side.

The danger of disturbing the public tranquillity by interesting too strongly the public passions is a still more serious objection against a frequent reference of constitutional questions to the decision of the whole society. Notwithstanding the success which has attended the revisions of our established forms of government and which does so much honor to the virtue and intelligence of the people of America, it must be confessed that the experiments are of too ticklish a nature to be unnecessarily multiplied. We are to recollect that all the existing constitutions were formed in the midst of a danger which repressed the passions most unfriendly to order and concord; of an enthusiastic confidence of the people in their patriotic leaders, which stifled the ordinary diversity of opinions on great national questions; of a universal ardor for new and opposite forms, produced by a universal resentment and indignation against the ancient government; and whilst no spirit of party connected with the changes to be made, or the abuses to be reformed, could mingle its leaven in the operation. The future situations in which we must expect to be usually placed do not present any equivalent security against the danger which is apprehended.

But the greatest objection of all is that the decisions which would probably result from such appeals would not answer the purpose of maintaining the constitutional equilibrium of the government. We have seen that the tendency of republican governments is to an aggrandizement of the legislative at the expense of the other departments. The appeals to the people, therefore, would usually be made by the executive and judiciary departments. But whether made by one side or the other, would each side enjoy equal advantages on the trial? Let us view their different situations. The members of the executive and judiciary departments are few in number, and can be personally known to a small part only of the people. The latter, by the mode of their appointment, as well as by the nature and permanency of it, are too far removed from the people to share much in their prepossessions. The former are generally the objects of jealousy and their administration is always liable to be discolored and rendered unpopular. The members of the legislative department, on the other hand, are numerous. They are distributed and dwell among the people at large. Their connections of blood, of friendship, and of acquaintance embrace a great proportion of the most influential part of the society. The nature of their public trust implies a personal influence among the people, and that they are more immediately the confidential guardians of the rights and liberties of the people. With these advantages it can hardly be supposed that the adverse party would have an equal chance for a favorable issue.

But the legislative party would not only be able to plead their cause most successfully with the people. They would probably be constituted themselves the judges. The same influence which had gained them an election into the legislature would gain them a seat in the convention. If this should not be the case with all, it would probably be the case with many, and pretty certainly with those leading characters, on whom everything depends in such bodies. The convention, in short, would be composed chiefly of men who had been, who actually were, or who expected to be, members of the department whose conduct was arraigned. They would consequently be parties to the very question to be decided by them.

It might, however, sometimes happen, that appeals would be made under circumstances less adverse to the executive and judiciary departments. The usurpations of the legislature might be so flagrant and so sudden, as to admit of no specious coloring. A strong party among themselves might take side with the other branches. The executive power might be in the hands of a peculiar favorite of the people. In such a posture of things, the public decision might be less swayed by prepossessions in favor of the legislative party. But still it could never be expected to turn on the true merits of the question. It would inevitably be connected with the spirit of pre-existing parties, or of parties springing out of the question itself. It would be connected with persons of distinguished character and extensive influence in the community. It would be pronounced by the very men who had been agents in, or opponents of, the measures to which the decision would relate. The *passions*, therefore, not the *reason*, of the public would sit in judgment. But it is the reason, alone, of the public, that ought to control and regulate the government. The passions ought to be controlled and regulated by the government.

We found in the last paper that mere declarations in the written Constitution are not sufficient to restrain the several departments within their legal rights. It appears in this that occasional appeals to the people would be neither a proper nor an effectual provision for that purpose. How far the provisions of a different nature contained in the plan above quoted might be adequate I do not examine. Some of them are unquestionably founded on sound political principals, and all of them are framed with singular ingenuity and precision.   PUBLIUS

No. 51: Madison

To what expedient, then, shall we finally resort, for maintaining in practice the necessary partition of power among the several departments as laid down in the Constitution? The only answer that can be given is that as all these exterior provisions are found to be inadequate the defect must be supplied, by so contriving the interior structure of the government as that its several constituent parts may, by their mutual relations, be the means of keeping each other in their proper places. Without presuming to undertake a full development of this important idea I will hazard a few general observations which may perhaps place it in a clearer light, and enable us to form a more correct judgment of the principles and structure of the government planned by the convention.

In order to lay a due foundation for that separate and distinct exercise of the different powers of government, which to a certain extent is admitted on all hands to be essential to the preservation of liberty, it is evident that each department should have a will of its own; and consequently should be so constituted that the members of each should have as little agency as possible in the appointment of the members of the others. Were this principle rigorously adhered to, it would require that all the appointments for the supreme executive, legislative, and judiciary magistracies should be drawn from the same fountain of authority, the people, through channels having no communication whatever with one another. Perhaps such a plan of constructing the several departments would be less difficult in practice than it may in contemplation appear. Some difficulties, however, and some additional expense would attend the execution of it. Some deviations, therefore, from the principle must be admitted. In the constitution of the judiciary department in particular, it might be inexpedient to insist rigorously on the principle: first, because peculiar qualifications being essential in the members, the primary consideration ought to be to select that mode of choice which best secures these qualifications; second, because the permanent tenure by which the appointments are held in that department must soon destroy all sense of dependence on the authority conferring them.

It is equally evident that the members of each department should be as little dependent as possible on those of the others for the emoluments annexed to their offices. Were the executive magistrate, or the judges, not independent of the legislature in this particular, their independence in every other would be merely nominal.

But the great security against a gradual concentration of the several powers in the same department consists in giving to those who administer each department the necessary constitutional means and personal motives to resist encroachments of the others. The provision for defense must in this, as in all other cases, be made commensurate to the danger of attack. Ambition must be made to counteract ambition. The interest of the man must be connected with the constitutional rights of the place. It may be a reflection on human nature that such devices should be necessary to control the abuses of government. But what is government itself but the greatest of all reflections on human nature? If men were angels, no government would be necessary. If angels were to govern men, neither external nor internal controls on government would be necessary. In framing a government which is to be administered by men over men, the great difficulty lies in this: you must first enable the government to control the governed; and in the next place oblige it to control itself. A dependence on the people is, no doubt, the primary control on the government; but experience has taught mankind the necessity of auxiliary precautions.

This policy of supplying, by opposite and rival interests, the defect of better motives, might be traced through the whole system of human affairs, private as well as public. We see it particularly displayed in all the subordinate distributions of power, where the constant aim is to divide and arrange the several offices in such a manner as that each may be a check on the other—that the private interest of every individual may be a sentinel over the public rights. These inventions of prudence cannot be less requisite in the distribution of the supreme powers of the State.

But it is not possible to give to each department an equal power of self-defense. In republican government, the legislative authority necessarily predominates. The remedy for this inconveniency is to divide the legislature into different branches; and to render them, by different modes of election and different principles of action, as little connected with each other as the nature of their common functions and their common dependence on the society will admit. It may even be necessary to guard against dangerous encroachments by still further precautions. As the weight of the legislative authority requires that it should be thus divided, the weakness of the executive may require, on the other hand, that it should be fortified. An absolute negative on the legislature appears, at first view, to be the natural defense with which the executive magistrate should be armed. But perhaps it would be neither altogether safe nor alone sufficient. On ordinary occasions it might not be exerted with the requisite firmness, and on extraordinary occasions it might be perfidiously abused. May not this defect of an absolute negative be supplied by some qualified connection between this weaker department and the weaker branch of the stronger department, by which the latter may be led to support the constitutional rights of the former, without being too much detached from the rights of its own department?

If the principles on which these observations are founded be just, as I persuade myself they are, and they be applied as a criterion to the several State constitutions, and to the federal Constitution, it will be found that if the latter does not perfectly correspond with them, the former are infinitely less able to bear such a test.

There are, moreover, two considerations particularly applicable to the federal system of America, which place that system in a very interesting point of view.

First. In a single republic, all the power surrendered by the people is submitted to the administration of a single government; and the usurpations are guarded against by a division of the government into distinct and separate departments. In the compound republic of America, the power surrendered by the people is first divided between two distinct governments, and then the portion allotted to each subdivided among distinct and separate departments. Hence a double security arises to the rights of the people. The different governments will control each other, at the same time that each will be controlled by itself.

Second. It is of great importance in a republic not only to guard the society against the oppression of its rulers, but to guard one part of the society against the injustice of the other part. Different interests necessarily exist in different classes of citizens. If a majority be united by a common interest, the rights of the minority will be insecure. There are but two methods of providing against this evil: the one by creating a will in the community independent of the majority—that is, of the society itself; the other, by comprehending in the society so many separate descriptions of citizens as will render an unjust combination of a majority of the whole very improbable, if not impracticable. The first method prevails in all governments possessing an hereditary or self-appointed authority. This, at best, is but a precarious security; because a power independent of the society may as well espouse the unjust views of the major as the rightful interests of the minor party, and may possibly be turned against both parties. The second method will be exemplified in the federal republic of the United States. Whilst all authority in it will be derived from and dependent on the society, the society itself will be broken into so many parts, interests and classes of citizens, that the rights of individuals, or of the minority, will be in little danger from interested combinations of the majority. In a free government the security for civil rights must be the same as that for religious rights. It consists in the one case in the multiplicity of interests, and in the other in the multiplicity of sects. The degree of security in both cases will depend on the number of interests and sects; and this may be presumed to depend on the extent of country and number of people comprehended under the same government. This view of the subject must particularly recommend a proper federal system to all the sincere and considerate friends of republican government, since it shows that in exact proportion as the territory of the Union may be formed into more circumscribed Confederacies, or States, oppressive combinations of a majority will be facilitated; the best security, under the republican forms, for the rights of every class of citizen, will be diminished; and consequently the stability and independence of some member of the government, the only other security, must be proportionally increased. Justice is the end of government. It is the end of civil society. It ever has been and ever will be pursued until it be obtained, or until liberty be lost in the pursuit. In a society under the forms of which the stronger faction can readily unite and oppress the weaker, anarchy may as truly be said to reign as in a state of nature, where the weaker individual is not secured against the violence of the stronger; and as, in the latter state, even the stronger individuals are prompted, by the uncertainty of their condition, to submit to a government which may protect the weak as well as themselves; so, in the former state, will the more powerful factions or parties be gradually induced, by a like motive, to wish for a government which will protect all parties, the weaker as well as the more powerful. It can be little doubted that if the State of Rhode Island was separated from the Confederacy and left to itself, the insecurity of rights under the popular form of government within such narrow limits would be displayed by such reiterated oppressions of factious majorities that some power altogether independent of the people would soon be called for by the voice of the very factions whose misrule had proved the necessity of it. In the extended republic of the United States, and among the great variety of interests, parties, and sects which it embraces, a coalition of a majority of the whole society could seldom take place on any other principles than those of justice and the general good; whilst there being thus less danger to a minor from the will of a major party, there must be less pretext, also, to provide for the security of the former, by introducing into the government a will not dependent on the latter, or, in other words, a will independent of the society itself. It is no less certain than it is important, notwithstanding the contrary opinions which have been entertained, that the larger the society, provided it lie within a practicable sphere, the more duly capable it will be of self-government. And happily for the *republican cause*, the practicable sphere may be carried to a very great extent by a judicious modification and mixture of the *federal principle*.   PUBLIUS

Georg Wilhelm Friedrich Hegel (1770–1831 C.E.)

A German philosopher with appointments to the University of Heidelberg and the University of Berlin, he was a victim of the cholera epidemic of 1831. Hegel's metaphysical views became quite influential throughout most of the nineteenth century and well into the twentieth, and were a key influence on Marx. He edited *The Critical Journal of Philosophy* with the philosopher Schelling. His chief publications are *The Phenomenology of the Spirit* (1807), *Encyclopedia of Philosophy* (1817), and *Outlines of the Philosophy of Right* (1820), excerpted here.

From The Philosophy of Right*

Idea and Aim of the State

The State is the realization of the ethical idea. It is the ethical spirit as revealed, self-conscious, substantial will. It is the will which thinks and knows itself, and carries out what it knows, and in so far as it knows. The unreflected existence of the State rests on custom, and its reflected existence on the self-consciousness of the individual, on his knowledge and activity. The individual, in return, has his substantial freedom in the State, as the essence, purpose, and product of his activity.

   The true State is the ethical whole and the realization of freedom. It is the absolute purpose of reason that freedom should be realized. The State is the spirit, which lives in the world and there realizes itself consciously; while in nature it is actual only as its own other or as dormant spirit. Only as present in consciousness, knowing itself as an existing object, is it the State. The State is the march of God through the world, its ground is the power of reason realizing itself as will. The idea of the State should not denote any particular State, or particular institution; one must rather consider the Idea only, this actual God, by itself. Because it is more easy to find defects than to grasp the positive meaning, one readily falls into the mistake of emphasizing so much the particular nature of the State as to overlook its inner organic essence. The State is no work of art. It exists in the world, and thus in the realm of caprice, accident, and error. Evil behavior toward it may disfigure it on many sides. But the ugliest man, the criminal, the invalid, and the cripple, are still living human beings. The affirmative, life, persists in spite of defects, and it is this affirmative which alone is here in question.

   In the State, everything depends upon the unity of the universal and the particular. In the ancient States the subjective purpose was absolutely one with the will of the State. In modern times, on the contrary, we demand an individual opinion, an individual will and conscience. The ancients had none of these in the modern sense; the final thing for them was the will of the State. While in Asiatic despotisms the individual had no inner

---

*An Excerpt.

self and no self-justification, in the modern world man demands to be honored for the sake of his subjective individuality.

The union of duty and right has the twofold aspect that what the State demands as duty should directly be the right of the individual, since the State is nothing but the organization of the concept of freedom. The determinations of the individual will are given by the State objectivity, and it is through the State alone that they attain truth and realization. The State is the sole condition of the attainment of the particular end and good.

Political disposition, called patriotism—the assurance resting in truth and the will which has become a custom—is simply the result of the institutions subsisting in the State, institutions in which reason is actually present.

Under patriotism one frequently understands a mere willingness to perform extraordinary acts and sacrifices. But patriotism is essentially the sentiment of regarding, in the ordinary circumstances and ways of life, the weal of the community as the substantial basis and the final end. It is upon this consciousness, present in the ordinary course of life and under all circumstances, that the disposition to heroic effort is founded. But as people are often rather magnanimous than just, they easily persuade themselves that they possess the heroic kind of patriotism, in order to save themselves the trouble of having the truly patriotic sentiment, or to excuse the lack of it.

Political sentiment, as appearance, must be distinguished from what people truly will. What they at bottom will is the real cause, but they cling to particular interests and delight in the vain contemplation of improvements. The conviction of the necessary stability of the State in which alone the particular interests can be realized, people indeed possess, but custom makes invisible that upon which our whole existence rests; it does not occur to any one, when he safely passes through the streets at night, that it could be otherwise. The habit of safety has become a second nature, and we do not reflect that it is the result of the activity of special institutions. It is through force—this is frequently the superficial opinion—that the State coheres, but what alone holds it together is the fundamental sense of order, which is possessed by all.

The State is an organism or the development of the idea into its differences. These different sides are the different powers of the State with their functions and activities, by means of which the universal is constantly and necessarily producing itself, and, being presupposed in its own productive function, it is thus always actively present. This organism is the political constitution. It eternally springs from the State, just as the State in turn maintains itself through the constitution. If these two things fall asunder, if both different sides become independent of each other, then the unity which the constitution produces is no longer operative; the fable of the stomach and the other organs may be applied to it. It is the nature of an organism that all its parts must constitute a certain unity; if one part asserts its independence the other parts must go to destruction. No predicates, principles, and the like suffice to express the nature of the State; it must be comprehended as an organism.

The State is real, and its reality consists in the interest of the whole being realized in particular ends. Actuality is always the unity of universality and particularity, and the differentiation of the universal into particular ends. These particular ends seem independent, though they are borne and sustained by the whole only. In so far as this unity is absent, no thing is real, though it may exist. A bad State is one which merely exists. A sick body also exists, but it has no true reality. A hand, which is cut off, still looks like a hand and exists, but it has no reality. True reality is necessity. What is real is eternally necessary.

To the complete State belongs, essentially, consciousness and thought. The State knows thus what it wills, and it knows it under the form of thought.

The essential difference between the State and religion consists in that the commands of the State have the form of legal duty, irrespective of the feelings accompanying their performance; the sphere of religion, on the other hand, is in the inner life. Just as the State, were it to frame its commands as religion does, would endanger the right of the inner life, so the church, if it acts as a State and imposes punishment, degenerates into a tyrannical religion.

In the State one must want nothing which is not an expression of rationality. The State is the world which the spirit has made for itself; it has therefore a determinate and self-conscious course. One often speaks of the wisdom of God in nature, but one must not believe that the physical world of nature is higher than the world of spirit. Just as spirit is superior to nature, so is the State superior to the physical life. We must therefore worship the State as the manifestation of the divine on earth, and consider that, if it is difficult to comprehend nature, it is infinitely harder to grasp the essence of the State. It is an important fact that we, in modern times, have attained definite insight into the State in general and are much engaged in discussing and making constitutions; but that does not advance the problem much. It is necessary to treat a rational matter in the light of reason, in order to learn its essential nature and to know that the obvious does not always constitute the essential.

When we speak of the different functions of the powers of the State, we must not fall into the enormous error of supposing each power to have an abstract, independent existence, since the powers are rather to be differentiated as elements in the conception of the State. Were the powers to be in abstract independence, however, it is clear that two independent things could never constitute a unity, but must produce war, and the result would be destruction of the whole or restoration of unity by force. Thus, in the French Revolution, at one time the legislative power had swallowed up the executive, at another time the executive had usurped the legislative power.

The Constitution

The constitution is rational, in so far as the State defines and differentiates its functions according to the nature of its concept.

Who shall make the constitution? This question seems intelligible, yet on closer examination reveals itself as meaningless, for it presupposes the existence of no constitution, but only a mere mass of atomic individuals. How a mass of individuals is to come by a constitution, whether by its own efforts or by those of others, whether by goodness, thought, or force, it must decide for itself, for with a disorganized mob the concept of the State has nothing to do. But if the question does presuppose an already existing constitution, then to make a constitution means only to change it. The presupposition of a constitution implies, however, at once, that any modification in it must take place constitutionally. It is absolutely essential that the constitution, though having a temporal origin, should not be regarded as made. It (the principle of constitution) is rather to be conceived as absolutely perpetual and rational, and therefore as divine, substantial, and above and beyond the sphere of what is made.

Subjective freedom is the principle of the whole modern world—the principle that all essential aspects of the spiritual totality should develop and attain their right. From this point of view one can hardly raise the idle question as to which form is the better, monarchy or democracy. One can but say that the forms of all constitutions are one-sided that are not able to tolerate the principle of free subjectivity and that do not know how to conform to the fully developed reason.

Since spirit is real only in what it knows itself to be, and since the State, as the nation's spirit, is the law permeating all its affairs, its ethical code, and the consciousness of its individuals, the constitution of a people chiefly depends upon the kind and the character of its self-consciousness. In it lies both its subjective freedom and the reality of the constitution.

To think of giving people a constitution *a priori,* though according to its content a more or less rational one—such a whim would precisely overlook that element which renders a constitution more than a mere abstract object. Every nation, therefore, has the constitution which is appropriate to it and belongs to it.

The State must, in its constitution, permeate all situations. A constitution is not a thing just made; it is the work of centuries, the idea and the consciousness of what is rational, in so far as it is developed in a people. No constitution, therefore, is merely created by the subjects of the State. The nation must feel that its constitution embodies its right and its status, otherwise the constitution may exist externally, but has no meaning or value. The need and the longing for a better constitution may often indeed be present in individuals, but that is quite different from the whole multitude being permeated with such an idea—that comes much later. The principle of morality, the inwardness of Socrates originated necessarily in his day, but it took time before it could pass into general self-consciousness. . . .

Karl Heinrich Marx (1818–1883 C.E.)

Marx was a German philosopher, educated at the Universities of Bonn and Berlin. Falling under the influence of Hegel, Marx initially followed Ludwig Feuerbach in rejecting theological interpretations of the Absolute, revising Hegel's dialectical *Idealism* into a dialectical *Materialism*. Marx took his Doctorate in Philosophy at the University of Jena, defending a thesis on Democritus and Epicurus. His early works include the "Economic and Philosophical Manuscripts" of 1844. Expelled from France in 1845 and then from Brussels in 1848, he spent the rest of his life in London. Marx involved himself in the politics of the socialist movement, supporting himself through free-lance writings for European and American newspapers. Of his book-length manuscripts many went unpublished in his lifetime. His major publications include *The Communist Manifesto* (1848, with Friedrich Engels), *Critique of the Gotha Programme*, and his chief lifetime publication, *Capital* (1867). Important posthumously published works include the *Grundrisse* and (with Engels) *The German Ideology*.

From Grundrisse*

General Introduction

I. Production

The subject of our discussion is first of all *material* production. Individuals producing in society, thus the socially determined production of individuals, naturally constitutes the starting-point. The individual and isolated hunter or fisher who forms the starting-point with Smith and Ricardo belongs to the insipid illusions of the eighteenth century. They are Robinson Crusoe stories which do not by any means represent, as students of the history of civilization imagine, a reaction against over-refinement and a return to a misunderstood natural life. They are no more based on such a naturalism than is Rousseau's *contrat social* which makes naturally independent individuals come in contact and have mutual intercourse by contract. They are the fiction and only the aesthetic fiction of the small and great adventure stories. They are, rather, the anticipation of 'civil society', which had been in the course of development since the sixteenth century and made gigantic strides towards maturity in the eighteenth. In this society of free competition the individual appears free from the bonds of nature, etc., which in former epochs of history made him part of a definite, limited human conglomeration. To the prophets of the eighteenth century, on whose shoulders Smith and Ricardo are still standing, this eighteenth-century individual, constituting the joint product of the dissolution of the feudal form of society and of the new forces of production which had developed since the sixteenth century, appears as an ideal

---

*An Excerpt.

whose existence belongs to the past; not as a result of history, but as its starting-point. Since that individual appeared to be in conformity with nature and corresponded to their conception of human nature, he was regarded not as developing historically, but as posited by nature. This illusion has been characteristic of every new epoch in the past. Steuart, who, as an aristocrat, stood more firmly on historical ground and was in many respects opposed to the spirit of the eighteenth century, escaped this simplicity of view.

The farther back we go into history, the more the individual and, therefore, the producing individual seems to depend on and belong to a larger whole: at first it is, quite naturally, the family and the clan, which is but an enlarged family; later on, it is the community growing up in its different forms out of the clash and the amalgamation of clans. It is only in the eighteenth century, in 'civil society', that the different forms of social union confront the individual as a mere means to his private ends, as an external necessity. But the period in which this standpoint—that of the isolated individual—became prevalent is the very one in which the social relations of society (universal relations according to that standpoint) have reached the highest state of development. Man is in the most literal sense of the word a *zoon politikon,* not only a social animal, but an animal which can develop into an individual only in society. Production by isolated individuals outside society—something which might happen as an exception to a civilized man who by accident got into the wilderness and already potentially possessed within himself the forces of society—is as great an absurdity as the idea of the development of language without individuals living together and talking to one another. We need not dwell on this any longer. It would not be necessary to touch upon this point at all, had not this nonsense—which, however, was justified and made sense in the eighteenth century—been transplanted, in all seriousness, into the field of political economy by Bastiat, Carey, Proudhon, and others. Proudhon and others naturally find it very pleasant, when they do not know the historical origin of a certain economic phenomenon, to give it a quasi-historico-philosophical explanation by going into mythology. Adam or Prometheus hit upon the scheme cut and dried, whereupon it was adopted, etc. Nothing is more tediously dry than the dreaming platitude.

Whenever we speak, therefore, of production, we always have in mind production at a certain stage of social development, or production by social individuals. Hence, it might seem that in order to speak of production at all, we must either trace the historical process of development through its various phases, or declare at the outset that we are dealing with a certain historical period, as, for example, with modern capitalist production, which, as a matter of fact, constitutes the proper subject of this work. But all stages of production have certain landmarks in common, common purposes. 'Production in general' is an abstraction, but it is a rational abstraction, in so far as it singles out and fixes the common features, thereby saving us repetition. Yet these general or common features discovered by comparison constitute something very complex, whose constituent elements have different destinations. Some of these elements belong to all epochs, others are common to a few. Some of them are common to the most modern as well as to the most ancient epochs. No production is conceivable without them; but while even the most completely developed languages have laws and conditions in common with the least developed ones, what is characteristic of their development are the points of departure from the general and common. The conditions which generally govern production must be differentiated in order that the essential points of difference should not be lost sight of in view of the general uniformity which is due to the fact that the subject, mankind, and the object, nature, remain the same. The failure to remember this one fact is the source of all the wisdom of modern economists who are trying to prove the eternal nature and harmony of existing social conditions. Thus they say, for example, that no production is possible without some instrument of production, let that instrument be only the hand; that none is possible without past accumulated labour, even if that labour should consist of mere skill which has been accumulated and concentrated in the hand of the savage by repeated exercise. Capital is, among other things, also an instrument of production, also past impersonal labour. Hence capital is a universal, eternal, natural phenomenon; which is true if we disregard the specific properties which turn an 'instrument of production' and 'stored up labour' into capital. The entire history of the relationships of production appears to a man like Carey, for example, as a malicious perversion on the part of governments.

If there is no production in general there is also no general production. Production is always either some special branch of production, as, for example, agriculture, stock-raising, manufactures, etc., or an aggregate. But political economy is not technology. The connection between the general determinations of productions at a given stage of social development and the particular forms of production is to be developed elsewhere (later on).

Finally, production is never only of a particular kind. It is always a certain social body or a social subject that is engaged on a larger or smaller aggregate of branches of production. The connection between the real process and its scientific presentation also falls outside of the scope of this treatise. Production in general. Special branches of production. Production as a whole.

It is the fashion with economists to open their works with a general introduction, which is entitled 'production' (see, for example, John Stuart Mill) and deals with the general 'requisites of production'. This general introductory part consists of (or is supposed to consist of):

1. The conditions without which production is impossible, i.e. the essential conditions of all production. As a matter of fact, however, it can be reduced, as we shall see, to a few very simple definitions, which flatten out into shallow tautologies.

2. Conditions which further production more or less, as, for example, Adam Smith's discussion of a progressive and stagnant state of society.

In order to give scientific value to what serves with him as a mere summary, it would be necessary to study the degree of productivity by periods in the development of individual nations; such a study falls outside the scope of the present subject, and in so far as it does belong here is to be brought out in connection with the discussion of competition, accumulation, etc. The commonly accepted view of the matter gives a general answer to the effect that an industrial nation is at the height of its production at the moment when it reaches its historical climax in all respects. As a matter of fact a nation is at its industrial height so long as its main object is not gain, but the process of gaining. In that respect the Yankees stand above the English. Or, that certain races, climates, natural conditions, such as distance from the sea, fertility of the soil, etc., are more favourable to production than others. That again comes down to the tautology that the facility of creating wealth depends on the extent to which its elements are present both subjectively and objectively.

But all that is not what the economists are really concerned with in this general part. Their object is rather to represent production in contradistinction to distribution—see Mill, for example—as subject to eternal laws independent of history, and then to substitute bourgeois relations, in an underhand way, as immutable natural laws of society *in abstracto*. This is the more or less conscious aim of the entire proceeding. When it comes to distribution, on the contrary, mankind is supposed to have indulged in all sorts of arbitrary action. Quite apart from the fact that they violently break the ties which bind production and distribution together, so much must be clear from the outset: that, no matter how greatly the systems of distribution may vary at different stages of society, it should be possible here, as in the case of production, to discover the common features and to confound and eliminate all historical differences in formulating general human laws. For example, the slave, the serf, the wage-labourer—all receive a quantity of food, which enables them to exist as slave, serf, and wage-labourer. The conqueror, the official, the landlord, the monk or the Levite, who respectively live on tribute, taxes, rent, alms, and the tithe—all receive a part of the social product which is determined by laws different from those which determine the part received by the slave, etc. The two main points which all economists place under this head are, first, property; secondly, the protection of the latter by the administration of justice, police, etc. The objections to these two points can be stated very briefly.

1. All production is appropriation of nature by the individual within and through a definite form of society. In that sense it is a tautology to say that property (appropriation) is a condition of production. But it becomes ridiculous, when from that one jumps at once to a definite form of property, e.g. private property (which implies, besides, as a prerequisite the existence of an opposite form, viz. absence of property). History points rather to common property (e.g. among the Hindus, Slavs, ancient Celts, etc.) as the primitive form, which still plays an important part at a much later period as communal property. The question as to whether wealth grows more rapidly under this or that form of property is not even raised here as yet. But that there can be no such thing as production, nor, consequently, society, where property does not exist in any form, is a tautology. Appropriation which does not appropriate is a contradictio in subjecto.

2. Protection of gain, etc. Reduced to their real meaning, these commonplaces express more than their preachers know, namely, that every form of production creates its own legal relations, forms of government, etc. The crudity and the shortcomings of the conception lie in the tendency to see only an accidental reflective connection in what constitutes an organic union. The bourgeois economists have a vague notion that production is better carried on under the modern police than it was, for example, under club law. They forget that club law is also law, and that the right of the stronger continues to exist in other forms even under their 'government of law'.

When the social conditions corresponding to a certain stage of production are in a state of formation or disappearance, disturbances of production naturally arise, although differing in extent and effect.

To sum up: all the stages of production have certain destinations in common, which we generalize in thought: but the so-called general conditions of all production are nothing but abstract conceptions which do not go to make up any real stage in the history of production.

2. The General Relation of Production to Distribution, Exchange, and Consumption

Before going into a further analysis of production, it is necessary to look at the various divisions which economists put side by side with it. The most shallow conception is as follows: by production, the members of society appropriate (produce and shape) the products of nature to human wants; distribution determines the proportion in which the individual participates in this production; exchange brings him the particular products into which he wishes to turn the quantity secured by him through distribution; finally, through consumption the products become objects of use and enjoyment, of individual appropriation. Production yields goods adapted to our needs; distribution distributes them according to social laws; exchange distributes further what has already been distributed, according to individual wants; finally, in consumption the product drops out of the social movement, becoming the direct object of the individual want which it serves and satisfies in use. Production thus appears as the starting-point; consumption as the final end; and distribution and exchange as the middle; the latter has a double aspect, distribution being defined as a process carried on by society, exchange as one proceeding from the individual. The person is objectified in production; the material thing is subjectified in the person. In distribution, society assumes the part of go-between for production and consumption in the form of generally prevailing rules; in exchange this is accomplished by the accidental make-up of the individual.

Distribution determines what proportion (quantity) of the products the individual is to receive; exchange determines the products in which the individual desires to receive his share allotted to him by distribution.

Production, distribution, exchange, and consumption thus form a perfect connection, production standing for the general, distribution and exchange for the special, and consumption for the individual, in which all are joined together. To be sure this is a connection, but it does not go very deep. Production is determined according to the economists by universal natural laws, while distribution depends on social chance: distribution can, therefore, have a more or less stimulating effect on production: exchange lies between the two as a formal social movement, and the final act of consumption, which is considered not only as a final purpose but also as a final aim, falls properly outside the scope of economics, except in so far as it reacts on the starting-point and causes the entire process to begin all over again.

The opponents of the economists—whether economists themselves or not—who reproach them with tearing apart, like barbarians, what is an organic whole, either stand on common ground with them or are below them. Nothing is more common than the charge that the economists have been considering production as an end in itself, too much to the exclusion of everything else. The same has been said with regard to distribution. This accusation is itself based on the economic conception that distribution exists side by side with production as a self-contained, independent sphere. Or, it is said, the various factors are not grasped in their unity. As though it were the textbooks that impress this separation upon life and not life upon the textbooks; and as though the subject at issue were a dialectical balancing of conceptions and not an analysis of real conditions.

Exchange and Circulation. The result we arrive at is not that production, distribution, exchange, and consumption are identical, but that they are all members of one entity, different aspects of one unit. Production predominates not only over production itself in the opposite sense of that term, but over the other elements as well. With production the process constantly starts over again. That exchange and consumption cannot be the predominating elements is self-evident. The same is true of distribution in the narrow sense of distribution of products; as for distribution in the sense of distribution of the agents of production, it is itself but a factor of production. A definite form of production thus determines the forms of consumption, distribution, exchange, and also the mutual relations between these various elements. Of course, production in its one-sided form is in its turn influenced by other elements, i.e. with the expansion of the market, i.e. of the sphere of exchange, production grows in volume and is subdivided to a greater extent.

With a change in distribution, production undergoes a change; as for example in the case of concentration of capital, of a change in the distribution of population in city and country, etc. Finally the demands of consumption also influence production. A mutual interaction takes place between the various elements. Such is the case with every organic body.

3. The Method of Political Economy

When we consider a given country from a politico-economic stand-point, we begin with its population, its subdivision into classes, location in city, country, or by the sea, occupation in different branches of production; then we study its exports and imports, annual production and consumption, prices of commodities, etc. It seems to be the correct procedure to commence with the real and the concrete, the actual prerequisites; in the case of political economy, to commence with population, which is the basis and the author of the entire productive activity of society. Yet on closer consideration it proves to be wrong. Population is an abstraction, if we leave out for example the classes of which it consists. These classes, again, are but an empty word unless we know what are the elements on which they are based, such as wage-labour, capital, etc. These imply, in their turn, exchange, division of labour, prices, etc. Capital, for example, does not mean anything without wage-labour, value, money, price, etc. If we start out, therefore, with population, we do so with a chaotic conception of the whole, and by closer analysis we will gradually arrive at simpler ideas; thus we shall proceed from the imaginary concrete to less and less complex abstractions, until we arrive at the simplest determinations. This once attained, we might start on our return journey until we finally came back to population, but this time not as a chaotic notion of an integral whole, but as a rich aggregate of many determinations and relations. The former method is the one which political economy had adopted in the past as its inception. The economists of the seventeenth century, for example, always started out with the living aggregate: population, nation, state, several states, etc., but in the end they invariably arrived by means of analysis at certain leading abstract general principles such as division of labour, money, value, etc. As soon as these separate elements had been more or less established by abstract reasoning, there arose the systems of political economy which start from simple conceptions such as labour, division of labour, demand, exchange value, and conclude with state, international exchange, and world market. The latter is manifestly the scientifically correct method. The concrete is concrete because it is a combination of many determinations, i.e. a unity of diverse elements. In our thought it therefore appears as a process of synthesis, as a result, and not as a starting-point, although it is the real starting-point and, therefore, also the starting-point of observation and conception. By the former method the complete conception passes into an abstract definition; by the latter the abstract definitions lead to the reproduction of the concrete subject in the course of reasoning. Hegel fell into the error, therefore, of considering the real as the result of self-coordinating, self-absorbed, and spontaneously operating thought, while the method of advancing from the abstract to the concrete is but the way of thinking by which the concrete is grasped and is reproduced in our mind as concrete. It is by no means, however, the process which itself generates the concrete. The simplest economic category, say, exchange value, implies the existence of population, population that is engaged in production under certain conditions; it also implies the existence of certain types of family, clan, or state, etc. It can have no other existence except as an abstract one-sided relation of an already given concrete and living aggregate.

As a category, however, exchange value leads an antediluvian existence. Thus the consciousness for which comprehending thought is what is most real in man, for which the world is only real when comprehended (and philosophical consciousness is of this nature), mistakes the movement of categories for the real act of production (which unfortunately receives only its impetus from outside), whose result is the world; that is true—here we have, however, again a tautology—in so far as the concrete aggregate, as a thought aggregate, the concrete subject of our thought, is in fact a product of thought, of comprehension; not, however, in the sense of a product of a self-emanating conception which works outside of and stands above observation and imagination, but of a conceptual working-over of observation and imagination. The whole, as it appears in our heads as a thought-aggregate, is the product of a thinking mind which grasps the world in the only way open to it, a way which differs from the one employed by the artistic, religious, or practical mind. The concrete subject continues to lead an independent existence after it has been grasped, as it did before, outside the head, so long as the head contemplates it only speculatively, theoretically. So that in the employment of the theoretical method in political economy, the subject, society, must constantly be kept in mind as the premiss from which we start.

But have these simple categories no independent historical or natural existence antedating the more concrete ones? That depends. For instance, in his *Philosophy of Right* Hegel rightly starts out with possession, as the simplest legal relation of individuals. But there is no such thing as possession before the family or the relations of lord and serf, which relations are a great deal more concrete, have come into existence. On the other hand, one would be right in saying that there are families and clans which only *possess*, but do not *own* things. The simpler category thus appears as a relation of simple family and clan communities with respect to property. In society the category appears as a simple relation of a developed organization, but the concrete substratum from which the relation of possession springs is always implied. One can imagine an isolated savage in possession of things. But in that case possession is no legal relation. It is not true that the family came as the result of the historical evolution of possession. On the contrary, the latter always implies the existence of this 'more concrete category of law'. Yet this much may be said, that the simple categories are the expression of relations in which the less developed concrete entity may have been realized without entering into the manifold relations and bearings which are mentally expressed in the concrete category; but when the concrete entity attains fuller development it will retain the same category as a subordinate relation.

Money may exist and actually had existed in history before capital or banks or wage-labour came into existence. With that in mind, it may be said that the more simple category can serve as an expression of the predominant relations of an undeveloped whole or of the subordinate relations of a more developed whole, relations which had historically existed before the whole developed in the direction expressed in the more concrete category. To this extent, the course of abstract reasoning, which ascends from the most simple to the complex, corresponds to the actual process of history.

On the other hand, it may be said that there are highly developed but historically less mature forms of society in which the highest economic forms are to be found, such as co-operation, advanced division of labour, etc., and yet there is no money in existence, e.g. Peru. In Slav communities also, money, as well as exchange to which it owes its existence, does not appear at all or very little within the separate communities, but it appears on their boundaries in their intercommunal traffic; in general, it is erroneous to consider exchange as a constituent element originating within the community. It appears at first more in the mutual relations between different communities than in those between the members of the same community. Furthermore, although money begins to play its part everywhere at an early stage, it plays in antiquity the part of a predominant element only in unidirectionally developed nations, viz. trading nations, and even in the most cultured antiquity, in Greece and Rome, it attains its full development, which constitutes the prerequisite of modern bourgeois society, only in the period of their decay. Thus this quite simple category attained its culmination in the past only at the most advanced stages of society. Even then it did not pervade all economic relations; in Rome, for example, at the time of its highest development, taxes and payments in kind remained the basis. As a matter of fact, the money system was fully developed there only so far as the army was concerned; it never came to dominate the entire system of labour. Thus, although the simple category may have existed historically before the more concrete one, it can attain its complete internal and external development only in complex forms of society, while the more concrete category has reached its full development in a less advanced form of society.

Labour is quite a simple category. The idea of labour in that sense, as labour in general, is also very old. Yet 'labour' thus simply defined by political economy is as much a modern category as the conditions which have given rise to this simple abstraction. The monetary system, for example, defines wealth quite objectively, as a thing external to itself in money. Compared with this point of view, it was a great step forward when the industrial or commercial system came to see the source of wealth not in the object but in the activity of persons, viz. in commercial and industrial labour. But even the latter was thus considered only in the limited sense of a money-producing activity. The physiocratic system marks still further progress in that it considers a certain form of labour, viz. agriculture, as the source of wealth, and wealth itself not in the disguise of money, but as a product in general, as the general result of labour. But corresponding to the limitations of the activity, this product is still only a natural product. Agriculture is productive, land is the source of production *par excellence.* It was a tremendous advance on the part of Adam Smith to throw aside all the limitations which mark wealth-producing activity and to define it as labour in general, neither industrial nor commercial nor agricultural, or one any more than the other. Along with the universal character of wealth-creating activity we now have the universal character of the object defined as wealth, viz. product in general, or labour in general, but as past, objectified labour. How difficult and how great was the transition is evident from the way Adam Smith himself falls back from time to time into the physiocratic system. Now it might seem as though this amounted simply to finding an abstract expression for the simplest relation into which men have been mutually entering as producers from times of yore, no matter under what form of society. In one sense this is true. In another it is not.

The indifference as to the particular kind of labour implies the existence of a highly developed aggregate of different species of concrete labour, none of which is any longer the predominant one. So the most general abstractions commonly arise only where there is the highest concrete development, where one feature appears to be jointly possessed by many and to be common to all. Then it cannot be thought of any longer in one particular form. On the other hand, this abstraction of labour is only the result of a concrete aggregate of different kinds of labour. The indifference to the particular kind of labour corresponds to a form of society in which individuals pass with ease from one kind of work to another, which makes it immaterial to them what particular kind of work may fall to their share. Labour has become here, not only categorially but really, a means of creating wealth in general and has no longer coalesced with the individual in one particular manner. This state of affairs has found its highest development in the most modern of bourgeois societies, the United States. It is only here that the abstraction of the category 'labour', 'labour in general', labour *sans phrase*, the starting-point of modern political economy, becomes realized in practice. Thus the simplest abstraction which modern political economy sets up as its starting-point, and which expresses a relation dating back to antiquity and prevalent under all forms of society, appears truly realized in this abstraction only as a category of the most modern society. It might be said that what appears in the United States as a historical product—viz. the indifference as to the particular kind of labour—appears among the Russians, for example, as a spontaneously natural disposition. But it makes all the difference in the world whether barbarians have a natural predisposition which makes them capable of applying themselves alike to everything, or whether civilized people apply themselves to everything. And, besides, this indifference of the Russians as to the kind of work they do corresponds to their traditional practice of remaining in the rut of a quite definite occupation until they are thrown out of it by external influences.

This example of labour strikingly shows how even the most abstract categories, in spite of their applicability to all epochs—just because of their abstract character—are by the very definiteness of the abstraction a product of historical conditions as well, and are fully applicable only to and under those conditions.

Bourgeois society is the most highly developed and most highly differentiated historical organization of production. The categories which serve as the expression of its conditions and the comprehension of its own organization enable it at the same time to gain an insight into the organization and the relationships of production which have prevailed under all the past forms of society, on the ruins and constituent elements of which it has arisen, and of which it still drags along some unsurmounted remains, while what had formerly been mere intimation has now developed to complete significance. The anatomy of the human being is the key to the anatomy of the ape. But the intimations of a higher animal in lower ones can be understood only if the animal of the higher order is already known. The bourgeois economy furnishes a key to ancient economy, etc. This is, however, by no means true of the method of those economists who blot out all historical differences and see the bourgeois form in all forms of society. One can understand the nature of tribute, tithes, etc., after one has learned the nature of rent. But they must not be considered identical.

Since, furthermore, bourgeois society is only a form resulting from the development of antagonistic elements, some relations belonging to earlier forms of society are frequently to be found in it, though in a crippled state or as a travesty of their former self, as for example communal property. While it may be said, therefore, that the categories of bourgeois economy contain what is true of all other forms of society, the statement is to be taken *cum grano salis* [with a grain of salt]. They may contain these in a developed or crippled or caricatured form, but always essentially different. The so-called historical development amounts in the last analysis to this, that the last form considers its predecessors as stages leading up to itself and always perceives them from a single point of view, since it is very seldom and only under certain conditions that it is capable of self-criticism; of course, we do not speak here of such historical periods as appear to their own contemporaries to be periods of decay. The Christian religion became capable of assisting us to an objective view of past mythologies as soon as it was ready for self-criticism to a certain extent, *dynamei*, so to speak. In the same way bourgeois political economy first came to understand the feudal, the ancient, and the oriental societies as soon as the self-criticism of bourgeois society had commenced. In as far as bourgeois political economy has not gone into the mythology of identifying the bourgeois system purely with the past, its criticism of the feudal system against which it still had to wage war resembled Christian criticism of the heathen religions or Protestant criticism of Catholicism.

In the study of economic categories, as in the case of every historical and social science, it must be borne in mind that, as in reality so in our mind, the subject, in this case modern bourgeois society, is given, and that the categories are therefore only forms of being, manifestations of existence, and frequently only one-sided aspects of this subject, this definite society; and that, expressly for that reason, the origin of political economy *as a science* does not by any means date from the time to which it is referred to *as such*. This is to be firmly kept in mind because it has an immediate and important bearing on the matter of the subdivisions of the science.

For instance, nothing seems more natural than to start with rent, with landed property, since it is bound up with land, the source of all production and all existence, and with the first form of production in all more or less settled communities, viz. agriculture. But nothing would be more erroneous. Under all forms of society there is a certain industry which predominates over all the rest and whose condition therefore determines the rank and influence of all the rest.

It is the universal light with which all the other colours are tinged and by whose peculiarity they are modified. It is a special ether which determines the specific gravity of everything that appears in it.

Let us take for example pastoral nations (mere hunting and fishing tribes are not as yet at the point from which real development commences). They engage in a certain form of agriculture, sporadically. The nature of land ownership is determined thereby. It is held in common and retains this form more or less according to the extent to which these nations hold on to traditions; such, for example, is land ownership among the Slavs. Among nations whose agriculture is carried on by a settled population—the settled state constituting a great advance—where agriculture is the predominant industry, such as in ancient and feudal societies, even the manufacturing industry and its organizations, as well as the forms of property which pertain to it, have more or less the characteristic features of the prevailing system of land ownership; society is then either entirely dependent upon agriculture, as in the case of ancient Rome, or, as in the Middle Ages, it imitates in its civic relations the forms or organization prevailing in the country. Even capital, with the exception of pure money capital, has, in the form of the traditional working tool, the characteristics of land ownership in the Middle Ages.

The reverse is true of bourgeois society. Agriculture comes to be more and more merely a branch of industry and is completely dominated by capital. The same is true of rent. In all the forms of society in which land ownership is the prevalent form, the influence of the natural element is the predominant one. In those where capital predominates, the prevailing element is the one historically created by society. Rent cannot be understood without capital, whereas capital can be understood without rent. Capital is the all-dominating economic power of bourgeois society. It must form the starting-point as well as the end and be developed before land ownership. After each has been considered separately, their mutual relation must be analysed.

It would thus be impractical and wrong to arrange the economic categories in the order in which they were the determining factors in the course of history. Their order of sequence is rather determined by the relation which they bear to one another in modern bourgeois society, and which is the exact opposite of what seems to be their natural order or the order of their historical development. What we are interested in is not the place which economic relations occupy in the historical succession of different forms of society. Still less are we interested in the order of their succession 'in the idea' (*Proudhon*), which is but a hazy conception of the course of history. We are interested in their organic connection within modern bourgeois society.

The sharp line of demarcation (abstract precision) which so clearly distinguished the trading nations of antiquity, such as the Phoenicians and the Carthaginians, was due to that very predominance of agriculture. Capital as trading or money capital appears in that abstraction where capital does not constitute as yet the predominating element of society. The Lombards and the Jews occupied the same position among the agricultural societies of the Middle Ages.

As a further illustration of the fact that the same category plays different parts at different stages of society, we may mention the following: one of the latest forms of bourgeois society, viz. joint stock companies, appears also at its beginning in the form of the great chartered monopolistic trading companies.

The concept of national wealth which is imperceptibly formed in the minds of the economists of the seventeenth century, and which in part continues to be entertained by those of the eighteenth century, is that wealth is produced solely for the state, but that the power of the latter is proportional to that wealth. It was as yet an unconsciously hypocritical way in which wealth announced itself and its own production as the aim of modern states, considering the latter merely as a means to the production of wealth.

The order of treatment must manifestly be as follows: first, the general abstract definitions which are more or less applicable to all forms of society, but in the sense indicated above. Secondly, the categories which go to make up the inner organization of bourgeois society and constitute the foundations of the principal classes: capital, wage-labour, landed property; their mutual relations; city and country; the three great social classes, the exchange between them; circulation, credit (private). Thirdly, the organization of bourgeois society in the form of the state, considered in relation to itself; the 'unproductive' classes; taxes; public debts; public credit; population; colonies; emigration. Fourthly, the international organization of production; international division of labour; international exchange; import and export; rate of exchange. Fifthly, the world market and crises.

4. Production, Means of Production, and Conditions of Production: the Relations of Production and Distribution; the Connection between Form of State and Consciousness on the One Hand and Relations of Production and Distribution on the Other: Legal Relations: Family Relations

Notes on the points to be mentioned here and not to be omitted:

1. *War* attains complete development before peace; how certain economic phenomena, such as wage-labour, machinery, etc., are developed at an earlier date through war and in armies than within bourgeois society. The connection between productive force and commercial relationships is made especially plain in the case of the army.

2. The relation between the previous idealistic methods of writing history and the realistic method; namely, the so-called history of civilization, which is all a history of religion and states. In this connection something may be said of the different methods hitherto employed in writing history. The so-called objective method. The subjective (the moral and others). The philosophical.

3. *Secondary and tertiary.* Conditions of production which have been taken over or transplanted; in general, those that are not original. Here the effect of international relations must be introduced.

4. Objections to the materialistic character of this view. Its relation to naturalistic materialism.

5. The dialectic of the conception of productive force (means of production) and relation of production, a dialectic whose limits are to be determined and which does not do away with the concrete difference.

6. The unequal relation between the development of material production and art, for instance. In general, the conception of progress is not to be taken in the sense of the usual abstraction. In the case of art, etc., it is not so important and difficult to understand this disproportion as in that of practical social relations, e.g. the relation between education in the United States and Europe. The really difficulty point, however, that is to be discussed here is that of the unequal development of relations of production as legal relations. As, for example, the connection between Roman civil law (this is less true of criminal and public law) and modern production.

7. This conception of development appears to imply necessity. On the other hand, justification of accident. How. (Freedom and other points.) (The effect of means of communication.) World history has not always existed; history as world history is a result.

8. The starting-point is to be found in certain facts of nature embodied subjectively and objectively in clans, races, etc.

It is well known that certain periods of the highest development of art stand in no direct connection to the general development of society, or to the material basis and skeleton structure of its organization. Witness the example of the Greeks as compared with the modern nations, or even Shakespeare. As regards certain forms of art, e.g. the epos, it is admitted that they can never be produced in the universal epoch-making form as soon as art as such has come into existence; in other words, that in the domain of art certain important forms of it are possible only at a low stage of its development. If that be true of the mutual relations of different forms of art within the domain of art itself, it is far less surprising that the same is true of the relation of art as a whole to the general development of society. The difficulty lies only in the general formulation of these contradictions. No sooner are they specified than they are explained.

Let us take for instance the relation of Greek art, and that of Shakespeare's time, to our own. It is a well-known fact that Greek mythology was not only the arsenal of Greek art, but also the very ground from which it had sprung. Is the view of nature and of social relations which shaped Greek imagination and Greek art possible in the age of automatic machinery and railways and locomotives and electric telegraphs? Where does Vulcan come in as against Roberts & Co.? Jupiter, as against the lightning conductor? and Hermes, as against the *Crédit Mobilier*? All mythology masters and dominates and shapes the forces of nature in and through the imagination; hence it disappears as soon as man gains mastery over the forces of nature. What becomes of the Goddess Fama side by side with Printing House Square? Greek art presupposes the existence of Greek mythology, i.e. that nature and even the form of society are wrought up in popular fancy in an unconsciously artistic fashion. That is its material. Not, however, any mythology taken at random, nor any accidental unconsciously artistic elaboration of nature (including under the latter all objects, hence also society). Egyptian mythology could never be the soil or womb which would give birth to Greek art. But in any event there had to be a mythology. In no event could Greek art originate in a society which excludes any mythological explanation of nature, any mythological attitude towards it, or which requires of the artist an imagination free from mythology.

Looking at it from another side: is Achilles possible side by side with powder and lead? Or is the *Iliad* at all compatible with the printing press and even printing machines? Do not singing and reciting and the muses necessarily go out of existence with the appearance of the printer's bar, and do not, therefore, the prerequisites of epic poetry disappear?

But the difficulty is not in grasping the idea that Greek art and epos are bound up with certain forms of social development. It lies rather in understanding why they still constitute for us a source of aesthetic enjoyment and in certain respects prevail as the standard and model beyond attainment.

A man cannot become a child again unless he becomes childish. But does he not enjoy the artless ways of the child, and must he not strive to reproduce its truth on a higher plane? Is not the character of every epoch revived, perfectly true to nature, in the child's nature? Why should the childhood of human society, where it had obtained its most beautiful development, not exert an eternal charm as an age that will never return? There are ill-bred children and precocious children. Many of the ancient nations belong to the latter class. The Greeks were normal children. The charm their art has for us does not conflict with the primitive character of the social order from which it had sprung. It is rather the product of the latter, and is due rather to the fact that the immature social conditions under which the art arose and under which alone it could appear can never return.

The Social Character of Production

Considered in the act of production itself, the labour of the individual is used by him as money to buy the product directly, that is, the object of his own activity; but it is particular money, used to buy this particular product. In order to be money in general, it must originate from general and not special labour; that is, it must originally be established as an element of general production. But on this presupposition it is not basically exchange that gives it its general character, but its presupposed social character will determine its participation in the products. The social character of production would make the product from the start a collective and general product. The exchange originally found in production—which is an exchange not of exchange values but of activities determined by communal needs and communal aims—would from the start imply the participation of individuals in the collective world of products.

On the basis of exchange values, it is exchange that first makes of labour something general. In the other system labour is established as such before the exchange; that is, the exchange of products is not at all the medium by which participation of the individual in general production is brought about. There must of course be mediation. In the first case, we start with the autonomous production of private individuals (however much it is determined and modified subsequently by complex relationships), and mediation is carried out by the exchange of goods, exchange value and money, which are all expressions of one and the same relationship. In the second case, the presupposition itself is mediated, i.e. the precondition is collective production; the community is the foundation of production. The labour of the individual is established from the start as collective labour. But whatever the particular form of the product which he creates or helps to create, what he has bought with his labour is not this or that product, but a definite participation in collective production. Therefore he has no special product to exchange. His product is not an exchange value. The product does not have to change into any special form in order to have a general character for the individual. Instead of a division of labour necessarily engendered by the exchange of values, there is an organization of labour, which has as its consequence the participation of the individual in collective consumption.

In the first case, the social character of producion is established subsequently by the elevation of products to exchange values, and the exchange of these values. In the second case, the social character of production is a precondition, and participation in the world of production and in consumption is not brought about by the exchange of labour or the products of labour which are independent of it. It is brought about by the social conditions of production, within which the individual acts.

Thus the desire to turn individual labour directly into money (which also includes the product of labour), i.e. into a realized exchange value, means that the worker's labour must be designated as general labour. In other words, this means that those conditions are denied in which he must necessarily become money and exchange value, and is dependent on private exchange. This requirement can be satisfied only in conditions in which it is no longer set. On the basis of exchange values, neither the labour of the individual nor his product are directly general; to obtain this character, an objective mediation is required, money distinct from the product.

If we suppose communal production, the determination of time remains, of course, essential. The less time society requires in order to produce wheat, cattle, etc., the more time it gains for other forms of production, material or intellectual. As with a single individual, the universality of its development, its enjoyment, and its activity depends on saving time. In the final analysis, all forms of economics can be reduced to an economics of time. Likewise, society must divide up its time purposefully in order to achieve a production suited to its general needs; just as the individual has to divide his time in order to acquire, in suitable proportions, the knowledge he needs or to fulfil the various requirements of his activity.

On the basis of community production, the first economic law thus remains the economy of time, and the methodical distribution of working time between the various branches of production; and this law becomes indeed of much greater importance. But all this differs basically from the measurement of exchange values (labour and the products of labour) by labour time. The work of individuals participating in the same branch of activity, and the different kinds of labour are not only quantitatively but also qualitatively different. What is the precondition of a merely quantitative difference between things? The fact that their quality is the same. Thus units of labour can be measured quantitatively only if they are of equal and identical quality.

The Rise and Downfall of Capitalism

It is necessary to produce a precise analysis of the concept of capital, since it is the basic concept of modern economics just as capital itself, which is its abstract reflection, is the basis of bourgeois society. From a clear perception of the basic premiss of the relationship all the contradictions of bourgeois production must emerge as also the limit at which it progresses beyond itself.

It is important to notice that wealth as such, i.e. bourgeois wealth, is always most powerfully expressed in exchange value where it is established as a mediator between the extremes itself and use value. This mid-point always appears as the completed economic relationship because it unites the opposites and always appears in the end as a unilateral and superior power over and against the extremes. The movement or relationship that originally appears as a mediator between the extremes progresses in a necessary dialectic to the following result: it appears as its own mediator, as the subject whose moments are merely the extremes, whose status as independent preconditions it abolishes in order thus to establish itself as the only autonomous factor. Similarly, in the religious sphere, Christ the mediator between God and man—simple means of circulation between one and the other—becomes their unity, the God-man and then, as such, becomes more important than God; the saints become more important than Christ; and the priests more important than the saints.

The total economic expression, itself unilateral in relation to the extremes, is always exchange value when it is established as an intermediate link; as, for example, gold in simple circulation, or capital itself as a mediator between production and circulation. Inside capital itself one of its forms adopts the position of exchange value against another which is use value. Thus, for example, industrial capital appears as a producer in relation to the trader who represents circulation. Thus industrial capital represents the material side, and the other the formal side, wealth as such. At the same time, mercantile capital is itself again mediator between production (industrial capital) and circulation (the consuming public) or between exchange value and use value. For both sides mutually establish each other: production as money and circulation as use value (consuming public), the first as use value (product) and the second as exchange value (money). It is the same inside trade itself: the wholesaler, as mediator between producer and retailer or between producer and agriculturalist or between different producers, plays the same role of superior centre. It is also the case of the middleman in relation to the wholesaler; of the banker in relation to industrialists and businessmen; of the joint stock company in relation to simple production, and of the financier as mediator between the state and bourgeois society at its highest stage. Wealth as such presents itself all the more distinctly and broadly the farther it is removed from direct production and itself acts as mediator between sides which, considered in themselves, are already forms of economic relationship. Note that money becomes an end instead of a means and that capital, as the superior form of mediation, everywhere establishes the inferior form, labour, simply as a source of surplus value. For example, the bill-broker, banker etc., in relation to producers and farmers who are established relative to the former as labour (use value), whereas the banker situates himself in relation to them as capital, creation of surplus value etc. This appears in its weirdest form with financiers.

Capital is the immediate unity of product and money or, better, of production and circulation. Thus it is itself something immediate and its development consists in establishing itself and going beyond itself on this unity which is a determined and therefore a simple relationship. At first this unity appears in capital as something simple. . . .

Thus on the one hand production which is founded on capital creates universal industry—i.e. surplus labour, value-producing labour; on the other hand it creates a system of general exploitation of natural human attributes, a system of general profitability, whose vehicles seem to be just as much science as all the physical and intellectual characteristics. There is nothing which can escape, by its own elevated nature or self-justifying characteristics, from this cycle of social production and exchange. Thus capital first creates bourgeois society and the universal appropriation of nature and of social relationships themselves by the members of society. Hence the great civilizing influence of capital, its production of a stage of society compared with which all earlier stages appear to be merely local progress and idolatory of nature. Nature becomes for the first time simply an object for mankind, purely a matter of utility; it ceases to be recognized as a power in its own right; and the theoretical knowledge of its independent laws appears only as a stratagem designed to subdue it to human requirements, whether as the object of consumption or as the means of production. Pursuing this tendency, capital has pushed beyond national boundaries and prejudices, beyond the deification of nature and the inherited, self-sufficient satisfaction of existing needs confined within well-defined bounds, and the reproduction of the traditional way of life. It is destructive of all this, and permanently revolutionary, tearing down all obstacles that impede the development of productive forces, the expansion of needs, the diversity of production and the exploitation and exchange of natural and intellectual forces.

But because capital sets up any such boundary as a limitation, and is thus ideally over and beyond it, it does not in any way follow that it has really surmounted it, and since any such limitation contradicts its vocation, capitalist production moves in contradictions which are constantly overcome, only to be, again, constantly re-established. Still more so. The universality towards which it is perpetually driving finds limitations in its own nature, which at a certain stage of its development will make it appear as itself the greatest barrier to this tendency, leading thus to its own self-destruction.

To come closer to the heart of the question: first, there is a limit not inherent to production generally, but to production founded on capital. This limit is dual, or rather revealed one and the same when considered from two angles. It is sufficient here, in order to have discovered the basis of overproduction—the fundamental contradiction of developed capitalism—to show that capital contains a particular limitation on production, a limitation which contradicts its general tendency to push beyond any barrier on its production. This is the discovery in general that capital is not, as the economists think, the absolute form for the development of productive forces, that is, not the absolute form of wealth coinciding absolutely with the development of productive forces. Viewed from the standpoint of capital, the stages of production that preceded it appear as so many fetters on the productive forces. But, correctly understood, capital itself appears as a condition for the development of productive forces so long as they need an external stimulant which is at the same time a brake. Capital disciplines productive forces, but becomes a superfluous burden at a certain stage of their development, in exactly the same way as the corporations were. These immanent limits must be identical with the nature of capital, with the essential determinations of its concept. These necessary limitations are:

1. Necessary labour as a limit to the exchange value of living labour power or of the salary of the industrial population.

2. Surplus value as a limit to surplus working time; and, in relation to relative surplus working time as a barrier to the development of productive forces.

3. What amounts to the same thing, transformation into money—exchange value in general—as a limit on production; or exchange based on value, or value based on exchange, as a limit on production.

4. Still the same point viewed as a limitation of the production of use values through exchange value; in other words, in order to become in general an object of production real wealth must adopt a determinate form, different from itself and thus absolutely not identical with it.

Hence over-production, which is the sudden recall of all these necessary moments of production based on capital; their neglect therefore brings a general depreciation in value. At the same time capital has the task imposed on it of beginning from a higher stage of the development of productive forces, etc. and renewing its search with a consequent ever greater collapse as capital. It is therefore clear that the higher the development of capital, the more it appears as a barrier to production, and therefore also to consumption, quite apart from the other contradictions which make it appear as a burdensome barrier to production and commerce. . . .

Alienated Labour

The additional value is thus again established as capital, as objectified labour entering into the exchange process with living labour, and thence dividing itself into a constant part—the objective conditions of labour, the existence of living labour power, the necessaries, food for the worker. In this second appearance of capital in this form, some points are cleared up which in its first appearance—as money, which is changing from the form of value into that of capital—were completely obscure. They are now solved through the process of valorization and production. At their first occurrence, the prerequisites themselves seemed to be exterior and derived from circulation; thus they did not arise from its internal nature, nor were they explained by it. These external prerequisites will now appear as elements in the movement of capital itself, so that capital itself has presupposed them as its own elements, irrespective of how they arose historically.

Within the production process itself, surplus value—the surplus value solicited as a result of the constraint of capital—appeared as surplus labour and even as living labour, which, however, since it cannot produce anything from nothing, finds its own objective conditions in advance. Now this surplus labour appears objectified as surplus product, and this surplus product, in order to valorize itself as capital, divides itself into a double form: as objective labour conditions (material and instrument) and as subjective labour conditions (food) for the living labour now to be put to work. The general form of value—objectified labour—and objectified labour arising from circulation is, naturally, the general and self-evident presupposition. Further: the surplus product in its totality—which objectifies surplus labour in its totality—now appears as surplus capital (as compared with the original capital, before it had undertaken this circulation), i.e as autonomous exchange value, which is opposed to the living labour power as its specific use all value. All the factors which were opposed to the living labour power as forces which were alien, external, and which consumed and utilized the living labour power under definite conditions which were themselves independent of it, are now established as its own product and result.

1. The surplus value or surplus product is nothing but a definite amount of objectified living labour—the sum of the surplus labour. This new value, which is opposed to living labour as an independent value to be exchanged against it, in fact as capital, is the product of labour. It is itself nothing but the general superfluity of labour over necessary labour—in an objective form, and thus as a value.

2. The special shapes that are assumed by this value in order to revalorize itself, i.e. to establish itself as capital—on the one hand as raw material and instrument, on the other as means of subsistence for labour during the act of production—are likewise, therefore, only special forms of surplus labour itself. Raw material and instrument are produced from it in such circumstances—or it itself becomes objective as raw material and instrument in such a proportion—that a definite sum of necessary work (necessary in the sense that it is living, and produces the means of subsistence which are its value) can be objectified in the surplus labour, and indeed incessantly objectified, in other words it can again continue the division of the objective and subjective conditions of its self-maintenance and self-reproduction. Moreover, while living labour is executing the process that reproduces its objective conditions, it has at the same time established raw material and instrument in such proportions that—as surplus labour, as labour beyond what is necessary—it can realize itself in them, and thus make them into material to create new values. The objective conditions of surplus labour—which are limited to the proportion of raw material and instrument above the requirements of necessary labour, while the objective conditions of necessary labour are divided within their objectivity into objective and subjective, into material elements of labour and subjective elements (means of subsistence for living labour)—thus now appear and are thus established as the product, the result, the objective form, the external existence of surplus labour itself. Originally, on the other hand, this seemed alien to living labour itself, as though capital was responsible for the fact that instrument and means of subsistence were present to such an extent that it was possible for living labour to realize itself not only as necessary labour but as surplus labour.

3. The independent and autonomous existence of value as against living labour power—

hence its existence as capital—

the objective, self-centred indifference, the alien nature of objective conditions of labour as against living labour power, reaching the point that—

(1) these conditions face the worker, as a person, in the person of the capitalist (as personifications with their own will and interest), this absolute separation and divorce of ownership (i.e. of the material conditions of labour from living labour power); these conditions are opposed to the worker as alien property, as the reality of another legal person and the absolute domain of their will—

and that

(2) labour hence appears as alien labour as opposed to the value personified in the capitalist or to the conditions of labour—

this absolute divorce between property and labour, between living labour power and the conditions of its realization, between objectified and living labour, between the value and the activity that creates value—

hence also the alien nature of the content of the work *vis-à-vis* the worker himself—

this separation now also appears as the product of labour itself, as an objectification of its own elements.

For through the new act of production itself (which merely confirmed the exchange between capital and living labour that had preceded it), surplus labour and thus surplus value, surplus product, in brief, the total result of labour (that of surplus labour as well as of necessary labour) is established as capital, as exchange value which is independently and indifferently opposed both to living labour power and to its mere use value.

Labour power has only adopted the subjective conditions of necessary labour—subsistence indispensable for productive labour power, i.e. its reproduction merely as labour power divorced from the conditions of its realization—and it has itself set up these conditions as objects and values, which stand opposed to it in an alien and authoritarian personification.

It comes out of this process not only no richer but actually poorer than when it entered it. For not only do the conditions of necessary labour that it has produced belong to capital; but also the possibility of creating values which is potentially present in labour power now likewise exists as surplus value, surplus product, in a word, as capital, as dominion over living labour power, as valued endowed with its own strength and will as opposed to the abstract, purposeless, purely subjective poverty of labour power. Labour power has not only produced alien wealth and its own poverty, but also the relationship of this wealth (as wealth concerned exclusively with itself) to itself as poverty, through the consumption of which wealth puts new life into itself and again makes itself fruitful. This all arose from the exchange in which labour power exchanged its living power for a quantity of objectified labour, except that this objectified labour—these conditions of its existence which exist outside it, and the independent external nature of these material conditions—appears as its own product. These conditions appear as though set up by labour power itself, both as its own objectification, and as the objectification of its own power which has an existence independent of it and, even more, rules over it, rules over it by its own doing.

'Thou shalt labour by the sweat of thy brow!' was Jehovah's curse that he bestowed upon Adam. A. Smith conceives of labour as such a curse. 'Rest' appears to him to be the fitting state of things, and identical with 'liberty' and 'happiness'. It seems to be far from A. Smith's thoughts that the individual, 'in his normal state of health, strength, activity, skill, and efficiency', might also require a normal portion of work, and of cessation from rest. It is true that the quantity of labour to be provided seems to be conditioned by external circumstances, by the purpose to be achieved, and the obstacles to its achievement that have to be overcome by labour. But neither does it occur to A. Smith that the overcoming of such obstacles may itself constitute an exercise in liberty, and that these external purposes lose their character of mere natural necessities and are established as purposes which the individual himself fixes. The result is the self-realization and objectification of the subject, therefore real freedom, whose activity is precisely labour. Of course he is correct in saying that labour has always seemed to be repulsive, and forced upon the worker from outside, in its historical forms of slave-labour, bond-labour and wage-labour, and that in this sense non-labour could be opposed to it as 'liberty and happiness'. This is doubly true of this contradictory labour which has not yet created the subjective and objective conditions (which it lost when it abandoned pastoral conditions) which make it into attractive labour and individual self-realization. This does not mean that labour can be made merely a joke, or amusement, as Fourier naïvely expressed it in shop-girl terms. Really free labour, the composing of music for example, is at the same time damned serious and demands the greatest effort. The labour concerned with material production can only have this character if (1) it is of a social nature, (2) it has a scientific character and at the same time is general work, i.e. if it ceases to be human effort as a definite, trained natural force, gives up its purely natural, primitive aspects and becomes the activity of a subject controlling all the forces of nature in the production process. Moreover, A. Smith is thinking only of the slaves of capital. For example, even the semi-artistic worker of the Middle Ages cannot be included in his definition. However, my immediate concern is not to discuss his philosophic view of labour, but only its economic aspect. Labour considered purely as a sacrifice and therefore as establishing a value, labour as the price to be paid for things and thus giving them a price according as they cost more or less labour, is a purely negative definition. In this way Mr. Senior was able, for example, to make capital into a source of production *sui generis* in the same sense as labour is a source of production of value, since the capitalist too is making a sacrifice, the sacrifice of abstinence, for, instead of directly consuming his produce, he is enriching himself. A pure negative accomplishes nothing. When the worker takes pleasure in his work—as, certainly, Senior's miser takes pleasure in his abstinence—the product loses nothing of its value. It is labour alone that produces; it is the only substance of products considered as values. This is why working time (supposing it is of the same intensity) is the measure of value. The qualitative differences among workers—in so far as they are not the natural ones of sex, age, physical strength, etc., and express, fundamentally, not the qualitative value of labour, but its division and differentiation—are the result of historical processes. For the great majority of workers, these differences disappear again, since the work that they perform is simple; work that is of a higher quality, however, can be measured by economics in terms of simple labour. To say that working time, or the quantity of labour, measures values, means only that labour and values are measured by the same standard. Two things can be measured by the same standard only when they are of the same nature. Therefore products can be measured only by the standard of labour (working time) because they are by nature made from labour. They are objectified labour. As objects they may assume forms that show they were produced by labour and that finality has been imposed on them from the outside. This does not always occur; it is not possible to see objectified labour in an ox, nor in the products of nature that man reproduces. These forms, however, have nothing in common with each other; they exist as something constant so long as they have an existence as an activity measured by time, which can thus also be used to measure objectified labour. We shall examine later how far this measurement is linked to exchange, and to labour that is not yet socially organized, as a definite state of the social productive process. Use value is not connected with human activity as the source and creation of the product, it aims at producing an object that is useful for man. In so far as the product has a measure of its own, it is measured in terms of its natural properties—size, weight, length, capacity, measures of usefulness, etc. But as an effect, or as the static form of the force that has created it, is measured only by the volume of this force itself. The measure of labour is time. Simply because products are labour, they can be measured by the measure of labour, by the working time, or the quantity of labour consumed in them. The negation of rest, as a pure negation, as an ascetic sacrifice, accomplishes nothing. An individual may mortify the flesh and make a martyr of himself from morning to night, like the monks, but the amount of sacrifice that he makes will get him nowhere. The natural price of things is not the sacrifice made to obtain them. This is reminiscent of the pre-industrial era, in which riches were to be obtained by sacrifices to the gods. There must be something else besides the sacrifice. Instead of speaking of a sacrifice of rest, one might speak of a sacrifice of laziness, of lack of freedom, of unhappiness—in fact, the negation of a negative condition. A. Smith considers labour from the psychological point of view, in relation to the pleasure or opposite that it gives to the individual. But in addition to being a feeling concerning his activity, work is something else: in the first place, in relationship to other people, for the mere sacrifice of A would be no use to B. Secondly, there is the worker's own particular relationship towards the object that he is making, and towards his own talents for work. Work is a positive, creative activity. The standard by which work is measured—i.e. time—naturally does not depend on its productivity. The measure consists of a unity, whose aliquot parts express a certain quantity. It certainly does not follow from this that the value of labour is constant; it is so only in so far as equal quantities of labour have the same unity of measurement. Pursuing this analysis further, we find that the values of products are measured by labour, not the labour actually employed, but the labour that is necessary for their production. Thus the condition of production is not the sacrifice but the labour. The equation expresses the condition of its reproduction given in the exchange, in other words, the possibility of renewing productive activity created by its own product.

Moreover, if A. Smith's idea of sacrifice correctly expresses the subjective relationship of the wage-earner to his own work, it still will not yield what he wishes it to—namely, that value is determined by means of the time worked. From the worker's point of view, even one hour of work may represent a great sacrifice. But the value of his work does not in the slightest depend on his feelings; nor does the value of the hour he has worked. A. Smith admits that this sacrifice may sometimes be bought more cheaply, sometimes more dearly: in which case one is struck by the fact that it must always be sold at the same price. In this also he is illogical. Farther on, he declares wages to be the standard by which value is measured, not the quantity of labour. To go to the slaughter is always the same sacrifice for the ox; this is no reason for beef to have a constant value.

Machinery, Automation, Free Time, and Communism

Historically, competition meant the abolition of guild coercion, governmental regulations, and the abolition of frontiers, tolls, etc., within a state—and in the world market it meant the abolition of tariffs, protection, and prohibition. In short, it was historically a negation of the limits and obstacles peculiar to the levels of production that obtained before the development of capital. These were described quite correctly, historically speaking, by the physiocrats as *laissez faire, laissez passer*, and advocated by them as such. Competition, however, has never been considered from the purely negative and purely historical aspect; indeed, even more stupid interpretations have been put forward, for example that competition represents the clash between individuals released from their chains and acting only in their own interests; or that it represents the repulsion and attraction of free individuals in relation to one another, and thus is the absolute form of individual liberty in the sphere of production and exchange. Nothing could be more wrong.

Although free competition has abolished the obstacles created by the relationships and means of pre-capitalist production, it should first be remembered that what were restrictions for capital were inherent frontiers for earlier means of production, within which they developed and moved naturally. These frontiers became obstacles only after productive forces and commercial relationships had sufficiently developed for capital to be the ruling principle of production. The frontiers that it tore down were obstacles to its own movement, development, and realization. It did not abolish all frontiers by any means, or all obstacles; only those that did not correspond to its needs, those that were obstacles for it. Within its own limitations—however much these may seem, from a higher point of view, to be obstacles in production, and have been fixed as such by the historical development of capital—it feels itself free and unhampered, that is, bounded only by itself, but its own conditions of existence.

In the same way the industry of the guilds in its heyday found that the guild organization gave it the freedom it needed, i.e. the production relationships corresponding to it. Guild industry gave rise to these relationships, developing them as its own inherent conditions, and thus not at all as external, restricting obstacles. The historical aspect of the negation of guild industry, etc., by capital, by means of free competition, means nothing more than that capital, sufficiently strengthened by a means of circulation adequate for its nature, tore down the historical barriers which interfered with and restricted its movement. But competition is far removed from possessing merely this historical significance, or from playing merely this negative role. *Free competition* is the relation of capital to itself as another capital, i.e. it is the real behaviour of capital as such. It is only then that the internal laws of capital—which appear only as tendencies in the early historical stages of its evolution—can be established; production founded on capital only establishes itself in so far as free competition develops, since free competition is the free development of the conditions and means of production founded on capital and of the process which constantly reproduces these conditions. It is not individuals but capital that establishes itself freely in free competition. So long as production founded on capital is the necessary and therefore the most suitable form in which social productive forces can develop, the movement of individuals within the pure conditions of capital will seem to be free. This liberty is then assured dogmatically by constant reference to the barriers that have been torn down by free competition. Free competition expresses the real development of capital. Because of it, individual capital finds imposed upon itself an external necessity that corresponds to the nature of capital, to the means of production founded on it, to the concept of capital. The mutual constraint that different portions of capital impose on each other, on labour, etc. (the competition of workers between themselves is only another form of the competition of capital), is the free and at the same time the real development of wealth as capital. So much so, that the profoundest economic theorists, Ricardo for example, begin by presuming the absolute domination of free competition, in order to study and formulate the laws that are suitable to capital, laws which at the same time appear as the vital tendencies that dominate it. Free competition, however, is the form suitable to the productive process of capital. The more it develops, the more clearly the shape of its movement is seen. What Ricardo, for example, has thus recognized (despite himself) is the historical nature of capital, and the limited character of free competition, which is still only the free movement of portions of capital, i.e. their movement within conditions that have nothing in common with those of any dissolved preliminary stages, but are their own conditions. The domination of capital is the prerequisite of free competition, just as the despotism of the Roman emperors was the prerequisite of the free Roman civil law. So long as capital is weak, it will rely on crutches taken from past means of production or from means of production that are disappearing as it comes onto the scene. As soon as it feels strong, it throws the crutches away and moves according to its own laws. As soon as it begins to feel and to be aware that it is itself an obstacle to development, it takes refuge in forms that, although they appear to complete the mastery of capital, are at the same time, by curbing free competition, the heralds of its dissolution, and of the dissolution of the means of production which are based on it. What lies in the nature of capital is only expressed in reality as an external necessity through competition, which means no more than that the various portions of capital impose the inherent conditions of capital on one another and on themselves. No category of the bourgeois economy—not even the first one, the determination of value—can become real by means of free competition, i.e. through the real process of capital, which appears as the interaction of portions of capital on one another and of all the other relationships of production and circulation that are determined by capital.

Hence the absurdity of considering free competition as being the final development of human liberty, and the negation of free competition as being the negation of individual liberty and of social production founded on individual liberty. It is only free development on a limited foundation—that of the dominion of capital. This kind of individual liberty is thus at the same time the most complete suppression of all individual liberty and total subjugation of individuality to social conditions which take the form of material forces—and even of all-powerful objects that are independent of the individuals relating to them. The only rational answer to the deification of free competition by the middle-class prophets, or its diabolization by the socialists, lies in its own development. If it is said that, within the limits of free competition, individuals by following their pure self-interest realize their social, or rather their general, interest, this means merely that they exert pressure upon one another under the conditions of capitalist production and that this clash between them can only give rise to the conditions under which their interaction took place. Moreover, once the illusion that competition is the supposedly absolute form of free individuality disappears, this proves that the conditions of competition, i.e. of production founded on capital, are already felt and thought of as a barrier, that they indeed already are such and will increasingly become so. The assertion that free competition is the final form of the development of productive forces, and thus of human freedom, means only that the domination of the middle class is the end of the world's history—of course quite a pleasant thought for yesterday's parvenus!

So long as the means of labour remains a means of labour, in the proper sense of the word, as it has been directly and historically assimilated by capital into its valorization process, it only undergoes a formal change, in that it appears to be the means of labour not only from its material aspect, but at the same time as a special mode of existence of capital determined by the general process of capital—it has become fixed capital. But once absorbed into the production process of capital, the means of labour undergoes various metamorphoses, of which the last is the machine, or rather an automatic system of machinery ('automatic' meaning that this is only the most perfected and most fitting form of the machine, and is what transforms the machinery into a system).

This is set in motion by an automaton, a motive force that moves of its own accord. The automaton consists of a number of mechanical and intellectual organs, so that the workers themselves can be no more than the conscious limbs of the automaton. In the machine, and still more in machinery as an automatic system, the means of labour is transformed as regards its use value, i.e. as regards its material existence, into an existence suitable for fixed capital and capital in general; and the form in which it was assimilated as a direct means of labour into the production process of capital is transformed into one imposed by capital itself and in accordance with it. In no respect is the machine the means of labour of the individual worker. Its distinctive character is not at all, as with the means of labour, that of transmitting the activity of the worker to its object; rather this activity is so arranged that it now only transmits and supervises and protects from damage the work of the machine and its action on the raw material.

With the tool it was quite the contrary. The worker animated it with his own skill and activity; his manipulation of it depended on his dexterity. The machine, which possesses skill and force in the worker's place, is itself the virtuoso, with a spirit of its own in the mechanical laws that take effect in it; and, just as the worker consumes food, so the machine consumes coal, oil, etc. (instrumental material) for its own constant self-propulsion. The worker's activity, limited to a mere abstraction, is determined and regulated on all sides by the movement of the machinery, not the other way round. The knowledge that obliges the inanimate parts of the machine, through their construction, to work appropriately as an automaton, does not exist in the consciousness of the worker, but acts upon him through the machine as an alien force, as the power of the machine itself. The appropriation of living labour by objectified labour—of valorizing strength or activity by self-sufficient value—which is inherent in the concept of capital, is established as the character of the production process itself—when production is based on machinery—as a function of its material elements and material movement. The production process has ceased to be a labour process in the sense that labour is no longer the unity dominating and transcending it. Rather labour appears merely to be a conscious organ, composed of individual living workers at a number of points in the mechanical system; dispersed, subjected to the general process of the machinery itself, it is itself only a limb of the system, whose unity exists not in the living workers but in the living (active) machinery, which seems to be a powerful organism when compared to their individual, insignificant activities. With the stage of machinery, objectified labour appears in the labour process itself as the dominating force opposed to living labour, a force represented by capital in so far as it appropriates living labour.

That the labour process is no more than a simple element in the valorization process is confirmed by the transformation on the material plane of the working tool into machinery, and of the living worker into a mere living accessory of the machine; they become no more than the means whereby its action can take place.

As we have seen, capital necessarily tends towards an increase in the productivity of labour and as great a diminution as possible in necessary labour. This tendency is realized by means of the transformation of the instrument of labour into the machine. In machinery, objectified labour is materially opposed to living labour as its own dominating force; it subordinates living labour to itself not only by appropriating it, but in the real process of production itself. The character of capital as value that appropriates value-creating activity is established by fixed capital, existing as machinery, in its relationship as the use value of labour power. Further, the value objectified in machinery appears as a prerequisite, opposed to which the valorizing power of the individual worker disappears, since it has become infinitely small.

In the large-scale production created by machines, any relationship of the product to the direct requirements of the producer disappears, as does any immediate use value. The form of production and the circumstances in which production takes place are so arranged that it is only produced as a vehicle for value, its use value being only a condition for this.

In machinery, objectified labour appears not only in the form of a product, or of a product utilized as a means of labour, but also in the force of production itself. The development of the means of labour into machinery is not fortuitous for capital; it is the historical transformation of the traditional means of labour into means adequate for capitalism. The accumulation of knowledge and skill, of the general productive power of society's intelligence, is thus absorbed into capital in opposition to labour and appears as the property of capital, or more exactly of fixed capital, to the extent that it enters into the production process as an actual means of production. Thus machinery appears as the most adequate form of fixed capital; and the latter, in so far as capital can be considered as being related to itself, is the most adequate form of capital in general. On the other hand, in so far as fixed capital is firmly tied to its existence as a particular use value, it no longer corresponds to the concept of capital which, as a value, can take up or throw off any particular form of use value, and incarnate itself in any of them indifferently. Seen from this aspect of the external relationships of capital, circulating capital seems to be the most adequate form of capital as opposed to fixed capital.

In so far as machinery develops with the accumulation of social knowledge and productive power generally, it is not in labour but in capital that general social labour is represented. Society's productivity is measured in fixed capital, exists within it in an objectified form; and conversely, the productivity of capital evolves in step with this general progress that capital appropriates gratis. We shall not go into the development of machinery in detail here. We are considering it only from the general aspect, to the extent that the means of labour, in its material aspect, loses its immediate form and opposes the worker materially as capital. Science thus appears, in the machine, as something alien and exterior to the worker; and living labour is subsumed under objectified labour, which acts independently. The worker appears to be superfluous in so far as his action is not determined by the needs of capital.

Thus the full development of capital does not take place—in other words, capital has not set up the means of production corresponding to itself—until the means of labour is not only formally determined as fixed capital, but has been transcended in its direct form, and fixed capital in the shape of a machine is opposed to labour within the production process. The production process as a whole, however, is not subordinated to the direct skill of the worker; it has become a technological application of science.

The tendency of capital is thus to give a scientific character to production, reducing direct labour to a simple element in this process. As with the transformation of value into capital, we see when we examine the development of capital more closely that on the one hand it presupposes a definite historical development of the productive forces (science being included among these forces), and on the other hand accelerates and compels this development.

The quantitative volume, and the efficiency (intensity) with which capital develops as fixed capital, thus shows in general the degree to which capital has developed as capital, as domination over living labour, and the degree to which it dominates the production process in general. It also expressed the accumulation of objectified productive forces and likewise of objectified labour.

But if capital only adequately displays its nature as use value within the production process in the form of machinery and other material forms of fixed capital, railways, for example (we shall return to this later), this never means that this use value (machinery by itself) is capital, or that machinery can be regarded as synonymous with capital; any more than gold would cease to have usefulness as gold if it were no longer used as money. Machinery does not lose its use value when it ceases to be capital. From the fact that machinery is the most suitable form of the use value of fixed capital, it does not follow that its subordination to the social relations of capitalism is the most suitable and final social production relationship for the utilization of machinery.

To the same degree that working time—the mere quantity of labour—is established by capital as the sole determining element, direct labour and its quantity cease to be the determining element in production and thus in the creation of use value. It is reduced quantitatively to a smaller proportion, just as qualitatively it is reduced to an indispensable but subordinate role as compared with scientific labour in general, the technological application of the natural sciences, and the general productive forces arising from the social organization of production. This force appears to be a natural gift of community labour, although it is a historical product. In this way capital works for its own dissolution as the dominant form of production.

The transformation of the process of production from the simple labour process into a scientific process, which subjects the forces of nature and converts them to the service of human needs, appears to be a property of fixed capital as opposed to living labour. Individual labour ceases altogether to be productive as such; or rather, it is productive only in collective labour, which subjects the forces of nature. This promotion of immediate labour to the level of community labour shows that individual work is reduced to helplessness *vis-à-vis* the concentration of common interest represented in capital. On the other hand, a property of circulating capital is the retention of labour in one branch of production thanks to coexisting labour in another branch.

In small-scale circulation, capital advances the worker his wages, which he exchanges for products necessary for his own consumption. The money that he receives only has this power because, at the same time, work is being carried out alongside him. It is only because capital has appropriated his labour that it can give him, with the money, control over the labour of others. This exchange of worker's own labour for that of others does not seem to be determined and conditioned by the simultaneous coexistence of the others' labour, but by the advance that capital has made to him.

It appears to be a property of the part of the circulating capital that is assigned to the worker, and of circulating capital in general, that the worker can proceed to the assimilation of what he himself needs during the process of production. This exchange appears as the material exchange not of simultaneous forces, but of capital; because of the existence of circulating capital. Thus all the forces of labour are transposed into forces of capital; in its fixed part, the productive force of labour (which is placed outside it and exists materially independently of it); and in its circulating part, we find first of all that the worker has himself produced the conditions for the renewal of his work, and secondly that the exchange of his labour is mediated through the coexisting labour of others in such a way that capital appears to make him the advance and to ensure the existence of labour in other branches. (Both the latter statements really belong to the chapter on accumulation.) Capital sets itself up as a mediator between the various labourers in the form of circulating capital.

Fixed capital, considered as a means of production, whose most adequate form is machinery, only produces value (i.e. increases the value of the product) in two cases: (1) in so far as it has value, i.e. in so far as it is itself the product of labour, a definite quantity of labour in an objectified form; (2) in so far as it increases the proportion of surplus labour to necessary labour by making it possible for labour, by increasing its productivity, to create more quickly a larger amount of the products needed for the sustenance of living labour power. To say that the worker is in co-operation with the capitalist because the latter makes the worker's labour easier by means of fixed capital, or shortens his labour, is a bourgeois phrase of the greatest absurdity. Fixed capital is in any case the product of labour, and is merely alien labour that has been appropriated by capital; and the capitalist could be said, rather, to be robbing labour of all its independent and attractive character by means of the machine. On the contrary, capital only uses machinery in so far as it enables the worker to devote more of his working time to the capitalist, to work longer for others and experience a larger part of his time as not belonging to him. Through this process, in fact, the quantity of labour necessary for the production of a particular object is reduced to a minimum, so that a maximum of labour can be valorized into the maximum number of such objects. The first aspect is important, because capital in this instance has quite unintentionally reduced human labour, the expenditure of energy, to a minimum. This will be to the advantage of emancipated labour, and is the condition of its emancipation.

All this shows the absurdity of Lauderdale's statement that fixed capital is independent of working time, and a self-contained source of value. It is such a source only in so far as it is itself objectified labour time, and establishes surplus labour time. The introduction of machines historically presupposes superfluous hands. Machinery only replaces labour when there is a superfluity of labour force. Only in the imagination of economists does it come to the aid of the individual worker. It can only take effect with masses of workers, whose concentration as opposed to capital is one of its historical prerequisites, as we have seen. It does not arise in order to replace deficient labour power, but to reduce the mass of labour available to the necessary quantity. Only when labour power is present *en masse* is machinery introduced. (We shall return to this later.)

Lauderdale thinks he has made a great discovery when he says that machinery does not increase the productive power of labour but replaces it, or does what labour is unable to do by its own power. It is inherent in the concept of capital that the greater productive power of labour is seen as an increase of a force external to labour and as the enfeeblement of labour itself. The tools of labour make the worker independent—establish him as a proprietor. Machinery—as fixed capital—makes him dependent, expropriates him. Machinery only produces this effect to the extent that it is fixed capital, and it only has this character so long as the worker is related to the machine as a wage-earner, and the active individual in general as a mere worker.

Up to this point, fixed and circulating capital have appeared to be merely different, transitory determinations of capital; but now they are crystallized into special forms of existence of capital and circulating capital occurs alongside fixed capital. There are now two different kinds of capital. If we consider capital in a particular branch of production we see that it is divided into two parts, or that it is divided in a determined proportion into these two kinds of capital.

The difference within the production process—originally between the means of labour and labour material, and finally the product of labour—now appears as that between circulating capital (the first two) and fixed capital. The division of capital in its purely material aspect is now assimilated into its own form, which appears as what makes the distinction.

The mistake of such writers as Lauderdale, who state that capital, as such and independently of labour, creates value, and thus also surplus value (or profit), arises from their superficial view of the matter. Fixed capital, whose material form or use value is machinery, gives most appearance of truth to their fallacies. But against this, e.g. in *Labour Defended*, we see that the constructor of a road is willing to share it with the road user, but that the road itself cannot do this.

Circulating capital—provided only that it proceeds through its various stages—may decrease or increase, shorten or lengthen the circulation time, make the various stages of capitalist circulation easier or more difficult. Consequently, the surplus value that may be produced within a given time may be diminished without these interruptions—either because the number of reproductions is smaller, or because the quantity of capital constantly engaged in the process of production has contracted. In both cases there is no diminution of the presupposed value, but a decrease in its rate of growth.

As we have noted, the extent to which capital has developed is a measure of the development of heavy industry in general, and as soon as it has developed to a certain point, and thus has increased relative to the development of its productive forces (it being itself the objectification of these productive forces and their presupposed product), from this point onwards any interruption of the process of production will cause a diminution of capital itself and its presupposed value. The value of fixed capital is only reproduced to the extent that it is used upon the production process. If it is not used, it loses its use value without its value being transferred to the product. Thus the more fixed capital develops on a large scale, in the sense in which we have been considering it, the more the continuity of the production process or the constant flow of reproduction will become a condition and an external form of coercion of the means of production founded on capitalism.

From this standpoint, too, the appropriation of living labour by capital is directly expressed in machinery. It is a scientifically based analysis, together with the application of mechanical and chemical laws, that enables the machine to carry out the work formerly done by the worker himself. The development of machinery only follows this path, however, once heavy industry has reached an advanced stage, and the various sciences have been pressed into the service of capital, and, on the other hand, when machinery itself has yielded very considerable resources. Invention then becomes a branch of business, and the application of science to immediate production aims at determining the inventions at the same time as it solicits them. But this is not the way in which machinery in general came into being, still less the way that it progresses in detail. This way is a process of analysis—by subdivisions of labour, which transforms the worker's operations more and more into mechanical operations, so that, at a certain point, the mechanism can step into his place.

Thus we can see directly here how a particular means of labour is transferred from the worker to capital in the form of the machine and his own labour power devalued as a result of this transposition. Hence we have the struggle of the worker against machinery. What used to be the activity of the living worker has become that of the machine.

Thus the appropriation of his labour by capital is bluntly and brutally presented to the worker: capital assimilates living labour into itself 'as though love possessed its body'.

Real wealth develops much more (as is disclosed by heavy industry) in the enormous disproportion between the labour time utilized and its products, and also in the qualitative disproportion between labour that has been reduced to a mere abstraction, and the power of the production process that it supervises. Labour does not seem any more to be an essential part of the process of production. The human factor is restricted to watching and supervising the production process. (This applies not only to machinery, but also to the combination of human activities and the development of human commerce.)

The worker no longer inserts transformed natural objects as intermediaries between the material and himself; he now inserts the natural process that he has transformed into an industrial one between himself and inorganic nature, over which he has achieved mastery. He is no longer the principal agent of the production process: he exists alongside it. In this transformation, what appears as the mainstay of production and wealth is neither the immediate labour performed by the worker, nor the time that he works—but the appropriation by man of his own general productive force, his understanding of nature and the mastery of it; in a word, the development of the social individual. The theft of others' labour time upon which wealth depends today seems to be a miserable basis compared with this newly developed foundation that has been created by heavy industry itself. As soon as labour, in its direct form, has ceased to be the main source of wealth, then labour time ceases, and must cease, to be its standard of measurement, and thus exchange value must cease to be the measurement of use value. The surplus labour of the masses has ceased to be a condition for the development of wealth in general; in the same way that the non-labour of the few has ceased to be a condition for the development of the general powers of the human mind. Production based on exchange value therefore falls apart, and the immediate process of material production finds itself stripped of its impoverished, antagonistic form. Individuals are then in a position to develop freely. It is no longer a question of reducing the necessary labour time in order to create surplus labour, but of reducing the necessary labour of society to a minimum. The counterpart of this reduction is that all members of society can develop their education in the arts, sciences, etc., thanks to the free time and means available to all.

Capital is itself contradiction in action, since it makes an effort to reduce labour time to the minimum, while at the same time establishing labour time as the sole measurement and source of wealth. Thus it diminishes labour time in its necessary form, in order to increase its superfluous form; therefore it increasingly establishes superfluous labour time as a condition (a question of life and death) for necessary labour time. On the one hand it calls into life all the forces of science and nature, as well as those of social co-operation and commerce, in order to create wealth which is relatively independent of the labour time utilized. On the other hand it attempts to measure, in terms of labour time, the vast social forces thus created and imprisons them within the narrow limits that are required in order to retain the value already created *as* value. Productive forces and social relationships—the two different sides of the development of the social individual—appear to be, and are, only a means for capital, to enable it to produce from its own cramped base. But in fact they are the material conditions that will shatter this foundation.

Nature does not construct machines, locomotives, railways, electric telegraphs, self-acting mules, etc. These are products of human industry; natural material transformed into organs of the human will to dominate nature or to realize itself therein. They are organs of the human brain, created by human hands; the power of knowledge made into an object.

The development of fixed capital shows to what extent general social knowledge had become an immediate productive force, and thus up to what point the conditions for the social life process are themselves subjected to the control of the general intellect, and are remodelled to suit it, and to what extent social productive forces are produced not only in the form of knowledge but also as the direct organs of social practice; of the real life process.

Capital creates a great deal of disposable time, apart from the labour time that is needed for society in general and for each sector of society (i.e. space for the development of the individual's full productive forces, and thus also for those of society). This creation of non-working time is, from the capitalist standpoint, and from that of all earlier stages of development, non-working time or free time for the few. What is new in capital is that it also increases the surplus labour time of the masses by all artistic and scientific means possible, since its wealth consists directly in the appropriation of surplus labour time, since its direct aim is value, not use value. Thus, despite itself, it is instrumental in creating the means of social disposable time, and so in reducing working time for the whole of society to a minimum and thus making everyone's time free for their own development. But although its tendency is always to create disposable time, it also converts it into surplus labour. If it succeeds too well with the former, it will suffer from surplus production, and then the necessary labour will be interrupted as soon as no surplus labour can be valorized from capital. The more this contradiction develops, the clearer it becomes that the growth of productive forces can no longer be limited by the appropriation of the surplus labour of others; the masses of the workers must appropriate their own surplus labour.

When this has been done, disposable time ceases to have a contradictory character. Thus firstly, the labour time necessary will be measured by the requirements of the social individual, and secondly, social productivity will grow so rapidly that, although production is reckoned with a view to the wealth of all, the disposable time of all will increase. For real wealth is the developed productive force of all individuals. It is no longer the labour time but the disposable time which is the measure of wealth. Labour time as the measurement of wealth implies that wealth is founded on poverty, and that disposable time exists in and through opposition to surplus labour time; it implies that all an individual's time is working time, and degrades him to the level of a mere worker, and an instrument of labour. This is why the most developed machinery forces the worker to work longer hours than the savage does, or than the labourer himself when he only had the simplest and most primitive tools to work with. . . .

The development of heavy industry means that the basis upon which it rests—the appropriation of the labour time of others—ceases to constitute or to create wealth; and at the same time direct labour as such ceases to be the basis of production, since it is transformed more and more into a supervisory and regulating activity; and also because the product ceases to be made by individual direct labour, and results more from the combination of social activity. 'As the division of labour develops, almost all the work of any individual is a part of the whole, having no value or utility of itself. There is nothing on which the labourer can seize: this is my produce, this I will keep to myself.' In direct exchange between producers, direct individual labour is found to be realized in a particular product, or part of a product, and its common social character—as the objectification of general labour and the satisfaction of general need—is only established through exchange. The opposite takes place in the production process of heavy industry: on the one hand, once the productive forces of the means of labour have reached the level of an automatic process, the prerequisite is the subordination of the natural forces to the intelligence of society, while on the other hand individual labour in its direct form is transformed into social labour. In this way the other basis of this mode of production vanishes.

The labour time used for the production of fixed capital is related, within the production process of capital, to the time used for the production of circulating capital, as surplus labour time to necessary time. To the extent that production directed towards the satisfaction of immediate needs becomes more productive, a larger part of production can be directed towards the satisfaction of the needs of production itself, or the manufacture of means of production. In so far as the production of fixed capital is not materially directed either towards the production of immediate use values, or towards the production of values indispensable for the immediate reproduction of capital—which would again be an indirect representation of use value—but towards the production of means that serve to create value and not towards value as an immediate object; in other words, in so far as fixed capital concentrates on the creation of values and the means of valorization as the immediate object of production (the production of value is established materially in the object of production itself as the aim of production, the objectification of productive force, and the value-producing force of capital)—to that extent it is in the production of fixed capital that capital is established as an end in itself to a more powerful degree than in the production of circulating capital, and becomes effective as capital. Thus, in this sense too, the volume already possessed by fixed capital and the part occupied by its production in general production indicate the standard of development of wealth based on the mode of production of capital.

'The number of workers depends so far on circulating capital, as it depends on the quantity of products of coexisting labour, which labourers are allowed to consume.'

The passages that we have quoted from various economists all refer to fixed capital as the part of capital which is included in the production process. 'Flotating capital is consumed; fixed capital is merely used in the great process of production.' This is wrong, since it applies only to the part of the circulating capital that is itself consumed by fixed capital, by the material instruments. Only fixed capital is consumed 'in the great process of production', considered as the immediate production process.

Consumption within the production process is, however, in fact use. Moreover, the greater durability of fixed capital cannot be understood as a purely material phenomenon. The iron and wood of which my bed is made, the bricks out of which my house is constructed, or the marble statue that adorns a palace, are as durable as the iron and wood that are transformed into machinery. But it is not only for the technical reason that metal, etc., is most often used in machinery that durability is a necessary quality of the instrument and of the means of production, but because the instrument is intended constantly to play the same role in repeated processes of production. The solidity or durability of the means of production is a direct part of its use value. The more often it has to be renewed, the more expensive it becomes, and the greater the part of capital that must be transformed into it unprofitably. Its durability is thus its existence as a means of production. Its durability implies an increase in its productivity. With circulating capital on the other hand, if it is not transformed into fixed capital, durability does not in any way depend on the productive act itself; and therefore it is not a conceptually established element of it. . . .

'Since the general introduction of soulless machines into British factories, men have been treated, with a few exceptions, as secondary and subordinate machines, and much more attention has been given to the perfecting of raw material made of wood and metals than that made of bodies and minds.' [Robert Owen, *Essays on the Formation of the Human Character*, London, 1840, p. 31.]

Real economy—savings—consists in the saving of working time (the minimum, and reduction to the minimum, of production costs); but this saving is identical with the development of productivity. Economizing, therefore, does not mean the giving up of pleasure, but the development of power and productive capacity, and thus both the capacity for and the means of enjoyment. The capacity for enjoyment is a condition of enjoyment and therefore its primary means; and this capacity is the development of an individual's talents, and thus of the productive force. To economize on labour time means to increase the amount of free time, i.e. time for the complete development of the individual, which again reacts as the greatest productive force on the productive force of labour. From the standpoint of the immediate production process it may be considered as production of fixed capital; this fixed capital being man himself. It is also self-evident that immediate labour time cannot remain in its abstract contradiction to free time—as in the bourgeois economy. Work cannot become a game, as Fourier would like it to be; his great merit was that he declared that the ultimate object must be to raise to a higher level not distribution but the mode of production. Free time—which includes leisure time as well as time for higher activities—naturally transforms anyone who enjoys it into a different person, and it is this different person who then enters the direct process of production. The man who is being formed finds discipline in this process, while for the man who is already formed it is practice, experimental science, materially creative and self-objectifying knowledge, and he contains within his own head the accumulated wisdom of society. Both of them find exercise in it, to the extent that labour requires practical manipulation and free movement, as in agriculture.

As, little by little, the system of bourgeois economy develops, there develops also its negation, which is its final result. We are now still concerned with the direct process of production. If we consider bourgeois society as a whole, society itself seems to be the final result of the social process of production, i.e. man himself in his relation to society. Everything (such as the product, etc.) which has a fixed form appears only as an element, a vanishing element, in this movement. Even the immediate production process appears here only as an element. The conditions and objectifications of the process are themselves likewise elements of it, the subjects of which are only the individuals, but individuals who are related to one another, in relations which are both reproduced and created anew. It is their own constant process of movement in which they renew both themselves and the world of wealth which they create.

It is a fact that as the productive forces of labour develop, the objective conditions of labour (objectified labour) must grow in proportion to living labour. This is actually a tautology, for the growth of the productive forces of labour means merely that less direct labour is required in order to make a larger product, so that social wealth expresses itself more and more in the labour conditions that have been created by labour itself. From the point of view of capital, it does not appear that one of the elements of social activity (objectified labour) has become the ever more powerful body of the other element (subjective, living labour); rather it appears (and this is important for wage-labour) that the objective conditions of labour become more and more colossally independent of living labour—which is shown by their very extent—and social wealth becomes, in ever greater and greater proportions, an alien and dominating force opposing the worker. Stress is placed not on the state of objectification but on the state of alienation, estrangement, and abandonment, on the fact that the enormous objectified power which social labour has opposed to itself as one of its elements belongs not to the worker but to the conditions of production that are personified in capital. So long as the creation of this material form of activity, objectified in contrast to immediate labour power, occurs on the basis of capital and wage-labour, and so long as this process of objectification in fact seems to be a process of alienation as far as the worker is concerned, or to be the appropriation of alien labour from the capitalist's point of view, so long will this distortion and this inversion really exist and not merely occur in the imagination of both workers and capitalists. But this process of inversion is obviously merely a historical necessity, a necessity for the development of productive forces from a definite historical starting-point, or basis, but in no way an absolute necessity of production; it is, rather, ephemeral. The result and the immanent aim of the process is to destroy and transform this basis itself, as well as this form of the process. Bourgeois economists are so bogged down in their traditional ideas of the historical development of society in a single stage that the necessity of the objectification of the social forces of labour seems to them inseparable from the necessity of its alienation in relation to living labour.

But as living labour loses its immediate, individual character, whether subjective or entirely external, as individual activity becomes directly general or social, the objective elements of production lose this form of alienation. They are then produced as property, as the organic social body in which individuals are reproduced as individuals, but as social individuals. The conditions for their being such in the reproduction of their life, in their productive life process, have only been established by the historical economic process; these conditions are both objective and subjective conditions, which are the only two different forms of the same conditions.

The fact that the workers possess no property and the fact that objectified labour has property in living labour (in other words, that capital appropriates the labour of others) constitute the two opposite poles of the same relationship, and are the fundamental conditions of the bourgeois means of production and are in no sense a matter of indifference or chance. These means of distribution are the relations of production themselves, but *sub specie distributionis* (from the point of view of distribution). Thus it is quite absurd to say, as J. S. Mill does for example . . . that: 'The laws and conditions of the production of wealth partake of the character of physical truths . . . It is not so with the distribution of wealth. This is a matter of human institutions solely.' The 'laws and conditions' of the production of wealth and the laws of 'distribution of wealth' are the same laws in a different form; they both change and undergo the same historical process; they are, in general, never more than elements in a historical process.

No special sagacity is required in order to understand that, beginning with free labour or wage-labour for example, which arose after the dissolution of serfdom, machines can only develop in opposition to living labour, as a hostile power and alien property, i.e. they must, as capital, oppose the worker. But it is equally easy to see that machines do not cease to be agents of social production, once they become, for example, the property of associated workers. But in the first case, their means of distribution (the fact that they do not belong to the workers) is itself a condition of the means of production that is founded on wage-labour. In the second case, an altered means of distribution will derive from a new, altered basis of production emerging from the historical process.

Of the laws of modern political economy, the law of the tendency of the rate of profit to fall is, in every respect, the most important and the most essential for the understanding of the most difficult problems. From the historical point of view, also, it is the most important law, one which, in spite of its simplicity, has never yet been understood and still less been consciously enunciated. This fall in the rate of profit is bound up with (1) the already existing forces of production and the material foundation that it creates for a new production which in turn presupposes an enormous development of scientific powers; (2) the diminution of that part of capital already produced that has to be exchanged for direct labour, in other words a diminution in the direct labour which is necessary to reproduce an enormous quantity of values, which is expressed in a greater mass of products at low prices, since the sum total of prices equals the capital reproduced plus the profit; (3) the dimension of capital in general, including the portion of it that is not fixed capital. This implies great development in commerce, in exchange operations, and the market; the universality of simultaneous labour; means of communication; the presence of the necessary consumer funds to undertake this gigantic process (food, lodging for the workers, etc.). This being the case, it is plain that the already existing force of production that has been acquired as fixed capital, as well as scientific power, population—in short all the conditions of wealth—the most important conditions for the reproduction of wealth, that is, the rich development of the social individual, the development of the productive forces produced by capital itself in its historical development—all these factors, when they arrive at a certain stage, abolish the self-valorization of capital instead of establishing it. Beyond a certain point the development of productive forces becomes a barrier for capital. Thus capitalist relationships become a barrier for the development of the productive force of labour. On arrival at the point, capital, i.e. wage-labour, enters into the same relationship to the development of social wealth and productive forces as the guild system, serfdom, slavery, and is necessarily rejected as a fetter. Thus the last form of enslavement taken on by human activity—wage-labour on one side and capital on the other—is sloughed off and this process is in itself the result of the capitalist mode of production. The material and spiritual conditions of the negation of wage-labour and capital (which themselves are already the negation of earlier forms of unfree social production) are themselves the results of its process of production. The growing incompatibility of the productive development of society with its established relationships of production is expressed in acute contradictions, crises, and convulsions. The violent annihilation of capital, not through external relationships, but as the condition of its own self-preservation, is the most striking form in which notice is given to it to be gone and give room to a higher state of social production.

From Critique of the Gotha Programme*

. . . Free state—what is this?

It is by no means the aim of the workers, who have got rid of the narrow mentality of humble subjects, to set the state free. In the German Empire the 'state' is almost as 'free' as in Russia. Freedom consists in converting the state from an organ superimposed upon society into one completely subordinate to it, and today, too, the forms of state are more free or less free to the extent that they restrict the 'freedom of the state'.

The German workers' party—at least if it adopts the programme—shows that its socialist ideas are not even skin-deep; in that, instead of treating existing society (and this holds good for any future one) as the basis of the existing state (or of the future state in the case of future society), it treats the state rather as an independent entity that possesses its own intellectual, ethical, and libertarian bases.

And what of the riotous misuse which the programme makes of the words 'present-day state', 'present-day society', and of the still more riotous misconception it creates in regard to the state to which it addresses its demands?

'Present-day society' is capitalist society, which exists in all civilized countries, more or less free from medieval admixture, more or less modified by the particular historical development of each country, more or less developed. On the other hand, the 'present-day state' changes with a country's frontier. It is different in the Prusso-German Empire

---

*An Excerpt.

from what it is in Switzerland, and different in England from what it is in the United States. 'The present-day state' is, therefore, a fiction.

Nevertheless, the different states of the different civilized countries, in spite of their motley diversity of form, all have this in common, that they are based on modern bourgeois society, only one more or less capitalistically developed. They have, therefore, also certain essential characteristics in common. In this sense it is possible to speak of the 'present-day states', in contrast with the future, in which its present root, bourgeois society, will have died off.

The question then arises: what transformation will the state undergo in communist society? In other words, what social functions will remain in existence there that are analogous to present state functions? This question can only be answered scientifically, and one does not get a flea-hop nearer to the problem by a thousandfold combination of the word people with the word state.

Between capitalist and communist society lies the period of the revolutionary transformation of the one into the other. Corresponding to this is also a political transition period in which the state can be nothing but the revolutionary dictatorship of the proletariat.

Now the programme does not deal with this nor with the future state of communist society.

Its political demands contain nothing beyond the old democratic litany familiar to all: universal suffrage, direct legislation, popular rights, a people's militia, etc. They are a mere echo of the bourgeois People's party, of the League of Peace and Freedom. They are all demands which, in so far as they are not exaggerated in fantastic presentation, have already been realized. Only the state to which they belong does not lie within the borders of the German Empire, but in Switzerland, the United States, etc. This sort of 'state of the future' is a present-day state, although existing outside the 'framework' of the German Empire.

But one thing has been forgotten. Since the German workers' party expressly declares that it acts within 'the present-day national state', hence within its own state, the Prusso-German Empire—its demands would indeed otherwise be largely meaningless, since one only demands what one has not got—it should not have forgotten the chief thing, namely, that all those pretty little gewgaws rest on the recognition of the so-called sovereignty of the people and hence are appropriate only in a democratic republic.

Since one has not the courage—and wisely so, for the circumstances demand caution—to demand the democratic republic, as the French workers' programmes under Louis Philippe and under Louis Napoleon did, one should not have resorted, either, to the subterfuge, neither 'honest' nor decent, of demanding things which have meaning only in a democratic republic from a state which is nothing but a police-guarded military despotism, embellished with parliamentary forms, alloyed with a feudal admixture, already influenced by the bourgeoisie and bureaucratically carpentered, and then to assure this state into the bargain that one imagines one will be able to force such things upon it 'by legal means'.

Even vulgar democracy, which sees the millennium in the democratic republic and has no suspicion that it is precisely in this last form of state of bourgeois society that the class struggle has to be fought out to a confusion—even it towers mountains above this kind of democratism which keeps within the limits of what is permitted by the police and not permitted by logic.

That, in fact, by the word 'state' is meant the government machine, or the state in so far as it forms a special organism separated from society through division of labour, is shown by the words 'the German workers' party demands as the economic basis of the state: a single progressive income tax', etc. Taxes are the economic basis of the government machinery and of nothing else. In the state of the future, existing in Switzerland, this demand has been pretty well fulfilled. Income tax presupposes various sources of income of the various social classes, and hence capitalist society. It is, therefore, nothing remarkable that the Liverpool financial reformers, bourgeois headed by Gladstone's brother, are putting forward the same demand as the programme....

'The emancipation of labour demands the promotion of the instruments of labour to the common property of society and the co-operative regulation of the total labour with a fair distribution of the proceeds of labour.'

'Promotion of the instruments of labour to the common property' ought obviously to read their 'conversion into the common property'; but this only in passing.

What are 'proceeds of labour'? The product of labour or its value? And in the latter case, is it the total value of the product or only that part of the value which labour has newly added to the value of the means of production consumed?

'Proceeds of labour' is a loose notion which Lassalle has put in the place of definite economic conceptions.

What is 'a fair distribution'?

Do not the bourgeois assert that the present-day distribution is 'fair'? And is it not, in fact, the only 'fair' distribution on the basis of the present-day mode of production? Are economic relations regulated by legal conceptions or do not, on the contrary, legal relations arise from economic ones? Have not also the socialist sectarians the most varied notions about 'fair' distribution?

To understand what is implied in this connection by the phrase 'fair distribution', we must take the first paragraph and this one together. The latter presupposes a society wherein 'the instruments of labour are common property and the total labour is co-operatively regulated', and from the first paragraph we learn that 'the proceeds of labour belong undiminished with equal right to all members of society'.

'To all members of society'? To those who do not work as well? What remains then of the 'undiminished proceeds of labour'? Only to those members of society who work? What remains then of the 'equal right' of all members of society?

But 'all members of society' and 'equal right' are obviously mere phrases. The kernel consists in this, that in this communist society every worker must receive the 'undiminished' Lassallean 'proceeds of labour'.

Let us take first of all the words 'proceeds of labour' in the sense of the product of labour; then the co-operative proceeds of labour are the total social product.

From this must now be deducted:

First, cover for replacement of the means of production used up.

Secondly, additional portion for expansion of production.

Thirdly, reserve or insurance funds to provide against accidents, dislocations caused by natural calamities, etc.

These deductions from the 'undiminished proceeds of labour' are an economic necessity and their magnitude is to be determined according to available means and forces, and partly by computation of probabilities, but they are in no way calculable by equity.

There remains the other part of the total product, intended to serve as means of consumption.

Before this is divided among the individuals, there has to be deducted again from it:

First, the general costs of administration not belonging to production.

This part will, from the outset, be very considerably restricted in comparison with present-day society and it diminishes in proportion as the new society develops.

Secondly, that which is intended for the common satisfaction of needs, such as schools, health services, etc.

From the outset this part grows considerably in comparison with present-day society and it grows in proportion as the new society develops.

Thirdly, funds for those unable to work, etc., in short, for what is included under so-called official poor relief today.

Only now do we come to the 'distribution' which the programme, under Lassallean influence, alone has in view in its narrow fashion, namely, to that part of the means of consumption which is divided among the individual producers of the co-operative society.

The 'undiminished proceeds of labour' have already unnoticeably become converted into the 'diminished' proceeds, although what the producer is deprived of in his capacity as a private individual benefits him directly or indirectly in his capacity as a member of society.

Just as the phrase of the 'undiminished proceeds of labour' has disappeared, so now does the phrase of the 'proceeds of labour' disappear altogether.

Within the co-operative society based on common ownership of the means of production, the producers do not exchange their products; just as little does the labour employed on the products appear here as the value of these products, as a material quality possessed by them, since now, in contrast to capitalist society, individual labour no longer exists in an indirect fashion but directly as a component part of the total labour. The phrase 'proceeds of labour', objectionable also today on account of its ambiguity, thus loses all meaning.

What we have to deal with here is a communist society, not as it has developed on its own foundations, but, on the contrary, just as it emerges from capitalist society; which is thus in every respect, economically, morally, and intellectually, still stamped with the birth marks of the old society from whose womb it emerges. Accordingly, the individual producer receives back from society—after the deductions have been made—exactly what he gives to it. What he has given to it is his individual quantum of labour. For example, the social working day consists of the sum of the individual hours of work; the individual labour time of the individual producer is the part of the social working day contributed by him, his share in it. He receives a certificate from society that he has furnished such and such an amount of labour (after deducting his labour for the common funds), and with this certificate he draws from the social stock of means of consumption as much as costs the same amount of labour. The same amount of labour which he has given to society in one form he receives back in another.

Here obviously the same principle prevails as that which regulates the exchange of commodities, as far as this is exchange of equal values. Content and form are changed, because under the altered circumstances no one can give anything except his labour, and because, on the other hand, nothing can pass to the ownership of individuals except individual means of consumption. But, as far as the distribution of the latter among the individual producers is concerned, the same principle prevails as in the exchange of commodity-equivalents: a given amount of labour in one form is exchanged for an equal amount of labour in another form.

Hence, equal right here is still in principle—bourgeois right, although principle and practice are no longer at loggerheads, while the exchange of equivalents in commodity exchange only exists on the average and not in the individual case.

In spite of this advance, this equal right is still constantly stigmatized by a bourgeois limitation. The right of the producers is proportional to the labour they supply; the equality consists in the fact that measurement is made with an equal standard, labour.

But one man is superior to another physically or mentally and so supplies more labour in the same time, or can labour for a longer time; and labour, to serve as a measure, must be defined by its duration or intensity, otherwise it ceases to be a standard of measurement. This equal right is an unequal right for unequal labour. It recognizes no class differences, because everyone is only a worker like everyone else; but it tacitly recognizes unequal individual endowment and thus productive capacity as natural privileges. It is, therefore, a right of inequality, in its content, like every right. Right by its very nature can consist only in the application of an equal standard; but unequal individuals (and they would not be different individuals if they were not unequal) are measurable only by an equal standard in so far as they are brought under an equal point of view, are taken from one definite side only, for instance, in the present case, are regarded only as workers and nothing more is seen in them, everything else being ignored. Further, one worker is married, another not; one has more children than another, and so on and so forth. Thus, with an equal performance of labour, and hence an equal share in the social consumption fund, one will in fact receive more than another, one will be richer than another, and so on. To avoid all these defects, right instead of being equal would have to be unequal.

But these defects are inevitable in the first phase of communist society as it is when it has just emerged after prolonged birth pangs from capitalist society. Right can never be higher than the economic structure of society and its cultural development conditioned thereby.

In a higher phase of communist society, after the enslaving subordination of the individual to the division of labour, and therewith also the antithesis between mental and physical labour, has vanished; after labour has become not only a means of life but life's prime want; after the productive forces have also increased with the all-round development of the individual, and all the springs of co-operative wealth flow more abundantly—only then can the narrow horizon of bourgeois right be crossed in its entirety and society inscribe on its banners: from each according to his ability, to each according to his needs!

I have dealt more at length with the 'undiminished proceeds of labour', on the one hand, and with 'equal right' and 'fair distribution', on the other, in order to show what a crime it is to attempt, on the one hand, to force on our Party again, as dogmas, ideas which in a certain period had some meaning but have now become obsolete verbal rubbish, while again perverting, on the other, the realistic outlook, which it cost so much effort to instil into the Party but which has now taken root in it, by means of ideological nonsense about right and other trash so common among the democrats and French Socialists.

Quite apart from the analysis so far given, it was in general a mistake to make a fuss about so-called distribution and put the principal stress on it.

Any distribution whatever of the means of consumption is only a consequence of the distribution of the conditions of production themselves. The latter distribution, however, is a feature of the mode of production itself. The capitalist mode of production, for example, rests on the fact that the material conditions of production are in the hands of non-workers in the form of property in capital and land, while the masses are only owners of the personal condition of production, of labour power. If the elements of production are so distributed, then the present-day distribution of the means of consumption results automatically. If the material conditions of production are the co-operative property of the workers themselves, then there likewise results a distribution of the means of consumption different from the present one. Vulgar socialism (and from it in turn a section of the democracy) has taken over from the bourgeois economists the consideration and treatment of distribution as independent of the mode of production and hence the presentation of socialism as turning principally on distribution. After the real relation has long been made clear, why retrogress again? . . .

John Stuart Mill (1806–1873 C.E.)

An Englishman educated by his father James Mill (a political theorist who was an associate of Jeremy Bentham), John Stuart Mill was to become one of the most learned thinkers ever. He was trained in Latin and Greek from age three, and studied classics, logic, philosophy, economics, science, and history. Mill was influenced by his father and Bentham from early on, and was sympathetic to the general principles of utilitarianism. However, Mill wanted to reconcile the principle of utility with intuitive notions of justice and rights. While it seems like an incompatibility, Mill reconceived of utility in such a way as to make individual liberty a necessary condition of social well-being. The essay "On Liberty" (1859), from which the following is excerpted, explains what Mill has in mind.

From On Liberty*

Chapter I

Introductory

The subject of this essay is not the so-called "liberty of the will," so unfortunately opposed to the misnamed doctrine of philosophical necessity; but civil, or social liberty: the nature and limits of the power which can be legitimately exercised by society over the individual. A question seldom stated, and hardly ever discussed in general terms, but which profoundly influences the practical controversies of the age by its latent presence, and is likely soon to make itself recognized as the vital question of the future. It is so far from being new that, in a certain sense, it has divided mankind almost from the remotest ages; but in the stage of progress into which the more civilized portions of the species have now entered, it presents itself under new conditions and requires a different and more fundamental treatment.

The struggle between liberty and authority is the most conspicuous feature in the portions of history with which we are earliest familiar, particularly in that of Greece, Rome, and England. But in old times this contest was between subjects, or some classes of subjects, and the government. By liberty was meant protection against the tyranny of the political rulers. The rulers were conceived (except in some of the popular governments of Greece) as in a necessarily antagonistic position to the people whom they ruled. They consisted of a governing One, or a governing tribe or caste, who derived their authority from inheritance or conquest, who, at all events, did not hold it at the pleasure of the governed, and whose supremacy men did not venture, perhaps did not desire, to contest, whatever precautions might be taken against its oppressive exercise. Their power was regarded as necessary, but also as highly dangerous; as a weapon which they would attempt to use against their subjects, no less than against external enemies. To prevent

---

*An Excerpt.

the weaker members of the community from being preyed upon by innumerable vultures, it was needful that there should be an animal of prey stronger than the rest, commissioned to keep them down. But as the king of the vultures would be no less bent upon preying on the flock than any of the minor harpies, it was indispensable to be in a perpetual attitude of defense against his beak and claws. The aim, therefore, of patriots was to set limits to the power which the ruler should be suffered to exercise over the community; and this limitation was what they meant by liberty. It was attempted in two ways. First, by obtaining a recognition of certain immunities, called political liberties or rights, which it was to be regarded as a breach of duty in the ruler to infringe, and which if he did infringe, specific resistance or general rebellion was held to be justifiable. A second, and generally a later, expedient was the establishment of constitutional checks by which the consent of the community, or of a body of some sort, supposed to represent its interests, was made a necessary condition to some of the more important acts of the governing power. To the first of these modes of limitation, the ruling power, in most European countries, was compelled, more or less, to submit. It was not so with the second; and, to attain this, or, when already in some degree possessed, to attain it more completely, became everywhere the principal object of the lovers of liberty. And so long as mankind were content to combat one enemy by another, and to be ruled by a master on condition of being guaranteed more or less efficaciously against his tyranny, they did not carry their aspirations beyond this point.

A time, however, came, in the progress of human affairs, when men ceased to think it a necessity of nature that their governors should be an independent power opposed in interest to themselves. It appeared to them much better that the various magistrates of the state should be their tenants or delegates, revocable at their pleasure. In that way alone, it seemed, could they have complete security that the powers of government would never be abused to their disadvantage. By degrees this new demand for elective and temporary rulers became the prominent object of the exertions of the popular party wherever any such party existed, and superseded, to a considerable extent, the previous efforts to limit the power of rulers. As the struggle proceeded for making the ruling power emanate from the periodical choice of the ruled, some persons began to think that too much importance had been attached to the limitation of the power itself. *That* (it might seem) was a resource against rulers whose interests were habitually opposed to those of the people. What was now wanted was that the rulers should be identified with the people, that their interest and will should be the interest and will of the nation. The nation did not need to be protected against its own will. There was no fear of its tyrannizing over itself. Let the rulers be effectually responsible to it, promptly removable by it, and it could afford to trust them with power of which it could itself dictate the use to be made. Their power was but the nation's own power, concentrated and in a form convenient for exercise. This mode of thought, or rather perhaps of feeling, was common among the last generation of European liberalism, in the Continental section of which it still apparently predominates. Those who admit any limit to what a government may do, except in the case of such governments as they think ought not to exist, stand out as brilliant exceptions among the political thinkers of the Continent. A similar tone of sentiment might by this time have been prevalent in our own country if the circumstances which for a time encouraged it had continued unaltered.

But, in political and philosophical theories as well as in persons, success discloses faults and infirmities which failure might have concealed from observation. The notion that the people have no need to limit their power over themselves might seem axiomatic, when popular government was a thing only dreamed about, or read of as having existed at some distant period of the past. Neither was that notion necessarily disturbed by such temporary aberrations as those of the French Revolution, the worst of which were the work of a usurping few, and which, in any case, belonged, not to the permanent working of popular institutions, but to a sudden and convulsive outbreak against monarchical and aristocratic despotism. In time, however, a democratic republic came to occupy a large portion of the earth's surface and made itself felt as one of the most powerful members of the community of nations;[1] and elective and responsible government became subject to the observations and criticisms which wait upon a great existing fact. It was now perceived that such phrases as "self-government," and "the power of the people over themselves," do not express the true state of the case. The "people" who exercise the power are not always the same people with those over whom it is exercised; and the "self-government" spoken of is not the government of each by himself, but of each by all the rest. The will of the people, moreover, practically means the will of the most numerous or the most active *part* of the people—the majority, or those who succeed in making themselves accepted as the majority; the people, consequently, *may* desire to oppress a part of their number, and precautions are as much needed against this as against any other abuse of power. The limitation, therefore, of the power of government over individuals loses none of its importance when the holders of power are regularly accountable to the community, that is, to the strongest party therein. This view of things, recommending itself equally to the intelligence of thinkers and to the inclination of those important classes in European society to whose real or supposed interests democracy is adverse, has had no difficulty in establishing itself; and in political speculations "the tyranny of the majority" is now generally included among the evils against which society requires to be on its guard.

Like other tyrannies, the tyranny of the majority was at first, and is still vulgarly, held in dread, chiefly as operating through the acts of the public authorities. But reflecting persons perceived that when society is itself the tyrant—society collectively over the separate individuals who compose it—its means of tyrannizing are not restricted to the acts which it may do by the hands of its political functionaries. Society can and does execute its own mandates; and if it issues wrong mandates instead of right, or any mandates at all in things with which it ought not to meddle, it practices a social tyranny more formidable than many kinds of political oppression, since, though not usually upheld by such extreme penalties, it leaves fewer means of escape, penetrating much more deeply into the details of life, and enslaving the soul itself. Protection, therefore, against the tyranny of the magistrate is not enough; there needs protection also against the tyranny of the prevailing opinion and feeling, against the tendency of society to impose, by other means than civil penalties, its own ideas and practices as rules of conduct on those who dissent from them; to fetter the development and, if possible, prevent the formation of any in-

---

[1]Reference is to the United States of America.

dividuality not in harmony with its ways, and compel all characters to fashion themselves upon the model of its own. There is a limit to the legitimate interference of collective opinion with individual independence; and to find that limit, and maintain it against encroachment, is as indispensable to a good condition of human affairs as protection against political despotism.

But though this proposition is not likely to be contested in general terms, the practical question where to place the limit—how to make the fitting adjustment between individual independence and social control—is a subject on which nearly everything remains to be done. All that makes existence valuable to anyone depends on the enforcement of restraints upon the actions of other people. Some rules of conduct, therefore, must be imposed—by law in the first place, and by opinion on many things which are not fit subjects for the operation of law. What these rules should be is the principal question in human affairs; but if we except a few of the most obvious cases, it is one of those which least progress has been made in resolving. No two ages, and scarcely any two countries, have decided it alike; and the decision of one age or country is a wonder to another. Yet the people of any given age and country no more suspect any difficulty in it than if it were a subject on which mankind had always been agreed. The rules which obtain among themselves appear to them self-evident and self-justifying. This all but universal illusion is one of the examples of the magical influence of custom, which is not only, as the proverb says, a second nature but is continually mistaken for the first. The effect of custom, in preventing any misgiving respecting the rules of conduct which mankind impose on one another, is all the more complete because the subject is one on which it is not generally considered necessary that reasons should be given, either by one person to others or by each to himself. People are accustomed to believe, and have been encouraged in the belief by some who aspire to the character of philosophers, that their feelings on subjects of this nature are better than reasons and render reasons unnecessary. The practical principle which guides them to their opinions on the regulation of human conduct is the feeling in each person's mind that everybody should be required to act as he, and those with whom he sympathizes, would like them to act. No one, indeed, acknowledges to himself that his standard of judgment is his own liking; but an opinion on a point of conduct, not supported by reasons, can only count as one person's preference; and if the reasons, when given, are a mere appeal to a similar preference felt by other people, it is still only many people's liking instead of one. To an ordinary man, however, his own preference, thus supported, is not only a perfectly satisfactory reason but the only one he generally has for any of his notions of morality, taste, or propriety, which are not expressly written in his religious creed, and his chief guide in the interpretation even of that. Men's opinions, accordingly, on what is laudable or blamable are affected by all the multifarious causes which influence their wishes in regard to the conduct of others, and which are as numerous as those which determine their wishes on any other subject. Sometimes their reason; at other times their prejudices or superstitions; often their social affections, not seldom their antisocial ones, their envy or jealousy, their arrogance or contemptuousness; but most commonly their desires or fears for themselves—their legitimate or illegitimate self-interest. Wherever there is an ascendant class, a large portion of the morality of the country emanates from its class interests and its feelings of class superiority. The morality between Spartans and Helots, between planters and Negroes, between princes and subjects, between nobles and roturiers,[2] between men and women has been for the most part the creation of these class interests and feelings; and the sentiments thus generated react in turn upon the moral feelings of the members of the ascendant class, in their relations among themselves. Where, on the other hand, a class, formerly ascendant, has lost its ascendancy, or where its ascendancy is unpopular, the prevailing moral sentiments frequently bear the impress of an impatient dislike of superiority. Another grand determining principle of the rules of conduct, both in act and forbearance, which have been enforced by law or opinion, has been the servility of mankind toward the supposed preferences or aversions of their temporal masters or of their gods. This servility, though essentially selfish, is not hypocrisy; it gives rise to perfectly genuine sentiments of abhorrence; it made men burn magicians and heretics. Among so many baser influences, the general and obvious interests of society have, of course, had a share, and a large one, in the direction of the moral sentiments; less, however, as a matter of reason, and on their own account, than as a consequence of the sympathies and antipathies which grew out of them; and sympathies and antipathies which had little or nothing to do with the interests of society have made themselves felt in the establishment of moralities with quite as great force.

The likings and dislikings of society, or of some powerful portion of it, are thus the main thing which has practically determined the rules laid down for general observance, under the penalties of law or opinion. And in general, those who have been in advance of society in thought and feeling have left this condition of things unassailed in principle, however they may have come into conflict with it in some of its details. They have occupied themselves rather in inquiring what things society ought to like or dislike than in questioning whether its likings or dislikings should be a law to individuals. They preferred endeavoring to alter the feelings of mankind on the particular points on which they were themselves heretical rather than make common cause in defense of freedom with heretics generally. The only case in which the higher ground has been taken on principle and maintained with consistency, by any but an individual here and there, is that of religious belief: a case instructive in many ways, and not least so as forming a most striking instance of the fallibility of what is called the moral sense; for the *odium theologicum,* in a sincere bigot, is one of the most unequivocal cases of moral feeling. Those who first broke the yoke of what called itself the Universal Church were in general as little willing to permit difference of religious opinion as that church itself. But when the heat of the conflict was over, without giving a complete victory to any party, and each church or sect was reduced to limit its hopes to retaining possession of the ground it already occupied, minorities, seeing that they had no chance of becoming majorities, were under the necessity of pleading to those whom they could not convert for permission to differ. It is accordingly on this battlefield, almost solely, that the rights of the individual against society have been asserted on broad grounds of principle, and the claim of society to exercise authority over dissentients openly controverted. The great writers to whom the world owes what religious liberty it possesses have mostly asserted freedom of conscience as an indefeasible right,

---

[2]Freemen holding land through payment of rent.

and denied absolutely that a human being is accountable to others for his religious belief. Yet so natural to mankind is intolerance in whatever they really care about that religious freedom has hardly anywhere been practically realized, except where religious indifference, which dislikes to have its peace disturbed by theological quarrels, has added its weight to the scale. In the minds of almost all religious persons, even in the most tolerant countries, the duty of toleration is admitted with tacit reserves. One person will bear with dissent in matters of church government, but not of dogma; another can tolerate everybody, short of a Papist or a Unitarian; another, everyone who believes in revealed religion; a few extend their charity a little further, but stop at the belief in a God and in a future state. Wherever the sentiment of the majority is still genuine and intense, it is found to have abated little of its claim to be obeyed.

In England, from the peculiar circumstances of our political history, though the yoke of opinion is perhaps heavier, that of law is lighter than in most other countries of Europe; and there is considerable jealousy of direct interference by the legislative or the executive power with private conduct, not so much from any just regard for the independence of the individual as from the still subsisting habit of looking on the government as representing an opposite interest to the public. The majority have not yet learned to feel the power of the government their power, or its opinions their opinions. When they do so, individual liberty will probably be as much exposed to invasion from the government as it already is from public opinion. But, as yet, there is a considerable amount of feeling ready to be called forth against any attempt of the law to control individuals in things in which they have not hitherto been accustomed to be controlled by it; and this with very little discrimination as to whether the matter is, or is not, within the legitimate sphere of legal control; insomuch that the feeling, highly salutary on the whole, is perhaps quite as often misplaced as well grounded in the particular instances of its application. There is, in fact, no recognized principle by which the propriety or impropriety of government interference is customarily tested. People decide according to their personal preferences. Some, whenever they see any good to be done, or evil to be remedied, would willingly instigate the government to undertake the business, while others prefer to bear almost any amount of social evil rather than add one to the departments of human interests amenable to governmental control. And men range themselves on one or the other side in any particular case, according to this general direction of their sentiments, or according to the degree of interest which they feel in the particular thing which it is proposed that the government should do, or according to the belief they entertain that the government would, or would not, do it in the manner they prefer; but very rarely on account of any opinion to which they consistently adhere, as to what things are fit to be done by a government. And it seems to me that in consequence of this absence of rule or principle, one side is at present as often wrong as the other; the interference of government is, with about equal frequency, improperly invoked and improperly condemned.

The object of this essay is to assert one very simple principle, as entitled to govern absolutely the dealings of society with the individual in the way of compulsion and control, whether the means used be physical force in the form of legal penalties or the moral coercion of public opinion. That principle is that the sole end for which mankind are warranted, individually or collectively, in interfering with the liberty of action of any of their number is self-protection. That the only purpose for which power can be rightfully exercised over any member of a civilized community, against his will, is to prevent harm to others. His own good, either physical or moral, is not a sufficient warrant. He cannot rightfully be compelled to do or forbear because it will be better for him to do so, because it will make him happier, because, in the opinions of others, to do so would be wise or even right. These are good reasons for remonstrating with him, or reasoning with him, or persuading him, or entreating him, but not for compelling him or visiting him with any evil in case he do otherwise. To justify that, the conduct from which it is desired to deter him must be calculated to produce evil to someone else. The only part of the conduct of anyone for which he is amenable to society is that which concerns others. In the part which merely concerns himself, his independence is, of right, absolute. Over himself, over his own body and mind, the individual is sovereign.

It is, perhaps, hardly necessary to say that this doctrine is meant to apply only to human beings in the maturity of their faculties. We are not speaking of children or of young persons below the age which the law may fix as that of manhood or womanhood. Those who are still in a state to require being taken care of by others must be protected against their own actions as well as against external injury. For the same reason we may leave out of consideration those backward states of society in which the race itself may be considered as in its nonage. The early difficulties in the way of spontaneous progress are so great that there is seldom any choice of means for overcoming them; and a ruler full of the spirit of improvement is warranted in the use of any expedients that will attain an end perhaps otherwise unattainable. Despotism is a legitimate mode of government in dealing with barbarians, provided the end be their improvement and the means justified by actually effecting that end. Liberty, as a principle, has no application to any state of things anterior to the time when mankind have become capable of being improved by free and equal discussion. Until then, there is nothing for them but implicit obedience to an Akbar or a Charlemagne, if they are so fortunate as to find one. But as soon as mankind have attained the capacity of being guided to their own improvement by conviction or persuasion (a period long since reached in all nations with whom we need here concern ourselves), compulsion, either in the direct form or in that of pains and penalties for noncompliance, is no longer admissible as a means to their own good, and justifiable only for the security of others.

It is proper to state that I forego any advantage which could be derived to my argument from the idea of abstract right as a thing independent of utility. I regard utility as the ultimate appeal on all ethical questions; but it must be utility in the largest sense, grounded on the permanent interests of man as a progressive being. Those interests, I contend, authorize the subjection of individual spontaneity to external control only in respect to those actions of each which concern the interest of other people. If anyone does an act hurtful to others, there is a *prima facie* case for punishing him by law or, where legal penalties are not safely applicable, by general disapprobation. There are also many positive acts for the benefit of others which he may rightfully be compelled to perform, such as to give evidence in a court of justice, to bear his fair share in the common defense or in any other joint work necessary to the interest of the society of which he enjoys the protection, and to perform certain acts of individual beneficence, such as saving a fellow creature's life or interposing to protect the defenseless against ill usage—things which whenever it is obviously a man's duty to do he may rightfully be made responsible to society for not doing. A person may cause evil to others not only by his actions but by his inaction, and in either case he is justly accountable to them for the injury. The latter case, it is true, requires a much more cautious exercise of compulsion than the former. To make anyone answerable for doing evil to others is the rule; to make him answerable for not preventing evil is, comparatively speaking, the exception. Yet there are many cases clear enough and grave enough to justify that exception. In all things which regard the external relations of the individual, he is *de jure* amenable to those whose interests are concerned, and, if need be, to society as their protector. There are often good reasons for not holding him to the responsibility; but these reasons must arise from the special expediencies of the case: either because it is a kind of case in which he is on the whole likely to act better when left to his own discretion than when controlled in any way in which society have it in their power to control him; or because the attempt to exercise control would produce other evils, greater than those which it would prevent. When such reasons as these preclude the enforcement of responsibility, the conscience of the agent himself should step into the vacant judgment seat and protect those interests of others which have no external protection; judging himself all the more rigidly, because the case does not admit of his being made accountable to the judgment of his fellow creatures.

But there is a sphere of action in which society, as distinguished from the individual, has, if any, only an indirect interest: comprehending all that portion of a person's life and conduct which affects only himself or, if it also affects others, only with their free, voluntary, and undeceived consent and participation. When I say only himself, I mean directly and in the first instance; for whatever affects himself may affect others through himself; and the objection which may be grounded on this contingency will receive consideration in the sequel. This, then, is the appropriate region of human liberty. It comprises, first, the inward domain of consciousness, demanding liberty of conscience in the most comprehensive sense, liberty of thought and feeling, absolute freedom of opinion and sentiment on all subjects, practical or speculative, scientific, moral, or theological. The liberty of expressing and publishing opinions may seem to fall under a different principle, since it belongs to that part of the conduct of an individual which concerns other people, but, being almost of as much importance as the liberty of thought itself and resting in great part on the same reasons, is practically inseparable from it. Secondly, the principle requires liberty of tastes and pursuits, of framing the plan of our life to suit our own character, of doing as we like, subject to such consequences as may follow, without impediment from our fellow creatures, so long as what we do does not harm them, even though they should think our conduct foolish, perverse, or wrong. Thirdly, from this liberty of each individual follows the liberty, within the same limits, of combination among individuals; freedom to unite for any purpose not involving harm to others: the persons combining being supposed to be of full age and not forced or deceived.

No society in which these liberties are not, on the whole, respected is free, whatever may be its form of government; and none is completely free in which they do not exist absolute and unqualified. The only freedom which deserves the name is that of pursuing our own good in our own way, so long as we do not attempt to deprive others of theirs or impede their efforts to obtain it. Each is the proper guardian of his own health, whether bodily *or* mental and spiritual. Mankind are greater gainers by suffering each other to live as seems good to themselves than by compelling each to live as seems good to the rest.

Though this doctrine is anything but new and, to some persons, may have the air of a truism, there is no doctrine which stands more directly opposed to the general tendency of existing opinion and practice. Society has expended fully as much effort in the attempt (according to its lights) to compel people to conform to its notions of personal as of social excellence. The ancient commonwealths thought themselves entitled to practice, and the ancient philosophers countenanced, the regulation of every part of private conduct by public authority, on the ground that the State had a deep interest in the whole bodily and mental discipline of every one of its citizens—a mode of thinking which may have been admissible in small republics surrounded by powerful enemies, in constant peril of being subverted by foreign attack or internal commotion, and to which even a short interval of relaxed energy and self-command might so easily be fatal that they could not afford to wait for the salutary permanent effects of freedom. In the modern world, the greater size of political communities and, above all, the separation between spiritual and temporal authority (which placed the direction of men's consciences in other hands than those which controlled their worldly affairs) prevented so great an interference by law in the details of private life; but the engines of moral repression have been wielded more strenuously against divergence from the reigning opinion in self-regarding than even in social matters; religion, the most powerful of the elements which have entered into the formation of moral feeling, having almost always been governed either by the ambition of a hierarchy seeking control over every department of human conduct, or by the spirit of Puritanism. And some of those modern reformers who have placed themselves in strongest opposition to the religions of the past have been noway behind either churches or sects in their assertion of the right of spiritual domination: M. Comte, in particular, whose social system, as unfolded in his *Système de Politique Positive*, aims at establishing (though by moral more than by legal appliances) a despotism of society over the individual surpassing anything contemplated in the political ideal of the most rigid disciplinarian among the ancient philosophers.

Apart from the peculiar tenets of individual thinkers, there is also in the world at large an increasing inclination to stretch unduly the powers of society over the individual both by the force of opinion and even by that of legislation; and as the tendency of all the changes taking place in the world is to strengthen society and diminish the power of the individual, this encroachment is not one of the evils which tend spontaneously to disappear, but, on the contrary, to grow more and more formidable. The disposition of mankind, whether as rulers or as fellow citizens, to impose their own opinions and inclinations as a rule of conduct on others is so energetically supported by some of the best and by some of the worst feelings incident to human nature that it is hardly ever kept under restraint by anything but want of power; and as the power is not declining, but growing, unless a strong barrier of moral conviction can be raised against the mischief, we must expect, in the present circumstances of the world, to see it increase.

It will be convenient for the argument if, instead of at once entering upon the general thesis, we confine ourselves in the first instance to a single branch of it on which the principle here stated is, if not fully, yet to a certain point, recognized by the current opinions. This one branch is the Liberty of Thought, from which it is impossible to separate the cognate liberty of speaking and of writing. Although these liberties, to some considerable amount, form part of the political morality of all countries which profess religious toleration and free institutions, the grounds, both philosophical and practical, on which they rest are perhaps not so familiar to the general mind, nor so thoroughly appreciated by many, even of the leaders of opinion, as might have been expected. Those grounds, when rightly understood, are of much wider application than to only one division of the subject, and a thorough consideration of this part of the question will be found the best introduction to the remainder. Those to whom nothing which I am about to say will be new may therefore, I hope, excuse me if on a subject which for now three centuries has been so often discussed I venture on one discussion more.

Chapter II

Of the Liberty of Thought and Discussion

The time, it is to be hoped, is gone by when any defense would be necessary of the "liberty of the press" as one of the securities against corrupt or tyrannical government. No argument, we may suppose, can now be needed against permitting a legislature or an executive, not identified in interest with the people, to prescribe opinions to them and determine what doctrines or what arguments they shall be allowed to hear. This aspect of the question, besides, has been so often and so triumphantly enforced by preceding writers that it needs not be specially insisted on in this place. Though the law of England, on the subject of the press, is as servile to this day as it was in the time of the Tudors, there is little danger of its being actually put in force against political discussion except during some temporary panic when fear of insurrection drives ministers and judges from their propriety; and, speaking generally, it is not, in constitutional countries, to be apprehended that the government, whether completely responsible to the people or not, will often attempt to control the expression of opinion, except when in doing so it makes itself the organ of the general intolerance of the public. Let us suppose, therefore, that the government is entirely at one with the people, and never thinks of exerting any power of coercion unless in agreement with what it conceives to be their voice. But I deny the right of the people to exercise such coercion, either by themselves or by their government. The power itself is illegitimate. The best government has no more title to it than the worst. It is as noxious, or more noxious, when exerted in accordance with public opinion than when in opposition to it. If all mankind minus one were of one opinion, mankind would be no more justified in silencing that one person than he, if he had the power, would be justified in silencing mankind. Were an opinion a personal possession of no value except to the owner, if to be obstructed in the enjoyment of it were simply a private injury, it would make some difference whether the injury was inflicted only on a few persons or on many. But the peculiar evil of silencing the expression of an opinion is that it is robbing the human race, posterity as well as the existing generation—those who dissent from the opinion, still more than those who hold it. If the opinion is right, they are deprived of the opportunity of exchanging error for truth; if wrong, they lose, what is almost as great a benefit, the clearer perception and livelier impression of truth produced by its collision with error.

It is necessary to consider separately these two hypotheses, each of which has a distinct branch of the argument corresponding to it. We can never be sure that the opinion we are endeavoring to stifle is a false opinion; and if we were sure, stifling it would be an evil still.

First, the opinion which it is attempted to suppress by authority may possibly be true. Those who desire to suppress it, of course, deny its truth; but they are not infallible. They have no authority to decide the question for all mankind and exclude every other person from the means of judging. To refuse a hearing to an opinion because they are sure that it is false is to assume that *their* certainty is the same thing as *absolute* certainty. All silencing of discussion is an assumption of infallibility. Its condemnation may be allowed to rest on this common argument, not the worse for being common.

Unfortunately for the good sense of mankind, the fact of their fallibility is far from carrying the weight in their practical judgment which is always allowed to it in theory; for while everyone well knows himself to be fallible, few think it necessary to take any precautions against their own fallibility, or admit the supposition that any opinion of which they feel very certain may be one of the examples of the error to which they acknowledge themselves to be liable. Absolute princes, or others who are accustomed to unlimited deference, usually feel this complete confidence in their own opinions on nearly all subjects. People more happily situated, who sometimes hear their opinions disputed and are not wholly unused to be set right when they are wrong, place the same unbounded reliance only on such of their opinions as are shared by all who surround them, or to whom they habitually defer; for in proportion to a man's want of confidence in his own solitary judgment does he usually repose, with implicit trust, on the infallibility of "the world" in general. And the world, to each individual, means the part of it with which he comes in contact: his party, his sect, his church, his class of society; the man may be called, by comparison, almost liberal and large-minded to whom it means anything so comprehensive as his own country or his own age. Nor is his faith in this collective authority at all shaken by his being aware that other ages, countries, sects, churches, classes, and parties have thought, and even now think, the exact reverse. He devolves upon his own world the responsibility of being in the right against the dissentient worlds of other people; and it never troubles him that mere accident has decided which of these numerous worlds is the object of his reliance, and that the same causes which make him a churchman in London would have made him a Buddhist or a Confucian in Peking. Yet it is as evident in itself, as any amount of argument can make it, that ages are no more infallible than individuals—every age having held many opinions which subsequent ages have deemed not only false but absurd; and it is as certain that many opinions, now general, will be rejected by future ages, as it is that many, once general, are rejected by the present.

The objection likely to be made to this argument would probably take some such form as the following. There is no greater assumption of infallibility in forbidding the propagation of error than in any other thing which is done by public authority on its own judgment and responsibility. Judgment is given to men that they may use it. Because it may be used erroneously, are men to be told that they ought not to use it at all? To prohibit what they think pernicious is not claiming exemption from error, but fulfilling the duty incumbent on them, although fallible, of acting on their conscientious conviction. If we were never to act on our opinions, because those opinions may be wrong, we should leave all our interests uncared for, and all our duties unperformed. An objection which applies to all conduct can be no valid objection to any conduct in particular. It is the duty of governments, and of individuals, to form the truest opinions they can; to form them carefully, and never impose them upon others unless they are quite sure of being right. But when they are sure (such reasoners may say), it is not conscientiousness but cowardice to shrink from acting on their opinions and allow doctrines which they honestly think dangerous to the welfare of mankind, either in this life or in another, to be scattered abroad without restraint, because other people, in less enlightened times, have persecuted opinions now believed to be true. Let us take care, it may be said, not to make the same mistake; but governments and nations have made mistakes in other things which are not denied to be fit subjects for the exercise of authority: they have laid on bad taxes, made unjust wars. Ought we therefore to lay on no taxes and, under whatever provocation, make no wars? Men and governments must act to the best of their ability. There is no such thing as absolute certainty, but there is assurance sufficient for the purposes of human life. We may, and must, assume our opinion to be true for the guidance of our own conduct; and it is assuming no more when we forbid bad men to pervert society by the propagation of opinions which we regard as false and pernicious.

I answer, that it is assuming very much more. There is the greatest difference between presuming an opinion to be true because, with every opportunity for contesting it, it has not been refuted, and assuming its truth for the purpose of not permitting its refutation. Complete liberty of contradicting and disproving our opinion is the very condition which justifies us in assuming its truth for purposes of action; and on no other terms can a being with human faculties have any rational assurance of being right.

When we consider either the history of opinion or the ordinary conduct of human life, to what is it to be ascribed that the one and the other are no worse than they are? Not certainly to the inherent force of the human understanding, for on any matter not self-evident there are ninety-nine persons totally incapable of judging of it for one who is capable; and the capacity of the hundredth person is only comparative, for the majority of the eminent men of every past generation held many opinions now known to be erroneous, and did or approved numerous things which no one will now justify. Why is it, then, that there is on the whole a preponderance among mankind of rational opinions and rational conduct? If there really is this preponderance—which there must be unless human affairs are, and have always been, in an almost desperate state—it is owing to a quality of the human mind, the source of everything respectable in man either as an intellectual or as a moral being, namely, that his errors are corrigible. He is capable of rectifying his mistakes by discussion and experience. Not by experience alone. There must be discussion to show how experience is to be interpreted. Wrong opinions and practices gradually yield to fact and argument; but facts and arguments, to produce any effect on the mind, must be brought before it. Very few facts are able to tell their own story, without comments to bring out their meaning. The whole strength and value, then, of human judgment depending on the one property, that it can be set right when it is wrong, reliance can be placed on it only when the means of setting it right are kept constantly at hand. In the case of any person whose judgment is really deserving of confidence, how has it become so? Because he has kept his mind open to criticism of his opinions and conduct. Because it has been his practice to listen to all that could be said against him; to profit by as much of it as was just, and to expound to himself, and upon occasion to others, the fallacy of what was fallacious. Because he has felt that the only way in which a human being can make some approach to knowing the whole of a subject is by hearing what can be said about it by persons of every variety of opinion, and studying all modes in which it can be looked at by every character of mind. No wise man ever acquired his wisdom in any mode but this; nor is it in the nature of human intellect to become wise in any other manner. The steady habit of correcting and completing his own opinion by collating it with those of others, so far from causing doubt and hesitation in carrying it into practice, is the only stable foundation for a just reliance on it; for, being cognizant of all that can, at least obviously, be said against him, and having taken up his position against all gainsayers—knowing that he has sought for objections and difficulties instead of avoiding them, and has shut out no light which can be thrown upon the subject from any quarter—he has a right to think his judgment better than that of any person, or any multitude, who have not gone through a similar process.

It is not too much to require that what the wisest of mankind, those who are best entitled to trust their own judgment, find necessary to warrant their relying on it, should be submitted to by that miscellaneous collection of a few wise and many foolish individuals called the public. The most intolerant of churches, the Roman Catholic Church, even at the canonization of a saint admits, and listens patiently to, a "devil's advocate." The holiest of men, it appears, cannot be admitted to posthumous honors until all that the devil could say against him is known and weighed. If even the Newtonian philosophy were not permitted to be questioned, mankind could not feel as complete assurance of its truth as they now do. The beliefs which we have most warrant for have no safeguard to rest on but a standing invitation to the whole world to prove them unfounded. If the challenge is not accepted, or is accepted and the attempt fails, we are far enough from certainty still, but we have done the best that the existing state of human reason admits of: we have neglected nothing that could give the truth a chance of reaching us; if the lists are kept open, we may hope that, if there be a better truth, it will be found when the human mind is capable of receiving it; and in the meantime we may rely on having attained such approach to truth as is possible in our own day. This is the amount of certainty attainable by a fallible being, and this the sole way of attaining it.

Strange it is that men should admit the validity of the arguments for free discussion, but object to their being "pushed to an extreme," not seeing that unless the reasons are good for an extreme case, they are not good for any case. Strange that they should imagine that they are not assuming infallibility when they acknowledge that there should be free discussion on all subjects which can possibly be *doubtful*, but think that some particular principle or doctrine should be forbidden to be questioned because it is so *certain*, that is, because *they are certain* that it is certain. To call any proposition certain, while there is anyone who would deny its certainty if permitted, but who is not permitted, is to assume that we ourselves, and those who agree with us, are the judges of certainty, and judges without hearing the other side.

In the present age—which has been described as "destitute of faith, but terrified at skepticism"—in which people feel sure, not so much that their opinions are true as that they should not know what to do without them—the claims of an opinion to be protected from public attack are rested not so much on its truth as on its importance to society. There are, it is alleged, certain beliefs so useful, not to say indispensable, to well-being that it is as much the duty of governments to uphold those beliefs as to protect any other of the interests of society. In a case of such necessity, and so directly in the line of their duty, something less than infallibility may, it is maintained, warrant, and even bind, governments to act on their own opinion confirmed by the general opinion of mankind. It is also often argued, and still oftener thought, that none but bad men would desire to weaken these salutary beliefs; and there can be nothing wrong, it is thought, in restraining bad men and prohibiting what only such men would wish to practice. This mode of thinking makes the justification of restraints on discussion not a question of the truth of doctrines but of their usefulness, and flatters itself by that means to escape the responsibility of claiming to be an infallible judge of opinions. But those who thus satisfy themselves do not perceive that the assumption of infallibility is merely shifted from one point to another. The usefulness of an opinion is itself matter of opinion—as disputable, as open to discussion, and requiring discussion as much as the opinion itself. There is the same need of an infallible judge of opinions to decide an opinion to be noxious as to decide it to be false, unless the opinion condemned has full opportunity of defending itself. And it will not do to say that the heretic may be allowed to maintain the utility or harmlessness of his opinion, though forbidden to maintain its truth. The truth of an opinion is part of its utility. If we would know whether or not it is desirable that a proposition should be believed, is it possible to exclude the consideration of whether or not it is true? In the opinion, not of bad men, but of the best men, no belief which is contrary to truth can be really useful; and can you prevent such men from urging that plea when they are charged with culpability for denying some doctrine which they are told is useful, but which they believe to be false? Those who are on the side of received opinions never fail to take all possible advantage of this plea; you do not find *them* handling the question of ability as if it could be completely abstracted from that of truth; on the contrary, it is, above all, because their doctrine is "the truth" that the knowledge or the belief of it is held to be so indispensable. There can be no fair discussion of the question of usefulness when an argument so vital may be employed on one side, but not on the other. And in point of fact, when law or public feeling do not permit the truth of an opinion to be disputed, they are just as little tolerant of a denial of its usefulness. The utmost they allow is an extenuation of its absolute necessity, or of the positive guilt of rejecting it.

In order more fully to illustrate the mischief of denying a hearing to opinions because we, in our own judgment, have condemned them, it will be desirable to fix down the discussion to a concrete case; and I choose, by preference, the cases which are least favorable to me—in which the argument against freedom of opinion, both on the score of truth and on that of utility, is considered the strongest. Let the opinions impugned be the belief in a God and in a future state, or any of the commonly received doctrines of morality. To fight the battle on such ground gives a great advantage to an unfair antagonist, since he will be sure to say (and many who have no desire to be unfair will say it internally), Are these the doctrines which you do not deem sufficiently certain to be taken under the protection of law? Is the belief in a God one of the opinions to feel sure of which you hold to be assuming infallibility? But I must be permitted to observe that it is not the feeling sure of a doctrine (be it what it may) which I call an assumption of infallibility. It is the undertaking to decide that question *for others*, without allowing them to hear what can be said on the contrary side. And I denounce and reprobate this pretension not the less if put forth on the side of my most solemn convictions. However positive anyone's persuasion may be, not only of the falsity but of the pernicious consequences— not only of the pernicious consequences, but (to adopt expressions which I altogether condemn) the immorality and impiety of an opinion—yet if, in pursuance of that private judgment, though backed by the public judgment of his country or his contemporaries, he prevents the opinion from being heard in its defense, he assumes infallibility. And so far from the assumption being less objectionable or less dangerous because the opinion is called immoral or impious, this is the case of all others in which it is most fatal. These are exactly the occasions on which the men of one generation commit those dreadful mistakes which excite the astonishment and horror of posterity. It is among such that we find the instances memorable in history, when the arm of the law has been employed to root out the best men and the noblest doctrines; with deplorable success as to the men, though some of the doctrines have survived to be (as if in mockery) invoked in defense of similar conduct toward those who dissent from *them*, or from their received interpretation.

Mankind can hardly be too often reminded that there was once a man called Socrates, between whom and the legal authorities and public opinion of his time there took place a memorable collision. Born in an age and country abounding in individual greatness, this man has been handed down to us by those who best knew both him and the age as the most virtuous man in it; while *we* know him as the head and prototype of all subsequent teachers of virtue, the source equally of the lofty inspiration of Plato and the judicious utilitarianism of Aristotle, "*i maestri di color che sanno*," the two headsprings of ethical as of all other philosophy. This acknowledged master of all the eminent thinkers who have since lived—whose fame, still growing after more than two thousand years, all but outweighs the whole remainder of the names which make his native city illustrious— was put to death by his countrymen, after a judicial conviction, for impiety and immorality. Impiety, in denying the gods recognized by the State; indeed, his accuser asserted (see the *Apologia*) that he believed in no gods at all. Immorality, in being, by his doctrines and instructions, a "corruptor of youth." Of these charges the tribunal, there is every ground for believing, honestly found him guilty, and condemned the man who probably of all then born had deserved best of mankind to be put to death as a criminal.

To pass from this to the only other instance of judicial iniquity, the mention of which, after the condemnation of Socrates, would not be an anticlimax: the event which took place on Calvary rather more than eighteen hundred years ago. The man who left on the memory of those who witnessed his life and conversation such an impression of his moral grandeur that eighteen subsequent centuries have done homage to him as the

Almighty in person, was ignominiously put to death, as what? As a blasphemer. Men did not merely mistake their benefactor, they mistook him for the exact contrary of what he was and treated him as that prodigy of impiety which they themselves are now held to be for their treatment of him. The feelings with which mankind now regard these lamentable transactions, especially the later of the two, render them extremely unjust in their judgment of the unhappy actors. These were, to all appearance, not bad men—not worse than men commonly are, but rather the contrary; men who possessed in a full, or somewhat more than a full measure, the religious, moral, and patriotic feelings of their time and people: the very kind of men who, in all times, our own included, have every chance of passing through life blameless and respected. The high priest who rent his garments when the words were pronounced, which, according to all the ideas of his country, constituted the blackest guilt, was in all probability quite as sincere in his horror and indignation as the generality of respectable and pious men now are in the religious and moral sentiments they profess; and most of those who now shudder at his conduct, if they had lived in his time, and been born Jews, would have acted precisely as he did. Orthodox Christians who are tempted to think that those who stoned to death the first martyrs must have been worse men than they themselves are ought to remember that one of those persecutors was Saint Paul.

Let us add one more example, the most striking of all, if the impressiveness of an error is measured by the wisdom and virtue of him who falls into it. If ever anyone possessed of power had grounds for thinking himself the best and most enlightened among his contemporaries, it was the Emperor Marcus Aurelius. Absolute monarch of the whole civilized world, he preserved through life not only the most unblemished justice, but what was less to be expected from his Stoical breeding, the tenderest heart. The few failings which are attributed to him were all on the side of indulgence, while his writings, the highest ethical product of the ancient mind, differ scarcely perceptibly, if they differ at all, from the most characteristic teachings of Christ. This man, a better Christian in all but the dogmatic sense of the word than almost any of the ostensibly Christian sovereigns who have since reigned, persecuted Christianity. Placed at the summit of all the previous attainments of humanity, with an open, unfettered intellect, and a character which led him of himself to embody in his moral writings the Christian ideal, he yet failed to see that Christianity was to be a good and not an evil to the world, with his duties to which he was so deeply penetrated. Existing society he knew to be in a deplorable state. But such as it was, he saw, or thought he saw, that it was held together, and prevented from being worse, by belief and reverence of the received divinities. As a ruler of mankind, he deemed it his duty not to suffer society to fall in pieces; and saw not how, if its existing ties were removed, any others could be formed which could again knit it together. The new religion openly aimed at dissolving these ties; unless, therefore, it was his duty to adopt that religion, it seemed to be his duty to put it down. Inasmuch then as the theology of Christianity did not appear to him true or of divine origin, inasmuch as this strange history of a crucified God was not credible to him, and a system which purported to rest entirely upon a foundation to him so wholly unbelievable, could not be foreseen by him to be that renovating agency which, after all abatements, it has in fact proved to be; the gentlest and most amiable of philosophers and rulers, under a solemn sense of duty, authorized the persecution of Christianity. To my mind this is one of the most tragical facts in all history. It is a bitter thought how different a thing the Christianity of the world might have been if the Christian faith had been adopted as the religion of the empire under the auspices of Marcus Aurelius instead of those of Constantine. But it would be equally unjust to him and false to truth to deny that no one plea which can be urged for punishing anti-Christian teaching was wanting to Marcus Aurelius for punishing, as he did, the propagation of Christianity. No Christian more firmly believes that atheism is false and tends to the dissolution of society than Marcus Aurelius believed the same things of Christianity; he who, of all men then living, might have been thought the most capable of appreciating it. Unless anyone who approves of punishment for the promulgation of opinions flatters himself that he is a wiser and better man than Marcus Aurelius—more deeply versed in the wisdom of his time, more elevated in his intellect above it, more earnest in his search for truth, or more single-minded in his devotion to it when found—let him abstain from that assumption of the joint infallibility of himself and the multitude which the great Antoninus [Aurelius] made with so unfortunate a result.

Aware of the impossibility of defending the use of punishment for restraining irreligious opinions by any argument which will not justify Marcus Antoninus, the enemies of religious freedom, when hard pressed, occasionally accept this consequence and say, with Dr. Johnson, that the persecutors of Christianity were in the right, that persecution is an ordeal through which truth ought to pass, and always passes successfully, legal penalties being, in the end, powerless against truth, though sometimes beneficially effective against mischievous errors. This is a form of the argument for religious intolerance sufficiently remarkable not to be passed without notice.

A theory which maintains that truth may justifiably be persecuted because persecution cannot possibly do it any harm cannot be charged with being intentionally hostile to the reception of new truths; but we cannot commend the generosity of its dealing with the persons to whom mankind are indebted for them. To discover to the world something which deeply concerns it, and of which it was previously ignorant, to prove to it that it had been mistaken on some vital point of temporal or spiritual interest, is as important a service as a human being can render to his fellow creatures, and in certain cases, as in those of the early Christians and of the Reformers, those who think with Dr. Johnson believe it to have been the most precious gift which could be bestowed on mankind. That the authors of such splendid benefits should be requited by martyrdom, that their reward should be to be dealt with as the vilest of criminals, is not, upon this theory, a deplorable error and misfortune for which humanity should mourn in sackcloth and ashes, but the normal and justifiable state of things. The propounder of a new truth, according to this doctrine, should stand, as stood, in the legislation of the Locrians, the proposer of a new law, with a halter round his neck, to be instantly tightened if the public assembly did not, on hearing his reasons, then and there adopt his proposition. People who defend this mode of treating benefactors cannot be supposed to set much value on the benefit; and I believe this view of the subject is mostly confined to the sort of persons who think that new truths may have been desirable once, but that we have had enough of them now.

But, indeed, the dictum that truth always triumphs over persecution is one of those pleasant falsehoods which men repeat after one another till they pass into commonplaces, but which all experience refutes. History teems with instances of truth put down by persecution. If not suppressed forever, it may be thrown back for centuries. To speak only of religious opinions: the Reformation broke out at least twenty times before Luther, and was put down. Arnold of Brescia was put down. Fra Dolcino was put down. Savonarola was put down. The Albigeois were put down. The Vaudois were put down. The Lollards were put down. The Hussites were put down. Even after the era of Luther, wherever persecution was persisted in, it was successful. In Spain, Italy, Flanders, the Austrian empire, Protestantism was rooted out; and, most likely, would have been so in England had Queen Mary lived or Queen Elizabeth died. Persecution has always succeeded save where the heretics were too strong a party to be effectually persecuted. No reasonable person can doubt that Christianity might have been extirpated in the Roman Empire. It spread and became predominant because the persecutions were only occasional, lasting but a short time, and separated by long intervals of almost undisturbed propagandism. It is a piece of idle sentimentality that truth, merely as truth, has any inherent power denied to error of prevailing against the dungeon and the stake. Men are not more zealous for truth than they often are for error, and a sufficient application of legal or even of social penalties will generally succeed in stopping the propagation of either. The real advantage which truth has consists in this, that when an opinion is true, it may be extinguished once, twice, or many times, but in the course of ages there will generally be found persons to rediscover it, until some one of its reappearances falls on a time when from favorable circumstances it escapes persecution until it has made such head as to withstand all subsequent attempts to suppress it.

It will be said that we do not now put to death the introducers of new opinions: we are not like our fathers who slew the prophets; we even build sepulchers to them. It is true we no longer put heretics to death; and the amount of penal infliction which modern feeling would probably tolerate, even against the most obnoxious opinions, is not sufficient to extirpate them. But let us not flatter ourselves that we are yet free from the stain even of legal persecution. Penalties for opinion, or at least for its expression, still exist by law; and their enforcement is not, even in these times, so unexampled as to make it at all incredible that they may some day be revived in full force. In the year 1857, at the summer assizes of the county of Cornwall, an unfortunate man, said to be of unexceptionable conduct in all relations of life, was sentenced to twenty-one months' imprisonment for uttering, and writing on a gate, some offensive words concerning Christianity. Within a month of the same time, at the Old Bailey, two persons, on two separate occasions, were rejected as jurymen, and one of them grossly insulted by the judge and by one of the counsel, because they honestly declared that they had no theological belief; and a third, a foreigner, for the same reason, was denied justice against a thief. This refusal of redress took place in virtue of the legal doctrine that no person can be allowed to give evidence in a court of justice who does not profess belief in a God (any god is sufficient) and in a future state, which is equivalent to declaring such persons to be outlaws, excluded from the protection of the tribunals; who may not only be robbed or assaulted with impunity, if no one but themselves, or persons of similar opinions, be present, but anyone else may be robbed or assaulted with impunity if the proof of the fact depends on their evidence. The assumption on which this is grounded is that the oath is worthless of a person who does not believe in a future state—a proposition which betokens much ignorance of history in those who assent to it (since it is historically true that a large proportion of infidels in all ages have been persons of distinguished integrity and honor), and would be maintained by no one who had the smallest conception how many of the persons in greatest repute with the world, both for virtues and attainments, are well known, at least to their intimates, to be unbelievers. The rule, besides, is suicidal and cuts away its own foundation. Under pretense that atheists must be liars, it admits the testimony of all atheists who are willing to lie, and rejects only those who brave the obloquy of publicly confessing a detested creed rather than affirm a falsehood. A rule thus self-convicted of absurdity so far as regards its professed purpose can be kept in force only as a badge of hatred, a relic of persecution—a persecution, too, having the peculiarity that the qualification for undergoing it is the being clearly proved not to deserve it. The rule and the theory it implies are hardly less insulting to believers than to infidels. For if he who does not believe in a future state necessarily lies, it follows that they who do believe are only prevented from lying, if prevented they are, by the fear of hell. We will not do the authors and abettors of the rule the injury of supposing that the conception which they have formed of Christian virtue is drawn from their own consciousness.

These, indeed, are but rags and remnants of persecution, and may be thought to be not so much an indication of the wish to persecute, as an example of that very frequent infirmity of English minds, which makes them take a preposterous pleasure in the assertion of a bad principle, when they are no longer bad enough to desire to carry it really into practice. But unhappily there is no security in the state of the public mind that the suspension of worse forms of legal persecution, which has lasted for about the space of a generation, will continue. In this age the quiet surface of routine is as often ruffled by attempts to resuscitate past evils as to introduce new benefits. What is boasted of at the present time as the revival of religion is always, in narrow and uncultivated minds, at least as much the revival of bigotry; and where there is the strong permanent leaven of intolerance in the feelings of a people, which at all times abides in the middle classes of this country, it needs but little to provoke them into actively persecuting those whom they have never ceased to think proper objects of persecution. For it is this—it is the opinions men entertain, and the feelings they cherish, respecting those who disown the beliefs they deem important which makes this country not a place of mental freedom. For a long time past, the chief mischief of the legal penalties is that they strengthen the social stigma. It is that stigma which is really effective, and so effective is it that the profession of opinions which are under the ban of society is much less common in England than is, in many other countries, the avowal of those which incur risk of judicial punishment. In respect to all persons but those whose pecuniary circumstances make them independent of the good will of other people, opinion, on this subject, is as efficacious as law; men might as well be imprisoned as excluded from the means of earning their bread. Those whose bread is already secured, and who desire no favors from men in power, or from bodies of men, or from the public, have nothing to fear from the open avowal of any opinions but to be ill-thought of and ill-spoken of, and this it ought not to require a very heroic mold to enable them to bear. There is no room for any appeal *ad misericordiam* in behalf of such persons. But though we do not now inflict so much evil on those who think differently from us as it was formerly our custom to do, it may be that we do ourselves as much evil as ever by our treatment of them. Socrates was put to death, but the Socratic philosophy rose like the sun in heaven and spread its illumination over the whole intellectual firmament. Christians were cast to the lions, but the Christian church grew up a stately and spreading tree, overtopping the older and less vigorous growths, and stifling them by its shade. Our merely social intolerance kills no one, roots out no opinions, but induces men to disguise them or to abstain from any active effort for their diffusion. With us, heretical opinions do not perceptibly gain, or even lose, ground in each decade or generation; they never blaze out far and wide, but continue to smolder in the narrow circles of thinking and studious persons among whom they originate, without ever lighting up the general affairs of mankind with either a true or a deceptive light. And thus is kept up a state of things very satisfactory to some minds, because, without the unpleasant process of fining or imprisoning anybody, it maintains all prevailing opinions outwardly undisturbed, while it does not absolutely interdict the exercise of reason by dissentients afflicted with the malady of thought. A convenient plan for having peace in the intellectual world, and keeping all things going on therein very much as they do already. But the price paid for this sort of intellectual pacification is the sacrifice of the entire moral courage of the human mind. A state of things in which a large portion of the most active and inquiring intellects find it advisable to keep the general principles and grounds of their convictions within their own breasts, and attempt, in what they address to the public, to fit as much as they can of their own conclusions to premises which they have internally renounced, cannot send forth the open, fearless characters and logical, consistent intellects who once adorned the thinking world. The sort of men who can be looked for under it are either mere conformers to commonplace, or timeservers for truth, whose arguments on all great subjects are meant for their hearers, and are not those which have convinced themselves. Those who avoid this alternative do so by narrowing their thoughts and interest to things which can be spoken of without venturing within the region of principles, that is, to small practical matters which would come right of themselves, if but the minds of mankind were strengthened and enlarged, and which will never be made effectually right until then, while that which would strengthen and enlarge men's minds—free and daring speculation on the highest subjects—is abandoned.

Those in whose eyes this reticence on the part of heretics is no evil should consider, in the first place, that in consequence of it there is never any fair and thorough discussion of heretical opinions; and that such of them as could not stand such a discussion, though they may be prevented from spreading, do not disappear. But it is not the minds of heretics that are deteriorated most by the ban placed on all inquiry which does not end in the orthodox conclusions. The greatest harm done is to those who are not heretics, and whose whole mental development is cramped and their reason cowed by the fear of heresy. Who can compute what the world loses in the multitude of promising intellects combined with timid characters, who dare not follow out any bold, vigorous, independent train of thought, lest it should land them in something which would admit of being considered irreligious or immoral? Among them we may occasionally see some man of deep conscientiousness and subtle and refined understanding, who spends a life in sophisticating with an intellect which he cannot silence, and exhausts the resources of ingenuity in attempting to reconcile the promptings of his conscience and reason with orthodoxy, which yet he does not, perhaps, to the end succeed in doing. No one can be a great thinker who does not recognize that as a thinker it is his first duty to follow his intellect to whatever conclusions it may lead. Truth gains more even by the errors of one who, with due study and preparation, thinks for himself than by the true opinions of those who only hold them because they do not suffer themselves to think. Not that it is solely, or chiefly, to form great thinkers that freedom of thinking is required. On the contrary, it is as much and even more indispensable to enable average human beings to attain the mental stature which they are capable of. There have been, and may again be, great individual thinkers in a general atmosphere of mental slavery. But there never has been, nor ever will be, in that atmosphere an intellectually active people. Where any people has made a temporary approach to such a character, it has been because the dread of heterodox speculation was for a time suspended. Where there is a tacit convention that principles are not to be disputed, where the discussion of the greatest questions which can occupy humanity is considered to be closed, we cannot hope to find that generally high scale of mental activity which has made some periods of history so remarkable. Never when controversy avoided the subjects which are large and important enough to kindle enthusiasm was the mind of a people stirred up from its foundations, and the impulse given which raised even persons of the most ordinary intellect to something of the dignity of thinking beings. Of such we have had an example in the condition of Europe during the times immediately following the Reformation; another, though limited to the Continent and to a more cultivated class, in the speculative movement of the latter half of the eighteenth century; and a third, of still briefer duration, in the intellectual fermentation of Germany during the Goethian and Fichtean period. These periods differed widely in the particular opinions which they developed, but were alike in this, that during all three the yoke of authority was broken. In each, an old mental despotism had been thrown off, and no new one had yet taken its place. The impulse given at these three periods has made Europe what it now is. Every single improvement which has taken place either in the human mind or in institutions may be traced distinctly to one or other of them. Appearances have for some time indicated that all three impulses are well-nigh spent; and we can expect no fresh start until we again assert our mental freedom.

Let us now pass to the second division of the argument, and dismissing the supposition that any of the received opinions may be false, let us assume them to be true and examine into the worth of the manner in which they are likely to be held when their truth is not freely and openly canvassed. However unwillingly a person who has a strong opinion may admit the possibility that his opinion may be false, he ought to be moved by the consideration that, however true it may be, if it is not fully, frequently, and fearlessly discussed, it will be held as a dead dogma, not a living truth.

There is a class of persons (happily not quite so numerous as formerly) who think it enough if a person assents undoubtingly to what they think true, though he has no knowledge whatever of the grounds of the opinion and could not make a tenable defense of it against the most superficial objections. Such persons, if they can once get their creed taught from authority, naturally think that no good, and some harm, comes of its being allowed to be questioned. Where their influence prevails, they make it nearly impossible for the received opinion to be rejected wisely and considerately, though it may still be rejected rashly and ignorantly; for to shut out discussion entirely is seldom possible, and when it once gets in, beliefs not grounded on conviction are apt to give way before the slightest semblance of an argument. Waiving, however, this possibility—assuming that the true opinion abides in the mind, but abides as a prejudice, a belief independent of, and proof against, argument—this is not the way in which truth ought to be held by a rational being. This is not knowing the truth. Truth, thus held, is but one superstition the more, accidentally clinging to the words which enunciate a truth.

If the intellect and judgment of mankind ought to be cultivated, a thing which Protestants at least do not deny, on what can these faculties be more appropriately exercised by anyone than on the things which concern him so much that it is considered necessary for him to hold opinions on them? If the cultivation of the understanding consists in one thing more than in another, it is surely in learning the grounds of one's own opinions. Whatever people believe, on subjects on which it is of the first importance to believe rightly, they ought to be able to defend against at least the common objections. But, someone may say, "Let them be *taught* the grounds of their opinions. It does not follow that opinions must be merely parroted because they are never heard controverted. Persons who learn geometry do not simply commit the theorems to memory, but understand and learn likewise the demonstrations; and it would be absurd to say that they remain ignorant of the grounds of geometrical truths because they never hear anyone deny and attempt to disprove them." Undoubtedly; and such teaching suffices on a subject like mathematics, where there is nothing at all to be said on the wrong side of the question. The peculiarity of the evidence of mathematical truths is that all the argument is on one side. There are no objections, and no answers to objections. But on every subject on which difference of opinion is possible, the truth depends on a balance to be struck between two sets of conflicting reasons. Even in natural philosophy, there is always some other explanation possible of the same facts; some geocentric theory instead of heliocentric, some phlogiston instead of oxygen; and it has to be shown why that other theory cannot be the true one; and until this is shown, and until we know how it is shown, we do not understand the grounds of our opinion. But when we turn to subjects infinitely more complicated, to morals, religion, politics, social relations, and the business of life, three-fourths of the arguments for every disputed opinion consist in dispelling the appearances which favor some opinion different from it. The greatest orator, save one, of antiquity, has left it on record that he always studied his adversary's case with as great, if not still greater, intensity than even his own. What Cicero practiced as the means of forensic success requires to be imitated by all who study any subject in order to arrive at the truth. He who knows only his own side of the case knows little of that. His reasons may be good, and no one may have been able to refute them. But if he is equally unable to refute the reasons on the opposite side, if he does not so much as know what they are, he has no ground for preferring either opinion. The rational position for him would be suspension of judgment, and unless he contents himself with that, he is either led by authority or adopts, like the generality of the world, the side to which he feels most inclination. Nor is it enough that he should hear the arguments of adversaries from his own teachers, presented as they state them, and accompanied by what they offer as refutations. That is not the way to do justice to the arguments or bring them into real contact with his own mind.

He must be able to hear them from persons who actually believe them, who defend them in earnest and do their very utmost for them. He must know them in their most plausible and persuasive form; he must feel the whole force of the difficulty which the true view of the subject has to encounter and dispose of, else he will never really possess himself of the portion of truth which meets and removes that difficulty. Ninety-nine in a hundred of what are called educated men are in this condition, even of those who can argue fluently for their opinions. Their conclusion may be true, but it might be false for anything they know; they have never thrown themselves into the mental position of those who think differently from them, and considered what such persons may have to say; and, consequently, they do not, in any proper sense of the word, know the doctrine which they themselves profess. They do not know those parts of it which explain and justify the remainder—the considerations which show that a fact which seemingly conflicts with another is reconcilable with it, or that, of two apparently strong reasons, one and not the other ought to be preferred. All that part of the truth which turns the scale and decides the judgment of a completely informed mind, they are strangers to; nor is it ever really known but to those who have attended equally and impartially to both sides and endeavored to see the reasons of both in the strongest light. So essential is this discipline to a real understanding of moral and human subjects that, if opponents of all-important truths do not exist, it is indispensable to imagine them and supply them with the strongest arguments which the most skillful devil's advocate can conjure up.

To abate the force of these considerations, an enemy of free discussion may be supposed to say that there is no necessity for mankind in general to know and understand all that can be said against or for their opinions by philosophers and theologians. That it is not needful for common men to be able to expose all the misstatements or fallacies of an ingenious opponent. That it is enough if there is always somebody capable of answering them, so that nothing likely to mislead uninstructed persons remains unrefuted. That simple minds, having been taught the obvious grounds of the truths inculcated in them, may trust to authority for the rest and, being aware that they have neither knowledge nor talent to resolve every difficulty which can be raised, may repose in the assurance that all those which have been raised have been or can be answered by those who are specially trained to the task.

Conceding to this view of the subject the utmost that can be claimed for it by those most easily satisfied with the amount of understanding of truth which ought to accompany the belief of it, even so, the argument for free discussion is noway weakened. For even this doctrine acknowledges that mankind ought to have a rational assurance that all objections have been satisfactorily answered; and how are they to be answered if that which requires to be answered is not spoken? Or how can the answer be known to be satisfactory if the objectors have no opportunity of showing that it is unsatisfactory? If not the public, at least the philosophers and theologians who are to resolve the difficulties must make themselves familiar with those difficulties in their most puzzling form; and this cannot be accomplished unless they are freely stated and placed in the most advantageous light which they admit of. The Catholic Church has its own way of dealing with this embarrassing problem. It makes a broad separation between those who can be permitted to receive its doctrines on conviction and those who must accept them on trust. Neither, indeed, are allowed any choice as to what they will accept; but the clergy, such at least as can be fully confided in, may admissibly and meritoriously make themselves acquainted with the arguments of opponents, in order to answer them, and may, therefore, read heretical books; the laity, not unless by special permission, hard to be obtained. This discipline recognizes a knowledge of the enemy's case as beneficial to the teachers, but finds means, consistent with this, of denying it to the rest of the world, thus giving to the *élite* more mental culture, though not more mental freedom, than it allows to the mass. By this device it succeeds in obtaining the kind of mental superiority which its purposes require: for though culture without freedom never made a large and liberal mind, it can make a clever *nisi prius* advocate of a cause. But in countries professing Protestantism, this resource is denied, since Protestants hold, at least in theory, that the responsibility for the choice of a religion must be borne by each for himself and cannot be thrown off upon teachers. Besides, in the present state of the world, it is practically impossible that writings which are read by the instructed can be kept from the uninstructed. If the teachers of mankind are to be cognizant of all that they ought to know, everything must be free to be written and published without restraint.

If, however, the mischievous operation of the absence of free discussion, when the received opinions are true, were confined to leaving men ignorant of the grounds of those opinions, it might be thought that this, if an intellectual, is no moral evil and does not affect the worth of the opinions, regarded in their influence on the character. The fact, however, is that not only the grounds of the opinion are forgotten in the absence of discussion, but too often the meaning of the opinion itself. The words which convey it cease to suggest ideas, or suggest only a small portion of those they were originally employed to communicate. Instead of a vivid conception and a living belief, there remain only a few phrases retained by rote; or, if any part, the shell and husk only of the meaning is retained, the finer essence being lost. The great chapter in human history which this fact occupies and fills cannot be too earnestly studied and meditated on. . . .

It still remains to speak of one of the principal causes which make diversity of opinion advantageous, and will continue to do so until mankind shall have entered a stage of intellectual advancement which at present seems at an incalculable distance. We have hitherto considered only two possibilities: that the received opinion may be false, and some other opinion, consequently, true; or that, the received opinion being true, a conflict with the opposite error is essential to a clear apprehension and deep feeling of its truth. But there is a commoner case than either of these: when the conflicting doctrines, instead of being one true and the other false, share the truth between them, and the nonconforming opinion is needed to supply the remainder of the truth of which the received doctrine embodies only a part. Popular opinions, on subjects not palpable to sense, are often true, but seldom or never the whole truth. They are a part of the truth, sometimes a greater, sometimes a smaller part, but exaggerated, distorted, and disjointed from the truths by which they ought to be accompanied and limited. Heretical opinions, on the other hand, are generally some of these suppressed and neglected truths, bursting the bonds which kept them down, and either seeking reconciliation with the truth contained in the common opinion, or fronting it as enemies, and setting themselves up, with similar exclusiveness, as the whole truth. The latter case is hitherto the most frequent, as, in the human mind, one-sidedness has always been the rule, and many-sidedness the exception. Hence, even in revolutions of opinion, one part of the truth usually sets while another rises. Even progress, which ought to superadd, for the most part only substitutes one partial and incomplete truth for another; improvement consisting chiefly in this, that the new fragment of truth is more wanted, more adapted to the needs of the time than that which it displaces. Such being the partial character of prevailing opinions, even when resting on a true foundation, every opinion which embodies somewhat of the portion of truth which the common opinion omits ought to be considered precious, with whatever amount of error and confusion that truth may be blended. No sober judge of human affairs will feel bound to be indignant because those who force on our notice truths which we should otherwise have overlooked, overlook some of those which we see. Rather, he will think that so long as popular truth is one-sided, it is more desirable than otherwise that unpopular truth should have one-sided assertors, too, such being usually the most energetic and the most likely to compel reluctant attention to the fragment of wisdom which they proclaim as if it were the whole.

Thus, in the eighteenth century, when nearly all the instructed, and all those of the uninstructed who were led by them, were lost in admiration of what is called civilization, and of the marvels of modern science, literature, and philosophy, and while greatly overrating the amount of unlikeness between the men of modern and those of ancient times, indulged the belief that the whole of the difference was in their own favor; with what a salutary shock did the paradoxes of Rousseau explode like bombshells in the midst, dislocating the compact mass of one-sided opinion and forcing its elements to recombine in a better form and with additional ingredients. Not that the current opinions were on the whole farther from the truth than Rousseau's were; on the contrary, they were nearer to it; they contained more of positive truth, and very much less of error. Nevertheless there lay in Rousseau's doctrine, and has floated down the stream of opinion along with it, a considerable amount of exactly those truths which the popular opinion wanted; and these are the deposit which was left behind them when the flood subsided. The superior worth of simplicity of life, the enervating and demoralizing effect of the trammels and hypocrisies of artificial society are ideas which have never been entirely absent from cultivated minds since Rousseau wrote; and they will in time produce their due effect, though at present needing to be asserted as much as ever, and to be asserted by deeds; for words, on this subject, have nearly exhausted their power.

In politics, again, it is almost a commonplace that a party of order or stability and a party of progress or reform are both necessary elements of a healthy state of political life, until the one or the other shall have so enlarged its mental grasp as to be a party equally of order and of progress, knowing and distinguishing what is fit to be preserved from what ought to be swept away. Each of these modes of thinking derives its utility from the deficiencies of the other; but it is in a great measure the opposition of the other that keeps each within the limits of reason and sanity. Unless opinions favorable to democracy and to aristocracy, to property and to equality, to cooperation and to competition, to luxury and to abstinence, to sociality and individuality, to liberty and discipline, and all the other standing antagonisms of practical life, are expressed with equal freedom and enforced and defended with equal talent and energy, there is no chance of both elements obtaining their due; one scale is sure to go up, and the other down. Truth, in the great practical concerns of life, is so much a question of the reconciling and combining of opposites that very few have minds sufficiently capacious and impartial to make the adjustment with an approach to correctness, and it has to be made by the rough process of a struggle between combatants fighting under hostile banners. On any of the great open questions just enumerated, if either of the two opinions has a better claim than the other, not merely to be tolerated, but to be encouraged and countenanced, it is the one which happens at the particular time and place to be in a minority. That is the opinion which, for the time being, represents the neglected interests, the side of human well-being which is in danger of obtaining less than its share. I am aware that there is not, in this country, any intolerance of differences of opinion on most of these topics. They are adduced to show, by admitted and multiplied examples, the universality of the fact that only through diversity of opinion is there, in the existing state of human intellect, a chance of fair play to all sides of the truth. When there are persons to be found who form an exception to the apparent unanimity of the world on any subject, even if the world is in the right, it is always probable that dissentients have something worth hearing to say for themselves, and that truth would lose something by their silence. . . .

We have now recognized the necessity to the mental well-being of mankind (on which all their other well-being depends) of freedom of opinion, and freedom of the expression of opinion, on four distinct grounds, which we will now briefly recapitulate:

First, if any opinion is compelled to silence, that opinion may, for aught we can certainly know, be true. To deny this is to assume our own infallibility.

Secondly, though the silenced opinion be an error, it may, and very commonly does, contain a portion of truth; and since the general or prevailing opinion on any subject is rarely or never the whole truth, it is only by the collision of adverse opinions that the remainder of the truth has any chance of being supplied.

Thirdly, even if the received opinion be not only true, but the whole truth; unless it is suffered to be, and actually is, vigorously and earnestly contested, it will, by most of those who receive it, be held in the manner of a prejudice, with little comprehension or feeling of its rational grounds. And not only this, but, fourthly, the meaning of the doctrine itself will be in danger of being lost or enfeebled, and deprived of its vital effect on the character and conduct: the dogma becoming a mere formal profession, inefficacious for good, but cumbering the ground and preventing the growth of any real and heartfelt conviction from reason or personal experience.

Before quitting the subject of freedom of opinion, it is fit to take some notice of those who say that the free expression of all opinions should be permitted on condition that the manner be temperate, and do not pass the bounds of fair discussion. Much might be said on the impossibility of fixing where these supposed bounds are to be placed; for if the test be offense to those whose opinions are attacked, I think experience testifies that this offense is given whenever the attack is telling and powerful, and that every opponent who pushes them hard, and whom they find it difficult to answer, appears to them, if he shows any strong feeling on the subject, an intemperate opponent. But this, though an important consideration in a practical point of view, merges in a more fundamental objection. Undoubtedly, the manner of asserting an opinion, even though it be a true one, may be very objectionable and may justly incur severe censure. But the principal offenses of the kind are such as it is mostly impossible, unless by accidental self-betrayal, to bring home to conviction. The gravest of them is, to argue sophistically, to suppress facts or arguments, to misstate the elements of the case, or misrepresent the opposite opinion. But all this, even to the most aggravated degree, is so continually done in perfect good faith by persons who are not considered, and in many other respects may not deserve to be considered, ignorant or incompetent, that it is rarely possible, on adequate grounds, conscientiously to stamp the misrepresentation as morally culpable, and still less could law presume to interfere with this kind of controversial misconduct. With regard to what is commonly meant by intemperate discussion, namely invective, sarcasm, personality, and the like, the denunciation of these weapons would deserve more sympathy if it were ever proposed to interdict them equally to both sides; but it is only desired to restrain the employment of them against the prevailing opinion; against the unprevailing they may not only be used without general disapproval, but will be likely to obtain for him who uses them the praise of honest zeal and righteous indignation. Yet whatever mischief arises from their use is greatest when they are employed against the comparatively defenseless; and whatever unfair advantage can be derived by any opinion from this mode of asserting it accrues almost exclusively to received opinions. The worst offense of this kind which can be committed by a polemic is to stigmatize those who hold the contrary opinion as bad and immoral men. To calumny of this sort, those who hold any unpopular opinion are peculiarly exposed, because they are in general few and uninfluential, and nobody but themselves feels much interested in seeing justice done them; but this weapon is, from the nature of the case, denied to those who attack a prevailing opinion: they can neither use it with safety to themselves, nor, if they could, would it do anything but recoil on their own cause. In general, opinions contrary to those commonly received can only obtain a hearing by studied moderation of language and the most cautious avoidance of unnecessary offense, from which they hardly ever deviate even in a slight degree without losing ground, while unmeasured vituperation employed on the side of the prevailing opinion really does deter people from professing contrary opinions and from listening to those who profess them. For the interest, therefore, of truth and justice it is far more important to restrain this employment of vituperative language than the other; and, for example, if it were necessary to choose, there would be much more need to discourage offensive attacks on infidelity than on religion. It is, however, obvious that law and authority have no business with restraining either, while opinion ought, in every instance, to determine its verdict by the circumstances of the individual case—condemning everyone, on whichever side of the argument he places himself, in whose mode of advocacy either want of candor, or malignity, bigotry, or intolerance of feeling manifest themselves; but not inferring these vices from the side which a person takes, though it be the contrary side of the question to our own; and giving merited honor to everyone, whatever opinion he may hold, who has calmness to see and honesty to state what his opponents and their opinions really are, exaggerating nothing to their discredit, keeping nothing back which tells, or can be supposed to tell, in their favor. This is the real morality of public discussion; and if often violated, I am happy to think that there are many controversialists who to a great extent observe it, and a still greater number who conscientiously strive toward it.

Mary Wollstonecraft (1759–1797 C.E.)

Mary Wollstonecraft's book *Vindication of the Rights of Woman* (1792), from which the following selection is taken, is an essential source not only for feminist thought, but also for egalitarian liberalism generally. Wollstonecraft was a schoolteacher and a private tutor as well as a novelist, and she wrote often on politics. It is of historical interest that she married the anarchist philosopher William Godwin, whose work, while not included in this collection, is a valuable source for those interested in the history of that movement, and that their daughter Mary was the author of the novel *Frankenstein*. Wollstonecraft died soon after Mary's birth.

From Vindication of the Rights of Woman*

Chapter 9

Of the Pernicious Effects which Arise from the Unnatural Distinctions Established in Society

From the respect paid to property flow, as from a poisoned fountain, most of the evils and vices which render this world such a dreary scene to the contemplative mind. For it is in the most polished society that noisome reptiles and venomous serpents lurk under the rank herbage; and there is voluptuousness pampered by the still sultry air, which relaxes every good disposition before it ripens into virtue.

One class presses on another, for all are aiming to procure respect on account of their property; and property once gained will procure the respect due only to talents and virtue. Men neglect the duties incumbent on man, yet are treated like demigods. Religion is also separated from morality by a ceremonial veil, yet men wonder that the world is almost, literally speaking, a den of sharpers or oppressors.

There is a homely proverb, which speaks a shrewd truth, that whoever the devil finds idle he will employ. And what but habitual idleness can hereditary wealth and titles produce? For man is so constituted that he can only attain a proper use of his faculties by exercising them, and will not exercise them unless necessity of some kind first set the wheels in motion. Virtue likewise can only be acquired by the discharge of relative duties; but the importance of these sacred duties will scarcely be felt by the being who is cajoled out of his humanity by the flattery of sycophants. There must be more equality established in society, or morality will never gain ground, and this virtuous equality will not rest firmly even when founded on a rock, if one-half of mankind be chained to its bottom by fate, for they will be continually undermining it through ignorance or pride.

It is vain to expect virtue from women till they are in some degree independent of men; nay, it is vain to expect that strength of natural affection which would make them

---

*An Excerpt.

good wives and mothers. Whilst they are absolutely dependent on their husbands they will be cunning, mean, and selfish; and the men who can be gratified by the fawning fondness of spaniel-like affection have not much delicacy, for love is not to be bought; in any sense of the words, its silken wings are instantly shrivelled up when anything beside a return in kind is sought. Yet whilst wealth enervates men, and women live, as it were, by their personal charms, how can we expect them to discharge those ennobling duties which equally require exertion and self-denial? Hereditary property sophisticates the mind, and the unfortunate victims to it—if I may so express myself—swathed from their birth, seldom exert the locomotive faculty or body of mind, and thus viewing everything through one medium, and that a false one, they are unable to discern in what true merit and happiness consist. False, indeed, must be the light when the drapery of situation hides the man, and makes him stalk in masquerade, dragging from one scene of dissipation to another the nerveless limbs that hang with stupid listlessness, and rolling round the vacant eye, which plainly tells us that there is no mind at home.

I mean therefore to infer that the society is not properly organized which does not compel men and women to discharge their respective duties by making it the only way to acquire that countenance from their fellow-creatures, which every human being wishes some way to attain. The respect consequently which is paid to wealth and mere personal charms is a true north-east blast that blights the tender blossoms of affection and virtue. Nature has wisely attached affections to duties to sweeten toil, and to give that vigour to the exertions of reason which only the heart can give. But the affections which is put on merely because it is the appropriated insignia of a certain character, when its duties are not fulfilled, is one of the empty compliments which vice and folly are obliged to pay to virtue and the real nature of things.

To illustrate my opinion, I need only observe that when a woman is admired for her beauty, and suffers herself to be so far intoxicated by the admiration she receives as to neglect to discharge the indispensable duty of a mother, she sins against herself by neglecting to cultivate an affection that would equally tend to make her useful and happy. True happiness—I mean all the contentment and virtuous satisfaction that can be snatched in this imperfect state—must arise from well-regulated affections, and an affection includes a duty. Men are not aware of the misery they cause, and the vicious weakness they cherish, by only inciting women to render themselves pleasing; they do not consider that they thus make natural and artificial duties clash by sacrificing the comfort and respectability of a woman's life to voluptuous notions of beauty when in nature they all harmonize.

Cold would be the heart of a husband, were he not rendered unnatural by early debauchery, who did not feel more delight at seeing his child suckled by its mother than the most artful wanton tricks could ever raise, yet this natural way of cementing the matrimonial tie, and twisting esteem with fonder recollections, wealth leads women to spurn. To preserve their beauty, and wear the flowery crown of the day, which gives them a kind of right to reign for a short time over the sex, they neglect to stamp impressions on their husbands' hearts that would be remembered with more tenderness when the snow on the head began to chill the bosom than even their virgin charms. The maternal solicitude of a reasonable affectionate woman is very interesting, and the chastened dignity with which a mother returns the caresses that she and her child receive from a father who has been fulfilling the serious duties of his station is not only a respectable, but a beautiful sight. So singular, indeed, are my feelings—and I have endeavoured not to catch factitious ones—that after having been fatigued with the sight of insipid grandeur and the slavish ceremonies that with cumbrous pomp supplied the place of domestic affections, I have turned to some other scene to relieve my eye by resting it on the refreshing green everywhere scattered by Nature. I have then viewed with pleasure a woman nursing her children, and discharging the duties of her station with perhaps merely a servant-maid to take off her hands the servile part of the household business. I have seen her prepare herself and children, with only the luxury of cleanliness, to receive her husband, who, returning weary home in the evening, found smiling babes and a clean hearth. My heart has loitered in the midst of the group, and has even throbbed with sympathetic emotion when the scraping of the well-known foot has raised a pleasing tumult.

Whilst my benevolence has been gratified by contemplating this artless picture, I have thought that a couple of this description, equally necessary and independent of each other, because each fulfilled the respective duties of their station, possessed all that life could give. Raised sufficiently above abject poverty not to be obliged to weigh the consequence of every farthing they spend, and having sufficient to prevent their attending to a frigid system of economy which narrows both heart and mind, I declare, so vulgar are my conceptions, that I know not what is wanted to render this the happiest as well as the most respectable situation in the world, but a taste for literature, to throw a little variety and interest into social converse, and some superfluous money to give to the needy and to buy books. For it is not pleasant when the heart is opened by compassion, and the head active in arranging plans of usefulness, to have a prim urchin continually twitching back the elbow to prevent the hand from drawing out an almost empty purse, whispering at the same time some prudential maxim about the priority of justice.

Destructive, however, as riches and inherited honours are to the human character, women are more debased and cramped, if possible, by them than men, because men may still in some degree unfold their faculties by becoming soldiers and statesmen.

As soldiers, I grant they can now only gather for the most part vain-glorious laurels, whilst they adjust to a hair the European balance, taking especial care that no bleak northern nook or sound incline the beam. But the days of true heroism are over, when a citizen fought for his country like a Fabricius or a Washington, and then returned to his farm to let his virtuous fervour run in a more placid, but not a less salutary, stream. No, our British heroes are oftener sent from the gaming-table than from the plough; and their passions have been rather inflamed by hanging with dumb suspense on the turn of a die, than sublimated by panting after the adventurous march of virtue in the historic page.

The statesman, it is true, might with more propriety quit the faro bank, or card-table, to guide the helm, for he has still but to shuffle and trick—the whole system of British politics, if system it may courteously be called, consisting in multiplying dependents and contriving taxes which grind the poor to pamper the rich. Thus a war, or any wild-goose chase, is, as the vulgar use the phrase, a lucky turn-up of patronage for the minister, whose chief merit is the art of keeping himself in place. It is not necessary then that he should have bowels for the poor, so he can secure for his family the odd trick. Or should some show of respect, for what is termed with ignorant ostentation an Englishman's birthright, be expedient to bubble the gruff mastiff that he has to lead by the nose, he can make an empty show, very safely, by giving his single voice, and suffering his light squadron to file off to the other side. And when a question of humanity is agitated, he may dip a sop in the milk of human kindness to silence Cerberus, and talk of the interest which his heart takes in an attempt to make the earth no longer cry for vengeance as it sucks in its children's blood, though his cold hand may at the very moment rivet their chains, by sanctioning the abominable traffic. A minister is no longer a minister, than while he can carry a point, which he is determined to carry. Yet it is not necessary that a minister should feel like a man, when a bold push might shake his seat.

But, to have done with these episodical observations, let me return to the more specious slavery which chains the very soul of woman, keeping her for ever under the bondage of ignorance.

The preposterous distinctions of rank, which render civilization a curse, by dividing the world between voluptuous tyrants and cunning envious dependents, corrupt, almost equally, every class of people, because respectability is not attached to the discharge of the relative duties of life, but to the station, and when the duties are not fulfilled the affections cannot gain sufficient strength to fortify the virtue of which they are the natural reward. Still there are some loop-holes out of which a man may creep, and dare to think and act for himself; but for a woman it is an herculean task, because she has difficulties peculiar to her sex to overcome, which require almost superhuman powers.

A truly benevolent legislator always endeavours to make it the interest of each individual to be virtuous; and thus private virtue becoming the cement of public happiness, an orderly whole is consolidated by the tendency of all the parts towards a common centre. But the private or public virtue of woman is very problematical, for Rousseau, and a numerous list of male writers, insist that she should all her life be subjected to a severe restraint, that of propriety. Why subject her to propriety—blind propriety—if she be capable of acting from a nobler spring, if she be an heir of immortality? Is sugar always to be produced by vital blood? Is one half of the human species, like the poor African slaves, to be subjected to prejudices that brutalize them, when principles would be a surer guard, only to sweeten the cup of man? Is not this indirectly to deny woman reason? for a gift is a mockery, if it be unfit for use.

Women are, in common with men, rendered weak and luxurious by the relaxing pleasures which wealth procures; but added to this they are made slaves to their persons, and must render them alluring that man may lend them his reason to guide their tottering steps aright. Or should they be ambitious, they must govern their tyrants by sinister tricks, for without rights there cannot be any incumbent duties. The laws respecting woman, which I mean to discuss in a future part, make an absurd unit of a man and his wife; and then, by the easy transition of only considering him as responsible, she is reduced to a mere cipher.

The being who discharges the duties of its station is independent; and, speaking of women at large, their first duty is to themselves as rational creatures, and the next, in point of importance, as citizens, is that, which includes so many, of a mother. The rank in life which dispenses with their fulfilling this duty, necessarily degrades them by making them mere dolls. Or should they turn to something more important than merely fitting drapery upon a smooth block, their minds are only occupied by some soft platonic attachment; or the actual management of an intrigue may keep their thoughts in motion; for when they neglect domestic duties, they have it not in their power to take the field and march and counter-march like soldiers, or wrangle in the senate to keep their faculties from rusting.

I know that, as a proof of the inferiority of the sex, Rousseau has exultingly exclaimed, How can they leave the nursery for the camp! And the camp has by some moralists been proved the school of the most heroic virtues; though I think it would puzzle a keen casuist to prove the reasonableness of the greater number of wars that have dubbed heroes. I do not mean to consider this question critically; because, having frequently viewed these freaks of ambition as the first natural mode of civilization, when the ground must be torn up, and the woods cleared by fire and sword, I do not choose to call them pests; but surely the present system of war has little connection with virtue of any denomination, being rather the school of *finesse* and effeminacy than of fortitude.

Yet, if defensive war, the only justifiable war, in the present advanced state of society, where virtue can show its face and ripen amidst the rigours which purify the air on the mountain's top, were alone to be adopted as just and glorious, the true heroism of antiquity might again animate female bosoms. But fair and softly, gentle reader, male or female, do not alarm thyself, for though I have compared the character of a modern soldier with that of a civilized woman, I am not going to advise them to turn their distaff into a musket, though I sincerely wish to see the bayonet converted into a pruning-hook. I only re-created an imagination, fatigued by contemplating the vices and follies which all proceed from a feculent stream of wealth that has muddied the pure rills of natural affection, by supposing that society will some time or other be so constituted, that man must necessarily fulfil the duties of a citizen, or be despised, and that while he was employed in any of the departments of civil life, his wife, also an active citizen, should be equally intent to manage her family, educate her children, and assist her neighbours.

But to render her really virtuous and useful, she must not, if she discharge her civil duties, want individually the protection of civil laws; she must not be dependent on her husband's bounty for her subsistence during his life, or support after his death; for how can a being be generous who has nothing of its own? or virtuous who is not free? The wife, in the present state of things, who is faithful to her husband, and neither suckles not educates her children, scarcely deserves the name of a wife, and has no right to that of a citizen. But take away natural rights, and duties become null.

Women then must be considered as only the wanton solace of men, when they become so weak in mind and body that they cannot exert themselves unless to pursue some frothy pleasure, or to invent some frivolous fashion. What can be a more melancholy sight to a thinking mind, than to look into the numerous carriages that drive helter-skelter about this metropolis in a morning full of pale-faced creatures who are flying from themselves! I have often wished, with Dr Johnson, to place some of them in a little shop with half a dozen children looking up to their languid countenances for support. I am much mistaken, if some latent vigour would not soon give health and spirit to their eyes, and some lines drawn by the exercise of reason on the blank cheeks, which before were only undulated by dimples, might restore lost dignity to the character, or rather enable it to attain the true dignity of its nature. Virtue is not to be acquired even by speculation, much less by the negative supineness that wealth naturally generates.

Besides, when poverty is more disgraceful than even vice, is not morality cut to the quick? Still to avoid misconstruction, though I consider that women in the common walks of life are called to fulfil the duties of wives and mothers, by religion and reason, I cannot help lamenting that women of a superior cast have not a road open by which they can pursue more extensive plans of usefulness and independence. I may excite laughter, by dropping a hint, which I mean to pursue, some future time, for I really think that women ought to have representatives, instead of being arbitrarily governed without having any direct share allowed them in the deliberations of government.

But, as the whole system of representation is now, in this country, only a convenient handle for despotism, they need not complain, for they are as well represented as a numerous class of hard-working mechanics, who pay for the support of royalty when they can scarcely stop their children's mouths with bread. How are they represented whose very sweat supports the splendid stud of an heir-apparent, or varnishes the chariot of some female favourite who looks down on shame? Taxes on the very necessaries of life, enable an endless tribe of idle princes and princesses to pass with stupid pomp before a gaping crowd, who almost worship the very parade which costs them so dear. This is mere gothic grandeur, something like the barbarous useless parade of having sentinels on horseback at Whitehall, which I could never view without a mixture of contempt and indignation.

How strangely must the mind be sophisticated when this sort of state impresses it! But, till these monuments of folly are levelled by virtue, similar follies will leaven the whole mass. For the same character, in some degree, will prevail in the aggregate of society; and the refinements of luxury, or the vicious repinings of envious poverty, will equally banish virtue from society, considered as the characteristic of that society, or only allow it to appear as one of the stripes of the harlequin coat, worn by the civilized man.

In the superior ranks of life, every duty is done by deputies, as if duties could ever be waived, and the vain pleasures which consequent idleness forces the rich to pursue, appear so enticing to the next rank, that the numerous scramblers for wealth sacrifice everything to tread on their heels. The most sacred trusts are then considered as sinecures, because they were procured by interest, and only sought to enable a man to keep *good company*. Women, in particular, all want to be ladies. Which is simply to have nothing to do, but listlessly to go they scarcely care where, for they cannot tell what.

But what have women to do in society? I may be asked, but to loiter with easy grace; surely you would not condemn them all to suckle fools and chronicle small beer! No. Women might certainly study the art of healing and be physicians as well as nurses. And midwifery, decency seems to allot to them though I am afraid the word midwife, in our dictionaries, will soon give place to *accoucheur*, and one proof of the former delicacy of the sex be effaced from the language.

They might also study politics, and settle their benevolence on the broadest basis; for the reading of history will scarcely be more useful than the perusal of romances, if read as mere biography; if the character of the times, the political improvements, arts, etc., be not observed. In short, if it be not considered as the history of man; and not of particular men, who filled a niche in the temple of fame, and dropped into the black rolling stream of time, that silently sweeps all before it into the shapeless void called—eternity.—For shape, can it be called, "that shape hath none"?

Business of various kinds, they might likewise pursue, if they were educated in a more orderly manner, which might save many from common and legal prostitution. Women would not then marry for a support, as men accept of places under Government, and neglect the implied duties; nor would an attempt to earn their own subsistence, a most laudable one! sink them almost to the level of those poor abandoned creatures who live by prostitution. For are not milliners and mantua-makers reckoned the next class? The few employments open to women, so far, from being liberal, are menial; and when a superior education enables them to take charge of the education of children as governesses, they are not treated like the tutors of sons, though even clerical tutors are not always treated in a manner calculated to render them respectable in the eyes of their pupils, to say nothing of the private comfort of the individual. But as women educated like gentlewomen, are never designed for the humiliating situation which necessity sometimes forces them to fill; these situations are considered in the light of a degradation; and they know little of the human heart, who need to be told, that nothing so painfully sharpens sensibility as such a fall in life.

Some of these women might be restrained from marrying by a proper spirit of delicacy, and others may not have had it in their power to escape in this pitiful way from servitude; is not that Government then very defective, and very unmindful of the happiness of one-half of its members, that does not provide for honest, independent women, by encouraging them to fill respectable stations? But in order to render their private virtue a public benefit, they must have a civil existence in the State, married or single; else we shall continually see some worthy woman, whose sensibility has been rendered painfully acute by undeserved contempt, droop like "the lily broken down by a plowshare."

It is a melancholy truth; yet such is the blessed effect of civilization! the most respectable women are the most oppressed; and, unless they have understandings far superior to the common run of understandings, taking in both sexes, they must, from being treated like contemptible beings, become contemptible. How many women thus waste life away the prey of discontent, who might have practised as physicians, regulated a farm, managed a shop, and stood erect, supported by their own industry, instead of hanging their heads surcharged with the dew of sensibility, that consumes the beauty to which it at first gave lustre; nay, I doubt whether pity and love are so near akin as poets feign, for I have seldom seen much compassion excited by the helplessness of females, unless they were fair; then, perhaps, pity was the soft handmaid of love, or the harbinger of lust.

How much more respectable is the woman who earns her own bread by fulfilling any duty, than the most accomplished beauty!—beauty did I say!—so sensible am I of the beauty of moral loveliness, or the harmonious propriety that attunes the passions of a well-regulated mind, that I blush at making the comparison; yet I sigh to think how few women aim at attaining this respectability by withdrawing from the giddy whirl of pleasure, or the indolent calm that stupefies the good sort of women it sucks in.

Proud of their weakness, however, they must always be protected, guarded from care, and all the rough toils that dignify the mind. If this be the fiat of fate, if they will make themselves insignificant and contemptible, sweetly to waste "life away," let them not expect to be valued when their beauty fades, for it is the fate of the fairest flowers to be admired and pulled to pieces by the careless hand that plucked them. In how many ways do I wish, from the purest benevolence, to impress this truth on my sex; yet I fear that they will not listen to a truth that dear bought experience has brought home to many an agitated bosom, nor willingly resign the privileges of rank and sex for the privileges of humanity, to which those have no claim who do not discharge its duties.

Those writers are particularly useful, in my opinion, who make man feel for man, independent of the station he fills, or the drapery of factitious sentiments. I then would fain convince reasonable men of the importance of some of my remarks; and prevail on them to weigh dispassionately the whole tenor of my observations. I appeal to their understandings; and, as a fellow-creature, claim, in the name of my sex, some interest in their hearts. I entreat them to assist to emancipate their companion, to make her a *help-meet* for them.

Would men but generously snap our chains, and be content with rational fellowship instead of slavish obedience, they would find us more observant daughters, more affectionate sisters, more faithful wives, more reasonable mothers—in a word, better citizens. We should then love them with true affection, because we should learn to respect ourselves; and the peace of mind of a worthy man would not be interrupted by the idle vanity of his wife, nor the babes sent to nestle in a strange bosom, having never found a home in their mother's.

Thomas Hill Green (1836–1882 C.E.)

Green, the son of a clergyman of the Church of England, was a philosopher trained at Oxford's Balliol College. His career spanned both academe and public service (he became a leader of the temperance movement in 1876). He became the first secular tutor at Balliol, and eventually was elected Whyte's Professor of moral philosophy. His work was hampered by illness, so that his manuscript *Prolegomena to Ethics* had not been finished by the time of his death. Green was trained in the methods of Kant and Hegel. He saw applications of transcendental idealism in his notions of an interventionist state. Green represents a departure from the liberalism and utilitarianism of his day, and was influential in shaping British social policy in the late nineteenth century.

From Justice and the Common Good*

Prolegomena to Ethics
Book 3: The Moral Ideal and Moral Progress

Chapter 3: The Origin and Development of the Moral Ideal

A. Reason as Source of the Idea of a Common Good

. . .

202. . . . The conception of a moral law, in its strict philosophical form, is no doubt an analogical adaptation of the notion of law in the more primary sense—the notion of it as a command enforced by a political superior, or by some power to which obedience is habitually rendered by those to whom the command is addressed. But there is an idea which equally underlies the conception both of moral duty and of legal right; which is prior, so to speak, to the distinction between them; which must have been at work in the minds of men before they could be capable of recognising any kind of action as one that *ought* to be done, whether because it is enjoined by law or authoritative custom, or because, though not thus enjoined, a man owes it to himself or to his neighbour or to God. This is the idea of an absolute and a common good; a good common to the person conceiving it with others, and good for him and them, whether at any moment it answers their likings or no. As affected by such an idea, a man's attitude to his likes and dislikes will be one of which, in his inward converse, the "Thou shalt" or "Thou must" of command is the natural expression, though of law, in the sense either of the command of a political superior or of a self-imposed rule of life, he may as yet have no definite conception.

And so affected by it he must be, before the authority either of custom or of law can have any meaning for him. Simple fear cannot constitute the sense of such authority nor

---

*An Excerpt.

by any process of development, properly so called, become it. It can only spring from a conviction, on the part of those recognising the authority, that a good which is really their good, though in constant conflict with their inclinations, is really served by the power in which they recognise authority. Whatever force may be employed in maintaining custom or law, however "the interest of the stronger," whether an individual or the few or the majority of some group of people, may be concerned in maintaining it, only some persuasion of its contribution to a recognised common good can yield that sort of obedience to it which, equally in the simpler and the more complex stages of society, forms the social bond.

203. The idea, then, of a possible well-being of himself, that shall not pass away with this, that, or the other pleasure; and relation to some group of persons whose well-being he takes to be as his own, and in whom he is interested in being interested in himself—these two things must condition the life of any one who is to be a creator or sustainer either of law or of that prior authoritative custom out of which law arises. Without them there might be instruments of law and custom; intelligent cooperating subjects of law and custom there could not be. They are conditions at once of might being so exercised that it can be recognised as having right, and of that recognition itself. It is in this sense that the old language is justified, which speaks of Reason as the parent of Law. . . .

. . .

205. The foundation of morality, then, in the reason or self-objectifying consciousness of man, is the same thing as its foundation in the institutions of a common life—in these as directed to a common good, and so directed not mechanically but with consciousness of the good on the part of those subject to the institutions. Such institutions are, so to speak, the form and body of reason, as practical in men. Without them the rational or self-conscious or moral man does not exist, nor without them can any being have existed from whom such a man could be developed, if any continuity of nature is implied in development. No development of morality can be conceived, nor can any history of it be traced (for that would imply such a conception), which does not presuppose some idea of a common good, expressing itself in some elementary effort after a regulation of life. Without such an idea the development would be as impossible as it is impossible that sight should be generated when there is no optic nerve. With it, however restricted in range the idea may be, there is given "in promise and potency" the ideal of which the realisation would be perfect morality, the ideal of a society in which every one shall treat every one else as his neighbour, in which to every rational agent the well-being or perfection of every other such agent shall be included in that perfection of himself for which he lives. And as the most elementary notion in a rational being of a personal good, common to himself with another who is as himself, is in possibility such an ideal, so the most primitive institutions for the regulation of a society with reference to a common good are already a school for the character which shall be responsive to the moral ideal.

. . .

B. The Extension of the Area of Common Good

. . .

211. For an abstract expression of the notion that there is something due from every man to every man, simply as men, we may avail ourselves of the phrase employed in the famous definition of Justice in the Institutes:—"Justitia est constans et perpetua voluntas suum cuique tribuendi." Every man both by law and common sentiment is recognised as having a "suum," whatever the "suum" may be, and is thus effectually distinguished from the animals (at any rate according to our treatment of them) and from things. He is deemed capable of having something of his own, as animals and things are not. He is treated as an end, not merely as a means. It is obvious indeed that the notion expressed by the "suum cuique," even when it carries with it the admission that every man, as such, has a "suum," is a most insufficient guide to conduct till we can answer the question what the "suum" in each case is, and that no such answer is deducible from the mere principle that every one has a "suum." In fact, of course, this principle is never wrought into law or general sentiment without very precise, though perhaps insufficient and ultimately untenable, determinations of what is due from one to another in the ordinary intercourse of those habitually associated. Particular duties to this man and that have been recognised long before reflection has reached the stage in which a duty to man as such can be recognised. How far upon reflection we can find in these particular duties—in the detail of conventional morality—a permanent and universal basis for right conduct, is a separate question. For the present we wish to follow out the effect exerted upon the responsive conscience by life in a society where a capacity for rights, some claim on his fellow-men, has come to be ascribed to every man. Given that readiness to recognise a duty and to act upon the recognition, which is the proper outcome in the individual of family and civil discipline as governed by an idea of common good, what sort of rule of conduct will the individual, upon unbiassed reflection, obtain for himself from the establishment in law and general sentiment of the principle that every man can claim something as his due? How will it tend to define for him the absolutely desirable, and the ideal of conduct as directed thereto?

212. The great result will be to fix it in his mind, as a condition of such conduct, that it should be *alike* for the real good of all men concerned in or affected by it, as estimated on the same principle. This rule has indeed become so familiarised to our consciences, however frequently we violate it, that at first sight it may seem to some too trivial to be worthy a philosopher's attention, while by others it may be remarked that, till we have decided what the real good of all men is, and have at least some general knowledge of the effect upon it, under certain conditions, of certain lines of conduct, the rule will not tell us how we ought to act in particular cases. Such a remark would be plainly true. For the present, however, we are considering the importance to the conscientious man of this recognition of a like claim in all men, taken simply by itself, irrespectively of those criteria of the good and of those convictions as to the means of arriving at it by which the recognition is in fact always accompanied. It is the source of the refinement in his sense of justice. It is that which makes him so over-curious, as it seems to the ordinary man of the world, in enquiring, as to any action that may suggest itself to him, whether the benefit which he might gain by it for himself or for some one in whom he is interested, would be gained at the expense of any one else, however indifferent to him personally, however separated from him in family, status, or nation. It makes the man, in short, who will be just before he is generous; who will not merely postpone his own interest to his friend's, but who, before he gratifies an "altruistic" inclination, will be careful to enquire how in doing so he would affect others who are not the object of the inclination. This characteristic of the man who is just in the full light of the idea of human equality is independent of any theory of well-being on his part. Whether he has any theory on the matter at all, whether he is theoretically an "Ascetic" or a "Hedonist," makes little practical difference. The essential thing is that he applies no other standard in judging of the well-being of others than in judging of his own, and that he will not promote his own well-being or that of one whom he loves or likes, from whom he has received service or expects it, at the cost of impeding in any way the well-being of one who is nothing to him but a man, or whom he involuntarily dislikes; that he will not do this knowingly, and that he is habitually on the look-out to know whether his actions will have this effect or not.

. . .

217. . . . Thus in the conscientious citizen of modern Christendom reason without and reason within, reason as objective and reason as subjective, reason as the better spirit of the social order in which he lives, and reason as his loyal recognition and interpretation of that spirit—these being but different aspects of one and the same reality, which is the operation of the divine mind in man—combine to yield both the judgment, and obedience to the judgment, which we variously express by saying that every human person has an absolute value; that humanity in the person of every one is always to be treated as an end, never merely as a means; that in the estimate of that well-being which forms the true good every one is to count for one and no one for more than one; that every one has a "suum" which every one else is bound to render him.

Lectures on the Principles of Political Obligation

. . .

G. Will, Not Force, Is the Basis of the State

. . .

114. To ask why I am to submit to the power of the state, is to ask why I am to allow my life to be regulated by that complex of institutions without which I literally should not have a life to call my own, nor should be able to ask for a justification of what I am called on to do. For that I may have a life which I can call my own, I must not only be conscious of myself and of ends which I present to myself as mine; I must be able to reckon on a certain freedom of action and acquisition for the attainment of those ends, and this can only be secured through common recognition of this freedom on the part of each other by members of a society, as being for a common good. Without this, the very consciousness of having ends of his own and a life which he can direct in a certain way, a life of which he can make something, would remain dormant in a man. It is true that slaves have been found to have this consciousness in high development; but a slave even at his lowest has been partly made what he is by an ancestral life which was not one of slavery pure and simple, a life in which certain elementary rights were secured to the members of a society through their recognition of a common interest. He retains certain spiritual aptitudes from that state of family or tribal freedom. . . . Slavery, moreover, implies the establishment of some regular system of rights in the slave-owning society. The slave, especially the domestic slave, has the signs and effects of this system all about him. . . . Thus the appearance in slaves of the conception that they should be masters of themselves, does not conflict with the proposition that only so far as a certain freedom of action and acquisition is secured to a body of men through their recognition of the exercise of that freedom by each other as being for the common good, is there an actualisation of the individual's consciousness of having life and ends of his own. The exercise, manifestation, expression of this consciousness through a freedom secured in the way described is necessary to its real existence, just as language of some sort is necessary to the real existence of thought, and bodily movement to that of the soul.

115. The demand, again, for a justification of what one is called on by authority to do presupposes some standard of right, recognised as equally valid for and by the person making the demand and others who form a society with him, and such a recognised standard in turn implies institutions for the regulation of men's dealings with each other, institutions of which the relation to the consciousness of right may be compared, as above, to that of language to thought. It cannot be said that the most elementary consciousness of right is prior to them, or they to it. They are the expressions in which it becomes real. As conflicting with the momentary inclinations of the individual, these institutions are a power which he obeys unwillingly; which he has to, or is made to, obey. But it is only through them that the consciousness takes shape and form which expresses itself in the question, "Why should I thus be constrained? By what right is my natural right to do as I like overborne?"

116. The doctrine that the rights of government are founded on the consent of the governed is a confused way of stating the truth, that the institutions by which man is moralised, by which he comes to do what he sees that he must, as distinct from what he would like, express a conception of a common good; that through them that conception takes form and reality; and that it is in turn through its presence in the individual that they have a constraining power over him, a power which is not that of mere fear, still less a physical compulsion, but which leads him to do what he is not inclined to because there is a law that he should.

Rousseau, it will be remembered, speaks of the "social pact" not merely as the foundation of sovereignty or civil government, but as the foundation of morality. Through it man becomes a moral agent; for the slavery to appetite he substitutes the freedom of subjection to a self-imposed law. If he had seen at the same time that rights do not begin till duties begin, and that if there was no morality prior to the pact there could not be rights, he might have been saved from the error which the notion of there being natural rights introduces into his theory. But though he does not seem himself to have been aware of the full bearing of his own conception, the conception itself is essentially true. Setting aside the fictitious representation of an original covenant as having given birth to that common "ego" or general will, without which no such covenant would have been possible, and of obligations arising out of it, as out of a bargain made between one man and another, it remains true that only through a recognition by certain men of a common interest, and through the expression of that recognition in certain regulations of their dealings with each other, could morality originate, or any meaning be gained for such terms as "ought" and "right" and their equivalents.

117. Morality, in the first instance, is the observance of such regulations, and though a higher morality, the morality of the character governed by "disinterested motives," i.e., by interest in some form of human perfection, comes to differentiate itself from this primitive morality consisting in the observance of rules established for a common good, yet this outward morality is the presupposition of the higher morality. Morality and political subjection thus have a common source, "*political* subjection" being distinguished from that of a slave, as a subjection which secures rights to the subject. That common source is the rational recognition by certain human beings—it may be merely by children of the same parent—of a common well-being which is their well-being, and which they conceive as their well-being whether at any moment any one of them is inclined to it or no, and the embodiment of that recognition in rules by which the inclinations of the individuals are restrained, and a corresponding freedom of action for the attainment of well-being on the whole is secured.

. . .

M. The Right of the State to Promote Morality

207. The right of the individual man as such to free life is constantly gaining on its negative side more general recognition. It is the basis of the growing scrupulosity in regard to punishments which are not reformatory, which put rights finally out of the reach of a criminal instead of qualifying him for their renewed exercise. But the only rational foundation for the ascription of this right is the ascription of capacity for free contribution to social good. We treat this capacity in the man whose crime has given proof of its having been overcome by anti-social tendencies, as yet giving him a title to a further chance of its development; on the other hand, we act as if it conferred no title on its possessors, before a crime has been committed, to be placed under conditions in which its realisation would be possible. Is this reasonable? Yet are not all modern states so acting? Are they not allowing their ostensible members to grow up under conditions which render the development of social capacity practically impossible? Was it not more reasonable, as in the ancient states, to deny the right to life in the human subject as such, than to admit it under conditions which prevent the realisation of the capacity that forms the ground of its admission? This brings us to the fourth of the questions that arose out of the assertion of the individual's right to free life. What is the nature and extent of the individual's claim to be enabled positively to realise that capacity for freely contributing to social good which is the foundation of his right to free life?

208. In dealing with this question, it is important to bear in mind that the capacity we are considering is essentially a free or (what is the same) a moral capacity. It is a capacity, not for action determined by relation to a certain end, but for action determined by a conception of the end to which it is relative. Only thus is it a foundation of rights. The action of an animal or plant may be made contributory to social good, but it is not therefore a foundation of rights on the part of an animal or plant, because they are not affected by the conception of the good to which they contribute. A right is a power of acting for his own ends,—for what he conceives to be his good,—secured to an individual by the community, on the supposition that its exercise contributes to the good of the community. But the exercise of such a power cannot be so contributory, unless the individual, in acting for his own ends, is at least affected by the conception of a good as common to himself with others. The condition of making the animal contributory to human good is that we do not leave him free to determine the exercise of his powers; that we determine them for him; that we use him merely as an instrument; and this means that we do not, because we cannot, endow him with rights. We cannot endow him with rights because there is no conception of a good common to him with us which we can treat as a motive to him to do to us as he would have us do to him. It is not indeed necessary to a capacity for rights, as it is to true moral goodness, that interest in a good conceived as common to himself with others should be a man's dominant motive. It is enough if that which he presents to himself from time to time as his good, and which accordingly determines his action, is so far affected by consideration of the position in which he stands to others,—of the way in which this or that possible action of his would affect them, and of what he would have to expect from them in return,—as to result habitually, without force or fear of force, in action not incompatible with conditions necessary to the pursuit of a common good on the part of others. In other words, it is the presumption that a man in his general course of conduct will of his own motion have respect to the common good, which entitles him to rights at the hands of the community. The question of the moral value of the motive which may induce this respect—whether an unselfish interest in common good or the wish for personal pleasure and fear of personal pain—does not come into the account at all. An agent, indeed, who could only be induced by fear of death or bodily harm to behave conformably to the requirements of the community, would not be a subject of rights, because this influence could never be brought to bear on him so constantly, if he were free to regulate his own life, as to secure the public safety. But a man's desire for pleasure to himself and aversion from pain to himself, though dissociated from any desire for a higher object, for any object that is desired because good for others, may constitute a capacity for rights, if his imagination of pleasure and pain is so far affected by sympathy with the feeling of others about him as to make him, independently of force or fear of punishment, observant of established rights. In such a case the fear of punishment may be needed to neutralise antisocial impulses under circumstances of special temptation, but by itself it could never be

a sufficiently uniform motive to qualify a man, in the absence of more spontaneously social feelings, for the life of a free citizen. The qualification for such a life is a spontaneous
habit of acting with reference to a common good, whether that habit be founded on an
imagination of pleasures and pains or on a conception of what ought to be. In either case
the habit implies at least an understanding that there is such a thing as a common good,
and a regulation of egoistic hopes and fears, if not an inducing of more "disinterested"
motives, in consequence of that understanding.

209. The capacity for rights, then, being a capacity for spontaneous action regulated
by a conception of a common good, either so regulated through an interest which flows
directly from that conception, or through hopes and fears which are affected by it
through more complex channels of habit and association, is a capacity which cannot be
generated—which on the contrary is neutralised—by any influences that interfere with
the spontaneous action of social interests. Now any direct enforcement of the outward
conduct, which ought to flow from social interests, by means of threatened penalties—
and a law requiring such conduct necessarily implies penalties for disobedience to it—
does interfere with the spontaneous action of those interests, and consequently checks the
growth of the capacity which is the condition of the beneficial exercise of rights. For this
reason the effectual action of the state, i.e., the community as acting through law, for the
promotion of habits of true citizenship, seems necessarily to be confined to the removal
of obstacles. Under this head, however, there may and should be included much that most
states have hitherto neglected, and much that at first sight may have the appearance of
an enforcement of moral duties, e.g., the requirement that parents have their children
taught the elementary arts. To educate one's children is no doubt a moral duty, and it is
not one of those duties, like that of paying debts, of which the neglect directly interferes
with the rights of someone else. It might seem, therefore, to be a duty with which positive law should have nothing to do, any more than with the duty of striving after a noble
life. On the other hand, the neglect of it does tend to prevent the growth of the capacity for beneficially exercising rights on the part of those whose education is neglected,
and it is on this account, not as a purely moral duty on the part of a parent, but as the
prevention of a hindrance to the capacity for rights on the part of children, that education should be enforced by the state. It may be objected, indeed, that in enforcing it we
are departing in regard to the parents from the principle above laid down; that we are
interfering with the spontaneous action of social interests, though we are doing so with a
view to promoting this spontaneous action in another generation. But the answer to this
objection is, that a law of compulsory education, if the preferences, ecclesiastical or otherwise, of those parents who show any practical sense of their responsibility are duly respected, is from the beginning only felt as compulsion by those in whom, so far as this
social function is concerned, there is no spontaneity to be interfered with; and that in the
second generation, though the law with its penal sanctions still continues, it is not felt as
a law, as an enforcement of action by penalties, at all.

210. On the same principle the freedom of contract ought probably to be more restricted in certain directions than is at present the case. The freedom to do as they like
on the part of one set of men may involve the ultimate disqualification of many others,

or of a succeeding generation, for the exercise of rights. This applies most obviously to such kinds of contract or traffic as affect the health and housing of the people, the growth of population relatively to the means of subsistence, and the accumulation or distribution of landed property. In the hurry of removing those restraints on free dealing between man and man, which have arisen partly perhaps from some confused idea of maintaining morality, but much more from the power of class-interests, we have been apt to take too narrow a view of the range of persons—not one generation merely, but succeeding generations—whose freedom ought to be taken into account, and of the conditions necessary to their freedom ("freedom" here meaning their qualification for the exercise of rights). Hence the massing of population without regard to conditions of health; unrestrained traffic in deleterious commodities; unlimited upgrowth of the class of hired labourers in particular industries which circumstances have suddenly stimulated, without any provision against the danger of an impoverished proletariate in following generations. Meanwhile, under pretence of allowing freedom of bequest and settlement, a system has grown up which prevents the landlords of each generation from being free either in the government of their families or in the disposal of their land, and aggravates the tendency to crowd into towns, as well as the difficulties of providing healthy house-room, by keeping land in a few hands. It would be out of place here to consider in detail the remedies for these evils, or to discuss the question how far it is well to trust to the initiative of the state or of individuals in dealing with them. It is enough to point out the directions in which the state may remove obstacles to the realisation of the capacity for beneficial exercise of rights, without defeating its own object by vitiating the spontaneous character of that capacity.

Lecture on Liberal Legislation and Freedom of Contract

. . .

We shall probably all agree that freedom, rightly understood, is the greatest of blessings; that its attainment is the true end of all our effort as citizens. But when we thus speak of freedom, we should consider carefully what we mean by it. We do not mean merely freedom from restraint or compulsion. We do not mean merely freedom to do as we like irrespectively of what it is that we like. We do not mean a freedom that can be enjoyed by one man or one set of men at the cost of a loss of freedom to others. When we speak of freedom as something to be so highly prized, we mean a positive power or capacity to doing or enjoying something worth doing or enjoying, and that, too, something that we do or enjoy in common with others. We mean by it a power which each man exercises through the help or security given him by his fellow-men, and which he in turn helps to secure for them. When we measure the progress of a society by its growth in freedom, we measure it by the increasing development and exercise on the whole of those powers of contributing to social good with which we believe the members of the society to be endowed; in short, by the greater power on the part of the citizens as a body to make the most and best of themselves. Thus, though of course there can be no freedom among men who act not willingly but under compulsion, yet on the other hand the mere removal of compulsion, the mere enabling a man to do as he likes, is in itself no contribution to true freedom. In one sense no man is so well able to do as he likes as the wandering savage. He has no master. There is no one to say him nay. Yet we do not count him really free, because the freedom of savagery is not strength, but weakness. The actual powers of the noblest savage do not admit of comparison with those of the humblest citizen of a law-abiding state. He is not the slave of man, but he is the slave of nature. Of compulsion by natural necessity he has plenty of experience, though of restraint by society none at all. Nor can he deliver himself from that compulsion except by submitting to this restraint. So to submit is the first step in true freedom, because the first step towards the full exercise of the faculties with which man is endowed. But we rightly refuse to recognise the highest development on the part of an exceptional individual or exceptional class, as an advance towards the true freedom of man, if it is founded on a refusal of the same opportunity to other men. . . .

If I have given a true account of that freedom which forms the goal of social effort, we shall see that freedom of contract, freedom in all the forms of doing what one will with one's own, is valuable only as a means to an end. That end is what I call freedom in the positive sense: in other words, the liberation of the powers of all men equally for contributions to a common good. No one has a right to do what he will with his own in such a way as to contravene this end. It is only through the guarantee which society gives him that he has property at all, or, strictly speaking, any right to his possessions. This guarantee is founded on a sense of common interest. Every one has an interest in securing to every one else the free use and enjoyment and disposal of his possessions, so long as that freedom on the part of one does not interfere with a like freedom on the part of others, because such freedom contributes to that equal development of the faculties of all which is the highest good for all. This is the true and the only justification of rights of property. Rights of property, however, have been and are claimed which cannot be thus justified. We are all now agreed that men cannot rightly be the property of men. The institution of property being only justifiable as a means to the free exercise of the social capabilities of all, there can be no true right to property of a kind which debars one class of men from such free exercise altogether. We condemn slavery no less when it arises out of a voluntary agreement on the part of the enslaved person. A contract by which any one agreed for a certain consideration to become the slave of another we should reckon a void contract. Here, then, is a limitation upon freedom of contract which we all recognise as rightful. No contract is valid in which human persons, willingly or unwillingly, are dealt with as commodities, because such contracts of necessity defeat the end for which alone society enforces contracts at all.

Are there no other contracts which, less obviously perhaps but really, are open to the same objection? In the first place, let us consider contracts affecting labour. Labour, the economist tells us, is a commodity exchangeable like other commodities. This is in a certain sense true, but it is a commodity which attaches in a peculiar manner to the person of man. Hence restrictions may need to be placed on the sale of this commodity which would be unnecessary in other cases, in order to prevent labour from being sold under conditions which make it impossible for the person selling it ever to become a free contributor to social good in any form. This is most plainly the case when a man bargains to work under conditions fatal to health, e.g., in an unventilated factory. Every injury to the health of the individual is, so far as it goes, a public injury. It is an impediment to the general freedom; so much deduction from our power, as members of society, to make the best of ourselves. Society is, therefore, plainly within its right when it limits freedom of contract for the sale of labour, so far as is done by our laws for the sanitary regulations of factories, workshops, and mines. It is equally within its right in prohibiting the labour of women and young persons beyond certain hours. If they work beyond those hours, the result is demonstrably physical deterioration; which, as demonstrably, carries with it a lowering of the moral forces of society. For the sake of that general freedom of its members to make the best of themselves, which it is the object of civil society to secure, a prohibition should be put by law, which is the deliberate voice of society, on all such contracts of service as in a general way yield such a result. The purchase or hire of unwholesome dwellings is properly forbidden on the same principle. Its application to compulsory education may not be quite so obvious, but it will appear on a little reflection. Without a command of certain elementary arts and knowledge, the individual in modern society is as effectually crippled as by the loss of a limb or a broken constitution. He is not free to develop his faculties. With a view to securing such freedom among its members it is as certainly within the province of the state to prevent children from growing up in that kind of ignorance which practically excludes them from a free career in life, as it is within its province to require the sort of building and drainage necessary for public health.

Our modern legislation then with reference to labour, and education, and health, involving as it does manifold interference with freedom of contract, is justified on the ground that it is the business of the state, not indeed directly to promote moral goodness, for that, from the very nature of moral goodness, it cannot do, but to maintain the conditions without which a free exercise of the human faculties is impossible. It does not indeed follow that it is advisable for the state to do all which it is justified in doing. We are often warned nowadays against the danger of over-legislation; or, as I heard it put in a speech of the present home secretary in days when he was sowing his political wild oats, of "grandmotherly government." There may be good ground for the warning, but at any rate we should be quite clear what we mean by it. The outcry against state interference is often raised by men whose real objection is not to state interference but to centralisation, to the constant aggression of the central executive upon local authorities. . . . But there are some political speculators whose objection is not merely to centralisation, but to the extended action of law altogether. They think that the individual ought to be left much more to himself than has of late been the case. . . . Might not all the rules, . . . which legislation of the kind we have been discussing is intended to attain, have been attained without it; not so quickly, perhaps, but without tampering so dangerously with the independence and self-reliance of the people?

Now, we shall probably all agree that a society in which the public health was duly protected, and necessary education duly provided for, by the spontaneous action of individuals, was in a higher condition than one in which the compulsion of law was needed to secure these ends. But we must take men as we find them. Until such a condition of society is reached, it is the business of the state to take the best security it can for the young citizens' growing up in such health and with so much knowledge as is necessary for their real freedom. In so doing it need not at all interfere with the independence and self-reliance of those whom it requires to do what they would otherwise do for themselves. . . . But it was not their case that the laws we are considering were especially meant to meet. It was the overworked women, the ill-housed and untaught families, for whose benefit they were intended. And the question is whether without these laws the suffering classes could have been delivered quickly or slowly from the condition they were in. Could the enlightened self-interest or benevolence of individuals, working under a system of unlimited freedom of contract, have ever brought them into a state compatible with the free development of the human faculties? No one considering the facts can have any doubt as to the answer to this question. Left to itself, or to the operation of casual benevolence, a degraded population perpetuates and increases itself. . . .

As there is practically no danger of a reversal of our factory and school laws, it may seem needless to dwell at such length on their justification. I do so for two reasons; partly to remind the younger generation of citizens of the great blessing which they inherited in those laws, and of the interest which they still have in their completion and extension; but still more in order to obtain some clear principles for our guidance when we approach those difficult questions of the immediate future. . . .

Herbert Spencer (1820–1903 C.E.)

Spencer was born in Derby, England, and was self-educated, primarily in mathematics and sciences. After a three-month venture as a school headmaster, Spencer took a job as civil engineer with the London and Birmingham Railroad and later with the Birmingham and Gloucester Railroad (1837-1841). In this period he read on politics, religion, and education. When laid off in 1841 he got involved in politics and journalism through the Complete Suffrage Movement. From 1848 to 1853 he was a sub-editor at *The Economist* magazine and published his first book, *Social Statics*, excerpted here, in 1851. In this work Spencer developed a form of evolutionary theory applied to social issues. After Darwin's *Origin of Species* made evolution dramatically central in biology, Spencer undertook a project to generalize the mechanisms of evolution to all of science. His other key publications include *Principles of Psychology* (1855), *The Man Versus the State* (1884), and *Data of Ethics* (1879).

From Social Statics*

Chapter XIX

The Right to Ignore the State

1. As a corollary to the proposition that all institutions must be subordinated to the law of equal freedom, we cannot choose but admit the right of the citizen to adopt a condition of voluntary outlawry. If every man has freedom to do all that he wills, provided he infringes not the equal freedom of any other man, then he is free to drop connection with the state—to relinquish its protection and to refuse paying toward its support. It is self-evident that in so behaving he in no way trenches upon the liberty of others, for his position is a passive one, and while passive he cannot become an aggressor. It is equally self-evident that he cannot be compelled to continue one of a political corporation without a breach of the moral law, seeing that citizenship involves payment of taxes; and the taking away of a man's property against his will is an infringement of his rights. Government being simply an agent employed in common by a number of individuals to secure to them certain advantages, the very nature of the connection implies that it is for each to say whether he will employ such an agent or not. If any one of them determines to ignore this mutual-safety confederation, nothing can be said except that he loses all claim to its good offices and exposes himself to the danger of maltreatment—a thing he is quite at liberty to do if he likes. He cannot be coerced into political combination without a breach of the law of equal freedom; he can withdraw from it without committing any such breach, and he has therefore a right so to withdraw.

---

*An Excerpt.

2. "No human laws are of any validity if contrary to the law of nature; and such of them as are valid derive all their force and all their authority mediately or immediately from this original." Thus writes Blackstone, to whom let all honor be given for having so far outseen the ideas of his time and, indeed, we may say of our time. A good antidote, this, for those political superstitions which so widely prevail. A good check upon that sentiment of power worship which still misleads us by magnifying the prerogatives of constitutional governments as it once did those of monarchs. Let men learn that a legislature is not "our God upon earth," though, by the authority they ascribe to it and the things they expect from it, they would seem to think it is. Let them learn rather that it is an institution serving a purely temporary purpose, whose power, when not stolen, is at the best borrowed.

Nay, indeed, have we not seen that government is essentially immoral? Is it not the offspring of evil, bearing about it all the marks of its parentage? Does it not exist because crime exists? Is it not strong—or, as we say, despotic—when crime is great? Is there not more liberty—that is, less government—as crime diminishes? And must not government cease when crime ceases, for very lack of objects on which to perform its function? Not only does magisterial power exist *because* of evil, but it exists *by* evil. Violence is employed to maintain it, and all violence involves criminality. Soldiers, policemen, and jailers; swords, batons, and fetters are instruments for inflicting pain; and all inflection of pain is in the abstract wrong. The state employs evil weapons to subjugate evil and is alike contaminated by the objects with which it deals and the means by which it works. Morality cannot recognize it, for morality, being simply a statement of the perfect law, can give no countenance to anything growing out of, and living by, breaches of that law. Wherefore, legislative authority can never be ethical—must always be conventional merely.

Hence, there is a certain inconsistency in the attempt to determine the right position, structure, and conduct of a government by appeal to the first principles of rectitude. For, as just pointed out, the acts of an institution which is in both nature and origin imperfect cannot be made to square with the perfect law. All that we can do is to ascertain, firstly, in what attitude a legislature must stand to the community to avoid being by its mere existence an embodied wrong; secondly, in what manner it must be constituted so as to exhibit the least incongruity with the moral law; and thirdly, to what sphere its actions must be limited to prevent it from multiplying those breaches of equity it is set up to prevent.

The first condition to be conformed to before a legislature can be established without violating the law of equal freedom is the acknowledgment of the right now under discussion—the right to ignore the state.

3. Upholders of pure despotism may fitly believe state control to be unlimited and unconditional. They who assert that men are made for governments and not governments for men may consistently hold that no one can remove himself beyond the pale of political organization. But they who maintain that the people are the only legitimate source of power—that legislative authority is not original, but deputed—cannot deny the right to ignore the state without entangling themselves in an absurdity.

For, if legislative authority is deputed, it follows that those from whom it proceeds are the masters of those on whom it is conferred; it follows further that as masters they confer the said authority voluntarily; and this implies that they may give or withhold it as they please. To call that deputed which is wrenched from men, whether they will or not, is nonsense. But what is here true of all collectively is equally true of each separately. As a government can rightly act for the people only when empowered by them, so also can it rightly act for the individual only when empowered by him. If A, B, and C debate whether they shall employ an agent to perform for them a certain service, and if while A and B agree to do so C dissents, C cannot equitably be made a party to the agreement in spite of himself. And this must be equally true of thirty as of three; and if of thirty, why not of three hundred, or three thousand, or three million?

4. Of the political superstitions lately alluded to, none is so universally diffused as the notion that majorities are omnipotent. Under the impression that the preservation of order will ever require power to be wielded by some party, the moral sense of our time feels that such power cannot rightly be conferred on any but the largest moiety of society. It interprets literally the saying that "the voice of the people is the voice of God," and, transferring to the one the sacredness attached to the other, it concludes that from the will of the people—that is, of the majority—there can be no appeal. Yet is this belief entirely erroneous.

Suppose, for the sake of argument, that, struck by some Malthusian panic, a legislature duly representing public opinion were to enact that all children born during the next ten years should be drowned. Does anyone think such an enactment would be warrantable? If not, there is evidently a limit to the power of a majority. Suppose, again, that of two races living together—Celts and Saxons, for example—the most numerous determined to make the others their slaves. Would the authority of the greatest number be in such case valid? If not, there is something to which its authority must be subordinate. Suppose, once more, that all men having incomes under £50 a year were to resolve upon reducing every income above that amount to their own standard, and appropriating the excess for public purposes. Could their resolution be justified? If not, it must be a third time confessed that there is a law to which the popular voice must defer. What, then, is that law, if not the law of pure equity—the law of equal freedom? These restraints, which all would put to the will of the majority, are exactly the restraints set up by that law. We deny the right of a majority to murder, to enslave, or to rob, simply because murder, enslaving, and robbery are violations of that law—violations too gross to be overlooked. But if great violations of it are wrong, so also are smaller ones. If the will of the many cannot supersede the first principle of morality in these cases, neither can it in any. So that, however insignificant the minority, and however trifling the proposed trespass against their rights, no such trespass is permissible.

When we have made our constitution purely democratic, thinks to himself the earnest reformer, we shall have brought government into harmony with absolute justice. Such a faith, though perhaps needful for the age, is a very erroneous one. By no process can coercion be made equitable. The freest form of government is only the least objectional form. The rule of the many by the few we call tyranny; the rule of the few by the many is tyranny also, only of a less intense kind. "You shall do as we will, and not as you will," is in either case the declaration; and if the hundred make it to the ninety-nine, instead of the ninety-nine to the hundred, it is only a fraction less immoral. Of two such parties, whichever fulfills this declaration necessarily breaks the law of equal freedom: the only difference being that by the one it is broken in the persons of ninety-nine, while by the other it is broken in the persons of a hundred. And the merit of the democratic form of government consists solely in this, that it trespasses against the smallest number.

The very existence of majorities and minorities is indicative of an immoral state. The man whose character harmonizes with the moral law, we found to be one who can obtain complete happiness without diminishing the happiness of his fellows. But the enactment of public arrangements by vote implies a society consisting of men otherwise constituted—implies that the desires of some cannot be satisfied without sacrificing the desires of others—implies that in the pursuit of their happiness the majority inflict a certain amount of unhappiness on the minority—implies, therefore, organic immorality. Thus, from another point of view, we again perceive that even in its most equitable form it is impossible for government to dissociate itself from evil; and further, that unless the right to ignore the state is recognized, its acts must be essentially criminal.

5. That a man is free to abandon the benefits and throw off the burdens of citizenship may indeed be inferred from the admissions of existing authorities and of current opinion. Unprepared as they probably are for so extreme a doctrine as the one here maintained, the radicals of our day yet unwittingly profess their belief in a maxim which obviously embodies this doctrine. Do we not continually hear them quote Blackstone's assertion that "no subject of England can be constrained to pay any aids or taxes even for the defence of the realm or the support of government, but such as are imposed by his own consent, or that of his representative in parliament?" And what does this mean? It means, say they, that every man should have a vote. True, but it means much more. If there is any sense in words it is a distinct enunciation of the very right now contended for. In affirming that a man may not be taxed unless he has directly or indirectly given his consent, it affirms that he may refuse to be so taxed; and to refuse to be taxed is to cut all connection with the state. Perhaps it will be said that this consent is not a specific, but a general one, and that the citizen is understood to have assented to everything his representative may do when he voted for him. But suppose he did not vote for him, and on the contrary did all in his power to get elected someone holding opposite views—what then? The reply will probably be that, by taking part in such an election, he tacitly agreed to abide by the decision of the majority. And how if he did not vote at all? Why, then he cannot justly complain of any tax, seeing that he made no protest against its imposition. So, curiously enough, it seems that he gave his consent in whatever way he acted—whether he said yes, whether he said no, or whether he remained neuter! A rather awkward doctrine, this. Here stands an unfortunate citizen who is asked if he will pay money for a certain proffered advantage; and whether he employs the only means of expressing his refusal or does not employ it, we are told that he practically agrees, if only the number of others who agree is greater than the number of those who dissent. And thus we are introduced to the novel principle that A's consent to a thing is not determined by what A says, but by what B may happen to say!

It is for those who quote Blackstone to choose between this absurdity and the doctrine above set forth. Either his maxim implies the right to ignore the state, or it is sheer nonsense.

6. There is a strange heterogeneity in our political faiths. Systems that have had their day and are beginning here and there to let the daylight through are patched with modern notions utterly unlike in quality and color; and men gravely display these systems, wear them, and walk about in them, quite unconscious of their grotesqueness. This transition state of ours, partaking as it does equally of the past and the future, breeds hybrid theories exhibiting the oddest union of bygone despotism and coming freedom. Here are types of the old organization curiously disguised by germs of the new, peculiarities showing adaptation to a preceding state modified by rudiments that prophesy of something to come, making altogether so chaotic a mixture of relationships that there is no saying to what class these births of the age should be referred.

As ideas must of necessity bear the stamp of the time, it is useless to lament the contentment with which these incongruous beliefs are held. Otherwise it would seem unfortunate that men do not pursue to the end the trains of reasoning which have led to these partial modifications. In the present case, for example, consistency would force them to admit that, on other points besides the one just noticed, they hold opinions and use arguments in which the right to ignore the state is involved.

For what is the meaning of Dissent? The time was when a man's faith and his mode of worship were as much determinable by law as his secular acts; and, according to provisions extant in our statute book, are so still. Thanks to the growth of a Protestant spirit, however, we have ignored the state in this matter—wholly in theory, and partly in practice. But how have we done so? By assuming an attitude which, if consistently maintained, implies a right to ignore the state entirely. Observe the positions of the two parties. "This is your creed," says the legislator; "you must believe and openly profess what is here set down for you." "I shall not do anything of the kind," answers the nonconformist; "I will go to prison rather." "Your religious ordinances," pursues the legislator, "shall be such as we have prescribed. You shall attend the churches we have endowed and adopt the ceremonies used in them." "Nothing shall induce me to do so," is the reply; "I altogether deny your power to dictate to me in such matters, and mean to resist to the uttermost." "Lastly," adds the legislator, "we shall require you to pay such sums of money toward the support of these religious institutions as we may see fit to ask." "Not a farthing will you have from me," exclaims our sturdy Independent; "even did I believe in the doctrines of your church (which I do not), I should still rebel against your interference; and if you take my property, it shall be by force and under protest."

What now does this proceeding amount to when regarded in the abstract? It amounts to an assertion by the individual of the right to exercise one of his faculties—the religious sentiment—without let or hindrance, and with no limit save that set up by the equal claims of others. And what is meant by ignoring the state? Simply an assertion of the right similarly to exercise *all* the faculties. The one is just an expansion of the other—rests on the same footing with the other—must stand or fall with the other. Men do indeed speak of civil and religious liberty as different things: but the distinction is quite arbitrary. They are parts of the same whole and cannot philosophically be separated.

"Yes, they can," interposes an objector; "assertion of the one is imperative as being a religious duty. The liberty to worship God in the way that seems to him right is a liberty without which a man cannot fulfill what he believes to be Divine commands, and therefore conscience requires him to maintain it." True enough; but how if the same can be asserted of all other liberty? How if maintenance of this also turns out to be a matter of conscience? Have we not seen that human happiness is the Divine will—that only by exercising our faculties is this happiness obtainable—and that it is impossible to exercise them without freedom? And if this freedom for the exercise of faculties is a condition without which the Divine will cannot be fulfilled, the preservation of it is, by our objector's own showing, a duty. Or, in other words, it appears not only that the maintenance of liberty of action *may* be a point of conscience, but that it *ought* to be one. And thus we are clearly shown that the claims to ignore the state in religious and in secular matters are in essence identical.

The other reason commonly assigned for nonconformity admits of similar treatment. Besides resisting state dictation in the abstract, the dissenter resists it from disapprobation of the doctrines taught. No legislative injunction will make him adopt what he considers an erroneous belief; and, bearing in mind his duty toward his fellow men, he refuses to help through the medium of his purse in disseminating this erroneous belief. The position is perfectly intelligible. But it is one which either commits its adherents to civil nonconformity also, or leaves them in a dilemma. For why do they refuse to be instrumental in spreading error? Because error is adverse to human happiness. And on what ground is any piece of secular legislation disapproved? For the same reason—because thought adverse to human happiness. How, then, can it be shown that the state ought to be resisted in the one case and not in the other? Will anyone deliberately assert that if a government demands money from us to aid in *teaching* what we think will produce evil we ought to refuse it, but that if the money is for the purpose of *doing* what we think will produce evil we ought not to refuse it? Yet such is the hopeful proposition which those have to maintain who recognize the right to ignore the state in religious matters but deny it in civil matters.

7. The substance of this chapter once more reminds us of the incongruity between a perfect law and an imperfect state. The practicability of the principle here laid down varies directly as social morality. In a thoroughly vicious community its admission would be productive of anarchy. In a completely virtuous one its admission will be both innocuous and inevitable. Progress toward a condition of social health—a condition, that is, in which the remedial measures of legislation will no longer be needed—is progress toward a condition in which those remedial measures will be cast aside and the authority prescribing them disregarded. The two changes are of necessity co-ordinate. That moral sense whose supremacy will make society harmonious and government unnecessary is the same moral sense which will then make each man assert his freedom even to the extent of ignoring the state—is the same moral sense which, by deterring the majority from coercing the minority, will eventually render government impossible. And as what are merely different manifestations of the same sentiment must bear a constant ratio to each other, the tendency to repudiate governments will increase only at the same rate that governments become needless.

Let not any be alarmed, therefore, at the promulgation of the foregoing doctrine. There are many changes yet to be passed through before it can begin to exercise much influence. Probably a long time will elapse before the right to ignore the state will be generally admitted, even in theory. It will be still longer before it receives legislative recognition. And even then there will be plenty of checks upon the premature exercise of it. A sharp experience will sufficiently instruct those who may too soon abandon legal protection. While, in the majority of men, there is such a love of tried arrangements and so great a dread of experiments that they will probably not act upon this right until long after it is safe to do so.

Mikhail Bakunin (1814–1876 C.E.)

Bakunin was a Russian social theorist who was among the group of anarchists who broke from the Marxists over the issue of the state. Attracted early on to socialism, he later came to the view that Marx's plans would entail state coercion, and he split, with several others, from socialism. Periodically imprisoned and exiled to Siberia, Bakunin combined a critique of the state with a critique of religion, which he saw as twin oppressors of the human spirit.

From God and the State*

... Christianity is precisely the religion *par excellence,* because it exhibits and manifests, to the fullest extent, the very nature and essence of every religious system, which is *the impoverishment, enslavement, and annihilation of humanity for the benefit of divinity.*

God being everything, the real world and man are nothing. God being truth, justice, goodness, beauty, power, and life, man is falsehood, iniquity, evil, ugliness, impotence, and death. God being master, man is the slave. Incapable of finding justice, truth, and eternal life by his own effort, he can attain them only through a divine revelation. But whoever says revelation says revealers, messiahs, prophets, priests, and legislators inspired by God himself; and these, once recognized as the representatives of divinity on earth, as the holy instructors of humanity, chosen by God himself to direct it in the path of salvation, necessarily exercise absolute power. All men owe them passive and unlimited obedience; for against the divine reason there is no human reason, and against the justice of God no terrestrial justice holds. Slaves of God, men must also be slaves of Church and State, *in so far as the State is consecrated by the Church.* This truth Christianity, better than all other religions that exist or have existed, understood, not excepting even the old Oriental religions, which included only distinct and privileged nations, while Christianity aspires to embrace entire humanity; and this truth Roman Catholicism, alone among all the Christian sects, has proclaimed and realized with rigorous logic. That is why Christianity is the absolute religion, the final religion; why the Apostolic and Roman Church is the only consistent, legitimate, and divine church.

With all due respect, then, to the metaphysicians and religious idealists, philosophers, politicians, or poets: *The idea of God implies the abdication of human reason and justice; it is the most decisive negation of human liberty, and necessarily ends in the enslavement of mankind, both in theory and practice.*

Unless, then, we desire the enslavement and degradation of mankind, as the Jesuits desire it, as the *mômiers,* pietists, or Protestant Methodists desire it, we may not, must not make the slightest concession either to the God of theology or to the God of metaphysics. He who, in this mystical alphabet, begins with A will inevitably end with Z; he who desires

---

*An Excerpt.

to worship God must harbor no childish allusions about the matter, but bravely renounce his liberty and humanity.

If God is, man is a slave; now, man can and must be free; then, God does not exist.

I defy anyone whomsoever to avoid this circle; now, therefore, let all choose.

Is it necessary to point out to what extent and in what manner religions debase and corrupt the people? They destroy their reason, the principal instrument of human emancipation, and reduce them to imbecility, the essential condition of their slavery. They dishonor human labor, and make it a sign and source of servitude. They kill the idea and sentiment of human justice, ever tipping the balance to the side of triumphant knaves, privileged objects of divine indulgence. They kill human pride and dignity, protecting only the cringing and humble. They stifle in the heart of nations every feeling of human fraternity, filling it with divine cruelty instead.

All religions are cruel, all founded on blood; for all rest principally on the idea of sacrifice—that is, on the perpetual immolation of humanity to the insatiable vengeance of divinity. In this bloody mystery man is always the victim, and the priest—a man also, but a man privileged by grace—is the divine executioner. That explains why the priests of all religions, the best, the most humane, the gentlest, almost always have at the bottom of their hearts—and, if not in their hearts, in their imaginations, in their minds (and we know the fearful influence of either on the hearts of men)—something cruel and sanguinary.

None know all this better than our illustrious contemporary idealists. They are learned men, who know history by heart; and, as they are at the same time living men, great souls penetrated with a sincere and profound love for the welfare of humanity, they have cursed and branded all these misdeeds, all these crimes of religion with an eloquence unparalleled. They reject with indignation all solidarity with the God of positive religions and with his representatives, past, present, and on earth.

The God whom they adore, or whom they think they adore, is distinguished from the real gods of history precisely in this—that he is not at all a positive god, defined in any way whatever, theologically or even metaphysically. He is neither the supreme being of Robespierre and J. J. Rousseau, nor the pantheistic god of Spinoza, nor even the at once immanent, transcendental, and very equivocal god of Hegel. They take good care not to give him any positive definition whatever, feeling very strongly that any definition would subject him to the dissolving power of criticism. They will not say whether he is a personal or impersonal god, whether he created or did not create the world; they will not even speak of his divine providence. All that might compromise him. They content themselves with saying "God" and nothing more. But, then, what is their God? Not even an idea; it is an aspiration.

It is the generic name of all that seems grand, good, beautiful, noble, human to them. But why, then, do they not say, "Man." Ah! because King William of Prussia and Napoleon III and all their compeers are likewise men: which bothers them very much. Real humanity presents a mixture of all that is most sublime and beautiful with all that is vilest and most monstrous in the world. How do they get over this? Why, they call one *divine* and the other *bestial,* representing divinity and animality as two poles, between which they place humanity. They either will not or cannot understand that these three terms are really but one, and that to separate them is to destroy them.

They are not strong on logic, and one might say that they despise it. That is what distinguishes them from the pantheistical and deistical metaphysicians, and gives their ideas the character of a practical idealism, drawing its inspiration much less from the severe development of a thought than from the experiences, I might almost say the emotions, historical and collective as well as individual, of life. This gives their propaganda an appearance of wealth and vital power, but an appearance only; for life itself becomes sterile when paralyzed by a logical contradiction.

This contradiction lies here: they wish God, and they wish humanity. They persist in connecting two terms which, once separated, can come together again only to destroy each other. They say in a single breath: "God and the liberty of man," "God and the dignity, justice, equality, fraternity, prosperity of men"—regardless of the fatal logic by virtue of which, if God exists, all these things are condemned to non-existence. For, if God is, he is necessarily the eternal, supreme, absolute master, and, if such a master exists, man is a slave; now, if he is a slave, neither justice, nor equality, nor fraternity, nor prosperity are possible for him. In vain, flying in the face of good sense and all the teachings of history, do they represent their God as animated by the tenderest love of human liberty: a master, whoever he may be and however liberal he may desire to show himself, remains none the less always a master. His existence necessarily implies the slavery of all that is beneath him. Therefore, if God existed, only in one way could he serve human liberty—by ceasing to exist.

A jealous lover of human liberty, and deeming it the absolute condition of all that we admire and respect in humanity, I reverse the phrase of Voltaire, and say that, *if God really existed, it would be necessary to abolish him.*

The severe logic that dictates these words is far too evident to require a development of this argument. And it seems to me impossible that the illustrious men, whose names so celebrated and so justly respected I have cited, should not have been struck by it themselves, and should not have perceived the contradiction in which they involve themselves in speaking of God and human liberty at once. To have disregarded it, they must have considered this inconsistency or logical license *practically* necessary to humanity's well-being.

Perhaps, too, while speaking of *liberty* as something very respectable and very dear in their eyes, they give the term a meaning quite different from the conception entertained by us, materialists and Revolutionary Socialists. Indeed, they never speak of it without immediately adding another word, *authority*—a word and a thing which we detest with all our heart.

What is authority? Is it the inevitable power of the natural laws which manifest themselves in the necessary concatenation and succession of phenomena in the physical and social worlds? Indeed, against these laws revolt is not only forbidden—it is even impossible. We may misunderstand them or not know them at all, but we cannot disobey them; because they constitute the basis and fundamental conditions of our existence; they envelop us, penetrate us, regulate all our movements, thoughts, and acts; even when we believe that we disobey them, we only show their omnipotence.

Yes, we are absolutely the slaves of these laws. But in such slavery there is no humiliation, or, rather, it is not slavery at all. For slavery supposes an external master, a legislator outside of him whom he commands, while these laws are not outside of us; they are inherent in us; they constitute our being, our whole being, physically, intellectually, and morally: we live, we breathe, we act, we think, we wish only through these laws. Without them we are nothing, *we are not*. Whence, then, could we derive the power and the wish to rebel against them?

In his relation to natural laws but one liberty is possible to man—that of recognizing and applying them on an ever-extending scale in conformity with the object of collective and individual emancipation or humanization which he pursues. These laws, once recognized, exercise an authority which is never disputed by the mass of men. One must, for instance, be at bottom either a fool or a theologian or at least a metaphysician, jurist, or bourgeois economist to rebel against the law by which twice two make four. One must have faith to imagine that fire will not burn nor water drown, except, indeed, recourse be had to some subterfuge founded in its turn on some other natural law. But these revolts, or, rather, these attempts at or foolish fancies of an impossible revolt, are decidedly the exception; for, in general, it may be said that the mass of men, in their daily lives, acknowledge the government of common sense—that is, of the sum of the natural laws generally recognized—in an almost absolute fashion.

The great misfortune is that a large number of natural laws, already established as such by science, remain unknown to the masses, thanks to the watchfulness of these tutelary governments that exist, as we know, only for the good of the people. There is another difficulty—namely, that the major portion of the natural laws connected with the development of human society, which are quite as necessary, invariable, fatal, as the laws that govern the physical world, have not been duly established and recognized by science itself.

Once they shall have been recognized by science, and then from science, by means of an extensive system of popular education and instruction, shall have passed into the consciousness of all, the question of liberty will be entirely solved. The most stubborn authorities must admit that then there will be no need either of political organization or direction or legislation, three things which, whether they emanate from the will of the sovereign or from the vote of a parliament elected by universal suffrage, and even should they conform to the system of natural laws—which has never been the case and never will be the case—are always equally fatal and hostile to the liberty of the masses from the very fact that they impose upon them a system of external and therefore despotic laws.

The liberty of man consists solely in this: that he obeys natural laws because he has *himself* recognized them as such, and not because they have been externally imposed upon him by any extrinsic will whatever, divine or human, collective or individual.

Suppose a learned academy, composed of the most illustrious representatives of science; suppose this academy charged with legislation for and the organization of society, and that, inspired only by the purest love of truth, it frames none but laws in absolute harmony with the latest discoveries of science. Well, I maintain, for my part, that such legislation and such organization would be a monstrosity, and that for two reasons: first, that human science is always and necessarily imperfect, and that, comparing what it has discovered with what remains to be discovered, we may say that it is still in its cradle. So that were we to try to force the practical life of men, collective as well as individual, into strict and exclusive conformity with the latest data of science, we should condemn society as well as individuals to suffer martyrdom on a bed of Procrustes, which would soon end by dislocating and stifling them, life ever remaining an infinitely greater thing than science.

The second reason is this: a society which should obey legislation emanating from a scientific academy, not because it understood itself the rational character of this legislation (in which case the existence of the academy would become useless), but because this legislation, emanating from the academy, was imposed in the name of a science which it venerated without comprehending—such a society would be a society, not of men, but of brutes. It would be a second edition of those missions in Paraguay which submitted so long to the government of the Jesuits. It would surely and rapidly descend to the lowest stage of idiocy.

But there is still a third reason which would render such a government impossible—namely that a scientific academy invested with a sovereignty, so to speak, absolute, even if it were composed of the most illustrious men, would infallibly and soon end in its own moral and intellectual corruption. Even to-day, with the few privileges allowed them, such is the history of all academies. The greatest scientific genius, from the moment that he becomes an academician, an officially licensed *savant,* inevitably lapses into sluggishness. He loses his spontaneity, his revolutionary hardihood, and that troublesome and savage energy characteristic of the grandest geniuses, ever called to destroy old tottering worlds and lay the foundations of new. He undoubtedly gains in politeness, in utilitarian and practical wisdom, what he loses in power of thought. In a word, he becomes corrupted.

It is the characteristic of privilege and of every privileged position to kill the mind and heart of men. The privileged man, whether politically or economically, is a man depraved in mind and heart. That is a social law which admits of no exception, and is as applicable to entire nations as to classes, corporations, and individuals. It is the law of equality, the supreme condition of liberty and humanity. The principal object of this treatise is precisely to demonstrate this truth in all the manifestations of human life.

A scientific body to which had been confided the government of society would soon end by devoting itself no longer to science at all, but to quite another affair; and that affair, as in the case of all established powers, would be its own eternal perpetuation by rendering the society confided to its care ever more stupid and consequently more in need of its government and direction.

But that which is true of scientific academies is also true of all constituent and legislative assemblies, even those chosen by universal suffrage. In the latter case they may renew their composition, it is true, but this does not prevent the formation in a few years' time of a body of politicians, privileged in fact though not in law, who, devoting themselves exclusively to the direction of the public affairs of a country, finally form a sort of political aristocracy or oligarchy. Witness the United States of America and Switzerland.

Consequently, no external legislation and no authority—one, for that matter, being inseparable from the other, and both tending to the servitude of society and the degradation of the legislators themselves.

Does it follow that I reject all authority? Far from me such a thought. In the matter of boots, I refer to the authority of the bootmaker; concerning houses, canals, or railroads, I consult that of the architect or engineer. For such or such special knowledge I apply to such or such a *savant.* But I allow neither the bootmaker nor the architect nor the *savant* to impose his authority upon me. I listen to them freely and with all the respect merited by their intelligence, their character, their knowledge, reserving always my incontestable right of criticism and censure. I do not content myself with consulting a single authority in any special branch; I consult several; I compare their opinions, and choose that which seems to me the soundest. But I recognize no infallible authority, even in special questions; consequently, whatever respect I may have for the honesty and the sincerity of such or such an individual, I have no absolute faith in any person. Such a faith would be fatal to my reason, to my liberty, and even to the success of my undertakings; it would immediately transform me into a stupid slave, an instrument of the will and interests of others.

If I bow before the authority of the specialists and avow my readiness to follow, to a certain extent and as long as may seem to me necessary, their indications and even their directions, it is because their authority is imposed upon me by no one, neither by men nor by God. Otherwise I would repel them with horror, and bid the devil take their counsels, their directions, and their services, certain that they would make me pay, by the loss of my liberty and self-respect, for such scraps of truth, wrapped in a multitude of lies, as they might give me.

I bow before the authority of special men because it is imposed upon me by my own reason. I am conscious of my inability to grasp, in all its details and positive developments, any very large portion of human knowledge. The greatest intelligence would not be equal to a comprehension of the whole. Thence results, for science as well as for industry, the necessity of the division and association of labor. I receive and I give—such is human life. Each directs and is directed in his turn. Therefore there is no fixed and constant authority, but a continual exchange of mutual, temporary, and, above all, voluntary authority and subordination.

This same reason forbids me, then, to recognize a fixed, constant, and universal authority, because there is no universal man, no man capable of grasping in that wealth of detail, without which the application of science to life is impossible, all the sciences, all the branches of social life. And if such universality could ever be realized in a single man, and if he wished to take advantage thereof to impose his authority upon us, it would be necessary to drive this man out of society, because his authority would inevitably reduce all the others to slavery and imbecility. I do not think that society ought to maltreat men of genius as it has done hitherto; but neither do I think it should indulge them too far, still less accord them any privileges or exclusive rights whatsoever; and that for three reasons: first, because it would often mistake a charlatan for a man of genius; second, because, through such a system of privileges, it might transform into a charlatan even a real man of genius, demoralize him, and degrade him; and, finally, because it would establish a master over itself.

To sum up. We recognize, then, the absolute authority of science, because the sole object of science is the mental reproduction, as well-considered and systematic as possible, of the natural laws inherent in the material, intellectual, and moral life of both the physical and the social worlds, these two worlds constituting, in fact, but one and the same natural world. Outside of this only legitimate authority, legitimate because rational and in harmony with human liberty, we declare all other authorities false, arbitrary and fatal.

We recognize the absolute authority of science, but we reject the infallibility and universality of the *savant*. In our church—if I may be permitted to use for a moment an expression which I so detest: Church and State are my two *bêtes noires*—in our church, as in the Protestant church, we have a chief, an invisible Christ, science; and, like the Protestants, more logical even than the Protestants, we will suffer neither pope, nor council, nor conclaves of infallible cardinals, nor bishops, nor even priests. Our Christ differs from the Protestant and Christian Christ in this—that the latter is a personal being, ours impersonal; the Christian Christ, already completed in an eternal past, presents himself as a perfect being, while the completion and perfection of our Christ, science, are ever in the future: which is equivalent to saying that they will never be realized. Therefore, in recognizing *absolute science* as the only absolute authority, we in no way compromise our liberty.

I mean by the words "absolute science," the truly universal science which would reproduce ideally, to its fullest extent and in all its infinite detail, the universe, the system or co-ordination of all the natural laws manifested by the incessant development of the world. It is evident that such a science, the sublime object of all the efforts of the human mind, will never be fully and absolutely realized. Our Christ, then, will remain eternally unfinished, which must considerably take down the pride of his licensed representatives among us. Against that God the Son in whose name they assume to impose upon us their insolent and pedantic authority, we appeal to God the Father, who is the real world, real life, of which he (the Son) is only a too imperfect expression, whilst we real beings, living, working, struggling, loving, aspiring, enjoying, and suffering, are its immediate representatives.

But, while rejecting the absolute, universal, and infallible authority of men of science, we willingly bow before the respectable, although relative, quite temporary, and very restricted authority of the representatives of special sciences, asking nothing better than to consult them by turns, and very grateful for such precious information as they may extend to us, on condition of their willingness to receive from us on occasions when, and concerning matters about which, we are more learned than they. In general, we ask nothing better than to see men endowed with great knowledge, great experience, great minds, and, above all, great hearts, exercise over us a natural and legitimate influence, freely accepted, and never imposed in the name of any official authority whatsoever, celestial or terrestrial. We accept all natural authorities and all influences of fact, but none of right; for every authority or every influence of right, officially imposed as such, becoming directly an oppression and a falsehood, would inevitably impose upon us, as I believe I have sufficiently shown, slavery and absurdity.

In a word, we reject all legislation, all authority, and all privileged, licensed, official, and legal influence, even though arising from universal suffrage, convinced that it can turn only to the advantage of a dominant minority of exploiters against the interests of the immense majority in subjection to them.

This is the sense in which we are really Anarchists. . . .

Part IV

Contemporary Political Philosophy

The twentieth century has seen the political triumph of liberal democracies over nations committed to such theories as fascism, socialism, and communism. Yet those theories—sometimes refigured or redesigned—remain active parts of the intellectual landscape of political philosophy. Indeed, most extant regimes incorporate elements of all of these theories. Political philosophy, of course, continues to concern itself with questions about the nature of justice, the proper relationship between the individual and society, and the justification and scope of political authority. Further explorations into the nature and extent of equality for women occupy a significant place. Radical theories about rights and their scope, welfare, power, community, and other concepts of political relevance are being discussed.

This chapter exhibits contemporary work in liberalism, socialism, libertarianism, anarchism, and feminism, as well as other sorts of inquiries. The debates continue.

John Dewey (1859–1952 C.E.)

This American philosopher did not invent the Dewey decimal library system, but did bring together the pragmatist theories of earlier Americans C. S. Peirce and William James, bringing this approach to bear on logical analysis, educational theory, and ethics. He studied under Peirce at the Johns Hopkins University. Later he was a colleague of G. H. Mead at the University of Michigan. He taught at the University of Chicago and at Columbia University. The following selection, from *Ethics* (1932), raises issues that continue to be controversial in political philosophy.

From Ethics*

3. If Capitalism Is to Continue

The extreme individualism of *laissez faire*, with competition as the only regulator of the economic process, has been shown to be no longer tolerable in present conditions. Just as the congested traffic of a modern city demands a traffic officer to regulate the streams of rushing automobiles and to protect pedestrians—so the necessities of public welfare, and of the large numbers who are economically in the status of pedestrians, require the supremacy of an authority which aims at justice and not at profits; and which interprets justice, not merely as keeping order while the contestants fight it out, but as revising the rules of the contest in the interest of the common good when this is made necessary by the changed conditions of industrial life.

The issue is then between a modified capitalism—in which the democratic principle, embodied in our political and educational systems, shall have increasing recognition, and in which liberty, efficiency, and justice shall be combined so far as possible—as over against policies of a more radical character, such as are on trial in Russia and Italy.

In another aspect the issue is one between the democratic principle of equality, which has more and more gained recognition in the modern world in political, religious, and educational life; and the principle of inequality which formerly obtained in the three areas just mentioned, and which now seems to be essential to efficiency in economic life.

Perhaps the deepest reason for distrust in Western Europe, and particularly in the United States, of either the Russian or the Fascist system is unwillingness to be subject to *absolute control of a single master*. In Russia this master is an economic class; in Italy it is a nationalist group. Both profess to be acting for the general welfare, but the fact remains that a single master is in absolute control. In a system such as obtains in Western Europe and the United States, the masters of the economic system and those of the political system form two distinct groups selected on different principles. Economic leaders are chosen principally by competition in the market. This selects men of certain types of ability,

---

*An Excerpt.

and gives them wide scope for the exercise of that ability to organize which is so largely responsible for the efficiency of modern business and industry. Leaders in the political sphere are selected by votes on the basis of their ability to win public approval. They represent a distinctly different phase of society, and a distinctly different interest from that represented by economic leaders. Perhaps the interests of the public are safer when control is thus divided than when it is concentrated in one hand.

It is probably safe to assume that in the immediate future a modified capitalism is likely to continue. The present owners of the vast proportion of the national wealth in Western Europe and America, even though a small minority of the total population, wield a power and influence proportionate to their wealth rather than to their numbers. The agricultural group, although in the United States the least prosperous as measured by income (the per capita income of those engaged in agriculture for 1926 was estimated by Professor Copeland to be $265.00, as contrasted with the average income of the whole population for that same year estimated at $750.00), nevertheless have a relatively large investment in land and are therefore favorable to private property, which is one of the fundamentals of the existing system. The industrial workers are the class which might be supposed to be most inclined toward change. In European countries this class has been largely favorable to a socialistic trend, although for the most part committed to constitutional and legal methods of change toward State control, rather than to a violent social revolution. In the United States, however, the American Federation of Labor has been strongly opposed to socialism. There has been a widespread feeling among industrial workers that it is a more prudent and wiser policy to give a free hand to owners and employers in developing improved methods of production, distribution, and selling of goods; and to concentrate efforts rather upon obtaining as large a share as possible of the increasingly profitable returns from such efficient industry. In other words, it may be better to let the capitalist make money and to depend upon coming in on an increasing share of the income, than to take the risks of making a mess of things if either workmen themselves or the State should displace the capitalist in ownership and control of the productive, distributing, and financial machinery.

A further and perhaps the main reason why economic socialism has as yet made little headway in the United States is the great and liberal scale on which public education has been conceived and measurably carried out in the United States. The aim, as stated by the late President Angell of the University of Michigan, that every child might see a path from the door of his home to the state university, has been generously furthered, particularly in the newer states. And despite the expressed fears of some, that too many are seeking higher education, it is not likely that the public system will close its doors to its young people.

If then the present economic system is likely to continue, it is all the more important to consider how some of its worst abuses, wastes, injustices, may be remedied at least partially. We have already noted six points at which organized society has interfered with the extreme individualistic program based on private property, free enterprise, free contract, and free competition. Some of these measures—notably factory laws, stabilization of finance and to some extent of public utility charges, the income tax—have marked progress. Others such as the Sherman Act have been of doubtful value. It is moreover evident that though for certain ends we may properly rely upon law and public administration, there are other ends which can be gained only through education and a change of attitude both in producers and in consumers. We may roughly divide the field into (1) problems of increasing production and decreasing waste; (2) problems of security; (3) problems of protecting workmen and especially women and children against dangerous processes and machinery, against excessive hours, fatigue, and unsanitary conditions; (4) problems of improving the wisdom and good taste of consumers of goods, and of raising standards for recreation, as contrasted with commercialized standards; (5) problems of juster distribution of the enormous gains in economic processes—juster both as measured by service to the community, and as measured by the requirements of a functional society.

4. Improvements Needed

1. Increasing production and decreasing waste. Increasing production is largely an engineering problem. Great strides have been made in this direction. A constantly increasing ratio of power—hydraulic, steam, electric—available through tapping new sources of supply and through its more efficient utilization, constantly improved organization, and in many cases better cooperation between management and workmen, have resulted in a rising rate of efficiency. The profit motive is of course enlisted toward this end. It is not wholly an engineering problem in the ordinary sense of the term, because the willingness of workmen to cooperate in increased production, is dependent in part upon their expectation of sharing in the returns created by this cooperation. Yet if we take engineering in the most inclusive sense this may well comprise such a consideration of the human factor as will lead to juster distribution.

Prevention of waste might also be thought to be an engineering problem. As regards methods, it is such. Extraordinary savings have been made in electric lighting, in the generation of power from steam, in the means of transportation. And these economies have resulted in lowering of costs, in preventing waste of coal, and in many cases in the lowering of prices to consumers, and thus to a wider market. But the engineer under capitalism does not always have a free hand. Whether he is permitted to save or not depends on whether it is more profitable to save or to waste. In the case of the management of forests and the reforestation of cut-over areas, it has thus far seemed more profitable to waste than to save or reforest. European countries have been successful in keeping forests and their management under public ownership and control. The Federal government still has a considerable area under the charge of a national forestry system, and a few experiments have been made in state or municipal forestry. Even in Massachusetts, where the courts have been extremely conservative in protecting private business from public competition, towns are allowed to own forests. In the extraction of oil a recent movement of owners to cooperate in reducing waste has promise. But natural gas has for the most part been recklessly wasted.

2. A further field in which up to the present time the engineer has been unable to prevent waste is that of unemployment. In this case his inability is not due directly to the profit motive, because the recurring periods of depression in industry and business are as yet imperfectly understood. Government supervision of banking has indeed reduced the "money panics" which private management was utterly incapable to prevent. But the business cycle is still not under control. Certain shrewd and powerful individuals may very likely profit by the opportunity to buy back at a low price the securities which at the crest of a prosperity wave they sold to the trustful public. Yet they cannot be charged with total responsibility for depressions. The heaviest burden rests upon the shoulders of those who are thrown out of employment, and who never had sufficient margin of income over expense to lay by for the rainy day. The American plan has been to let them look out for themselves, and to let their families suffer except as relieved by charity. Europe has provided for the risks of unemployment, as well as for those of accident, illness, and old age. Mr. Rubinow says:

> Every period of unemployment in this country [the United States] results in increased mendicancy, increased applications to charitable organizations, both private and public, increased crime, disease, and general demoralization, a sum total of social results which surely is much graver than the presumed demoralizing effect of the English so-called dole system.

And a measure for old age has been adopted by seventeen state legislatures. But the very fact that American workmen have been able to be more provident than those of Europe has delayed measures to remove the manifest injustice of allowing the calamity of unemployment to rest upon those least able to bear it. Until scientists and engineers have discovered the way to prevent unemployment and its wastes, social insurance or some form of large public works undertaken by the state is the only practicable remedy. It is absurd to object to a national plan for mitigating suffering and injustice on the ground that it was first tried in Europe. The argument that social insurance is "paternalistic" or "socialistic" or "German" is convenient hokum.

3. The principle that life and health should not be sacrificed to profits is seldom denied openly. Much has been done both by private initiative and by public control to safeguard workmen, and especially women and children. Much, however, still remains to be done. Since the Great War some of the states have undertaken to rehabilitate and reeducate those crippled in industry, following the example of the nation in rehabilitating those crippled in war. The general reaction against liberal and humanitarian activities on the part of government, which was manifest in many directions, has apparently postponed any successful attempt to establish a national protection of children against premature employment. Nevertheless it may be doubted whether state action will be adequate. In the meantime, however, those who live in states which have no protection against child labor, or inadequate protection, may work to improve local standards. The whole movement for labor legislation is scarcely more than a generation old in the United States, and it is premature to despair of further progress. Some form of public health insurance is probably also necessary to provide adequate medical and hospital service for those with small incomes.

4. Improvement of taste on the part of consumers, and of better standards of goods. If problems under (1) were primarily for the engineer, and problems under (2) primarily for government, problems of improving the taste of consumers and the standards of goods are primarily problems of education. The profit motive is not adequate as we have already seen. This has worked well in the case of automobiles, for these have improved in both beauty and utility.

On the other hand, this motive has failed almost utterly in providing dwellings of better quality. No doubt modern dwellings are better equipped as to plumbing, lighting, and heating, than those available a generation ago. But the congestion of cities, the hideous surroundings of the ordinary workingman's home which is near a factory or a railroad, the almost universal practice under the profit motive of covering the ground in cities with multiple dwellings, leaving no space for the play of children or for the recreation of adults, except in so far as the city itself has stepped in to provide parks and playgrounds—these show the profit motive nearly at its worst. As engineers are limited by profits, so architects who would like to plan generously are restricted by rents and profits. Courts do not allow the government to supply more healthful dwellings, and hence the ultimate remedy appears to be in the general education of the consumer to demand a different type of dwelling. The sphere of government is limited to preventing, under housing and zoning laws, the more outrageous violations of sanitation and good taste, and to the positive provision of free spaces for public parks and playgrounds. The newer parts of the country have been able to secure far more adequate space for children's play, than the older portions in which it was assumed that no provision need be made by the public. Adulteration of foods is another instance in which the profit motive cannot be trusted. Law in this case has stopped some of the worst practices in the case of foods. It is, however, impossible to prevent by law all kinds of trickery and deception.

Education, with the increased application of scientific standards for quality, is indispensable. Above all, it is education to which we must look for improvement in standards of art, literature, and recreation. Legislation may prevent some of those practices of commercial recreation, and commercial art and literature, which are most shocking to morality. But it cannot insure a more healthful taste. In this field, as distinguished from that of the automobile, the greater profit seems to lie in the worse products. The moving pictures, the jazz music, the comic strips, and various other forms of popular entertainment, are not an object of pride to those who have learned to know good art, good music, and good literature. A civilization, in which the average man spends his day in a factory and his evening at a movie, has still a long way to go.

5. Just distribution. As already noted, the conception of just distribution may be approached in several ways. We found it extremely difficult and indeed impossible to say how much each contributes, and hence that it is impracticable to determine how much each deserves to receive from the great pool into which go the accumulated knowledge and skill of past generations, the genius of the discoverer and inventor, the patient labors of the scientist, the order and tranquillity and social standards so necessary for peaceful production, and the taste and sensitiveness to color, form, and sound which are our in-heritage from the past. The only promising approach is rather by the path which Plato suggested when he asked what was necessary for a good society. On behalf of inequality in wealth it may be argued that more capital will be available for business enterprise if wealth is distributed as at present, and it may be granted that in the past this has in many if not in all cases been true. If we take the illustration of dividing a thousand dollars among one hundred men it is probable that if each received $10.00 he would expend it on some present need; whereas if ninety men received $1.00 each, and if nine more received $40.00 each, and the one hundredth man received the balance of $550.00, it is probable that the last named man would be inclined to use at least a part of the $550.00 for some new venture. But at present we recognize that this may be overdone. If the great mass have only sufficient income to maintain a meager standard of living, the market for goods will be correspondingly limited. The rich man cannot consume indefinitely. The mass of men provide the great market. It is by the constant education of greater and greater numbers to use more and better goods that the market is widened and sustained. The movement, which some far-sighted employers have initiated, of paying better wages in order to increase the number of consumers is commended by economists as tending in a wise direction.

Unfortunately the case of the farmer is more difficult. There are many advantages from the point of view of the general welfare in the continuance of small holdings and independent farms. On the other hand, it may be that it will prove impossible to resist the trend toward larger units, which has gone so far in the industrial world. In the meantime the farmer receives low prices for his goods, and pays high prices for what he must buy; while if he needs help he must compete with the wages paid by industry.

Efforts toward a juster distribution of gains need not be limited to better wages. Society through public agencies is constantly doing more for its members. The outstanding example is of course the system of public education. Most communities provide books as well as buildings and teachers. Public libraries, public parks and playgrounds, have done much to counteract the evils of city congestion. Such inventions as the automobile and the radio have made available to the multitude the advances of science. Generous gifts to hospitals and education, and endowments for research in all lines, are continually making better standards of life possible.

It is sometimes objected that such activities by the public tend to limit private enterprise, with the self-help and independence which has been so important a factor in modern society. On the other hand, it is more probable that the opening of wider doors, to all sorts and conditions of men, by education and acquaintance with the finer things of life, will more than even the balance.

Looking at our economic life in the light of what we have learned from Hebrew and Greek, and from modern conceptions of scientific method and fuller life—we may say that a good society should aim to secure justice, should keep a right perspective as to the various goods which are desirable, should take account of all the human relations, and should move toward raising all men toward that measure of equality and democracy which has been the ideal and aspiration not only of the finer spirits but of increasing multitudes in the modern world.

5. A Distorted Perspective

We have considered some of the merits and defects of our present order with respect to justice, liberty, and equality. In conclusion, we note what is perhaps the most serious question of all, namely, that of the proper perspective. If the economic dominates life—and if the economic order relies chiefly upon the profit motive as distinguished from the motive of professional excellence, i.e., craftsmanship, and from the functional motive of giving a fair return for what is received—there is danger that a part of life, which should be subordinate or at most coordinate with other interests and values, may become supreme. It is as true now as when the words were uttered that life is more than meat. And when wealth is made a chief if not the sole interest, some of the precious and finer things of life—love, justice, knowledge, beauty—are liable to be displaced. Referring to the unlimited exercise of powers in the acquisition of wealth, and the conception that to this pursuit there is no limit other than that which individuals think advisable, Mr. Tawney says:

> Under the impulse of such ideas men do not become religious or wise or artistic; for religion and wisdom and art imply the acceptance of limitations. But they become powerful and rich.

It is by no means intended that all men who engage in business and industry become absorbed wholly in the pursuit of wealth. Every one knows conspicuous instances which would refute such a judgment. The point which it is intended to urge is that exclusive reliance upon the profit motive and upon the supreme importance of wealth tends to distort the proper perspective for life as a whole.

Benito Mussolini (1883–1945 C.E.)

Mussolini was a political activist and a journalist before he became a political leader. His movement, known as Fascism, grew to such popularity in the disarray following the First World War that he was able to become dictator in 1922. Initially supported by the Italian public, he lost favor with them and was eventually assassinated following his disastrous alliance with Hitler's Germany in the Second World War. He was also one of the few leaders of a Fascist society who produced some serious theoretical work on the nature of such regimes, a sample of which is presented here.

From Fascism: Doctrine and Institutions*

Like all sound political conceptions, Fascism is action and it is thought; action in which doctrine is immanent, and doctrine arising from a given system of historical forces in which it is inserted, and working on them from within. It has therefore a form correlated to contingencies of time and space; but it has also an ideal content which makes it an expression of truth in the higher region of the history of thought. There is no way of exercising a spiritual influence in the world as a human will dominating the will of others, unless one has a conception both of the transient and the specific reality on which that action is to be exercised, and of the permanent and universal reality in which the transient dwells and has its being. To know men one must know man; and to know man one must be acquainted with reality and its laws. There can be no conception of the State which is not fundamentally a conception of life: philosophy or intuition, system of ideas evolving within the framework of logic or concentrated in a vision or a faith, but always, at least potentially, an organic conception of the world.

Thus many of the practical expressions of Fascism—such as party organisation, system of education, discipline—can only be understood when considered in relation to its general attitude toward life. A spiritual attitude. Fascism sees in the world not only those superficial, material aspects in which man appears as an individual, standing by himself, self-centred, subject to natural law which instinctively urges him toward a life of selfish momentary pleasure; it sees not only the individual but the nation and the country; individuals and generations bound together by a moral law, with common traditions and a mission which suppressing the instinct for life closed in a brief circle of pleasure, builds up a higher life, founded on duty, a life free from the limitations of time and space, in which the individual, by self-sacrifice, the renunciation of self-interest, by death itself, can achieve that purely spiritual existence in which his value as a man consists.

The conception is therefore a spiritual one, arising from the general reaction of the century against the flacid materialistic positivism of the XIXth century. Anti-positivistic but positive; neither sceptical nor agnostic; neither pessimistic nor supinely optimistic as

---

*An Excerpt.

are, generally speaking, the doctrines (all negative) which place the centre of life outside man; whereas, by the exercise of his free will, man can and must create his own world.

Fascism wants man to be active and to engage in action with all his energies; it wants him to be manfully aware of the difficulties besetting him and ready to face them. It conceives of life as a struggle in which it behoves a man to win for himself a really worthy place, first of all by fitting himself (physically, morally, intellectually) to become the implement required for winning it. As for the individual, so for the nation, and so for mankind. Hence the high value of culture in all its forms (artistic, religious, scientific), and the outstanding importance of education. Hence also the essential value of work, by which man subjugates nature and creates the human world (economic, political, ethical, intellectual).

This positive conception of life is obviously an ethical one. It invests the whole field of reality as well as the human activities which master it. No action is exempt from moral judgement; no activity can be despoiled of the value which a moral purpose confers on all things. Therefore life, as conceived of by the Fascist, is serious, austere, religious; all its manifestations are poised in a world sustained by moral forces and subject to spiritual responsibilities. The Fascist disdains an "easy" life.

The Fascist conception of life is a religious one, in which man is viewed in his immanent relation to a higher law, endowed with an objective will transcending the individual and raising him to conscious membership of a spiritual society. Those who perceive nothing beyond opportunistic considerations in the religious policy of the Fascist régime fail to realise that Fascism is not only a system of government but also and above all a system of thought.

In the Fascist conception of history, man is man only by virtue of the spiritual process to which he contributes as a member of the family, the social group, the nation, and in function of history to which all nations bring their contribution. Hence the great value of tradition in records, in language, in customs, in the rules of social life. Outside history man is a nonentity. Fascism is therefore opposed to all individualistic abstractions based on eighteenth century materialism. . . . It does not believe in the possibility of "happiness" on earth as conceived by the economistic literature of the XVIIIth century, and it therefore rejects the teleological notion that at some future time the human family will secure a final settlement of all its difficulties. This notion runs counter to experience which teaches that life is in continual flux and in process of evolution. In politics Fascism aims at realism; in practice it desires to deal only with those problems which are the spontaneous product of historic conditions and which find or suggest their own solutions. Only by entering in to the process of reality and taking possession of the forces at work within it, can man act on man and on nature.

Anti-individualistic, the Fascist conception of life stresses the importance of the State and accepts the individual only in so far as his interests coincide with those of the State, which stands for the conscience and the universal will of man as a historic entity. It is opposed to classical liberalism which arose as a reaction to absolutism and exhausted its historical function when the State became the expression of the conscience and will of the people. Liberalism denied the State in the name of the individual; Fascism reasserts the rights of the State as expressing the real essence of the individual. And if liberty is to be the attribute of living men and not of abstract dummies invented by individualistic liberalism, then Fascism stands for liberty, and for the only liberty worth having, the liberty of the State and of the individual within the State. The Fascist conception of the State is all-embracing; outside of it no human or spiritual values can exist, much less have value. Thus understood, Fascism, is totalitarian, and the Fascist State—a synthesis and a unit inclusive of all values—interprets, develops, and potentiates the whole life of a people.

No individuals or groups (political parties, cultural associations, economic unions, social classes) outside the State. Fascism is therefore opposed to Socialism to which unity within the State (which amalgamates classes into a single economic and ethical reality) is unknown, and which sees in history nothing but the class struggle. Fascism is likewise opposed to trade-unionism as a class weapon. But when brought within the orbit of the State, Fascism recognises the real needs which gave rise to socialism and trade-unionism, giving them due weight in the guild or corporative system in which divergent interests are coordinated and harmonised in the unity of the State.

Grouped according to their several interests, individuals form classes; they form trade-unions when organised according to their several economic activities; but first and foremost they form the State, which is no mere matter of numbers, the sum of the individuals forming the majority. Fascism is therefore opposed to that form of democracy which equates a nation to the majority, lowering it to the level of the largest number; but it is the purest form of democracy if the nation be considered—as it should be—from the point of view of quality rather than quantity, as an idea, the mightiest because the most ethical, the most coherent, the truest, expressing itself in a people as the conscience and will of the few, if not, indeed, of one, and ending to express itself in the conscience and the will of the mass, of the whole group ethnically moulded by natural and historical conditions into a nation, advancing, as one conscience and one will, along the self-same line of development and spiritual formation. Not a race, nor a geographically defined region, but a people, historically perpetuating itself; a multitude unified by an idea and imbued with the will to live, the will to power, self-consciousness, personality.

In so far as it is embodied in a State, this higher personality becomes a nation. It is not the nation which generates the State; that is an antiquated naturalistic concept which afforded a basis for XIXth century publicity in favor of national governments. Rather is it the State which creates the nation, conferring volition and therefore real life on a people made aware of their moral unity.

The right to national independence does not arise from any merely literary and idealistic form of self-consciousness; still less from a more or less passive and unconscious *de facto* situation, but from an active, self-conscious, political will expressing itself in action and ready to prove its rights. It arises, in short, from the existence, at least *in fieri*, of a State. Indeed, it is the State which, as the expression of a universal ethical will, creates the right to national independence.

A nation, as expressed in the State, is a living, ethical entity only in so far as it is progressive. Inactivity is death. Therefore the State is not only Authority which governs and confers legal form and spiritual value on individual wills, but it is also Power which makes its will felt and respected beyond its own frontiers, thus affording practical proof of the universal character of the decisions necessary to ensure its development. This implies organisation and expansion, potential if not actual. Thus the State equates itself to the will of man, whose development cannot be checked by obstacles and which, by achieving self-expression, demonstrates its own infinity.

The Fascist State, as a higher and more powerful expression of personality, is a force, but a spiritual one. It sums up all the manifestations of the moral and intellectual life of man. Its functions cannot therefore be limited to those of enforcing order and keeping the peace, as the liberal doctrine had it. It is no mere mechanical device for defining the sphere within which the individual may duly exercise his supposed rights. The Fascist State is an inwardly accepted standard and rule of conduct, a discipline of the whole person; it permeates the will no less than the intellect. It stands for a principle which becomes the central motive of man as a member of civilised society, sinking deep down into his personality; it dwells in the heart of the man of action and of the thinker, of the artist and of the man of science: soul of the soul.

Fascism, in short, is not only a law-giver and a founder of institutions, but an educator and a promoter of spiritual life. It aims at refashioning not only the forms of life but their content—man, his character, and his faith. To achieve this purpose it enforces discipline and uses authority, entering into the soul and ruling with undisputed sway. . . .

Vladimir Ilich Lenin (1870–1924 C.E.)

Lenin was a Russian political theorist who became a revolutionary leader. After the Bolshevik victory in 1917, he became leader of the governing faction, eventually becoming the head of the Communist party, which ruled Russia as part of the Soviet Union. Lenin's theoretical contributions are as important as his actual participation, as he expanded Marxist doctrine in politically useful ways. He also produced analytical writings on economic systems and world politics.

From On Soviet Socialist Democracy*

"The Immediate Tasks of the Soviet Government"

The resolution adopted by the recent Moscow Congress of Soviets advanced as the primary task of the moment the establishment of a "harmonious organization," and the tightening of discipline. Everyone now readily "votes for" and "subscribes to" resolutions of this kind; but usually people do not think over the fact that the application of such resolutions calls for coercion—coercion precisely in the form of dictatorship. And yet it would be extremely stupid and absurdly utopian to assume that the transition from capitalism to socialism is possible without coercion and without dictatorship. Marx's theory very definitely opposed this petty-bourgeois-democratic and anarchist absurdity long ago. And Russia of 1917-18 confirms the correctness of Marx's theory in this respect so strikingly, palpably and imposingly that only those who are hopelessly dull or who have obstinately decided to turn their backs on the truth can be under any misapprehension concerning this. Either the dictatorship of Kornilov (if we take him as the Russian type of bourgeois Cavaignac), or the dictatorship of the proletariat—any other choice is out of the question for a country which is developing at an extremely rapid rate with extremely sharp turns and amidst desperate ruin created by one of the most horrible wars in history. Every solution that offers a middle path is either a deception of the people by the bourgeoisie—. . . who chatter about the unity of democracy, the dictatorship of democracy, the general democratic front, and similar nonsense. Those whom even the progress of the Russian Revolution of 1917-18 has not taught that a middle course is impossible, must be given up for lost.

On the other hand, it is not difficult to see that during every transition from capitalism to socialism, dictatorship is necessary for two main reasons, or along two main channels. Firstly, capitalism cannot be defeated and eradicated without the ruthless suppression of the resistance of the exploiters, who cannot at once be deprived of their wealth, of their advantages of organization and knowledge, and consequently for a fairly long period will inevitably try to overthrow the hated rule of the poor; secondly, every great revolution, and a socialist revolution in particular, even if there is no external war,

*An Excerpt.

is inconceivable without internal war, i.e., civil war, which is even more devastating than external war, and involves thousands and millions of cases of wavering and desertion from one side to another, implies a state of extreme indefiniteness, lack of equilibrium and chaos. And of course, all the elements of disintegration of the old society, which are inevitably very numerous and connected mainly with the petty bourgeoisie (because it is the petty bourgeoisie that every war and every crisis ruins and destroys first), are bound to "reveal themselves" during such a profound revolution. And these elements of disintegration *cannot* "reveal themselves" otherwise than in an increase of crime, hooliganism, corruption, profiteering and outrages of every kind. To put these down requires time and *requires an iron hand.*

There has not been a single great revolution in history in which the people did not instinctively realize this and did not show salutary firmness by shooting thieves on the spot. The misfortune of previous revolutions was that the revolutionary enthusiasm of the people, which sustained them in their state of tension and gave them the strength to suppress ruthlessly the elements of disintegration, did not last long. The social, i.e., the class, reason for this instability of the revolutionary enthusiasm of the people was the weakness of the proletariat, which alone is able (if it is sufficiently numerous, class-conscious and disciplined) to win over to its side the majority of the working and exploited people (the majority of the poor, to speak more simply and popularly) and retain power sufficiently long to suppress completely all the exploiters as well as all the elements of disintegration.

It was this historical experience of all revolutions, it was this world-historic—economic and political—lesson that Marx summed up when he gave his short, sharp, concise and expressive formula: dictatorship of the proletariat. And the fact that the Russian-revolution has been correct in its approach to this world-historic task *has been proved* by the victorious progress of the Soviet form of organization among all the peoples and tongues of Russia. For Soviet power is nothing but an organizational form of the dictatorship of the proletariat, the dictatorship of the advanced class, which raises to a new democracy and to independent participation in the administration of the state tens upon tens of millions of working and exploited people, who by their own experience learn to regard the disciplined and class-conscious vanguard of the proletariat as their most reliable leader.

Dictatorship, however, is a big word, and big words should not be thrown about carelessly. Dictatorship is iron rule, government that is revolutionary bold, swift and ruthless in suppressing both exploiters and hooligans. But our government is excessively mild, very often it resembles jelly more than iron. . . . The nearer we approach the complete military suppression of the bourgeoisie, the more dangerous does the element of petty-bourgeois anarchy become. And the fight against this element cannot be waged solely with the aid of propaganda and agitation, solely by organizing competition and by selecting organizers. The struggle must also be waged by means of coercion. . . .

It is not yet sufficiently realized that the courts are an organ which enlists precisely the poor, every one of them, in the work of state administration (for the work of the courts is one of the functions of state administration), that the courts are an *organ of the power* of the proletariat and of the poor peasants, that the courts are an instrument *for inculcating discipline.* There is not yet sufficient appreciation of the simple and obvious fact that if the principal misfortunes of Russia at the present time are hunger and unemployment, these misfortunes cannot be overcome by spurts, but only by comprehensive, all-embracing, country-wide organization and discipline in order to increase the output of bread for the people and bread for industry (fuel), to transport these in good time to the places where they are required, and to distribute them properly; and it is not fully appreciated that, consequently, it is *those* who violate labour discipline at any factory, in any undertaking, in any matter, who are *responsible* for the sufferings caused by the famine and unemployment, that we must know how to find the guilty ones, to bring them to trial and ruthlessly punish them. Where the petty-bourgeois anarchy against which we must now wage a most persistent struggle makes itself felt is in the failure to appreciate the economic and political connection between famine and unemployment, on the one hand, and general laxity in matters of organization and discipline, on the other. . . .

Here and there, among Left Socialist-Revolutionaries, a positively hooligan agitation, i.e., agitation appealing to the base instincts and to the small proprietor's urge to "grab all he can," has been developed against the dictatorship decree. The question has become one of really enormous significance. Firstly, the question of principle, namely, is the appointment of individuals, dictators with unlimited powers, in general compatible with the fundamental principles of Soviet government? Secondly, what relation has this case—this precedent, if you will—to the special tasks of government in the present concrete situation? We must deal very thoroughly with both these questions.

That in the history of revolutionary movements the dictatorship of individuals was very often the expression, the vehicle, the channel of the dictatorship of the revolutionary classes has been shown by the irrefutable experience of history. Undoubtedly, the dictatorship of individuals was compatible with bourgeois democracy. On this point, however, the bourgeois denigrators of the Soviet system, as well as their petty-bourgeois henchmen, always display sleight of hand: on the one hand, they declare the Soviet system to be something absurd, anarchistic and savage, and carefully pass over in silence all our historical examples and theoretical arguments which prove that the Soviets are a higher form of democracy, and what is more, the beginning of a *socialist* form of democracy; on the other hand, they demand of us a higher democracy than bourgeois democracy and say: personal dictatorship is absolutely incompatible with your, Bolshevik (i.e., not bourgeois, *but socialist,* Soviet democracy.

These are exceedingly poor arguments. If we are not anarchists, we must admit that the state, *that is, coercion,* is necessary for the transition from capitalism to socialism. The form of coercion is determined by the degree of development of the given revolutionary class, and also by special circumstances, such as, for example, the legacy of a long and reactionary war and the forms of resistance put up by the bourgeoisie and the petty bourgeoisie. There is, therefore, absolutely *no* contradiction in principle between Soviet (*that is,* socialist) democracy and the exercise of dictatorial powers by individuals. The difference between proletarian dictatorship and bourgeois dictatorship is that the former strikes at the exploiting minority in the interests of the exploited majority, and that it is exercised—*also through individuals*—not only by the working and exploited people, but also by organizations which are built in such a way as to rouse these people to history-making activity. (The Soviet organizations are organizations of this kind.)

In regard to the second question, concerning the significance of individual dictatorial powers from the point of view of the specific tasks of the present moment, it must be said that large-scale machine industry—which is precisely the material source, the productive source, the foundation of socialism—calls for absolute and strict *unity of will*, which directs the joint labours of hundreds, thousands and tens of thousands of people. The technical, economic and historical necessity of this is obvious, and all those who have thought about socialism have always regarded it as one of the conditions of socialism. But how can strict unity of will be ensured? By thousands subordinating their will to the will of one.

Given ideal class-consciousness and discipline on the part of those participating in the common work, this subordination would be something like the mild leadership of a conductor of an orchestra. It may assume the sharp forms of a dictatorship if ideal discipline and class-consciousness are lacking. But be that as it may, *unquestioning subordination* to a single will is absolutely necessary for the success of processes organized on the pattern of large-scale machine industry. . . .

We have successfully fulfilled the first task of the revolution; we have seen how the mass of working people evolved in themselves the fundamental condition for its success: they united their efforts against the exploiters in order to overthrow them. . . .

We have successfully fulfilled the second task of the revolution: to awaken, to raise those very "lower ranks" of society whom the exploiters had pushed down, and who only after October 25, 1917, obtained complete freedom to overthrow the exploiters and to begin to take stock of things and arrange life in their own way. The airing of questions at public meetings by the most oppressed and downtrodden, by the least educated mass of working people, their coming over to the side of the Bolsheviks, their setting up everywhere of their own Soviet organizations—this was the second great stage of the revolution.

The third stage is now beginning. We must consolidate what we ourselves have won, what we ourselves have decreed, made law, discussed, planned—consolidate all this in stable forms of *everyday labour discipline*. This is the most difficult, but the most gratifying task, because only its fulfillment will give us a socialist system. We must learn to combine the "public meeting" democracy of the working people—turbulent, surging, overflowing its banks like a spring flood—with *iron* discipline while at work, with *unquestioning obedience* to the will of a single person, the Soviet leader, while at work. . . .

We must work unremittingly to develop the organization of the Soviets and of the Soviet government. There is a petty-bourgeois tendency to transform the members of the Soviets into "parliamentarians," or else into bureaucrats. We must combat this by drawing *all* the members of the Soviets into the practical work of administration. In many places the departments of the Soviets are gradually merging with the Commissariats. Our aim is to draw *the whole of the poor* into the practical work of administration, and all steps that are taken in this direction—the more varied they are, the better—should be carefully recorded, studied, systematized, tested by wider experience and embodied in law. Our aim is to ensure that *every* toiler, having finished his eight hours' "task" in productive labour, shall perform state duties *without pay*; the transition to this is particularly difficult, but this transition alone can guarantee the final consolidation of socialism. Naturally, the novelty and difficulty of the change lead to an abundance of steps being taken, as it were, gropingly, to an abundance of mistakes, vacillation—without this, any marked progress is impossible. The reason why the present position seems peculiar to many of those who would like to be regarded as socialists is that they have been accustomed to contrasting capitalism with socialism abstractly, and that they profoundly put between the two the word "leap" (some of them, recalling fragments of what they have read of Engels's writings, still more profoundly add the phrase "leap from the realm of necessity into the realm of freedom"). . . .

The fight against the bureaucratic distortion of the Soviet form of organization is assured by the firmness of the connection between the Soviets and the "people," meaning by that the working and exploited people, and by the flexibility and elasticity of this connection. Even in the most democratic capitalist republics in the world, the poor never regard the bourgeois parliament as "their" institution. But the Soviets are "theirs" and not alien institutions to the mass of workers and peasants. . . .

It is the closeness of the Soviets to the "people," to the working people, that creates the special forms of recall and other means of control from below which must be most zealously developed now. The more resolutely we now have to stand for a ruthlessly firm government, for the dictatorship of individuals *in definite processes of work*, in definite aspects of *purely executive* functions, the more varied must be the forms and methods of control from below in order to counteract every shadow of a possibility of distorting the principles of Soviet government, in order repeatedly and tirelessly to weed out bureaucracy.

Friedrich August von Hayek (1899–1992 C.E.)

Hayek was born in Vienna, and after post-doctoral work in the United States he returned to Austria. In 1931, he relocated to England, where he was appointed the Tooke Professor of Economics and Statistics at the University of London (1931-50). He became a British citizen in 1938. In 1950 he joined the faculty of the University of Chicago. In 1962 he took a professorship in economics at the University of Freiburg, where he remained until he retired in 1969. Although he wrote widely on law and political theory, Hayek is best known for his work in economics, which earned him the Nobel Prize in 1974. Among his principal political works are *The Road to Serfdom* (1944), *The Constitution of Liberty* (1960), excerpted here, and *Law, Legislation, and Liberty* (1979).

From The Constitution of Liberty*

Freedom, Reason, and Tradition

1. Though freedom is not a state of nature but an artifact of civilization, it did not arise from design. The institutions of freedom, like everything freedom has created, were not established because people foresaw the benefits they would bring. But, once its advantages were recognized, men began to perfect and extend the reign of freedom and, for that purpose, to inquire how a free society worked. This development of a theory of liberty took place mainly in the eighteenth century. It began in two countries, England and France. The first of these knew liberty; the second did not.

As a result, we have had to the present day two different traditions in the theory of liberty: one empirical and unsystematic, the other speculative and rationalistic—the first based on an interpretation of traditions and institutions which had spontaneously grown up and were but imperfectly understood, the second aiming at the construction of a utopia, which has often been tried but never successfully. Nevertheless, it has been the rationalist, plausible, and apparently logical argument of the French tradition, with its flattering assumptions about the unlimited powers of human reason, that has progressively gained influence, while the less articulate and less explicit tradition of English freedom has been on the decline.

This distinction is obscured by the facts that what we have called the "French tradition" of liberty arose largely from an attempt to interpret British institutions and that the conceptions which other countries formed of British institutions were based mainly on their description by French writers. The two traditions became finally confused when they merged in the liberal movement of the nineteenth century and when even leading British liberals drew as much on the French as on the British tradition. It was, in the end, the vic-

---

*An Excerpt.

tory of the Benthamite Philosophical Radicals over the Whigs in England that concealed the fundamental difference which in more recent years has reappeared as the conflict between liberal democracy and "social" or totalitarian democracy.

This difference was better understood a hundred years ago than it is today. In the year of the European revolutions in which the two traditions merged, the contrast between "Anglican" and "Gallican" liberty was still clearly described by an eminent German-American political philosopher. "Gallican Liberty," wrote Francis Lieber in 1848, "is sought in the *government,* and according to an Anglican point of view, it is looked for in a wrong place, where it cannot be found. Necessary consequences of the Gallican view are, that the French look for the highest degree of political civilization in *organization,* that is, in the highest degree of interference by public power. The question whether this interference be despotism or liberty is decided solely by the fact *who* interferes, and for the benefit of which class the interference takes place, while according to the Anglican view this interference would always be either absolutism or aristocracy, and the present dictatorship of the *ouvriers* would appear to us an uncompromising aristocracy of the *ouvriers.*"

Since this was written, the French tradition has everywhere progressively displaced the English. To disentangle the two traditions it is necessary to look at the relatively pure forms in which they appeared in the eighteenth century. What we have called the "British tradition" was made explicit mainly by a group of Scottish moral philosophers led by David Hume, Adam Smith, and Adam Ferguson, seconded by their English contemporaries Josiah Tucker, Edmund Burke, and William Paley, and drawing largely on a tradition rooted in the jurisprudence of the common law. Opposed to them was the tradition of the French Enlightenment, deeply imbued with Cartesian rationalism: the Encyclopedists and Rousseau, the Physiocrats and Condorcet, are their best-known representatives. Of course, the division does not fully coincide with national boundaries. Frenchmen like Montesquieu and, later, Benjamin Constant and, above all, Alexis de Tocqueville are probably nearer to what we have called the "British" than to the "French" tradition. And, in Thomas Hobbes, Britain has provided at least one of the founders of the rationalist tradition, not to speak of the whole generation of enthusiasts for the French Revolution, like Godwin, Priestley, Price, and Paine, who (like Jefferson after his stay in France) belong entirely to it.

2. Though these two groups are now commonly lumped together as the ancestors of modern liberalism, there is hardly a greater contrast imaginable than that between their respective conceptions of the evolution and functioning of a social order and the role played in it by liberty. The difference is directly traceable to the predominance of an essentially empiricist view of the world in England and a rationalist approach in France. The main contrast in the practical conclusions to which these approaches led has recently been well put, as follows: "One finds the essence of freedom in spontaneity and the absence of coercion, the other believes it to be realized only in the pursuit and attainment of an absolute collective purpose"; and "one stands for organic, slow, half-conscious growth, the other for doctrinaire deliberateness; one for trial and error procedure, the other for an enforced solely valid pattern." It is the second view, as J. S. Talmon has shown in an important book from which this description is taken, that has become the origin of totalitarian democracy.

The sweeping success of the political doctrines that stem from the French tradition is probably due to their great appeal to human pride and ambition. But we must not forget that the political conclusions of the two schools derive from different conceptions of how society works. In this respect the British philosophers laid the foundations of a profound and essentially valid theory, while the rationalist school was simply and completely wrong.

Those British philosophers have given us an interpretation of the growth of civilization that is still the indispensable foundation of the argument for liberty. They find the origin of institutions, not in contrivance or design, but in the survival of the successful. Their view is expressed in terms of "how nations stumble upon establishments which are indeed the result of human action but not the execution of human design." It stresses that what we call political order is much less the product of our ordering intelligence than is commonly imagined. As their immediate successors saw it, what Adam Smith and his contemporaries did was "to resolve almost all that has been ascribed to positive institution into the spontaneous and irresistible development of certain obvious principles, and to show with how little contrivance or political wisdom the most complicated and apparently artificial schemes of policy might have been erected."

This "anti-rationalistic insight into historical happenings that Adam Smith shares with Hume, Adam Ferguson, and others" enabled them for the first time to comprehend how institutions and morals, language and law, have evolved by a process of cumulative growth and that it is only with and within this framework that human reason has grown and can successfully operate. Their argument is directed throughout against the Cartesian conception of an independently and antecedently existing human reason that invented these institutions and against the conception that civil society was formed by some wise original legislator or an original "social contract." The latter idea of intelligent men coming together for deliberation about how to make the world anew is perhaps the most characteristic outcome of those design theories. It found its perfect expression when the leading theorist of the French Revolution, Abbé Sieyès, exhorted the revolutionary assembly "to act like men just emerging from the state of nature and coming together for the purpose of signing a social contract."

The ancients understood the conditions of liberty better than that. Cicero quotes Cato as saying that the Roman constitution was superior to that of other states because it "was based upon the genius, not of one man, but of many: it was founded, not in one generation, but in a long period of several centuries and many ages of men. For, said he, there never has lived a man possessed of so great a genius that nothing could escape him, nor could the combined powers of all men living at one time possibly make all the necessary provisions for the future without the aid of actual experience and the test of time." Neither republican Rome nor Athens—the two free nations of the ancient world—could thus serve as an example for the rationalists. For Descartes, the fountainhead of the rationalist tradition, it was indeed Sparta that provided the model; for her greatness "was due not the pre-eminence of each of its laws in particular . . . but to the circumstance that, originated by a single individual, they all tended to a single end." And it was Sparta which became the ideal of liberty for Rousseau as well as for Robespierre and Saint-Just and for most of the later advocates of "social" or totalitarian democracy.

Like the ancient, the modern British conceptions of liberty grew against the background of a comprehension, first achieved by the lawyers, of how institutions had developed. "There are many things specially in laws and governments," wrote Chief Justice Hale in the seventeenth century in a critique of Hobbes, "that mediately, remotely, and consequentially are reasonable to be approved, though the reason of the party does not presently or immediately and distinctly see its reasonableness. . . . Long experience makes more discoveries touching conveniences or inconveniences of laws than is possible for the wisest council of men at first to foresee. And that those amendments and supplements that through the various experiences of wise and knowing men have been applied to any law must needs be better suited to the convenience of laws, than the best invention of the most pregnant wits not aided by such a series and tract of experience. . . . This adds to the difficulty of a present fathoming of the reason of laws, because they are the production of long and iterated experience which, though it be commonly called the mistress of fools, yet certainly it is the wisest expedient among mankind, and discovers those defects and supplies which no wit of man could either at once foresee or aptly remedy. . . . It is not necessary that the reasons of the institution should be evident unto us. It is sufficient that they are instituted laws that give a certainty to us, and it is reasonable to observe them though the particular reason of the institution appear not."

3. From these conceptions gradually grew a body of social theory that showed how, in the relations among men, complex and orderly and, in a very definite sense, purposive institutions might grow up which owed little to design, which were not invented but arose from the separate actions of many men who did not know what they were doing. This demonstration that something greater than man's individual mind may grow from men's fumbling efforts represented in some ways an even greater challenge to all design theories than even the later theory of biological evolution. For the first time it was shown that an evident order which was not the product of a designing human intelligence need not therefore be ascribed to the design of a higher, supernatural intelligence, but that there was a third possibility—the emergence of order as the result of adaptive evolution.

Since the emphasis we shall have to place on the role that selection plays in this process of social evolution today is likely to create the impression that we are borrowing the idea from biology, it is worth stressing that it was, in fact, the other way round: there can be little doubt that it was from the theories of social evolution that Darwin and his contemporaries derived the suggestion for their theories. Indeed, one of those Scottish philosophers who first developed these ideas anticipated Darwin even in the biological field; and the later application of these conceptions by the various "historical schools" in law and language rendered the idea that similarity of structure might be accounted for by a common origin a commonplace in the study of social phenomena long before it was applied to biology. It is unfortunate that at a later date the social sciences, instead of building on these beginnings in their own field, re-imported some of these ideas from biology and with them brought in such conceptions as "natural selection," "struggle for existence," and "survival of the fittest," which are not appropriate in their field; for in social evolution, the decisive factor is not the selection of the physical and inheritable properties of the individuals but the selection by imitation of successful institutions and habits.

Though this operates also through the success of individuals and groups, what emerges is not an inheritable attribute of individuals, but ideas and skills—in short, the whole cultural inheritance which is passed on by learning and imitation.

4. A detailed comparison of the two traditions would require a separate book; here we can merely single out a few of the crucial points on which they differ.

While the rationalist tradition assumes that man was originally endowed with both the intellectual and the moral attributes that enabled him to fashion civilization deliberately, the evolutionists made it clear that civilization was the accumulated hard earned result of trial and error; that it was the sum of experience, in part handed from generation to generation as explicit knowledge, but to a larger extent embodied in tools and institutions which had proved themselves superior—institutions whose significance we might discover by analysis but which will also serve men's ends without men's understanding them. The Scottish theorists were very much aware how delicate this artificial structure of civilization was which rested on man's more primitive and ferocious instincts being tamed and checked by institutions that he neither had designed nor could control. They were very far from holding such naïve views, later unjustly laid at the door of their liberalism, as the "natural goodness of man," the existence of a "natural harmony of interests," or the beneficent effects of "natural liberty" (even though they did sometimes use the last phrase). They knew that it required the artifices of institutions and traditions to reconcile the conflicts of interest. Their problem was how "that universal mover in human nature, self love, may receive such direction in this case (as in all others) as to promote the public interest by those efforts it shall make towards pursuing its own." It was not "natural liberty" in any literal sense, but the institutions evolved to secure "life, liberty, and property," which made those individual efforts beneficial. Not Locke, nor Hume, nor Smith, nor Burke, could ever have argued, as Bentham did, that "every law is an evil for every law is an infraction of liberty." Their argument was never a complete laissez faire argument, which, as the very words show, is also part of the French rationalist tradition and in its literal sense was never defended by any of the English classical economists. They knew better than most of their later critics that it was not some sort of magic but the evolution of "well-constructed institutions," where the "rules and principles of contending interests and compromised advantages" would be reconciled, that had successfully channeled individual efforts to socially beneficial aims. In fact, their argument was never antistate as such, or anarchistic, which is the logical outcome of the rationalistic laissez faire doctrine; it was an argument that accounted both for the proper functions of the state and for the limits of state action.

The difference is particularly conspicuous in the respective assumptions of the two schools concerning individual human nature. The rationalistic design theories were necessarily based on the assumption of the individual man's propensity for rational action and his natural intelligence and goodness. The evolutionary theory, on the contrary, showed how certain institutional arrangements would induce man to use his intelligence to the best effect and how institutions could be framed so that bad people could do least harm. The antirationalist tradition is here closer to the Christian tradition of the fallibility and sinfulness of man, while the perfectionism of the rationalist is in irreconcilable conflict with it. Even such a celebrated figment as the "economic man" was not an original part of the British evolutionary tradition. It would be only a slight exaggeration to say that, in the view of those British philosophers, man was by nature lazy and indolent, improvident and wasteful, and that it was only by the force of circumstances that he could be made to behave economically or would learn carefully to adjust his means to his ends. The *homo oeconomicus* was explicitly introduced, with much else that belongs to the rationalist rather than to the evolutionary tradition, only by the younger Mill.

5. The greatest difference between the two views, however, is in their respective ideas about the role of traditions and the value of all the other products of unconscious growth proceeding throughout the ages. It would hardly be unjust to say that the rationalistic approach is here opposed to almost all that is the distinct product of liberty and that gives liberty its value. Those who believe that all useful institutions are deliberate contrivances and who cannot conceive of anything serving a human purpose that has not been consciously designed are almost of necessity enemies of freedom. For them freedom means chaos.

To the empiricist evolutionary tradition, on the other hand, the value of freedom consists mainly in the opportunity it provides for the growth of the undesigned, and the beneficial functioning of a free society rests largely on the existence of such freely grown institutions. There probably never has existed a genuine belief in freedom, and there has certainly been no successful attempt to operate a free society, without a genuine reverence for grown institutions, for customs and habits and "all those securities of liberty which arise from regulation of long prescription and ancient ways." Paradoxical as it may appear, it is probably true that a successful free society will always in a large measure be a tradition-bound society.

This esteem for tradition and custom, of grown institutions, and of rules whose origins and rationale we do not know does not, of course, mean—as Thomas Jefferson believed with a characteristic rationalist misconception that we "ascribe to men of preceding age a wisdom more than human, and . . . suppose what they did beyond amendment." Far from assuming that those who created the institutions were wiser than we are, the evolutionary view is based on the insight that the result of the experimentation of many generations may embody more experience than any one man possesses.

6. We have already considered the various institutions and habits, tools and methods of doing things, which have emerged from this process and constitute our inherited civilization. But we have yet to look at those rules of conduct which have grown as part of it, which are both a product and a condition of freedom. Of these conventions and customs of human intercourse, the moral rules are the most important but by no means the only significant ones. We understand one another and get along with one another, are able to act successfully on our plans, because, most of the time, members of our civilization conform to unconscious patterns of conduct, show a regularity in their actions that is not the result of commands or coercion, often not even of any conscious adherence to known rules, but of firmly established habits and traditions. The general observance of these conventions is a necessary condition of the orderliness of the world in which we live, of our being able to find our way in it, though we do not know their significance and may not even be consciously aware of their existence. In some instances it would be necessary, for the smooth running of society, to secure a similar uniformity by coercion, if such conventions or rules were not observed often enough. Coercion, then, may sometimes be avoidable only because a high degree of voluntary conformity exists, which means that voluntary conformity may be a condition of a beneficial working of freedom. It is indeed a truth, which all the great apostles of freedom outside the rationalistic school have never tired of emphasizing, that freedom has never worked without deeply ingrained moral beliefs and that coercion can be reduced to a minimum only where individuals can be expected as a rule to conform voluntarily to certain principles.

There is an advantage in obedience to such rules not being coerced, not only because coercion as such is bad, but because it is, in fact, often desirable that rules should be observed only in most instances and that the individual should be able to transgress them when it seems to him worthwhile to incur the odium which this will cause. It is also important that the strength of the social pressure and of the force of habit which insures their observance is variable. It is this flexibility of voluntary rules which in the field of morals makes gradual evolution and spontaneous growth possible, which allows further experience to lead to modifications and improvements. Such an evolution is possible only with rules which are neither coercive nor deliberately imposed—rules which, though observing them is regarded as merit and though they will be observed by the majority, can be broken by individuals who feel that they have strong enough reasons to brave the censure of their fellows. Unlike any deliberately imposed coercive rules, which can be changed only discontinuously and for all at the same time, rules of this kind allow for gradual and experimental change. The existence of individuals and groups simultaneously observing partially different rules provides the opportunity for the selection of the more effective ones.

It is this submission to undesigned rules and conventions whose significance and importance we largely do not understand, this reverence for the traditional, that the rationalistic type of mind finds so uncongenial, though it is indispensable for the working of a free society. It has its foundation in the insight which David Hume stressed and which is of decisive importance for the antirationalist, evolutionary tradition—namely, that "the rules of morality are not the conclusions of our reason." Like all other values, our morals are not a product but a presupposition of reason, part of the ends which the instrument of our intellect has been developed to serve. At any one stage of our evolution, the system of values into which we are born supplies the ends which our reason must serve. This givenness of the value framework implies that, although we must always strive to improve our institutions, we can never aim to remake them as a whole and that, in our efforts to improve them, we must take for granted much that we do not understand. We must always work inside a framework of both values and institutions which is not of our own making. In particular, we can never synthetically construct a new body of moral rules or make our obedience of the known rules dependent on our comprehension of the implications of this obedience in a given instance.

7. The rationalistic attitude to these problems is best seen in its views on what it calls "superstition." I do not wish to underestimate the merit of the persistent and relentless fight of the eighteenth and nineteenth centuries against beliefs which are demonstrably false. But we must remember that the extension of the concept of superstition to all beliefs which are not demonstrably true lacks the same justification and may often be harmful. That we ought not to believe anything which has been shown to be false does not mean that we ought to believe only what has been demonstrated to be true. There are good reasons why any person who wants to live and act successfully in society must accept many common beliefs, though the value of these reasons may have little to do with their demonstrable truth. Such beliefs will also be based on some past experience but not on experience for which anyone can produce the evidence. The scientist, when asked to accept a generalization in his field, is of course entitled to ask for the evidence on which it is based. Many of the beliefs which in the past expressed the accumulated experience of the race have been disproved in this manner. This does not mean, however, that we can reach the stage where we can dispense with all beliefs for which such scientific evidence is lacking. Experience comes to man in many more forms than are commonly recognized by the professional experimenter or the seeker after explicit knowledge. We would destroy the foundations of much successful action if we disdained to rely on ways of doing things evolved by the process of trial and error simply because the reason for their adoption has not been handed down to us. The appropriateness of our conduct is not necessarily dependent on our knowing why it is so. Such understanding is one way of making our conduct appropriate, but not the only one. A sterilized world of beliefs, purged of all elements whose value could not be positively demonstrated, would probably be not less lethal than would an equivalent state in the biological sphere.

While this applies to all our values, it is most important in the case of moral rules of conduct. Next to language, they are perhaps the most important instance of an undesigned growth, of a set of rules which govern our lives but of which we can say neither why they are what they are nor what they do to us: we do not know what the consequences of observing them are for us as individuals and as a group. And it is against the demand for submission to such rules that the rationalistic spirit is in constant revolt. It insists on applying to them Descartes's principle which was "to reject as absolutely false all opinions in regard to which I could suppose the least ground for doubt." The desire of the rationalist has always been for the deliberately constructed, synthetic system of morals, for the system in which, as Edmund Burke has described it, "the practice of all moral duties, and the foundations of society, rested upon their reasons made clear and demonstrative to every individual." The rationalists of the eighteenth century, indeed, explicitly argued that, since they knew human nature, they "could easily find the morals which suited it." They did not understand that what they called "human nature" is very largely the result of those moral conceptions which every individual learns with language and thinking.

8. An interesting symptom of the growing influence of this rationalist conception is the increasing substitution, in all languages known to me, of the word "social" for the word "moral" or simply "good." It is instructive to consider briefly the significance of this. When people speak of a "social conscience" as against mere "conscience," they are presumably referring to an awareness of the particular effects of our actions on other people, to an endeavor to be guided in conduct not merely by traditional rules but by explicit consideration of the particular consequences of the action in question. They are in effect saying that our action should be guided by a full understanding of the functioning of the social process and that it should be our aim, through conscious assessment of the concrete facts of the situation, to produce a foreseeable result which they describe as the "social good."

The curious thing is that this appeal to the "social" really involves a demand that individual intelligence, rather than rules evolved by society, should guide individual action—that men should dispense with the use of what could truly be called "social" (in the sense of being a product of the impersonal process of society) and should rely on their individual judgment of the particular case. The preference for "social considerations" over the adherence to moral rules is, therefore, ultimately the result of a contempt for what really is a social phenomenon and of a belief in the superior powers of individual human reason.

The answer to these rationalistic demands is, of course, that they require knowledge which exceeds the capacity of the individual human mind and that, in the attempt to comply with them, most men would become less useful members of society than they are while they pursue their own aims within the limits set by the rules of law and morals.

The rationalist argument here overlooks the point that, quite generally, the reliance on abstract rules is a device we have learned to use because our reason is insufficient to master the full detail of complex reality. This is as true when we deliberately formulate an abstract rule for our individual guidance as when we submit to the common rules of action which have been evolved by a social process.

We all know that, in the pursuit of our individual aims, we are not likely to be successful unless we lay down for ourselves some general rules to which we will adhere without reexamining their justification in every particular instance. In ordering our day, in doing disagreeable but necessary tasks at once, in refraining from certain stimulants, or in suppressing certain impulses, we frequently find it necessary to make such practices an unconscious habit, because we know that without this the rational grounds which make such behavior desirable would not be sufficiently effective to balance temporary desires and to make us do what we should wish to do from a long-term point of view. Though it sounds paradoxical to say that in order to make ourselves act rationally we often find it necessary to be guided by habit rather than reflection, or to say that to prevent ourselves from making the wrong decision we must deliberately reduce the range of choice before us, we all know that this is often necessary in practice if we are to achieve our long-range aims.

The same considerations apply even more where our conduct will directly affect not ourselves but others and where our primary concern, therefore, is to adjust our actions to the actions and expectations of others so that we avoid doing them unnecessary harm. Here it is unlikely that any individual would succeed in rationally constructing rules which would be more effective for their purpose than those which have been gradually evolved; and, even if he did, they could not really serve their purpose unless they were observed by all. We have thus no choice but to submit to rules whose rationale we often do not know, and to do so whether or not we can see that anything important depends on their being observed in the particular instance. The rules of morals are instrumental in the sense that they assist mainly in the achievement of other human values; however, since we only rarely can know what depends on their being followed in the particular instance, to observe them must be regarded as a value in itself, a sort of intermediate end which we must pursue without questioning its justification in the particular case.

9. These considerations, of course, do not prove that all the sets of moral beliefs which have grown up in a society will be beneficial. Just as a group may owe its rise to the morals which its members obey, and their values in consequence be ultimately imitated by the whole nation which the successful group has come to lead, so may a group or nation destroy itself by the moral beliefs to which it adheres. Only the eventual results can show whether the ideals which guide a group are beneficial or destructive. The fact that a society has come to regard the teaching of certain men as the embodiment of goodness is no proof that it might not be the society's undoing if their precepts were generally followed. It may well be that a nation may destroy itself by following the teaching of what it regards as its best men, perhaps saintly figures unquestionably guided by the most unselfish ideals. There would be little danger of this in a society whose members were still free to choose their way of practical life, because in such a society such tendencies would be self-corrective: only the groups guided by "impractical" ideals would decline, and others, less moral by current standards, would take their place. But this will happen only in a free society in which such ideals are not enforced on all. Where all are made to serve the same ideals and where dissenters are not allowed to follow different ones, the rules can be proved inexpedient only by the decline of the whole nation guided by them.

The important question that arises here is whether the agreement of a majority on a moral rule is sufficient justification for enforcing it on a dissenting minority or whether this power ought not also to be limited by more general rules—in other words, whether ordinary legislation should be limited by general principles just as the moral rules of individual conduct preclude certain kinds of action, however good may be their purpose. There is as much need of moral rules in political as in individual action, and the consequences of successive collective decisions as well as those of individual decisions will be beneficial only if they are all in conformity with common principles.

Such moral rules for collective action are developed only with difficulty and very slowly. But this should be taken as an indication of their preciousness. The most important among the few principles of this kind that we have developed is individual freedom, which it is most appropriate to regard as a moral principle of political action. Like all moral principles, it demands that it be accepted as a value in itself, as a principle that must be respected without our asking whether the consequences in the particular instance will be beneficial. We shall not achieve the results we want if we do not accept it as a creed or presumption so strong that no considerations of expediency can be allowed to limit it.

The argument for liberty, in the last resort, is indeed an argument for principles and against expediency in collective action, which, as we shall see, is equivalent to saying that only the judge and not the administrator may order coercion. When one of the intellectual leaders of nineteenth-century liberalism, Benjamin Constant, described liberalism as the *système de principes,* he pointed to the heart of the matter. Not only is liberty a system under which all government action is guided by principles, but it is an ideal that will not be preserved unless it is itself accepted as an overriding principle governing all particular acts of legislation. Where no such fundamental rule is stubbornly adhered to as an ultimate ideal about which there must be no compromise for the sake of material advantages—as an ideal which, even though it may have to be temporarily infringed during a passing emergency, must form the basis of all permanent arrangements—freedom is

almost certain to be destroyed by piecemeal encroachments. For in each particular instance it will be possible to promise concrete and tangible advantages as the result of a
curtailment of freedom, while the benefits sacrificed will in their nature always be unknown and uncertain. If freedom were not treated as the supreme principle, the fact that
the promises which a free society has to offer can always be only chances and not cer-
tainties, only opportunities and not definite gifts to particular individuals, would inevitably
prove a fatal weakness and lead to its slow erosion.

10. The reader will probably wonder by now what role there remains to be played
by reason in the ordering of social affairs, if a policy of liberty demands so much refraining from deliberate control, so much acceptance of the undirected and spontaneously grown. The first answer is that, if it has become necessary to seek appropriate
limits to the uses of reason here, to find these limits is itself a most important and difficult exercise of reason. Moreover, if our stress here has been necessarily on those limits,
we have certainly not meant to imply thereby that reason has no important positive task.
Reason undoubtedly is man's most precious possession. Our argument is intended to
show merely that it is not all-powerful and that the belief that it can become its own master and control its own development may yet destroy it. What we have attempted is a defense of reason against its abuse by those who do not understand the conditions of its
effective functioning and continuous growth. It is an appeal to men to see that we must
use our reason intelligently and that, in order to do so, we must preserve that indispensable matrix of the uncontrolled and non-rational which is the only environment wherein
reason can grow and operate effectively.

The antirationalistic position here taken must not be confounded with irrationalism
or any appeal to mysticism. What is advocated here is not an abdication of reason but a
rational examination of the field where reason is appropriately put in control. Part of this
argument is that such an intelligent use of reason does not mean the use of deliberate
reason in the maximum possible number of occasions. In opposition to the naïve rationalism which treats our present reason as an absolute, we must continue the efforts which
David Hume commenced when he "turned against the enlightenment its own weapons"
and undertook "to whittle down the claims of reason by the use of rational analysis."

The first condition for such an intelligent use of reason in the ordering of human
affairs is that we learn to understand what role it does in fact play and can play in the
working of any society based on the co-operation of many separate minds. This means
that, before we can try to remold society intelligently, we must understand its functioning; we must realize that, even when we believe that we understand it, we may be mistaken. What we must learn to understand is that human civilization has a life of its own,
that all our efforts to improve things must operate within a working whole which we cannot entirely control, and the operation of whose forces we can hope merely to facilitate
and assist so far as we understand them. Our attitude ought to be similar to that of the
physician toward a living organism: like him, we have to deal with a self-maintaining whole
which is kept going by forces which we cannot replace and which we must therefore use
in all we try to achieve. What can be done to improve it must be done by working with
these forces rather than against them. In all our endeavor at improvement we must always
work inside this given whole, aim at piecemeal, rather than total, construction, and use

at each stage the historical material at hand and improve details step by step rather than attempt to redesign the whole.

None of these conclusions are arguments against the use of reason, but only arguments against such uses as require any exclusive and coercive powers of government; not arguments against experimentation, but arguments against all exclusive, monopolistic power to experiment in a particular field—power which brooks no alternative and which lays a claim to the possession of superior wisdom—and against the consequent preclusion of solutions better than the ones to which those in power have committed themselves.

The Origins of the Rule of Law

1. Individual liberty in modern times can hardly be traced back farther than the England of the seventeenth century. It appeared first, as it probably always does, as a by-product of a struggle for power rather than as the result of deliberate aim. But it remained long enough for its benefits to be recognized. And for over two hundred years the preservation and perfection of individual liberty became the guiding ideal in that country, and its institutions and traditions the model for the civilized world.

This does not mean that the heritage of the Middle Ages is irrelevant to modern liberty. But its significance is not quite what it is often thought to be. True, in many respects medieval man enjoyed more liberty than is now commonly believed. But there is little ground for thinking that the liberties of the English were then substantially greater than those of many Continental peoples. But if men of the Middle Ages knew many liberties in the sense of privileges granted to estates or persons, they hardly knew liberty as a general condition of the people. In some respects the general conceptions that prevailed then about the nature and sources of law and order prevented the problem of liberty from arising in its modern form. Yet it might also be said that it was because England retained more of the common medieval ideal of the supremacy of law, which was destroyed elsewhere by the rise of absolutism, that she was able to initiate the modern growth of liberty.

This medieval view, which is profoundly important as background for modern developments, though completely accepted perhaps only during the early Middle Ages, was that "the state cannot itself create or make law, and of course as little abolish or violate law, because this would mean to abolish justice itself, it would be absurd, a sin, a rebellion against God who alone creates law." For centuries it was recognized doctrine that kings or any other human authority could only declare or find the existing law, or modify abuses that had crept in, and not create law. Only gradually, during the later Middle Ages, did the conception of deliberate creation of new law—legislation as we know it—come to be accepted. In England, Parliament thus developed from what had been mainly a law-finding body to a law-creating one. It was finally in the dispute about the authority to legislate in which the contending parties reproached each other for acting arbitrarily—acting, that is, not in accordance with recognized general laws—that the cause of individual freedom was inadvertently advanced. The new power of the highly organized national state which arose in the fifteenth and sixteenth centuries used legislation for the first time as an instrument of deliberate policy. For a while it seemed as if this new power would lead in England, as on the Continent, to absolute monarchy, which would destroy the medieval liberties. The conception of limited government which arose from the English struggle of the seventeenth century was thus a new departure, dealing with new problems. If earlier English doctrine and the great medieval documents, from Magna Carta, the great "Constitutio Libertatis," downward, are significant in the development of the modern, it is because they served as weapons in that struggle.

Yet if for our purposes we need not dwell longer on the medieval doctrine, we must look somewhat closer at the classical inheritance which was revived at the beginning of the modern period. It is important, not only because of the great influence it exercised on the political thought of the seventeenth century, but also because of the direct significance that the experience of the ancients has for our time.

2. Though the influence of the classical tradition of the modern ideal of liberty is indisputable, its nature is often misunderstood. It has often been said that the ancients did not know liberty in the sense of individual liberty. This is true of many places and periods even in ancient Greece, but certainly not of Athens at the time of its greatness (or of late republican Rome); it may be true of the degenerate democracy of Plato's time, but surely not of those Athenians to whom Pericles said that "the freedom which we enjoy in our government extends also to our ordinary life [where], far from exercising a jealous surveillance over each other, we do not feel called upon to be angry with our neighbour for doing what he likes" and whose soldiers, at the moment of supreme danger during the Sicilian expedition, were reminded by their general that, above all, they were fighting for a country in which they had "unfettered discretion to live as they pleased." What were the main characteristics of that freedom of the "freest of free countries," as Nicias called Athens on the same occasion, as seen both by the Greeks themselves and by Englishmen of the later Tudor and Stuart times?

The answer is suggested by a word which the Elizabethans borrowed from the Greeks but which has since gone out of use. "Isonomia" was imported into England from Italy at the end of the sixteenth century as a word meaning "equality of laws to all manner of persons"; shortly afterward it was freely used by the translator of Livy in the Englished form "isonomy" to describe a state of equal laws for all and responsibility of the magistrates. It continued in use during the seventeenth century until "equality before the law," "government of law," or "rule of law" gradually displaced it.

The history of the concept in ancient Greece provides an interesting lesson because it probably represents the first instance of a cycle that civilizations seem to repeat. When it first appeared, it described a state which Solon had earlier established in Athens when he gave the people "equal laws for the noble and the base" and thereby gave them "not so much control of public policy as the certainty of being governed legally in accordance with known rules." Isonomy was contrasted with the arbitrary rule of tyrants and became a familiar expression in popular drinking songs celebrating the assassination of one of these tyrants. The concept seems to be older than that of *demokratia*, and the demand for equal participation of all in the government appears to have been one of its consequences. To Herodotus it is still isonomy rather than democracy which is the "most beautiful of all names of a political order." The term continued in use for some time after democracy had been achieved, at first in its justification and later, as has been said, increasingly in order to disguise the character it assumed; for democratic government soon came to disregard that very equality before the law from which it had derived its justification. The Greeks clearly understood that the two ideals, though related, were not the same: Thucydides speaks without hesitation about an "isonomic oligarchy," and Plato even uses the term "isonomy" in deliberate contrast to democracy rather than in justification of it. By the end of the fourth century it had come to be necessary to emphasize that "in a democracy the laws should be masters."

Against this background certain famous passages in Aristotle, though he no longer uses the term "isonomia," appear as a vindication of that traditional ideal. In the *Politics* he stresses that "it is more proper that the law should govern than any of the citizens," that the persons holding supreme power "should be appointed only guardians and servants of the law," and that "he who would place supreme power in mind, would place it in God and the laws." He condemns the kind of government in which "the people govern and not the law" and in which "everything is determined by majority vote and not by law." Such a government is to him not that of a free state, "for, when government is not in the laws, then there is no free state, for the law ought to be supreme over all things." A government that "centers all power in the votes of the people cannot, properly speaking, be a democracy: for their decrees cannot be general in their extent." If we add to this the following passage in the *Rhetoric,* we have indeed a fairly complete statement of the ideal of government by law: "It is of great moment that well drawn laws should themselves define all the points they possibly can, and leave as few as possible to the decision of the judges, [for] the decision of the lawgiver is not particular but prospective and general, whereas members of the assembly and the jury find it their duty to decide on definite cases brought before them."

There is clear evidence that the modern use of the phrase "government by laws and not by men" derives directly from this statement of Aristotle. Thomas Hobbes believed that it was "just another error of Aristotle's politics that in a well-ordered commonwealth not men should govern but the law," whereupon James Harrington retorted that "the art whereby a civil society is instituted and preserved upon the foundations of common rights and interest . . . [is], to follow Aristotle and Livy, the empire of laws, not of men."

3. In the course of the seventeenth century the influence of Latin writers largely replaced the direct influence of the Greeks. We should therefore take a brief look at the tradition derived from the Roman Republic. The famous Laws of the Twelve Tables, reputedly drawn up in conscious imitation of Solon's laws, form the foundation of its liberty. The first of the public laws in them provides that "no privileges, or statutes shall be enacted in favour of private persons, to the injury of others contrary to the law common to all citizens, and which individuals, no matter of what rank, have a right to make use of." This was the basic conception under which there was gradually formed, by a process very similar to that by which the common law grew, the first fully developed system of private law—in spirit very different from the later Justinian code, which determined the legal thinking of the Continent.

This spirit of the laws of free Rome has been transmitted to us mainly in the works of the historians and orators of the period, who once more became influential during the Latin Renaissance of the seventeenth century. Livy—whose translator made people familiar with the term "isonomia" (which Livy himself did not use) and who supplied Harrington with the distinction between the government of law and the government of men—Tacitus and, above all, Cicero became the chief authors through whom the classical tradition spread. Cicero indeed became the main authority for modern liberalism, and we owe to him many of the most effective formulations of freedom under the law. To him is due the conception of general rules or *leges legum*, which govern legislation, the conception that we obey the law in order to be free, and the conception that the judge ought to be merely the mouth through whom the law speaks. No other author shows more clearly that during the classical period of Roman law it was fully understood that there is no conflict between law and freedom and that freedom is dependent upon certain attributes of the law, its generality and certainty, and the restrictions it places on the discretion of authority.

This classical period was also a period of complete economic freedom, to which Rome largely owed its prosperity and power. From the second century A.D., however, state socialism advanced rapidly. In this development the freedom which equality before the law had created was progressively destroyed as demands for another kind of equality arose. During the later empire the strict law was weakened as, in the interest of a new social policy, the state increased its control over economic life. The outcome of this process, which culminated under Constantine, was, in the words of a distinguished student of Roman law, that "the absolute empire proclaimed together with the principle of equity the authority of the empirical will unfettered by the barrier of law. Justinian with his learned professors brought this process to its conclusions." Thereafter, for a thousand years, the conception that legislation should serve to protect the freedom of the individual was lost. And when the art of legislation was rediscovered, it was the code of Justinian with its conception of a prince who stood above the law that served as the model on the Continent.

4. In England, however, the wide influence which the classical authors enjoyed during the reign of Elizabeth helped to prepare the way for a different development. Soon after her death the great struggle between king and Parliament began, from which emerged as a by-product the liberty of the individual. It is significant that the disputes began largely over issues of economic policy very similar to those which we again face today. To the nineteenth-century historian the measures of James I and Charles I which provoked the conflict might have seemed antiquated issues without topical interest. To us the problems caused by the attempts of the kings to set up industrial monopolies have a familiar ring: Charles I even attempted to nationalize the coal industry and was dissuaded from this only by being told that this might cause a rebellion.

Ever since a court had laid down in the famous Case of Monopolies that the grant of exclusive rights to produce any article was "against the common law and the liberty of the subject," the demand for equal laws for all citizens became the main weapon of Parliament in its opposition to the king's aims. Englishmen then understood better than they do today that the control of production always means the creation of privilege: that Peter is given permission to do what Paul is not allowed to do.

It was another kind of economic regulation, however, that occasioned the first great statement of the basic principle. The Petition of Grievances of 1610 was provoked by new regulations issued by the king for building in London and prohibiting the making of starch from wheat. This celebrated plea of the House of Commons states that, among all the traditional rights of British subjects, "there is none which they have accounted more dear and precious than this, to be guided and governed by the certain rule of law, which giveth to the head and the members that which of right belongeth to them, and not by any uncertain and arbitrary form of government. . . . Out of this root has grown the indubitable right of the people of this kingdom, not to be made subject to any punishment that shall extend to their lives, lands, bodies, or goods, other than such as are ordained by the common laws of this land, or the statutes made by their common consent in parliament."

It was, finally, in the discussion occasioned by the Statute of Monopolies of 1624 that Sir Edward Coke, the great fountain of Whig principles, developed his interpretation of Magna Carta that became one of the cornerstones of the new doctrine. In the second part of his *Institutes of the Laws of England,* soon to be printed by order of the House of Commons, he not only contended (with reference to the Case of Monopolies) that "if a grant be made to any man, to have the sole making of cards, or the sole dealing with any other trade, that grant is against the liberty and freedom of the subject, that before did, or lawfully might have used that trade, and consequently against this great charter"; but he went beyond such opposition to the royal prerogative to warn Parliament itself "to leave all causes to be measured by the golden and straight mete-wand of the law, and not to the incertain and crooked cord of discretion."

Out of the extensive and continuous discussion of these issues during the Civil War, there gradually emerged all the political ideals which were thenceforth to govern English political evolution. We cannot attempt here to trace their evolution in the debates and pamphlet literature of the period, whose extraordinary wealth of ideas has come to be seen only since their re-publication in recent times. We can only list the main ideas that appeared more and more frequently until, by the time of the Restoration, they had become part of an established tradition and, after the Glorious Revolution of 1688, part of the doctrine of the victorious party.

The great event that became for later generations the symbol of the permanent achievements of the Civil War was the abolition in 1641 of the prerogative courts and especially the Star Chamber which had become, in F. W. Maitland's often quoted words, "a court of politicians enforcing a policy, not a court of judges administering the law." At almost the same time an effort was made for the first time to secure the independence of the judges. In the debates of the following twenty years the central issue became increasingly the prevention of arbitrary action of government. Though the two meanings of "arbitrary" were long confused, it came to be recognized, as Parliament began to act as arbitrarily as the king, that whether or not an action was arbitrary depended not on the source of the authority but on whether it was in conformity with pre-existing general principles of law. The points most frequently emphasized were that there must be no punishment without a previously existing law providing for it, that all statutes should have only prospective and not retrospective operation, and that the discretion of all magistrates should be strictly circumscribed by law. Throughout, the governing idea was that the law should be king or, as one of the polemical tracts of the period expressed it, *Lex, Rex.*

Gradually, two crucial conceptions emerged as to how these basic ideals should be safeguarded: the idea of a written constitution and the principle of the separation of powers. When in January, 1660, just before the Restoration, a last attempt was made in the "Declaration of Parliament Assembled at Westminister" to state in a formal document the essential principles of a constitution, this striking passage was included: "There being nothing more essential to the freedom of a state, than that the people should be governed by the laws, and that justice be administered by such only as are accountable for mal-administration, it is hereby further declared that all proceedings touching the lives, liberties and estates of all the free people of this commonwealth, shall be according to the laws of the land, and that the Parliament will not meddle with ordinary administration, or the executive part of the law: it being the principle [*sic*] part of this, as it hath been of all former Parliaments, to provide for the freedom of the people against arbitrariness in government." If thereafter the principle of the separation of powers was perhaps not quite "an accepted principle of constitutional law," it at least remained part of the governing political doctrine.

5. All these ideas were to exercise a decisive influence during the next hundred years, not only in England but also in America and on the Continent, in the summarized form they were given after the final expulsion of the Stuarts in 1688. Though at the time perhaps some other works were equally and perhaps even more influential, John Locke's *Second Treatise on Civil Government* is so outstanding in its lasting effects that we must confine our attention to it.

Locke's work has come to be known mainly as a comprehensive philosophical justification of the Glorious Revolution, and it is mostly in his wider speculations about the philosophical foundations of government that his original contribution lies. Opinions may differ about their value. The aspect of his work which was at least as important at the time and which mainly concerns us here, however, is his codification of the victorious political doctrine, of the practical principles which, it was agreed, should thenceforth control the powers of government.

While in his philosophical discussion Locke's concern is with the source which makes power legitimate and with the aim of government in general, the practical problem with which he is concerned is how power, whoever exercises it, can be prevented from becoming arbitrary: "Freedom of men under government is to have a standing rule to live by, common to every one of that society, and made by the legislative power erected in it; a liberty to follow my own will in all things, where that rule prescribes not: and not to be subject to the inconstant, uncertain, arbitrary will of another man." It is against the "irregular and uncertain exercise of the power" that the argument is mainly directed: the important point is that "whoever has the legislative or supreme power of any commonwealth is bound to govern by established standing laws promulgated and known to the people, and not by extemporary decrees; by indifferent and upright judges, who are to decide controversies by those laws; and to employ the forces of the community at home only in the execution of such laws." Even the legislature has no "absolute arbitrary power," "cannot assume to itself a power to rule by extemporary arbitrary decrees, but is bound to dispense justice, and decide the rights of the subject by promulgated standing laws, and known authorized judges," while the "supreme executor of the law . . . has no will, no power, but that of the law." Locke is loath to recognize any sovereign power, and the *Treatise* has been described as an assault upon the very idea of sovereignty. The main practical safeguard against the abuse of authority proposed by him is the separation of powers, which he expounds somewhat less clearly and in a less familiar form than did some of his predecessors. His main concern is how to limit the discretion of "him that has the executive power," but he has no special safeguards to offer. Yet his ultimate aim throughout is what today is often called the "taming of power": the end why men "choose and authorize a legislative is that there may be laws made, and rules set, as guards and fences to the properties of all the members of society, to limit the power and moderate the dominion of every part and member of that society."

6. It is a long way from the acceptance of an ideal by public opinion to its full realization in policy; and perhaps the ideal of the rule of law had not yet been completely put into practice when the process was reversed two hundred years later. At any rate, the main period of consolidation, during which it progressively penetrated everyday practice, was the first half of the eighteenth century. From the final confirmation of the independence of the judges in the Act of Settlement of 1701, through the occasion when the last bill of attainder ever passed by Parliament in 1706 led not only to a final restatement of all the arguments against such arbitrary action of the legislature but also to a reaffirmation of the principle of the separation of powers, the period is one of slow but steady extension of most of the principles for which the Englishmen of the seventeenth century had fought.

A few significant events of the period may be briefly mentioned, such as the occasion when a member of the House of Commons (at a time when Dr. Johnson was reporting the debates) restated the basic doctrine of *nulla poena sine lege*, which even now is sometimes alleged not to be part of English law: "That where there is no law there is no transgression, is a maxim not only established by universal consent, but in itself evident and undeniable; and it is, Sir, surely no less certain that where there is no transgression there can be no punishment." Another is the occasion when Lord Camden in the Wilkes case made it clear that courts are concerned only with general rules and not with the particular aims of government or, as his position is sometimes interpreted, that public policy is not an argument in a court of law. In other respects progress was more slow, and it is probably true that, from the point of view of the poorest, the ideal of equality before the law long remained a somewhat doubtful fact. But if the process of reforming the laws in the spirit of those ideals was slow, the principles themselves ceased to be a matter of dispute: they were no longer a party view but had come to be fully accepted by the Tories. In some respects, however, evolution moved away rather than toward the ideal. The principle of the separation of powers in particular, though regarded throughout the century as the most distinctive feature of the British constitution, became less and less a fact as modern cabinet government developed. And Parliament with its claim to unlimited power was soon to depart from yet another of the principles.

7. The second half of the eighteenth century produced the coherent expositions of the ideals which largely determined the climate of opinion for the next hundred years. As is so often the case, it was less the systematic expositions by political philosophers and lawyers than the interpretations of events by the historians that carried these ideas to the public. The most influential among them was David Hume, who in his works again and again stressed the crucial points and of whom it has justly been said that for him the real meaning of the history of England was the evolution from a "government of will to a government of law." At least one characteristic passage from his *History of England* deserves to be quoted. With reference to the abolition of the Star Chamber he writes: "No government, at that time, appeared in the world, nor is perhaps to be found in the records of any history, which subsisted without the mixture of some arbitrary authority, committed to some magistrate; and it might reasonably, beforehand, appear doubtful, whether human society could ever arrive at that state of perfection, as to support itself with no other control, than the general and rigid maxims of law and equity. But the parliament justly thought, that the King was too eminent a magistrate to be trusted with discretionary power, which he might so easily turn to the destruction of liberty. And in the event it has been found, that, though some inconveniencies arise from the maxim of adhering strictly to law, yet the advantages so much overbalance them, as should render the English forever grateful to the memory of their ancestors, who, after repeated contests, at last established that noble principle."

Later in the century these ideals are more often taken for granted than explicitly stated, and the modern reader has to infer them when he wants to understand what men like Adam Smith and his contemporaries meant by "liberty." Only occasionally, as in Blackstone's *Commentaries*, do we find endeavors to elaborate particular points, such as the significance of the independence of the judges and of the separation of powers, or to clarify the meaning of "law" by its definition as "a rule, not a transient sudden order from a superior or concerning a particular person; but something permanent, uniform and universal."

Many of the best-known expressions of those ideals are, of course, to be found in the familiar passages of Edmund Burke. But probably the fullest statement of the doctrine of the rule of law occurs in the work of William Paley, the "great codifier of thought in an age of codification." It deserves quoting at some length: "The first maxim of a free state," he writes, "is, that the laws be made by one set of men, and administered by another; in other words, that the legislative and the judicial character be kept separate. When these offices are unified in the same person or assembly, particular laws are made for particular cases, springing often times from partial motives, and directed to private ends: whilst they are kept separate, general laws are made by one body of men, without foreseeing whom they may affect; and, when made, must be applied by the other, let them affect whom they will. . . . When the parties and interests to be affected by the laws were known, the inclination of the law makers would inevitably attach to one side or the other; and where there were neither any fixed rules to regulate their determinations, nor any superior power to control their proceedings, these inclinations would interfere with the integrity of public justice. The consequence of which must be, that the subjects of such a constitution would live either without constant laws, that is, without any known preestablished rules of adjudication whatever; or under laws made for particular persons, and partaking of the contradictions and iniquity of the motives to which they owed their origin.

"Which dangers, by the division of the legislative and judicial functions, are in this country effectually provided against. Parliament knows not the individuals upon whom its acts will operate; it has no case or parties before it; no private designs to serve: consequently, its resolutions will be suggested by the considerations of universal effects and tendencies, which always produce impartial, and commonly advantageous regulations."

8. With the end of the eighteenth century, England's major contributions to the development of the principles of freedom come to a close. Though Macaulay did once more for the nineteenth century what Hume had done for the eighteenth, and though the Whig intelligentsia of the *Edinburgh Review* and economists in the Smithian tradition, like J. R. MacCulloch and N. W. Senior, continued to think of liberty in classical terms, there was little further development. The new liberalism that gradually displaced Whiggism came more and more under the influence of the rationalist tendencies of the philosophical radicals and the French tradition. Bentham and his Utilitarians did much to destroy the beliefs which England had in part preserved from the Middle Ages, by their scornful treatment of most of what until then had been the most admired features of the British constitution. And they introduced into Britain what had so far been entirely absent—the desire to remake the whole of her law and institutions on rational principles.

The lack of understanding of the traditional principles of English liberty on the part of the men guided by the ideals of the French Revolution is clearly illustrated by one of the early apostles of that revolution in England, Dr. Richard Price. As early as 1778 he argued: "Liberty is too imperfectly defined when it is said to be 'a Government of LAWS and not by MEN.' If the laws are made by one man, or a junto of men in a state, and not by common CONSENT, a government by them is not different from slavery." Eight years later he was able to display a commendatory letter from Turgot: "How comes it that you are almost the first of the writers of your country, who has given a just idea of liberty, and shown the falsity of the notion so frequently repeated by almost all Republican Writers, 'that liberty consists in being subject only to the laws'?" From then onward, the essentially French concept of political liberty was indeed progressively to displace the English ideal of individual liberty, until it could be said that "in Great Britain, which, little more than a century ago, repudiated the ideas on which the French Revolution was based, and led the resistance to Napoleon, those ideas have triumphed." Though in Britain most of the achievements of the seventeenth century were preserved beyond the nineteenth, we must look elsewhere for the further development of the ideals underlying them.

Ayn Rand (1905–1982 C.E.)

Ayn Rand was born Alissa Rosenbaum in St. Petersburg, Russia, in 1905 and emigrated to the United States in 1926, where she changed her name. She worked as a screenwriter, and wrote the novels *We, the Living* (1936), *Anthem* (1938), and *The Fountainhead* (1943), which became a best seller and contained the earliest statement of her moral philosophy. In 1957 Rand published her big philosophical novel *Atlas Shrugged*, which was also a best seller. She launched the Objectivist movement with Nathaniel Branden thereafter and began to promulgate her philosophy through lectures, journals, and non-fiction books such as *The Virtue of Selfishness* (1964), where the following essay appeared, *Capitalism: The Unknown Ideal* (1966), and *Introduction to Objectivist Epistemology* (1970). Her philosophical work, especially in epistemology, ethics, and politics, has since gained some attention in professional philosophical circles.

Man's Rights

If one wishes to advocate a free society—that is, capitalism—one must realize that its indispensable foundation is the principle of individual rights. If one wishes to uphold individual rights, one must realize that capitalism is the only system that can uphold and protect them. And if one wishes to gauge the relationship of freedom to the goals of today's intellectuals, one may gauge it by the fact that the concept of individual rights is evaded, distorted, perverted and seldom discussed, most conspicuously seldom by the so-called "conservatives."

"Rights" are a moral concept—the concept that provides a logical transition from the principles guiding an individual's actions to the principles guiding his relationship with others—the concept that preserves and protects individual morality in a social context—the link between the moral code of a man and the legal code of a society, between ethics and politics. *Individual rights are the means of subordinating society to moral law.*

Every political system is based on some code of ethics. The dominant ethics of mankind's history were variants of the altruist-collectivist doctrine which subordinated the individual to some higher authority, either mystical or social. Consequently, most political systems were variants of the same statist tyranny, differing only in degree, not in basic principle, limited only by the accidents of tradition, of chaos, of bloody strife and periodic collapse. Under all such systems, morality was a code applicable to the individual, but not to society. Society was placed *outside* the moral law, as its embodiment or source or exclusive interpreter—and the inculcation of self-sacrificial devotion to social duty was regarded as the main purpose of ethics in man's earthly existence.

Since there is no such entity as "society," since society is only a number of individual men, this meant, in practice, that the rulers of society were exempt from moral law; subject only to traditional rituals, they held total power and exacted blind obedience—on the implicit principle of: "The good is that which is good for society (or for the tribe, the race, the nation), and the ruler's edicts are its voice on earth."

This was true of all statist systems, under all variants of the altruist-collectivist ethics, mystical or social. "The Divine Right of Kings" summarizes the political theory of the first—"*Vox populi, vox dei*" of the second. As witness: the theocracy of Egypt, with the Pharaoh as an embodied god—the unlimited majority rule or *democracy* of Athens—the welfare state run by the Emperors of Rome—the Inquisition of the late Middle Ages—the absolute monarchy of France—the welfare state of Bismarck's Prussia—the gas chambers of Nazi Germany—the slaughterhouse of the Soviet Union.

All these political systems were expressions of the altruist-collectivist ethics—and their common characteristic is the fact that society stood above the moral law, as an omnipotent, sovereign whim worshiper. Thus, politically, all these systems were variants of an *amoral* society.

The most profoundly revolutionary achievement of the United States of America was *the subordination of society to moral law.*

The principle of man's individual rights represented the extension of morality into the social system—as a limitation on the power of the state, as man's protection against the brute force of the collective, as the subordination of *might* to *right*. The United States was the first *moral* society in history.

All previous systems had regarded man as a sacrificial means to the ends of others, and society as an end in itself. The United States regarded man as an end in himself, and society as a means to the peaceful, orderly, *voluntary* co-existence of individuals. All previous systems had held that man's life belongs to society, that society can dispose of him in any way it pleases, and that any freedom he enjoys is his only by favor, by the *permission* of society, which may be revoked at any time. The United States held that man's life is his by *right* (which means: by moral principle and by his nature), that a right is the property of an individual, that society as such has no rights, and that the only moral purpose of a government is the protection of individual rights.

A "right" is a moral principle defining and sanctioning a man's freedom of action in a social context. There is only *one* fundamental right (all the others are its consequences or corollaries): a man's right to his own life. Life is a process of self-sustaining and self-generated action; the right to life means the right to engage in self-sustaining and self-generated action—which means: the freedom to take all the actions required by the nature of a rational being for the support, the furtherance, the fulfillment and the enjoyment of his own life. (Such is the meaning of the right to life, liberty and the pursuit of happiness.)

The concept of a "right" pertains only to action—specifically, to freedom of action. It means freedom from physical compulsion, coercion or interference by other men.

Thus, for every individual, a right is the moral sanction of a *positive*—of his freedom to act on his own judgment, for his own goals, by his own *voluntary, uncoerced* choice. As to his neighbors, his rights impose no obligations on them except of a *negative* kind: to abstain from violating his rights.

The right to life is the source of all rights—and the right to property is their only implementation. Without property rights, no other rights are possible. Since man has to sustain his life by his own effort, the man who has no right to the product of his effort has no means to sustain his life. The man who produces while others dispose of his product, is a slave.

Bear in mind that the right to property is a right to action, like all the others: it is not the right *to an object* but to the action and the consequences of producing or earning that object. It is not a guarantee that a man *will* earn any property, but only a guarantee that he will own it if he earns it. It is the right to gain, to keep, to use and to dispose of material values.

The concept of individual rights is so new in human history that most men have not grasped it fully to this day. In accordance with the two theories of ethics, the mystical or the social, some men assert that rights are a gift of God—others, that rights are a gift of society. But, in fact, the source of rights is man's nature.

The Declaration of Independence stated that men "are endowed by their Creator with certain unalienable rights." Whether one believes that man is the product of a Creator or of nature, the issue of man's origin does not alter the fact that he is an entity of a specific kind—a rational being—that he cannot function successfully under coercion, and that rights are a necessary condition of his particular mode of survival.

"The source of man's rights is not divine law or congressional law, but the law of identity. A is A—and Man is Man. *Rights* are conditions of existence required by man's nature for his proper survival. If man is to live on earth, it is *right* for him to use his mind, it is *right* to act on his own free judgment, it is *right* to work for his values and to keep the product of his work. If life on earth is his purpose, he has a *right* to live as a rational being: nature forbids him the irrational." (*Atlas Shrugged*)

To violate man's rights means to compel him to act against his own judgment, or to expropriate his values. Basically, there is only one way to do it: by the use of physical force. There are two potential violators of man's rights: the criminals and the government. The great achievement of the United States was to draw a distinction between these two—by forbidding to the second the legalized version of the activities of the first.

The Declaration of Independence laid down the principle that "to secure these rights, governments are instituted among men." This provided the only valid justification of a government and defined its only proper purpose: to protect man's rights by protecting him from physical violence.

Thus the government's function was changed from the role of ruler to the role of servant. The government was set to protect man from criminals—and the Constitution was written to protect man from the government. The Bill of Rights was not directed against private citizens, but against the government—as an explicit declaration that individual rights supersede any public or social power.

The result was the pattern of a civilized society which—for the brief span of some hundred and fifty years—America came close to achieving. A civilized society is one in which physical force is banned from human relationships—in which the government, acting as a policeman, may use force *only* in retaliation and *only* against those who initiate its use.

This was the essential meaning and intent of America's political philosophy, implicit in the principle of individual rights. But it was not formulated explicitly, nor fully accepted nor consistently practiced.

America's inner contradiction was the altruist-collectivist ethics. Altruism is incompatible with freedom, with capitalism and with individual rights. One cannot combine the pursuit of happiness with the moral status of a sacrificial animal.

It was the concept of individual rights that had given birth to a free society. It was with the destruction of individual rights that the destruction of freedom had to begin.

A collectivist tyranny dare not enslave a country by an outright confiscation of its values, material or moral. It has to be done by a process of internal corruption. Just as in the material realm the plundering of a country's wealth is accomplished by inflating the currency—so today one may witness the process of inflation being applied to the realm of rights. The process entails such a growth of newly promulgated "rights" that people do not notice the fact that the meaning of the concept is being reversed. Just as bad money drives out good money, so these "printing-press rights" negate authentic rights.

Consider the curious fact that never has there been such a proliferation, all over the world, of two contradictory phenomena: of alleged new "rights" and of slave-labor camps.

The "gimmick" was the switch of the concept of rights from the political to the economic realm.

The Democratic Party platform of 1960 summarizes the switch boldly and explicitly. It declares that a Democratic Administration "will reaffirm the economic bill of rights which Franklin Roosevelt wrote into our national conscience sixteen years ago."

Bear clearly in mind the meaning of the concept of "*rights*" when you read the list which that platform offers:

"**1.** The right to a useful and remunerative job in the industries or shops or farms or mines of the nation.

"**2.** The right to earn enough to provide adequate food and clothing and recreation.

"**3.** The right of every farmer to raise and sell his products at a return which will give him and his family a decent living.

"**4.** The right of every businessman, large and small, to trade in an atmosphere of freedom from unfair competition and domination by monopolies at home and abroad.

"**5.** The right of every family to a decent home.

"**6.** The right to adequate medical care and the opportunity to achieve and enjoy good health.

"**7.** The right to adequate protection from the economic fears of old age, sickness, accidents and unemployment.

"**8.** The right to a good education."

A single question added to each of the above eight clauses would make the issue clear: *At whose expense?*

Jobs, food, clothing, recreation (!), homes, medical care, education, etc., do not grow in nature. These are man-made values—goods and services produced by men. *Who* is to provide them?

If some men are entitled *by right* to the products of the work of others, it means that those others are deprived of rights and condemned to slave labor.

Any alleged "right" of one man, which necessitates the violation of the rights of another, is not and cannot be a right.

No man can have a right to impose an unchosen obligation, an unrewarded duty or an involuntary servitude on another man. There can be no such thing as "*the right to enslave.*"

A right does not include the material implementation of that right by other men; it includes only the freedom to earn that implementation by one's own effort.

Observe, in this context, the intellectual precision of the Founding Fathers: they spoke of the right to *the pursuit* of happiness—*not* of the right to happiness. It means that a man has the right to take the actions he deems necessary to achieve his happiness; it does *not* mean that others must make him happy.

The right to life means that a man has the right to support his life by his own work (on any economic level, as high as his ability will carry him); it does *not* mean that others must provide him with the necessities of life.

The right to property means that a man has the right to take the economic actions necessary to earn property, to use it and to dispose of it; it does *not* mean that others must provide him with property.

The right of free speech means that a man has the right to express his ideas without danger of suppression, interference or punitive action by the government. It does *not* mean that others must provide him with a lecture hall, a radio station or a printing press through which to express his ideas.

Any undertaking that involves more than one man, requires the *voluntary* consent of every participant. Every one of them has the *right* to make his own decision, but none has the right to force his decision on the others.

There is no such thing as "a right to a job"—there is only the right of free trade, that is: a man's right to take a job if another man chooses to hire him. There is no "right to a home," only the right of free trade: the right to build a home or to buy it. There are no "rights to a 'fair' wage or a 'fair' price" if no one chooses to pay it, to hire a man or to buy his product. There are no "rights of consumers" to milk, shoes, movies or champagne if no producers choose to manufacture such items (there is only the right to manufacture them oneself). There are no "rights" of special groups, there are no "rights of farmers, of workers, of businessmen, of employees, of employers, of the old, of the young, of the unborn." There are only *the Rights of Man*—rights possessed by every individual man and by *all* men as individuals.

Property rights and the right of free trade are man's only "economic rights" (they are, in fact, *political* rights)—and there can be no such thing as "an *economic* bill of rights." But observe that the advocates of the latter have all but destroyed the former.

Remember that rights are moral principles which define and protect a man's freedom of action, but impose no obligations on other men. Private citizens are not a threat to one another's rights or freedom. A private citizen who resorts to physical force and violates the rights of others is a criminal—and men have legal protection against him.

Criminals are a small minority in any age or country. And the harm they have done to mankind is infinitesimal when compared to the horrors—the bloodshed, the wars, the persecutions, the confiscations, the famines, the enslavements, the wholesale destructions—perpetrated by mankind's governments. Potentially, a government is the most dangerous threat to man's rights: it holds a legal monopoly on the use of physical force against legally disarmed victims. When unlimited and unrestricted by individual rights, a government is men's deadliest enemy. It is not as protection against *private* actions, but against governmental actions that the Bill of Rights was written.

Now observe the process by which that protection is being destroyed.

The process consists of ascribing to private citizens the specific violations constitutionally forbidden to the government (which private citizens have no power to commit) and thus freeing the government from all restrictions. The switch is becoming progressively more obvious in the field of free speech. For years, the collectivists have been propagating the notion that a private individual's refusal to finance an opponent is a violation of the opponent's right of free speech and an act of "censorship."

It is "censorship," they claim, if a newspaper refuses to employ or publish writers whose ideas are diametrically opposed to its policy.

It is "censorship," they claim, if businessmen refuse to advertise in a magazine that denounces, insults and smears them.

It is "censorship," they claim, if a TV sponsor objects to some outrage perpetrated on a program he is financing—such as the incident of Alger Hiss being invited to denounce former Vice-President Nixon.

And then there is Newton N. Minow who declares: "There is censorship by ratings, by advertisers, by networks, by affiliates which reject programming offered to their areas." It is the same Mr. Minow who threatens to revoke the license of any station that does not comply with his views on programming—and who claims that *that* is not censorship.

Consider the implications of such a trend.

"Censorship" is a term pertaining only to governmental action. No private action is censorship. No private individual or agency can silence a man or suppress a publication; only the government can do so. The freedom of speech of private individuals includes the right not to agree, not to listen and not to finance one's own antagonists.

But according to such doctrines as the "economic bill of rights," an individual has no right to dispose of his own material means by the guidance of his own convictions—and must hand over his money indiscriminately to any speakers or propagandists, who have a "right" to his property.

This means that the ability to provide the material tools for the expression of ideas deprives a man of the right to hold any ideas. It means that a publisher has to publish books he considers worthless, false or evil—that a TV sponsor has to finance commentators who choose to affront his convictions—that the owner of a newspaper must turn his editorial pages over to any young hooligan who clamors for the enslavement of the press. It means that one group of men acquires the "right" to unlimited license—while another group is reduced to helpless irresponsibility.

But since it is obviously impossible to provide every claimant with a job, a microphone or a newspaper column, *who* will determine the "distribution" of "economic rights" and select the recipients, when the owners' right to choose has been abolished? Well, Mr. Minow has indicated *that* quite clearly.

And if you make the mistake of thinking that this applies only to big property owners, you had better realize that the theory of "economic rights" includes the "right" of every would-be playwright, every beatnik poet, every noise-composer and every nonob-jective artist (who have political pull) to the financial support you did not give them when you did not attend their shows. What else is the meaning of the project to spend your tax money on subsidized art?

And while people are clamoring about "economic rights," the concept of political rights is vanishing. It is forgotten that the right of free speech means the freedom to ad-vocate one's views and to bear the possible consequences, including disagreement with others, opposition, unpopularity and lack of support. The political function of "the right of free speech" is to protect dissenters and unpopular minorities from forcible suppres-sion—*not* to guarantee them the support, advantages and rewards of a popularity they have not gained.

The Bill of Rights reads: "Congress shall make no law . . . abridging the freedom of speech, or of the press . . ." It does not demand that private citizens provide a microphone for the man who advocates their destruction, or a passkey for the burglar who seeks to rob them, or a knife for the murderer who wants to cut their throats.

Such is the state of one of today's most crucial issues: *political* rights versus "*economic* rights." It's either-or. One destroys the other. But there are, in fact, no "economic rights," no "collective rights," no "public-interest rights." The term "individual rights" is a redun-dancy: there is no other kind of rights and no one else to possess them.

Those who advocate *laissez-faire* capitalism are the only advocates of man's rights.

(*April 1963*)

Leo Strauss (1899–1973 C.E.)

Strauss was born and educated in Germany and emigrated to the United States in 1938. He taught political science and philosophy at the New School for Social Research, and later became Professor of Political Philosophy at the University of Chicago and at Claremont Men's College. From 1969 to his death he was the Scott Buchanan Scholar in Residence at Saint John's in Annapolis, MD. Strauss' influential theories are still discussed today. His major publications include *The City and Man* (1964), *Natural Right and History* (1965), and *What Is Political Philosophy?* (1959), from which the following is taken.

From What Is Political Philosophy?*

1. The Problem
of Political Philosophy

. . . The meaning of political philosophy and its meaningful character is as evident today as it always has been since the time when political philosophy came to light in Athens. All political action aims at either preservation or change. When desiring to preserve, we wish to prevent a change to the worse; when desiring to change, we wish to bring about something better. All political action is then guided by some thought of better and worse. But thought of better or worse implies thought of the good. The awareness of the good which guides all our actions has the character of opinion: it is no longer questioned but, on reflection, it proves to be questionable. The very fact that we can question it directs us towards such a thought of the good as is no longer questionable—towards a thought which is no longer opinion but knowledge. All political action has then in itself a directedness towards knowledge of the good: of the good life, or of the good society. For the good society is the complete political good.

If this directedness becomes explicit, if men make it their explicit goal to acquire knowledge of the good life and of the good society, political philosophy emerges. By calling this pursuit political philosophy, we imply that it forms a part of a larger whole: of philosophy; or that political philosophy is a branch of philosophy. In the expression "political philosophy," "philosophy" indicates the manner of treatment: a treatment which both goes to the roots and is comprehensive; "political" indicates both the subject matter and the function: political philosophy deals with political matters in a manner that is meant to be relevant for political life; therefore its subject must be identical with the goal, the ultimate goal of political action. The theme of political philosophy is mankind's great objectives, freedom and government or empire—objectives which are capable of lifting all men beyond their poor selves. Political philosophy is that branch of philosophy which is closest to political life, to non-philosophic life, to human life. Only in his *Politics* does Aristotle make use of oaths—the almost inevitable accompaniment of passionate speech.

---

*An Excerpt.

Since political philosophy is a branch of philosophy, even the most provisional explanation of what political philosophy is cannot dispense with an explanation, however provisional, of what philosophy is. Philosophy, as quest for wisdom, is quest for universal knowledge, for knowledge of the whole. The quest would not be necessary if such knowledge were immediately available. The absence of knowledge of the whole does not mean, however, that men do not have thoughts about the whole: philosophy is necessarily preceded by opinions about the whole. It is, therefore, the attempt to replace opinions about the whole by knowledge of the whole. Instead of "the whole" the philosophers also say "all things": the whole is not a pure ether or an unrelieved darkness in which one cannot distinguish one part from the other, or in which one cannot discern anything. Quest for knowledge of "all things" means quest for knowledge of God, the world, and man—or rather quest for knowledge of the natures of all things: the natures in their totality are "the whole."

Philosophy is essentially not possession of the truth, but quest for the truth. The distinctive trait of the philosopher is that "he knows that he knows nothing," and that his insight into our ignorance concerning the most important things induces him to strive with all his power for knowledge. He would cease to be a philosopher by evading the questions concerning these things or by disregarding them because they cannot be answered. It may be that as regards the possible answers to these questions, the pros and cons will always be in a more or less even balance, and therefore that philosophy will never go beyond the stage of discussion or disputation and will never reach the stage of decision. This would not make philosophy futile. For the clear grasp of a fundamental question requires understanding of the nature of the subject matter with which the question is concerned. Genuine knowledge of a fundamental question, thorough understanding of it, is better than blindness to it, or indifference to it, be that indifference or blindness accompanied by knowledge of the answers to a vast number of peripheral or ephemeral questions or not. *Minimum quod potest haberi de cognitione rerum altissimarum, desiderabilius est quam certissima cognitio quae habetur de minimis rebus.* (Thomas Aquinas, *Summa Theologica,* I, qu. 1a.5)

Of philosophy thus understood, political philosophy is a branch. Political philosophy will then be the attempt to replace opinion about the nature of political things by knowledge of the nature of political things. Political things are by their nature subject to approval and disapproval, to choice and rejection, to praise and blame. It is of their essence not to be neutral but to raise a claim to men's obedience, allegiance, decision or judgment. One does not understand them as what they are, as political things, if one does not take seriously their explicit or implicit claim to be judged in terms of goodness or badness, of justice or injustice, i.e., if one does not measure them by some standard of goodness or justice. To judge soundly one must know the true standards. If political philosophy wishes to do justice to its subject matter, it must strive for genuine knowledge of these standards. Political philosophy is the attempt truly to know both the nature of political things and the right, or the good, political order.

Political philosophy ought to be distinguished from political thought in general. In our times, they are frequently identified. People have gone so far in debasing the name of philosophy as to speak of the philosophies of vulgar impostors. By political thought we understand the reflection on, or the exposition of, political ideas; and by a political idea we may understand any politically significant "phantasm, notion, species, or whatever it is about which the mind can be employed in thinking" concerning the political fundamentals. Hence, all political philosophy is political thought but not all political thought is political philosophy. Political thought is, as such, indifferent to the distinction between opinion and knowledge; but political philosophy is the conscious, coherent and relentless effort to replace opinions about the political fundamentals by knowledge regarding them. Political thought may not be more, and may not even intend to be more, than the expounding or the defense of a firmly held conviction or of an invigorating myth; but it is essential to political philosophy to be set in motion, and be kept in motion, by the disquieting awareness of the fundamental difference between conviction, or belief, and knowledge. A political thinker who is not a philosopher is primarily interested in, or attached to, a specific order or policy; the political philosopher is primarily interested in, or attached to, the truth. Political thought which is not political philosophy finds its adequate expression in laws and codes, in poems and stories, in tracts and public speeches *inter alia;* the proper form of presenting political philosophy is the treatise. Political thought is as old as the human race; the first man who uttered a word like "father" or an expression like "thou shalt not . . ." was the first political thinker; but political philosophy appeared at a knowable time in the recorded past.

By political theory, people frequently understand today comprehensive reflections on the political situation which lead up to the suggestion of a broad policy. Such reflections appeal in the last resort to principles accepted by public opinion or a considerable part of it; i.e., they dogmatically assume principles which can well be questioned. Works of political theory in this sense would be Pinsker's *Autoemancipation* and Herzl's *Judenstaat.* Pinsker's *Autoemancipation* carries as its motto the words: "If I am not for myself, who will be for me? And if not now, when?" It omits the words: "And if I am only for myself, what am I?" Pinsker's silent rejection of the thought expressed in the omitted words is a crucial premise of the argument developed in his tract. Pinsker does not justify this rejection. For a justification, one would have to turn to the 3rd and 16th chapters of Spinoza's *Tractatus theologicopoliticus,* to a work of a political philosopher.

We are compelled to distinguish political philosophy from political theology. By political theology we understand political teachings which are based on divine revelation. Political philosophy is limited to what is accessible to the unassisted human mind. As regards social philosophy, it has the same subject matter as political philosophy, but it regards it from a different point of view. Political philosophy rests on the premise that the political association—one's country or one's nation—is the most comprehensive or the most authoritative association, whereas social philosophy conceives of the political association as a part of a larger whole which it designates by the term "society."

Finally, we must discuss the relation of political philosophy to political science. "Political science" is an ambiguous term: it designates such investigations of political things as are guided by the model of natural science, and it designates the work which is being done by the members of political science departments. As regards the former, or what we may call "scientific" political science, it conceives of itself as *the* way towards genuine knowledge of political things. Just as genuine knowledge of natural things began when people turned from sterile and vain speculation to empirical and experimental study, the genuine knowledge of political things will begin when political philosophy will have given way completely to the scientific study of politics. Just as natural science stands on its own feet, and at most supplies unintentionally materials for the speculations of natural philosophers, political science stands on its own feet, and at most supplies unintentionally materials for the speculations of political philosophers. Considering the contrast between the solidity of the one pursuit and the pitiful pretentiousness characteristic of the other, it is however more reasonable to dismiss the vague and inane speculations of political philosophy altogether than to go on paying lip service to a wholly discredited and decrepit tradition. The sciences, both natural and political, are frankly non-philosophic. They need philosophy of a kind: methodology or logic. But these philosophic disciplines have obviously nothing in common with political philosophy. "Scientific" political science is in fact incompatible with political philosophy. . . .

All political knowledge is surrounded by political opinion and interspersed with it. By political opinion we understand here opinion as distinguished from knowledge of political things: errors, guesses, beliefs, prejudices, forecasts, and so on. It is of the essence of political life to be guided by a mixture of political knowledge and political opinion. Hence, all political life is accompanied by more or less coherent and more or less strenuous efforts to replace political opinion by political knowledge. Even governments which lay claim to more than human knowledge are known to employ spies.

The character of political knowledge and of the demands made on it has been profoundly affected by a fairly recent change in the character of society. In former epochs, intelligent men could acquire the political knowledge, the political understanding they needed, by listening to wise old men or, which is the same thing, by reading good historians, as well as by looking around and by devoting themselves to public affairs. These ways of acquiring political knowledge are no longer sufficient because we live in "dynamic mass societies," i.e., in societies which are characterized by both immense complexity and rapid change. Political knowledge is more difficult to come by and it becomes obsolete more rapidly than in former times. Under these conditions it becomes necessary that a number of men should devote themselves entirely to the task of collecting and digesting knowledge of political things. It is this activity which today is frequently called political science. It does not emerge if it has not been realized among other things that even such political matters as have no bearing on the situation of the day deserve to be studied, and that their study must be carried on with the greatest possible care: a specific care which is designed to counteract the specific fallacies to which our judgment on political things is exposed. Furthermore, the men we speak of invest much toil in giving political knowledge the form of teachings which can be transmitted in classrooms. Moreover, while even the most unscrupulous politician must constantly try to replace in his own mind political opinion by political knowledge in order to be successful, the scholarly student of political things will go beyond this by trying to state the results of his investigations in public without any concealment and without any partisanship: he will act the part of the enlightened and patriotic citizen who has no axe of his own to grind. Or, differently expressed, the scholarly quest for political knowledge is essentially animated by a moral impulse, the love of truth. But however one may conceive of the difference between the scholarly and the non-scholarly quest for political knowledge, and however important these differences may be, the scholarly and the non-scholarly quest for political knowledge are identical in the decisive respect: their center of reference is the given political situation, and even in most cases the given political situation in the individual's own country. It is true that a botanist in Israel pays special attention to the flora of Israel, whereas the botanist in Canada pays special attention to the flora of Canada. But this difference, which is not more than the outcome of a convenient and even indispensable division of labor, has an entirely different character than the only apparently similar difference between the preoccupation of the Israeli political scientist and the Canadian political scientist. It is only when the Here and Now ceases to be the center of reference that a philosophic or scientific approach to politics can emerge.

All knowledge of political things implies assumptions concerning the nature of political things; i.e., assumptions which concern not merely the given political situation, but political life or human life as such. One cannot know anything about a war going on at a given time without having some notion, however dim and hazy, of war as such and its place within human life as such. One cannot see a policeman as a policeman without having made an assumption about law and government as such. The assumptions concerning the nature of political things, which are implied in all knowledge of political things, have the character of opinions. It is only when these assumptions are made the theme of critical and coherent analysis that a philosophic or scientific approach to politics emerges.

The cognitive status of political knowledge is not different from that of the knowledge possessed by the shepherd, the husband, the general, or the cook. Yet the pursuits of these types of man do not give rise to a pastoral, marital, military, or culinary philosophy because their ultimate goals are sufficiently clear and unambiguous. The ultimate political goal, on the other hand, urgently calls for coherent reflection. The goal of the general is victory, whereas the goal of the statesman is the common good. What victory means is not essentially controversial, but the meaning of the common good is essentially controversial. The ambiguity of the political goal is due to its comprehensive character. Thus the temptation arises to deny, or to evade, the comprehensive character of politics and to treat politics as one compartment among many. But this temptation must be resisted if it is necessary to face our situation as human beings, i.e., the whole situation. . . .

II. The Classical Solution

When we describe the political philosophy of Plato and of Aristotle as classical political philosophy, we imply that it is the classic form of political philosophy. The classic was once said to be characterized by noble simplicity and quiet grandeur. This suggestion guides us in the right direction. It is an attempt to articulate what was formerly also called the "natural" character of classical thought. "Natural" is here understood in contradistinction to what is merely human, all too human. A human being is said to be natural if he is guided by nature rather than by convention, or by inherited opinion, or by tradition, to say nothing of mere whims. Classical political philosophy is non-traditional, because it belongs to the fertile moment when all political traditions were shaken, and there was not yet in existence a tradition of political philosophy. In all later epochs, the philosophers' study of political things was mediated by a tradition of political philosophy which acted like a screen between the philosopher and political things, regardless of whether the individual philosopher cherished or rejected that tradition. From this it follows that the classical philosophers see the political things with a freshness and directness which have never been equalled. They look at political things in the perspective of the enlightened citizen or statesman. They see things clearly which the enlightened citizens or statesmen do not see clearly, or do not see at all. But this has no other reason but the fact that they look further afield in the same direction as the enlightened citizens or statesmen. They do not look at political things from the outside, as spectators of political life. They speak the language of the citizens or statesmen: they hardly use a single term which is not familiar to the market place. Hence their political philosophy is comprehensive; it is both political theory and political skill; it is as open minded to the legal and institutional aspects of political life as it is to that which transcends the legal and institutional; it is equally free from the narrowness of the lawyer, the brutality of the technician, the vagaries of the visionary, and the baseness of the opportunist. It reproduces, and raises to its perfection, the magnanimous flexibility of the true statesman, who crushes the insolent and spares the vanquished. It is free from all fanaticism because it knows that evil cannot be eradicated and therefore that one's expectations from politics must be moderate. The spirit which animates it may be described as serenity or sublime sobriety.

Compared with classical political philosophy, all later political thought, whatever else its merits may be, and in particular modern political thought, has a derivative character. This means that in later times there has occurred an estrangement from the simple and primary issues. This has given to political philosophy the character of "abstractness," and has therefore engendered the view that the philosophic movement must be a movement, not from opinion to knowledge, not from the here and now to what is always or eternal, but from the abstract towards the concrete. It was thought that by virtue of this movement towards the concrete, recent philosophy has overcome the limitations not only of modern political philosophy, but of classical political philosophy as well. It was overlooked, however, that this change of orientation perpetuated the original defect of modern philosophy because it accepted abstractions as its starting point, and that the concrete at which one eventually arrived was not at all the truly concrete, but still an abstraction. . . .

The character of classical political philosophy appears with the greatest clarity from Plato's *Laws*, which is his political work *par excellence*. The *Laws* is a conversation about law, and political things in general, between an old Athenian stranger, an old Cretan, and an old Spartan. The conversation takes place on the island of Crete. At the beginning one receives the impression that the Athenian has come to Crete in order to study there the best laws. For if it is true that the good is identical with the ancestral, the best laws for a Greek would be the oldest Greek laws, and these are the Cretan laws. But the equation of the good with the ancestral is not tenable if the first ancestors were not gods, or sons of gods, or pupils of gods. Hence, the Cretans believed that their laws were originated by Zeus, who instructed his son Minos, the Cretan legislator. The *Laws* opens with an expression of this belief. It appears immediately afterwards that this belief has no other ground, no better ground, than a saying of Homer—and the poets are of questionable veracity—as well as what the Cretans say—and the Cretans were famous for their lack of veracity. However this may be, very shortly after its beginning, the conversation shifts from the question of the origins of the Cretan laws and the Spartan laws to the question of their intrinsic worth: a code given by a god, by a being of superhuman excellence, must be unqualifiedly good. Very slowly, very circumspectly does the Athenian approach this grave question. To begin with he limits his criticism of the principle underlying the Cretan and the Spartan codes by criticizing not these codes, but a poet, a man without authority and, in addition, an expatriate, who had praised the same principle. In the sequel, the philosopher attacks not yet the Cretan and the Spartan codes, but the interpretation of these codes which had been set forth by his two interlocutors. He does not begin to criticize these venerable codes explicitly until he has appealed to a presumed Cretan and Spartan law which permits such criticism under certain conditions—under conditions which are fulfilled, to some extent, in the present conversation. According to that law, all must say with one voice and with one mouth that all the laws of Crete, or of Sparta, are good because they are god-given, and no one is suffered to say something different; but an old citizen may utter a criticism of an allegedly divine law before a magistrate of his own age if no young men are present. By this time it has become clear to the reader that the Athenian has not come to Crete in order to study there the best laws, but rather in order to introduce into Crete new laws and institutions, truly good laws and institutions. These laws and institutions will prove to be, to a considerable extent, of Athenian origin. It seems that the Athenian, being the son of a highly civilized society, has embarked on the venture of civilizing a rather uncivilized society. Therefore he has to apprehend that his suggestions will be odious, not only as innovations, but above all as foreign, as Athenian: deep-seated, old animosities and suspicions will be aroused by his recommendations. He begins his explicit criticism with a remark about the probable connection between certain Cretan and Spartan institutions and the practice of homosexuality in these cities. The Spartan, rising in defense of his fatherland, does not, indeed, defend homosexuality, but, turning to the offensive, rebukes the Athenians for their excessive drinking. The Athenian is thus given a perfect excuse for recommending the introduction of the Athenian institution of banquets: he is compelled to defend that institution; by defending it he acts the part, not of a civilizing philosopher who, being a philosopher, is a philanthropist, but of the patriot. He acts in a way which is perfectly understandable to his interlocutors and perfectly respectable in their opinion. He attempts to show that wine-drinking, and even drunkenness, if it is practiced in well-presided banquets, is conducive to education in temperance or moderation. This speech about wine forms the bulk of the first two books of the *Laws*. Only after the speech about wine has been brought to its conclusion does the Athenian turn to the question of the beginning of political life, to a question which is the true beginning of his political theme. The speech about wine appears to be *the* introduction to political philosophy.

Why does *the* Platonic dialogue about politics and laws begin with such an extensive conversation about wine? What is the artistic or logographic necessity demanding this? The proper interlocutors in a conversation about laws are old citizens of communities famous for their laws, for their obedience and allegiance to their old laws. Such men understand best what living under laws, living in laws, means. They are the perfect incarnation of the spirit of laws: of lawfulness, of law-abidingness. But their very virtue becomes a defect if there is no longer a question of preserving old laws, but of seeking the best laws or introducing new and better ones. Their habits and their competence make these men impervious to suggestions for improvement. The Athenian induces them to participate in a conversation about wine-drinking, about a pleasure that is forbidden to them by their old laws. The talk about wine-drinking is a kind of vicarious enjoyment of wine, especially since wine-drinking is a forbidden pleasure. Perhaps the talk reminds the two old interlocutors of secret and pleasurable transgressions of their own. The effect of the talk about wine is therefore similar to the effect of actual wine-drinking; it loosens their tongues; it makes them young; it makes them bold, daring, willing to innovate. They must not actually drink wine, since this would impair their judgment. They must drink wine, not in deed, but in speech.

But this means that wine-drinking educates to boldness, to courage, and not to moderation, and yet wine-drinking was said to be conducive to moderation. Let us therefore consider the other partner in the conversation, the Athenian philosopher. To doubt the sacredness of the ancestral means to appeal from the ancestral to the natural. It means to transcend all human traditions, nay, the whole dimension of the merely human. It means to learn to look down on the human as something inferior or to leave the cave. But by leaving the cave one loses sight of the city, of the whole political sphere. If the philosopher is to give political guidance, he must return to the cave: from the light of the sun to the world of shadows; his perception must be dimmed; his mind must undergo an obfuscation. The vicarious enjoyment of wine through a conversation about wine, which enlarges the horizon of the law-bred old citizens, limits the horizon of the philosopher. But this obfuscation, this acceptance of the political perspective, this adoption of the language of political man, this achievement of harmony between the excellence of man and the excellence of the citizen, or between wisdom and law-abidingness is, it seems, the most noble exercise of the virtue of moderation: wine-drinking educates to moderation. For moderation is not a virtue of thought: Plato likens philosophy to madness, the very opposite of sobriety or moderation; thought must be not moderate, but fearless, not to say shameless. But moderation is a virtue controlling the philosopher's speech.

We have suggested that the Athenian stranger had gone to Crete in order to civilize an uncivilized society, and that he had done this out of philanthropy. But does not philanthropy begin at home? Did he not have more pressing duties to perform at home? What kind of man is the Athenian stranger? The *Laws* begins with the word "God": it is the only Platonic dialogue which begins in that manner. There is one and only one Platonic dialogue which ends with the word "God": the *Apology of Socrates*. In the *Apology of Socrates* an old Athenian philosopher, Socrates, defends himself against the charge of impiety, of not believing that the gods worshiped by the city of Athens exist. It seems that there is a conflict between philosophy and accepting the gods of the city. In the *Laws* an old Athenian philosopher recommends a law about impiety which renders impossible the conflict between philosophy and the city, or which brings about harmony between philosophy and the city. The gods whose existence is to be admitted by every citizen of the city of the *Laws* are beings whose existence can be demonstrated. That old Athenian philosopher of the *Apology of Socrates* was condemned to death by the city of Athens. He was given an opportunity to escape from prison: he refused to avail himself of this opportunity. His refusal was not based on an appeal to a categorical imperative demanding passive obedience, without if's and but's. His refusal was based on a deliberation, on a prudential consideration of what was the right thing to do in the circumstances. One of the circumstances was Socrates' old age: we are forced to wonder how Socrates would have decided if he had been 30 or 40 years old instead of 70. Another circumstance was the unavailability of a proper place of exile: where should he flee? He seems to have a choice between law-abiding cities nearby, where his life would be unbearable, since he would be known as a fugitive from justice, and a lawless country far away, where the prevailing lack of order would make his life miserable. The disjunction is obviously incomplete: there were law-abiding cities far away, for instance on Crete, which is mentioned as a law-abiding place in the very deliberation in question. We are entitled to infer that if Socrates had fled, he would have gone to Crete. The *Laws* tells us what he would have done in Crete after his arrival: he would have brought the blessings of Athens, Athenian laws, Athenian institutions, banquets, and philosophy to Crete. (When Aristotle speaks about Plato's *Laws*, he takes it for granted that the chief character of the *Laws* is Socrates.) Escaping to Crete, living in Crete, was the alternative to dying in Athens. But Socrates chose to die in Athens. Socrates preferred to sacrifice his life in order to preserve philosophy in Athens rather than to preserve his life in order to introduce philosophy into Crete. If the danger to the future of philosophy in Athens had been less great, he might have chosen to flee to Crete. His choice was a political choice of the highest order. It did not consist in the simple subsumption of his case under a simple, universal, and unalterable rule.

But let us return after this long story to the beginning of Plato's *Laws*. If the originator of the Cretan laws, or any other laws, is not a god, the cause of laws must be human beings, the human legislator. There is a variety of types of human legislators: the legislator has a different character in a democracy, in an oligarchy, in a monarchy. The legislator is the governing body, and the character of the governing body depends on the whole social and political order, the *politeia,* the regime. The cause of the laws is the regime. Therefore the guiding theme of political philosophy is the regime rather than the laws. Regime becomes the guiding theme of political thought when the derivative or questionable character of laws has been realized. There are a number of Biblical terms which can be properly translated by "law"; there is no Biblical equivalent to "regime."

Regime is the order, the form, which gives society its character. Regime is therefore a specific manner of life. Regime is the form of life as living together, the manner of living of society and in society, since this manner depends decisively on the predominance of human beings of a certain type, on the manifest domination of society by human beings of a certain type. Regime means that whole, which we today are in the habit of viewing primarily in a fragmentized form: regime means simultaneously the form of life of a society, its style of life, its moral taste, form of society, form of state, form of government, spirit of laws. We may try to articulate the simple and unitary thought, that expresses itself in the term *politeia,* as follows: life is activity which is directed towards some goal; social life is an activity which is directed towards such a goal as can be pursued only by society; but in order to pursue a specific goal, as its comprehensive goal, society must be organized, ordered, constructed, constituted in a manner which is in accordance with that goal; this, however, means that the authoritative human beings must be akin to that goal.

There is a variety of regimes. Each regime raises a claim, explicitly or implicitly, which extends beyond the boundaries of any given society. These claims conflict, therefore, with each other. There is a variety of conflicting regimes. Thus the regimes themselves, and not any preoccupation of mere bystanders, force us to wonder which of the given conflicting regimes is better, and ultimately, which regime is the best regime. Classical political philosophy is guided by the question of the best regime.

The actualization of the best regime depends on the coming together, on the coincidence of, things which have a natural tendency to move away from each other (e.g., on the coincidence of philosophy and political power); its actualization depends therefore on chance. Human nature is enslaved in so many ways that it is almost a miracle if an individual achieves the highest: what can one expect of society! The peculiar manner of being of the best regime—namely, its lacking actuality while being superior to all actual regimes—has its ultimate reason in the dual nature of man, in the fact that man is the in-between being: in between brutes and gods.

The practical meaning of the notion of the best regime appears most clearly, when one considers the ambiguity of the term "good citizen." Aristotle suggests two entirely different definitions of the good citizen. In his more popular *Constitution of Athens* he suggests that the good citizen is a man who serves his country well, without any regard to the difference of regimes—who serves his country well in fundamental indifference to the change of regimes. The good citizen, in a word, is the patriotic citizen, the man whose loyalty belongs first and last to his fatherland. In his less popular *Politics,* Aristotle says that there is not *the* good citizen without qualification. For what it means to be a good citizen depends entirely on the regime. A good citizen in Hitler's Germany would be a bad citizen elsewhere. But whereas good citizen is relative to the regime, good man does not have such a relativity. The meaning of good man is always and everywhere the same. The good man is identical with the good citizen only in one case—in the case of the best regime. For only in the best regime is the good of the regime and the good of the good man identical, that goal being virtue. This amounts to saying that in his *Politics* Aristotle questions the proposition that patriotism is enough. From the point of view of the patriot, the fatherland is more important than any difference of regimes. From the point of view of the patriot, he who prefers any regime to the fatherland is a partisan, if not a traitor. Aristotle says in effect that the partisan sees deeper than the patriot but that only one kind of partisan is superior to the patriot; this is the partisan of virtue. One can express Aristotle's thought as follows: patriotism is not enough for the same reason that the most doting mother is happier if her child is good than if he is bad. A mother loves her child because he is her own; she loves what is her own. But she also loves the good. All human love is subject to the law that it be both love of one's own and love of the good, and there is necessarily a tension between one's own and the good, a tension which may well lead to a break, be it only the breaking of a heart. The relation between one's own and the good finds its political expression in the relation between the fatherland and the regime. In the language of classical metaphysics, the fatherland or the nation is the matter whereas the regime is the form. The classics held the view that the form is higher in dignity than the matter. One may call this view "idealism." The practical meaning of this idealism is that the good is of higher dignity than one's own, or that the best regime is a higher consideration than the fatherland. The Jewish equivalent of this relation might be said to be the relation between the Torah and Israel.

Classical political philosophy is today exposed to two very common objections, the raising of which requires neither originality nor intelligence, nor even erudition. The objections are these: (1) classical political philosophy is anti-democratic and hence bad; (2) classical political philosophy is based on classical natural philosophy or on classical cosmology, and this basis has been proven to be untrue by the success of modern natural science.

To speak first of the classics' attitude towards democracy, the premises: "the classics are good," and "democracy is good" do not validate the conclusion "hence the classics were good democrats." It would be silly to deny that the classics rejected democracy as an inferior kind of regime. They were not blind to its advantages. The severest indictment of democracy that ever was written occurs in the eighth book of Plato's *Republic.* But even there, and precisely there, Plato makes it clear—by coordinating his arrangement of regimes with Hesiod's arrangement of the ages of the world—that democracy is, in a very important respect, equal to the best regime, which corresponds to Hesiod's golden age: since the principle of democracy is freedom, all human types can develop freely in a democracy, and hence in particular the best human type. It is true that Socrates was killed by a democracy; but he was killed when he was 70; he was permitted to live for 70 long years. Yet Plato did not regard this consideration as decisive. For he was concerned not only with the possibility of philosophy, but likewise with a stable political order that would be congenial to moderate political courses; and such an order, he thought, depends on the predominance of old families. More generally, the classics rejected democracy because they thought that the aim of human life, and hence of social life, is not freedom but virtue. Freedom as a goal is ambiguous, because it is freedom for evil as well as for good. Virtue emerges normally only through education, that is to say, through the formation of character, through habituation, and this requires leisure on the part of both parents and children. But leisure in its turn requires some degree of wealth—more specifically a kind of wealth whose acquisition or administration is compatible with leisure. Now, as regards wealth, it so happens, as Aristotle observes, that there is always a minority of well-to-do people and a majority of the poor, and this strange coincidence will last forever because there is a kind of natural scarcity. "For the poor shall never cease out of the land." It is for this reason that democracy, or rule of the majority, is government by the uneducated. And no one in his senses would wish to live under such a government. This classical argument would not be stringent if men did not need education in order to acquire a firm adhesion to virtue. It is no accident that it was Jean-Jacques Rousseau who taught that all knowledge which men need in order to live virtuously is supplied by the conscience, the preserve of the simple souls rather than of other men: man is sufficiently equipped by nature for the good life; man is by nature good. But the same Rousseau was compelled to develop a scheme of education which very few people could financially afford. On the whole the view has prevailed that democracy must become rule by the educated, and this goal will be achieved by universal education. But universal education presupposes that the economy of scarcity has given way to an economy of plenty. And the economy of plenty presupposes the emancipation of technology from moral and political control. The essential difference between our view and the classical view consists then, not in a difference regarding moral principle, not in a different understanding of justice: we, too, even our communist coexistents, think that it is just to give equal things to equal people and unequal things to people of unequal merit. The difference between the classics and us with regard to democracy consists exclusively in a different estimate of the virtues of technology. But we are not entitled to say that the classical view has been refuted. Their implicit prophecy that the emancipation of technology, of the arts, from moral and political control would lead to disaster or to the dehumanization of man has not yet been refuted.

Nor can we say that democracy has found a solution to the problem of education. In the first place, what is today called education, very frequently does not mean education proper, i.e., the formation of character, but rather instruction and training. Secondly, to the extent to which the formation of character is indeed intended, there exists a very dangerous tendency to identify the good man with the good sport, the cooperative fellow, the "regular guy," i.e., an overemphasis on a certain part of social virtue and a corresponding neglect of those virtues which mature, if they do not flourish, in privacy, not to say in solitude: by educating people to cooperate with each other in a friendly spirit, one does not yet educate non-conformists, people who are prepared to stand alone, to fight alone, "rugged individualists." Democracy has not yet found a defense against the creeping conformism and the ever-increasing invasion of privacy which it fosters. Beings who look down on us from a star might find that the difference between democracy and communism is not quite as great as it appears to be when one considers exclusively the doubtless very important question of civil and political liberties, although only people of exceptional levity or irresponsibility say that the difference between communism and democracy is negligible in the last analysis. Now to the extent to which democracy is aware of these dangers, to the same extent it sees itself compelled to think of elevating its level and its possibilities by a return to the classics' notions of education: a kind of education which can never be thought of as mass-education, but only as higher and highest education of those who are by nature fit for it. It would be an understatement to call it royal education.

Yet granted that there are no valid moral or political objections to classical political philosophy—is that political philosophy not bound up with an antiquated cosmology? Does not the very question of the nature of man point to the question of the nature of the whole, and therewith to one or the other specific cosmology? Whatever the significance of modern natural science may be, it cannot affect our understanding of what is human in man. To understand man in the light of the whole means for modern natural science to understand man in the light of the sub-human. But in that light man as man is wholly unintelligible. Classical political philosophy viewed man in a different light. It was originated by Socrates. And Socrates was so far from being committed to a specific cosmology that his knowledge was knowledge of ignorance. Knowledge of ignorance is not ignorance. It is knowledge of the elusive character of the truth, of the whole. Socrates, then, viewed man in the light of the mysterious character of the whole. He held therefore that we are more familiar with the situation of man as man than with the ultimate causes of that situation. We may also say he viewed man in the light of the unchangeable ideas, i.e., of the fundamental and permanent problems. For to articulate the situation of man means to articulate man's openness to the whole. This understanding of the situation of man which includes, then, the quest for cosmology rather than a solution to the cosmological problem, was the foundation of classical political philosophy.

To articulate the problem of cosmology means to answer the question of what philosophy is or what a philosopher is. Plato refrained from entrusting the thematic discussion of this question to Socrates. He entrusted it to a stranger from Elea. But even that stranger from Elea did not discuss explicitly what a philosopher is. He discussed explicitly two kinds of men which are easily mistaken for the philosopher, the sophist and the statesman: by understanding both sophistry (in its highest as well as in its lower meaning) and statesmanship, one will understand what philosophy is. Philosophy strives for knowledge of the whole. The whole is the totality of the parts. The whole eludes us but we know parts: we possess partial knowledge of parts. The knowledge which we possess is characterized by a fundamental dualism which has never been overcome. At one pole we find knowledge of homogeneity: above all in arithmetic, but also in the other branches of mathematics, and derivatively in all productive arts or crafts. At the opposite pole we find knowledge of heterogeneity, and in particular of heterogeneous ends; the highest form of this kind of knowledge is the art of the statesman and of the educator. The latter kind of knowledge is superior to the former for this reason. As knowledge of the ends of human life, it is knowledge of what makes human life complete or whole; it is therefore knowledge of a whole. Knowledge of the ends of man implies knowledge of the human soul; and the human soul is the only part of the whole which is open to the whole and therefore more akin to the whole than anything else is. But this knowledge—the political art in the highest sense—is not knowledge of *the* whole. It seems that knowledge of the whole would have to combine somehow political knowledge in the highest sense with knowledge of homogeneity. And this combination is not at our disposal. Men are therefore constantly tempted to force the issue by imposing unity on the phenomena, by absolutizing either knowledge of homogeneity or knowledge of ends. Men are constantly attracted and deluded by two opposite charms: the charm of competence which is engendered by mathematics and everything akin to mathematics, and the charm of humble awe, which is engendered by meditation on the human soul and its experiences. Philosophy is characterized by the gentle, if firm, refusal to succumb to either charm. It is the highest form of the mating of courage and moderation. In spite of its highness or nobility, it could appear as Sisyphean or ugly, when one contrasts its achievement with its goal. Yet it is necessarily accompanied, sustained and elevated by *eros*. It is graced by nature's grace. . . .

John Rawls (b. 1921)

After decades of logical analysis dominating philosophy, Rawls' 1971 book *A Theory of Justice* restored political philosophy to mainstream acceptance. Rawls' conception of justice as fairness has been very influential, although the resurgence of political philosophy has also brought about many criticisms of this theory. Robert Nozick put it this way: "Political philosophers now must either work within Rawls' theory or explain why not." The following excerpts are from *A Theory of Justice*.

From A Theory of Justice*

Chapter I. Justice as Fairness

In this introductory chapter I sketch some of the main ideas of the theory of justice I wish to develop. The exposition is informal and intended to prepare the way for the more detailed arguments that follow. Unavoidably there is some overlap between this and later discussions. I begin by describing the role of justice in social cooperation and with a brief account of the primary subject of justice, the basic structure of society. I then present the main idea of justice as fairness, a theory of justice that generalizes and carries to a higher level of abstraction the traditional conception of the social contract. The compact of society is replaced by an initial situation that incorporates certain procedural constraints on arguments designed to lead to an original agreement on principles of justice. I also take up, for purposes of clarification and contrast, the classical utilitarian and intuitionist conceptions of justice and consider some of the differences between these views and justice as fairness. My guiding aim is to work out a theory of justice that is a viable alternative to these doctrines which have long dominated our philosophical tradition.

1. The Role of Justice

Justice is the first virtue of social institutions, as truth is of systems of thought. A theory however elegant and economical must be rejected or revised if it is untrue; likewise laws and institutions no matter how efficient and well-arranged must be reformed or abolished if they are unjust. Each person possesses an inviolability founded on justice that even the welfare of society as a whole cannot override. For this reason justice denies that the loss of freedom for some is made right by a greater good shared by others. It does not allow that the sacrifices imposed on a few are outweighed by the larger sum of advantages enjoyed by many. Therefore in a just society the liberties of equal citizenship are taken as settled; the rights secured by justice are not subject to political bargaining or to the calculus of social interests. The only thing that permits us to acquiesce in an erroneous theory is the

---

*An Excerpt.

lack of a better one; analogously, an injustice is tolerable only when it is necessary to avoid an even greater injustice. Being first virtues of human activities, truth and justice are uncompromising.

These propositions seem to express our intuitive conviction of the primacy of justice. No doubt they are expressed too strongly. In any event I wish to inquire whether these contentions or others similar to them are sound, and if so how they can be accounted for. To this end it is necessary to work out a theory of justice in the light of which these assertions can be interpreted and assessed. I shall begin by considering the role of the principles of justice. Let us assume, to fix ideas, that a society is a more or less self-sufficient association of persons who in their relations to one another recognize certain rules of conduct as binding and who for the most part act in accordance with them. Suppose further that these rules specify a system of cooperation designed to advance the good of those taking part in it. Then, although a society is a cooperative venture for mutual advantage, it is typically marked by a conflict as well as by an identity of interests. There is an identity of interests since social cooperation makes possible a better life for all than any would have if each were to live solely by his own efforts. There is a conflict of interests since persons are not indifferent as to how the greater benefits produced by their collaboration are distributed, for in order to pursue their ends they each prefer a larger to a lesser share. A set of principles is required for choosing among the various social arrangements which determine this division of advantages and for underwriting an agreement on the proper distributive shares. These principles are the principles of social justice: they provide a way of assigning rights and duties in the basic institutions of society and they define the appropriate distribution of the benefits and burdens of social cooperation.

Now let us say that a society is well-ordered when it is not only designed to advance the good of its members but when it is also effectively regulated by a public conception of justice. That is, it is a society in which (1) everyone accepts and knows that the others accept the same principles of justice, and (2) the basic social institutions generally satisfy and are generally known to satisfy these principles. In this case while men may put forth excessive demands on one another, they nevertheless acknowledge a common point of view from which their claims may be adjudicated. If men's inclination to self-interest makes their vigilance against one another necessary, their public sense of justice makes their secure association together possible. Among individuals with disparate aims and purposes a shared conception of justice establishes the bonds of civic friendship; the general desire for justice limits the pursuit of other ends. One may think of a public conception of justice as constituting the fundamental charter of a well-ordered human association.

Existing societies are of course seldom well-ordered in this sense, for what is just and unjust is usually in dispute. Men disagree about which principles should define the basic terms of their association. Yet we may still say, despite this disagreement, that they each have a conception of justice. That is, they understand the need for, and they are prepared to affirm, a characteristic set of principles for assigning basic rights and duties and for determining what they take to be the proper distribution of the benefits and burdens of social cooperation. Thus it seems natural to think of the concept of justice as distinct from the various conceptions of justice and as being specified by the role which these different sets of principles, these different conceptions, have in common. Those who hold different conceptions of justice can, then, still agree that institutions are just when no arbitrary distinctions are made between persons in the assigning of basic rights and duties and when the rules determine a proper balance between competing claims to the advantages of social life. Men can agree to this description of just institutions since the notions of an arbitrary distinction and of a proper balance, which are included in the concept of justice, are left open for each to interpret according to the principles of justice that he accepts. These principles single out which similarities and differences among persons are relevant in determining rights and duties and they specify which division of advantages is appropriate. Clearly this distinction between the concept and the various conceptions of justice settles no important questions. It simply helps to identify the role of the principles of social justice.

Some measure of agreement in conceptions of justice is, however, not the only prerequisite for a viable human community. There are other fundamental social problems, in particular those of coordination, efficiency, and stability. Thus the plans of individuals need to be fitted together so that their activities are compatible with one another and they can all be carried through without anyone's legitimate expectations being severely disappointed. Moreover, the execution of these plans should lead to the achievement of social ends in ways that are efficient and consistent with justice. And finally, the scheme of social cooperation must be stable: it must be more or less regularly complied with and its basic rules willingly acted upon; and when infractions occur, stabilizing forces should exist that prevent further violations and tend to restore the arrangement. Now it is evident that these three problems are connected with that of justice. In the absence of a certain measure of agreement on what is just and unjust, it is clearly more difficult for individuals to coordinate their plans efficiently in order to insure that mutually beneficial arrangements are maintained. Distrust and resentment corrode the ties of civility, and suspicion and hostility tempt men to act in ways they would otherwise avoid. So while the distinctive role of conceptions of justice is to specify basic rights and duties and to determine the appropriate distributive shares, the way in which a conception does this is bound to affect the problems of efficiency, coordination, and stability. We cannot, in general, assess a conception of justice by its distributive role alone, however useful this role may be in identifying the concept of justice. We must take into account its wider connections; for even though justice has a certain priority, being the most important virtue of institutions, it is still true that, other things equal, one conception of justice is preferable to another when its broader consequences are more desirable.

2. The Subject of Justice

Many different kinds of things are said to be just and unjust: not only laws, institutions, and social systems, but also particular actions of many kinds, including decisions, judgments, and imputations. We also call the attitudes and dispositions of persons, and persons themselves, just and unjust. Our topic, however, is that of social justice. For us the primary subject of justice is the basic structure of society, or more exactly, the way in which the major social institutions distribute fundamental rights and duties and determine the division of advantages from social cooperation. By major institutions I understand the political constitution and the principal economic and social arrangements. Thus the legal protection of freedom of thought and liberty of conscience, competitive markets, private property in the means of production, and the monogamous family are examples of major social institutions. Taken together as one scheme, the major institutions define men's rights and duties and influence their life-prospects, what they can expect to be and how well they can hope to do. The basic structure is the primary subject of justice because its effects are so profound and present from the start. The intuitive notion here is that this structure contains various social positions and that men born into different positions have different expectations of life determined, in part, by the political system as well as by economic and social circumstances. In this way the institutions of society favor certain starting places over others. These are especially deep inequalities. Not only are they pervasive, but they affect men's initial chances in life; yet they cannot possibly be justified by an appeal to the notions of merit or desert. It is these inequalities, presumably inevitable in the basic structure of any society, to which the principles of social justice must in the first instance apply. These principles, then, regulate the choice of a political constitution and the main elements of the economic and social system. The justice of a social scheme depends essentially on how fundamental rights and duties are assigned and on the economic opportunities and social conditions in the various sectors of society.

The scope of our inquiry is limited in two ways. First of all, I am concerned with a special case of the problem of justice. I shall not consider the justice of institutions and social practices generally, nor except in passing the justice of the law of nations and of relations between states. Therefore, if one supposes that the concept of justice applies whenever there is an allotment of something rationally regarded as advantageous or disadvantageous, then we are interested in only one instance of its application. There is no reason to suppose ahead of time that the principles satisfactory for the basic structure hold for all cases. These principles may not work for the rules and practices of private associations or for those of less comprehensive social groups. They may be irrelevant for the various informal conventions and customs of everyday life; they may not elucidate the justice, or perhaps better, the fairness of voluntary cooperative arrangements or procedures for making contractual agreements. The conditions for the law of nations may require different principles arrived at in a somewhat different way. I shall be satisfied if it is possible to formulate a reasonable conception of justice for the basic structure of society conceived for the time being as a closed system isolated from other societies. The significance of this special case is obvious and needs no explanation. It is natural to conjecture that once we have a sound theory for this case, the remaining problems of justice will prove more tractable in the light of it. With suitable modifications such a theory should provide the key for some of these other questions.

The other limitation on our discussion is that for the most part I examine the principles of justice that would regulate a well-ordered society. Everyone is presumed to act justly and to do his part in upholding just institutions. Though justice may be, as Hume remarked, the cautious, jealous virtue, we can still ask what a perfectly just society would be like. Thus I consider primarily what I call strict compliance as opposed to partial compliance theory. The latter studies the principles that govern how we are to deal with injustice. It comprises such topics as the theory of punishment, the doctrine of just war, and the justification of the various ways of opposing unjust regimes, ranging from civil disobedience and militant resistance to revolution and rebellion. Also included here are questions of compensatory justice and of weighing one form of institutional injustice against another. Obviously the problems of partial compliance theory are the pressing and urgent matters. These are the things that we are faced with in everyday life. The reason for beginning with ideal theory is that it provides, I believe, the only basis for the systematic grasp of these more pressing problems. The discussion of civil disobedience, for example, depends upon it. At least, I shall assume that a deeper understanding can be gained in no other way, and that the nature and aims of a perfectly just society is the fundamental part of the theory of justice.

Now admittedly the concept of the basic structure is somewhat vague. It is not always clear which institutions or features thereof should be included. But it would be premature to worry about this matter here. I shall proceed by discussing principles which do apply to what is certainly a part of the basic structure as intuitively understood; I shall then try to extend the application of these principles so that they cover what would appear to be the main elements of this structure. Perhaps these principles will turn out to be perfectly general, although this is unlikely. It is sufficient that they apply to the most important cases of social justice. The point to keep in mind is that a conception of justice for the basic structure is worth having for its own sake. It should not be dismissed because its principles are not everywhere satisfactory.

A conception of social justice, then, is to be regarded as providing in the first instance a standard whereby the distributive aspects of the basic structure of society are to be assessed. This standard, however, is not to be confused with the principles defining the other virtues, for the basic structure, and social arrangements generally, may be efficient or inefficient, liberal or illiberal, and many other things, as well as just or unjust. A complete conception defining principles for all the virtues of the basic structure, together with their respective weights when they conflict, is more than a conception of justice; it is a social ideal. The principles of justice are but a part, although perhaps the most important part, of such a conception. A social ideal in turn is connected with a conception of society, a vision of the way in which the aims and purposes of social cooperation are to be understood. The various conceptions of justice are the outgrowth of different notions of society against the background of opposing views of the natural necessities and opportunities of human life. Fully to understand a conception of justice we must make explicit the conception of social cooperation from which it derives. But in doing this we should not lose sight of the special role of the principles of justice or of the primary subject to which they apply.

In these preliminary remarks I have distinguished the concept of justice as meaning a proper balance between competing claims from a conception of justice as a set of related principles for identifying the relevant considerations which determine this balance. I have also characterized justice as but one part of a social ideal, although the theory I shall propose no doubt extends its everyday sense. This theory is not offered as a description of ordinary meanings but as an account of certain distributive principles for the basic structure of society. I assume that any reasonably complete ethical theory must include principles for this fundamental problem and that these principles, whatever they are, constitute its doctrine of justice. The concept of justice I take to be defined, then, by the role of its principles in assigning rights and duties and in defining the appropriate division of social advantages. A conception of justice is an interpretation of this role.

Now this approach may not seem to tally with tradition. I believe, though, that it does. The more specific sense that Aristotle gives to justice, and from which the most familiar formulations derive, is that of refraining from *pleonexia*, that is, from gaining some advantage for oneself by seizing what belongs to another, his property, his reward, his office, and the like, or by denying a person that which is due to him, the fulfillment of a promise, the repayment of a debt, the showing of proper respect, and so on. It is evident that this definition is framed to apply to actions, and persons are thought to be just insofar as they have, as one of the permanent elements of their character, a steady and effective desire to act justly. Aristotle's definition clearly presupposes, however, an account of what properly belongs to a person and of what is due to him. Now such entitlements are, I believe, very often derived from social institutions and the legitimate expectations to which they give rise. There is no reason to think that Aristotle would disagree with this, and certainly he has a conception of social justice to account for these claims. The definition I adopt is designed to apply directly to the most important case, the justice of the basic structure. There is no conflict with the traditional notion.

3. The Main Idea of the Theory of Justice

My aim is to present a conception of justice which generalizes and carries to a higher level of abstraction the familiar theory of the social contract as found, say, in Locke, Rousseau, and Kant. In order to do this we are not to think of the original contract as one to enter a particular society or to set up a particular form of government. Rather, the guiding idea is that the principles of justice for the basic structure of society are the object of the original agreement. They are the principles that free and rational persons concerned to further their own interests would accept in an initial position of equality as defining the fundamental terms of their association. These principles are to regulate all further agreements; they specify the kinds of social cooperation that can be entered into and the forms of government that can be established. This way of regarding the principles of justice I shall call justice as fairness.

Thus we are to imagine that those who engage in social cooperation choose together, in one joint act, the principles which are to assign basic rights and duties and to determine the division of social benefits. Men are to decide in advance how they are to regulate their claims against one another and what is to be the foundation charter of their society. Just as each person must decide by rational reflection what constitutes his good, that is, the system of ends which it is rational for him to pursue, so a group of persons must decide once and for all what is to count among them as just and unjust. The choice which rational men would make in this hypothetical situation of equal liberty, assuming for the present that this choice problem has a solution, determines the principles of justice.

In justice as fairness the original position of equality corresponds to the state of nature in the traditional theory of the social contract. This original position is not, of course, thought of as an actual historical state of affairs, much less as a primitive condition of culture.

It is understood as a purely hypothetical situation characterized so as to lead to a certain conception of justice. Among the essential features of this situation is that no one knows his place in society, his class position or social status, nor does any one know his fortune in the distribution of natural assets and abilities, his intelligence, strength, and the like. I shall even assume that the parties do not know their conceptions of the good or their special psychological propensities. The principles of justice are chosen behind a veil of ignorance. This ensures that no one is advantaged or disadvantaged in the choice of principles by the outcome of natural chance or the contingency of social circumstances. Since all are similarly situated and no one is able to design principles to favor his particular condition, the principles of justice are the result of a fair agreement or bargain. For given the circumstances of the original position, the symmetry of everyone's relations to each other, this initial situation is fair between individuals as moral persons, that is, as rational beings with their own ends and capable, I shall assume, of a sense of justice. The original position is, one might say, the appropriate initial status quo, and thus the fundamental agreements reached in it are fair. This explains the propriety of the name "justice as fairness": it conveys the idea that the principles of justice are agreed to in an initial situation that is fair. The name does not mean that the concepts of justice and fairness are the same, any more than the phrase "poetry as metaphor" means that the concepts of poetry and metaphor are the same.

Justice as fairness begins, as I have said, with one of the most general of all choices which persons might make together, namely, with the choice of the first principles of a conception of justice which is to regulate all subsequent criticism and reform of institutions. Then, having chosen a conception of justice, we can suppose that they are to choose a constitution and a legislature to enact laws, and so on, all in accordance with the principles of justice initially agreed upon. Our social situation is just if it is such that by this sequence of hypothetical agreements we would have contracted into the general system of rules which defines it. Moreover, assuming that the original position does determine a set of principles (that is, that a particular conception of justice would be chosen), it will then be true that whenever social institutions satisfy these principles those engaged in them can say to one another that they are cooperating on terms to which they would agree if they were free and equal persons whose relations with respect to one another were fair. They could all view their arrangements as meeting the stipulations which they would acknowledge in an initial situation that embodies widely accepted and reasonable constraints on the choice of principles. The general recognition of this fact would provide the basis for a public acceptance of the corresponding principles of justice. No society can, of course, be a scheme of cooperation which men enter voluntarily in a literal sense; each person finds himself placed at birth in some particular position in some particular society, and the nature of this position materially affects his life prospects. Yet a society satisfying the principles of justice as fairness comes as close as a society can to being a voluntary scheme, for it meets the principles which free and equal persons would assent to under circumstances that are fair. In this sense its members are autonomous and the obligations they recognize self-imposed.

One feature of justice as fairness is to think of the parties in the initial situation as rational and mutually disinterested. This does not mean that the parties are egoists, that is, individuals with only certain kinds of interests, say in wealth, prestige, and domination. But they are conceived as not taking an interest in one another's interests. They are to presume that even their spiritual aims may be opposed, in the way that the aims of those of different religions may be opposed. Moreover, the concept of rationality must be interpreted as far as possible in the narrow sense, standard in economic theory, of taking the most effective means to given ends. I shall modify this concept to some extent, as explained later, but one must try to avoid introducing into it any controversial ethical elements. The initial situation must be characterized by stipulations that are widely accepted.

In working out the conception of justice as fairness one main task clearly is to determine which principles of justice would be chosen in the original position. To do this we must describe this situation in some detail and formulate with care the problem of choice which it presents. These matters I shall take up in the immediately succeeding chapters. It may be observed, however, that once the principles of justice are thought of as arising from an original agreement in a situation of equality, it is an open question whether the principle of utility would be acknowledged. Offhand it hardly seems likely that persons who view themselves as equals, entitled to press their claims upon one another, would agree to a principle which may require lesser life prospects for some simply for the sake of a greater sum of advantages enjoyed by others. Since each desires to protect his interests, his capacity to advance his conception of the good, no one has a reason to acquiesce in an enduring loss for himself in order to bring about a greater net balance of satisfaction. In the absence of strong and lasting benevolent impulses, a rational man would not accept a basic structure merely because it maximized the algebraic sum of advantages irrespective of its permanent effects on his own basic rights and interests. Thus it seems that the principle of utility is incompatible with the conception of social cooperation among equals for mutual advantage. It appears to be inconsistent with the idea of reciprocity implicit in the notion of a well-ordered society. Or, at any rate, so I shall argue.

I shall maintain instead that the persons in the initial situation would choose two rather different principles: the first requires equality in the assignment of basic rights and duties, while the second holds that social and economic inequalities, for example inequalities of wealth and authority, are just only if they result in compensating benefits for everyone, and in particular for the least advantaged members of society. These principles rule out justifying institutions on the grounds that the hardships of some are offset by a greater good in the aggregate. It may be expedient but it is not just that some should have less in order that others may prosper. But there is no injustice in the greater benefits earned by a few provided that the situation of persons not so fortunate is thereby improved. The intuitive idea is that since everyone's well-being depends upon a scheme of cooperation without which no one could have a satisfactory life, the division of advantages should be such as to draw forth the willing cooperation of everyone taking part in it, including those less well situated. Yet this can be expected only if reasonable terms are proposed. The two principles mentioned seem to be a fair agreement on the basis of which those better endowed, or more fortunate in their social position, neither of which we can be said to deserve, could expect the willing cooperation of others when some workable scheme is a necessary condition of the welfare of all. Once we decide to look for a conception of justice that nullifies the accidents of natural endowment and the contingencies of social circumstance as counters in quest for political and economic advantage, we are led to these principles. They express the result of leaving aside those aspects of the social world that seem arbitrary from a moral point of view.

The problem of the choice of principles, however, is extremely difficult. I do not expect the answer I shall suggest to be convincing to everyone. It is, therefore, worth noting from the outset that justice as fairness, like other contract views, consists of two parts: (1) an interpretation of the initial situation and of the problem of choice posed there, and (2) a set of principles which, it is argued, would be agreed to. One may accept the first part of the theory (or some variant thereof), but not the other, and conversely. The concept of the initial contractual situation may seem reasonable although the particular principles proposed are rejected. To be sure, I want to maintain that the most appropriate conception of this situation does lead to principles of justice contrary to utilitarianism and perfectionism, and therefore that the contract doctrine provides an alternative to these views. Still, one may dispute this contention even though one grants that the contractarian method is a useful way of studying ethical theories and of setting forth their underlying assumptions.

Justice as fairness is an example of what I have called a contract theory. Now there may be an objection to the term "contract" and related expressions, but I think it will serve reasonably well. Many words have misleading connotations which at first are likely to confuse. The terms "utility" and "utilitarianism" are surely no exception. They too have unfortunate suggestions which hostile critics have been willing to exploit; yet they are clear enough for those prepared to study utilitarian doctrine. The same should be true of the term "contract" applied to moral theories. As I have mentioned, to understand it one has to keep in mind that it implies a certain level of abstraction. In particular, the content of the relevant agreement is not to enter a given society or to adopt a given form of government, but to accept certain moral principles. Moreover, the undertakings referred to are purely hypothetical: a contract view holds that certain principles would be accepted in a well-defined initial situation.

The merit of the contract terminology is that it conveys the idea that principles of justice may be conceived as principles that would be chosen by rational persons, and that in this way conceptions of justice may be explained and justified. The theory of justice is a part, perhaps the most significant part, of the theory of rational choice. Furthermore, principles of justice deal with conflicting claims upon the advantages won by social cooperation; they apply to the relations among several persons or groups. The word "contract" suggests this plurality as well as the condition that the appropriate division of advantages must be in accordance with principles acceptable to all parties. The condition of publicity for principles of justice is also connoted by the contract phraseology. Thus, if these principles are the outcome of an agreement, citizens have a knowledge of the principles that others follow. It is characteristic of contract theories to stress the public nature of political principles. Finally there is the long tradition of the contract doctrine. Expressing the tie with this line of thought helps to define ideas and accords with natural piety. There are then several advantages in the use of the term "contract." With due precautions taken, it should not be misleading.

A final remark. Justice as fairness is not a complete contract theory. For it is clear that the contractarian idea can be extended to the choice of more or less an entire ethical system, that is, to a system including principles for all the virtues and not only for justice. Now for the most part I shall consider only principles of justice and others closely related to them; I make no attempt to discuss the virtues in a systematic way. Obviously if justice as fairness succeeds reasonably well, a next step would be to study the more general view suggested by the name "rightness as fairness." But even this wider theory fails to embrace all moral relationships, since it would seem to include only our relations with other persons and to leave out of account how we are to conduct ourselves toward animals and the rest of nature. I do not contend that the contract notion offers a way to approach these questions which are certainly of the first importance; and I shall have to put them aside. We must recognize the limited scope of justice as fairness and of the general type of view that it exemplifies. How far its conclusions must be revised once these other matters are understood cannot be decided in advance.

4. The Original Position and Justification

I have said that the original position is the appropriate initial status quo which insures that the fundamental agreements reached in it are fair. This fact yields the name "justice as fairness." It is clear, then, that I want to say that one conception of justice is more reasonable than another, or justifiable with respect to it, if rational persons in the initial situation would choose its principles over those of the other for the role of justice. Conceptions of justice are to be ranked by their acceptability to persons so circumstanced. Understood in this way the question of justification is settled by working out a problem of deliberation: we have to ascertain which principles it would be rational to adopt given the contractual situation. This connects the theory of justice with the theory of rational choice.

If this view of the problem of justification is to succeed, we must, of course, describe in some detail the nature of this choice problem. A problem of rational decision has a definite answer only if we know the beliefs and interests of the parties, their relations with respect to one another, the alternatives between which they are to choose, the procedure whereby they make up their minds, and so on. As the circumstances are presented in different ways, correspondingly different principles are accepted. The concept of the original position, as I shall refer to it, is that of the most philosophically favored interpretation of this initial choice situation for the purposes of a theory of justice.

But how are we to decide what is the most favored interpretation? I assume, for one thing, that there is a broad measure of agreement that principles of justice should be chosen under certain conditions. To justify a particular description of the initial situation one shows that it incorporates these commonly shared presumptions. One argues from widely accepted but weak premises to more specific conclusions. Each of the presumptions should by itself be natural and plausible; some of them may seem innocuous or even trivial. The aim of the contract approach is to establish that taken together they impose significant bounds on acceptable principles of justice. The ideal outcome would be that these conditions determine a unique set of principles; but I shall be satisfied if they suffice to rank the main traditional conceptions of social justice.

One should not be misled, then, by the somewhat unusual conditions which characterize the original position. The idea here is simply to make vivid to ourselves the restrictions that it seems reasonable to impose on arguments for principles of justice, and therefore on these principles themselves. Thus it seems reasonable and generally acceptable that no one should be advantaged or disadvantaged by natural fortune or social circumstances in the choice of principles. It also seems widely agreed that it should be impossible to tailor principles to the circumstances of one's own case. We should insure further that particular inclinations and aspirations, and persons' conceptions of their good do not affect the principles adopted. The aim is to rule out those principles that it would be rational to propose for acceptance, however little the chance of success, only if one knew certain things that are irrelevant from the standpoint of justice. For example, if a man knew that he was wealthy, he might find it rational to advance the principle that various taxes for welfare measures be counted unjust; if he knew that he was poor, he would most likely propose the contrary principle. To represent the desired restrictions one imagines a situation in which everyone is deprived of this sort of information. One excludes the knowledge of those contingencies which sets men at odds and allows them to be guided by their prejudices. In this manner the veil of ignorance is arrived at in a natural way. This concept should cause no difficulty if we keep in mind the constraints on arguments that it is meant to express. At any time we can enter the original position, so to speak, simply by following a certain procedure, namely, by arguing for principles of justice in accordance with these restrictions.

It seems reasonable to suppose that the parties in the original position are equal. That is, all have the same rights in the procedure for choosing principles; each can make proposals, submit reasons for their acceptance, and so on. Obviously the purpose of these conditions is to represent equality between human beings as moral persons, as creatures having a conception of their good and capable of a sense of justice. The basis of equality is taken to be similarity in these two respects. Systems of ends are not ranked in value; and each man is presumed to have the requisite ability to understand and to act upon whatever principles are adopted. Together with the veil of ignorance, these conditions define the principles of justice as those which rational persons concerned to advance their interests would consent to as equals when none are known to be advantaged or disadvantaged by social and natural contingencies.

There is, however, another side to justifying a particular description of the original position. This is to see if the principles which would be chosen match our considered convictions of justice or extend them in an acceptable way. We can note whether applying these principles would lead us to make the same judgments about the basic structure of society which we now make intuitively and in which we have the greatest confidence; or whether, in cases where our present judgments are in doubt and given with hesitation, these principles offer a resolution which we can affirm on reflection. There are questions which we feel sure must be answered in a certain way. For example, we are confident that religious intolerance and racial discrimination are unjust. We think that we have examined these things with care and have reached what we believe is an impartial judgment not likely to be distorted by an excessive attention to our own interests. These convictions are provisional fixed points which we presume any conception of justice must fit. But we have much less assurance as to what is the correct distribution of wealth and authority. Here we may be looking for a way to remove our doubts. We can check an interpretation of the initial situation, then, by the capacity of its principles to accommodate our firmest convictions and to provide guidance where guidance is needed.

In searching for the most favored description of this situation we work from both ends. We begin by describing it so that it represents generally shared and preferably weak conditions. We then see if these conditions are strong enough to yield a significant set of principles. If not, we look for further premises equally reasonable. But if so, and these principles match our considered convictions of justice, then so far well and good. But presumably there will be discrepancies. In this case we have a choice. We can either modify the account of the initial situation or we can revise our existing judgments, for even the judgments we take provisionally as fixed points are liable to revision. By going back and forth, sometimes altering the conditions of the contractual circumstances, at others withdrawing our judgments and conforming them to principle, I assume that eventually we shall find a description of the initial situation that both expresses reasonable conditions and yields principles which match our considered judgments duly pruned and adjusted. This state of affairs I refer to as reflective equilibrium. It is an equilibrium because at last our principles and judgments coincide; and it is reflective since we know to what principles our judgments conform and the premises of their derivation. At the moment everything is in order. But this equilibrium is not necessarily stable. It is liable to be upset by further examination of the conditions which should be imposed on the contractual situation and by particular cases which may lead us to revise our judgments. Yet for the time being we have done what we can to render coherent and to justify our convictions of social justice. We have reached a conception of the original position.

I shall not, of course, actually work through this process. Still, we may think of the interpretation of the original position that I shall present as the result of such a hypothetical course of reflection. It represents the attempt to accommodate within one scheme both reasonable philosophical conditions on principles as well as our considered judgments of justice. In arriving at the favored interpretation of the initial situation there is no point at which an appeal is made to self-evidence in the traditional sense either of general conceptions or particular convictions. I do not claim for the principles of justice proposed that they are necessary truths or derivable from such truths. A conception of justice cannot be deduced from self-evident premises or conditions on principles; instead, its justification is a matter of the mutual support of many considerations, of everything fitting together into one coherent view.

A final comment. We shall want to say that certain principles of justice are justified because they would be agreed to in an initial situation of equality. I have emphasized that this original position is purely hypothetical. It is natural to ask why, if this agreement is never actually entered into, we should take any interest in these principles, moral or otherwise. The answer is that the conditions embodied in the description of the original position are ones that we do in fact accept. Or if we do not, then perhaps we can be persuaded to do so by philosophical reflection. Each aspect of the contractual situation can be given supporting grounds. Thus what we shall do is to collect together into one conception a number of conditions on principles that we are ready upon due consideration to recognize as reasonable. These constraints express what we are prepared to regard as limits on fair terms of social cooperation. One way to look at the idea of the original position, therefore, is to see it as an expository device which sums up the meaning of these conditions and helps us to extract their consequences. On the other hand, this conception is also an intuitive notion that suggests its own elaboration, so that led on by it we are drawn to define more clearly the standpoint from which we can best interpret moral relationships. We need a conception that enables us to envision our objective from afar: the intuitive notion of the original position is to do this for us. . . .

11. Two Principles of Justice

I shall now state in a provisional form the two principles of justice that I believe would be chosen in the original position. In this section I wish to make only the most general comments, and therefore the first formulation of these principles is tentative. As we go on I shall run through several formulations and approximate step by step the final statement to be given much later. I believe that doing this allows the exposition to proceed in a natural way.

The first statement of the two principles reads as follows.

First: each person is to have an equal right to the most extensive basic liberty compatible with a similar liberty for others.

Second: social and economic inequalities are to be arranged so that they are both (a) reasonably expected to be to everyone's advantage, and (b) attached to positions and offices open to all. There are two ambiguous phrases in the second principle, namely "everyone's advantage" and "open to all." . . .

By way of general comment, these principles primarily apply, as I have said, to the basic structure of society. They are to govern the assignment of rights and duties and to regulate the distribution of social and economic advantages. As their formulation suggests, these principles presuppose that the social structure can be divided into two more or less distinct parts, the first principle applying to the one, the second to the other. They distinguish between those aspects of the social system that define and secure the equal liberties of citizenship and those that specify and establish social and economic inequalities. The basic liberties of citizens are, roughly speaking, political liberty (the right to vote and to be eligible for public office) together with freedom of speech and assembly; liberty of conscience and freedom of thought; freedom of the person along with the right to hold (personal) property; and freedom from arbitrary arrest and seizure as defined by the concept of the rule of law. These liberties are all required to be equal by the first principle, since citizens of a just society are to have the same basic rights.

The second principle applies, in the first approximation, to the distribution of income and wealth and to the design of organizations that make use of differences in authority and responsibility, or chains of command. While the distribution of wealth and income need not be equal, it must be to everyone's advantage, and at the same time, positions of authority and offices of command must be accessible to all. One applies the second principle by holding positions open, and then, subject to this constraint, arranges social and economic inequalities so that everyone benefits.

These principles are to be arranged in a serial order with the first principle prior to the second. This ordering means that a departure from the institutions of equal liberty required by the first principle cannot be justified by, or compensated for, by greater social and economic advantages. The distribution of wealth and income, and the hierarchies of authority, must be consistent with both the liberties of equal citizenship and equality of opportunity.

It is clear that these principles are rather specific in their content, and their acceptance rests on certain assumptions that I must eventually try to explain and justify. A theory of justice depends upon a theory of society in ways that will become evident as we proceed. For the present, it should be observed that the two principles (and this holds for all formulations) are a special case of a more general conception of justice that can be expressed as follows.

> All social values—liberty and opportunity, income and wealth, and the bases
> of self-respect—are to be distributed equally unless an unequal distribution of
> any, or all, of these values is to everyone's advantage.

Injustice, then, is simply inequalities that are not to the benefit of all. Of course, this conception is extremely vague and requires interpretation.

As a first step, suppose that the basic structure of society distributes certain primary goods, that is, things that every rational man is presumed to want. These goods normally have a use whatever a person's rational plan of life. For simplicity, assume that the chief primary goods at the disposition of society are rights and liberties, powers and opportunities, income and wealth. . . . These are the social primary goods. Other primary goods such as health and vigor, intelligence and imagination, are natural goods; although their possession is influenced by the basic structure, they are not so directly under its control. Imagine, then, a hypothetical initial arrangement in which all the social primary goods are equally distributed: everyone has similar rights and duties, and income and wealth are evenly shared. This state of affairs provides a benchmark for judging improvements. If certain inequalities of wealth and organizational powers would make everyone better off than in this hypothetical starting situation, then they accord with the general conception.

Now it is possible, at least theoretically, that by giving up some of their fundamental liberties men are sufficiently compensated by the resulting social and economic gains. The general conception of justice imposes no restrictions on what sort of inequalities are permissible; it only requires that everyone's position be improved. We need not suppose anything so drastic as consenting to a condition of slavery. Imagine instead that men forego certain political rights when the economic returns are significant and their capacity to influence the course of policy by the exercise of these rights would be marginal in any case. It is this kind of exchange which the two principles as stated rule out; being arranged in serial order they do not permit exchanges between basic liberties and economic and social gains. The serial ordering of principles expresses an underlying preference among primary social goods. When this preference is rational so likewise is the choice of these principles in this order.

In developing justice as fairness I shall, for the most part, leave aside the general conception of justice and examine instead the special case of the two principles in serial order. The advantage of this procedure is that from the first the matter of priorities is recognized and an effort made to find principles to deal with it. One is led to attend throughout to the conditions under which the acknowledgment of the absolute weight of liberty with respect to social and economic advantages, as defined by the lexical order of the two principles, would be reasonable. Offhand, this ranking appears extreme and too special a case to be of much interest; but there is more justification for it than would appear at first sight. Or at any rate, so I shall maintain. Furthermore, the distinction between fundamental rights and liberties and economic and social benefits marks a difference among primary social goods that one should try to exploit. It suggests an important division in the social system. Of course, the distinctions drawn and the ordering proposed are bound to be at best only approximations. There are surely circumstances in which they fail. But it is essential to depict clearly the main lines of a reasonable conception of justice; and under many conditions anyway, the two principles in serial order may serve well enough. When necessary we can fall back on the more general conception.

The fact that the two principles apply to institutions has certain consequences. Several points illustrate this. First of all, the rights and liberties referred to by these principles are those which are defined by the public rules of the basic structure. Whether men are free is determined by the rights and duties established by the major institutions of society. Liberty is a certain pattern of social forms. The first principle simply requires that certain sorts of rules, those defining basic liberties, apply to everyone equally and that they allow the most extensive liberty compatible with a like liberty for all. The only reason for circumscribing the rights defining liberty and making men's freedom less extensive than it might otherwise be is that these equal rights as institutionally defined would interfere with one another.

Another thing to bear in mind is that when principles mention persons, or require that everyone gain from an inequality, the reference is to representative persons holding the various social positions, or offices, or whatever, established by the basic structure. Thus in applying the second principle I assume that it is possible to assign an expectation of well-being to representative individuals holding these positions. This expectation indicates their life prospects as viewed from their social station. In general, the expectations of representative persons depend upon the distribution of rights and duties throughout the basic structure. When this changes, expectations change. I assume, then, that expectations are connected: by raising the prospects of the representative man in one position we presumably increase or decrease the prospects of representative men in other positions. Since it applies to institutional forms, the second principle (or rather the first part of it) refers to the expectations of representative individuals. As I shall discuss below, neither principle applies to distributions of particular goods to particular individuals who may be identified by their proper names. The situation where someone is considering how to allocate certain commodities to needy persons who are known to him is not within the scope of the principles. They are meant to regulate basic institutional arrangements. We must not assume that there is much similarity from the standpoint of justice between an administrative allotment of goods to specific persons and the appropriate design of society. Our common sense intuitions for the former may be a poor guide to the latter.

Now the second principle insists that each person benefit from permissible inequalities in the basic structure. This means that it must be reasonable for each relevant representative man defined by this structure, when he views it as a going concern, to prefer his prospects with the inequality to his prospects without it. One is not allowed to justify differences in income or organizational powers on the ground that the disadvantages of those in one position are outweighed by the greater advantages of those in another. Much less can infringements of liberty be counterbalanced in this way. Applied to the basic structure, the principle of utility would have us maximize the sum of expectations of representative men (weighted by the number of persons they represent, on the classical view); and this would permit us to compensate for the losses of some by the gains of others. Instead, the two principles require that everyone benefit from economic and social inequalities. It is obvious, however, that there are indefinitely many ways in which all may be advantaged when the initial arrangement of equality is taken as a benchmark. How then are we to choose among these possibilities? The principles must be specified so that they yield a determinate conclusion. I now turn to this problem. . . .

24. The Veil of Ignorance

The idea of the original position is to set up a fair procedure so that any principles agreed to will be just. The aim is to use the notion of pure procedural justice as a basis of theory. Somehow we must nullify the effects of specific contingencies which put men at odds and tempt them to exploit social and natural circumstances to their own advantage. Now in order to do this I assume that the parties are situated behind a veil of ignorance. They do not know how the various alternatives will affect their own particular case and they are obliged to evaluate principles solely on the basis of general considerations.

It is assumed, then, that the parties do not know certain kinds of particular facts. First of all, no one knows his place in society, his class position or social status; nor does he know his fortune in the distribution of natural assets and abilities, his intelligence and strength, and the like. Nor, again, does anyone know his conception of the good, the particulars of his rational plan of life, or even the special features of his psychology such as his aversion to risk or liability to optimism or pessimism. More than this, I assume that the parties do not know the particular circumstances of their own society. That is, they do not know its economic or political situation, or the level of civilization and culture it has been able to achieve. The persons in the original position have no information as to which generation they belong. These broader restrictions on knowledge are appropriate in part because questions of social justice arise between generations as well as within them, for example, the question of the appropriate rate of capital saving and of the conservation of natural resources and the environment of nature. There is also, theoretically anyway, the question of a reasonable genetic policy. In these cases too, in order to carry through the idea of the original position, the parties must not know the contingencies that set them in opposition. They must choose principles the consequences of which they are prepared to live with whatever generation they turn out to belong to.

As far as possible, then, the only particular facts which the parties know is that their society is subject to the circumstances of justice and whatever this implies. It is taken for granted, however, that they know the general facts about human society. They understand political affairs and the principles of economic theory; they know the basis of social organization and the laws of human psychology. Indeed, the parties are presumed to know whatever general facts affect the choice of the principles of justice. There are no limitations on general information, that is, on general laws and theories, since conceptions of justice must be adjusted to the characteristics of the systems of social cooperation which they are to regulate, and there is no reason to rule out these facts. It is, for example, a consideration against a conception of justice that, in view of the laws of moral psychology, men would not acquire a desire to act upon it even when the institutions of their society satisfied it. For in this case there would be difficulty in securing the stability of social cooperation. It is an important feature of a conception of justice that it should generate its own support. That is, its principles should be such that when they are embodied in the basic structure of society men tend to acquire the corresponding sense of justice. Given the principles of moral learning, men develop a desire to act in accordance with its principles. In this case a conception of justice is stable. This kind of general information is admissible in the original position.

The notion of the veil of ignorance raises several difficulties. Some may object that the exclusion of nearly all particular information makes it difficult to grasp what is meant by the original position. Thus it may be helpful to observe that one or more persons can at any time enter this position, or perhaps, better, simulate the deliberations of this hypothetical situation, simply by reasoning in accordance with the appropriate restrictions. In arguing for a conception of justice we must be sure that it is among the permitted alternatives and satisfies the stipulated formal constraints. No considerations can be advanced in its favor unless they would be rational ones for us to urge were we to lack the kind of knowledge that is excluded. The evaluation of principles must proceed in terms of the general consequences of their public recognition and universal application, it being assumed that they will be complied with by everyone. To say that a certain conception of justice would be chosen in the original position is equivalent to saying that rational deliberation satisfying certain conditions and restrictions would reach a certain conclusion. If necessary, the argument to this result could be set out more formally. I shall, however, speak throughout in terms of the notion of the original position. It is more economical and suggestive, and brings out certain essential features that otherwise one might easily overlook.

These remarks show that the original position is not to be thought of as a general assembly which includes at one moment everyone who will live at some time; or, much less, as an assembly of everyone who could live at some time. It is not a gathering of all actual or possible persons. To conceive of the original position in either of these ways is to stretch fantasy too far; the conception would cease to be a natural guide to intuition. In any case, it is important that the original position be interpreted so that one can at any time adopt its perspective. It must make no difference when one takes up this viewpoint, or who does so: the restrictions must be such that the same principles are always chosen. The veil of ignorance is a key condition in meeting this requirement. It insures not only that the information available is relevant, but that it is at all times the same.

It may be protested that the condition of the veil of ignorance is irrational. Surely, some may object, principles should be chosen in the light of all the knowledge available. There are various replies to this contention. Here I shall sketch those which emphasize the simplifications that need to be made if one is to have any theory at all. (Those based on the Kantian interpretation of the original position are given later.) To begin with, it is clear that since the differences among the parties are unknown to them, and everyone is equally rational and similarly situated, each is convinced by the same arguments. Therefore, we can view the choice in the original position from the standpoint of one person selected at random. If anyone after due reflection prefers a conception of justice to another, then they all do, and a unanimous agreement can be reached. We can, to make the circumstances more vivid, imagine that the parties are required to communicate with each other through a referee as intermediary, and that he is to announce which alternatives have been suggested and the reasons offered in their support. He forbids the attempt to form coalitions, and he informs the parties when they have come to an understanding. But such a referee is actually superfluous, assuming that the deliberations of the parties must be similar.

Thus there follows the very important consequence that the parties have no basis for bargaining in the usual sense. No one knows his situation in society nor his natural assets, and therefore no one is in a position to tailor principles to his advantage. We might imagine that one of the contractees threatens to hold out unless the others agree to principles favorable to him. But how does he know which principles are especially in his interests? The same holds for the formation of coalitions: if a group were to decide to band together to the disadvantage of the others, they would not know how to favor themselves in the choice of principles. Even if they could get everyone to agree to their proposal, they would have no assurance that it was to their advantage, since they cannot identify themselves either by name or description. The one case where this conclusion fails is that of saving. Since the persons in the original position know that they are contemporaries (taking the present time of entry interpretation), they can favor their generation by refusing to make any sacrifices at all for their successors; they simply acknowledge the principle that no one has a duty to save for posterity. Previous generations have saved or they have not; there is nothing the parties can now do to affect that. So in this instance the veil of ignorance fails to secure the desired result. Therefore I resolve the question of justice between generations in a different way by altering the motivation assumption. But with this adjustment no one is able to formulate principles especially designed to advance his own cause. Whatever his temporal position, each is forced to choose for everyone.

The restrictions on particular information in the original position are, then, of fundamental importance. Without them we would not be able to work out any definite theory of justice at all. We would have to be content with a vague formula stating that justice is what would be agreed to without being able to say much, if anything, about the substance of the agreement itself. The formal constraints of the concept of right, those applying to principles directly, are not sufficient for our purpose. The veil of ignorance makes possible a unanimous choice of a particular conception of justice. Without these limitations on knowledge the bargaining problem of the original position would be hopelessly complicated. Even if theoretically a solution were to exist, we would not, at present anyway, be able to determine it.

The notion of the veil of ignorance is implicit, I think, in Kant's ethics. Nevertheless the problem of defining the knowledge of the parties and of characterizing the alternatives open to them has often been passed over, even by contract theories. Sometimes the situation definitive of moral deliberation is presented in such an indeterminate way that one cannot ascertain how it will turn out. Thus Perry's doctrine is essentially contractarian: he holds that social and personal integration must proceed by entirely different principles, the latter by rational prudence, the former by the concurrence of persons of good will. He would appear to reject utilitarianism on much the same grounds suggested earlier: namely, that it improperly extends the principle of choice for one person to choices facing society. The right course of action is characterized as that which best advances social aims as these would be formulated by reflective agreement given that the parties have full knowledge of the circumstances and are moved by a benevolent concern for one another's interests. No effort is made, however, to specify in any precise way the possible outcomes of this sort of agreement. Indeed, without a far more elaborate account, no conclusions can be drawn. I do not wish here to criticize others; rather, I want to explain the necessity for what may seem at times like so many irrelevant details.

Now the reasons for the veil of ignorance go beyond mere simplicity. We want to define the original position so that we get the desired solution. If a knowledge of particulars is allowed, then the outcome is biased by arbitrary contingencies. As already observed, to each according to his threat advantage is not a principle of justice. If the original position is to yield agreements that are just, the parties must be fairly situated and treated equally as moral persons. The arbitrariness of the world must be corrected for by adjusting the circumstances of the initial contractual situation. Moreover, if in choosing principles we required unanimity even when there is full information, only a few rather obvious cases could be decided. A conception of justice based on unanimity in these circumstances would indeed be weak and trivial. But once knowledge is excluded, the requirement of unanimity is not out of place and the fact that it can be satisfied is of great importance. It enables us to say of the preferred conception of justice that it represents a genuine reconciliation of interests.

A final comment. For the most part I shall suppose that the parties possess all general information. No general facts are closed to them. I do this mainly to avoid complications.

Nevertheless a conception of justice is to be the public basis of the terms of social cooperation. Since common understanding necessitates certain bounds on the complexity of principles, there may likewise be limits on the use of theoretical knowledge in the original position. Now clearly it would be very difficult to classify and to grade for complexity the various sorts of general facts. I shall make no attempt to do this. We do however recognize an intricate theoretical construction when we meet one. Thus it seems reasonable to say that other things equal one conception of justice is to be preferred to another when it is founded upon markedly simpler general facts, and its choice does not depend upon elaborate calculations in the light of a vast array of theoretically defined possibilities. It is desirable that the grounds for a public conception of justice should be evident to everyone when circumstances permit. This consideration favors, I believe, the two principles of justice over the criterion of utility. . . .

Robert Nozick (b. 1938)

Although the Austrian economists and the Rand-influenced Objectivists had been working for some time to promote individual liberty as a priority in political theory, it was not until the publication in 1974 of *Anarchy, State, and Utopia* that libertarianism regained academic respectability. The idea that individual rights should not be infringed by the government can trace its lineage to nineteenth-century writers such as Mill and the American A. J. Nock, but in the twentieth century such ideas were often dismissed. Nozick argues that the classical minimal state, which protects individuals from force and fraud, can be justified, but no more extensive state can be. The following selections are from *Anarchy, State, and Utopia*.

From Anarchy, State, and Utopia*

Section I

The Entitlement Theory

The subject of justice in holdings consists of three major topics. The first is the *original acquisition of holdings*, the appropriation of unheld things. This includes the issues of how unheld things may come to be held, the process, or processes, by which unheld things may come to be held, the things that may come to be held by these processes, the extent of what comes to be held by a particular process, and so on. We shall refer to the complicated truth about this topic, which we shall not formulate here, as the principle of justice in acquisition. The second topic concerns the *transfer of holdings* from one person to another. By what processes may a person transfer holdings to another? How may a person acquire a holding from another who holds it? Under this topic come general descriptions of voluntary exchange, and gift and (on the other hand) fraud, as well as reference to particular conventional details fixed upon in a given society. The complicated truth about this subject (with placeholders for conventional details) we shall call the principle of justice in transfer. (And we shall suppose it also includes principles governing how a person may divest himself of a holding, passing it into an unheld state.)

If the world were wholly just, the following inductive definition would exhaustively cover the subject of justice in holdings.

1. A person who acquires a holding in accordance with the principle of justice in acquisition is entitled to that holding.

2. A person who acquires a holding in accordance with the principle of justice in transfer, from someone else entitled to the holding, is entitled to the holding.

3. No one is entitled to a holding except by (repeated) applications of 1 and 2.

---

* An Excerpt.

The complete principle of distributive justice would say simply that a distribution is just if everyone is entitled to the holdings they possess under the distribution.

A distribution is just if it arises from another just distribution by legitimate means. The legitimate means of moving from one distribution to another are specified by the principle of justice in transfer. The legitimate first "moves" are specified by the principle of justice in acquisition.* Whatever arises from a just situation by just steps is itself just. The means of change specified by the principle of justice in transfer preserve justice. As correct rules of inference are truth-preserving, and any conclusion deduced via repeated application of such rules from only true premises is itself true, so the means of transition from one situation to another specified by the principle of justice in transfer are justice-preserving, and any situation actually arising from repeated transitions in accordance with the principle from a just situation is itself just. The parallel between justice-preserving transformations and truth-preserving transformations illuminates where it fails as well as where it holds. That a conclusion could have been deduced by truth-preserving means from premises that are true suffices to show its truth. That from a just situation a situation *could* have arisen via justice-preserving means does *not* suffice to show its justice. The fact that a thief's victims voluntarily *could* have presented him with gifts does not entitle the thief to his ill-gotten gains. Justice in holdings is historical; it depends upon what actually has happened. We shall return to this point later.

Not all actual situations are generated in accordance with the two principles of justice in holdings: the principle of justice in acquisition and the principle of justice in transfer. Some people steal from others, or defraud them, or enslave them, seizing their product and preventing them from living as they choose, or forcibly exclude others from competing in exchanges. None of these are permissible modes of transition from one situation to another. And some persons acquire holdings by means not sanctioned by the principle of justice in acquisition. The existence of past injustice (previous violations of the first two principles of justice in holdings) raises the third major topic under justice in holdings: the rectification of injustice in holdings. If past injustice has shaped present holdings in various ways, some identifiable and some not, what now, if anything, ought to be done to rectify these injustices? What obligations do the performers of injustice have toward those whose position is worse than it would have been had the injustice not been done? Or, than it would have been had compensation been paid promptly? How, if at all, do things change if the beneficiaries and those made worse off are not the direct parties in the act of injustice, but, for example, their descendants? Is an injustice done to someone whose holding was itself based upon an unrectified injustice? How far back must one go in wiping clean the historical slate of injustices? What may victims of injustice permissibly do in order to rectify the injustices being done to them, including the many injustices done by persons acting through their government? I do not know of a thorough or theoretically sophisticated treatment of such issues. Idealizing greatly, let us suppose theoretical investigation will produce a principle of rectification. This principle uses historical

---

* Applications of the principle of justice in acquisition may also occur as part of the move from one distribution to another. You may find an unheld thing now and appropriate it. Acquisitions also are to be understood as included when, to simplify, I speak only of transitions by transfers.

information about previous situations and injustices done in them (as defined by the first two principles of justice and rights against interference), and information about the actual course of events that flowed from these injustices, until the present, and it yields a description (or descriptions) of holdings in the society. The principle of rectification presumably will make use of its best estimate of subjunctive information about what would have occurred (or a probability distribution over what might have occurred, using the expected value) if the injustice had not taken place. If the actual description of holdings turns out not to be one of the descriptions yielded by the principle, then one of the descriptions yielded must be realized.*

The general outlines of the theory of justice in holdings are that the holdings of a person are just if he is entitled to them by the principles of justice in acquisition and transfer, or by the principle of rectification of injustice (as specified by the first two principles). If each person's holdings are just, then the total set (distribution) of holdings is just. To turn these general outlines into a specific theory we would have to specify the details of each of the three principles of justice in holdings: the principle of acquisition of holdings, the principle of transfer of holdings, and the principle of rectification of violations of the first two principles. I shall not attempt that task here. (Locke's principle of justice in acquisition is discussed below.)

Historical Principles
and End-Result Principles

The general outlines of the entitlement theory illuminate the nature and defects of other conceptions of distributive justice. The entitlement theory of justice in distribution is *historical;* whether a distribution is just depends upon how it came about. In contrast, *current time-slice principles* of justice hold that the justice of a distribution is determined by how things are distributed (who has what) as judged by some *structural* principle(s) of just distribution. A utilitarian who judges between any two distributions by seeing which has the greater sum of utility and, if the sums tie, applies some fixed equality criterion to choose the more equal distribution, would hold a current time-slice principle of justice. As would someone who had a fixed schedule of trade-offs between the sum of happiness and equality. According to a current time-slice principle, all that needs to be looked at, in judging the justice of a distribution, is who ends up with what; in comparing any two distributions one need look only at the matrix presenting the distributions. No further information need be fed into a principle of justice. It is a consequence of such principles of justice that any two structurally identical distributions are equally just. (Two distributions are structurally identical if they present the same profile, but perhaps have different persons occupying the particular

---

* If the principle of rectification of violations of the first two principles yields more than one description of holdings, then some choice must be made as to which of these is to be realized. Perhaps the sort of considerations about distributive justice and equality that I argue against play a legitimate role in *this* subsidiary choice. Similarly, there may be room for such considerations in deciding which otherwise arbitrary features a statute will embody, when such features are unavoidable because other considerations do not specify a precise line; yet a line must be drawn.

slots. My having ten and your having five, and my having five and your having ten are structurally identical distributions.) Welfare economics is the theory of current time-slice principles of justice. The subject is conceived as operating on matrices representing only current information about distribution. This, as well as some of the usual conditions (for example, the choice of distribution is invariant under relabeling of columns), guarantees that welfare economics will be a current time-slice theory, with all of its inadequacies.

Most persons do not accept current time-slice principles as constituting the whole story about distributive shares. They think it relevant in assessing the justice of a situation to consider not only the distribution it embodies, but also how that distribution came about. If some persons are in prison for murder or war crimes, we do not say that to assess the justice of the distribution in the society we must look only at what this person has, and that person has, and that person has, . . . at the current time. We think it relevant to ask whether someone did something so that he *deserved* to be punished, deserved to have a lower share. Most will agree to the relevance of further information with regard to punishments and penalties. Consider also desired things. One traditional socialist view is that workers are entitled to the product and full fruits of their labor; they have earned it; a distribution is unjust if it does not give the workers what they are entitled to. Such entitlements are based upon some past history. No socialist holding this view would find it comforting to be told that because the actual distribution A happens to coincide structurally with the one he desires D, A therefore is no less just than D; it differs only in that the "parasitic" owners of capital receive under A what the workers are entitled to under D, and the workers receive under A what the owners are entitled to under D, namely very little. This socialist rightly, in my view, holds onto the notions of earning, producing, entitlement, desert, and so forth, and he rejects current time-slice principles that look only to the structure of the resulting set of holdings. (The set of holdings resulting from what? Isn't it implausible that how holdings are produced and come to exist has no effect at all on who should hold what?) His mistake lies in his view of what entitlements arise out of what sorts of productive processes.

We construe the position we discuss too narrowly by speaking of *current* time-slice principles. Nothing is changed if structural principles operate upon a time sequence of current time-slice profiles and, for example, give someone more now to counterbalance the less he has had earlier. A utilitarian or an egalitarian or any mixture of the two over time will inherit the difficulties of his more myopic comrades. He is not helped by the fact that *some* of the information others consider relevant in assessing a distribution is reflected, unrecoverably, in past matrices. Henceforth, we shall refer to such unhistorical principles of distributive justice, including the current time-slice principles, as *end-result principles* or *end-state principles*.

In contrast to end-result principles of justice, *historical principles* of justice hold that past circumstances or actions of people can create differential entitlements or differential deserts to things. An injustice can be worked by moving from one distribution to another structurally identical one, for the second, in profile the same, may violate people's entitlements or deserts; it may not fit the actual history.

Patterning

The entitlement principles of justice in holdings that we have sketched are historical principles of justice. To better understand their precise character, we shall distinguish them from another subclass of the historical principles. Consider, as an example, the principle of distribution according to moral merit. This principle requires that total distributive shares vary directly with moral merit; no person should have a greater share than anyone whose moral merit is greater. (If moral merit could be not merely ordered but measured on an interval or ratio scale, stronger principles could be formulated.) Or consider the principle that results by substituting "usefulness to society" for "moral merit" in the previous principle. Or instead of "distribute according to moral merit," or "distribute according to usefulness to society," we might consider "distribute according to the weighted sum of moral merit, usefulness to society, and need," with the weights of the different dimensions equal. Let us call a principle of distribution *patterned* if it specifies that a distribution is to vary along with some natural dimension, weighted sum of natural dimensions, or lexicographic ordering of natural dimensions. And let us say a distribution is patterned if it accords with some patterned principle. (I speak of natural dimensions, admittedly without a general criterion for them, because for any set of holdings some artificial dimensions can be gimmicked up to vary along with the distribution of the set.) The principle of distribution in accordance with moral merit is a patterned historical principle, which specifies a patterned distribution. "Distribute according to I.Q." is a patterned principle that looks to information not contained in distributional matrices. It is not historical, however, in that it does not look to any past actions creating differential entitlements to evaluate a distribution; it requires only distributional matrices whose columns are labeled by I.Q. scores. The distribution in a society, however, may be composed of such simple patterned distributions, without itself being simply patterned. Different sectors may operate different patterns, or some combination of patterns may operate in different proportions across a society. A distribution composed in this manner, from a small number of patterned distributions, we also shall term "patterned." And we extend the use of "pattern" to include the overall designs put forth by combinations of end-state principles.

Almost every suggested principle of distributive justice is patterned: to each according to his moral merit, or needs, or marginal product, or how hard he tries, or the weighted sum of the foregoing, and so on. The principle of entitlement we have sketched is *not* patterned.* There is no one natural dimension or weighted sum or combination of

---

* One might try to squeeze a patterned conception of distributive justice into the framework of the entitlement conception, by formulating a gimmicky obligatory "principle of transfer" that would lead to the pattern. For example, the principle that if one has more than the mean income one must transfer everything one holds above the mean to persons below the mean so as to bring them up to (but not over) the mean. We can formulate a criterion for a "principle of transfer" to rule out such obligatory transfers, or we can say that no correct principle of transfer, no principle of transfer in a free society will be like this. The former is probably the better course, though the latter also is true.

Alternatively, one might think to make the entitlement conception instantiate a pattern, by using matrix entries that express the relative strength of a person's entitlements as measured by some real-valued function. But even if the limitation to natural dimensions failed to exclude this function, the resulting edifice would *not* capture our system of entitlements to *particular* things.

a small number of natural dimensions that yields the distributions generated in accordance with the principle of entitlement. The set of holdings that results when some persons receive their marginal products, others win at gambling, others receive a share of their mate's income, others receive gifts from foundations, others receive interest on loans, others receive gifts from admirers, others receive returns on investment, others make for themselves much of what they have, others find things, and so on, will not be patterned. Heavy strands of patterns will run through it; significant portions of the variance in holdings will be accounted for by pattern-variables. If most people most of the time choose to transfer some of their entitlements to others only in exchange for something from them, then a large part of what many people hold will vary with what they held that others wanted. More details are provided by the theory of marginal productivity. But gifts to relatives, charitable donations, bequests to children, and the like, are not best conceived, in the first instance, in this manner. Ignoring the strands of pattern, let us suppose for the moment that a distribution actually arrived at by the operation of the principle of entitlement is random with respect to any pattern. Though the resulting set of holdings will be unpatterned, it will not be incomprehensible, for it can be seen as arising from the operation of a small number of principles. These principles specify how an initial distribution may arise (the principle of acquisition of holdings) and how distributions may be transformed into others (the principle of transfer of holdings). The process whereby the set of holdings is generated will be intelligible, though the set of holdings itself that results from this process will be unpatterned.

The writings of F. A. Hayek focus less than is usually done upon what patterning distributive justice requires. Hayek argues that we cannot know enough about each person's situation to distribute to each according to his moral merit (but would justice demand we do so if we did have this knowledge?); and he goes on to say, "our objection is against all attempts to impress upon society a deliberately chosen pattern of distribution, whether it be an order of equality or of inequality." However, Hayek concludes that in a free society there will be distribution in accordance with value rather than moral merit; that is, in accordance with the perceived value of a person's actions and services to others. Despite his rejection of a patterned conception of distributive justice, Hayek himself suggests a pattern he thinks justifiable: distribution in accordance with the perceived benefits given to others, leaving room for the complaint that a free society does not realize exactly this pattern. Stating this patterned strand of a free capitalist society more precisely, we get "To each according to how much he benefits others who have the resources for benefiting those who benefit them." This will seem arbitrary unless some acceptable initial set of holdings is specified, or unless it is held that the operation of the system over time washes out any significant effects from the initial set of holdings. As an example of the latter, if almost anyone would have bought a car from Henry Ford, the supposition that it was an arbitrary matter who held the money then (and so bought) would not place Henry Ford's earnings under a cloud. In any event, *his* coming to hold it is not arbitrary. Distribution according to benefits to others *is* a major patterned strand in a free capitalist society, as Hayek correctly points out, but it is only a strand and does not constitute the whole pattern of a system of entitlements (namely, inheritance, gifts for arbitrary reasons, charity, and so on) or a standard that one should insist a society fit. Will people tolerate for long a system yielding distributions that they believe are un-patterned? No doubt people will not long accept a distribution they believe is *unjust*. People want their society to be and to look just. But must the look of justice reside in a resulting pattern rather than in the underlying generating principles? We are in no po-sition to conclude that the inhabitants of a society embodying an entitlement conception of justice in holdings will find it unacceptable. Still, it must be granted that were peo-ple's reasons for transferring some of their holdings to others always irrational or arbi-trary, we would find this disturbing. (Suppose people always determined what holdings they would transfer, and to whom, by using a random device.) We feel more comfortable upholding the justice of an entitlement system if most of the transfers under it are done for reasons. This does not mean necessarily that all deserve what holdings they receive. It means only that there is a purpose or point to someone's transferring a holding to one person rather than to another; that usually we can see what the transferrer thinks he's gaining, what cause he thinks he's serving, what goals he thinks he's helping to achieve, and so forth. Since in a capitalist society people often transfer holdings to oth-ers in accordance with how much they perceive these others benefiting them, the fabric constituted by the individual transactions and transfers is largely reasonable and intelli-gible.* (Gifts to loved ones, bequests to children, charity to the needy also are non-arbitrary components of the fabric.) In stressing the large strand of distribution in accordance with benefit to others, Hayek shows the point of many transfers, and so shows that the system of transfer of entitlements is not just spinning its gears aimlessly. The sys-tem of entitlements is defensible when constituted by the individual aims of individual transactions. No overarching aim is needed, no distributional pattern is required.

To think that the task of a theory of distributive justice is to fill in the blank in "to each according to his _____" is to be predisposed to search for a pattern; and the sep-arate treatment of "from each according to his _____" treats production and distribu-tion as two separate and independent issues. On an entitlement view these are *not* two separate questions. Whoever makes something, having bought or contracted for all other held resources used in the process (transferring some of his holdings for these cooperat-ing factors), is entitled to it. The situation is *not* one of something's getting made, and there being an open question of who is to get it. Things come into the world already at-tached to people having entitlements over them. From the point of view of the historical entitlement conception of justice in holdings, those who start afresh to complete "to each according to his _____" treat objects as if they appeared from nowhere, out of noth-ing. A complete theory of justice might cover this limit case as well; perhaps here is a use for the usual conceptions of distributive justice.

---

* We certainly benefit because great economic incentives operate to get others to spend much time and energy to figure out how to serve us by providing things we will want to pay for. It is not mere paradox mongering to wonder whether capitalism should be criticized for most rewarding and hence encouraging, not individualists like Thoreau who go about their own lives, but people who are occupied with serving others and winning them as customers. But to defend capitalism one need not think businessmen are the finest human types. (I do not mean to join here the general maligning of businessmen, either.) Those who think the finest should acquire the most can try to convince their fellows to transfer resources in accordance with *that* principle.

So entrenched are maxims of the usual form that perhaps we should present the entitlement conception as a competitor. Ignoring acquisition and rectification, we might say:

> From each according to what he chooses to do, to each according to what he makes for himself (perhaps with the contracted aid of others) and what others choose to do for him and choose to give him of what they've been given previously (under this maxim) and haven't yet expended or transferred.

This, the discerning reader will have noticed, has its defects as a slogan. So as a summary and great simplification (and not as a maxim with any independent meaning) we have:

From each as they choose, to each as they are chosen.

How Liberty Upsets Patterns

It is not clear how those holding alternative conceptions of distributive justice can reject the entitlement conception of justice in holdings. For suppose a distribution favored by one of these non-entitlement conceptions is realized. Let us suppose it is your favorite one and let us call this distribution D_1; perhaps everyone has an equal share, perhaps shares vary in accordance with some dimension you treasure. Now suppose that Wilt Chamberlain is greatly in demand by basketball teams, being a great gate attraction. (Also suppose contracts run only for a year, with players being free agents.) He signs the following sort of contract with a team: In each home game, twenty-five cents from the price of each ticket of admission goes to him. (We ignore the question of whether he is "gouging" the owners, letting them look out for themselves.) The season starts, and people cheerfully attend his team's games; they buy their tickets, each time dropping a separate twenty-five cents of their admission price into a special box with Chamberlain's name on it. They are excited about seeing him play; it is worth the total admission price to them. Let us suppose that in one season one million persons attend his home games, and Wilt Chamberlain winds up with $250,000, a much larger sum than the average income and larger even than anyone else has. Is he entitled to this income? Is this new distribution D_2, unjust? If so, why? There is *no* question about whether each of the people was entitled to the control over the resources they held in D_1; because that was the distribution (your favorite) that (for the purposes of argument) we assumed was acceptable. Each of these persons *chose* to give twenty-five cents of their money to Chamberlain. They could have spent it on going to the movies, or on candy bars, or on copies of *Dissent* magazine, or of *Monthly Review*. But they all, at least one million of them, converged on giving it to Wilt Chamberlain in exchange for watching him play basketball. If D_1 was a just distribution, and people voluntarily moved from it to D_2, transferring parts of their shares they were given under D_1 (what was it for if not to do something with?), isn't D_2 also just? If the people were entitled to dispose of the resources to which they were entitled (under D_1), didn't this include their being entitled to give it to, or exchange it with, Wilt Chamberlain? Can anyone else complain on grounds of justice? Each other person already has his legitimate share under D_1. Under D_1, there is nothing that anyone has that anyone else has a claim of justice against. After someone transfers something to Wilt Chamberlain, third parties *still* have their legitimate shares; *their* shares are not changed. By what process could such a transfer among two persons give rise to a legitimate claim of distributive justice on a portion of what was transferred, by a third party who had no claim of justice on any holding of the others *before* the transfer? To cut off objections irrelevant here, we might imagine the exchanges occurring in a socialist society, after hours. After playing whatever basketball he does in his daily work, or doing whatever other daily work he does, Wilt Chamberlain decides to put in *overtime* to earn additional money. (First his work quota is set; he works time over that.) Or imagine it is a skilled juggler people like to see, who puts on shows after hours.

Why might someone work overtime in a society in which it is assumed their needs are satisfied? Perhaps because they care about things other than needs. I like to write in books that I read, and to have easy access to books for browsing at odd hours. It would be very pleasant and convenient to have the resources of Widener Library in my back yard. No society, I assume, will provide such resources close to each person who would like them as part of his regular allotment (under D_1). Thus, persons either must do without some extra things that they want, or be allowed to do something extra to get some of these things. On what basis could the inequalities that would eventuate be forbidden? Notice also that small factories would spring up in a socialist society, unless forbidden. I melt down some of my personal possessions (under D_1) and build a machine out of the material. I offer you, and others, a philosophy lecture once a week in exchange for your cranking the handle on my machine, whose products I exchange for yet other things, and so on. (The raw materials used by the machine are given to me by others who possess them under D_1, in exchange for hearing lectures.) Each person might participate to gain things over and above their allotment under D_1. Some persons even might want to leave their job in socialist industry and work full time in this private sector. I shall say something more about these issues in the next chapter. Here I wish merely to note how private property even in means of production would occur in a socialist society that did not forbid people to use as they wished some of the resources they are given under the socialist distribution D_1. The socialist society would have to forbid capitalist acts between consenting adults.

The general point illustrated by the Wilt Chamberlain example and the example of the entrepreneur in a socialist society is that no end-state principle or distributional patterned principle of justice can be continuously realized without continuous interference with people's lives. Any favored pattern would be transformed into one unfavored by the principle, by people choosing to act in various ways; for example, by people exchanging goods and services with other people, or giving things to other people, things the transferrers are entitled to under the favored distributional pattern. To maintain a pattern one must either continually interfere to stop people from transferring resources as they wish to, or continually (or periodically) interfere to take from some persons resources that others for some reason chose to transfer to them. (But if some time limit is to be set on how long people may keep resources others voluntarily transfer to them, why let them keep these resources for *any* period of time? Why not have immediate confiscation?) It might be objected that all persons voluntarily will choose to refrain from actions which would upset the pattern. This presupposes unrealistically (1) that all will most want to maintain the pattern (are those who don't, to be "reeducated" or forced to undergo "self-criticism"?), (2) that each can gather enough information about his own actions and the ongoing activities of others to discover which of his actions will upset the pattern, and (3) that diverse and far-flung persons can coordinate their actions to dove-tail into the pattern. Compare the manner in which the market is neutral among persons' desires, as it reflects and transmits widely scattered information via prices, and coordinates persons' activities.

It puts things perhaps a bit too strongly to say that every patterned (or end-state) principle is liable to be thwarted by the voluntary actions of the individual parties transferring some of their shares they receive under the principle. For perhaps some *very* weak patterns are not so thwarted. Any distributional pattern with any egalitarian component is overturnable by the voluntary actions of individual persons over time; as is every patterned condition with sufficient content so as actually to have been proposed as presenting the central core of distributive justice. Still, given the possibility that some weak conditions or patterns may not be unstable in this way, it would be better to formulate an explicit description of the kind of interesting and contentful patterns under discussion, and to prove a theorem about their instability. Since the weaker the patterning, the more likely it is that the entitlement system itself satisfies it, a plausible conjecture is that any patterning either is unstable or is satisfied by the entitlement system.

Sen's Argument

Our conclusions are reinforced by considering a recent general argument of Amartya K. Sen. Suppose individual rights are interpreted as the right to choose which of two alternatives is to be more highly ranked in a social ordering of the alternatives. Add the weak condition that if one alternative unanimously is preferred to another then it is ranked higher by the social ordering. If there are two different individuals each with individual rights, interpreted as above, over different pairs of alternatives (having no members in common), then for some possible preference rankings of the alternatives by the individuals, there is no linear social ordering. For suppose that person A has the right to decide among (X, Y) and person B has the right to decide among (Z, W); and suppose their individual preferences are as follows (and that there are no other individuals). Person A prefers W to X to Y to Z, and person B prefers Y to Z to W to X. By the unanimity condition, in the social ordering W is preferred to X (since each individual prefers it to X), and Y is preferred to Z (since each individual prefers it to Z). Also in the social ordering, X is preferred to Y, by person A's right of choice among these two alternatives. Combining these three binary rankings, we get W preferred to X preferred to Y preferred to Z, in the social ordering. However, by person B's right of choice, Z must be preferred to W in the social ordering. There is no transitive social ordering satisfying all these conditions, and the social ordering, therefore, is nonlinear. Thus far, Sen.

The trouble stems from treating an individual's right to choose among alternatives as the right to determine the relative ordering of these alternatives within a social ordering. The alternative which has individuals rank *pairs* of alternatives, and separately rank the individual alternatives is no better; their ranking of pairs feeds into some method of amalgamating preferences to yield a social ordering of pairs; and the choice among the alternatives in the highest ranked pair in the social ordering is made by the individual with the right to decide between this pair. This system also has the result that an alternative may be selected although *everyone* prefers some other alternative; for example, A selects X over Y, where (X, Y) somehow is the highest ranked *pair* in the social ordering of pairs, although everyone, including A, prefers W to X. (But the choice person A was given, however, was only between X and Y.)

A more appropriate view of individual rights is as follows. Individual rights are co-possible; each person may exercise his rights as he chooses. The exercise of these rights fixes some features of the world. Within the constraints of these fixed features, a choice may be made by a social choice mechanism based upon a social ordering; if there are any choices left to make! Rights do not determine a social ordering but instead set the constraints within which a social choice is to be made, by excluding certain alternatives, fixing others, and so on. (If I have a right to choose to live in New York or in Massachusetts, and I choose Massachusetts, then alternatives involving my living in New York are not appropriate objects to be entered in a social ordering.) Even if all possible alternatives are ordered first, apart from anyone's rights, the situation is not changed: for then the highest ranked alternative *that is not excluded by anyone's exercise of his rights* is instituted. Rights do not determine the position of an alternative or the relative position of two alternatives in a social ordering; they *operate upon* a social ordering to constrain the choice it can yield.

If entitlements to holdings are rights to dispose of them, then social choice must take place *within* the constraints of how people choose to exercise these rights. If any patterning is legitimate, it falls within the domain of social choice, and hence is constrained by people's rights. *How else can one cope with Sen's result?* The alternative of first having a social ranking with rights exercised within *its* constraints is no alternative at all. Why not just select the top-ranked alternative and forget about rights? If that top-ranked alternative itself leaves some room for individual choice (and here is where "rights" of choice is supposed to enter in) there must be something to stop these choices from transforming it into another alternative. Thus Sen's argument leads us again to the result that patterning requires continuous interference with individuals' actions and choices.

Redistribution and Property Rights

Apparently, patterned principles allow people to choose to expend upon themselves, but not upon others, those resources they are entitled to (or rather, receive) under some favored distributional pattern D_1. For if each of several persons chooses to expend some of his D_1 resources upon one other person, then that other person will receive more than his D_1 share, disturbing the favored distributional pattern. Maintaining a distributional pattern is individualism with a vengeance! Patterned distributional principles do not give people what entitlement principles do, only better distributed. For they do not give the right to choose what to do with what one has; they do not give the right to choose to pursue an end involving (intrinsically, or as a means) the enhancement of another's position. To such views, families are disturbing; for within a family occur transfers that upset the favored distributional pattern. Either families themselves become units to which distribution takes place, the column occupiers (on what rationale?), or loving behavior is forbidden. We should note in passing the ambivalent position of radicals toward the family. Its loving relationships are seen as a model to be emulated and extended across the whole society, at the same time that it is denounced as a suffocating institution to be broken and condemned as a focus of parochial concerns that interfere with achieving radical goals. Need we say that it is not appropriate to enforce across the wider society the relationships of love and care appropriate within a family, relationships which are voluntarily undertaken? Incidentally, love is an interesting instance of another relationship that is historical, in that (like justice) it depends upon what actually occurred. An adult may come to love another because of the other's characteristics; but it is the other person, and not the characteristics, that is loved. The love is not transferrable to someone else with the same characteristics, even to one who "scores" higher for these characteristics. And the love endures through changes of the characteristics that gave rise to it. One loves the particular person one actually encountered. Why love is historical, attaching to persons in this way and not to characteristics, is an interesting and puzzling question.

Proponents of patterned principles of distributive justice focus upon criteria for determining who is to receive holdings; they consider the reasons for which someone should have something, and also the total picture of holdings. Whether or not it is better to give than to receive, proponents of patterned principles ignore giving altogether. In considering the distribution of goods, income, and so forth, their theories are theories of recipient justice; they completely ignore any right a person might have to give something to someone. Even in exchanges where each party is simultaneously giver and recipient, patterned principles of justice focus only upon the recipient role and its supposed rights. Thus discussions tend to focus on whether people (should) have a right to inherit, rather than on whether people (should) have a right to bequeath or on whether persons who have a right to hold also have a right to choose that others hold in their place. I lack a good explanation of why the usual theories of distributive justice are so recipient oriented; ignoring givers and transferrers and their rights is of a piece with ignoring producers and their entitlements. But why is it *all* ignored?

Patterned principles of distributive justice necessitate *re*distributive activities. The likelihood is small that any actual freely-arrived-at set of holdings fits a given pattern; and the likelihood is nil that it will continue to fit the pattern as people exchange and give. From the point of view of an entitlement theory, redistribution is a serious matter indeed, involving, as it does, the violation of people's rights. (An exception is those takings that fall under the principle of the rectification of injustices.) From other points of view, also, it is serious.

Taxation of earnings from labor is on a par with forced labor. Some persons find this claim obviously true: taking the earnings of *n* hours labor is like taking *n* hours from the person; it is like forcing the person to work *n* hours for another's purpose. Others find the claim absurd. But even these, *if* they object to forced labor, would oppose forcing unemployed hippies to work for the benefit of the needy. And they would also object to forcing each person to work five extra hours each week for the benefit of the needy. But a system that takes five hours' wages in taxes does not seem to them like one that forces someone to work five hours, since it offers the person forced a wider range of choice in activities than does taxation in kind with the particular labor specified. (But we can imagine a gradation of systems of forced labor, from one that specifies a particular activity, to one that gives a choice among two activities, to . . . ; and so on up.) Furthermore, people envisage a system with something like a proportional tax on everything above the amount necessary for basic needs. Some think this does not force someone to work extra hours, since there is no fixed number of extra hours he is forced to work, and since he can avoid the tax entirely by earning only enough to cover his basic needs. This is a very uncharacteristic view of forcing for those who *also* think people are forced to do something *whenever* the alternatives they face are considerably worse. However, *neither* view is correct. The fact that others intentionally intervene, in violation of a side constraint against aggression, to threaten force to limit the alternatives, in this case to paying taxes or (presumably the worse alternative) bare subsistence, makes the taxation system one of forced labor and distinguishes it from other cases of limited choices which are not forcings.

The man who chooses to work longer to gain an income more than sufficient for his basic needs prefers some extra goods or services to the leisure and activities he could perform during the possible nonworking hours; whereas the man who chooses not to work the extra time prefers the leisure activities to the extra goods or services he could acquire by working more. Given this, if it would be illegitimate for a tax system to seize some of a man's leisure (forced labor) for the purpose of serving the needy, how can it be legitimate for a tax system to seize some of a man's goods for that purpose? Why should we treat the man whose happiness requires certain material goods or services differently from the man whose preferences and desires make such goods unnecessary for his happiness? Why should the man who prefers seeing a movie (and who has to earn money for a ticket) be open to the required call to aid the needy, while the person who prefers looking at a sunset (and hence need earn no extra money) is not? Indeed, isn't it surprising that redistributionists choose to ignore the man whose pleasures are so easily attainable without extra labor, while adding yet another burden to the poor unfortunate who must work for his pleasures? If anything, one would have expected the reverse. Why is the person with the nonmaterial or nonconsumption desire allowed to proceed unimpeded to his most favored feasible alternative, whereas the man whose pleasures or desires involve material things and who must work for extra money (thereby serving whomever considers his activities valuable enough to pay him) is constrained in what he can realize? Perhaps there is no difference in principle. And perhaps some think the answer concerns merely administrative convenience. (These questions and issues will not disturb those who think that forced labor to serve the needy or to realize some favored end-state pattern is acceptable.) In a fuller discussion we would have (and want) to extend our argument to include interest, entrepreneurial profits, and so on. Those who doubt that this extension can be carried through, and who draw the line here at taxation of income from labor, will have to state rather complicated patterned *historical* principles of distributive justice, since end-state principles would not distinguish *sources* of income in any way. It is enough for now to get away from end-state principles and to make clear how various patterned principles are dependent upon particular views about the sources or the illegitimacy or the lesser legitimacy of profits, interest, and so on; which particular views may well be mistaken.

What sort of right over others does a legally institutionalized end-state pattern give one? The central core of the notion of a property right in *X*, relative to which other parts of the notion are to be explained, is the right to determine what shall be done with *X;* the right to choose which of the constrained set of options concerning *X* shall be realized or attempted. The constraints are set by other principles or laws operating in the society; in our theory, by the Lockean rights people possess (under the minimal state). My property rights in my knife allow me to leave it where I will, but not in your chest. I may choose which of the acceptable options involving the knife is to be realized. This notion of property helps us to understand why earlier theorists spoke of people as having property in themselves and their labor. They viewed each person as having a right to decide what would become of himself and what he would do, and as having a right to reap the benefits of what he did.

This right of selecting the alternative to be realized from the constrained set of alternatives may be held by an *individual* or by a *group* with some procedure for reaching a joint decision; or the right may be passed back and forth, so that one year I decide what's to become of *X*, and the next year you do (with the alternative of destruction, perhaps, being excluded). Or, during the same time period, some types of decisions about *X* may be made by me, and others by you. And so on. We lack an adequate, fruitful, analytical apparatus for classifying the *types* of constraints on the set of options among which choices are to be made, and the *types* of ways decision powers can be held, divided, and amalgamated. A *theory* of property would, among other things, contain such a classification of constraints and decision modes, and from a small number of principles would follow a host of interesting statements about the *consequences* and effects of certain combinations of constraints and modes of decision.

When end-result principles of distributive justice are built into the legal structure of a society, they (as do most patterned principles) give each citizen an enforceable claim to some portion of the total social product; that is, to some portion of the sum total of the individually and jointly made products. This total product is produced by individuals laboring, using means of production others have saved to bring into existence, by people organizing production or creating means to produce new things or things in a new way. It is on this batch of individual activities that patterned distributional principles give each individual an enforceable claim. Each person has a claim to the activities and the products of other persons, independently of whether the other persons enter into particular relationships that give rise to these claims, and independently of whether they voluntarily take these claims upon themselves, in charity or in exchange for something.

Whether it is done through taxation on wages or on wages over a certain amount, or through seizure of profits, or through there being a big *social pot* so that it's not clear what's coming from where and what's going where, patterned principles of distributive justice involve appropriating the actions of other persons. Seizing the results of someone's labor is equivalent to seizing hours from him and directing him to carry on various activities. If people force you to do certain work, or unrewarded work, for a certain period of time, they decide what you are to do and what purposes your work is to serve apart from your decisions. This process whereby they take this decision from you makes them a *part-owner* of you; it gives them a property right in you. Just as having such partial control and power of decision, by right, over an animal or inanimate object would be to have a property right in it.

End-state and most patterned principles of distributive justice institute (partial) ownership by others of people and their actions and labor. These principles involve a shift from the classical liberals' notion of self-ownership to a notion of (partial) property rights in *other* people.

Considerations such as these confront end-state and other patterned conceptions of justice with the question of whether the actions necessary to achieve the selected pattern don't themselves violate moral side constraints. Any view holding that there are moral side constraints on actions, that not all moral considerations can be built into end states that are to be achieved, must face the possibility that some of its goals are not achievable by any morally permissible available means. An entitlement theorist will face such conflicts in a society that deviates from the principles of justice for the generation of holdings, if and only if the only actions available to realize the principles themselves violate some moral constraints. Since deviation from the first two principles of justice (in acquisition and transfer) will involve other persons' direct and aggressive intervention to violate rights, and since moral constraints will not exclude defensive or retributive action in such cases, the entitlement theorist's problem rarely will be pressing. And whatever difficulties he has in applying the principle of rectification to persons who did not themselves violate the first two principles are difficulties in balancing the conflicting considerations so as correctly to formulate the complex principle of rectification itself; he will not violate moral side constraints by applying the principle. Proponents of patterned conceptions of justice, however, often will face head-on clashes (and poignant ones if they cherish each party to the clash) between moral side constraints on how individuals may be treated and their patterned conception of justice that presents an end state or other pattern that *must* be realized.

May a person emigrate from a nation that has institutionalized some end-state or patterned distributional principle? For some principles (for example, Hayek's) emigration presents no theoretical problem. But for others it is a tricky matter. Consider a nation having a compulsory scheme of minimal social provision to aid the neediest (or one organized so as to maximize the position of the worst-off group); no one may opt out of participating in it. (None may say, "Don't compel me to contribute to others and don't provide for me via this compulsory mechanism if I am in need.") Everyone above a certain level is forced to contribute to aid the needy. But if emigration from the country were allowed, anyone could choose to move to another country that did not have compulsory social provision but otherwise was (as much as possible) identical. In such a case, the person's *only* motive for leaving would be to avoid participating in the compulsory scheme of social provision. And if he does leave, the needy in his initial country will receive no (compelled) help from him. What rationale yields the result that the person be permitted to emigrate, yet forbidden to stay and opt out of the compulsory scheme of social provision? If providing for the needy is of overriding importance, this does militate against allowing internal opting out; but it also speaks against allowing external emigration. (Would it also support, to some extent, the kidnapping of persons living in a place without compulsory social provision, who could be forced to make a contribution to the needy in your community?) Perhaps the crucial component of the position that allows emigration solely to avoid certain arrangements, while not allowing anyone internally to opt out of them, is a concern for fraternal feelings within the country. "We don't want anyone here who doesn't contribute, who doesn't care enough about the others to contribute." That concern, in this case, would have to be tied to the view that forced aiding tends to produce fraternal feelings between the aided and the aider (or perhaps merely to the view that the knowledge that someone or other voluntarily is not aiding produces unfraternal feelings).

Locke's Theory of Acquisition

Before we turn to consider other theories of justice in detail, we must introduce an additional bit of complexity into the structure of the entitlement theory. This is best approached by considering Locke's attempt to specify a principle of justice in acquisition. Locke views property rights in an unowned object as originating through someone's mixing his labor with it. This gives rise to many questions. What are the boundaries of what labor is mixed with? If a private astronaut clears a place on Mars, has he mixed his labor with (so that he comes to own) the whole planet, the whole uninhabited universe, or just a particular plot? Which plot does an act bring under ownership? The minimal (possibly disconnected) area such that an act decreases entropy in that area, and not elsewhere? Can virgin land (for the purposes of ecological investigation by high-flying airplane) come under ownership by a Lockean process? Building a fence around a territory presumably would make one the owner of only the fence (and the land immediately underneath it).

Why does mixing one's labor with something make one the owner of it? Perhaps because one owns one's labor, and so one comes to own a previously unowned thing that becomes permeated with what one owns. Ownership seeps over into the rest. But why isn't mixing what I own with what I don't own a way of losing what I own rather than a way of gaining what I don't? If I own a can of tomato juice and spill it in the sea so that its molecules (made radioactive, so I can check this) mingle evenly throughout the sea, do I thereby come to own the sea, or have I foolishly dissipated my tomato juice? Perhaps the idea, instead, is that laboring on something improves it and makes it more valuable; and anyone is entitled to own a thing whose value he has created. (Reinforcing this, perhaps, is the view that laboring is unpleasant. If some people made things effortlessly, as the cartoon characters in *The Yellow Submarine* trail flowers in their wake, would they have lesser claim to their own products whose making didn't *cost* them anything?) Ignore the fact that laboring on something may make it less valuable (spraying pink enamel paint on a piece of driftwood that you have found). Why should one's entitlement extend to the whole object rather than just to the *added value* one's labor has produced? (Such reference to value might also serve to delimit the extent of ownership; for example, substitute "increases the value of" for "decreases entropy in" in the above entropy criterion.) No workable or coherent value-added property scheme has yet been devised, and any such scheme presumably would fall to objections (similar to those) that fell the theory of Henry George.

It will be implausible to view improving an object as giving full ownership to it, if the stock of unowned objects that might be improved is limited. For an object's coming under one person's ownership changes the situation of all others. Whereas previously they were at liberty (in Hohfeld's sense) to use the object, they now no longer are. This change in the situation of others (by removing their liberty to act on a previously unowned object) need not worsen their situation. If I appropriate a grain of sand from Coney Island, no one else may now do as they will with *that* grain of sand. But there are plenty of other grains of sand left for them to do the same with. Or if not grains of sand, then other things. Alternatively, the things I do with the grain of sand I appropriate might improve the position of others, counterbalancing their loss of the liberty to use that grain. The crucial point is whether appropriation of an unowned object worsens the situation of others.

Locke's proviso that there be "enough and as good left in common for others" (sect. 27) is meant to ensure that the situation of others is not worsened. (If this proviso is met is there any motivation for his further condition of nonwaste?) It is often said that this proviso once held but now no longer does. But there appears to be an argument for the conclusion that if the proviso no longer holds, then it cannot ever have held so as to yield permanent and inheritable property rights. Consider the first person Z for whom there is not enough and as good left to appropriate. The last person Y to appropriate left Z without his previous liberty to act on an object, and so worsened Z's situation. So Y's appropriation is not allowed under Locke's proviso. Therefore the next to last person X to appropriate left Y in a worse position, for X's act ended permissible appropriation. Therefore X's appropriation wasn't permissible. But then the appropriator two from last, W ended permissible appropriation and so, since it worsened X's position, W's appropriation wasn't permissible. And so on back to the first person A to appropriate a permanent property right.

This argument, however, proceeds too quickly. Someone may be made worse off by another's appropriation in two ways: first, by losing the opportunity to improve his situation by a particular appropriation or any one; and second, by no longer being able to use freely (without appropriation) what he previously could. A *stringent* requirement that another not be made worse off by an appropriation would exclude the first way if nothing else counterbalances the diminution in opportunity, as well as the second. A *weaker* requirement would exclude the second way, though not the first. With the weaker requirement, we cannot zip back so quickly from Z to A, as in the above argument; for though person Z can no longer *appropriate*, there may remain some for him to *use* as before. In this case Y's appropriation would not violate the weaker Lockean condition. (With less remaining that people are at liberty to use, users might face more inconvenience, crowding, and so on; in that way the situation of others might be worsened, unless appropriation stopped far short of such a point.) It is arguable that no one legitimately can complain if the weaker provision is satisfied. However, since this is less clear than in the case of the more stringent proviso, Locke may have intended this stringent proviso by "enough and as good" remaining, and perhaps he meant the non-waste condition to delay the end point from which the argument zips back.

Is the situation of persons who are unable to appropriate (there being no more accessible and useful unowned objects) worsened by a system allowing appropriation and permanent property? Here enter the various familiar social considerations favoring private property: it increases the social product by putting means of production in the hands of those who can use them most efficiently (profitably); experimentation is encouraged, because with separate persons controlling resources, there is no one person or small group whom someone with a new idea must convince to try it out; private property enables people to decide on the pattern and types of risks they wish to bear, leading to specialized types of risk bearing; private property protects future persons by leading some to hold back resources from current consumption for future markets; it provides alternate sources of employment for unpopular persons who don't have to convince any one person or small group to hire them, and so on. These considerations enter a Lockean theory to support the claim that appropriation of private property satisfies the intent behind the "enough and as good left over" proviso, *not* as a utilitarian justification of property. They enter to rebut the claim that because the proviso is violated no natural right to private property can arise by a Lockean process. The difficulty in working such an argument to show that the proviso is satisfied is in fixing the appropriate base line for comparison. Lockean appropriation makes people no worse off than they would be *how?* This question of fixing the baseline needs more detailed investigation than we are able to give it here. It would be desirable to have an estimate of the general economic importance of original appropriation in order to see how much leeway there is for differing theories of appropriation and of the location of the baseline. Perhaps this importance can be measured by the percentage of all income that is based upon untransformed raw materials and given resources (rather than upon human actions), mainly rental income representing the unimproved value of land, and the price of raw material *in situ* and by the percentage of current wealth which represents such income in the past.

We should note that it is not only persons favoring *private* property who need a theory of how property rights legitimately originate. Those believing in collective property, for example those believing that a group of persons living in an area jointly own the territory, or its mineral resources, also must provide a theory of how such property rights arise; they must show why the persons living there have rights to determine what is done with the land and resources there that persons living elsewhere don't have (with regard to the same land and resources).

The Proviso

Whether or not Locke's particular theory of appropriation can be spelled out so as to handle various difficulties, I assume that any adequate theory of justice in acquisition will contain a proviso similar to the weaker of the ones we have attributed to Locke. A process normally giving rise to a permanent bequeathable property right in a previously unowned thing will not do so if the position of others no longer at liberty to use the thing is thereby worsened. It is important to specify *this* particular mode of worsening the situation of others, for the proviso does not encompass other modes. It does not include the worsening due to more limited opportunities to appropriate (the first way above, corresponding to the more stringent condition), and it does not include how I "worsen" a seller's position if I appropriate materials to make some of what he is selling, and then enter into competition with him. Someone whose appropriation otherwise would violate the proviso still may appropriate provided he compensates the others so that their situation is not thereby worsened; unless he does compensate these others, his appropriation will violate the proviso of the principle of justice in acquisition and will be an illegitimate one. A theory of appropriation incorporating this Lockean proviso will handle correctly the cases (objections to the theory lacking the proviso) where someone appropriates the total supply of something necessary for life.

A theory which includes this proviso in its principle of justice in acquisition must also contain a more complex principle of justice in transfer. Some reflection of the proviso about appropriation constrains later actions. If my appropriating all of a certain substance violates the Lockean proviso, then so does my appropriating some and purchasing all the rest from others who obtained it without otherwise violating the Lockean proviso. If the proviso excludes someone's appropriating all the drinkable water in the world, it also excludes his purchasing it all. (More weakly, and messily, it may exclude his charging certain prices for some of his supply.) This proviso (almost?) never will come into effect; the more someone acquires of a scarce substance which others want, the higher the price of the rest will go, and the more difficult it will become for him to acquire it all. But still, we can imagine, at least, that something like this occurs: someone makes simultaneous secret bids to the separate owners of a substance, each of whom sells assuming he can easily purchase more from the other owners; or some natural catastrophe destroys all of the supply of something except that in one person's possession. The total supply could not be permissibly appropriated by one person at the beginning. His later acquisition of it all does not show that the original appropriation violated the proviso (even by a reverse argument similar to the one above that tried to zip back from Z to A). Rather, it is the combination of the original appropriation *plus* all the later transfers and actions that violates the Lockean proviso.

Each owner's title to his holding includes the historical shadow of the Lockean proviso on appropriation. This excludes his transferring it into an agglomeration that does violate the Lockean proviso and excludes his using it in a way, in coordination with others or independently of them, so as to violate the proviso by making the situation of others worse than their baseline situation. Once it is known that someone's ownership runs afoul of the Lockean proviso, there are stringent limits on what he may do with (what it is difficult any longer unreservedly to call) "his property." Thus a person may not appropriate the only water hole in a desert and charge what he will. Nor may he charge what he will if he possesses one, and unfortunately it happens that all the water holes in the desert dry up, except for his. This unfortunate circumstance, admittedly no fault of his, brings into operation the Lockean proviso and limits his property rights. Similarly, an owner's property right in the only island in an area does not allow him to order a castaway from a shipwreck off his island as a trespasser, for this would violate the Lockean proviso.

Notice that the theory does not say that owners do have these rights, but that the rights are overridden to avoid some catastrophe. (Overridden rights do not disappear; they leave a trace of a sort absent in the cases under discussion.) There is no such external (and *ad hoc?*) overriding. Considerations internal to the theory of property itself, to its theory of acquisition and appropriation, provide the means for handling such cases. The results, however, may be coextensive with some condition about catastrophe, since the baseline for comparison is so low as compared to the productiveness of a society with private appropriation that the question of the Lockean proviso being violated arises only in the case of catastrophe (or a desert-island situation).

The fact that someone owns the total supply of something necessary for others to stay alive does *not* entail that his (or anyone's) appropriation of anything left some people (immediately or later) in a situation worse than the baseline one. A medical researcher who synthesizes a new substance that effectively treats a certain disease and who refuses to sell except on his terms does not worsen the situation of others by depriving them of whatever he has appropriated. The others easily can possess the same materials he appropriated; the researcher's appropriation or purchase of chemicals didn't make those chemicals scarce in a way so as to violate the Lockean proviso. Nor would someone else's purchasing the total supply of the synthesized substance from the medical researcher. The fact that the medical researcher uses easily available chemicals to synthesize the drug no more violates the Lockean proviso than does the fact that the only surgeon able to perform a particular operation eats easily obtainable food in order to stay alive and to have the energy to work. This shows that the Lockean proviso is not an "end-state principle"; it focuses on a particular way that appropriative actions affect others, and not on the structure of the situation that results.

Intermediate between someone who takes all of the public supply and someone who makes the total supply out of easily obtainable substances is someone who appropriates the total supply of something in a way that does not deprive the others of it. For example, someone finds a new substance in an out-of-the-way place. He discovers that it effectively treats a certain disease and appropriates the total supply. He does not worsen the situation of others; if he did not stumble upon the substance no one else would have, and the others would remain without it. However, as time passes, the likelihood increases that others would have come across the substance; upon this fact might be based a limit to his property right in the substance so that others are not below their baseline position; for example, its bequest might be limited. The theme of someone worsening another's situation by depriving him of something he otherwise would possess may also illuminate the example of patents. An inventor's patent does not deprive others of an object which would not exist if not for the inventor. Yet patents would have this effect on others who independently invent the object. Therefore, these independent inventors, upon whom the burden of proving independent discovery may rest, should not be excluded from utilizing their own invention as they wish (including selling it to others). Furthermore, a known inventor drastically lessens the chances of actual independent invention. For persons who know of an invention usually will not try to reinvent it, and the notion of independent discovery here would be murky at best. Yet we may assume that in the absence of the original invention, sometime later someone else would have come up with it. This suggests placing a time limit on patents, as a rough rule of thumb to approximate how long it would have taken, in the absence of knowledge of the invention, for independent discovery.

I believe that the free operation of a market system will not actually run afoul of the Lockean proviso. (Recall that crucial to our story in Part I of how a protective agency becomes dominant and a *de facto* monopoly is the fact that it wields force in situations of conflict, and is not merely in competition, with other agencies. A similar tale cannot be told about other businesses.) If this is correct, the proviso will not play a very important role in the activities of protective agencies and will not provide a significant opportunity for future state action. Indeed, were it not for the effects of previous *illegitimate* state action, people would not think the possibility of the proviso's being violated as of more interest than any other logical possibility. (Here I make an empirical historical claim; as does someone who disagrees with this.) This completes our indication of the complication in the entitlement theory introduced by the Lockean proviso. . . .

How Utopia Works Out

"Well, what exactly will it all turn out to be like? In what directions will people flower? How large will the communities be? Will there be some large cities? How will economies of scale operate to fix the size of the communities? Will all of the communities be geographical, or will there be many important secondary associations, and so on? Will most communities follow particular (though diverse) utopian visions, or will many communities themselves be open, animated by no such particular vision?"

I do not know, and you should not be interested in my guesses about what would occur under the framework in the near future. As for the long run, I would not attempt to guess.

"So is this all it comes to: Utopia is a free society?" Utopia is *not* just a society in which the framework is realized. For who could believe that ten minutes after the framework was established, we would have utopia? Things would be no different than now. It is what grows spontaneously from the individual choices of many people over a long period of time that will be worth speaking eloquently about. (Not that any particular stage of the process is an end state which all our desires are aimed at. The utopian process is substituted for the utopian end state of other static theories of utopias.) Many communities will achieve many different characters. Only a fool, or a prophet, would try to prophesy the range and limits and characters of the communities after, for example, 150 years of the operation of this framework.

Aspiring to neither role, let me close by emphasizing the dual nature of the conception of utopia being presented here. There is the framework of utopia, and there are the particular communities within the framework. Almost all of the literature on utopia is, according to our conception, concerned with the character of the particular communities within the framework. The fact that I have not propounded some particular description of a constituent community does *not* mean that (I think) doing so is unimportant, or less important, or uninteresting. How could that be? We *live* in particular communities. It is here that one's nonimperialistic vision of the ideal or good society is to be propounded and realized. Allowing us to do that is what the framework is *for*. Without such visions impelling and animating the creation of particular communities with particular desired characteristics, the framework will lack life. Conjoined with many persons' particular visions, the framework enables us to get the best of all possible worlds.

The position expounded here totally rejects planning in detail, in advance, one community in which everyone is to live yet sympathizes with voluntary utopian experimentation and provides it with the background in which it can flower; does this position fall within the utopian or the antiutopian camp? My difficulty in answering this question encourages me to think the framework captures the virtues and advantages of each position. (If instead it blunders into combining the errors, defects, and mistakes of both of them, the filtering process of free and open discussion will make this clear.)

Utopia and the Minimal State

The framework for utopia that we have described is equivalent to the minimal state. The argument of this chapter starts (and stands) independently of the argument of Parts I and II and converges to their result, the minimal state, from another direction. In our discussion in this chapter we did not treat the framework as more than a minimal state, but we made no effort to build explicitly upon our earlier discussion of protective agencies. (For we wanted the convergence of two independent lines of argument.) We need not mesh our discussion here with our earlier one of dominant protective agencies beyond noting that whatever conclusions people reach about the role of a central authority (the controls on it, and so forth) will shape the (internal) form and structure of the protective agencies they choose to be the clients of.

We argued in Part I that the minimal state is morally legitimate; in Part II we argued that no more extensive state could be morally justified, that any more extensive state would (will) violate the rights of individuals. This morally favored state, the only morally legitimate state, the only morally tolerable one, we now see is the one that best realizes the utopian aspirations of untold dreamers and visionaries. It preserves what we all can keep from the utopian tradition and opens the rest of that tradition to our individual aspirations. Recall now the question with which this chapter began. Is not the minimal state, the framework for utopia, an inspiring vision?

The minimal state treats us as inviolate individuals, who may not be used in certain ways by others as means or tools or instruments or resources; it treats us as persons having individual rights with the dignity this constitutes. Treating us with respect by respecting our rights, it allows us, individually or with whom we choose, to choose our life and to realize our ends and our conception of ourselves, insofar as we can, aided by the voluntary cooperation of other individuals possessing the same dignity. How *dare* any state or group of individuals do more. Or less.

Murray N. Rothbard (1926–1995 C.E.)

Murray Rothbard was the leading economist of his generation of the "Austrian school" and one of the most influential theoreticians of the American libertarian movement. He was educated at Columbia University; his last teaching position was as S. J. Hall Distinguished Professor of Economics at the University of Nevada at Las Vegas. Rothbard was the author of some twenty-five books (with translations into more than ten languages), including *Man, Economy, and State* (1962), *The Ethics of Liberty* (1982), and the posthumously published *An Austrian Perspective on the History of Economic Thought* (2 vols., 1995). Some of his hundreds of scholarly articles are collected in *The Logic of Action* (2 vols., 1997). The following article is a frequently cited short exposition of his theory about the relationship between society and political authority.

Society Without a State

In attempting to outline how a "society without a State"—that is, an anarchist society—might function successfully, I would first like to defuse two common but mistaken criticisms of this approach. First, is the argument that in providing for such defense or protection services as courts, police, or even law itself, I am simply smuggling the state back into society in another form, and that therefore the system I am both analyzing and advocating is not "really" anarchism. This sort of criticism can only involve us in an endless and arid dispute over semantics. Let me say from the beginning that I define the state as that institution which possesses one or both (almost always both) of the following properties: (1) it acquires its income by the physical coercion known as "taxation"; and (2) it asserts and usually obtains a coerced monopoly of the provision of defense service (police and courts) over a given territorial area. Any institution not possessing either of these properties is not and cannot be, in accordance with my definition, a State. On the other hand, I define anarchist society as one where there is no legal possibility for coercive aggression against the person or property of any individual. Anarchists oppose the state because it has its very being in such aggression, namely, the expropriation of private property through taxation, the coercive exclusion of other providers of defense service from its territory, and all of the other depredations and coercions that are built upon these twin foci of invasions of individual rights.

Nor is our definition of the state arbitrary, for these two characteristics have been possessed by what is generally acknowledged to be states throughout recorded history. The state, by its use of physical coercion, has arrogated to itself a compulsory monopoly of defense services over its territorial jurisdiction. But it is certainly conceptually possible for such services to be supplied by private, nonstate institutions, and indeed such services have historically been supplied by other organizations than the state. To be opposed to the state is then not necessarily to be opposed to services that have often been linked with it; to be opposed to the state does not necessarily imply that we must be opposed to police protection, courts, arbitration, the minting of money, postal service, or roads and highways. *Some* anarchists have indeed been opposed to police and to all physical coercion *in defense of* person and property, but this is not inherent in and is fundamentally irrelevant to the anarchist position, which is precisely marked by opposition to all physical coercion invasive of, or aggressing against, person and property.

The crucial role of taxation may be seen in the fact that the state is the only institution or organization in society which regularly and systematically acquires its income through the use of physical coercion. All other individuals or organizations acquire their income voluntarily, either (1) through the voluntary sale of goods and services to consumers on the market, or (2) through voluntary gifts or donations by members or other donors. If I cease or refrain from purchasing Wheaties on the market, the Wheaties producers do not come after me with a gun or the threat of imprisonment to force me to purchase; if I fail to join the American Philosophical Association, the association may not force me to join or prevent me from giving up my membership. Only the state can do so; only the state can confiscate my property or put me in jail if I do not pay its tax tribute. Therefore, only the state regularly exists and has its very being by means of coercive depredations on private property.

Neither is it legitimate to challenge this sort of analysis by claiming that in some other sense, the purchase of Wheaties or membership in the APA is in some way "coercive"; there again, we can only be trapped in an endless semantic dispute. Apart from other rebuttals which cannot be considered here, I would simply say that anarchists are interested in the abolition of this type of action: for example, aggressive physical violence against person and property, and that this is how we define "coercion." Anyone who is still unhappy with this use of the term "coercion" can simply eliminate the word from this discussion and substitute for it "physical violence or the threat thereof," with the only loss being in literary style rather than in the substance of the argument. What anarchism proposes to do, then, is to abolish the state, that is, to abolish the regularized institution of aggressive coercion.

It need hardly be added that the state habitually builds upon its coercive source of income by adding a host of other aggressions upon society, ranging from economic controls to the prohibition of pornography to the compelling of religious observance to the mass murder of civilians in organized warfare. In short, the state, in the words of Albert Jay Nock, "claims and exercises a monopoly of crime" over its territorial area.

The second criticism I would like to defuse before beginning the main body of the paper is the common charge that anarchists "assume that all people are good" and that without the state no crime would be committed. In short, that anarchism assumes that with the abolition of the state a New Anarchist Man will emerge, cooperative, humane, and benevolent, so that no problem of crime will then plague the society. I confess that I do not understand the basis for this charge. Whatever other schools of anarchism profess—and I do not believe that they are open to this charge—I certainly do not adopt this view. I assume with most observers that mankind is a mixture of good and evil, of cooperative and criminal tendencies. In my view, the anarchist society is one which maximizes the tendencies for the good and the cooperative, while it minimizes both the opportunity and the moral legitimacy of the evil and the criminal. If the anarchist view is correct and the state is indeed the great legalized and socially legitimated channel for all manner of antisocial crime—theft, oppression, mass murder—on a massive scale, then surely the abolition of such an engine of crime can do nothing but favor the good in man and discourage the bad.

A further point: in a profound sense, *no* social system, whether anarchist or statist, can work at all unless most people are "good" in the sense that they are not all hell-bent upon assaulting and robbing their neighbors. If everyone were so disposed, no amount of protection, whether state or private, could succeed in staving off chaos. Furthermore, the more that people are disposed to be peaceful and not aggress against their neighbors, the more successfully *any* social system will work, and the fewer resources will need to be devoted to police protection. The anarchist view holds that, given the "nature of man," given the degree of goodness or badness at any point of time, anarchism will maximize the opportunities for the good and minimize the channels for the bad. The rest depends on the values held by the individual members of society. The only further point that need be made is that by eliminating the living example and the social legitimacy of the massive legalized crime of the state, anarchism will to a large extent promote peaceful values in the minds of the public.

We cannot of course deal here with the numerous arguments in favor of anarchism or against the state, moral, political, and economic. Nor can we take up the various goods and services now provided by the state and show how private individuals and groups will be able to supply them far more efficiently on the free market. Here we can only deal with perhaps the most difficult area, the area where it is almost universally assumed that the state must exist and act, even if it is only a "necessary evil" instead of a positive good: the vital realm of defense or protection of person and property against aggression. Surely, it is universally asserted, the state is at least vitally necessary to provide police protection, the judicial resolution of disputes and enforcement of contracts, and the creation of the law itself that is to be enforced. My contention is that all of these admittedly necessary services of protection can be satisfactorily and efficiently supplied by private persons and institutions on the free market.

One important caveat before we begin the body of this paper: new proposals such as anarchism are almost always gauged against the implicit assumption that the present, or statist, system works to perfection. Any laucunae or difficulties with the picture of the anarchist society are considered net liabilities, and enough to dismiss anarchism out of hand. It is, in short, implicitly assumed that the state is doing its self-assumed job of protecting person and property to perfection. We cannot here go into the reasons why the state is bound to suffer inherently from grave flaws and inefficiencies in such a task. All we need do now is to point to the black and unprecedented record of the state through history: no combination of private marauders can possibly begin to match the state's unremitting record of theft, confiscation, oppression, and mass murder. No collection of Mafia or private bank robbers can begin to compare with all the Hiroshimas, Dresdens, and Lidices and their analogues through the history of mankind.

This point can be made more philosophically: it is illegitimate to compare the merits of anarchism and statism by starting with the present system as the implicit given and then critically examining only the anarchist alternative. What we must do is to begin at the zero point and then critically examine *both* suggested alternatives. Suppose, for example, that we were all suddenly dropped down on the earth *de novo* and that we were all then confronted with the question of what societal arrangements to adopt. And suppose then that someone suggested: "We are all bound to suffer from those of us who wish to aggress against their fellow men. Let us then solve this problem of crime by handing all of our weapons to the Jones family, over there, by giving all of our ultimate power to settle disputes to that family. In that way, with their monopoly of coercion and of ultimate decision making, the Jones family will be able to protect each of us from each other." I submit that this proposal would get very short shrift, except perhaps from the Jones family themselves. And yet this is precisely the common argument for the existence of the state. When we start from zero point, as in the case of the Jones family, the question of "who will guard the guardians?" becomes not simply an abiding lacuna in the theory of the state but an overwhelming barrier to its existence.

A final caveat: the anarchist is always at a disadvantage in attempting to forecast the shape of the future anarchist society. For it is impossible for observers to predict voluntary social arrangements, including the provision of goods and services, on the free market. Suppose, for example, that this were the year 1874 and that someone predicted that eventually there would be a radio-manufacturing industry. To be able to make such a forecast successfully, does he have to be challenged to state immediately how many radio manufacturers there would be a century hence, how big they would be, where they would be located, what technology and marketing techniques they would use, and so on? Obviously, such a challenge would make no sense, and in a profound sense the same is true of those who demand a precise portrayal of the pattern of protection activities on the market. Anarchism advocates the dissolution of the state into social and market arrangements, and these arrangements are far more flexible and less predictable than political institutions. The most that we can do, then, is to offer broad guidelines and perspectives on the shape of a projected anarchist society.

One important point to make here is that the advance of modern technology makes anarchistic arrangements increasingly feasible. Take, for example, the case of lighthouses, where it is often charged that it is unfeasible for private lighthouse operators to row out to each ship to charge it for use of the light. Apart from the fact that this argument ignores the successful existence of private lighthouses in earlier days, as in England in the eighteenth century, another vital consideration is that modern electronic technology makes charging each ship for the light far more feasible. Thus, the ship would have to have paid for an electronically controlled beam which could then be automatically turned on for those ships which had paid for the service.

II

Let us turn now to the problem of how disputes—in particular disputes over alleged violations of person and property—would be resolved in an anarchist society. First, it should be noted that all disputes involve two parties: the plaintiff, the alleged victim of the crime or tort; and the defendant, the alleged aggressor. In many cases of broken contract, of course, each of the two parties alleging that the other is the culprit is at the same time a plaintiff and a defendant.

An important point to remember is that *any* society, be it statist or anarchist, has to have *some* way of resolving disputes that will gain a majority consensus in society. There would be no need for courts or arbitrators if everyone were omniscient and knew instantaneously *which* persons were guilty of any given crime or violation of contract. Since none of us is omniscient, there has to be some method of deciding who is the criminal or lawbreaker which will gain legitimacy; in short, whose decision will be accepted by the great majority of the public.

In the first place, a dispute may be resolved voluntarily between the two parties themselves, either unaided or with the help of a third mediator. This poses no problem, and will automatically be accepted by society at large. It is so accepted even now, much less in a society imbued with the anarchistic values of peaceful cooperation and agreement. Secondly and similarly, the two parties, unable to reach agreement, may decide to submit voluntarily to the decision of an arbitrator. This agreement may arise either after a dispute has arisen, or be provided for in advance in the original contract. Again, there is no problem in such an arrangement gaining legitimacy. Even in the present statist era the notorious inefficiency and coercive and cumbersome procedures of the politically run government courts has led increasing numbers of citizens to turn to voluntary and expert arbitration for a speedy and harmonious settling of disputes.

Thus, William C. Wooldridge has written that

> arbitration has grown to proportions that make the courts a secondary recourse in many areas and completely superfluous in others. The ancient fear of the courts that arbitration would "oust" them of their jurisdiction has been fulfilled with a vengeance the common-law judges probably never anticipated. Insurance companies adjust over fifty thousand claims a year among themselves through arbitration, and the American Arbitration Association (AAA), with headquarters in New York and twenty-five regional offices across the country, last year conducted over twenty-two thousand arbitrations. Its twenty-three thousand associates available to serve as arbitrators may outnumber the total number of judicial personnel . . . in the United States. . . . Add to this the unknown number of individuals who arbitrate disputes within particular industries or in particular localities, without formal AAA affiliation, and the quantitatively secondary role of official courts begins to be apparent.

Wooldridge adds the important point that, in addition to the speed of arbitration procedures vis-à-vis the courts, the arbitrators can proceed as experts in disregard of the official government law; in a profound sense, then, they serve to create a voluntary body of private law. "In other words," states Wooldridge, "the system of extralegal, voluntary courts has progressed hand in hand with a body of private law; the rules of the state are circumvented by the same process that circumvents the forums established for the settlement of disputes over those rules. . . . In short, a private agreement between two people, a bilateral 'law,' has supplanted the official law. The writ of the sovereign has ceased to run, and for it is substituted a rule tacitly or explicitly agreed to by the parties." Wooldridge concludes that "if an arbitrator can choose to ignore a penal damage rule or the statute of limitations applicable to the claim before him (and it is generally conceded that he has that power), arbitration can be viewed as a practically revolutionary instrument for self-liberation from the law. . . ."

It may be objected that arbitration only works successfully because the courts enforce the award of the arbitrator. Wooldridge points out, however, that arbitration was unenforceable in the American courts before 1920, but that this did not prevent voluntary arbitration from being successful and expanding in the United States and in England. He points, furthermore, to the successful operations of merchant courts since the Middle Ages, those courts which successfully developed the entire body of the law merchant. None of those courts possessed the power of enforcement. He might have added the private courts of shippers which developed the body of admiralty law in a similar way.

How then did these private, "anarchistic," and voluntary courts ensure the acceptance of their decisions? By the method of social ostracism, and by the refusal to deal any further with the offending merchant. This method of voluntary "enforcement," indeed, proved highly successful. Wooldridge writes that "the merchants' courts were voluntary, and if a man ignored their judgment, he could not be sent to jail. . . . Nevertheless, it is apparent that . . . [their] decisions were generally respected even by the losers; otherwise people would never have used them in the first place. . . . Merchants made their courts work simply by agreeing to abide by the results. The merchant who broke the understanding would not be sent to jail, to be sure, but neither would he long continue to be a merchant, for the compliance exacted by his fellows . . . proved if anything more effective than physical coercion." Nor did this voluntary method fail to work in modern times. Wooldridge writes that it was precisely in the years before 1920, when arbitration awards could not be enforced in the courts,

> that arbitration caught on and developed a following in the American mercantile community. Its popularity, gained at a time when abiding by an agreement to arbitrate had to be as voluntary as the agreement itself, casts doubt on whether legal coercion was an essential adjunct to the settlement of most disputes. Cases of refusal to abide by an arbitrator's award were rare; one founder of the American Arbitration Association could not recall a single example. Like their medieval forerunners, merchants in the Americas did not have to rely on any sanctions other than those they could collectively impose on each other. One who refused to pay up might find access to his association's tribunal cut off in the future, or his name released to the membership of his trade association; these penalties were far more fearsome than the cost of the award with which he disagreed. Voluntary and private adjudications were voluntarily and privately adhered to, if not out of honor, out of the self-interest of businessmen who knew that the arbitral mode of dispute settlement would cease to be available to them very quickly if they ignored an award.

It should also be pointed out that modern technology makes even more feasible the collection and dissemination of information about people's credit ratings and records of keeping or violating their contracts or arbitration agreements. Presumably, an anarchist society would see the expansion of this sort of dissemination of data and thereby facilitate the ostracism or boycotting of contract and arbitration violators.

How would arbitrators be selected in an anarchist society? In the same way as they are chosen now, and as they were chosen in the days of strictly voluntary arbitration: the arbitrators with the best reputation for efficiency and probity would be chosen by the various parties on the market. As in other processes of the market, the arbitrators with the best record in settling disputes will come to gain an increasing amount of business, and those with poor records will no longer enjoy clients and will have to shift to another line of endeavor. Here it must be emphasized that parties in dispute will seek out those arbitrators with the best reputation for both expertise and impartiality and that inefficient or biased arbitrators will rapidly have to find another occupation.

Thus, the Tannehills emphasize:

> the advocates of government see initiated force (the legal force of government) as the only solution to social disputes. According to them, if everyone in society were not forced to use the same court system . . . disputes would be insoluble. Apparently it doesn't occur to them that disputing parties are capable of freely choosing their own arbiters. . . . They have not realized that disputants would, in fact, be far better off if they could choose among competing arbitration agencies so that they could reap the benefits of competition and specialization. It should be obvious that a court system which has a monopoly guaranteed by the force of statutory law will not give as good quality service as will free-market arbitration agencies which must compete for their customers. . . .
>
> Perhaps the least tenable argument for government arbitration of disputes is the one which holds that governmental judges are more impartial because they operate outside the market and so have no vested interests. . . . Owing political allegiance to government is certainly no guarantee of impartiality! A governmental judge is always impelled to be partial—in favor of the government, from whom he gets his pay and his power! On the other hand, an arbiter who sells his services in a free market knows that he must be as scrupulously honest, fair, and impartial as possible or no pair of disputants will buy his services to arbitrate their dispute. A free-market arbiter depends for his livelihood on his skill and fairness at settling disputes. A governmental judge depends on political pull.

If desired, furthermore, the contracting parties could provide in advance for a series of arbitrators:

> It would be more economical and in most cases quite sufficient to have only one arbitration agency to hear the case. But if the parties felt that a further appeal might be necessary and were willing to risk the extra expense, they could provide for a succession of two or even more arbitration agencies. The names of these agencies would be written into the contract in order from the "first court of appeal" to the "last court of appeal." It would be neither necessary nor

desirable to have one single, final court of appeal for every person in the society, as we have today in the United States Supreme Court.

Arbitration, then, poses little difficulty for a portrayal of the free society. But what of torts or crimes of aggression where there has been no contract? Or suppose that the breaker of a contract defies the arbitration award? Is ostracism enough? In short, how can courts develop in the free-market, anarchist society which will have the power to enforce judgments against criminals or contract breakers?

In the wide sense, defense service consists of guards or police who use force in defending person and property against attack, and judges or courts whose role is to use socially accepted procedures to determine *who* the criminals or tortfeasors are, as well as to enforce judicial awards, such as damages or the keeping of contracts. On the free market, many scenarios are possible on the relationship between the private courts and the police; they may be "vertically integrated," for example, or their services may be supplied by separate firms. Furthermore, it seems likely that police service will be supplied by insurance companies who will provide crime insurance to their clients. In that case, insurance companies will pay off the victims of crime or the breaking of contracts or arbitration awards and then pursue the aggressors in court to recoup their losses. There is a natural market connection between insurance companies and defense service, since they need pay out less benefits in proportion as they are able to keep down the rate of crime.

Courts might either charge fees for their services, with the losers of cases obliged to pay court costs, or else they may subsist on monthly or yearly premiums by their clients, who may be either individuals or the police or insurance agencies. Suppose, for example, that Smith is an aggrieved party, either because he has been assaulted or robbed, or because an arbitration award in his favor has not been honored. Smith believes that Jones is the party guilty of the crime. Smith then goes to a court, Court A, of which he is a client, and brings charges against Jones as a defendant. In my view, the hallmark of an anarchist society is one where no man may legally compel someone who is not a convicted criminal to do anything, since that would be aggression against an innocent man's person or property. Therefore, Court A can only invite rather than subpoena Jones to attend his trial. Of course, if Jones refused to appear or send a representative, his side of the case will not be heard. The trial of Jones proceeds. Suppose that Court A finds Jones innocent. In my view, part of the generally accepted law code of the anarchist society (on which see further below) is that this must end the matter unless Smith can prove charges of gross incompetence or bias on the part of the court.

Suppose, next, that Court A finds Jones guilty. Jones might accept the verdict, because he too is a client of the same court, because he knows he is guilty, or for some other reason. In that case, Court A proceeds to exercise judgment against Jones. Neither of these instances pose very difficult problems for our picture of the anarchist society. But suppose, instead, that Jones contests the decision; he, then, goes to his court, Court B, and the case is retried there. Suppose that Court B, too, finds Jones guilty. Again, it seems to me that the accepted law code of the anarchist society will assert that this ends the matter; both parties have had their say in courts which each has selected, and the decision for guilt is unanimous.

Suppose, however, the most difficult case: that Court B finds Jones innocent. The two courts, each subscribed to by one of the two parties, have split their verdicts. In that case, the two courts will submit the case to an appeals court, or arbitrator, which the two courts agree upon. There seems to be no real difficulty about the concept of an appeals court. As in the case of arbitration contracts, it seems very likely that the various private courts in the society will have prior agents to submit their disputes to a particular appeals court. How will the appeals judges be chosen? Again, as in the case of arbitrators or of the first judges on the free market, they will be chosen for their expertise and their reputation for efficiency, honesty, and integrity. Obviously, appeals judges who are inefficient or biased will scarcely be chosen by courts who will have a dispute. The point here is that there is no need for a legally established or institutionalized single, monopoly appeals court system, as states now provide. There is no reason why there cannot arise a multitude of efficient and honest appeals judges who will be selected by the disputant courts, just as there are numerous private arbitrators on the market today. The appeals court renders its decision, and the courts proceed to enforce it if, in our example, Jones is considered guilty—unless, of course, Jones can prove bias in some other court proceedings.

No society can have unlimited judicial appeals, for in that case there would be no point to having judges or courts at all. Therefore, every society, whether statist or anarchist, will have to have some socially accepted cutoff point for trials and appeals. My suggestion is the rule that the agreement *of any two courts* be decisive. "Two" is not an arbitrary figure, for it reflects the fact that there are two parties, the plaintiff and the defendant, to any alleged crime or contract dispute.

If the courts are to be empowered to enforce decisions against guilty parties, does this not bring back the state in another form and thereby negate anarchism? No, for at the beginning of this paper I explicitly defined anarchism in such a way as not to rule out the use of defensive force—force in defense of person and property—by privately supported agencies. In the same way, it is not bringing back the state to allow persons to use force to defend themselves against aggression, or to hire guards or police agencies to defend them.

It should be noted, however, that in the anarchist society there will be no "district attorney" to press charges on behalf of "society." Only the victims will press charges as the plaintiffs. If, then, these victims should happen to be absolute pacifists who are opposed even to defensive force, then they will simply not press charges in the courts or otherwise retaliate against those who have aggressed against them. In a free society that would be their right. If the victim should suffer from murder, then his heir would have the right to press the charges.

What of the Hatfield-and-McCoy problem? Suppose that a Hatfield kills a McCoy, and that McCoy's heir does not belong to a private insurance, police agency, or court, and decides to retaliate himself? Since under anarchism there can be no coercion of the noncriminal, McCoy would have the perfect right to do so. No one may be compelled to bring his case to a court. Indeed, since the right to hire police or courts flows from the right of self-defense against aggression, it would be inconsistent and in contradiction to the very basis of the free society to institute such compulsion. Suppose, then, that the surviving McCoy finds what he believes to be the guilty Hatfield and kills him in turn? What then? This is fine, except that McCoy may have to worry about charges being brought against him by a surviving Hatfield. Here it must be emphasized that in the law of the anarchist society based on defense against aggression, the courts would not be able to proceed against McCoy if in fact he killed the right Hatfield. His problem would arise if the courts should find that he made a grievous mistake and killed the wrong man; in that case, he in turn would be found guilty of murder. Surely, in most instances, individuals will wish to obviate such problems by taking their case to a court and thereby gain social acceptability for their defensive retaliation—not for the *act* of retaliation but for the correctness of deciding who the criminal in any given case might be. The purpose of the judicial process, indeed, is to find a way of general agreement on who might be the criminal or contract breaker in any given case. The judicial process is not a good in itself; thus, in the case of an assassination, such as Jack Ruby's murder of Lee Harvey Oswald, on public television, there is no need for a complex judicial process, since the name of the murderer is evident to all.

Will not the possibility exist of a private court that may turn venal and dishonest, or of a private police force that turns criminal and extorts money by coercion? Of course such an event may occur, given the propensities of human nature. Anarchism is not a moral cure-all. But the important point is that market forces exist to place severe checks on such possibilities, especially in contrast to a society where a state exists. For, in the first place, judges, like arbitrators, will prosper on the market in proportion to their reputation for efficiency and impartiality. Secondly, on the free market important checks and balances exist against venal courts or criminal police forces. Namely, that there are competing courts and police agencies to whom the victims may turn for redress. If the "Prudential Police Agency" should turn outlaw and extract revenue from victims by coercion, the latter would have the option of turning to the "Mutual" or "Equitable" Police Agency for defense and for pressing charges against Prudential. These are the *genuine* "checks and balances" of the free market, genuine in contrast to the phony checks and balances of a state system, where all the alleged "balancing" agencies are in the hands of one monopoly government. Indeed, given the monopoly "protection service" of a state, what is there to prevent a state from using its monopoly channels of coercion to extort money from the public? What are the checks and limits of the state? None, except for the extremely difficult course of revolution against a power with all of the guns in its hands. In fact, the state provides an easy, legitimated channel for crime and aggression, since it has its very being in the crime of tax theft, and the coerced monopoly of "protection." It is the state, indeed, that functions as a mighty "protection racket" on a giant and massive scale. It is the state that says: "Pay us for your 'protection' or else." In the light of the massive and inherent activities of the state, the danger of a "protection racket" emerging from one or more private police agencies is relatively small indeed.

Moreover, it must be emphasized that a crucial element in the power of the state is its legitimacy in the eyes of the majority of the public, the fact that after centuries of propaganda, the depredations of the state are looked upon rather as benevolent services. Taxation is generally not seen as theft, nor war as mass murder, nor conscription as slavery. Should a private police agency turn outlaw, should "Prudential" become a protection racket, it would then lack the social legitimacy which the state has managed to accrue to itself over the centuries. "Prudential" would be seen by all as bandits, rather than as legitimate or divinely appointed "sovereigns" bent on promoting the "common good" or the "general welfare." And lacking such legitimacy, "Prudential" would have to face the wrath of the public and the defense and retaliation of the other private defense agencies, the police and courts, on the free market. Given these inherent checks and limits, a successful transformation from a free society to bandit rule becomes most unlikely. Indeed, historically, it has been very difficult for a state to arise to supplant a stateless society; usually, it has come about through external conquest rather than by evolution from within a society.

Within the anarchist camp, there has been much dispute on whether the private courts would have to be bound by a basic, common law code. Ingenious attempts have been made to work out a system where the laws or standards of decision-making by the courts would differ completely from one to another. But in my view all would have to abide by the basic law code, in particular, prohibition of aggression against person and property, in order to fulfill our definition of anarchism as a system which provides no legal sanction for such aggression. Suppose, for example, that one group of people in society holds that all redheads are demons who deserve to be shot on sight. Suppose that Jones, one of this group, shoots Smith, a redhead. Suppose that Smith or his heir presses charges in a court, but that Jones's court, in philosophic agreement with Jones, finds him innocent therefore. It seems to me that in order to be considered legitimate, any court would have to follow the basic libertarian law code of the inviolate right of person and property. For otherwise, courts might legally subscribe to a code which sanctions such aggression in various cases, and which to that extent would violate the definition of anarchism and introduce, if not the state, then a strong element of statishness or legalized aggression into the society.

But again I see no insuperable difficulties here. For in that case, anarchists, in agitating for their creed, will simply include in their agitation the idea of a general libertarian law code as part and parcel of the anarchist creed of abolition of legalized aggression against person or property in the society.

In contrast to the general law code, other aspects of court decisions could legitimately vary in accordance with the market or the wishes of the clients; for example, the language the cases will be conducted in, the number of judges to be involved, and so on.

There are other problems of the basic law code which there is no time to go into here: for example, the definition of just property titles or the question of legitimate punishment of convicted offenders—though the latter problem of course exists in statist legal systems as well. The basic point, however, is that the state is not needed to arrive at legal principles or their elaboration: indeed, much of the common law, the law merchant, admiralty law, and private law in general, grew up apart from the state, by judges not making the law but finding it on the basis of agreed-upon principles derived either from custom or reason. The idea that the state is needed to *make* law is as much a myth as that the state is needed to supply postal or police services.

Enough has been said here, I believe, to indicate that an anarchist system for settling disputes would be both viable and self-subsistent: that once adopted, it could work and continue indefinitely. *How to arrive* at that system is of course a very different problem, but certainly at the very least it will not likely come about unless people are convinced of its workability, are convinced, in short, that the state is not a *necessary* evil.

Susan Mendus (b. 1951)

Born in Wales and educated at Oxford, Mendus is currently the Director of the MA program in Political Philosophy at York University. In 1985 she was named Morrell Fellow in Toleration. Working in political philosophy and feminist theory, she explores conceptions of the self, human nature, and the phenomenon of caring. She wrote *Toleration and the Limits of Liberalism* (1989) and is the author or editor of numerous other works. The following essay explores different conceptions of the self and how they might inform political theory.

Liberal Man

I begin with two quotations: one from Anthony Crosland's *Socialism Now*, the other from Thucydides' account of the Peloponnesian War. Crosland says:

> experience shows that only a small minority of the population wish to participate [in politics]. I repeat what I have often said—the majority prefer to lead a full family life and cultivate their gardens. And a good thing too ... we do not necessarily want a busy, bustling society in which everyone is politically active and fussing around in an interfering and responsible manner, and herding us all into participating groups. *The threat to privacy and freedom would be intolerable.*

This is the voice of twentieth-century liberal man—of a man whose values are the values of individual privacy and freedom. By contrast, Thucydides says (or, more accurately, reports Pericles as saying):

> Here [in the polis] each individual is interested not only in his own affairs but in the affairs of state as well ... we do not say that a man who takes no interest in politics is a man who minds his own business: we say that he has no business here at all.

The two quotations highlight the different roles played by privacy and community in twentieth-century liberal society and the Athenian polis respectively. Whereas in liberal society, the public or political sphere is a more or less necessary evil, secondary to the home, the family and private life, for the Athenians the situation was almost the reverse. As Crosland notes, the central values now are values of privacy and individual freedom, and the state exists to protect privacy and individual freedom. The state, in other words, is subordinate to individuals. In fifth century Athens, by contrast, the central values were the values of community, friendship, and citizenship, and the individual was fulfilled when he pursued those communal ends. Put crudely, the state did not exist to serve the individual; the individual existed as part of the state.

Here, then, is one characteristic of liberal man: liberal man is a private and retiring man. He cultivates his garden, protects his privacy, minds his own business, keeps himself largely to himself. His loyalties are to his family and friends, not to the state. He is a man to whom the notion of community, in any strong sense, is alien.

A second characteristic of liberal man may be identified via two further quotations: one from a recent speech by the Conservative politician, John Moore, the other from the ancient Greek poet, Pindar. Justifying government changes in the National Health Service, Moore says;

> a climate of dependence can in time corrupt the human spirit. Everyone knows the sullen apathy of dependence and can compare it with the sheer delight of personal achievement. To deliberately set up a system that creates the former instead of the latter is to act directly against the best interests and indeed the welfare of individuals and of society. The job therefore has been to change this depressing climate of dependence and revitalize the belief which has been such a powerful force throughout British history: that individuals *can* take action to change their lives; *can* do things to control what happens to them. We believe that dependence in the long run decreases human happiness and reduces human freedom. We believe that the well being of individuals is best protected and promoted when they are helped to be independent, to use their talents to take care of themselves, and to achieve things on their own which is one of the greatest satisfactions life can offer.

Twentieth-century liberal man aspires to make his own life, control his own fate, and triumph over the contingencies of background, circumstance, and environment. By contrast, Pindar adopts a more accepting and (some would say) submissive attitude. He writes;

> But human excellence
> grows like a vine tree,
> fed by the green dew,
> raised up among wise men and just
> to the liquid sky.
> We have all kinds of needs for those we love
> most of all in hardships, but joy, too,
> strains to track down eyes that it can trust.

Here the emphasis is (both literally and metaphorically) on roots: man is not a controlling creature, striving to triumph over circumstance, but a dependent and needy creature, sunk in the contingencies of fate and chance. Like the vine tree, his well-being is dictated by things over which he has little or no control—sunlight, water, the green dew and the liquid sky. Moreover, and most importantly, this is not a source of regret, for human flourishing in Pindar's eyes is not *opposed* to dependence, it is defined in terms of dependence. As Martha Nussbaum has put it; 'human excellence is seen in Pindar's poem, and pervasively in the Greek poetic tradition, as something whose very nature it is to be in need, a growing thing that could not be made invulnerable and keep its own peculiar fineness'. Again, there is a gulf between the twentieth-century liberal view and the Greek view: where liberal man aspires to create his own life and to control the world, the Greek character accepts his dependent status, his vulnerability as a *part of* the world.

The two sets of quotations provide the themes of this paper: liberal man is private and solitary (he is a free and independent self), whereas Greek man is essentially a member of a community (he is defined by his role in society). Liberal man is autonomous and controlling (he *chooses* the commitments which constitute the self—commitments to his wife, his friends, his children), whereas Greek man is dependent and determined (he *accepts* his role within the world—acknowledges obligations which are largely unchosen—obligations to siblings, parents, the city state). So, where liberalism extols the value of autonomy, Pindar extols the value of dependence. Where liberalism extols the value of privacy, Thucydides (Pericles) extols the value of community. Put generally, where liberalism extols the value of the *chosen*, the Greek world extols the value of the *given*.

My aim in this paper is to discuss the implications of these different views of human nature and human fulfilment. In particular, I shall discuss the liberal commitment to independence—to achieving things on one's own. My claims will be that in so far as this purports to present a picture of what life is like, it is false; in so far as it purports to present a picture of what life ought to be like, it is morally impoverished, and in so far as it aspires to explain the human condition it is partial and distorting. We are more like the vine tree than liberals would have us believe, and there is reason to be grateful that that is so. In general, then, I shall be arguing for the practical and moral necessity of a move away from the liberal language of choice and towards the language of dependence.

In pursuing my aim I shall follow two distinct but connected paths: firstly, I shall consider a twentieth-century literary example, the example of George and Lennie in John Steinbeck's novel, *Of Mice and Men*. My aim here is to indicate that the model of man as independent and controlling is false to the realities of all our lives. Moreover, there is an important sense in which we should not aspire to this ideal: achieving things on our own, far from being the greatest satisfaction life can offer, is an aspiration which often turns out to be hollow.

Secondly, I shall consider the example of Antigone in Sophocles' play of that name. My aim here is to suggest that the whole nature of tragic circumstances is distorted by the liberal perspective. Liberal emphasis on man as a free and independent chooser not only misrepresents the realities of our lives, it also renders tragic circumstances incomprehensible. So the Steinbeck case enables us to see how the liberal conception of man as independent and controlling is an unwarranted idealization (it presents a distorted picture of what human flourishing consists in); the Antigone case enables us to see how the liberal conception of man as a free and independent self is an unacceptable abstraction (it cannot accommodate central features of our lives).

Steinbeck and Human Dependence

I turn first, then, to Steinbeck's *Of Mice and Men* and to a discussion of human dependence. Steinbeck's novel tells of two characters—George and Lennie. George and Lennie are migrant labourers who roam the Salinas Valley, moving from ranch to ranch in constant search of work. Together, they make an incongruous pair: George is small, shrewd, alert; Lennie a cretinous giant, barely able to think or remember the simplest things. His massive strength leads him to destroy the objects of his affection, and George is his guardian, saving him from the worst consequences of his own idiocy. George aspires to be the independent man. His constant refrain is of how good it would be if he were able to control his own life, to achieve things on his own. 'God a'mighty,' he says,

> if I was alone I could live so easy. I could go get a job an' work, an' no trouble. No mess at all, and when the end of the month come I could take my fifty bucks and go into town and get whatever I want. Why, I could stay in a cat house all night. I could eat anyplace I want, hotel or any place, and order any damn thing I could think of. An' I could do that every damn month.

This is George's dream, the dream of discovering 'one of the greatest satisfactions life can offer', the dream of independence. But there is another dream too, a dream which he shares with Lennie. They speak of it by the river as the novel begins, and again at its pathetic conclusion.

> 'Someday—we're gonna get the jack together and gonna have a little house and a couple of acres an' a cow and some pigs and—' '*An' live off the fatta the lan*' Lennie shouted. 'An' have *rabbits* Go on George! Tell about what we're gonna have in the garden and about the rabbits in the cages and about the rain in the winter and the stove, and how thick the cream is on the milk, like you can hardly cut it. Tell about that, George . . .'

This second dream is their 'best laid scheme', their 'promis'd joy'. It comes to nothing. Once again Lennie kills the thing he loves—their new employer's daughter—and George is forced to shoot him to keep him from being lynched. The story displays, in graphic detail, the extent to which the two protagonists are dependent creatures. In particular, their dependency consists in their vulnerability to three distinct forms of luck—constitutional luck (luck in their character); circumstantial luck (luck in their world); and consequential luck (luck in the way things turn out for them). These forms of luck make them victims of the world, rather than controllers of it. Lennie, in particular, is a victim: of his character, which makes him kill the things he loves; of his circumstances, which force him to move from place to place looking for work; and of consequences, since his good will delivers disastrous outcomes quite the reverse of his intentions. Moreover, and most importantly, in Steinbeck's vision 'Lennie was to be, not a pathetic cretin, but a symbolic figure . . . a Lennie who was not to represent insanity at all, but the inarticulate and powerful yearnings of all men.' Lennie's best laid scheme is doomed to failure, but it is doomed not because he is Lennie the imbecilic giant, but because he is human. His fate is (potentially) the fate of us all in so far as we are vulnerable to things outside our control.

The story directs attention to a form of dependence which involves absence of control. It suggests that we cannot always, or with any degree of certainty, 'take action to change our lives', nor can we 'do things to control what happens to us'. Much of the pathos of the story lies in the very fact that George and Lennie are victims of the world in which they find themselves. And much of its power lies in the implication that the rest of us are, at root, no different from them. We are none of us in control of our 'best laid schemes'. But the story also draws attention to another form of dependence, which connects control and neediness. In the poem from Pindar this kind of dependence is also referred to: Pindar sees human beings as both vulnerable (subject to things outside their control) and needy. By contrast liberals characteristically assume not only that we *can* control our lives (that we are to some degree invulnerable), but also that we will flourish better if we *do* control our lives (that we are, to some degree, not in need of things external to us). Thus John Moore speaks of individuals' ability to 'achieve things *on their own*', which is, he says, 'one of the greatest satisfactions life can offer'. Similarly, John Stuart Mill speaks enthusiastically of the man who is active, energetic, controlling. 'It is', he says, 'the privilege *and proper condition* of a human being arrived at the maturity of his faculties, to use and interpret experience in his own way, to decide what part of recorded experience is properly applicable to his own circumstances and character.' Men should, in Mill's view 'choose their own plan of life', mould and fashion their own world. They should employ judgment, choice, discrimination. In general, Mill's vision is the vision of man as a controlling creature—one who does not allow others or the world to determine his plan of life, but who achieves things on his own. The first lesson of Steinbeck's novel is that this is not always possible: like George and Lennie we may be dependent on circumstances and on character in a way which will make independent achievement impossible.

But a second lesson of Steinbeck's novel is that such achievement will not necessarily satisfy. When George is forced to shoot Lennie, he does not discover the benefits of independence, but rather its hollowness. He discovers that his personal dream—his dream of freedom and self-determination—is in fact empty. 'George is left with the free life he claimed to want, but which he actually dreaded, recognizing, though never admitting, its utter futility and loneliness.' Independence (the ability to achieve things on his own) far from being one of the greatest satisfactions life can offer, destroys the possibility of satisfaction. Despite George's professed aspiration to independence, he is highly dependent on Lennie. It is this dependence which gives meaning to his life and which makes him a proper object of our admiration.

Here, then, are two ways in which we may understand dependence: as vulnerability, or susceptibility to luck, which determines how well or ill our plans go; and as neediness, or dependence on others for our own well-being, which determines what value our plans have for us. I have suggested that in the former case dependence is an ineradicable feature of human life, and that in the latter case dependence can be the thing which makes our plans and our lives meaningful. So at one and the same time we are dependent because we cannot control our 'best-laid schemes', and dependent because those schemes make essential reference to others for their significance and value. Put together, these two forms of dependence cast doubt both upon the claim that we can control our lives and upon the claim that such control is 'one of the greatest satisfactions life can offer'. They undermine the liberal idealization of independence as a way of life.

Before discussing the implications of these examples, I want to draw one further contrast between conceptions of human nature as dependent, and conceptions of human nature as controlling. Steinbeck's major novels, written in the late 1930s and early 1940s, make constant reference to the coming of the machine, and to the ways in which the machine destroys the American Dream of endeavour rewarded. *The Grapes of Wrath* is, of course, the most obvious place where antagonism between man and machine is discussed. The Joads of Oklahoma are the victims of a burgeoning technology which denies them their birthright of a chicken in every pot and a car in every garage. As 'man' becomes more powerful over nature, individual men become impotent, or they become 'machine men'. Steinbeck speaks of 'the machine man, driving a dead tractor on land he does not know and love, [he] understands only chemistry; and he is contemptuous of the land and of himself. When the corrugated iron doors are shut, he goes home, and his home is not the land'.

The pursuit of technological supremacy—of control over nature—makes man less human. The analogy now is not between man and things in nature, like the vine tree. Rather the analogy is between man and the things which tame nature—the tractor, the machinery of the new technology. Man is no longer a part of the natural world, but a being distinct from the natural world, who manipulates it for his own purposes. And in this, Steinbeck implies, there is a loss of something characteristically human, for men do not simply use the machinery of the new world, they become like machines themselves. In the pursuit of technological omnipotence man becomes more like a tool himself. His value is no longer an intrinsic value, defined by reference to his neediness, but an instrumental value, defined in terms of the power he can exert over other things.

In his *Groundwork for a Metaphysic of Morals* Kant tells us that everything in the world has either a price or a dignity. As we cease to see human beings as akin to things in the natural world (the vine tree), and construe them as akin to machines, we abandon dignity in favour of price: we lose a sense of distinctively human value, and reduce everything to instrumental value, forgetting that where everything has instrumental value, nothing has dignity at all.

Of Mice and Men thus indicates two ways in which human beings are dependent: we are vulnerable to luck, and we are needy. We cannot eradicate the former kind of dependence, and we should not seek to eradicate the latter. The former puts success and failure at least partly beyond our control. This is not necessarily a source of regret. Our dependence on other people is what gives value to the success of our projects. Without it, we might succeed in controlling our own lives, but the victory would be a hollow and empty one. The reason for this is given in the final example—the example from *The Grapes of Wrath*. Steinbeck's notorious 'earthiness' suggests that it is not dependence in itself which is either good or bad. Rather, value springs from what we are dependent on. There are forms of dependence which assert our value as human beings, and there are forms of dependence which deny it. The dependence which implies that, as human beings, we have only an instrumental value is the worst form of dependence. It is this which is implied in the move from an analogy between man and the natural world to an analogy between man and the inanimate objects of the new technology. It is the very rejection of dependency (the neediness and vulnerability of the vine tree) which brings with it the denial of humanity.

Sophocles and the Nature of Tragedy

The example of George and Lennie illustrates the extent to which liberal emphasis on control and independence presents a distorted picture of human life. It is false to the facts of our lives and false also to our values, for we are not merely and as a matter of fact vulnerable and dependent. It is also the case that dependence is often the thing which invests our lives with meaning. Our frailty is, in this respect, also part of our fineness.

This last thought draws attention to the sense in which the liberal conception of agency may be an idealization, rather than a mere abstraction. Liberals often employ the notion of independence to refer to the kind of people we should aspire to be. Thus, John Moore advocates achieving things on one's own (this is not only what we do do, but what we should do), Mill speaks of the importance of choosing one's own style of life ('the privilege and *proper condition* of a human being'), and similarly John Rawls appeals to 'an ideal' of persons as independent and autonomous. Writing about Rawls, Onora O'Neill says:

> *A Theory of Justice* was tailored to hide the interlocking structure of desires and attitudes that is typical of human agents. Once the social relations between agents were masked it could seem plausible to . . . build a determinate ideal of mutual independence into a conception of justice. This ideal is not met by any human agents. It isn't only deficient and backward human agents whose choosing would be misrepresented by these ideal agents of construction. The construction assumes a mutual independence which is false of all human beings. Such independence is as much an idealization of human social relations as an assumption of generalized altruism would be.

The Steinbeck story may be read as an attempt to express precisely this: that liberalism assumes a mutual independence which is in fact not ours. In so doing it idealizes a picture of man as an independent chooser, but man is not an independent chooser. Man exists within complex networks of dependency, many of which are nothing to do with choice at all.

All this, however, is an attack on the idealization of independence, but characteristically liberals deny that they are idealizing at all. Rather, they claim merely to be simplifying by removing the contingencies which clutter everyday life. The earlier references to Mill and Rawls cast doubt on whether this is really true, but even if it were true, a problem persists, which is to establish the criteria whereby some things are deemed to be contingent and others not. How, in other words, can we know how much to abstract? It is here that the cultural specificity of liberal thinking becomes clear. For even if the liberal conception of human agents as mutually independent is 'our' conception, it is not thereby a universal conception, and this fact can lead to a distortion of our understanding of other ways of thinking. Put simply, the form of my argument is this: either liberal appeal to independence is an idealization or it is an abstraction. If it is an idealization, it is one which is false to our lives. We are victims as often as we are choosers. If, on the other hand, it is an abstraction, what warrants the decision to cull *this* from the process of abstraction, rather than something else? Who says that when we have abstracted we will be left with man as an independent chooser and controller, rather than man as merely one needy thing amongst others? My second example is an attempt to grapple with this problem.

Sophocles' *Antigone* tells of the tragic choice which faces Antigone when the laws of the state and the laws of the gods conflict. Her brother, Polynices, has died a traitor's death attacking his own city. As dictated by convention, Creon, the ruler, declares that his body is to be left unburied. But Antigone cannot comply. Disobeying the laws of the state, she buries Polynices and her punishment is death.

Antigone is one of the most comprehensively studied of Sophocles' plays, and a major debate amongst commentators is whether the character of Antigone represents moral right and Creon moral wrong, or whether there is a sense in which both are wrong. Does Antigone have too narrow a vision of moral duty, or is she the true representation of moral innocence, uncorrupted by political considerations of power and control? There is a sense in which the terms of that debate are themselves suffused with the liberal vision of man (in this case woman) as an active chooser. It is far less clear that the question arises in quite that way from outside the liberal tradition—from the Greek perspective itself. Why is this so?

Three thoughts are relevant here: firstly, that the tragic nature of Antigone's situation is evident only if we assume (as liberalism does not) that individuals are not merely selves, but also the occupiers of roles. Secondly, that the very nature of tragedy presupposes a non-liberal conception of human nature as dependent, not controlling. Thirdly, that the concept of community plays a central role in generating and explaining the tragedy. These three themes are evident in the commentaries on *Antigone* presented by three modern philosophers: Martin Hollis, Martha Nussbaum, and Alasdair MacIntyre. I shall conclude by discussing these briefly.

Hollis adopts a characteristically liberal approach to the tragedy. He claims that, whilst Antigone and Creon are both '*dramatis personae* in the old sense of "masks" or complete embodiments of role. Yet they both *choose* their doomed paths . . . this need not imply', he says, 'that other choices would have saved them, but it does imply that Sophocles is thinking in terms of individual agency. This seems to me to be a misrepresentation of the situation: of course, in so far as Antigone does something (rather than nothing), it is appropriate to say that she chooses. But the whole force of the tragedy is to indicate that the choices she makes are not choices *qua* individual agent, but choices *qua* occupier of a role. The liberal conception of individual agency (of a self) is largely inappropriate here, for there is nothing in Antigone, as an individual agent, which is relevant to the tragedy. The whole genesis of the tragic situation is directly attributable to the seriousness with which she accepts her role.

Thus, for example, the play begins with the cry 'O sister!' and Antigone goes on immediately to describe 'the death of our two brothers', and how she and Ismene are doomed to suffer 'for our father'. It is the fact that she is circumscribed by these societal roles which determines Antigone's fate. She does not choose in the way the liberal man would choose—as an independent self; she 'chooses' as a sister. More properly, she accepts the duties which the role of sister impose her, and reminds Ismene that Polynices is their brother, 'whether we like it or not'. In brief, her situation is not one of an individual agent who decides, but of a sister who acknowledges and accepts. This, then, is one aspect of the tragedy of Antigone: it is central to the play that she does not act as a free and independent liberal self.

A second feature, emphasized by Alasdair MacIntyre, is the relationship between tragedy and value pluralism. It is a commonplace in modern political philosophy that liberals are committed to a plurality of goods, some of which conflict with others. The guiding vision of liberalism is the vision of society as an association of independent agents who have distinct and sometimes incompatible conceptions of the good. Liberal societies do not attempt to impose their conception of the good on their citizens, rather they provide a neutral arena within which the agents themselves may decide upon and pursue their own conception of the good. Thus, the liberal scheme of things assumes a plurality of values. In general, what legitimates the choice of values is just that—that it is a choice.

By contrast, MacIntyre urges that Sophocles' claim is *both* that goods are irreconcilable (there is a plurality of values) *and* that there is an objective moral order. The tragic heroine is not, like the liberal, simply confronted by a bewildering array of choices, some of which conflict with others. She is also haunted by the knowledge that there is a right choice. 'There are indeed crucial conflicts in which different virtues appear as making different and incompatible claims upon us. But our situation is tragic in that we have to recognize the authority of both claims'. Here is the locus of at least some liberal misunderstanding of tragedy. Ackerman, for example, argues that 'there are no moral meanings hidden in the bowels of the universe. There is only you and I struggling in a world which neither we nor any other thing created'. This certainly makes life difficult, but it cannot, I think, make life tragic. The problem for the liberal is to establish which is the rational choice amongst the many conflicting values. But the problem for the tragic hero is to know, to acknowledge, what is right. He cannot escape his predicament by choosing, because more than choice is required. Knowledge is required. And knowledge is precisely what he cannot have.

Finally, and connectedly, both Alasdair MacIntyre and Martha Nussbaum emphasize the central role of community in the Greek conception. Whereas, for us, the role of friendship, company, and city-state are contingent, in the Greek conception they are central. The entire ethical experience of tragedy, says Nussbaum, 'stresses the fundamental value of community and friendship. It does not invite or even permit us to seek for the good apart from these'. In so far, therefore, as modern liberal thinking abstracts from the values of friendship and community, it abstracts what may well be contingent in our lives, but is essential to the Greek tragedians. Moreover, the point can be generalized beyond the considerations thrown up by *Antigone:* Rawls' *Theory of Justice* offers a coherent articulation of the deep moral commitments of 'our' society. We are invited to read the book as a vindication of the principles of justice 'we' would discover in drawing on 'our' underlying conceptions of free and equal citizenship. But as has been pointed out, 'this vindication of justice does not address others who, unlike "us", do not start with such ideals of citizenship; it has nothing to say to those others'.

These three themes express three reservations about the role of abstraction in liberal theory: a reservation about how we can know what we should abstract; a reservation about what we are left with after we have abstracted (are we left with an agent who is a chooser, or a tragic character who acknowledges fate?), and a reservation about what, if anything, we can say to the inhabitant of a different culture whose process of abstraction proceeds differently.

Conclusion

I began by mentioning two features characteristic of liberal man: he is a private self rather than the occupier of a social role; and he is an independent agent, who aspires to control his world. Put together, these features generate a conception of human agents as essentially choosing and deciding, rather than accepting or acknowledging. This conception was then contrasted with an alternative conception implicit in some of the literature of ancient Greece. The point of the contrast, and of the subsequent examples, was two-fold: firstly to draw a distinction between independence as an abstraction and independence as an idealization. Secondly to suggest that neither of these is adequate. The Steinbeck example aims to show that in so far as independence is an ideal, it is not an ideal to which we either do or should subscribe. There are many circumstances in which dependence is both an ineradicable fact of life, and also something which gives value to our plans and projects. We are not essentially independent and controlling creatures, and we have reason to be glad that that is so.

By contrast, the Antigone example aims to show that in so far as independence is an abstraction, it is one which misrepresents the nature of some, tragic, circumstances, The decision to abstract from an agent's role as sister, mother, father, subject within the state, is a decision to assert liberal values. It is not a justification of those values.

Moreover, in abstracting, we run the risk of failing to see the truly tragic nature of some situations. Antigone's tragedy lies not in the fact that she is faced with a choice between competing values, but in the fact that she must be dishonoured. The liberal conception of man as agent—as independent free chooser—leaves room for difficult choices, even impossible choices. But it does not leave room for tragic *situations*. Commenting on this, one philosopher has written;

> Consider what might happen in a society where, increasingly, the limitations of character and the situations which limit moral endeavour are not recognized. It is probable that the idea that there must be a solution to every difficulty would become even more prevalent than it is already in certain circles today. If this were to happen, the very idea of what a difficulty is would have changed in important respects. Difficulties would be regarded as signs that something

had gone wrong, in much the same way as a flaw in a product shows that there is something wrong in the techniques of production.

At the limit, the language of independence and control leaves no room for the tragic or the pathetic. The thoughts that life was too hard, that fortune was fickle, that burdens were too great cannot sensibly be accommodated by this way of looking at the world. Independence and control require effort, not acceptance. They allow only bad judgments, faulty calculations, incomplete equations. Tragedy, however, works in quite the opposite way, directing our attention to cases where trying is precisely not what is required. To the extent that this is so, the language of liberal individualism, the language of control and independence robs us of the means to understand others, and it may also rob us of an understanding of an important part of ourselves.

Ronald Dworkin (b. 1931)

Born in Worcester, MA, he was educated at Harvard University and at Oxford University. A member of the New York Bar since 1959, he served as Law Clerk to the respected jurist Learned Hand (1957-58), and also practiced law. He later joined the faculty of Yale Law School, where he stayed until his 1969 appointment as Professor of Jurisprudence at Oxford University. Since 1975 he has held the Oxford post concurrently with a Professorship at the New York University Law School. His chief works include *Taking Rights Seriously* (1977), excerpted here, and *Law's Empire* (1986). Dworkin is also a frequent contributor to *The New York Review of Books*.

*From Taking Rights Seriously**

What Rights Do We Have?

1. No Right to Liberty

Do we have a right to liberty? Thomas Jefferson thought so, and since his day the right to liberty has received more play than the competing rights he mentioned to life and the pursuit of happiness. Liberty gave its name to the most influential political movement of the last century, and many of those who now despise liberals do so on the ground that they are not sufficiently libertarian. Of course, almost everyone concedes that the right to liberty is not the only political right, and that therefore claims to freedom must be limited, for example, by restraints that protect the security or property of others. Nevertheless the consensus in favor of some right to liberty is a vast one, though it is, as I shall argue in this chapter, misguided.

The right to liberty is popular all over this political spectrum. The rhetoric of liberty fuels every radical movement from international wars of liberation to campaigns for sexual freedom and women's liberation. But liberty has been even more prominent in conservative service. Even the mild social reorganizations of the anti-trust and unionization movements, and of the early New Deal, were opposed on the grounds that they infringed the right to liberty, and just now efforts to achieve some racial justice in America through techniques like the busing of black and white schoolchildren, and social justice in Britain through constraints in private education are bitterly opposed on that ground.

It has become common, indeed, to describe the great social issues of domestic politics, and in particular the racial issue, as presenting a conflict between the demands of liberty and equality. It may be, it is said, that the poor and the black and the uneducated and the unskilled have an abstract right to equality, but the prosperous and the whites and the educated and the able have a right to liberty as well and any efforts at social

---

* An Excerpt.

reorganization in aid of the first set of rights must reckon with and respect the second. Everyone except extremists recognizes, therefore, the need to compromise between equality and liberty. Every piece of important social legislation, from tax policy to integration plans, is shaped by the supposed tension between these two goals.

I have this supposed conflict between equality and liberty in mind when I ask whether we have a *right* to liberty, as Jefferson and everyone else has supposed. That is a crucial question. If freedom to choose one's schools, or employees, or neighborhood is simply something that we all want, like air conditioning or lobsters, then we are not entitled to hang on to these freedoms in the face of what we concede to be the rights of others to an equal share of respect and resources. But if we can say, not simply that we want these freedoms, but that we are ourselves entitled to them, then we have established at least a basis for demanding a compromise.

There is now a movement, for example, in favor of a proposed amendment to the constitution of the United States that would guarantee every school child the legal right to attend a 'neighborhood school' and thus outlaw busing. The suggestion, that neighborhood schools somehow rank with jury trials as constitutional values, would seem silly but for the sense many Americans have that forcing school children into buses is somehow as much an interference with the fundamental right to liberty as segregated schooling was an insult to equality. But that seems to me absurd; indeed it seems to me absurd to suppose that men and women have any general right to liberty at all, at least as liberty has traditionally been conceived by its champions.

I have in mind the traditional definition of liberty as the absence of constraints placed by a government upon what a man might do if he wants to. Isaiah Berlin, in the most famous modern essay on liberty, put the matter this way: 'The sense of freedom, in which I use this term, entails not simply the absence of frustration but the absence of obstacles to possible choices and activities — absence of obstructions on roads along which a man can decide to walk.' This conception of liberty as license is neutral amongst the various activities a man might pursue, the various roads he might wish to walk. It diminishes a man's liberty when we prevent him from talking or making love as he wishes, but it also diminishes his liberty when we prevent him from murdering or defaming others. These latter constraints may be justifiable, but only because they are compromises necessary to protect the liberty or security of others, and not because they do not, in themselves, infringe the independent value of liberty. Bentham said that any law whatsoever is an 'infraction' of liberty, and though some such infractions might be necessary, it is obscurantist to pretend that they are not infractions after all. In this neutral, all embracing sense of liberty as license, liberty and equality are plainly in competition. Laws are needed to protect equality, and laws are inevitably compromises of liberty.

Liberals like Berlin are content with this neutral sense of liberty, because it seems to encourage clear thinking. It allows us to identify just what is lost, though perhaps unavoidably, when men accept constraints on their actions for some other goal or value. It would be an intolerable muddle, on this view, to use the concept of liberty or freedom in such a way that we counted a loss of freedom only when men were prevented from doing something that we thought they ought to do. It would allow totalitarian governments to masquerade as liberal, simply by arguing that they prevent men from doing only what is wrong. Worse, it would obscure the most distinctive point of the liberal tradition, which is that interfering with a man's free choice to do what he might want to do is in and of itself an insult to humanity, a wrong that may be justified but can never be wiped away by competing considerations. For a true liberal, any constraint upon freedom is something that a decent government must regret, and keep to the minimum necessary to accommodate the other rights of its constituents.

In spite of this tradition, however, the neutral sense of liberty seems to me to have caused more confusion than it has cured, particularly when it is joined to the popular and inspiring idea that men and women have a right to liberty. For we can maintain that idea only by so watering down the idea of a right that the right to liberty is something hardly worth having at all.

The term "right" is used in politics and philosophy in many different senses, some of which I have tried to disentangle elsewhere. In order sensibly to ask whether we have a right to liberty in the neutral sense, we must fix on some one meaning of "right." It would not be difficult to find a sense of that term in which we could say with some confidence that men have a right to liberty. We might say, for example, that someone has a right to liberty if it is in his interest to have liberty, that is, if he either wants it or if it would be good for him to have it. In this sense, I would be prepared to concede that citizens have a right to liberty. But in this sense I would also have to concede that they have a right, at least generally, to vanilla ice cream. My concession about liberty, moreover, would have very little value in political debate. I should want to claim, for example, that people have a right to equality in a much stronger sense, that they do not simply want equality but that they are entitled to it, and I would therefore not recognize the claim that some men and women want liberty as requiring any compromise in the efforts that I believe are necessary to give other men and women the equality to which they are entitled.

If the right to liberty is to play the role cut out for it in political debate, therefore, it must be a right in a much stronger sense. . . . A successful claim of right, in the strong sense I described, has this consequence. If someone has a right to something, then it is wrong for the government to deny it to him even though it would be in the general interest to do so. This sense of a right (which might be called the anti-utilitarian concept of a right) seems to me very close to the sense of right principally used in political and legal writing and argument in recent years. It marks the distinctive concept of an individual right against the State which is the heart, for example, of constitutional theory in the United States.

I do not think that the right to liberty would come to very much, or have much power in political argument, if it relied on any sense of the right any weaker than that. If we settle on this concept of a right, however, then it seems plain that there exists no general right to liberty as such. I have no political right to drive up Lexington Avenue. If the government chooses to make Lexington Avenue one-way down town, it is a sufficient justification that this would be in the general interest, and it would be ridiculous for me to argue that for some reason it would nevertheless be wrong. The vast bulk of the laws which diminish my liberty are justified on utilitarian grounds, as being in the general interest or for the general welfare; if, as Bentham supposes, each of these laws diminishes my liberty, they nevertheless do not take away from me any thing that I have a right to have. It will not do, in the one-way street case, to say that although I have a right to drive up Lexington Avenue, nevertheless the government for special reasons is justified in overriding that right. That seems silly because the government needs no special justification—but only *a* justification—for this sort of legislation. So I can have a political right to liberty, such that every act of constraint diminishes or infringes that right, only in such a weak sense of right that the so called right to liberty is not competitive with strong rights, like the right to equality, at all. In any strong sense of right, which would be competitive with the right to equality, there exists no general right to liberty at all.

It may now be said that I have misunderstood the claim that there is a right to liberty. It does not mean to argue, it will be said, that there is a right to all liberty, but simply to important or basic liberties. Every law is, as Bentham said, an infraction of liberty, but we have a right to be protected against only fundamental or serious infractions. If the constraint on liberty is serious or severe enough, then it is indeed true that the government is not entitled to impose that constraint simply because that would be in the general interest; the government is not entitled to constrain liberty of speech, for example, whenever it thinks that would improve the general welfare. So there is, after all, a general right to liberty as such, provided that that right is restricted to important liberties or serious deprivations. This qualification does not affect the political arguments I described earlier, it will be said, because the rights to liberty that stand in the way of full equality are rights to basic liberties like, for example, the right to attend a school of one's choice.

But this qualification raises an issue of great importance for liberal theory, which those who argue for a right to liberty do not face. What does it mean to say that the right to liberty is limited to basic liberties, or that it offers protection only against serious infractions of liberty? That claim might be spelled out in two different ways, with very different theoretical and practical consequences. Let us suppose two cases in which government constrains a citizen from doing what he might want to do: the government prevents him from speaking his mind on political issues; from driving his car uptown on Lexington Avenue. What is the connection between these two cases, and the difference between them, such that though they are both cases in which a citizen is constrained and deprived of liberty, his right to liberty is infringed only in the first, and not in the second?

On the first of the two theories we might consider, the citizen is deprived of the same commodity, namely liberty, in both cases, but the difference is that in the first case the amount of that commodity taken away from him is, for some reason, either greater in amount or greater in its impact than in the second. But that seems bizarre. It is very difficult to think of liberty as a commodity. If we do try to give liberty some operational sense, such that we can measure the relative diminution of liberty occasioned by different sorts of laws or constraints, then the result is unlikely to match our intuitive sense of what are basic liberties and what are not. Suppose, for example, we measure a diminution in liberty by calculating the extent of frustration that it induces. We shall then have to face the fact that laws against theft, and even traffic laws, impose constraints that are felt more keenly by most men than constraints on political speech would be. We might take a different tack, and measure the degree of loss of liberty by the impact that a particular constraint has on future choices. But we should then have to admit that the ordinary criminal code reduces choice for most men more than laws which forbid fringe political activity. So the first theory—that the difference between cases covered and those not covered by our supposed right to liberty is a matter of degree—must fail.

The second theory argues that the difference between the two cases has to do, not with the degree of liberty involved, but with the special character of the liberty involved in the case covered by the right. On this theory, the offense involved in a law that limits free speech is of a different character, and not just different in degree, from a law that prevents a man from driving up Lexington Avenue. That sounds plausible, though as we shall see it is not easy to state what this difference in character comes to, or why it argues for a right in some cases though not in others. My present point, however, is that if the distinction between basic liberties and other liberties is defended in this way, then the notion of a general right to liberty as such has been entirely abandoned. If we have a right to basic liberties not because they are cases in which the commodity of liberty is somehow especially at stake, but because an assault on basic liberties injures us or demeans us in some way that goes beyond its impact on liberty, then what we have a right to is not liberty at all, but to the values or interests or standing that this particular constraint defeats.

This is not simply a question of terminology. The idea of a right to liberty is a misconceived concept that does a disservice to political thought in at least two ways. First, the idea creates a false sense of a necessary conflict between liberty and other values when social regulation, like the busing program, is proposed. Second, the idea provides too easy an answer to the question of why we regard certain kinds of restraints, like the restraint on free speech or the exercise of religion, as especially unjust. The idea of a right to liberty allows us to say that these constraints are unjust because they have a special impact on liberty as such. Once we recognize that this answer is spurious, then we shall have to face the difficult question of what is indeed at stake in these cases.

I should like to turn at once to that question. If there is no general right to liberty, then why do citizens in a democracy have rights to any specific kind of liberty, like freedom of speech or religion or political activity? It is no answer to say that if individuals have these rights, then the community will be better off in the long run as a whole. This idea—that individual rights may lead to overall utility—may or may not be true, but it is irrelevant to the defense of rights as such, because when we say that someone has a right to speak his mind freely, in the relevant political sense, we mean that he is entitled to do so even if this would not be in the general interest. If we want to defend individual rights in the sense in which we claim them, then we must try to discover something beyond utility that argues for these rights.

I mentioned one possibility earlier. We might be able to make out a case that individuals suffer some special damage when the traditional rights are invaded. On this argument, there is something about the liberty to speak out on political issues such that if that liberty is denied the individual suffers a special kind of damage which makes it wrong to inflict that damage upon him even though the community as a whole would benefit. This line of argument will appeal to those who themselves would feel special deprivation at the loss of their political and civil liberties, but it is nevertheless a difficult argument to pursue for two reasons.

First, there are a great many men and women and they undoubtedly form the majority even in democracies like Britain and the United States, who do not exercise political liberties that they have, and who would not count the loss of these liberties as especially grievous. Second, we lack a psychological theory which would justify and explain the idea that the loss of civil liberties, or any particular liberties, involves inevitable or even likely psychological damage. On the contrary, there is now a lively tradition in psychology, led by psychologists like Ronald Laing, who argue that a good deal of mental instability in modern societies may be traced to the demand for too much liberty rather than too little. In their account, the need to choose, which follows from liberty, is an unnecessary source of destructive tension. These theories are not necessarily persuasive, but until we can be confident that they are wrong, we cannot assume that psychology demonstrates the opposite, however appealing that might be on political grounds.

If we want to argue for a right to certain liberties, therefore, we must find another ground. We must argue on grounds of political morality that it is wrong to deprive individuals of these liberties, for some reason, apart from direct psychological damage, in spite of the fact that the common interest would be served by doing so. I put the matter this vaguely because there is no reason to assume, in advance, that only one kind of reason would support that moral position. It might be that a just society would recognize a variety of individual rights, some grounded on very different sorts of moral considerations from others. In what remains of this chapter I shall try to describe only one possible ground for rights. It does not follow that men and women in civil society have only the rights that the argument I shall make would support; but it does follow that they have at least these rights, and that is important enough.

2. The Right to Liberties

The central concept of my argument will be the concept not of liberty but of equality. I presume that we all accept the following postulates of political morality. Government must treat those whom it governs with concern, that is, as human beings who are capable of suffering and frustration, and with respect, that is, as human beings who are capable of forming and acting on intelligent conceptions of how their lives should be lived. Government must not only treat people with concern and respect, but with equal concern and respect. It must not distribute goods or opportunities unequally on the ground that some citizens are entitled to more because they are worthy of more concern. It must not constrain liberty on the ground that one citizen's conception of the good life of one group is nobler or superior to another's. These postulates, taken together, state what might be called the liberal conception of equality; but it is a conception of equality, not of liberty as license, that they state.

The sovereign question of political theory, within a state supposed to be governed by the liberal conception of equality, is the question of what inequalities in goods, opportunities and liberties are permitted in such a state, and why. The beginning of an answer lies in the following distinction. Citizens governed by the liberal conception of equality each have a right to equal concern and respect. But there are two different rights that might be comprehended by that abstract right. The first is the right to equal treatment, that is, to the same distribution of goods or opportunities as anyone else has or is given. The Supreme Court, in the Reapportionment Cases, held that citizens have a right to equal treatment in the distribution of voting power; it held that one man must be given one vote in spite of the fact that a different distribution of votes might in fact work for the general benefit. The second is the right to treatment as an equal. This is the right, not to an equal distribution of some good or opportunity, but the right to equal concern and respect in the political decision about how these goods and opportunities are to be distributed. Suppose the question is raised whether an economic policy that injures long-term bondholders is in the general interest. Those who will be injured have a right that their prospective loss be taken into account in deciding whether the general interest is served by the policy. They may not simply be ignored in that calculation. But when their interest is taken into account it may nevertheless be outweighed by the interests of others who will gain from the policy, and in that case their right to equal concern and respect, so defined, would provide no objection. In the case of economic policy, therefore, we might wish to say that those who will be injured if inflation is permitted have a right to treatment as equals in the decision whether that policy would serve the general interest, but no right to equal treatment that would outlaw the policy even if it passed that test.

I propose that the right to treatment as an equal must be taken to be fundamental under the liberal conception of equality, and that the more restrictive right to equal treatment holds only in those special circumstances in which, for some special reason, it follows from the more fundamental right, as perhaps it does in the special circumstance of the Reapportionment Cases. I also propose that individual rights to distinct liberties must be recognized only when the fundamental right to treatment as an equal can be shown to require these rights. If this is correct, then the right to distinct liberties does not conflict with any supposed competing right to equality, but on the contrary follows from a conception of equality conceded to be more fundamental.

I must now show, however, how the familiar rights to distinct liberties—those established, for example, in the United States constitution—might be thought to be required by that fundamental conception of equality. I shall try to do this, for present purposes, only by providing a skeleton of the more elaborate argument that would have to be made to defend any particular liberty on this basis, and then show why it would be plausible to expect that the more familiar political and civil liberties would be supported by such an argument if it were in fact made.

A government that respects the liberal conception of equality may properly constrain liberty only on certain very limited types of justification. I shall adopt, for purposes of making this point, the following crude typology of political justifications. There are, first, arguments of principle, which support a particular constraint on liberty on the argument that the constraint is required to protect the distinct right of some individual who will be injured by the exercise of the liberty. There are, second, arguments of policy, which support constraints on the different ground that such constraints are required to reach some overall political goal, that is, to realize some state of affairs in which the community as a whole, and not just certain individuals, are better off by virtue of the constraint. Arguments of policy might be further subdivided in this way. Utilitarian arguments of policy argue that the community as a whole will be better off because (to put the point roughly) more of its citizens will have more of what they want overall, even though some of them will have less. Ideal arguments of policy, on the other hand, argue that the community will be better off, not because more of its members will have more of what they want, but because the community will be in some way closer to an ideal community, whether its members desire the improvement in question or not.

The liberal conception of equality sharply limits the extent to which ideal arguments of policy may be used to justify any constraint on liberty. Such arguments cannot be used if the idea in question is itself controversial within the community. Constraints cannot be defended, for example, directly on the ground that they contribute to a culturally sophisticated community, whether the community wants the sophistication or not, because that argument would violate the canon of the liberal conception of equality that prohibits a government from relying on the claim that certain forms of life are inherently more valuable than others.

Utilitarian arguments of policy, however, would seem secure from that objection. They do not suppose that any form of life is inherently more valuable than any other, but instead base their claim, that constraints on liberty are necessary to advance some collective goal of the community, just on the fact that that goal happens to be desired more widely or more deeply than any other. Utilitarian arguments of policy, therefore, seem not to oppose but on the contrary to embody the fundamental right of equal concern and respect, because they treat the wishes of each member of the community on a par with the wishes of any other, with no bonus or discount reflecting the view that that member is more or less worthy of concern, or his views more or less worthy of respect, than any other.

This appearance of egalitarianism has, I think, been the principal source of the great appeal that utilitarianism has had, as a general political philosophy, over the last century. . . . however, . . . the egalitarian character of a utilitarian argument is often an illusion. . . .

Utilitarian arguments fix on the fact that a particular constraint on liberty will make more people happier, or satisfy more of their preferences, depending upon whether psychological or preference utilitarianism is in play. But people's overall preference for one policy rather than another may be seen to include, on further analysis, both preferences that are *personal*, because they state a preference for the assignment of one set of goods or opportunities to him and preferences that are *external*, because they state a preference for one assignment of goods or opportunities to others. But a utilitarian argument that assigns critical weight to the external preferences of members of the community will not be egalitarian in the sense under consideration. It will not respect the right of everyone to be treated with equal concern and respect.

Suppose, for example, that a number of individuals in the community holds racist rather than utilitarian political theories. They believe, not that each man is to count for one and no one for more than one in the distribution of goods, but rather that a black man is to count for less and a white man therefore to count for more than one. That is an external preference, but it is nevertheless a genuine preference for one policy rather than another, the satisfaction of which will bring pleasure. Nevertheless if this preference or pleasure is given the normal weight in a utilitarian calculation, and blacks suffer accordingly, then their own assignment of goods and opportunities will depend, not simply on the competition among personal preferences that abstract statements of utilitarianism suggest, but precisely on the fact that they are thought less worthy of concern and respect than others are.

Suppose, to take a different case, that many members of the community disapprove on moral grounds of homosexuality, or contraception, or pornography, or expressions of adherence to the Communist party. They prefer not only that they themselves do not indulge in these activities, but that no one else does so either, and they believe that a community that permits rather than prohibits these acts is inherently a worse community. These are external preferences, but, once again, they are no less genuine, nor less a source of pleasure when satisfied and displeasure when ignored, than purely personal preferences. Once again, however, if these external preferences are counted, so as to justify a constraint on liberty, then those constrained suffer, not simply because their personal preferences have lost in a competition for scarce resources with the personal preferences of others, but precisely because their conception of a proper or desirable form of life is despised by others.

These arguments justify the following important conclusion. If utilitarian arguments of policy are to be used to justify constraints on liberty, then care must be taken to insure that the utilitarian calculations on which the argument is based fix only on personal and ignore external preferences. That is an important conclusion for political theory because it shows, for example, why the arguments of John Stuart Mill in *On Liberty* are not counter-utilitarian but, on the contrary, arguments in service of the only defensible form of utilitarianism.

Important as that conclusion is at the level of political philosophy, however, it is in itself of limited practical significance, because it will be impossible to devise political procedures that will accurately discriminate between personal and external preferences. Representative democracy is widely thought to be the institutional structure most suited, in a complex and diverse society, to the identification and achievement of utilitarian policies. It works imperfectly at this, for the familiar reason that majoritarianism cannot sufficiently take account of the intensity, as distinct from the number, of particular preferences, and because techniques of political persuasion, backed by money, may corrupt the accuracy with which votes represent the genuine preferences of those who have voted. Nevertheless democracy seems to enforce utilitarianism more satisfactorily, in spite of these imperfections, than any alternative general political scheme would.

But democracy cannot discriminate, within the overall preferences imperfectly revealed by voting, distinct personal and external components, so as to provide a method for enforcing the former while ignoring the latter. An actual vote in an election or referendum must be taken to represent an overall preference rather than some component of the preference that a skillful cross-examination of the individual voter, if time and expense permitted, would reveal. Personal and external preferences are sometimes so inextricably combined, moreover, that the discrimination is psychologically as well as institutionally impossible. That will be true, for example, in the case of the associational preferences that many people have for members of one race, or people of one talent or quality, rather than another, for this is a personal preference so parasitic upon external preferences that it is impossible to say, even as a matter of introspection, what personal preferences would remain if the underlying external preference were removed. It is also true of certain self-denying preferences that many individuals have; that is preferences for less of a certain good on the assumption, or rather proviso, that other people will have more. That is also a preference, however noble, that is parasitic upon external preferences, in the shape of political and moral theories, and they may no more be counted in a defensible utilitarian argument than less attractive preferences rooted in prejudice rather than altruism.

I wish now to propose the following general theory of rights. The concept of an individual political right, in the strong anti-utilitarian sense I distinguished earlier, is a response to the philosophical defects of a utilitarianism that counts external preferences and the practical impossibility of a utilitarianism that does not. It allows us to enjoy the institutions of political democracy, which enforce overall or unrefined utilitarianism, and yet protect the fundamental right of citizens to equal concern and respect by prohibiting decisions that seem, antecedently, likely to have been reached by virtue of the external components of the preferences democracy reveals.

It should be plain how this theory of rights might be used to support the idea, which is the subject of this chapter, that we have distinct rights to certain liberties like the liberty of free expression and of free choice in personal and sexual relations. It might be shown that any utilitarian constraint on these liberties must be based on overall preferences in the community that we know, from our general knowledge of society, are likely to contain large components of external preferences, in the shape of political or moral theories, which the political process cannot discriminate and eliminate. It is not, as I said, my present purpose to frame the arguments that would have to be made to defend particular rights to liberty in this way, but only to show the general character such arguments might have.

I do wish, however, to mention one alleged right that might be called into question by my general argument, which is the supposed individual right to the free use of property. In chapter II I complained about the argument, popular in certain quarters, that it is inconsistent for liberals to defend a liberty of speech, for example, and not also concede a parallel right of some sort of property and its use. There might be force in that argument if the claim, that we have a right of free speech, depended on the more general proposition that we have a right to something called liberty as such. But that general idea is untenable and incoherent; there is no such thing as any general right to liberty. The argument for any given specific liberty may therefore be entirely independent of the argument for other, and there is no antecedent inconsistency or even implausibility in contending for one while disputing the other.

What can be said, on the general theory of rights I offer, for any particular right of property? What can be said, for example, in favor of the right to liberty of contract sustained by the Supreme Court in the famous *Lochner* case, and later regretted, not only by the court, but by liberals generally? I cannot think of any argument that a political decision to limit such a right, in the way in which minimum wage laws limited it, is antecedently likely to give effect to external preferences, and in that way offend the right of those whose liberty is curtailed to equal concern and respect. If, as I think, no such argument can be made out, then the alleged right does not exist; in any case there can be no inconsistency in denying that it exists while warmly defending a right to other liberties.

Jurgen Habermas (b. 1929)

Born in Gummersbach, Germany, Habermas attended the Universities of Gottingen, Bonn, and Zurich. He worked as a journalist first, and eventually became Theodor W. Adorno's associate at the University of Frankfurt. Later he taught philosophy at the University of Heidelberg and then philosophy and sociology at the University of Frankfurt. He is regarded as the leader of the Frankfurt School, a branch of neo-Marxian scholarship. He wrote *Knowledge and Human Interest* (1971), *Theory and Practice* (1973), and *The Theory of Communicative Action* (1984), among other works. The following is from 1993's *Justification and Application: Remarks on Discourse Ethics*.

From Justification and Application*

On the Pragmatic, the Ethical, and the Moral Employments of Practical Reason

Contemporary discussions in practical philosophy draw, now as before, on three main sources: Aristotelian ethics, utilitarianism, and Kantian moral theory. Two of the parties to these interesting debates also appeal to Hegel who tried to achieve a synthesis of the classical communal and modern individualistic conceptions of freedom with his theory of objective spirit and his "sublation" (*Aufhebung*) of morality into ethical life. Whereas the communitarians appropriate the Hegelian legacy in the form of an Aristotelian ethics of the good and abandon the universalism of rational natural law, discourse ethics takes its orientation for an intersubjective interpretation of the categorical imperative from Hegel's theory recognition but without incurring the cost of a historical *dissolution* of morality in ethical life. Like Hegel it insists, though in a Kantian spirit, on the internal relation between justice and solidarity. It attempts to show that the meaning of the basic principle of morality can be explicated in terms of the content of the unavoidable pre-suppositions of an argumentative practice that can be pursued only in common with others. The moral point of view from which we can judge practical questions impartially is indeed open to different interpretations. But because it is grounded in the communicative structure of rational discourse as such, we cannot simply dispose of it at will. It forces itself intuitively on anyone who is at all open to this reflective form of communicative action. With this fundamental assumption, discourse ethics situates itself squarely in the Kantian tradition yet without leaving itself vulnerable to the objections with which the abstract ethics of conviction has met from its inception. Admittedly, it adopts a narrowly circumscribed conception of morality that focuses on questions of justice. But it neither has

---

* An Excerpt.

to neglect the calculation of the consequences of actions rightly emphasized by utilitarianism nor exclude from the sphere of discursive problematization the questions of the good life accorded prominence by classical ethics, abandoning them to irrational emotional dispositions or decisions. The term *discourse ethics* may have occasioned a misunderstanding in this connection. The theory of discourse relates in different ways to moral, ethical, and pragmatic questions. It is this differentiation that I propose to clarify here.

Classical ethics, like modern theories, proceeds from the question that inevitably forces itself upon an individual in need of orientation faced with a perplexing practical task in a particular situation: how should I proceed, what should I do? The meaning of this "should" remains indeterminate as long as the relevant problem and the aspect under which it is to be addressed have not been more clearly specified. I will begin by taking the distinction between pragmatic, ethical, and moral questions as a guide to differentiating the various uses of practical reason. Different tasks are required of practical reason under the aspects of the purposive, the good, and the just. Correspondingly, the constellation of reason and volition changes as we move between pragmatic, ethical, and moral discourses. Finally, once moral theory breaks out of the investigative horizon of the first-person singular, it encounters the reality of an alien will, which generates problems of a different order.

I

Practical problems beset us in a variety of situations. They "have to be" mastered; otherwise we suffer consequences that are at very least annoying. We *must* decide what to do when the bicycle we use every day is broken, when we are afflicted with illness, or when we lack the money necessary to realize certain desires. In such cases we look for reasons for a rational choice between different available courses of action in the light of a task that we *must* accomplish if we *want* to achieve a certain goal. The goals themselves can also become problematic, as, for example, when holiday plans fall through or when we must make a career decision. Whether one travels to Scandinavia or to Elba or stays at home or whether one goes directly to college or first does an apprenticeship, becomes a physician or a salesperson—such things depend in the first instance on our preferences and on the options open to us in such situations. Once again we seek reasons for a rational choice but in this case for a choice between the goals themselves.

In both cases the rational thing to do is determined in part by what one wants: it is a matter of making a rational choice of means in the light of fixed purposes or of the rational assessment of goals in the light of existing preferences. Our will is already fixed as a matter of fact by our wishes and values; it is open to further determination only in respect of alternative possible choices of means or specifications of ends. Here we are exclusively concerned with appropriate techniques—whether for repairing bicycles or treating disease—with strategies for acquiring money or with programs for planning vacations and choosing occupations. In complex cases decision-making strategies themselves must be developed; then reason seeks reassurance concerning its own procedure by becoming reflective—for example, in the form of a theory of rational choice. As long as the question "What should I do?" has such pragmatic tasks in view, observations, investigations, comparisons, and assessments undertaken on the basis of empirical data with a view to efficiency or with the aid of other decision rules are appropriate. Practical reflection here proceeds within the horizon of purposive rationality, its goal being to discover appropriate techniques, strategies, or programs. It leads to recommendations that, in the most straightforward cases, are expressed in the semantic form of conditional imperatives. Kant speaks in this connection of rules of skill and of counsels of prudence and, correspondingly, of technical and pragmatic imperatives. These relate causes to effects in accordance with value preferences and prior goal determinations. The imperative meaning they express can be glossed as that of a *relative ought*, the corresponding directions for action specifying what one "ought" or "must" do when faced with a particular problem if one wants to realize certain values or goals. Of course, once the values themselves become problematic, the question "What should I do?" points beyond the horizon of purposive rationality.

In the case of complex decisions—for example, choosing a career—it may transpire that the question is not a pragmatic one at all. Someone who wants to become a manager of a publishing house might deliberate as to whether it is more expedient to do an apprenticeship first or go straight to college; but someone who is not clear about what he wants to do is in a completely different situation. In the latter case, the choice of a career or a direction of study is bound up with one's "inclinations" or interests, what occupation one would find fulfilling, and so forth. The more radically this question is posed, the more it becomes a matter of what life one would like to lead, and that means what kind of person one is and would like to be. When faced with crucial existential choices, someone who does not know what he wants to be will ultimately be led to pose the question, "Who am I, and who would I like to be?" Decisions based on weak or trivial preferences do not require justification; no one need give an account of his preferences in automobiles or sweaters, whether to himself or anyone else. In the contrasting case, I shall follow Charles Taylor in using the term *strong preferences* to designate preferences that concern not merely contingent dispositions and inclinations but the self-understanding of a person, his character and way of life; they are inextricably interwoven with each individual's identity. This circumstance not only lends existential decisions their peculiar weight but also furnishes them with a context in which they both admit and stand in need of justification. Since Aristotle, important *value decisions* have been regarded as clinical questions of the good life. A decision based on illusions—attaching oneself to the wrong partner or choosing the wrong career—can lead to a failed life. The exercise of practical reason directed in this sense to the good and not merely to the possible and expedient belongs, following classical usage, to the sphere of ethics.

Strong evaluations are embedded in the context of a particular self-understanding. How one understands oneself depends not only on how one describes oneself but also on the ideals toward which one strives. One's identity is determined simultaneously by how one sees oneself and how one would like to see oneself, by what one finds oneself to be and the ideals with reference to which one fashions oneself and one's life. This existential self-understanding is evaluative in its core and, like all evaluations, is Janus faced. Two components are interwoven in it: the descriptive component of the ontogenesis of the ego and the normative component of the ego-ideal. Hence, the clarification of one's self-understanding or the clinical reassurance of one's identity calls for an *appro-priative* form of understanding—the appropriation of one's own life history and the tra-ditions and circumstances of life that have shaped one's process of development. If illusions are playing a role, this hermeneutic self-understanding can be raised to the level of a form of reflection that dissolves self-deceptions. Bringing one's life history and its normative context to awareness in a critical manner does not lead to a value-neutral self-understanding; rather, the hermeneutically generated self-description is logically contin-gent upon a critical relation to self. A more profound self-understanding alters the attitudes that sustain, or at least imply, a life project with normative substance. In this way, strong evaluations can be justified through hermeneutic self-clarification.

One will be able to choose between pursuing a career in management and training to become a theologian on better grounds after one has become clear about who one is and who one would like to be. Ethical questions are generally answered by unconditional imperatives such as the following: "You must embark on a career that affords you the as-surance that you are helping other people." The meaning of this imperative can be un-derstood as an "ought" that is not dependent on subjective purposes and preferences and yet is not absolute. What you "should" or "must" do has here the sense that it is "good" for you to act in this way in the long run, all things considered. Aristotle speaks in this connection of paths to the good and happy life. Strong evaluations take their orientation from a goal posited absolutely for me, that is, from the highest good of a self-sufficient form of life that has its value in itself.

The meaning of the question "What should I do?" undergoes a further transforma-tion as soon as my actions affect the interests of others and lead to conflicts that should be regulated in an impartial manner, that is, from the moral point of view. A contrasting comparison will be instructive concerning the new discursive modality that thereby comes into play. Pragmatic tasks are informed by the perspective of an agent who takes his pref-erences and goals as his point of departure. Moral problems cannot even be conceived from this point of view because other persons are accorded merely the status of means or limiting conditions for the realization of one's own individual plan of action. In strategic action, the participants assume that each decides egocentrically in accordance with his own interests. Given these premises, there exists from the beginning at least a latent con-flict between adversaries. This can be played out or curbed and brought under control; it can also be resolved in the mutual interest of all concerned. But without a radical shift in perspective and attitude, an interpersonal conflict cannot be perceived by those in-volved *as* a moral problem. If I can secure a loan only by concealing pertinent informa-tion, then from a pragmatic point of view all that counts is the probability of my deception's succeeding. Someone who raises the issue of its permissibility is posing a *dif-ferent* kind of question—the moral question of whether we all could will that anyone in my situation should act in accordance with the same maxim.

Ethical questions by no means call for a complete break with the egocentric per-spective; in each instance they take their orientation from the telos of one's own life. From this point of view, other persons, other life histories, and structures of interests ac-quire importance only to the extent that they are interrelated or interwoven with my iden-tity, my life history, and my interests within the framework of an intersubjectively shared form of life. My development unfolds against a background of traditions that I share with other persons; moreover, my identity is shaped by collective identities, and my life history is embedded in encompassing historical forms of life. To that extent the life that is good for me also concerns the forms of life that are common to us. Thus, Aristotle viewed the *ethos* of the individual as embedded in the *polis* comprising the citizen body. But ethical questions point in a different direction from moral questions: the regulation of interpersonal conflicts of action resulting from opposed interests is not yet an issue. Whether I would like to be someone who in a case of acute need would be willing to defraud an anonymous insurance company just this one time is not a moral question, for it concerns my self-respect and possibly the respect that others show me, but not equal respect for all, and hence not the symmetrical respect that everyone should accord the integrity of all other persons.

We approach the moral outlook once we begin to examine our maxims as to their compatibility with the maxims of others. By maxims Kant meant the more or less trivial, situational rules of action by which an individual customarily regulates his actions. They relieve the agent of the burden of everyday decision making and fit together to constitute a more or less consistent life practice in which the agent's character and way of life are mirrored. What Kant had in mind were primarily the maxims of an occupationally stratified, early capitalist society. Maxims constitute in general the smallest units in a network of operative customs in which the identity and life projects of an individual (or group) are concretized; they regulate the course of daily life, modes of interaction, the ways in which problems are addressed and conflicts resolved, and so forth. Maxims are the plane in which ethics and morality intersect because they can be judged alternately from ethical and moral points of view. The maxim to allow myself just one trivial deception may not be *good* for me—for example, if it does not cohere with the picture of the person who I would like to be and would like others to acknowledge me to be. The same maxim may also be *unjust* if its general observance is not equally good for all. A mode of examining maxims or a heuristic for generating maxims guided by the question of how I want to live involves a *different* exercise of practical reason from reflection on whether from my perspective a generally observed maxim is suitable to regulate our communal existence. In the first case, what is being asked is whether a maxim is good for me and is appropriate in the given situation, and in the second, whether I can will that a maxim should be followed by everyone as a general law.

The former is a matter for ethical deliberation, the latter for moral deliberation, though still in a restricted sense, for the outcome of this deliberation remains bound to the personal perspective of a particular individual. My perspective is structured by my self-understanding, and a casual attitude toward deception may be compatible with my preferred way of life if others behave similarly in comparable situations and occasionally make me the victim of their manipulations. Even Hobbes recognizes a golden rule with reference to which such a maxim could be justified under appropriate circumstances. For him it is a "natural law" that each should accord everyone else the rights he demands for himself. But an egocentrically conceived universalizability test does not yet imply that a maxim would be accepted by all as the moral yardstick of their actions. This would follow only if my perspective necessarily cohered with that of everyone else. Only if my identity and my life project reflected a universally valid form of life would what from my perspective is equally good for all in fact be equally in the interest of all.

A categorical imperative that specifies that a maxim is just only if *all* could will that it should be adhered to by everyone in comparable situations first signals a break with the egocentric character of the golden rule ("Do not do unto others what you would not have them do unto you"). *Everyone* must be able to will that the maxims of our action should become a universal law. Only a maxim that can be generalized from the perspective of all affected counts as a norm that can command general assent and to that extent is worthy of recognition or, in other words, is morally binding. The question "What should I do?" is answered morally with reference to what *one* ought to do. Moral commands are categorical or unconditional imperatives that express valid norms or make implicit reference to them. The imperative meaning of these commands alone can be understood as an "ought" that is dependent on neither subjective goals and preferences nor on what is for me the absolute goal of a good, successful, or not-failed life. Rather, what one "should" or "must" do has here the sense that to act thus is just and therefore a duty.

II

Thus, the question "What should I do?" takes on a pragmatic, an ethical, or a moral meaning depending on how the problem is conceived. In each case it is a matter of justifying choices among alternative available courses of action, but pragmatic tasks call for a different *kind of action* and the corresponding question, a different *kind of answer*, from ethical or moral ones. Value-oriented assessments of ends and purposive assessments of available means facilitate rational decisions concerning how we must intervene in the objective world in order to bring about a desired state of affairs. This is essentially a matter of settling empirical questions and questions of rational choice, and the *terminus ad quem* of a corresponding pragmatic discourse is a recommendation concerning a suitable technology or a realizable program of action. The rational consideration of an important value decision that affects the whole course of one's life is quite a different matter. This latter involves hermeneutical clarification of an individual's self-understanding and clinical questions of a happy or not-failed life. The *terminus ad quem* of a corresponding ethical-existential discourse is advice concerning the correct conduct of life and the realization of a personal life project. Moral judgment of actions and maxims is again something different. It serves to clarify legitimate behavioral expectations in response to interpersonal conflicts resulting from the disruption of our orderly coexistence by conflicts of interests. Here we are concerned with the justification and application of norms that stipulate reciprocal rights and duties, and the *terminus ad quem* of a corresponding moral-practical discourse is an agreement concerning the just resolution of a conflict in the realm of norm-regulated action.

Thus, the pragmatic, ethical, and moral employments of practical reason have as their respective goals technical and strategic directions for action, clinical advice, and moral judgments. Practical reason is the ability to justify corresponding imperatives, where

not just the illocutionary meaning of "must" or "ought" changes with the practical relation and the kind of decision impending but also the *concept of the will* that is supposed
to be open to determination by rationally grounded imperatives in each instance. The
"ought" of pragmatic recommendations relativized to subjective ends and values is tai-
lored to the *arbitrary choice* (*Willkür*) of a subject who makes intelligent decisions on the
basis of contingent attitudes and preferences that form his point of departure; the faculty
of rational choice does not extend to the interests and value orientations themselves but
presupposes them as given. The "ought" of clinical advice relativized to the telos of the
good life is addressed to the striving for self-realization and thus to the *resoluteness*
(*Entschlußkraft*) of an individual who has committed himself to an authentic life; the capacity for existential decisions or radical choice of self always operates within the horizon
of a life history, in whose traces the individual can discern who he is and who he would
like to become. The categorical "ought" of moral injunctions, finally, is directed to the
free will (*freien Willen*), emphatically construed, of a person who acts in accordance with
self-given laws; this will alone is autonomous in the sense that it is completely open to determination by moral insights. In the sphere of validity of the moral law, neither contingent dispositions nor life histories and personal identities set limits to the determination
of the will by practical reason. Only a will that is guided by moral insight, and hence is
completely rational, can be called autonomous. All heteronomous elements of mere
choice or of commitment to an idiosyncratic way of life, however authentic it may be, have
been expunged from such a will. Kant confused the autonomous will with an omnipotent
will and had to transpose it into the intelligible realm in order to conceive of it as absolutely determinative. But in the world as we experience it, the autonomous will is efficacious only to the extent that it can ensure that the motivational force of good reasons
outweighs the power of other motives. Thus, in the plain language of everyday life, we
call a correctly informed but weak will a "good will."

To summarize, practical reason, according to whether it takes its orientation from
the purposive, the good, or the just, directs itself in turn to the choice of the purposively
acting subject, to the resoluteness of the authentic, self-realizing subject, or to the free
will of the subject capable of moral judgment. In each instance, the constellation of reason and volition and the concept of practical reason itself undergo alteration. Not only
the addressee, the will of the agent who seeks an answer, changes its status with the meaning of the question "What should I do?" but also the addresser, the capacity of practical
deliberation itself. According to the aspect chosen, there result three different though
complementary interpretations of practical reason. But in each of the three major philosophical traditions, just one of these interpretations has been thematized. For Kant practical reason is coextensive with morality; only in autonomy do reason (*Vernunft*) and the
will attain unity. Empiricism assimilates practical reason to its pragmatic use; in Kantian
terminology, it is reduced to the purposive exercise of the understanding (*Verstand*). And
in the Aristotelian tradition, practical reason assumes the role of a faculty of judgment
(*Urteilskraft*) that illuminates the life historical horizon of a customary *ethos*. In each case
a *different* exercise is attributed to practical reason, as will become apparent when we consider the respective discourses in which they operate.

III

Pragmatic discourses in which we justify technical and strategic recommendations have a certain affinity with empirical discourses. They serve to relate empirical knowledge to hypothetical goal determinations and preferences and to assess the consequences of (imperfectly informed) choices in the light of underlying maxims. Technical or strategic recommendations ultimately derive their validity from the empirical knowledge on which they rest. Their validity does not depend on whether an addressee decides to adopt their directives. Pragmatic discourses take their orientation from *possible contexts* of application. They are related to the actual volitions of agents only though subjective goal determinations and preferences. There is no *internal* relation between reason and the will. In ethical-existential discourses, this constellation is altered in such a way that justifications become rational motives for changes of attitude.

The roles of agent and participant in discourse overlap in such processes of self-clarification. Someone who wishes to attain clarity about his life as a whole—to justify important value decisions and to gain assurance concerning his identity—cannot allow himself to be represented by someone else in ethical-existential discourse, whether in his capacity as the one involved or as the one who must weigh competing claims. Nevertheless, there is room here for discourse because here too the steps in argumentation should not be idiosyncratic but must be comprehensible in intersubjective terms. The individual attains reflective distance from his own life history only within the horizon of forms of life that he shares with others and that themselves constitute the context for different individual life projects. Those who belong to a shared lifeworld are potential participants who can assume the catalyzing role of impartial critics in processes of self-clarification. This role can be refined into the therapeutic role of an analyst once generalizable clinical knowledge comes into play. Clinical knowledge of this sort is first generated in such discourses.

Self-clarification draws on the context of a specific life history and leads to evaluative statements about what is good for a particular person. Such evaluations, which rest on the reconstruction of a consciously appropriated life history, have a peculiar semantic status, for "reconstruction" here signifies not just the descriptive delineation of a developmental process through which one has become the individual one finds oneself to be; it signifies at the same time a critical sifting and rearrangement of the elements integrated in such a way that one's own past can be accepted in the light of existing possibilities of action as the developmental history of the person one would like to be and continue to be in the future. The existential figure of the "thrown projection" (*geworfener Entwurf*) illuminates the Janus-faced character of the strong evaluations justified by way of a critical appropriation of one's own life history. Here genesis and validity can no longer be separated as they can in the case of technical and strategic recommendations. Insofar as I recognize what is good for me, I also already in a certain sense make the advice my own; that is what it means to make a conscious decision. To the extent that I have become convinced of the soundness of clinical advice, I have also already made up my mind to transform my life in the manner suggested. On the other hand, my identity is only responsive to—even at the mercy of—the reflexive pressure of an altered self-understanding when it observes the same standards of authenticity as ethical-existential discourse itself. Such a discourse already presupposes, on the part of the addressee, a striving to live an authentic life or the suffering of a patient who has become conscious of the "sickness unto death." In this respect, ethical-existential discourse remains contingent on the *prior* telos of a *consciously* pursued way of life.

IV

In ethical-existential discourses, reason and the will condition one another reciprocally, though the latter remains embedded in the life-historical context thematized. Participants in processes of self-clarification cannot distance themselves from the life histories and forms of life in which they actually find themselves. Moral-practical discourses, by contrast, require a break with all of the unquestioned truths of an established, concrete ethical life, in addition to distancing oneself from the contexts of life with which one's identity is inextricably interwoven. The higher-level intersubjectivity characterized by an intermeshing of the perspective of each with the perspectives of all is constituted only under the communicative presuppositions of a universal discourse in which all those possibly affected could take part and could adopt a hypothetical, argumentative stance toward the validity claims of norms and modes of action that have become problematic. This impartial standpoint overcomes the subjectivity of the individual participant's perspective without becoming disconnected from the performative attitude of the participants. The objectivity of the so-called ideal observer would impede access to the intuitive knowledge of the lifeworld. Moral-practical discourse represents the ideal extension of each individual communication community from within. In this forum, only those norms proposed that express a common interest of all affected can win justified assent. To this extent, discursively justified norms bring to expression simultaneously both insight into what is equally in the interest of all and a general will that has absorbed into itself, *without repression*, the will of all. Understood in this way, the will determined by moral grounds does not remain external to argumentative reason; the autonomous will is completely internal to reason.

Hence, Kant believed that practical reason first completely comes into its own and becomes coextensive with morality in its role as a norm-testing court of appeal. Yet the discourse-ethical interpretation of the categorical imperative we have offered reveals the one-sidedness of a theory that concentrates exclusively on questions of justification. Once moral justifications rest on a principle of universalization constraining participants in discourse to examine whether disputed norms could command the well-considered assent of all concerned, detached from practical situations and without regard to current motives or existing institutions, the problem of how norms, thus grounded, could ever be *applied* becomes more acute. Valid norms owe their abstract universality to the fact that they withstand the universalization test only in a decontextualized form. But in this abstract formulation, they can be applied without qualification only to standard situations whose salient features have been integrated from the outset into the conditional components of the rule as conditions of application. Moreover, every justification of a norm is necessarily subject to the normal limitations of a finite, historically situated outlook that is provincial in regard to the future. Hence *a forteriori* it cannot already explicitly allow for all of the salient features that at some time in the future will characterize the constellations of unforeseen individual cases. For this reason, the *application* of norms calls for argumentative clarification in its own right. In this case, the impartiality of judgment cannot again be secured through a principle of universalization; rather, in addressing questions of context-sensitive application, practical reason must be informed by a principle of appropriateness (*Angemessenheit*). What must be determined here is which of the norms already accepted as valid is appropriate in a given case in the light of all the relevant features of the situation conceived as exhaustively as possible.

Of course, discourses of application, like justificatory discourses, are a purely cognitive undertaking and as such cannot compensate for the uncoupling of moral judgment from the concrete motives that inform actions. Moral commands are valid regardless of whether the addressee can also summon the resolve to do what is judged to be right. The autonomy of his will is a function of whether he is capable of acting from moral insight, but moral insights do not of themselves lead to autonomous actions. The validity claim we associate with normative propositions certainly has obligatory force, and duty, to borrow Kant's terminology, is the affection of the will by the validity claim of moral commands. That the reasons underlying such validity claims are not completely ineffectual is shown by the pangs of conscience that plague us when we act against our better judgment. Guilt feelings are a palpable indicator of transgressions of duty, but then they express only the recognition that we lack good reasons to act *otherwise*. Thus, feelings of guilt reflect a split within the will itself.

V

The empirical will that has split off from the autonomous will plays an important role in the dynamics of our moral learning processes. The division of the will is a symptom of weakness of will only when the moral demands against which it transgresses are in fact legitimate and it is *reasonable* (*zumutbar*) to expect adherence to them under the given circumstances. In the revolt of a dissident will, there all too often also come to expression, as we know, the voice of the other who is excluded by rigid moral principles, the violated integrity of human dignity, recognition refused, interests neglected, and differences denied.

Because the principles of a will that has attained autonomy embody a claim analogous to that associated with knowledge, validity and genesis once again diverge here as they do in pragmatic discourse. Thus, behind the facade of categorical validity may lurk a hidden, entrenched interest that is susceptible only of being pushed through. This facade can be erected all the more easily because the rightness of moral commands, unlike the truth of technical or strategic recommendations, does not stand in a contingent relation to the will of the addressee but is intended to bind the will rationally from within. Liberating ourselves from the merely presumptive generality of selectively employed universalistic principles applied in a context-insensitive manner has always required, and today still requires, social movements and political struggles; we have to learn from the painful experiences and the irreparable suffering of those who have been humiliated, insulted, injured, and brutalized that nobody may be excluded in the name of moral universalism—neither underprivileged classes nor exploited nations, neither domesticated women nor marginalized minorities. Someone who in the name of universalism excludes another who has the right to *remain* alien or other betrays his own guiding idea. The universalism of equal respect for all and of solidarity with everything that bears the mark of humanity is first put to the test by radical freedom in the choice of individual life histories and particular forms of life.

This reflection already oversteps the boundaries of individual will formation. Thus far we have examined the pragmatic, ethical, and moral employments of practical reason, taking as a guide the traditional question, "What should *I* do?" But with the shift in horizon of our questions from the first-person singular to the first-person plural, more changes than just the forum of reflection. Individual will formation by its very nature is already guided by public argumentation, which it simply reproduces *in foro interno.* Thus, where moral life runs up against the boundaries of morality, it is not a matter of a shift in perspective from internal monological thought to public discourse but of a transformation in the problem at issue; what changes is the role in which other subjects are encountered.

Moral-practical discourse detaches itself from the orientation to personal success and one's own life to which both pragmatic and ethical reflection remain tied. But norm-testing reason still encounters the other as an opponent in an *imaginary*—because counter-factually extended and virtually enacted—process of argumentation. Once the other appears as a *real* individual with his own unsubstitutable will, new problems arise. *This* reality of the alien will belongs to the primary conditions of collective will formation.

The fact of the plurality of agents and the twofold contingency under which the reality of one will confronts that of another generate the additional problem of the communal pursuit of collective goals, and the problem of the regulation of communal existence under the pressure of social complexity also takes on a new form. Pragmatic discourses point to the necessity of compromise as soon as one's own interests have to be brought into harmony with those of others. Ethical-political discourses have as their goal the clarification of a collective identity that must leave room for the pursuit of diverse individual life projects. The problem of the conditions under which moral commands are reasonable motivates the transition from morality to law. And, finally, the implementation of goals and programs gives rise to questions of the transfer and neutral exercise of power.

Modern rational natural law responded to this constellation of problems, but it failed to do justice to the intersubjective nature of collective will formation, which cannot be correctly construed as individual will formation writ large. Hence, we must renounce the premises of the philosophy of the subject on which rational natural law is based. From the perspective of a theory of discourse, the problem of agreement among parties whose wills and interests clash is shifted to the plane of institutionalized procedures and communicative presuppositions of processes of argumentation and negotiation that must be actually carried out.

It is only at the level of a discourse theory of law and politics that we can also expect an answer to the question invited by our analyses: Can we still speak of practical reason in the singular after it has dissolved into three different forms of argumentation under the aspects of the purposive, the good, and the right? All of these forms of argument are indeed related to the wills of possible agents, but as we have seen, concepts of the will change with the type of question and answer entertained. The unity of practical reason can no longer be grounded in the unity of moral argumentation in accordance with the Kantian model of the unity of transcendental consciousness, for there is no metadiscourse on which we could fall back to justify the choice between different forms of argumentation. Is the issue of whether we wish to address a given problem under the standpoint of the purposive, the good, or the just not then left to the arbitrary choice, or at best the prediscursive judgment, of the individual? Recourse to a faculty of judgment that "grasps" whether a problem is aesthetic rather than economic, theoretical rather than practical, ethical rather than moral, political rather than legal, must remain suspect for anyone who agrees that Kant had good grounds for abandoning the Aristotelian concept of judgment. In any case, it is not the faculty of reflective judgment, which subsumes particular cases under general rules, that is relevant here but an aptitude for discriminating problems into different kinds.

As Peirce and the pragmatists correctly emphasize, real problems are always rooted in something objective. The problems we confront thrust themselves upon us; they have a situation-defining power and engage our minds with their own logics. Nevertheless, if each problem followed a unique logic of its own that had nothing to do with the logic of the next problem, our minds would be led in a new direction by every new kind of problem. A practical reason that saw its unity only in the blind spot of such a reactive faculty of judgment would remain an opaque construction comprehensible only in phenomenological terms.

Moral theory must bequeath this question unanswered to the philosophy of law; the unity of practical reason can be realized in an unequivocal manner only within a network of public forms of communication and practices in which the conditions of rational collective will formation have taken on concrete institutional form.

Alison Mary Jaggar (b. 1942)

Born in Sheffield, England, she was educated at the University of London and the University of Edinburgh, receiving her doctorate from the State University of New York at Buffalo. She is currently Professor of Philosophy at the University of Colorado. Jaggar works in ethics, social, and political philosophy, attending closely to issues of feminism. She wrote *Feminist Politics and Human Nature* (1983), which is excerpted here, and is the author or editor of many books.

From Feminist Politics and Human Nature*

Socialist Feminism
and Human Nature

. . . Like radical feminism, socialist feminism is a daughter of the contemporary women's liberation movement. It is a slightly younger daughter, born in the 1970s and, like most younger daughters, impressed by its elder sister, while wanting at the same time to avoid her mistakes. The central project of socialist feminism is the development of a politial theory and practice that will synthesize the best insights of radical feminism and of the Marxist tradition and that simultaneously will escape the problems associated with each. So far, socialist feminism has made only limited progress toward this goal: "It is a commitment to the *development* of an analysis and political practice, rather than to one which already exists." In spite of the programmatic nature of its achievement so far, I believe that socialist feminism constitutes a distinctive approach to political life, one that offers the most convincing promise of constructing an adequate theory and practice for women's liberation.

Any attempt to define socialist feminism faces the same problems as attempts to define liberal feminism, radical feminism or Marxism. Feminist theorists and activists do not always wear labels and, even if they do, they are not always agreed on who should wear which label. Moreover, there are differences even between those wearing the same label and, in addition, dialogue between feminists of different tendencies has led to modifications in all their views. Most Marxists, for instance, now take the oppression of women much more seriously than they did prior to the emergence of the women's liberation movement, while radical feminists are paying increasing attention to class, ethnic and national differences between women. As a result, the line between socialist feminism and other feminist theories is increasingly blurred, at least on the surface. For all these reasons, it is inevitable that my account of socialist feminism, like my account of the other feminist theories, will be stipulative as well as reportive. As in defining the other theories, I shall identify socialist feminism primarily by reference to its distinctive, underlying conception of human nature.

---

*An Excerpt.

The easiest way to provide a preliminary outline of socialist feminism is in terms of its similarities and contrasts with the other feminist theories, especially with Marxism and radical feminism to which it is most closely linked. In a very general sense, all feminists address the same problem: what constitutes the oppression of women and how can that oppression be ended?. Both liberal feminists and traditional Marxists believe that this question can be answered in terms of the categories and principles that were formulated originally to deal with other problems. For them, the oppression of women is just one among a number of essentially similar types of problems. Socialist feminism shares with radical feminism the belief that older established political theories are incapable, in principle, of giving an adequate account of women's oppression and that, in order to do so, it is necessary to develop new political and economic categories.

Like radical feminists, socialist feminists believe that these new categories must reconceptualize not only the so-called public sphere, but also the hitherto private sphere of human life. They must give us a way of understanding sexuality, childbearing, child-rearing and personal maintenance in political and economic terms. Unlike many American radical feminists, however, socialist feminists attempt to conceptualize these activities in a deliberately historical, rather than a universal and sometimes biologistic, way. A defining feature of socialist feminism is that it attempts to interpret the historical materialist method of traditional Marxism so that it applies to the issues made visible by radical feminists. To revise Juliet Mitchell's comment, it uses a feminist version of the Marxist method to provide feminist answers to feminist questions.

Ever since its inception in the mid-1960s, the women's liberation movement has been split by a chronic dispute over the relation between feminism and Marxism. This dispute has taken a number of forms, but one of the most common ways of interpreting it has been in terms of political priorities. The political analysis of traditional Marxism has led to the position that the struggle for feminism should be subordinated to the class struggle, whereas a radical feminist analysis has implied that the struggle for women's liberation should take priority over the struggle for all other forms of liberation. Socialist feminism rejects this dilemma. Not only does it refuse to compromise socialism for the sake of feminism or feminism for the sake of socialism; it argues that either of these compromises ultimately would be self-defeating. On the socialist feminist analysis, capitalism, male dominance, racism and imperialism are intertwined so inextricably that they are inseparable; consequently the abolition of any of these systems of domination requires the end of all of them. Socialist feminists claim that a full understanding of the capitalist system requires a recognition of the way in which it is structured by male dominance and, conversely, that a full understanding of contemporary male dominance requires a recognition of the way it is organized by the capitalist division of labor. Socialist feminists believe that an adequate account of "capitalist patriarchy" requires the use of the historical materialist method developed originally by Marx and Engels. They argue, however, that the conceptual tools of Marxism are blunt and biased until they are ground into precision on the sharp edge of feminist consciousness.

One question that arises from this preliminary characterization is whether socialist feminism is or is not a variety of Marxism. Obviously, the answer to this question depends both on one's understanding of socialist feminism and on one's interpretation of Marxism.

Political motivations are also involved. Some Marxists do not want the honorific title of Marxism to be granted to what they see as heresy, others want to appropriate for Marxism at least those aspects of socialist feminism that they perceive as correct. Similarly, some socialist feminists want to define themselves as Marxists in opposition to other types of socialists; others see no reason to give Marx credit for a theory and a practice that reveals a social reality ignored and obscured by traditional Marxism. My own view is that socialist feminism is unmistakably Marxist, at least insofar as it utilizes the method of historical materialism. I shall argue that socialist feminism is in fact the most consistent application of Marxist method and therefore the most "orthodox" form of Marxism. . . .

The Socialist Feminist Conception of Human Nature

Socialist feminism is committed to the basic Marxist conception of human nature as created historically through the dialectical interrelation between human biology, human society and the physical environment. This interrelation is mediated by human labor or praxis. The specific form of praxis dominant within a given society creates the distinctive physical and psychological human types characteristic of that society.

Traditional political theory has given theoretical recognition only to a very limited number of human types. It is true that liberals acknowledge individual human variation; indeed, this acknowledgment is a necessary part of their arguments for a firm limitation on the extent of state power. As we have seen, Locke and Mill explain the reasons for at least some of this variation in terms of the social opportunities available to different classes, and liberal feminists explain psychological differences between the sexes in terms of sex-role socialization. Ultimately, however, liberals view the differences between people as relatively superficial, and they assume that underlying these superficial differences is a certain fixed human nature which is modified but not fundamentally created by social circumstances. Marxists, by contrast, view human nature as necessarily constituted in society: they believe that specific historical conditions create distinctive human types. Within contemporary capitalism, they give theoretical recognition to two such types, the capitalist and the proletariat. However, the traditional Marxist conception of human nature is flawed by its failure to recognize explicitly that all human beings in contemporary society belong not only to a specific class; they also have a specific sex and they are at a specific stage in the life cycle from infancy to death. In addition, although this point was not emphasized earlier because it is not a specifically feminist point, all humans in modern industrial society have specific racial, ethnic and national backgrounds. Contemporary society thus consists of groups of individuals, defined simultaneously by age, sex, class, nationality and by racial and ethnic origin, and these groups differ markedly from each other, both physically and psychologically. Liberal political theory has tended to ignore or minimize all these differences. Marxist political theory has tended to recognize only differences of class. The political theory of radical feminism has tended to recognize only differences of age and sex, to understand these in universal terms, and often to view them as determined biologically. By contrast, socialist feminism recognizes all these differences as constituent parts of contemporary human nature and seeks a way of understanding them that is not only materialist but also historical. In particular, it has insisted on the need for a more adequate theoretical understanding of the differences between women and men. Given that its methodological commitment is basically Marxist, it seeks this understanding through an examination of what it calls the sexual division of labor. In other words, it focuses on the different types of praxis undertaken by women and men in order to develop a fully historical materialist account of the social construction of sex and gender.

The differences between women and men are both physical and psychological. Socialist feminist have begun to look at both these aspects of human nature. Some theorists, for instance, have studied variations in menstruation and menopause and have discovered that often these variations are socially determined. Marian Lowe has begun to investigate the ways in which society influences women's sporting achievements, as well as their menstrual patterns. Iris Young has explored some of the socially determined ways in which men and women move differently from each other and experience space, objects, and even their own bodies differently. She has observed that women in sexist society are "physically handicapped." Interesting work has also been done on women's body language. In undertaking these sorts of investigations, socialist feminists focus on the dialectical relationship between sex and society as it emerges through activity organized by gender norms. The methodological approach of socialist feminists makes it obvious that they have abandoned an ahistorical conception of human biology. Instead, they view human biology as being, in part, socially constructed. Biology is "gendered" as well as sexed.

In spite of their interest in the physical differences between women and men, contemporary feminists have been far more concerned with psychological differences, and socialist feminist theory has reflected that priority. Its main focus has been on the social construction not of masculine and feminine physical types, but rather of masculine and feminine character types. Among the many socialist feminist theorists who have worked on this project are Juliet Mitchell, Jane Flax, Gayle Rubin, Nancy Chodorow and, perhaps, Dorothy Dinnerstein. All these theorists have been impressed by how early in life masculine and feminine character structures are established and by the relative rigidity of these structures, once established. To explain the mechanism by which psychological masculinity and feminity are imposed on infants and young children, all utilize some version of psychoanalysis. This is because they view psychoanalytic theory as providing the most plausible and systematic account of how the individual psyche is structured by gender. But unlike Freud, the father of psychoanalysis, socialist feminist theorists do not view psychological masculinity and femininity as the child's inevitable response to a fixed and universal biological endowment. Instead, they view the acquisition of gendered character types as the result of specific social practices, particularly procreative practices, that are not determined by biology and that in principle, therefore, are alterable. They want to debiologize Freud and to reinterpret him in historical materialist terms. As Gayle Rubin puts it: "Psychoanalysis provides a description of the mechanisms by which the sexes are divided and deformed, of how bisexual, androgynous infants are transformed into boys and girls." . . .

The distinctive aspect of the socialist feminist approach to human psychology is the way in which it synthesizes insights drawn from a variety of sources. Socialist feminism claims all of the following: that our "inner" lives, as well as our bodies and behavior, are structured by gender; that this gender-structuring is not innate but is socially imposed; that the specific characteristics that are imposed are related systematically to the historically prevailing system of organizing social production; that the gender-structuring of our "inner" lives occurs when we are very young and is reinforced throughout our lives in a variety of different spheres; and that these relatively rigid masculine and feminine character structures are a very important element in maintaining male dominance. Given this conception of human psychology, one of the major theoretical tasks that socialist feminism sets itself is to provide a historical materialist account of the relationship between our "inner" lives and our social praxis. It seeks to connect masculine and feminine psychology with the sexual division of labor. . . .

It is generally accepted, by non-feminists and feminists alike, that the most obvious manifestation of the sexual division of labor, in contemporary society if not in all societies, is marked by the division between the so-called public and private spheres of human life. The line between these two spheres has varied historically: in the political theory of ancient Greece, for instance, "the economy" fell within the private sphere, whereas in contemporary political theory, both liberal and Marxist, "the economy" is considered—in different ways—to be part of the public realm. Wherever the distinction has existed, the private realm has always included sexuality and procreation, has always been viewed as more "natural" and therefore less "human" than the public realm, and has always been viewed as the realm of women Although women have always done many kinds of work, they have been defined primarily by their sexual and procreative labor; throughout history, women have been defined as "sex objects" and as mothers.

Partly because of this definition of women's work and partly because of their conviction that an individual's gender identity is established very early in life, much socialist feminist theory has focused on the area of sexuality and procreation. Yet the theory has been committed to conceptualizing this area in terms that are historical, rather than biological, and specific, rather than universal. Socialist feminism has accepted the radical feminist insight that sexual activity, childbearing, and childrearing are social practices that embody power relations and are therefore appropriate subjects for political analysis. Because of its rejection of biological determinism, however, socialist feminism denies the radical feminist assumption that these practices are fundamentally invariant. On the contrary, socialist feminists have stressed historical variation both in the practices and in the categories by which they are understood. Zillah Eisenstein writes:

> None of the processes in which a woman engages can be understood separate from the relations of the society which she embodies and which are reflected in the ideology of society. For instance, the act of giving birth to a child is only termed an act of motherhood if it reflects the relations of marriage and the family. Otherwise the very same act can be termed adultery and the child is "illegitimate" or a "bastard." The term "mother" may have a significantly different meaning when different relations are involved—as in "unwed mother." It depends on what relations are embodied in the act.

In the same spirit, Ann Foreman writes that "fatherhood is a social invention . . . located in a series of functions rather than in biology." Rayna Rapp writes that even "being a child is a highly variable social relation." Using the same historical approach, Ann Ferguson has argued that the emergence of lesbianism, as a distinct sexual identity, is a recent rather than a universal phenomenon insofar as it presupposes an urban society with the possibility of economic independence for women. More generally, "It was only with the development of capitalist societies that 'sexuality' and 'the economy' became separable from other spheres of society and could be counter-posed to one another as realities of different sorts."

Other authors have claimed that there is no transhistorical definition of marriage in terms of which the marital institutions of different cultures can be compared usefully. Even within a single society, divisions of class mean that the working-class family unit is defined very differently from the upper-class family unit, and that it performs very different social functions. One author denies that the family is a "bounded universe" and suggests that "we should extend to the study of 'family' [a] thoroughgoing agnosticism." In general, socialist feminist theory has viewed human nature as constructed in part through the historically specific ways in which people have organized their sexual, childbearing and childrearing activities. The organization of these activities both affects and is affected by class and ethnic differences, but it is seen as particularly important in creating the masculine and feminine physiques and character structures that are considered appropriate in a given society.

The beginnings of this conception of human nature are already evident, to some extent, in the work of Marx and Engels. Engels' famous definition of the materialist conception of history in his introduction to *The Origin of the Family, Private Property and the State* states clearly:

> The social organization under which the people of a particular historical epoch and a particular country live is determined by both kinds of production: by the state of development of labor on the one hand and of the family on the other.

Moreover, Marx and Engels warn explicitly against conceptualizing procreation in an ahistorical way. In *The German Ideology*, they mock an ahistorical approach to "the concept of the family," and Engels' own work in *Origin* is designed precisely to demonstrate historical change in the social rules governing the eligibility of an individual's sexual partners. However, Marx and Engels view changes in the social organization of procreation as ultimately determined themselves by changes in the so-called mode of production, at least in postprimitive societies. Consequently, they see procreation as being now only of secondary importance in shaping human nature and society. One reason for this view may be that Marx and Engels still retain certain assumptions about the "natural," presumably biological, determination of much procreative activity. Thus, they do not give a symmetrical treatment to the human needs for food, shelter, and clothing, on the one hand, and to sexual, childbearing and childrearing needs, on the other. They view the former as changing historically, giving rise to new possibilities of social organization, but they regard human procreative needs as more "natural" and less open to historical transformation. Socialist feminists, by contrast, emphasize the social determination of sexual, childbearing and childrearing needs. They understand that these needs have developed historically in dialectical relation with changing procreative practices. Consequently, they are prepared to subject sexual and procreative practices to sustained political analysis and to reflect systematically on how changes in these practices could transform human nature.

Although socialist feminist theory stresses the importance of the so-called private sphere of procreation in constructing the historically appropriate types of masculinity and femininity, it does not ignore the so-called public sphere. It recognizes that women have always worked outside procreation, providing goods and services not only for their families but for the larger society as well. Socialist feminism claims that the conception of women as primarily sexual beings and/or as mothers is an ideological mystification that obscures the facts, for instance, that more than half the world's farmers are women, and that, in the United States, women now make up almost half the paid labor force. Indeed, the Department of Labor projects that women will constitute 51.4 percent of the U.S. paid labor force by 1990.

For socialist feminism, women, just as much as men, are beings whose labor transforms the non-human world. Socialist feminists view the slogan "A women's place is everywhere" as more than a call for change: for them, it is already a partial description of existing reality.

Only a partial description, however. Although socialist feminism recognizes the extent of women's productive work, it recognizes also that this work has rarely, if ever, been the same as men's. Even in contemporary market society, socialist feminism recognizes that the paid labor force is almost completely segregated by sex; at every level, there are "women's specialties." Within the contemporary labor force, moreover, women's work is invariably less prestigious, lower paid, and defined as being less skilled than men's, even when it involves such socially valuable and complex skills as dealing with children or sick people. Socialist feminism sees, therefore, that the sexual division of labor is not just a division *between* procreation and "production": it is also a division *within* procreation and *within* "production." Consequently, socialist feminism does not view contemporary masculinity and femininity as constructed entirely through the social organization of procreation; these constructs are elaborated and reinforced in nonprocreative labor as well. . . .

We can now summarize the socialist feminist view of human nature in general and of women's nature in particular. Unlike liberalism and some aspects of traditional Marxism, socialist feminism does not view humans as "abstract, genderless" (and ageless and colorless) individuals, with women essentially indistinguishable from men. Neither does it view women as irreducibly different from men, the same yesterday, today and forever. Instead, it views women as constituted essentially by the social relations they inhabit. "(T)he social relations of society define the particular activity a woman engages in at a given moment. Outside these relations, 'woman' becomes an abstraction."

Gayle Rubin paraphrases Marx thus:

> What is a domesticated woman? A female of the species. The one explanation is as good as the other. A woman is a woman. She only becomes a domestic, a

wife, a chattel, a playboy bunny, a prostitute, or a human dictaphone in certain relations. Torn from these relationships, she is no more the helpmate of a man than gold in itself is money.

To change these relationships is to change women's and so human nature.

Since history is never static, continuing changes in human nature are inevitable. As Marx himself remarked, "All history is nothing but a continuous transformation of human nature." Socialist feminists want women to participate fully in taking conscious social control of these changes. They deny that there is anything especially natural about women's relationships with each other, with children or with men. Instead, they seek to reconstitute those relationships in such a way as to liberate the full power of women's (and human) creative potential.

No contemporary feminist would deny this goal, stated in the abstract. Just as at one time everyone was against sin, so now everyone is in favor of liberating human potential. Just as people used to disagree over how to identify sin, however, so now there is disagreement over what are human potentialities, which ones should be developed and how this development should be undertaken. Every conception of human nature implies an answer to these questions, and socialist feminism has its own distinctive answer. Unlike liberalism, the socialist feminist ideal of human fulfilment is not individual autonomy; for reasons that will be explained more fully later, socialist feminism views the ideal of autonomy as characteristically masculine as well as characteristically capitalist. The socialist feminist conception of human fulfillment is closer to the Marxist ideal of the full development of human potentialities through free productive labor, but socialist feminism construes productive labor more broadly than does traditional Marxism. Consequently, the socialist feminist ideal of human well-being and fulfilment includes the full development of human potentialities for free sexual expression, for freely bearing children and for freely rearing them.

To many Marxists, the theory of alienation expresses Marx's conception of human nature in capitalist society. As the theory is traditionaly interpreted, alienation characterizes primarily workers' relation to wage labor; however, Marx saw that the way workers experience wage labor also affects the way they experience the rest of their lives. Because their wage labor is coerced, their activity outside wage labor seems free by contrast.

> We arrive at the result that man (the worker) feels himself to be freely active only in his animal functions—eating, drinking and procreating, or at most also in his dwelling and in personal adornment—while in his human functions he is reduced to an animal. The animal becomes human and the human becomes animal.

To socialist feminists, this conception of alienation is clearly male-biased. Men may feel free when eating, drinking, and procreating, but women do not. As the popular saying has it, "A woman's work is never done." An Englishman's home may be his castle, but it is his wife's prison. Women are compelled to do housework, to bear and raise children and to define themselves sexually in terms of men's wishes. The pressures on women to do this work are almost overwhelming:

When I say that women are subject to a form of compulsive labor, I mean that they may only resist with great difficulty, and that the majority succumb. The same may be said of non-owners when it comes to wage work. In both cases, it is not compulsive in the sense that one is driven to it with whips and chains (though that happens, too!), but in the sense that no real alternative is generally available to women, and that everything in society conspires to ensure that women do this work. While a nonowner may attempt small independent production, or simply refuse to work and live off begging or state welfare, that is not proof of his freedom. The same is true of women. While a woman may with great difficulty resist doing reproductive work, that is no proof that she is "free" not to do it.

One way in which socialist feminists are attempting to conceptualize contemporary women's lack of freedom is by extending the traditional Marxist theory of alienation. . . . Iris Young's reflections on "the struggle for our bodies," cited earlier in this chapter, suggest that women suffer a special form of alienation from their bodies. Similarly, Sandra Bartky claims that women are alienated in cultural production, as mothers and sexual beings. She believes that feminine narcissism is the paradigm of a specifically feminine form of sexual alienation. Ann Foreman argues that femininity as such is an alienated condition: "While alienation reduces the man to an instrument of labour within industry, it reduces the woman to an instrument for his sexual pleasure within the family." One may define the goal of socialist feminism as being to overcome all forms of alienation but especially those that are specific to women.

If it is difficult to envision what nonalienated industry would be like, it seems almost impossible to foresee the form of nonalienated sexuality or parenthood. Because of the ideological dogma that these are determined biologically, it is even harder to envision alternatives to prevailing sexual and procreative practices than it is to the capitalist mode of production. Alternative ways of organizing procreation tend to be viewed as science fiction; indeed, they are considered more often in fiction than in political theory. A number of socialist feminists are experimenting with alternatives in procreation, but the extent and validity of those experiments is limited, of course, by their context in a society that is emphatically neither socialist nor feminist.

The one solid basis of agreement among socialist feminists is that to overcome women's alienation, the sexual division of labor must be eliminated in every area of life. Just as sexual segregation in nonprocreative work must be eliminated, so men must participate fully in childrearing and, so far as possible, in childbearing. Normative heterosexuality must be replaced by a situation in which the sex of one's lovers is a matter of social indifference, so that the dualist categories of heterosexual, homosexual and bisexual may be abandoned. Some authors describe the ideal as androgyny, but even this term is implicitly dualistic. If it is retained for the present, we must remember that the ultimate transformation of human nature at which socialist feminists aim goes beyond the liberal conception of psychological androgyny to a possible transformation of "physical" human capacities, some of which, until now, have been seen as biologically limited to one sex. This transformation might even include the capacities for insemination, for lactation and for gestation so that, for instance, one woman could inseminate another, so that men and nonparturitive women could lactate and so that fertilized ova could be transplanted into women's or even into men's bodies. These developments may seem far-fetched, but in fact they are already on the technological horizon; however, what is needed much more immediately than technological development is a substantial reduction in the social domination of women by men. Only such a reduction can ensure that these or alternative technological possibilities are used to increase women's control over their bodies and thus over their lives, rather than being used as an additional means for women's subjugation. Gayle Rubin writes: "We are not only oppressed *as* women, we are oppressed by having to *be* women or men as the case may be." The goal of socialist feminism is to abolish the social relations that constitute humans not only as workers and capitalists but also as women and men. Whereas one version of radical feminism takes the human ideal to be a woman, the ideal of socialist feminism is that women (and men) will disappear as socially constituted categories.

Richard Rorty (b. 1931)

Born in New York City, he studied philosophy at the University of Chicago and at Yale University, where he received the Ph.D. After service in the U.S. Army, he taught philosophy at Yale, at Wellesley College, and at Princeton University. Since 1982, he has been a University Professor of Humanities at the University of Virginia. He has made contributions to most areas of philosophy, including social and political philosophy. His chief publications include *Philosophy and the Mirror of Nature* (1979), *The Consequences of Pragmatism* (1982), and *Contingency, Irony and Solidarity* (1989). Rorty has been a Guggenheim Fellow and a MacArthur Fellow.

From Objectivity, Relativism, and Truth*

Solidarity or Objectivity?

There are two principal ways in which reflective human beings try, by placing their lives in a larger context, to give sense to those lives. The first is by telling the story of their contribution to a community. This community may be the actual historical one in which they live, or another actual one, distant in time or place, or a quite imaginary one, consisting perhaps of a dozen heroes and heroines selected from history or fiction or both. The second way is to describe themselves as standing in immediate relation to a nonhuman reality. This relation is immediate in the sense that it does not derive from a relation between such a reality and their tribe, or their nation, or their imagined band of comrades. I shall say that stories of the former kind exemplify the desire for solidarity, and that stories of the latter kind exemplify the desire for objectivity. Insofar as a person is seeking solidarity, she does not ask about the relation between the practices of the chosen community and something outside that community. Insofar as she seeks objectivity, she distances herself from the actual persons around her not by thinking of herself as a member of some other real or imaginary group, but rather by attaching herself to something which can be described without reference to any particular human beings.

The tradition in Western culture which centers around the notion of the search for Truth, a tradition which runs from the Greek philosophers through the Enlightenment, is the clearest example of the attempt to find a sense in one's existence by turning away from solidarity to objectivity. The idea of Truth as something to be pursued for its own sake, not because it will be good for oneself, or for one's real or imaginary community, is the central theme of this tradition. It was perhaps the growing awareness by the Greeks of the sheer diversity of human communities which stimulated the emergence of this ideal. A fear of parochialism, of being confined within the horizons of the group into which one happens to be born, a need to see it with the eyes of a stranger, helps produce the skeptical and ironic tone characteristic of Euripides and Socrates. Herodotus'

---

*An Excerpt.

willingness to take the barbarians seriously enough to describe their customs in detail may have been a necessary prelude to Plato's claim that the way to transcend skepticism is to envisage a common goal of humanity—a goal set by human nature rather than by Greek culture. The combination of Socratic alienation and Platonic hope gives rise to the idea of the intellectual as someone who is in touch with the nature of things, not by way of the opinions of his community, but in a more immediate way.

Plato developed the idea of such an intellectual by means of distinctions between knowledge and opinion, and between appearance and reality. Such distinctions conspire to produce the idea that rational inquiry should make visible a realm to which nonintellectuals have little access, and of whose very existence they may be doubtful. In the Enlightenment, this notion became concrete in the adoption of the Newtonian physical scientist as a model of the intellectual. To most thinkers of the eighteenth century, it seemed clear that the access to Nature which physical science had provided should now be followed by the establishment of social, political, and economic institutions which were in accordance with Nature. Ever since, liberal social thought has centered around social reform as made possible by objective knowledge of what human beings are like—not knowledge of what Greeks or Frenchmen or Chinese are like, but of humanity as such. We are the heirs of this objectivist tradition, which centers around the assumption that we must step outside our community long enough to examine it in the light of something which transcends it, namely, that which it has in common with every other actual and possible human community. This tradition dreams of an ultimate community which will have transcended the distinction between the natural and the social, which will exhibit a solidarity which is not parochial because it is the expression of an ahistorical human nature. Much of the rhetoric of contemporary intellectual life takes for granted that the goal of scientific inquiry into man is to understand "underlying structures," or "culturally invariant factors," or "biologically determined patterns."

Those who wish to ground solidarity in objectivity—call them "realists"—have to construe truth as correspondence to reality. So they must construct a metaphysics which has room for a special relation between beliefs and objects which will differentiate true from false beliefs. They also must argue that there are procedures of justification of belief which are natural and not merely local. So they must construct an epistemology which has room for a kind of justification which is not merely social but natural, springing from human nature itself, and made possible by a link between that part of nature and the rest of nature. On their view, the various procedures which are thought of as providing rational justification by one or another culture may or may not really *be* rational. For to be truly rational, procedures of justification *must* lead to the truth, to correspondence to reality, to the intrinsic nature of things.

By contrast, those who wish to reduce objectivity to solidarity—call them "pragmatists"—do not require either a metaphysics or an epistemology. They view truth as, in William James' phrase, what is good for *us* to believe. So they do not need an account of a relation between beliefs and objects called "correspondence," nor an account of human cognitive abilities which ensures that our species is capable of entering into that relation. They see the gap between truth and justification not as something to be bridged by isolating a natural and transcultural sort of rationality which can be used to criticize certain cultures and praise others, but simply as the gap between the actual good and the possible better. From a pragmatist point of view, to say that what is rational for us now to believe may not be *true* is simply to say that somebody may come up with a better idea. It is to say that there is always room for improved belief, since new evidence, or new hypotheses, or a whole new vocabulary, may come along. For pragmatists, the desire for objectivity is not the desire to escape the limitations of one's community, but simply the desire for as much intersubjective agreement as possible, the desire to extend the reference of "us" as far as we can. Insofar as pragmatists make a distinction between knowledge and opinion, it is simply the distinction between topics on which such agreement is relatively easy to get and topics on which agreement is relatively hard to get.

"Relativism" is the traditional epithet applied to pragmatism by realists. Three different views are commonly referred to by this name. The first is the view that every belief is as good as every other. The second is the view that "true" is an equivocal term, having as many meanings as there are procedures of justification. The third is the view that there is nothing to be said about either truth or rationality apart from descriptions of the familiar procedures of justification which a given society—*ours*—uses in one or another area of inquiry. The pragmatist holds the ethnocentric third view. But he does not hold the self-refuting first view, nor the eccentric second view. He thinks that his views are better than the realists', but he does not think that his views correspond to the nature of things. He thinks that the very flexibility of the word "true"—the fact that it is merely an expression of commendation—insures its univocity. The term "true," on his account, means the same in all cultures, just as equally flexible terms like "here," "there," "good," "bad," "you," and "me" mean the same in all cultures. But the identity of meaning is, of course, compatible with diversity of reference, and with diversity of procedures for assigning the terms. So he feels free to use the term "true" as a general term of commendation in the same way as his realist opponent does—and in particular to use it to commend his own view.

However, it is not clear why "relativist" should be thought an appropriate term for the ethnocentric third view, the one which the pragmatist *does* hold. For the pragmatist is not holding a positive theory which says that something is relative to something else. He is, instead, making the purely *negative* point that we should drop the traditional distinction between knowledge and opinion, construed as the distinction between truth as correspondence to reality and truth as a commendatory term for well-justified beliefs. The reason that the realist calls this negative claim "relativistic" is that he cannot believe that anybody would seriously deny that truth has an intrinsic nature. So when the pragmatist says that there is nothing to be said about truth save that each of us will commend as true those beliefs which he or she finds good to believe, the realist is inclined to interpret this as one more positive theory about the nature of truth: a theory according to which truth is simply the contemporary opinion of a chosen individual or group. Such a theory would, of course, be self-refuting. But the pragmatist does not have a theory of truth, much less a relativistic one. As a partisan of solidarity, his account of the value of cooperative human inquiry has only an ethical base, not an epistemological or metaphysical one. Not having *any* epistemology, *a fortiori* he does not have a relativistic one.

The question of whether truth or rationality has an intrinsic nature, of whether we ought to have a positive theory about either topic, is just the question of whether our self-description ought to be constructed around a relation to human nature or around a relation to a particular collection of human beings, whether we should desire objectivity or solidarity. It is hard to see how one could choose between these alternatives by looking more deeply into the nature of knowledge, or of man, or of nature. Indeed, the proposal that this issue might be so settled begs the question in favor of the realist, for it presupposes that knowledge, man, and nature *have* real essences which are relevant to the problem at hand. For the pragmatist, by contrast, "knowledge" is, like "truth," simply a compliment paid to the beliefs which we think so well justified that, for the moment, further justification is not needed. An inquiry into the nature of knowledge can, on his view, only be a sociohistorical account of how various people have tried to reach agreement on what to believe.

The view which I am calling "pragmatism" is almost, but not quite, the same as what Hilary Putnam, in his recent *Reason, Truth, and History,* calls "the internalist conception of philosophy." Putnam defines such a conception as one which gives up the attempt at a God's eye view of things, the attempt at contact with the nonhuman which I have been calling "the desire for objectivity." Unfortunately, he accompanies his defense of the anti-realist views I am recommending with a polemic against a lot of the other people who hold these views—e.g., Kuhn, Feyerabend, Foucault, and myself. We are criticized as "relativists." Putnam presents "internalism" as a happy *via media* between realism and relativism. He speaks of "the plethora of relativistic doctrines being marketed today" and in particular of "the French philosophers" as holding "some fancy mixture of cultural relativism and 'structuralism.'" But when it comes to criticizing these doctrines all that Putnam finds to attack is the so-called "incommensurability thesis": viz., "terms used in another culture cannot be equated in meaning or reference with any terms or expressions *we* possess." He sensibly agrees with Donald Davidson in remarking that this thesis is self-refuting. Criticism of this thesis, however, is destructive of, at most, some incautious passages in some early writings by Feyerabend. Once this thesis is brushed aside, it is hard to see how Putnam himself differs from most of those he criticizes.

Putnam accepts the Davidsonian point that, as he puts it, "the whole justification of an interpretative scheme . . . is that it renders the behavior of others at least minimally reasonable by *our* lights." It would seem natural to go on from this to say that we cannot get outside the range of those lights, that we cannot stand on neutral ground illuminated only by the natural light of reason. But Putnam draws back from this conclusion. He does so because he construes the claim that we cannot do so as the claim that the range of our thought is restricted by what he calls "institutionalized norms," publicly available criteria for settling all arguments, including philosophical arguments. He rightly says that there are no such criteria, arguing that the suggestion that there are is as self-refuting as the "incommensurability thesis." He is, I think, entirely right in saying that the notion that philosophy is or should become such an application of explicit criteria contradicts the very idea of philosophy. One can gloss Putnam's point by saying that "philosophy" is precisely what a culture becomes capable of when it ceases to define itself in terms of explicit rules, and becomes sufficiently leisured and civilized to rely on inarticulate know-how, to substitute *phronesis* for codification, and conversation with foreigners for conquest of them.

But to say that we cannot refer every question to explicit criteria institutionalized by our society does not speak to the point which the people whom Putnam calls "relativists" are making. One reason these people are pragmatists is precisely that they share Putnam's distrust of the positivistic idea that rationality is a matter of applying criteria.

Such a distrust is common, for example, to Kuhn, Mary Hesse, Wittgenstein, Michael Polanyi, and Michael Oakeshott. Only someone who did think of rationality in this way would dream of suggesting that "true" means something different in different societies. For only such a person could imagine that there was anything to pick out to which one might make "true" relative. Only if one shares the logical positivists' idea that we all carry around things called "rules of language" which regulate what we say when, will one suggest that there is no way to break out of one's culture.

In the most original and powerful section of his book, Putnam argues that the notion that "rationality . . . is defined by the local cultural norms" is merely the demonic counterpart of positivism. It is, as he says, "a scientistic theory inspired by anthropology as positivism was a scientistic theory inspired by the exact sciences." By "scientism" Putnam means the notion that rationality consists in the application of criteria. Suppose we drop this notion, and accept Putnam's own Quinean picture of inquiry as the continual reweaving of a web of beliefs rather than as the application of criteria to cases. Then the notion of "local cultural norms" will lose its offensively parochial overtones. For now to say that we must work by our own lights, that we must be ethnocentric, is merely to say that beliefs suggested by another culture must be tested by trying to weave them together with beliefs we already have. It is a consequence of this holistic view of knowledge, a view *shared* by Putnam and those he criticizes as "relativists," that alternative cultures are not to be thought of on the model of alternative geometries. Alternative geometries are irreconcilable because they have axiomatic structures, and contradictory axioms. They are *designed* to be irreconcilable. Cultures are not so designed, and do not have axiomatic structures. To say that they have "institutionalized norms" is only to say, with Foucault, that knowledge is never separable from power—that one is likely to suffer if one does not hold certain beliefs at certain times and places. But such institutional backups for beliefs take the form of bureaucrats and policemen, not of "rules of language" and "criteria of rationality." To think otherwise is the Cartesian fallacy of seeing axioms where there are only shared habits, of viewing statements which summarize such practices as if they reported constraints enforcing such practices. Part of the force of Quine's and Davidson's attack on the distinction between the conceptual and the empirical is that the distinction between different cultures does not differ in kind from the distinction between different theories held by members of a single culture. The Tasmanian aborigines and the British colonists had trouble communicating, but this trouble was different only in extent from the difficulties in communication experienced by Gladstone and Disraeli. The trouble in all such cases is just the difficulty of explaining why other people disagree with us, of reweaving our beliefs so as to fit the fact of disagreement together with the other beliefs we hold. The same Quinean arguments which dispose of the positivists' distinction between analytic and synthetic truth dispose of the anthropologists' distinction between the inter-cultural and the intracultural.

On this holistic account of cultural norms, however, we do not need the notion of a universal transcultural rationality which Putnam invokes against those whom he calls "relativists." Just before the end of his book, Putnam says that once we drop the notion of a God's-eye point of view we realize that:

> we can only hope to produce a more rational *conception* of rationality or a bet-ter *conception* of morality if we operate from *within* our tradition (with its echoes of the Greek agora, of Newton, and so on, in the case of rationality, and with its echoes of scripture, of the philosophers, of the democratic revo-lutions, and so on . . . in the case of morality.) We are invited to engage in a truly human dialogue.

With this I entirely agree, and so, I take it, would Kuhn, Hesse, and most of the other so-called "relativists"—perhaps even Foucault. But Putnam then goes on to pose a further question:

> Does this dialogue have an ideal terminus? Is there a *true* conception of ratio-nality, an ideal morality, even if all we ever have are our conceptions of these?

I do not see the point of this question. Putnam suggests that a negative answer—the view that "there is only the dialogue"—is just another form of self-refuting relativism. But, once again, I do not see how a claim that something does not exist can be construed as a claim that something is relative to something else. In the final sentence of his book, Putnam says that "The very fact that we speak of our different conceptions as different concep-tions of *rationality* posits a *Grenzbegriff*, a limit-concept of ideal truth." But what is such a posit supposed to do, except to say that from God's point of view the human race is head-ing in the right direction? Surely Putnam's "internalism" should forbid him to say any-thing like that. To say that *we* think we're heading in the right direction is just to say, with Kuhn, that we can, by hindsight, tell the story of the past as a story of progress. To say that we still have a long way to go, that our present views should not be cast in bronze, is too platitudinous to require support by positing limit-concepts. So it is hard to see what difference is made by the difference between saying "there is only the dialogue" and say-ing "there is also that to which the dialogue converges."

I would suggest that Putnam here, at the end of the day, slides back into the scien-tism he rightly condemns in others. For the root of scientism, defined as the view that ra-tionality is a matter of applying criteria, is the desire for objectivity, the hope that what Putnam calls "human flourishing" has a transhistorical nature. I think that Feyerabend is right in suggesting that until we discard the metaphor of inquiry, and human activity gen-erally, as converging rather than proliferating, as becoming more unified rather than more diverse, we shall never be free of the motives which once led us to posit gods. Posit-ing *Grenzbegriffe* seems merely a way of telling ourselves that a nonexistent God would, if he did exist, be pleased with us. If we could ever be moved solely by the desire for solidarity, setting aside the desire for objectivity altogether, then we should think of human progress as making it possible for human beings to do more interesting things and be more interesting people, not as heading towards a place which has somehow been prepared for humanity in advance. Our self-image would employ images of making rather than finding, the images used by the Romantics to praise poets rather than the images used by the Greeks to praise mathematicians. Feyerabend seems to me right in trying to develop such a self-image for us, but his project seems misdescribed, by himself as well as by his critics, as "relativism."

Those who follow Feyerabend in this direction are often thought of as necessarily enemies of the Enlightenment, as joining in the chorus which claims that the traditional self-descriptions of the Western democracies are bankrupt, that they somehow have been shown to be "inadequate" or "self-deceptive." Part of the instinctive resistance to attempts by Marxists, Sartreans, Oakeshottians, Gadamerians and Foucauldians to reduce objectivity to solidarity is the fear that our traditional liberal habits and hopes will not survive the reduction. Such feelings are evident, for example, in Habermas' criticism of Gadamer's position as relativistic and potentially repressive, in the suspicion that Heidegger's attacks on realism are somehow linked to his Nazism, in the hunch that Marxist attempts to interpret values as class interests are usually just apologies for Leninist takeovers, and in the suggestion that Oakeshott's skepticism about rationalism in politics is merely an apology for the status quo.

I think that putting the issue in such moral and political terms, rather than in epistemological or metaphilosophical terms, makes clearer what is at stake. For now the question is not about how to define words like "truth" or "rationality" or "knowledge" or "philosophy," but about what self-image our society should have of itself. The ritual invocation of the "need to avoid relativism" is most comprehensible as an expression of the need to preserve certain habits of contemporary European life. These are the habits nurtured by the Enlightenment, and justified by it in terms of an appeal of Reason, conceived as a transcultural human ability to correspond to reality, a faculty whose possession and use is demonstrated by obedience to explicit criteria. So the real question about relativism is whether these same habits of intellectual, social, and political life can be justified by a conception of rationality as criterionless muddling through, and by a pragmatist conception of truth.

I think that the answer to this question is that the pragmatist cannot justify these habits without circularity, but then neither can the realist. The pragmatists' justification of toleration, free inquiry, and the quest for undistorted communication can only take the form of a comparison between societies which exemplify these habits and those which do not, leading up to the suggestion that nobody who has experienced both would prefer the latter. It is exemplified by Winston Churchill's defense of democracy as the worst form of government imaginable, except for all the others which have been tried so far. Such justification is not by reference to a criterion, but by reference to various detailed practical advantages. It is circular only in that the terms of praise used to describe liberal societies will be drawn from the vocabulary of the liberal societies themselves. Such praise has to be in *some* vocabulary, after all, and the terms of praise current in primitive or theocratic or totalitarian societies will not produce the desired result. So the pragmatist admits that he has no ahistorical standpoint from which to endorse the habits of modern democracies he wishes to praise. These consequences are just what partisans of solidarity expect. But among partisans of objectivity they give rise, once again, to fears of the dilemma formed by ethnocentrism on the one hand and relativism on the other. Either we attach a special privilege to our own community, or we pretend an impossible tolerance for every other group.

I have been arguing that we pragmatists should grasp the ethnocentric horn of this dilemma. We should say that we must, in practice, privilege our own group, even though there can be no noncircular justification for doing so. We must insist that the fact that nothing is immune from criticism does not mean that we have a duty to justify everything. We Western liberal intellectuals should accept the fact that we have to start from where we are, and that this means that there are lots of views which we simply cannot take seriously. To use Neurath's familiar analogy, we can *understand* the revolutionary's suggestion that a sailable boat can't be made out of the planks which make up ours, and that we must simply abandon ship. But we cannot take his suggestion seriously. We cannot take it as a rule for action, so it is not a live option. For some people, to be sure, the option *is* live. These are the people who have always hoped to become a New Being, who have hoped to be converted rather than persuaded. But we—the liberal Rawlsian searchers for consensus, the heirs of Socrates, the people who wish to link their days dialectically each to each—cannot do so. Our community—the community of the liberal intellectuals of the secular modern West—wants to be able to give a *post factum* account of any change of view. We want to be able, so to speak, to justify ourselves to our earlier selves. This preference is not built into us by human nature. It is just the way *we* live now.

This lonely provincialism, this admission that we are just the historical moment that we are, not the representatives of something ahistorical, is what makes traditional Kantian liberals like Rawls draw back from pragmatism. "Relativism," by contrast, is merely a red herring. The realist is, once again, projecting his own habits of thought upon the pragmatist when he charges him with relativism. For the realist thinks that the whole point of philosophical thought is to detach oneself from any particular community and look down at it from a more universal standpoint. When he hears the pragmatist repudiating the desire for such a standpoint he cannot quite believe it. He thinks that everyone, deep down inside, *must* want such detachment. So he attributes to the pragmatist a perverse form of his own attempted detachment, and sees him as an ironic, sneering aesthete who refuses to take the choice between communities seriously, a mere "relativist." But the pragmatist, dominated by the desire for solidarity, can only be criticized for taking his own community *too* seriously. He can only be criticized for ethnocentrism, not for relativism. To be ethnocentric is to divide the human race into the people to whom one must justify one's beliefs and the others. The first group—one's *ethnos*—comprises those who share enough of one's beliefs to make fruitful conversation possible. In this sense, everybody is ethnocentric when engaged in actual debate, no matter how much realist rhetoric about objectivity he produces in his study.

What is disturbing about the pragmatist's picture is not that it is relativistic but that it takes away two sorts of metaphysical comfort to which our intellectual tradition has become accustomed. One is the thought that membership in our biological species carries with it certain "rights," a notion which does not seem to make sense unless the biological similarities entail the possession of something nonbiological, something which links our species to a nonhuman reality and thus gives the species moral dignity. This picture of rights as biologically transmitted is so basic to the political discourse of the Western democracies that we are troubled by any suggestion that "human nature" is not a useful moral concept. The second comfort is provided by the thought that our community cannot wholly die. The picture of a common human nature oriented towards correspondence to reality as it is in itself comforts us with the thought that even if our civilization is destroyed, even if all memory of our political or intellectual or artistic community is erased, the race is fated to recapture the virtues and the insights and the achievements which were the glory of that community. The notion of human nature as an inner structure which leads all members of the species to converge to the same point, to recognize the same theories, virtues, and works of art as worthy of honor, assures us that even if the Persians had won, the arts and sciences of the Greeks would sooner or later have appeared elsewhere. It assures us that even if the Orwellian bureaucrats of terror rule for a thousand years the achievements of the Western democracies will someday be duplicated by our remote descendants. It assures us that "man will prevail," that something reasonably like *our* world-view, *our* virtues, *our* art, will bob up again whenever human beings are left alone to cultivate their inner natures. The comfort of the realist picture is the comfort of saying not simply that there is a place prepared for our race in our advance, but also that we now know quite a bit about what that place looks like. The inevitable ethnocentrism to which we are all condemned is thus as much a part of the realist's comfortable view as of the pragmatist's uncomfortable one.

The pragmatist gives up the first sort of comfort because he thinks that to say that certain people have certain rights is merely to say that we should treat them in certain ways. It is not to give a *reason* for treating them in those ways. As to the second sort of comfort, he suspects that the hope that something resembling *us* will inherit the earth is impossible to eradicate, as impossible as eradicating the hope of surviving our individual deaths through some satisfying transfiguration. But he does not want to turn this hope into a theory of the nature of man. He wants solidarity to be our *only* comfort, and to be seen not to require metaphysical support.

My suggestion that the desire for objectivity is in part a disguised form of the fear of the death of our community echoes Nietzsche's charge that the philosophical tradition which stems from Plato is an attempt to avoid facing up to contingency, to escape from time and chance. Nietzsche thought that realism was to be condemned not only by arguments from its theoretical incoherence, the sort of argument we find in Putnam and Davidson, but also on practical, pragmatic, grounds. Nietzsche thought that the test of human character was the ability to live with the thought that there was no convergence. He wanted us to be able to think of truth as:

> a mobile army of metaphors, metonyms, and anthromorphisms—in short a sum of human relations, which have been enhanced, transposed, and embellished poetically and rhetorically and which after long use seem firm, canonical, and obligatory to a people.

Nietzsche hoped that eventually there might be human beings who could and did think of truth in this way, but who still liked themselves, who saw themselves as *good* people for whom solidarity was *enough.*

I think that pragmatism's attack on the various structure-content distinctions which buttress the realist's notion of objectivity can best be seen as an attempt to let us think of truth in this Nietzschean way, as entirely a matter of solidarity. That is why I think we need to say, despite Putnam, that "there is only the dialogue," only *us,* and to throw out the last residues of the notion of "transcultural rationality." But this should not lead us to repudiate, as Nietzsche sometimes did, the elements in our movable host which embody the ideas of Socratic conversation, Christian fellowship, and Enlightenment science. Nietzsche ran together his diagnosis of philosophical realism as an expression of fear and resentment with his own resentful idiosyncratic idealizations of silence, solitude, and violence. Post-Nietzschean thinkers like Adorno and Heidegger and Foucault have run together Nietzsche's criticisms of the metaphysical tradition on the one hand with his criticisms of bourgeois civility, of Christian love, and of the nineteenth century's hope that science would make the world a better place to live, on the other. I do not think that there is any interesting connection between these two sets of criticisms. Pragmatism seems to me, as I have said, a philosophy of solidarity rather than of despair. From this point of view, Socrates' turn away from the gods, Christianity's turn from an Omnipotent Creator to the man who suffered on the Cross, and the Baconian turn from science as contemplation of eternal truth to science as instrument of social progress, can be seen as so many preparations for the act of social faith which is suggested by a Nietzschean view of truth.

The best argument we partisans of solidarity have against the realistic partisans of objectivity is Nietzsche's argument that the traditional Western metaphysico-epistemological way of firming up our habits simply isn't working anymore. It isn't doing its job. It has become as transparent a device as the postulation of deities who turn out, by a happy coincidence, to have chosen *us* as their people. So the pragmatist suggestion that we substitute a "merely" ethical foundation for our sense of community—or, better, that we think of our sense of community as having no foundation except shared hope and the trust created by such sharing—is put forward on practical grounds. It is *not* put forward as a corollary of a metaphysical claim that the objects in the world contain no intrinsically action-guiding properties, nor of an epistemological claim that we lack a faculty of moral sense, nor of a semantical claim that truth is reducible to justification. It is a suggestion about how we might think of ourselves in order to avoid the kind of resentful belatedness—characteristic of the bad side of Nietzsche—which now characterizes much of high culture. This resentment arises from the realization, which I referred to at the beginning of this chapter, that the Enlightenment's search for objectivity has often gone sour.

The rhetoric of scientific objectivity, pressed too hard and taken too seriously, has led us to people like B. F. Skinner on the one hand and people like Althusser on the other—two equally pointless fantasies, both produced by the attempt to be "scientific" about our moral and political lives. Reaction against scientism led to attacks on natural science as a sort of false god. But there is nothing wrong with science, there is only something wrong with the attempt to divinize it, the attempt characteristic of realistic philosophy. This reaction has also led to attacks on liberal social thought of the type common to Mill and Dewey and Rawls as a mere ideological superstructure, one which obscures the realities of our situation and represses attempts to change that situation. But there is nothing wrong with liberal democracy, nor with the philosophers who have tried to enlarge its scope. There is only something wrong with the attempt to see their efforts as failures to achieve something which they were not trying to achieve—a demonstration of the "objective" superiority of our way of life over all other alternatives. There is, in short, nothing wrong with the hopes of the Enlightenment, the hopes which created the Western democracies. The value of the ideals of the Enlightenment is, for us pragmatists, just the value of some of the institutions and practices which they have created. In this essay I have sought to distinguish these institutions and practices from the philosophical justifications for them provided by partisans of objectivity, and to suggest an alternative justification.

Suggestions for Further Reading

In addition to the works from which these selections have been drawn, we offer this incomplete list for further reading.

BECKER, LAWRENCE C. *Property Rights* (Routledge & Kegan Paul, 1977)

COHEN, MARSHALL, THOMAS NAGEL, AND THOMAS SCANLON, eds. *Marx, Justice, and History* (Princeton UP, 1980)

DANIELS, NORMAN, ed. *Reading Rawls* (Basic, 1975)

EVERDELL, WILLIAM. *The End of Kings: A History of Republics and Republicans* (Free Press, 1983)

FEINBERG, JOEL. *Social Philosophy* (Prentice-Hall, 1973)

GOLDING, MARTIN. *Philosophy of Law* (Prentice-Hall, 1975)

GUTMANN, AMY, AND DENNIS F. THOMPSON. *Democracy and Disagreement* (Belknap Press, 1996)

HART, H.L.A. *The Concept of Law* (Oxford UP, 1961)

HOLMES, STEPHEN. *The Anatomy of Antiliberalism* (Harvard UP, 1993)

KAVKA, GREGORY S. *Hobbesian Moral and Political Theory* (Princeton UP, 1986)

KRAUT, RICHARD. *Socrates and the State* (Princeton UP, 1984)

LERNER, RALPH, AND MUSHIN MAHDI, eds. *Medieval Political Philosophy* (Cornell UP, 1963)

LOMASKY, LOREN. *Persons, Rights, and the Moral Community* (Oxford UP, 1987)

LUKES, STEVEN. *Marxism and Morality* (Oxford UP, 1985)

MacCallum, Gerald. *Political Philosophy* (Prentice-Hall, 1987)

Machan, Tibor R., and Douglas Rasmussen, eds. *Liberty for the 21st Century: Contemporary Libertarian Thought* (Rowman & Littlefield, 1995)

Machan, Tibor. *Individuals and Their Rights* (Open Court, 1989)

Miller, Fred D., Jr. *Nature, Justice, and Rights in Aristotle's Politics* (Oxford UP, 1995)

Morgan, Michael L., ed. *Classics of Moral and Political Theory* (Hackett, 1992)

Narveson, Jan. *The Libertarian Idea* (Temple UP, 1988)

Oakeshott, Michael. *Rationalism in Politics and Other Essays* (Liberty Press, 1991)

Olen, Jeffrey, and Vincent Barry, eds. *Applying Ethics* (Wadsworth, 1996)

Paul, Jeffrey. *Reading Nozick* (Rowman & Littlefield, 1981)

Porter, Jene M., ed. *Classics in Political Philosophy* (Prentice-Hall, 1989)

Quinton, Anthony. "Political Philosophy," in *The Oxford History of Western Philosophy*, Anthony Kenny, ed. (Oxford UP, 1994)

Rasmussen, Douglas B., and Douglas J. Den Uyl. *Liberty and Nature: An Aristotelian Defense of Liberal Order* (Open Court, 1991)

Sandel, Michael J. *Liberalism and the Limits of Justice* (Cambridge UP, 1982)

Sanders, John T., and Jan Narveson, eds. *For and Against the State* (Rowman & Littlefield, 1996)

Schauer, Frederick, and Walter Sinnott-Armstrong, eds. *The Philosophy of Law* (Harcourt-Brace, 1996)

Schmitt, Carl, et. al. *The Concept of the Political* (University of Chicago Press, 1996)

Scheuerman, William E. *Between the Norm and the Exception: The Frankfurt School and the Rule of Law* (MIT Press, 1994)

Sen, Amartya, and Bernard Williams, eds. *Utilitarianism and Beyond* (Cambridge UP, 1982)

Sher, George, ed. *Moral Philosophy: Selected Readings* (Harcourt-Brace, 1996)

Simmons, A. John. *Moral Principles and Political Obligation* (Princeton UP, 1979)

Smart, J.J.C., and Bernard Williams. *Utilitarianism: For and Against* (Cambridge UP, 1973)

Smith, Elizabeth, and H. Gene Blocker, eds. *Applied Social and Political Philosophy* (Prentice-Hall, 1994)

Sterba, James P., ed. *Morality and Social Justice* (Rowman & Littlefield, 1995)

Sterba, James P., ed. *Justice: Alternative Political Perspectives* (Wadsworth, 1992)

Waldron, Jeremy. *Theories of Rights* (Oxford UP, 1984)

Walzer, Michael. *Spheres of Justice* (Basic, 1983)

Wertheimer, Alan. *Coercion* (Princeton UP, 1990)

Wolff, Robert Paul. *In Defense of Anarchism* (Harper & Row, 1970)

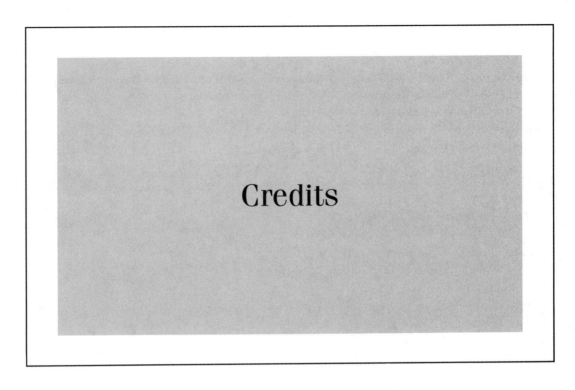

Credits

Part I:

Xenophon, from *Memorabilia*, tr. J.S. Watson.

Plato, from *Republic*, tr. B. Jowett.

Plato, from *Statesman*, tr. J. Skemp (New Haven: Yale University Press, 1952), pp. 294–311. By permission.

Aristotle, from *Politics*, tr. B. Jowett, rev. J. Barnes (Princeton University Press, 1984), pp. 1986–88, 2029–39. By permission.

Part II:

Saint Augustine of Hippo, from *The City of God*, tr. Henry Paolucci (Washington, D.C.: Regnery Publishers, 1985), from chapters 2, 3, 4, 14, 15, 18, 19, 22. By permission.

Saint Thomas Aquinas, from *The Treatise on Law*, questions 94–96 (Washington, D.C.: Regnery Publishers, 1987). By permission.

Marsilius of Padua, from *Defender of Peace*, tr. A. Gwirth (Columbia University Press, 1956), chapters 2–11. By permission.

Part III:

Niccolò Machiavelli, from *The Prince*, tr. C. Detmold.

Thomas Hobbes, from *Leviathan*.

Baruch Spinoza, from *The Theological-Political Treatise*, tr. R. Elwes (Dover Publications, 1951), pp. 200–36. By permission.

John Locke, from *Second Treatise of Government*.

David Hume, from *A Treatise of Human Nature*.

Immanuel Kant, "Perpetual Peace," H.S. Reiss (ed.); H.B. Nisbet (trans.), from *Kant's Political Writings* (Cambridge University Press, 1970), pp. 93–115. By permission.

Jean-Jacques Rousseau, from *On The Social Contract*.

Edmund Burke, from *Reflections on the Revolution in France*.

The Federalist Papers; nos. 10, 15, 31, 37, 49, 51.

G.W.F. Hegel, from *The Philosophy of Right*, tr. J. Loewenberg.

Karl Marx, from "Grundrisse," tr. D. McLellan.

Karl Marx, from "Critique of the Gotha Programme."

John Stuart Mill, from *On Liberty*.

Mary Wollstonecraft, from *Vindication of the Rights of Woman*.

Thomas Hill Green, from *Justice and the Common Good*.

Herbert Spencer, from *Social Statics*.

Mikhail Bakunin, from *God and The State*.

Part IV:

John Dewey, from *Ethics*, in *The Collected Works of John Dewey Later Works Vol. 7* (Carbondale: Southern Illinois University Press, 1932), pp. 428–37. By permission

Benito Mussolini, from *Fascism: Doctrine and Institutions*.

Vladimir Ilich Lenin, from "On Soviet Socialist Democracy."

Freidrich August von Hayek, from *The Constitution of Liberty* (University of Chicago Press, 1960), pp. 54–70, 162–75. By permission.

Ayn Rand, "Man's Rights," from *The Virtue of Selfishness* (Estate of Ayn Rand, 1963), pp. 92–100. By permission.

Leo Strauss, from *What Is Political Philosophy?* (The Free Press, A Division of Simon & Schuster, 1959), pp. 1–17, 27–40. By permission.

John Rawls, from *A Theory of Justice* (Harvard University Press, 1971), pp. 3–22, 60–65, 136–42. By permission of the President and Fellows of Harvard College.

Robert Nozick, from *Anarchy, State, and Utopia* (New York: Basic Books, 1974), pp. 150–64, 167–82, 331–34. By permission.

Murray N. Rothbard, "Society without a State," in *Nomos*, vol. XIX, ed. J. Pennock and J. Chapman (New York University Press, 1978). By permission.

Susan Mendus, "Liberal Man," from *Philosophy and Politics*, ed. G.M.K. Hunt (Cambridge University Press, 1990), pp. 45–57. By permission.

Ronald Dworkin, from *Taking Rights Seriously* (Harvard University Press, 1977), pp. 266–78. By permission.

Jurgen Habermas, from *Justification and Application*, tr. C. Cronin (Cambridge, MA: MIT Press, 1993), pp. 1–17. By permission.

Alison Jaggar, from *Feminist Politics and Human Nature* (Lanham, MD: Rowman and Littlefield, 1983), pp. 123–32. By permission.

Richard Rorty, from *Objectivity, Relativism, and Truth* (Cambridge University Press, 1991), pp. 1–8. By permission.